AN ENCYCLOPEDIA OF MACROECONOMICS

To Jean and Christine;
and in loving memory of Philip M. Vane (1920–98)

An Encyclopedia of Macroeconomics

Edited by

Brian Snowdon

Principal Lecturer in Economics, Divison of Economics, Newcastle Business School, University of Northumbria, UK

and

Howard R. Vane

Professor of Economics, School of Accounting, Finance and Economics, Liverpool John Moores University, UK

Edward Elgar
Cheltenham, UK • Northampton, MA, USA

Published by
Edward Elgar Publishing Limited
Glensanda House
Montpellier Parade
Cheltenham
Glos GL50 1UA
UK

Edward Elgar Publishing, Inc.
136 West Street
Suite 202
Northampton
Massachusetts 01060
USA

A catalogue record for this book is available from the British Library

Library of Congress Cataloguing in Publication Data
An encyclopedia of macroeconomics / edited by Brian Snowdon and Howard R. Vane.
    p. cm.
    1. Macroeconomics—Encyclopedias.   2. Economics—Encyclopedias.
    I. Snowdon, Brian.   II. Vane, Howard R.

HB172.5 .E55. 2003
339′.03—dc21   2002026392

ISBN 1 84064 3870

Printed and bound in Great Britain by MPG Books Ltd, Bodmin, Cornwall

Contents

* Main entries are in bold face.

Contributors of main entries

Ahmad, Syed (Prof.), McMaster University, Hamilton, Ontario, Canada

Demand for Money: Keynesian Approach

Backhouse, Roger E. (Prof.), University of Birmingham, Birmingham, UK

Keynesian Cross; Say's Law

Baddeley, Michelle (Dr), Gonville and Caius College, Cambridge, UK

Investment: Accelerator Theory of; Speculative Bubbles

Bain, Andrew D. (Hon. Prof.), University of Glasgow, Glasgow, Scotland, UK

Demand for Money: Friedman's Approach

Benz, Matthias, University of Zurich, Zurich, Switzerland

Business Cycles: Political Business Cycle Approach

Blaug, Mark (Vis. Prof.), University of Amsterdam, Amsterdam, Netherlands

Endogenous Growth Theory

Bleaney, Michael (Prof.), University of Nottingham, Nottingham, UK

Purchasing Power Parity Theory

Boumans, Marcel (Dr), University of Amsterdam, Amsterdam, Netherlands

Calibration

Burmeister, Edwin (Prof.), Duke University, Durham, NC, USA

Samuelson, Paul A.

Colander, David C. (Prof.), Middlebury College, Middlebury, VT, USA

Tobin, James

Cornwall, John L. (Prof.), Dalhousie University, Halifax, Nova Scotia, Canada

Catching Up and Convergence; Evolutionary Macroeconomics

Cornwall, Wendy (Prof.), Mount St. Vincent University, Halifax, Nova Scotia, Canada

Catching Up and Convergence; New Political Macroeconomics

Cross, Rod B. (Prof.), University of Strathclyde, Glasgow, Scotland, UK

Hysteresis

Davidson, Paul (Prof.), University of Tennessee, Knoxville, TN, USA

Post Keynesian Economics

Dawson, Graham J.A. (Dr), Open University, Milton Keynes, UK

Ecological Macroeconomics; Inflation: Costs of; Inflation: Costs of Reducing; Menu Costs

Demirbas, Dilek (Dr), University of Northumbria, Newcastle-upon-Tyne, UK

Optimum Currency Area

De Vanssay, Xavier (Assoc. Prof.), York University, Toronto, Ontario, Canada

Marshall–Lerner Condition

De Vroey, Michel (Dr), Université Catholique de Louvain, Louvain-La-Neuve, Belgium

Involuntary Unemployment in Keynes's General Theory; Involuntary Unemployment in Keynesian Economics; Keynesian Economics: Reappraisals of

Dimand, Robert W. (Prof.), Brock University, St. Catharine's, Ontario, Canada.

Balance of Payments: Keynesian Approach; *Hicks, John R.*; *Real Balance Effect*; *Ricardian Equivalence*; *Schools of Thought in Macroeconomics*

Dixon, Huw D. (Prof.), University of York, York, UK

Real Rigidity

Dore, Mohammed H.I. (Prof.), Brock University, St. Catharine's, Ontario, Canada

Representative Agent Model

Dow, Sheila C. (Prof.), University of Stirling, Stirling, Scotland, UK

Money Supply: Endogenous or Exogenous?

Dowd, Kevin (Prof.), University of Nottingham Business School, Nottingham, UK

Gold Standard; *Time Inconsistency*

Eijffinger, Sylvester C.W. (Prof.), Tilburg University, Tilburg, Netherlands.

Central Bank Accountability and Transparency; *Central Bank Independence*

Falvey, Rod (Prof.), University of Nottingham, Nottingham, UK

Comparative Advantage

Fender, John (Prof.), University of Birmingham, Birmingham, UK

Nominal Rigidity

Fletcher, Gordon (Dr), University of Liverpool, Liverpool, UK

Neoclassical Synthesis

Frazer, William (Prof.), University of Florida, Florida, Gainesville, FL, USA

Friedman, Milton

Frey, Bruno S. (Prof.), University of Zurich, Zurich, Switzerland

Business Cycles: Political Business Cycle Approach

Garrison, Roger W. (Prof.), Auburn University, Auburn, AL,USA

Business Cycles: Austrian Approach

Gausden, Robert (formerly at the University of Northumbria, Newcastle-upon-Tyne, UK)

Absolute Income Hypothesis; *Permanent Income Hypothesis*

Gerrard, Bill (Dr), University of Leeds, Leeds, UK

Keynes's General Theory

Grieve Smith, John, Robinson College, Cambridge, UK

Bretton Woods

Hammond, J. Daniel (Prof.), Wake Forest University, Winston-Salem, NC, USA

Business Cycles: Monetarist Approach

Hamouda, Omar F. (Prof.), York University, North York, Ontario, Canada

Keynes, John Maynard

Hargreaves Heap, Shaun P. (Dr), University of East Anglia, Norwich, UK

New Keynesian Economics

Harrington, Richard L., University of Manchester, Manchester, UK

Classical Dichotomy

Healey, Nigel M. (Prof.), Manchester Metropolitan University, Manchester, UK

AD–AS Model; Credibility and Reputation

Holden, Ken (Prof.), Liverpool John Moores University, Liverpool, UK

Forecasting; *Macroeconometric Models*; *Vector Autoregressions*

Howitt, Peter (Prof.), Brown University, Providence, RI, USA

Coordination Failures

Humphrey, Thomas M. (Vice President and Economist), Federal Reserve Bank of Richmond, Richmond, VA, USA

Adaptive Expectations; *Balance of Payments: Monetary Approach*

Hunt, Andrew, University of Northumbria, Newcastle-upon-Tyne, UK

Incomes Policy

Jackson, Peter M. (Prof.), University of Leicester, Leicester, UK

Budget Deficits: Cyclical and Structural

Junankar, P.N. Raja (Prof.), University of Western Sydney, Macarthur, Campbelltown, NSW, Australia

Investment: Neoclassical Theories of

Laidler, David E.W. (Prof.), University of Western Ontario, London, Ontario, Canada

Quantity Theory of Money

Leeson, Robert (Assoc. Prof.), Murdoch University, Perth, Australia

Expectations-augmented Phillips Curve

Mayer, Thomas (Prof.), University of California, Davis, CA, USA

Monetarism; *Monetary Policy: Role of*

McCombie, John (Dr), Downing College, Cambridge, UK

Balance of Payments-constrained Economic Growth

Middleton, Roger (Dr), University of Bristol, Bristol, UK

Solow, Robert M.

Minford, A. Patrick L. (Prof.), University of Wales, Cardiff, Wales, UK
Supply-side Economics

Mishkin, Frederic S. (Prof.), Columbia University, New York, NY, USA
Inflation Targeting

Mizen, Paul (Dr), University of Nottingham, Nottingham, UK
Credit Channels; *Demand for Money: Buffer Stocks*

Mulhearn, Chris J. (Dr), Liverpool John Moores University, Liverpool, UK
Expenditure Reducing Policy; *Expenditure Switching Policy*

O'Brien, Denis P. (Prof.), University of Durham, Durham, UK
Classical Economics

Peston, Maurice (Prof.), University of London, London, UK
Crowding Out; *IS–LM Model: Closed Economy*; *IS–LM Model: Open Economy*

Reuten, Geert (Dr), University of Amsterdam, Amsterdam, Netherlands
Business Cycles: Marxian Approach; *Marxian Macroeconomics: An Overview*; *Marxian Macroeconomics: Some Key Relationships*

Ryan, Cillian (Dr), University of Birmingham, Birmingham, UK
Business Cycles: Real Business Cycle Approach; *Business Cycles: Stylized Facts*

Sandilands, Roger J., University of Strathclyde, Glasgow, Scotland, UK
Great Depression

Setterfield, Mark (Assoc. Prof.), Trinity College, Hartford, CT, USA
Inflation: Alternative Theories of

Shaw, G.K. (Prof.), University of Buckingham, Buckingham, UK
Balanced Budget Multiplier; *Keynesian Economics*

Sheffrin, Steven M. (Prof.), University of California, Davis, CA, USA

Fiscal Policy: Role of

Shone, Ronald, University of Stirling, Stirling, Scotland, UK

Exchange Rate Determination: Monetary Approach

Simkins, Scott P. (Assoc. Prof.), North Carolina A and T State University, Greenboro, NC, USA

Lucas Critique; *Theory and Measurement in Macroeconomics: Role of*

Smithin, John (Prof.), York University, North York, Ontario, Canada

Phillips Curve

Snowdon, Brian, University of Northumbria, Newcastle-upon-Tyne, UK

Business Cycles: New Classical Approach; *Economic Growth and the Role of Institutions*; *Growth Accounting*; *Harrod–Domar Growth Model*; *Lucas, Robert E. Jr.*; *Modigliani, Franco*; *Multiplier; Mundell, Robert A.*; *New Classical Economics*; *Rules versus Discretion*

Solow, Robert M. (Prof.), Massachusetts Institute of Technology, Cambridge, MA, USA

Neoclassical Growth Model

Spindler, Zane A. (Prof.), Simon Fraser University, Burnably, British Columbia, Canada

Laffer Curve

Stevenson, Andrew (Honorary Senior Research Fellow), University of Glasgow, Glasgow, Scotland, UK

Fixed Exchange Rate System; *Flexible Exchange Rate System*

Thompson, John L. (Prof.), Liverpool John Moores University, Liverpool, UK

Natural Rate of Unemployment; *Rational Expectations*

Trautwein, Hans-Michael (Prof.), Carl von Ossietzky University Oldenburg, Germany

Credit Views in Macroeconomic Theory

Trigg, Andrew B., Open University, Milton Keynes, UK

Business Cycles: Keynesian Approach

Vane, Howard R. (Prof.), Liverpool John Moores University, Liverpool, UK

Business Cycles: New Classical Approach; Economic Growth and the Role of Institutions; Growth Accounting; Harrod–Domar Growth Model; Lucas, Robert E. Jr.; Modigliani, Franco; Multiplier; Mundell, Robert A.; New Classical Economics; Rules versus Discretion

Visser, Hans (Prof.), Free University of Amsterdam, Amsterdam, Netherlands

Neutrality of Money

Went, Robert (Dr), University of Amsterdam, Amsterdam, Netherlands

Globalization

Wray, L. Randall (Prof.), University of Missouri, Kansas City, MO, USA

Financial Instability

Preface

Over recent years we have collaborated in writing and/or editing a number of books on macroeconomics. In the first of these, *A Modern Guide to Macroeconomics: An Introduction to Competing Schools of Thought* (Edward Elgar, 1994), we sought to provide a comprehensive introduction to the central tenets underlying, and policy implications of, the main schools of thought in macroeconomics. That book, which is primarily aimed at intermediate undergraduates, traces the origins and development of modern macroeconomics in historical perspective. Adopting the same approach, our edited volume *A Macroeconomics Reader* (Routledge, 1997), contains a collection of 26 insightful and accessible articles for intermediate undergraduates which shed light on the development of, and selected important controversies within, modern macroeconomics. That book was followed by the publication of *Reflections on the Development of Modern Macroeconomics* (Edward Elgar, 1997), an edited book containing eight original essays which focus on a number of important issues relating to the development of modern macroeconomics. More recently, in our *Conversations with Leading Economists: Interpreting Modern Macroeconomics* (Edward Elgar, 1999) we sought to shed *new* light on the origins, development and current state of macroeconomics through interviewing 14 leading economists (including five Nobel Laureates) who have made a profound contribution to the controversies witnessed in the fields of macroeconomic theory and policy, the way macroeconomics is taught and the history and methodology of macroeconomic research.

The main idea behind the present volume is to provide a major *reference* book for intermediate undergraduates, postgraduates and lecturers in the field of macroeconomics. Within the alphabetically ordered book the reader will find two types of entry: short entries (written by ourselves) and main entries (mainly, but not exclusively, written by invited contributors). In the former case we have included three types of short entry: (a) definitions of important terms and concepts which appear in the macroeconomics literature; (b) brief biographical details of economists who have made important contributions to the research agenda in macroeconomics (many of these details were taken from Mark Blaug's monumental *Who's Who in Economics*, 3rd edn, Edward Elgar, 1999); and (c) cross-references to main entries. In the latter case, the main entries entail lengthier pieces on selected important topics and individuals associated with the development and current state of macroeconomics. The brief we set contributors in writing these main entries was that they should be between 1000 and 1500 words in length, but, in the course of commenting on first drafts of these entries, we soon came to realize that we had set many of our contributors an almost impossible task. In consequence, either as a result of editorial discretion or, in a few instances, owing to our inability to rein in some contributors (including ourselves at times), the length of a number of these main entries extends beyond that originally envisaged.

While other academics would no doubt have included topics not covered, and excluded topics from those covered, in the final list of entries, our intention has been to provide our target audience with an accessible and, it is hoped, valuable reference book. A project of this kind inevitably involves making compromises in terms of both breadth and depth of coverage, against a constraint of length of manuscript contracted with the publisher.

Finally, anyone who has ever been involved in a project of this kind will appreciate that it should contain a 'health warning' for the editors concerned. Establishing the list of contributors, commenting on their entries, answering queries and so on has involved more than 600 letters, 500 e-mails and numerous phone calls, all of which have helped maintain the profitability of the UK postal service and British Telecom. On a far more positive note, our word processing skills have been transformed beyond recognition. More importantly, we have gained in knowledge and as editors we would like to express our gratitude to the 73 contributors listed in the preliminary pages for their valuable contributions to this volume.

BRIAN SNOWDON
HOWARD R. VANE

Abramovitz, Moses (1912–2001)

Moses Abramovitz (b.1912, New York City, New York, USA) obtained his BA from Harvard University in 1932 and his PhD from Columbia University in 1939. His main past posts included the following: Research Associate at the National Bureau of Economic Research (NBER), 1938–42; Lecturer in Economics at Columbia University, 1940–42 and 1946–8; Principal Economist of the US War Production Board in 1942; Principal Economist at the US Office of Strategic Services in 1943; Director of Business Cycle Studies at the NBER, 1946–8; and Professor of Economics and Economic History at Stanford University, 1948–77. From 1977 until his death in 2001 he was the Coe Professor of American Economic History, Emeritus, at Stanford University. Between 1975–7 and 1981–5 he was managing editor of the *Journal of Economic Literature*.

He is best known for his work on inventories and business cycles, which helped to establish the importance of inventory accumulation in explaining fluctuations in output; and his study of economic growth in industrialized countries. In the latter case this included work showing that 'long swings' in growth can be attributed to the interaction between the intensities of resource use and the growth of factors of production. Abramovitz also emphasized social capability as a prerequisite for successful economic growth. Among his best known books are *Inventories and Business Cycles* (NBER, 1950) and *Capital Formation and Economic Growth* (ed.) (Princeton University Press, 1955). His most widely read articles include 'Resource and Output Trends in the United States since 1870' (*American Economic Review*, **46**, May 1956); 'Catching Up, Forging Ahead and Falling Behind' (*Journal of Economic History*, **46**, June 1986); and 'What Economists Don't Know About Growth' (*Challenge*, **42**, January–February 1999).

See also

Catching up and Convergence; National Bureau of Economic Research.

Absolute Income Hypothesis

The Absolute Income Hypothesis (AIM) is a theory of consumption that is closely associated with the work of Keynes – in particular, *The General Theory of Employment, Interest and Money* (GTEIM), published in 1936. Indeed, the AIH has the interpretation of a simple representation of the more quantitative aspects of Keynes's views concerning the determination of aggregate consumption expenditure. The AIH can be presented as the following four conjectures:

1

1. real consumption (C) is a stable function of real disposable income (Y);
2. the marginal propensity to consume (*mpc*) has a value which is greater than zero but less than one;
3. as the value of income increases, the value of the average propensity to consume (*apc*) falls, such that $apc > mpc$;
4. as the value of income increases, the value of *mpc* falls.

With respect to conjecture (1), Keynes maintained that 'aggregate income . . . is, as a rule, the principal variable upon which the consumption-constituent of the aggregate demand function will depend' (GTEIM, p. 96). Also, towards the end of section II of Chapter 8 of the *General Theory*, he concluded that 'the propensity to consume may be considered a fairly stable function' (GTEIM, p. 95). Furthermore, when discussing the first of the principal objective factors which influence consumption, Keynes's initial statement was that 'Consumption is obviously much more a function of (in some sense) *real* income than of money-income' (GTEIM, p. 91).

Conjecture (2) arises from Keynes's 'fundamental psychological law'. This stated that 'men are disposed, as a rule and on the average, to increase their consumption as their income increases, but not by as much as the increase in their income' (GTEIM, p. 96).

Keynes gave two reasons why, as a rule, as the value of real income increases, a greater proportion of income is saved. The first explanation related to short-run behaviour, whereas the second was of a more general nature. Keynes asserted that 'a man's habitual standard of life usually has the first claim on his income' (GTEIM, p. 97). Later, he maintained that 'the satisfaction of the immediate primary needs of a man and his family is usually a stronger motive than the motives towards accumulation, which only acquire effective sway when a margin of comfort has been attained' (GTEIM, p. 97).

Concerning conjecture (4), it was Keynes's view that *mpc* is not constant for all levels of employment or values of real income. More specifically, he alleged that 'it is probable that there will be, as a rule, a tendency for it to diminish as employment increases' (GTEIM, p. 120).

The most common mathematical representation of the AIH is the linear consumption function, shown below:

$$C = a + bY,$$

where $a > 0$ and $0 < b < 1$. The above equation is in accordance with the first three conjectures but not conjecture (4). The presence of a non-zero intercept term in the equation has the effect of making the relationship between consumption and income non-proportional. More specifically, an implication of the parameter, a, being positive is that, as the value of income increases, consumption increases but by a smaller percentage.

This linear consumption function represents a fundamental component of the Keynesian system of aggregate demand. A consequence of the linear functional form is that the value of *mpc* is constant across the different values of disposable income. The value of *mpc* influences the value of the autonomous expenditure multiplier, and so the effectiveness of fiscal policy in promoting a change in the equilibrium value of national income. More specifically, the larger is the value of *mpc*, the smaller is the increase in government expenditure that is required to achieve a stipulated higher level of national income.

The AIH has been tested using both cross-section data and time-series data. Analyses of cross-section data generated strong support for this theory of consumption. Various budget studies that have been performed (for example, Brady and Friedman, 1947) have shown that, across household income groups, the value of *apc* declines as the value of income increases. These studies have also indicated that low-income groups dissave. Furthermore, evidence was obtained of a non-linear relationship between consumption and income. More specifically, in accordance with conjecture (4), as the value of income increases, the value of *mpc* falls.

The AIH also received support from analyses of short-run time-series data. Early time-series studies involved producing estimates of the parameters of a consumption function using aggregate data for (predominantly) the 1930s. A typical result is that obtained by Davis (1952) using annual, real, per capita data on the United States, expressed in billions of dollars, for the period 1929–40:

$$C = 11.45 + 0.78\,Y.$$

It can be seen that the estimate of *mpc* is a positive fraction. Also the estimate of the intercept term is greater than zero. Moreover, the value of the coefficient of determination corresponding to this equation is 0.986, indicating that income can account for almost all of the variation in consumption about its mean over the specified interval.

However, the validity of the AIH was called into question as a consequence of pessimistic predictions about the level of demand for the period immediately after the end of World War II failing to be realized. The 'Keynes–Hansen secular stagnation thesis' was formed in the late 1930s (Hansen, 1939). Assume that a closed economy is initially operating at full employment. Were the value of income subsequently to increase, then, accepting conjecture (3) contributing to the AIH, the ratio of consumption expenditure to income would fall. Given that there is no reason to believe that the ratio of investment expenditure to income rises as income increases, then, to maintain full employment, it would be necessary for government expenditure to grow at a faster rate than income. In fact, after the end of the war, when government expenditure inevitably fell, the United States economy did not experience a recession. Consumption expenditure was considerably greater than had been predicted, such that not only was full employment maintained but also there occurred substantial price inflation.

Further evidence that was damaging to the AIH resulted from analyses of long-run time-series data. Simon Kuznets performed two studies, each of which examined the nature of the long-run relationship between constant-price consumers' expenditure and real national income in the United States. The data that were analysed took the form of overlapping ten-year averages. The earlier study (Kuznets, 1942) compared mean values of consumption and income over the period 1879–1938. It was discovered that, ignoring the depression decades, 1924–33 and 1929–38, the ratio of consumption to income fell within the narrow bounds, 0.83–0.90. Over the same period, though, there was observed a considerable increase in income, from $17.9 billion to $72.0 billion. The later study (Kuznets, 1946) extended the period of analysis to 1869–1938. Again, after having excluded the depression decades, it was found that the ratio of consumption to income was not less than 0.83 and did not exceed 0.90. Over the same period, though, national income increased substantially, from $9.3 billion to $72.0 billion.

Hence the evidence produced by Kuznets indicated that, as income increased significantly over a long period of time, the ratio of consumption to income was approximately constant. The suggestion was that the long-run relationship between consumption and income is proportional, rather than non-proportional, which is implied by the AIH. Having analysed time-series data spanning several business cycles, Goldsmith (1955) also obtained evidence of a proportional relationship between consumption and income. More specifically, Goldsmith investigated the relationship between personal saving and personal disposable income in the United States over the period 1896–1949. The data took the form of mean values over business cycles and showed little variation in *apc*. Over the same period, though, real personal disposable income grew threefold.

Quarterly data from the early post-World War II period on the United States were also seen to contradict the AIH. According to conjecture (2), *mpc* is greater than zero and less than one. Hence the theory maintains that consumption and income should always be moving in the same direction and the change in consumption should be smaller than the change in income. However, when Gardner Ackley (1961) examined 22 quarter-to-quarter changes in consumption and income, he found only seven instances of compliance with the AIH. For five quarters, consumption and income were moving in opposite directions. Also, for 10 quarters in which consumption and income changed in the same direction, the change in consumption was greater than the change in income.

In conclusion, then, although the evidence obtained from budget studies and analyses of short-run time-series data supported the AIH, the evidence arising from studies of long-run time-series data and an examination of quarterly movements of consumption and income refuted the theory. The failure of the AIH to receive support from all forms of data was evident by the end of the 1940s and led to alternative theories of consumption being proposed, namely, the Relative Income Hypothesis, the Life-Cycle Hypothesis and the Permanent Income Hypothesis.

ROBERT GAUSDEN

See also:

Consumption Function; Keynes's *General Theory*; Kuznets, Simon S.; Life Cycle Hypothesis; Multiplier; Permanent Income Hypothesis; Relative Income Hypothesis.

Bibliography

Ackley, G. (1961), *Macroeconomic Theory*, New York: Macmillan.
Brady, D.S. and R.D. Friedman (1947), 'Saving and the Income Distribution', in *Studies in Income and Wealth*, **10**, New York: National Bureau of Economic Research.
Davis, T.E. (1952), 'The Consumption Function as a Tool for Prediction', *Review of Economics and Statistics*, **34**, August, pp. 270–75.
Goldsmith, R.W. (1955), *A Study of Saving in the United States*, vol. 1 Princeton, NJ: Princeton University Press.
Hansen, A.H. (1939), 'Economic Progress and Declining Population Growth', *American Economic Review*, **29**, March, pp. 1–15.
Keynes, J.M. (1936), *The General Theory of Employment, Interest and Money*, London: Macmillan.
Kuznets, S. (1942), *Uses of National Income in Peace and War*, occasional paper no. 6, New York: National Bureau of Economic Research.
Kuznets, S. (1946), *National Product Since 1869*, New York: National Bureau of Economic Research.

Absorption Approach to the Balance of Payments

A method of analysing a country's balance of payments on its current account. The approach highlights the relationship between a country's total output (Y) and its domestic expenditure (or absorption, A) on goods (where $A = C + I + G$).

Rearranging, and substituting A for $C + I + G$, in $Y = C + I + G + X - M$ we obtain: $Y - A = X - M$. This shows that a balance of payments surplus

($X>M$) occurs when output exceeds absorption ($Y>A$). In this situation the excess of total output relative to absorption is sold abroad generating a current account surplus. Conversely, a balance of payments deficit ($X<M$) occurs when absorption is greater than total output ($Y<A$). If the current account of the balance of payments is to improve then there must be: (1) a reduction in absorption relative to output, (2) an increase in output relative to absorption, or (3) some combination of both. As such the absorption approach recognizes that in a situation of full employment, when output cannot be increased, devaluation alone will be insufficient to improve the current account of the balance of payments. At full employment the balance of payments will only improve if absorption is reduced relative to output.

See also:

Balance of Payments; Devaluation; Expenditure Reducing Policy; Expenditure Switching Policy.

Accelerator Principle

The theory that relates changes in net investment to changes in output.

See also:

Investment: Accelerator Theory of.

Activism

The active use of fiscal and monetary policy to offset changes in private sector expenditure in order to help stabilize the economy.

See also:

Countercyclical Policy; Discretionary Policy; Fine Tuning; Rough Tuning.

Activist Policy Rule

A pre-specified rule for the conduct of policy which is linked to the state of the economy; also known as a feedback rule. An example of an activist monetary policy rule would be one where the money supply is targeted to grow at a rate of, say, 3 per cent per annum if unemployment is 6 per cent, but monetary growth is automatically increased (or decreased) by 1 per cent per annum for every 1 per cent by which unemployment rises above (or falls below) 6 per cent. If unemployment rose to 8 per cent, monetary growth would be increased to 5 per cent. Conversely, if unemployment fell to 5 per cent, monetary growth would be reduced to 2 per cent.

See also:
Rules versus Discretion.

Acyclical Variable

A variable that moves in no consistent direction over the business cycle.

See also:
Business Cycles: Stylized Facts.

Adaptive Expectations

The adaptive expectations hypothesis states that people form their expectations of the future values of economic variables, notably the rate of price inflation, from the mean or weighted average of lagged past values of those same variables. Such expectations are entirely backward looking and predetermined inasmuch as they are formed from mechanical extrapolations of the past history of the particular variable being forecast.

Equivalently, the hypothesis states that forecasters periodically revise or adjust their expectations in corrective, error-learning fashion when those expectations turn out to be wrong; that is, when realized actual values of the variables differ from those expected. When applied to inflationary expectations the error-learning formula takes its name from the notion that inflation forecasters learn from their mistakes and so adapt their predictions by some fraction of their forecasting errors.

The basic idea of the lagged adjustment of expectations to experience dates back at least to David Hume, who described the slowness with which workers, employers and consumers perceive inflation rate changes and adapt to them. Irving Fisher, in the 1920s and the early 1930s, invented the concept of distributed lags to model the output, employment and real interest rate effects of sluggishly adjusting inflation perceptions and expectations. But the modern origins of the hypothesis begin in the early 1950s. It was then that Philip Cagan (1956), who with Milton Friedman was studying the behaviour of money's circulation velocity in hyperinflations, sought to find an empirical proxy for expected inflation, an unobservable variable

that measures the depreciation cost of holding money. Friedman described
Cagan's problem to the New Zealand economist A.W. Phillips, who suggested relating changes in the expected rate of inflation to the difference
between actual inflation and expected inflation (see Leeson, 2000).
Friedman conveyed Phillips's suggestion to Cagan who, upon converting
the implied differential equation into an exponentially weighted average of
past inflation rates, found it worked well as an empirical proxy for inflationary expectations in money demand functions. Thus was born the adaptive
expectations hypothesis, with Phillips its originator and Cagan its influential early propagator.

Phillips expressed the hypothesis in its error-learning form,

$$dp^*/dt = b(p - p^*),$$

where the differential operator d/dt applied to the expected rate of inflation
p^* indicates the rate of change (time derivative) of that variable, $p - p^*$ is
the expectations or forecast error (that is, the difference between actual and
expected price inflation) and b is the adjustment fraction or coefficient of
adaptation. Assuming, for example, an adjustment fraction of 1/2,
Phillips's equation says that if the actual and expected rates of inflation are
10 per cent and 4 per cent, respectively – that is, the expectational error is
six percentage points – then forecasters will revise upwards their predictions
of the expected rate by an amount equal to half the error, or three percentage points. Provided the actual inflation rate remains unchanged, such revision will continue until the expectational error is eliminated and inflation
predictions are fully realized. The closer the adjustment fraction, or coefficient of adaptation, is to unity the faster the adjustment – a unit coefficient
implying instantaneous adjustment and a zero coefficient no adjustment at
all.

Solving Phillips's error-learning equation, Cagan obtained the equivalent equation

$$p_t^* = \sum_{i=0}^{T} (1 - e^{-b})e^{-bi} \, p_{t-i},$$

expressing expected inflation p^* as a weighted average of all past rates of
inflation p_{t-i} with the weights $(1 - e^{-b})e^{-bi}$ declining exponentially and
summing to unity. The exponentially declining weights imply that forecasters give more attention to recent than to older price history in forming their
forecasts. How fast the weights decline depends on the rate at which forecasters' memories of inflation decay. Rapidly declining weights indicate
that memories are short, so that expected inflation depends primarily on
recent inflation experience. Slowly declining weights imply long memories,

so that expectations are influenced significantly by inflation rates in the more distant past. As for the unit-sum-of-weights property, it ensures that any stable (constant) rate of inflation will eventually be fully anticipated as expectations catch up with reality.

As mentioned, Cagan used adaptive expectations to represent the depreciation-cost-of-holding-money variable in money demand, or velocity, functions. In the 1960s and 1970s, Milton Friedman (1968), Edmund Phelps (1967) and others used adaptive expectations to represent anticipated inflation in the augmented Phillips curve equation

$$p - p^* = f(U - U_N),$$

expressing a functional, trade-off relationship between unexpected inflation $p - p^*$ (the difference between actual and expected inflation) and the unemployment rate U measured in terms of deviations from its natural equilibrium rate, U_N. Here adaptive expectations proved instrumental in the derivation of three propositions that dominated macroeconomic policy discussion in the 1970s and early 1980s.

First was the natural rate hypothesis according to which no permanent trade-offs exist between inflation and unemployment. Such trade-offs necessarily vanish when expectations fully adjust, as the unit-sum-of-weights property ensures they must, to any stable rate of inflation established by the central bank. At this point, the expectations error $p - p^*$ goes to zero and unemployment returns to its natural rate such that no trade-offs remain to be exploited.

Second was the accelerationist proposition asserting that, whereas adaptive expectations rule out permanent trade-offs between inflation and unemployment, they permit permanent trade-offs between unemployment and the *rate of acceleration* of the inflation rate. That is, because adaptive expectations adjust to actual inflation with a lag, policy makers can permanently peg unemployment below its natural level by continually raising the inflation rate so that it always stays a step ahead of expectations and frustrates their attempt to catch up.

Third was the costly-disinflation proposition that adaptive expectations, which posit that agents revise their inflation expectations downwards only when actual inflation turns out to be lower than expected, might render disinflationary policy too painful to pursue. For if the policy makers sought to eradicate inflationary expectations – an absolute necessity of any successful disinflationary policy – they would have to force actual inflation below expected inflation in order to induce the latter to adjust to the former as it converged to the desired target rate. To achieve such disinflation, the authorities would apply contractionary measures to raise unemployment above its natural level. The resulting excess unemployment would put downward pressure on the actual rate of inflation to which the expected rate would adjust with a lag. Through this long and painful error-learning adjustment process, both actual and anticipated inflation eventually would be squeezed out of the economy, albeit at the cost of much lost output and employment. Small wonder that some economists in the 1970s and 1980s thought it might be better to learn to live with inflation than to fight it.

The foregoing accelerationist and costly-disinflation propositions, however, proved only as convincing as the expectations hypothesis underlying them. The propositions lost credence when adaptive expectations came under attack in the 1970s. On at least three grounds, critics faulted adaptive expectations for constituting an irrational and therefore unrealistic means of forecasting.

First, why would profit-maximizing forecasters look only at past inflation when other relevant and freely available information, especially information on current and likely future policy moves, would improve their inflation predictions?

Second, given that adaptive expectations systematically underpredict accelerating inflation, why would forecasters seeing such persistent and predictable series of one-way errors not abandon the mechanism producing them for more accurate expectations-generating schemes?

Third, why indeed would forecasters resort to any formula that is inconsistent with the way inflation is actually generated in the economy? Why would they not discover the true inflation-generating process and then use all information pertinent to it in forming their expectations? For example, suppose central banks generate inflation by creating excess money growth when currently observed unemployment rises above its natural rate. Would not rational forecasters learn to form their expectations of future inflation by looking, not at past inflation, but rather at the same unemployment variable that central banks respond to?

The upshot of these criticisms was to discredit the adaptive expectations hypothesis and render it unreliable in policy analysis. By the mid-1980s, economists had largely abandoned it for the rival rational expectations hypothesis (Muth, 1961) according to which agents form their expectations in a way that avoids all systematic (predictable) errors. With adaptive expectations in retreat, so too were the associated accelerationist and costly-disinflation propositions. Rational expectations, with their capacity to foresee all systematic inflationary processes, including those involving higher time derivatives, promised to render accelerationist policy null and void. Ever-rising inflation had no power to stimulate real activity as long as agents could anticipate the rate of rise of the inflation rate and never be fooled by it (see Lucas, 1972). As for fears of costly disinflation, they too were laid to rest by the rational expectations undertaker. Provided central bankers conducted disinflationary policy in a systematic, predictable manner, rational expectations implied that agents would anticipate such policy actions and incorporate them in their forecasts. Actual and expected rates of inflation and disinflation would coincide, leaving no gap to develop between them. With no gap, there would be no need for excess unemployment to generate it. Inflation, actual and expected, could be brought to its target level with only minor costs in terms of excess unemployment.

Today, the adaptive expectations hypothesis finds few adherents. The once-popular notion of expected inflation as a backward-looking, pre-determined (by past history) phenomenon has given way to the notion of inflationary expectations as forward-looking phenomena determined by current and anticipated future events.

THOMAS M. HUMPHREY

See also:

Cagan, Philip D.; Expectations-augmented Phillips Curve; Inflation: Costs of Reducing; Natural Rate of Unemployment; Phillips, A. William H.; Rational Expectations.

Bibliography

Cagan, P. (1956), 'The Monetary Dynamics of Hyperinflation', in M. Friedman (ed.), *Studies in the Quantity Theory of Money*, Chicago: University of Chicago Press.
Friedman, M. (1968), 'The Role of Monetary Policy', *American Economic Review*, **58**, March, pp. 1–17.
Leeson, R. (ed.) (2000), *A.W.H.Phillips: Collected Works in Contemporary Perspective*, Cambridge: Cambridge University Press.
Lucas, R.E. Jr. (1972), 'Expectations and the Neutrality of Money', *Journal of Economic Theory*, **4**, April, pp. 103–24.
Muth, J.F. (1961), 'Rational Expectations and the Theory of Price Movements', *Econometrica*, **29**, July, pp. 315–35.
Phelps, E.S. (1967), 'Phillips Curves, Expectations of Inflation and Optimal Inflation Over Time', *Economica*, **34**, August, pp. 254–81.

AD–AS Model

'Keynesianism' became the dominant macroeconomic paradigm in the post-World War II era. Based on interpretations of the macroeconomic theories propounded by Keynes (1936), two basic textbook models emerged as standard Keynesian teaching and analytical tools: the introductory income–expenditure (45 degree line) framework invented by Samuelson (1939) and the more advanced IS–LM approach pioneered by Hicks (1937). The essential insight of the Keynesian school of thought is that output is determined by effective (aggregate) demand and that, owing to price and wage stickiness, effective demand may be insufficient to support the full-employment level of output. This analysis provided a compelling explanation for the prolonged depression in the United States and the United Kingdom in the 1930s. Reflecting the growing political influence of Keynesianism, the UK wartime coalition government published its famous 'White Paper on Employment Policy' in 1944, committing future peacetime governments to stabilize output at its full-employment level. Over the following three decades, 'discretionary' macroeconomic policy was used in an attempt to maintain the economy at a permanently high rate of employment.

The Keynesian income–expenditure and IS–LM frameworks shared two limitations, which were steadily exposed by changes in macroeconomic performance across the developed world. First, these models did not explicitly deal with aggregate supply. Given the primacy of aggregate demand in determining output, aggregate supply was assumed to respond passively to changes in aggregate demand up to the full-employment level of output. Second, these models did not explain the price level, which was assumed to be constant below the full-employment level of output and to rise only when aggregate demand exceeded the full-employment level of output (so that there was an 'inflationary gap'). Major supply-side shocks, most notably the 1973 rise in oil prices, and rapidly increasing inflation throughout the developed world in the late 1960s and 1970s, presented major challenges to the relevance of these simple versions of the Keynesian model. The aggregate demand (AD) and aggregate supply (AS) model was developed in direct response and, while it is theoretically flawed, it has subsequently become the standard textbook model for analysing the macro economy (see, Colander, 1995).

The aggregate demand and supply model is presented in its early (Keynesian) form in Figure 1. The vertical axis measures the aggregate price level, P (the GDP deflator), while the horizontal axis measures aggregate output, Y (or real GDP). The supply schedule, AS, represents the aggregate supply of final goods and services by all firms in the economy. In this simple Keynesian version, the aggregate supply schedule is horizontal up to the full-employment level of income, Y_F, at which point it becomes vertical.

The demand schedule, AD, represents the aggregate demand for domestic goods and services by households (C), firms (I), government (G) and the foreign sector (net exports, $X - M$); that is, $AD = C + I + G + X - M$. The aggregate demand schedule may be derived formally from either the income-expenditure or IS–LM models. In simple terms, however, when the price level rises, households demand a smaller quantity of real goods and services for three main reasons:

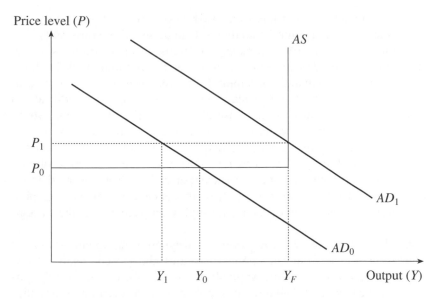

Figure 1

1. the 'real balance (or Pigou wealth) effect' (as prices rise, the real value
    of wealth declines and households reduce current spending to rebuild
    their savings);
2. the 'interest rate (or Keynes) effect' (as prices rise, the demand for
    money increases, interest rates rise and firms and households reduce
    borrowing and spending); and
3. the 'open economy (or net export) effect' (as domestic prices rise, con-
    sumers switch from domestically produced goods to relatively lower
    priced foreign goods, reducing net exports).

On this basis, the behaviour of the economy can be easily modelled.
Below full employment fluctuations in aggregate demand result in changes
in output. If, for example, the government cuts income tax, the aggregate
demand schedule will shift to the right, from AD_0 to AD_1, and output will
increase until the economy reaches full capacity at Y_F. Prices will then
begin to rise until equilibrium is reached with prices higher at P_1. This
model can also be used to capture the impact of a supply-side shock. For
example, an oil price hike will shift the aggregate supply schedule upwards
– for example, from P_0 to P_1. If aggregate demand is unchanged at AD_0, the
effect of the adverse supply-side shock is to reduce output to Y_1 and
increase prices to P_1.

Recasting the Keynesian model in terms of aggregate demand and supply provided an accessible framework within which both supply-side shocks and inflation could be analysed. It highlighted the possibility that inflation could emanate on the supply side ('cost-push' inflation) as well as the demand side ('demand-pull' inflation) of the economy and this form of the aggregate demand and supply framework was quickly adopted in the late 1970s as a standard teaching tool. A common modification, designed to reflect the commonsense observation that bottlenecks would begin to appear in some parts of the economy before others, was to assume that the aggregate supply schedule is horizontal (perfectly elastic) at low levels of output, but becomes positively sloped as the economy approaches Y_F, before becoming vertical (perfectly inelastic) when the full-employment level of output is reached (this is certainly more in keeping with Keynes's discussion of aggregate supply on page 296 of the *General Theory*).

By the end of the 1970s, however, the Keynesian paradigm was under increasing attack from the monetarists and the closely related 'New Classical' school of thought. Arguably, the reason for the enduring popularity of the aggregate demand and supply model has been that it provides a common framework within which competing perspectives on macroeconomic theory can be presented and assessed. For example, the New Classical counter-revolution stressed the centrality of the 'invisible hand' in coordinating economic activity. While prices and wages were clearly sticky in the real world, it was argued that such stickiness was transitory and resulted from incomplete information rather than persistent market failure.

By focusing on the microfoundations of aggregate supply, the monetarist school (see Friedman, 1968) linked the shape and position of the aggregate supply schedule, via the aggregate production function (in which output is a function of, *inter alia*, labour employed), to the labour market. In the labour market, both the supply of, and demand for, labour are functions of the real wage (that is, the nominal, or money, wage deflated by the aggregate price level). In the short run, there is an information asymmetry, insofar as firms know precisely the real wages they are paying their workers from day to day (the money wage deflated by the current price of their product), whereas workers know the money wages they are receiving, but have to make some assumption about the behaviour of the aggregate price level to gauge their real wages.

In the basic, expectations-augmented aggregate demand and supply model, workers perceive their real wages to be their actual money wages deflated by the expected price level over the next time period. If the actual price level increases above the expected level, real wages fall. Because this fall is not immediately apparent to workers, they continue to offer the same quantity of labour at a lower real wage. This amounts to a (temporary) rightwards shift in the supply schedule for labour (relative to real wages) and the labour market clears at a higher quantity of labour. In terms of the aggregate supply schedule, a higher price level calls forth higher output, but only because workers are 'fooled' into accepting lower real wages. In the next time period, price expectations adapt to the higher actual price level and the labour supply schedule returns to its original position.

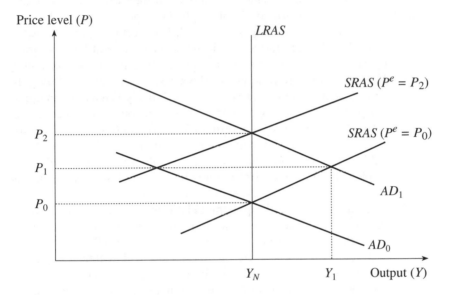

Figure 2

Figure 2 illustrates the dynamics of the model. Y_N is the natural level of output, which is the level of output consistent with full equilibrium in the labour market, with the expected and actual price level equal at P_0. If the price level rises above P_0, in the short run the economy will slide up the short-run aggregate supply schedule, $SRAS (P^e = P_0)$. Thus an increase in aggregate demand from AD_0 to AD_1 will move the economy to P_1, Y_1. As the higher price level is subsequently built into wage bargains to restore real wages (that is, as price expectations catch up with the actual price level), so the short-run aggregate supply schedule shifts leftwards to $SRAS (P^e = P_2)$, until equilibrium is finally restored at the natural level of output, Y_N, with the price level stabilizing at P_2 (the long-run price level consistent with the new, higher level of aggregate demand). The long-run aggregate supply schedule ($LRAS$) is vertical at the natural level of output.

The introduction of price expectations into the aggregate demand and supply model fundamentally changes its policy implications. The Keynesian version suggests that, by flexible, discretionary demand management, the government can respond to aggregate demand and supply shocks by adjusting aggregate demand and stabilizing the economy at the full-employment level of output, with little or no cost in terms of rising prices. The expectations-augmented monetarist version implies, in stark contrast, that there is no long-run trade-off between prices and output. Indeed, depending upon the way in which workers form their expectations of the price level, even the short-run trade-off implied by a positively sloped short-run aggregate supply curve may be qualified. If expectations are adaptive, in the sense that they are formed by looking backwards at historic price levels, there is scope to exploit a short-run trade-off at the cost of ever-rising prices. If expectations are rational, in the sense that agents are forward-looking and take account of the policy maker's likely behaviour, any predictable expansion of aggregate demand will be built into their price expectations. The only way of exploiting the short-run trade-off is by 'surprising' workers and firms by engineering an unpredicted price increase, which implies that anticipated macroeconomic policy pursued according to the principles of optimal control cannot have even short-run effects on output.

The aggregate demand and supply model is often presented in a dynamic form, with inflation replacing the price level on the vertical axis, the aggregate supply schedule representing the level of output at different inflation rates and the demand schedule relating to the growth of aggregate demand. The attraction of this conversion is that it makes the model more intuitively appealing, since it operates in terms of inflation, rather than the more unfamiliar, artificial construct of the general price level. In this formulation, the short-run aggregate supply schedule is simply the Lucas 'surprise function':

$$Y = Y_N + \pi - \pi^e + \varepsilon,$$

where π is inflation, π^e is expected inflation and ε is a random disturbance term with a mean of zero. Figure 3 illustrates the dynamic version of the aggregate demand and supply model. Figure 3 shows that, with a given rate of growth of aggregate demand, AD_0, the economy is in equilibrium with inflation at π_0 and output at its natural level, Y_N. Faster demand growth of AD_1 leads, with adaptive expectations, to a temporary output gain at the cost of higher inflation, π_1, but ultimately only to higher inflation, π_2, as expectations (and nominal wages) adjust. With rational expectations, this short-run expansion in output only occurs to the extent that the increase in the growth of aggregate demand is not anticipated by workers and firms, given their knowledge of the government's policy objectives.

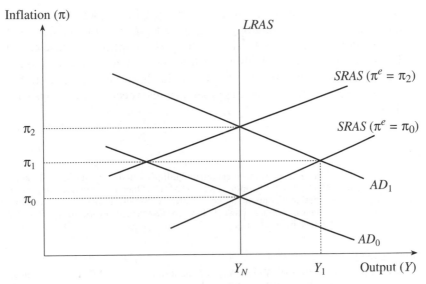

Figure 3

A key advantage of this version of aggregate demand and supply is that it can be directly linked, via 'Okun's Law' (that there is an inverse relationship between changes in output and unemployment), to the expectations-augmented Phillips curve model, which relates unemployment to inflation. For any given set of inflationary expectations, there is a short-run aggregate supply schedule, $SRAS\,(\pi^e = \pi_\alpha)$. which shows the rate of output associated with any actual inflation rate, and this corresponds with a unique, short-run Phillips Curve, $SRPC\,(\pi^e = \pi_\alpha)$, which shows the rate of unemployment associated with different actual inflation rates (see also Romer, 2000; Taylor, 2000).

The main problem with the aggregate demand and supply framework from a Keynesian perspective is that, despite its intuitive appeal, it conflicts with the key insight of the Keynesian approach. The aggregate supply curve assumes that firms can sell all their output at the going price, whereas the income–expenditure and *IS–LM* models preserve the essential Keynesian idea that producers and workers may be quantity-constrained by insufficient, effective aggregate demand. In other words, the underlying Keynesian model explicitly assumes that aggregate demand and supply are interlinked and co-determined (that is, households are both producers and consumers), rather than representing – as in the microeconomic parallel – independent sets of producers and consumers brought together in the market place to interact. From a monetarist perspective, there are also weaknesses. For example, the positively sloped short-run aggregate supply schedule depends critically upon workers having incomplete information about the price level (or inflation), but the model ignores the possibility of the same informational problems distorting consumption and investment decisions on the demand side. Nevertheless, the simplicity and tractability of the aggregate demand and supply model have ensured that it has remained the standard textbook approach to macroeconomic analysis for the last two decades.

NIGEL M. HEALEY

See also:

Adaptive Expectations; Expectations-augmented Phillips Curve; Inflation: Alternative Theories of; *IS–LM* Model: Closed Economy; *IS–LM* Model: Open Economy; Keynes Effect; Keynesian Cross; Keynesian Economics; Lucas 'Surprise' Supply Function; Monetarism; New Classical Economics; Okun's Law; Policy Ineffectiveness Proposition; Rational Expectations; Real Balance Effect.

Bibliography

Colander, D. (1995), 'The Stories We Tell: A Reconsideration of the AS/AD Analysis', *Journal of Economic Perspectives*, **9**, Summer, pp. 169–88.
Friedman, M. (1968), 'The Role of Monetary Policy', *American Economic Review*, **58**, March, pp. 1–17.
Hicks, J. (1937), 'Mr Keynes and the "Classics": A Suggested Interpretation', *Econometrica*, **5**, April, pp. 147–59.
Keynes, J.M. (1936), *The General Theory of Employment, Interest, and Money*, New York: Harcourt Brace.
Romer, D. (2000), 'Keynesian Macroeconomics Without the LM Curve', *Journal of Economic Perspectives*, **14**, Spring, pp. 149–69.
Samuelson, P. (1939), 'A Synthesis of the Principle of Acceleration and the Multiplier', *Journal of Political Economy*, **47**, December, pp 786–97.
Taylor, J.B. (2000), 'Teaching Macroeconomics at the Principles Level', *American Economic Review*, **90**, May, pp. 90–94.

Adjustable Peg System

An exchange rate system where the exchange rate is fixed or pegged, but where the exchange rate can be adjusted or changed according to certain rules. The Bretton Woods system provides the best example of such a system. The rules of the system permitted devaluations and revaluations of up to 10 per cent, but permission had to be obtained from the International Monetary Fund if the change in the exchange rate was greater than 10 per cent.

See also:

Bretton Woods; Devaluation; Fixed Exchange Rate System; International Monetary Fund; Revaluation.

Adverse Selection Model

A model in which firms that offer higher wages will not only attract the best or most productive applicants, but will also deter the most productive workers from quitting. In the labour market asymmetric information predominates, with applicants having more information about their abilities, honesty and commitment than potential employers. Given the non-trivial costs associated with hiring and training new employees, firms clearly prefer not to hire workers only later to find that they need to fire those with low productivity, incurring an additional set of firing costs. One way to avoid this potential problem is to offer higher wages. If workers' abilities are closely related to their reservation wage then high wage offers will attract the most productive applicants. Indeed, any applicant who offers to work for less than the efficiency wage will be regarded as a potential 'lemon'. Higher wages will also deter the most productive workers from quitting.

See also:
Asymmetric Information; Efficiency Wage Theory.

Aggregate Demand

The total demand for goods and services comprising consumer expenditure (C), investment expenditure (I), government expenditure (G) and exports (X) minus imports (M). In the Keynesian cross model the level of output and employment is determined by aggregate demand.

See also:
AD–AS Model; Aggregate Demand Management; Keynesian Cross.

Aggregate Demand Management

The discretionary use of fiscal and/or monetary policy to influence the level of aggregate demand in order to reduce the severity of short-term cyclical fluctuations in aggregate economic activity and help stabilize the economy. Aggregate demand management may entail (1) the frequent use of fiscal and monetary policy in an attempt to maintain output and employment at, or near, their full employment or natural levels (so-called 'fine tuning') or (2) the occasional use of fiscal and monetary policy in response to a large divergence in output and employment from their full employment or natural levels (so-called 'rough tuning').

Activist aggregate demand management is synonymous with Keynesian economics. In the Keynesian view the economy is inherently unstable, experiencing shocks that cause undesirable and inefficient economic fluctuations. Not only do Keynesians stress the need for stabilization policy but they also contend that the authorities can, and therefore should, stabilize the economy via aggregate demand management. New Keynesians do not support attempts (popular in the 1950s and 1960s among orthodox Keynesians) to fine tune the economy, but have instead championed the case for rough tuning. In particular, hysteresis effects provide new Keynesians with a strong case that the authorities should be given the discretionary power to stimulate aggregate demand during a prolonged recession.

In contrast, the view held by monetarists and new classicists is that there is no need for activist stabilization policy involving the management of aggregate demand and that discretionary fiscal and monetary policy cannot, and therefore should not, be used to stabilize the economy. Believing the economy to be inherently stable, in that it will fairly rapidly self-equilibrate around the natural rate of output and employment after being subjected to some disturbance, they question the need for stabilization policy involving the management of aggregate demand. Highlighting a number of problems associated with attempts to stabilize the economy (including those associated with time lags, forecasting and uncertainty over reliable estimates of the natural rate of unemployment), monetarists argue that discretionary policy activism may make matters worse. Instead they advocate that discretionary aggregate demand policies should be replaced by policy based on rules. New classicists' support for rules over discretion is based on the insights provided by the policy ineffectiveness proposition, the problem of time inconsistency and the Lucas critique. Finally, in the real business cycle view there is no role for the authorities to stabilize fluctuations in output and employment through aggregate demand management.

See also:

Hysteresis; Keynesian Economics; Lucas Critique; Monetarism; Natural Rate of Unemployment; New Classical Economics; New Keynesian Economics; Policy Ineffectiveness Proposition; Real Business Cycle Model; Rules versus Discretion; Time Inconsistency.

Aggregate Production Function

A functional relationship between the quantity of aggregate output produced in an economy and the quantities of inputs used in production. This relationship can be written as:

$$Y = A(t)\, F(K, L),$$

where Y is real output, $A(t)$ represents technological know-how at time t, and F is a function that relates real output to K, the quantity of capital inputs, and L, the quantity of labour inputs. Real output will increase over time if there is an increase in the quantity of factors inputs (capital and/or labour) and/or if there is an increase in the productivity of capital and labour inputs (that is, an increase in output per unit of factor input) due to an increase in technological know-how.

In the neoclassical growth model developed by Robert Solow in the mid-1950s, the aggregate production function obeys three key properties. First, factor inputs of labour and capital can be smoothly substituted for each other in the production process (that is, firms can use more capital inputs and fewer labour inputs, or vice versa) to produce the same quantity of output. Second, factor inputs experience diminishing returns. For example, while an increase in the quantity of labour inputs with the quantity of capital inputs held constant will result in an increase in real output, output will increase at an ever-declining rate. Similarly, diminishing returns will result from an increase in the capital stock to a fixed labour force. Third, the aggregate production function exhibits constant returns to scale, meaning that, when all factor inputs increase in some proportion, real output will increase in the same proportion. For example, if both the quantity of labour and capital inputs were doubled, the amount of real output would also be doubled. Given the assumption of constant returns to scale, then, for a given technology, the aggregate production function can also be expressed in per worker terms. This relationship can be written as:

$$Y/L = A(t)\, f(K/L),$$

where output per worker (Y/L) depends on the amount of capital input per worker (K/L).

See also:

Neoclassical Growth Model; Solow, Robert M.

Aggregate Supply

The total amount of output firms produce in an economy.

See also:

AD–AS model.

Akerlof, George A.

George Akerlof (b.1940, New Haven, Connecticut, USA) obtained his BA from Yale University in 1962 and his PhD from Massachusetts Institute of Technology (MIT) in 1966. His main past posts have included Assistant Professor (1960–70) and Associate Professor (1970–71) at the University of California, Berkeley; Senior Economist, US President's Council of Economic Advisers, 1973–4; Visiting Research Economist, Board of Governors, Federal Reserve Board, 1977–8; and Professor at the London School of Economics, 1978–80. Since 1977 he has been Professor at the University of California, Berkeley. In 2001 he was jointly awarded, with Joseph Stiglitz and Michael Spence, the Nobel Prize in Economics 'for their analyses of markets with asymmetric information'. He is best known for his important contributions to the new Keynesian literature. His books include *Efficiency Wage Models of the Labour Market* (ed. with J.L. Yellen) (Cambridge University Press, 1986). His most widely read articles include 'The Market for "Lemons": Quality Uncertainty and the Market Mechanism' (*Quarterly Journal of Economics*, **84**, August 1970); 'Labour Contracts as Partial Gift Exchange' (*Quarterly Journal of Economics*, **97**, November 1982); 'Can Small Deviations from Rationality Make Significant Differences to Economic Equilibria?' (co-authored with J.L. Yellen) (*American Economic Review*, **75**, September 1985); and 'A Near-Rational Model of the Business Cycle, with Wage and Price Inertia' (co-authored with J.L. Yellen) (*Quarterly Journal of Economics*, **100**, Supplement 1985).

See also:

Council of Economic Advisers; Efficiency Wage Theory; New Keynesian Economics; Nobel Prize in Economics.

Alesina, Alberto

Alberto Alesina (b.1957, Broni, Italy) obtained his Laurea from the Universita Bocconi, Milan in 1981 and his PhD from Harvard University in 1986. His main past posts have included the following: Assistant Professor of Economics at Carnegie-Mellon University, 1987–8; Assistant Professor of Economics and Government (1988–90) and Associate Professor of Political Economy (1991–3) at Harvard University. Since 1993 he has been Professor of Economics and Government at Harvard University. He is best known for his contributions, in terms of both theoretical analysis and of empirical investigation, to the various forms of interaction between politics and macroeconomics; and his influential work on politicoeconomic cycles, the origin and implications of fiscal deficits, and the relationship between political stability and economic growth. Among his best known books are *Partisan Politics, Divided Government and the Economy* (co-authored with H. Rosenthal) (Cambridge University Press, 1995); *Political Cycles and the Macroeconomy* (co-authored with N. Roubini) (MIT Press, 1997); and *The Size of Nations* (co-authored with E. Spolare) (MIT Press, 2002). His most widely read articles include 'Macroeconomic Policy in a Two-Party System as a Repeated Game' (*Quarterly Journal of Economics*, **102**, August 1987); 'Political Cycles in OECD Economies' (co-authored with N. Roubini) (*Review of Economic Studies*, **59**, October 1992); 'Central Bank Independence and Macroeconomic Performance: Some Comparative Evidence' (co-authored with L.Summers) (*Journal of Money, Credit and Banking*, **25**, May 1993); 'Distributive Politics and Economic Growth' (co-authored with D. Rodrik) (*Quarterly Journal of Economics*, **109**, May 1994); and 'The Political Economy of the Budget Surplus in the US' (*Journal of Economic Perspectives*, **14**, Summer 2000).

See also:
Business Cycles: Political Business Cycle Approach; New Political Macroeconomics)

American Economic Association

The AEA was organized in 1885 at Saratoga, New York. Currently based at Nashville, Tennessee its present-day mission statement includes (1) the encouragement of economic research, (2) the issue of publications on economic subjects, and (3) the encouragement of perfect freedom of economic discussion, including an annual meeting. Among its publications are the prestigious *American Economic Review* (first published in 1911) and the *Journal of Economic Literature* (first published in 1963). Approximately 22 000 economists are members of, and 5500 institutes subscribe to, the AEA. Over half of its membership is associated with academic institutions, just over a third with business and industry, and the balance largely with federal, state and local government agencies. For more information the reader is referred to the official website of the AEA at (*http://www. vanderbilt.edu/AEA*).

Animal Spirits

A term first used by John Maynard Keynes in *The General Theory of Employment, Interest and Money* (Macmillan, 1936) to describe how, in Keynes's view, investment decisions depend on the whims or spontaneous urges (optimistic or pessimistic) of entrepreneurs – see also Keynes's article 'The General Theory of Employment' (*Quarterly Journal of Economics*, **51**, February 1937). The term was subsequently popularized by the Cambridge University economist Joan Robinson (1903–83) who emphasized Chapter 12 'The State of Long-Term Expectation', where the term appears, as the key chapter in the *General Theory*.

See also:
Keynes's *General Theory*; Keynes, John Maynard; Robinson, Joan.

Anticipated Inflation

The rate of inflation which is expected over some future time period. In a hypothetical situation in which the actual rate of inflation is equal to the expected rate, inflation is said to be perfectly anticipated. In reality inflation is imperfectly anticipated as the actual rate of inflation will rarely coincide with the anticipated or expected rate. Debate exists about how best to model the way economic agents form expectations.

See also:
Adaptive Expectations; Inflation: Costs of; Rational Expectations; Unanticipated Inflation.

Appreciation (Nominal) of a Currency

An increase in the price of one currency in terms of other currencies in a flexible exchange rate system; an increase in the nominal exchange rate in a flexible exchange rate system.

See also:
Flexible Exchange Rate System; Nominal Exchange Rate.

Assignment Problem

The problem of assigning each policy instrument to the ultimate policy objective or target on which it has the most influence. For example, in the IS–LM (Mundell–Fleming) model of the open economy this involves the assignment of monetary policy to attain external balance (balance of payments equilibrium on the combined current and capital accounts) and fiscal policy to attain internal balance (full employment).

See also:
IS–LM model: Open Economy; Mundell, Robert A.

Asymmetric Information

Asymmetric information occurs where parties to a market transaction possess different information about the good, service or asset that is being traded. The labour market is a good example of a market where asymmetric information predominates. Applicants for a job will, for example, have more information about their abilities, honesty and commitment than potential employers. Asymmetric information is one reason why firms may offer higher wages not only to attract the best or most productive applicants but also to deter the most productive workers from quitting, in line with the adverse selection model. The reader is referred to B. Hillier, *The Economics of Asymmetric Information* (Macmillan, 1997) for an accessible discussion of recent developments in the economics of asymmetric information, including the markets for investment, insurance and labour.

See also:
Adverse Selection Model; Akerlof, George A.; Stiglitz, Joseph E.

Automatic Stabilizers

Automatic stabilizers exist within an economy where there is a built-in mechanism that *automatically* produces offsetting changes to current movements in GNP. The most important examples arise from the government's budget position and include progressive income tax and unemployment insurance. For example, in a recession when GNP falls the government's tax receipts fall, while at the same time unemployment insurance payments increase as unemployment rises. These arrangements prevent the fall (or rise in the case of an upturn in economic activity) in

GNP from being as large as it would otherwise have been in their absence. As a result, they reduce the severity of cyclical fluctuations in the economy. One of the main advantages of built-in stabilizers is that they operate automatically without a planned or discretionary policy change being initiated by the government. In other words, with automatic stabilizers there is no inside lag. Furthermore, by reducing the size of the multiplier, automatic stabilizers reduce the extent of economic fluctuations due to autonomous disturbances in aggregate demand.

See also:
Budget Balance; Inside Lag; Multiplier.

Autonomous Expenditure

Expenditure that does not depend on the level of income. For example, in the Keynesian cross model government expenditure (G), investment expenditure (I) and exports (X) are assumed to be independent of the level of income.

See also:
Keynesian Cross.

Average Propensity to Consume

Aggregate consumption (C) expressed as a proportion of aggregate income (Y). The average propensity to consume (C/Y) can be expressed as the ratio of aggregate consumer expenditure to either aggregate disposable income or national income. The average propensity to consume will equal the marginal propensity to consume when the consumption function (a) is linear and (b) passes through the origin.

See also:
Absolute Income Hypothesis; Consumption Function; Disposable Income; Marginal Propensity to Consume; National Income; Permanent Income Hypothesis; Relative Income Hypothesis.

Average Propensity to Save

Aggregate savings (S) expressed as a proportion of aggregate income (Y). The average propensity to save (S/Y) can be expressed as the ratio of savings to either aggregate disposable income or national income.

See also:
Disposable Income; National Income.

Average Tax Rate

Total tax payments expressed as a proportion of total income. While the concept can be applied in the context of a variety of taxes, more often than not it is used to express the fraction of total income paid in income tax.

Balance of Payments

The balance of payments is an accounting record of a country's international transactions with the rest of the world over a given time period (for example, a year). All receipts from non-residents are termed credits and give rise to supplies of foreign currency and a demand for domestic currency. In contrast, all payments by residents to non-residents are termed debits and give rise to a demand for foreign currency and supplies of domestic currency. Credits and debits in the balance of payments can arise from transactions in (a) goods and services, which are recorded in the current account, and (b) capital assets (both real and financial), which are recorded in the capital account. The current account will be in deficit when the total value of imported goods and services is greater than the total value of goods and services exported, and vice versa. The capital account will be in deficit when outflows of capital (for example to finance overseas investment) are greater than inflows of capital, and vice versa. In both cases a deficit corresponds to a situation where payments (debits) to non-residents are greater than receipts (credits) from abroad. Conversely, a surplus corresponds to a situation where receipts (credits) from non-residents are greater than payments (debits) abroad. As a financial statement, the overall balance of payments (on the combined current and capital accounts) should sum to zero, with a deficit on the current account offset by a surplus on the capital account, and vice versa.

Under a system of flexible exchange rates the exchange rate adjusts to clear the foreign exchange market, ensuring overall balance of payments equilibrium. In contrast, under a system of fixed exchange rates it is possible for a country, at least in the short run, to experience balance of payments disequilibria (deficits and surpluses). Deficits may be financed by running down gold and foreign currency reserves and/or government borrowing from abroad, while surpluses allow a country to add to its reserves and/or repay official government debt. Three main approaches to remedy balance of payments disequilibria can be found in the literature. The elasticities approach examines the conditions under which devaluation will be successful in remedying a balance of payments deficit on the current account. The absorption approach also examines the way in which government policy intervention can improve the current account of the balance of payments. In contrast, the monetary approach concentrates on the sum of the current and capital accounts and views the balance of payments as essentially a monetary phenomenon with an automatic adjustment mechanism.

See also:

Absorption Approach to the Balance of Payments; Balance of Payments: Keynesian Approach; Balance of Payments: Monetary Approach; Devaluation; Elasticities Approach to the Balance of Payments; Fixed Exchange Rate System; Flexible Exchange Rate System.

Balance of Payments-constrained Economic Growth

The balance of payments-constrained growth model provides a Keynesian demand-oriented explanation of why growth rates differ. This approach stands in marked contrast to the neoclassical growth theory (whether of the Solow–Swan or the endogenous variety), with the latter's emphasis on the role of the supply side. The central tenet of the balance of payments-constrained growth model is that a country cannot run a balance of payments deficit for any length of time that has to be financed by short-term capital flows and which results in an increasing net foreign debt-to-GDP ratio. If a country attempts to do this, the operation of the international financial markets will lead to increasing downward pressure on the currency, with the danger of a collapse in the exchange rate and the risk of a resulting depreciation/inflation spiral. There is also the possibility that the country's international credit rating will be downgraded. Consequently, in the long run, the basic balance (current account plus long-term capital flows) has to be in equilibrium. An implication of this approach is that there is nothing that guarantees that this rate will be the one consistent with the full employment of resources or the growth of the productive potential.

The main elements of this approach are set out in Thirlwall's (1979) seminal paper, which has its antecedents in the cumulative causation growth model as set out by Myrdal (1957) and subsequently developed by Kaldor (1966, 1970). (Toner, 1999, provides a detailed discussion of the development of this approach from Young's 1928 influential paper to Kaldor.) Kaldor emphasized, in particular, the role of the Verdoorn law (the empirical relationship between industrial productivity and output growth) in explaining disparities in productivity growth rates (see Verdoorn, 1949; McCombie and Thirlwall, 1994, ch. 2). The law is interpreted as showing that a faster growth of manufacturing output causes a faster growth of productivity through induced capital accumulation and economies of scale. The latter are defined broadly to include not only static but also dynamic increasing returns to scale (for example, those arising from learning-by-doing). A key assumption of this approach is that output growth is fundamentally determined by the growth of demand, most notably that derived from the growth of exports through the Harrod foreign trade multiplier. The growth of exports, in turn, is specified as a function of the growth of world income and the rate of change of relative prices. A formalization of this approach is to be found in Dixon and Thirlwall (1975). However, as Thirlwall and Dixon (1979) noted, there was no balance of payments constraint in this model and so there was nothing to ensure that exports could not grow indefinitely faster than imports, or vice versa.

The subsequent model of Thirlwall (1979) and Thirlwall and Dixon (1979) expressly addressed this shortcoming. The growth of exports is again determined by the growth of world income and the rate of change of relative prices. The growth of imports is specified as a function of the growth of domestic income, together with the rate of change of relative prices. Substituting these into the definitional equation for the balance of payments, expressed in growth rate form, gives the growth of domestic income as a function of the growth of world income, the rate of change of relative prices and the growth of net international capital flows.

If the impact of the last two on economic growth is quantitatively negligible (as empirically is the case), the growth rate of income consistent with balance of payments equilibrium is given by $y_B = \varepsilon z/\pi = x/\pi$ where ε, π, z and x are the world income elasticity of demand for exports, the domestic income elasticity of demand for imports, the growth of world income, and the growth of exports. These two equations for y_B are alternative specifications of what has come to be known as 'Thirlwall's law'. It can be seen that once again the key factor determining the growth of a country is the growth of the exogenous component of demand, that is, exports, which in turn is determined by the growth of world markets. Thus the model is an extension of the export-led growth hypothesis, but where the balance of payments constraint is now explicitly incorporated.

There are substantial differences between countries in their values of ε (and of π) and hence in how fast these economies can grow without encountering balance of payments problems. The disparities in ε and π are interpreted as reflecting differences in non-price competitiveness (for example, differences in the quality of goods and services, the effectiveness of a country's distribution network, delivery dates, and so on). Thus the supply side is important to the extent that these supply characteristics play a crucial role in explaining the growth of exports and, hence, income. This stands in marked contrast to the way in which the neoclassical approach emphasizes the supply side, where technical change and the growth of factor inputs are the causal factors in the growth process.

A necessary condition for the balance of payments constraint to be binding is that the rate of change of the exchange rate is ineffective in determining the growth of exports and imports. If this were not the case, real exchange rate adjustments could ensure that the balance of payments was brought into equilibrium at any given rate of the growth of income, including the growth of productive potential. However, it should be emphasized that the balance of payments-constrained growth model does not imply that changes in relative prices have *no* effect on the current account. It may be that changes in these are sufficient to bring a current account deficit back into equilibrium when, for example, the economy is growing at or near its balance of payments equilibrium rate, but they are unlikely to be sufficient to raise the balance of payments equilibrium growth rate, *per se*. Given the multiplicative nature of the export and import demand functions, to achieve the latter would require a sustained real depreciation.

This approach thus differs from the earlier cumulative causation models where changes in relative prices are important in providing a positive feedback from productivity to output growth. While the Verdoorn law does not explicitly appear in Thirlwall's law, this does not mean that it does not have an important role to play. The benefits of a faster growth of productivity are not passed on through improving relative price competitiveness, but lead to a faster growth of the real wage. While the ratio of the income elasticity of demand for exports to that of imports is taken as exogenous in the balance of payments-constrained equilibrium growth model, in the long run it is likely to be a function of the rate of growth of output (that is, the value of the ratio is 'deeply endogenous'). A faster growth of output and capital accumulation is likely to lead not only to greater process, but also product, inventions and innovations. This may lead to increased non-price competitiveness and consequently further raise the growth rate. On the other hand, it is possible that a faster growth of output could eventually lead to the economy becoming 'locked-in' to what eventually proves to be an inferior technology (Setterfield, 1997). In this way, virtuous and vicious circles of growth may result.

Thirlwall's law may be regarded as a dynamic version of Harrod's foreign trade multiplier. Harrod (1933) in his book, *International Economics*, put forward the view that the level of output of industrial economies is explained by the principle of the foreign trade multiplier, which at the same time provides the mechanism for keeping the balance of payments in equilibrium. In the simplest case with no government and no saving and investment, trade is always balanced and, in the absence of any change in relative prices, the level of income Y is given by $Y = X/m$, where X is the volume of exports and m is the marginal propensity to import. Thirlwall has shown that the expression for the balance of payments equilibrium growth rate is essentially a dynamic version of the Harrod foreign trade multiplier. (Thirlwall, 1997, provides a discussion of the history of the development of the law and its antecedents.)

McCombie (1985) demonstrated that, in a more complex Keynesian model, Thirlwall's law could be more generally regarded as the workings of the Hicks 'super-multiplier'. An increase in export growth from, for example, a position of current account equilibrium would increase the growth of income directly through the Harrod foreign trade multiplier. Moreover, at the same time, by generating an increasing current account surplus, it allows a further increase in the growth of other domestic components of demand to occur, thereby raising the growth rate even further, until the balance of payments is brought back into equilibrium again. The combined effect of these two mechanisms represents the operation of the Hicks 'super-multiplier' in dynamic form.

There have been an increasing number of studies that have tested this approach to economic growth. The general methodology is to estimate the values ε and π for a particular country from export and import demand functions (which include relative price terms) using time-series data. In the original studies, ordinary least squares was used, but recently more sophisticated econometric techniques have been adopted, such as those that test for stationarity and cointegration of the data. From the estimates of ε and π, a value for the balance of payments equilibrium growth rate can be obtained using the expression for Thirlwall's law, $y_B = \varepsilon z / \pi$ (alternatively, $y_B = x / \pi$ is sometimes used). The balance of payments equilibrium growth rate, when calculated over a period of a decade or longer, is often found to be very close to the actual growth rate and this has been confirmed by a variety of statistical tests. It is also commonly found that the estimates of the price elasticities in the export and import demand functions are either small or statistically insignificant, or both. This provides further evidence of the unimportance of price competition in international trade. See McCombie and Thirlwall (1994) and the minisymposium in the 1997 edition of the *Journal of Post Keynesian Economics* (Davidson, 1997).

Of course, all countries will not necessarily be simultaneously balance of payments-constrained. At any one time, some countries (or trading blocs) may be 'policy constrained', where demand management policies have resulted in the actual growth of income being below the balance of payments equilibrium growth rate. This occurred in the 1970s and 1980s in some advanced countries where governments attempted to curtail the rate of growth of inflation by using deflationary policies. Other countries may be growing so fast that they are 'resource constrained', as with Japan in the early post-World War II period. The problem is that the balance of payments-constrained countries find that their growth rates are effectively limited by the growth of these policy- and resource-constrained countries. If, for example, a particular country curtails its growth for policy reasons, its major trading partners are going to find that their balance of payments

equilibrium growth rates fall. Their actual rate of growth will then be curtailed, regardless of whether or not the conditions in their domestic market
warrant this (McCombie, 1993).

The approach does not just apply to countries with national currencies,
but the principle holds at the regional level (Thirlwall, 1980). This suggests
that the formation of a monetary union, such as the EMU, will not remove
the importance of export growth and the balance of payments in determining the overall growth rate of a country.

There have been a number of criticisms of this approach to economic
growth. McCombie and Thirlwall (1994) contains a lively interchange with
McGregor & Swales, that first appeared in *Applied Economics*, over such
issues as the direction of causation, whether the model captures non-price
competitiveness, and whether the 'law of one price' renders the model incoherent. (It is important not to confuse the small variation in relative prices
due to the reasons set out above with the neoclassical 'law of one price'. The
latter, with its assumptions of competitive markets and that the price elasticity of demand of exports is infinite for a small open economy, does imply
that countries cannot be balance of payments-constrained. However, in
practice, prices are determined in oligopolistic markets and are sticky for
the reasons noted above.)

Krugman (1989) rediscovered the law, which he termed 'the 45-degree
rule'. This is because one country's growth relative to all others will be equiproportional to the ratio of the income elasticity of demand for its exports
to the income elasticity of demand for its imports. The relationship between
a country's growth rate and the values of ε and π are interpreted in a neoclassical manner and not as reflecting the Harrod foreign trade multiplier.
Krugman develops a model based on monopolistic competition and
increasing returns to scale. The number of product varieties produced in a
country is assumed to be proportional to its effective labour force, where
the latter is taken to be a measure of resource availability. As a country's
growth rate increases, so does the number of varieties it produces, and this
increases both its share in world markets and its value of ε. Hence the latter
is assumed to be determined endogenously. If this were true, it would mean
that a faster growth of the UK would suddenly raise the growth of its
exports and reduce the income elasticity of demand for imports such as to
prevent a deficit from arising with no downward pressure on the exchange
rate. This is implausible and contrary to the historical experience.

Crafts (1988) notes that if, for example, the UK had maintained its share
in its overseas markets, its 'hypothetical' or 'constant-market-share' income
elasticity of demand for its exports would have been comparable in size
with those of the other advanced countries (which all tend to be roughly
equal). Consequently, its hypothetical growth rate of exports would have

been the same as those of the other countries. Hence, using the constant-market-share estimates of ε, it is argued that the UK's balance of payments equilibrium growth rate is approximately the same as those of the other advanced countries, including Japan. But all this shows is that, if the UK had matched, say, Japan in terms of its non-price competitiveness, its hypo-thetical balance-of-payments growth rate would have been the same as Japan's. But the fact is that it did not, and the estimates of the hypothetical income elasticities have no relevance at all as to whether the UK's growth was actually balance of payments constrained. All these critiques are assessed in greater detail in McCombie and Thirlwall (1997).

In conclusion, Davidson (1990–91) has summarized this approach as a significant contribution to Post Keynesian economic theory in its demon-stration that 'international payments imbalances can have severe real growth consequences, i.e. money is not neutral in an open economy'.

JOHN S.L. McCOMBIE

See also:

Balance of Payments; Marshall–Lerner Condition; Multiplier; Neoclassical Growth Model; Post Keynesian Economics.

Bibliography

Crafts, N. (1988), 'The Assessment: British Economic Growth over the Long Run', *Oxford Review of Economic Policy*, **4**, Spring, pp. i–xxi.
Davidson, P. (1990–91), 'A Post Keynesian Positive Contribution to "Theory"', *Journal of Post Keynesian Economics*, **13**, Winter, pp. 298–303.
Davidson, P. (1997), 'Minisymposium on Thirlwall's Law and Economic Growth in an Open Economy Context', *Journal of Post Keynesian Economics*, **19**, Spring pp. 318–85.
Dixon, R.J. and A.P. Thirlwall (1975), 'A Model of Regional Growth-Rate Differences on Kaldorian Lines', *Oxford Economic Papers*, **27**, July, pp. 201–14.
Harrod, R.F. (1933), *International Economics*, Cambridge: Cambridge University Press.
Kaldor, N. (1966), *The Causes of the Slow Rate of Economic Growth of the United Kingdom: An Inaugural Lecture*, Cambridge: Cambridge University Press.
Kaldor, N. (1970), 'The Case for Regional Policies', *Scottish Journal of Political Economy*, **17**, November, pp. 337–48.
Krugman, P. (1989), 'Differences in Income Elasticities and Trends in Real Exchange Rates', *European Economic Review*, **33**, May, pp. 1031–46.
McCombie, J.S.L. (1985), 'Economic Growth, the Harrod Foreign Trade Multiplier and the Hicks Super-Multiplier', *Applied Economics*, **17**, February, pp. 52–72.
McCombie, J.S.L. (1993), 'Economic Growth, Trade Interlinkages, and the Balance-of-Payments Constraint', *Journal of Post Keynesian Economics*, **15**, Summer, pp. 471–505.
McCombie J.S.L. and A.P. Thirlwall (1994), *Economic Growth and the Balance-of-Payments Constraint*, Basingstoke: Macmillan.
McCombie J.S.L. and A.P. Thirlwall (1997), 'The Dynamic Harrod Foreign Trade Multiplier and the Demand-Oriented Approach to Economic Growth', *International Review of Applied Economics*, **11**, January, pp. 5–25.
Myrdal, G. (1957), *Economic Theory and the Underdeveloped Countries*, London: Duckworth.
Setterfield, M. (1997), *Rapid Growth and Relative Decline: Modelling Macroeconomic Dynamics with Hysteresis*, Basingstoke: Macmillan.
Thirlwall, A.P. (1979), 'The Balance of Payments Constraint as an Explanation of

International Growth Rate Differences', *Banca Nazionale del Lavoro Quarterly Review*, **128**, March, pp. 45–53.

Thirlwall, A.P. (1980), 'Regional Problems are 'Balance-of-Payments' Problems', *Regional Studies*, **14**, July, pp. 419–26.

Thirlwall, A.P. (1997), 'Reflections on the Concept of Balance-of-Payments-Constrained Growth', *Journal of Post Keynesian Economics*, **19**, Spring, pp. 375–85.

Thirlwall A.P. and R.J. Dixon (1979), 'A Model of Export-Led Growth with a Balance of Payments Constraint', in J.K. Bowers (ed.), *Inflation, Development and Integration*, Leeds: Leeds University Press.

Toner, P. (1999), *Main Currents in Cumulative Causation: The Dynamics of Growth and Development*, Basingstoke: Macmillan.

Verdoorn P.J. (1949), 'Fattori che Regolano lo Sviluppo della Produttività del Lavoro', *L'Industria*, 1, pp. 3–10; English translation by A.P. Thirlwall, 'Factors Governing the Growth of Labour Productivity', in D. Ironmonger, J.O.N. Perkins and T. Van Hoa (eds) (1988), *National Income and Economic Progress*, London: Macmillan Press.

Young, A.A. (1928), 'Increasing Returns and Economic Progress', *Economic Journal*, **38**, December, pp. 527–42.

Balance of Payments: Keynesian Approach

The balance of payments, summarizing a country's transactions with the rest of the world, consists of the current account (net sales of goods and services to the rest of the world), the capital account (net sales of assets to the rest of the world) and the official settlements balance (change in official reserves of gold and foreign currency). The Keynesian approach to international macroeconomic adjustment emphasizes the determination of real national income and its effect on the current account, in contrast to the emphasis of the monetary approach on the supply of and demand for money.

Although Keynes's *General Theory* dealt formally with a closed economy, Keynes had a longstanding concern with balance of payments constraints on national stabilization policies, with the deflationary bias of the gold standard and with the avoidance of international monetary disorder. In *A Tract on Monetary Reform* (1923), Keynes, still writing as an orthodox follower of Alfred Marshall, applied the Cambridge cash balance version of the quantity theory of money to explain the collapsing exchange rates of German and other Central European currencies after World War I, introducing the concept of covered interest parity (the premium or discount in the forward exchange market equals the nominal interest differential between two countries). He discussed how observed deviations from purchasing power parity could occur despite arbitrage, because the same goods have different weights in the price indexes of different countries. Keynes (1925) protested against Britain's return to the gold standard at the prewar parity because the resulting price deflation would increase unemployment, given downward stickiness of nominal wages (as well as redistributing wealth from taxpayers to bondholders). Ironically, Keynes (1929), analysing the balance of payments problems of German reparations payments, emphasized changes in prices in paying and receiving countries, while Bertil Ohlin (1929) stressed the equilibrating role of changes in national income. Above all, Keynes (1983) was one of the principal architects of the Bretton Woods monetary settlement establishing the International Monetary Fund and the World Bank after World War II, with a system of fixed exchange rates with adjustable pegs. However, the settlement did not go nearly as far as he wished in ensuring the liquidity of the international monetary system or in placing the burden of balance of payments adjustment on surplus countries as well as on deficit countries (Thirlwall, 1976). Keynes favoured controls on international portfolio investment to preserve national autonomy of interest rates, and wished to dampen speculation (Dimand and Dore, 2000). Keynes (1946) doubted that the dollar shortage was a permanent problem, and saw a role for policy in accelerating the classical forces of balance of payments adjustment, rather than replacing them.

Fritz Machlup (1943) extended the multiplier analysis of income determination to open economies, incorporating net exports in aggregate expenditure and adding the marginal propensity to import to the tax rate and the marginal propensity to save in the denominator of the multiplier, which reduced the multiplier from what it would be in a closed economy. (Some of the earliest formulations of the multiplier by R.G. Hawtrey and L.F. Giblin had included only the marginal propensity to import in the denominator.) Exports increase with foreign income and with the real exchange rate, the terms of trade eP^*/P (where P^* is the foreign price level, P the domestic price level and e the domestic currency price of foreign exchange). Imports increase with domestic income and decrease with eP^*/P. Machlup's framework, which remains standard in introductory macroeconomics courses, permitted analysis of the international transmission of spending shocks through the trade balance. In this model, income can be at its equilibrium level without the current account being zero.

The absorption, internal balance/external balance, and elasticities approaches of Joan Robinson (1947), James Meade (1951) and Sidney Alexander (1952) extended this multiplier analysis by equating the trade balance to the difference between output and domestic absorption, and by considering the effect on the trade balance of a change in terms of trade (for instance, due to devaluation of the currency). Empirical studies in the late 1940s and the 1950s often expressed 'elasticity pessimism', finding the price elasticities of imports and exports were too small in absolute value to satisfy the Marshall–Lerner condition for stability, so devaluation of a fixed exchange rate or depreciation of a flexible exchange rate could not eliminate a current account deficit. In contrast, the later monetary approach to the balance of payments, viewing foreign and domestic goods as perfect or near-perfect substitutes, has considered the long-run price elasticity of exports and imports as tending towards infinity for small open economies. The Keynesian approach has treated foreign and domestic goods as substitutes but imperfect ones since, by comparative advantage and the international division of labour, countries specialize in producing different goods. Keynesian analyses in the 1950s pointed to a need for expenditure-reducing or expenditure-switching fiscal policy to remedy a persistent current account deficit and for expenditure switching to achieve compatibility of internal balance (full employment equilibrium) with external balance.

In the early 1960s, the IS–LM model was extended to open economies by J. Marcus Fleming (1962) and Robert Mundell (papers collected in Mundell, 1968). The resulting IS–LM–BP diagram in interest and income space had curves representing equilibrium for the goods market (the *IS* curve, investment = saving), the money market (the *LM* curve, liquidity preference = money supply) and the foreign exchange market (the *BP* curve, balance of payments = excess supply of foreign exchange = zero). If there is perfect capital mobility (perfect substitution between foreign and domestic assets), the *BP* curve of a small open economy will be horizontal at the foreign interest rate (a small economy being one that has no effect on foreign variables). With a fixed exchange rate, the equilibrium levels of income and interest (for a given price level) are given by the intersection of the *IS* and *BP* curves. Monetary policy has no effect on aggregate demand under fixed exchange rates because a balance of payments surplus or deficit equates to purchases or sales of foreign exchange by the central bank, changing the money supply and shifting the *LM* curve to pass through the *IS/BP* intersection (assuming no offsetting trades by the central bank in the domestic bond market). Fiscal policy is effective in changing aggregate demand under fixed exchange rates, with the only crowding out reflecting an upward slope of the *BP* curve. If the *BP* curve is horizontal (perfect substitution between foreign and domestic assets) and exchange rates are fixed, fiscal policy has its full multiplier effect on aggregate demand with no crowding out of private investment. With flexible exchange rates, monetary policy determines aggregate demand, affecting net exports through exchange depreciation or appreciation. With a fixed money supply and flexible exchange rate, external shocks to the current account (but not changes in foreign interest rates) are wholly absorbed by the exchange rate. Fiscal policy, on the other hand, crowds out net exports under flexible exchange rates (see Frenkel and Razin, 1987). Tobin and de Macedo (1980) show that these strong propositions about the effectiveness of monetary and fiscal policy and insulation about external shocks are sensitive to the way in which asset markets are modelled, and depend on the exclusion of exchange rates from asset demand functions.

Such Keynesian approaches treat the exchange rate as part of the relative price of foreign and domestic goods, and emphasize income and relative price effects on the current account. The monetary approach (to which Mundell contributed later in the 1960s) takes $eP^*/P = 1$ (purchasing power parity) and, at least in later New Classical versions, $Y = Y^*$ (potential output), so it excludes such income and relative price effects and relates the current account balance to the excess demand for money. The monetary approach treats the exchange rate as the relative price of two assets. The Keynesian approach pays more attention to the determination of real national income, the monetary approach to the international transmission of inflation. Aspects of both approaches can be incorporated in a more general portfolio model with more asset markets (Frenkel *et al.*, 1980; Gylfason and Helliwell, 1983). In addition to the challenge from the monetary approach, the Mundell–Fleming IS–LM–BP Keynesian approach has been criticized by Post Keynesians such as Davidson (1992) for neglect of uncertainty and of the fragility of the international financial system in the face of speculation.

ROBERT W. DIMAND

See also:

Absorption Approach to the Balance of Payments; Balance of Payments; Balance of Payments-constrained Economic Growth; Balance of Payments: Monetary Approach; Bretton Woods; Elasticities Approach to the Balance of Payments; Expenditure Reducing Policy; Expenditure Switching Policy; Fixed Exchange Rate System; Flexible Exchange Rate System; Gold Standard; IS–LM Model: Open Economy; Marshall–Lerner Condition; Multiplier; Mundell, Robert A.; Purchasing Power Parity Theory.

Bibliography

Alexander, S.S. (1952), 'Effects of a Devaluation on a Trade Balance', *International Monetary Fund Staff Papers*, **2**, pp. 263–78.
Arize, A., T.H. Bonitsis, I. Kallianiotis, K. Kasibhatla and J. Malindretos (eds) (2000), *Balance of Payments Adjustment: Macro Facets of International Finance Revisited*, Westport, CT: Greenwood Press.
Davidson, P. (1992), *International Money and the Real World*, 2nd edn, London: Macmillan.
Dimand, R.W., and M.H.I. Dore (2000), 'Keynes's Casino Capitalism, Bagehot's International Currency, and the Tobin Tax: Historical Notes on Preventing Currency Fires', *Journal of Post Keynesian Economics*, **22**, Summer, pp. 515–28.
Fleming, J.M. (1962), 'Domestic Financial Policies Under Fixed and Floating Exchange Rates', *International Monetary Fund Staff Papers*, **9**, November, pp. 369–79.
Frenkel, J., and A. Razin (1987), 'The Mundell–Fleming Model a Quarter Century Later: A Unified Exposition', *International Monetary Fund Staff Papers*, **34**, December, pp. 567–620.
Frenkel, J., T. Gylfason and J. Helliwell (1980), 'A Synthesis of Monetary and Keynesian Approaches to Short-Run Balance of Payments Theory', *Economic Journal*, **90**, September, pp. 582–92.

Gylfason, T. and J. Helliwell (1983), 'A Synthesis of Keynesian, Monetary and Portfolio Approaches to Flexible Exchange Rates', *Economic Journal*, **93**, December, pp. 820–31.

Keynes, J.M. (1923), *A Tract on Monetary Reform*, London: Macmillan.

Keynes, J.M. (1925), *The Economic Consequences of Mr. Churchill*, London: Hogarth Press.

Keynes, J.M. (1929), 'The German Transfer Problem', *Economic Journal*, **39**, March, pp. 1–7.

Keynes, J.M. (1946), 'The Balance of Payments of the United States', *Economic Journal*, **56**, April, pp. 172–87.

Keynes, J.M. (1983), *Collected Writings*, eds D.E. Moggridge and E.A.G. Robinson, vols 25 and 26, ed. D.E. Moggridge, London: Macmillan and New York: Cambridge University Press, for the Royal Economic Society.

Machlup, F. (1943), *International Trade and the National Income Multiplier*, Philadelphia: Blakiston; reprinted in R.W. Dimand (ed.), *Origins of Macroeconomics*, London and New York: Routledge, 2001.

Meade, J.E. (1951), *The Theory of International Economic Policy*, vol. 1: *The Balance of Payments*, London: Oxford University Press.

Mundell, R.A. (1968), *International Economics*, New York: Macmillan.

Ohlin, B. (1929), 'The Reparation Problem: A Discussion', *Economic Journal*, **39**, June, pp. 172–8.

Robinson, J. (1947), 'The Foreign Exchanges', *Essays in the Theory of Employment*, 2nd edn, Oxford: Basil Blackwell.

Thirlwall, A.P. (ed.) (1976), *Keynes and International Monetary Relations*, London: Macmillan and New York: St Martin's.

Tobin, J. and J.B. de Macedo (1980), 'The Short-Run Macroeconomics of Floating Exchange Rates: An Exposition', in J. Chipman and C. Kindleberger (eds), *Flexible Exchange Rates and the Balance of Payments: Essays In Memory of Egon Sohmen*, Amsterdam: North-Holland, pp. 5–28.

Balance of Payments: Monetary Approach

With intellectual roots tracing back at least to Adam Smith's *Wealth of Nations*, the monetary approach to the balance of payments consists of a conceptual framework for analysing how integrated open national economies eliminate their excess money supplies and demands in a regime of fixed exchange rates. The framework, as developed by James Meade in 1952, by Jacques J. Polak and his associates at the International Monetary Fund in the late 1950s, and by Robert A. Mundell and Harry G. Johnson and their students at the University of Chicago in the 1960s and 1970s, distinguishes between the individual small open economy and the closed world aggregate of which it is a part.

In the case of the closed world aggregate, all the familiar propositions of the closed-economy quantity theory hold. World money supply (the sum of the national money stocks expressed in terms of a common monetary unit at the fixed exchange rate) and world money demand determine the world price level. That price level adjusts to clear the world market for money balances by equating the real, or price-deflated, value of the nominal money stock with the real demand for it so that all money is willingly held. Any rise in the nominal money stock such that actual real money balances exceed desired ones produces a rise in world prices that restores monetary equilibrium by adjusting actual to desired real balances. For the closed world economy, price-level changes constitute the adjustment mechanism that equilibrates money supply and demand, and the quantity theory holds in the sense of causation running unidirectionally from money to prices.

In the case of the small open economy operating under fixed exchange rates and trading its goods on unified world markets, however, adjustment cannot occur solely through price-level changes since prices are determined on world markets and given exogenously to the small open economy. Instead, adjustment takes place through the balance of payments as domestic residents export money in exchange for imports of goods and securities to rid themselves of an excess money supply just as they export goods and securities for imports of money to eliminate an excess money demand. In short, for the small open economy, a rise in the nominal money supply such that actual real cash balances exceed desired ones generates a balance of payments deficit and a corresponding monetary outflow that eliminates the monetary excess and restores monetary equilibrium. Conversely, a rise in the world (and hence domestic) price level such that actual real cash balances fall short of desired real cash balances induces a temporary balance of payments surplus as domestic residents act to correct the monetary shortfall by exporting goods in exchange for imports of money. Here, flows of money through the balance of payments constitute the adjustment mechanism that equilibrates money supply and demand and causality runs from prices to money rather than vice versa as in the quantity theory.

To illustrate how the small open economy achieves monetary equilibrium through the balance of payments, proponents of the monetary approach employ a simple small-economy expository model consisting of the following four equations:

$$D = kPY. \tag{1}$$

$$M = C + R. \tag{2}$$

$$P = eP^*. \tag{3}$$

$$M = D. \tag{4}$$

Equation (1) expresses the public's demand for money D as the product of the domestic price level P, the level of real output Y and the fraction k of nominal income PY that people want to hold in the form of cash balances. The price level P is treated as given on the grounds that the small open economy is too small to influence world prices and thus is a price taker on world markets. Likewise, real output *Y* is treated as given on the grounds that the small open economy can sell all it wishes on the world market at given world prices and thus always produces the full-capacity level of output.

Equation (2) defines the money stock *M* in terms of its source components, or assets backing it, namely domestic credit *C* extended by the consolidated banking system (commercial banks plus the central bank) and foreign exchange reserves *R* acquired through the balance of payments. Of these two components, only domestic credit *C* is exogenous and under the control of the central bank. By contrast, the foreign reserve component *R* is endogenous and responds passively through the balance of payments to changes in money demand.

Equation (3) expresses the purchasing power parity condition, or law of one price, according to which the price-equalizing effect of commodity arbitrage renders the prices *P* of domestic goods (all of which are traded) the same as their world prices *P** expressed in terms of domestic currency units at the fixed exchange rate *e*. Both world prices *P** and the exchange rate *e* (the home currency price of a unit of foreign currency) are taken as given, which means that domestic prices *P* are determined on world markets and given exogenously to the small open economy.

Equation (4) is the monetary equilibrium condition according to which money supply *M* must equal money demand *D* so that all money is willingly held and the market for cash balances clears. With the stock of domestic credit *C* given, monetary demand-and-supply equilibrium is achieved via flows of foreign reserves through the balance of payments according to the equation

$$R = keP^*Y - C, \tag{5}$$

obtained by substituting equations (1) to (3) into equation (4) and then solving for reserves *R*. This equation says that, under fixed exchange rates, the small open economy's stock of foreign exchange reserves *R* must adjust to accommodate changes in real output *Y*, world prices *P**, the public's cash balance ratio *k*, and domestic credit *C*. In short, the model states that reserve flows through the balance of payments adjust to maintain monetary equilibrium in the face of autonomous shifts in the determinants of money supply and demand.

Recognizing that the change in reserves *dR/dt* is by definition the state of the balance of payments *B*, advocates of the monetary approach summarize the self-equilibrating role of reserve flows through the balance of payments in the form of the expression

$$B = dR/dt = b(D - M). \tag{6}$$

Equation (6) says that the state of the balance of payments B and the associated change in reserves dR/dt depends upon the excess demand for money $D - M$, being positive when there is excess money demand, negative when there is excess money supply and zero in the absence of excess money supply or demand. In short, the equation implies that reserve flows act to correct the very monetary disequilibrium that precipitates them and do so at a pace represented by the speed-of-adjustment parameter b. Here then is the key idea of the monetary approach, namely that when actual cash balances fall short of desired ones people correct the discrepancy by exporting domestic goods and securities in exchange for imports of money. In this way, for example, real growth in the open economy, if unaccommodated by domestic credit expansion, attracts from abroad the extra money necessary to support it. Such growth, by raising real output Y and thus the demand for money relative to the money supply, produces a temporary trade balance surplus financed by reserve inflows that restore equality between monetary demand and supply.

The foregoing model yields six hallmark propositions that characterize and identify the monetary approach.

Price level exogeneity
The price level is determined in world markets and given exogenously to the small open economy, which operates as a price taker when buying and selling its goods internationally.

Money stock endogeneity
A small open economy's money stock is an endogenous variable that adapts to money demand through reserve flows through the balance of payments.

Money stock composition
Monetary authorities in the small open economy can control the composition but not the total of the money stock. Given the public's demand for money D, a policy-engineered rise in the domestic credit component C of the money stock induces an equal and offsetting fall in the foreign reserve component R, leaving the total stock unchanged as indicated by the expression $D = C + R$.

Price-to-money causality
Causality runs from prices to money in the small open economy. Determined on world markets, prices are given exogenously to the small open economy by the operation of commodity arbitrage, which ensures that prices tend to be everywhere the same. Money then flows in through the balance of payments to support or validate the given prices. In this way,

causality runs in reverse direction from prices to money in the small open economy, contrary to the predictions of the quantity theory. That is, while the quantity theory applies at the level of the closed world economy, it does not apply to the small open economy operating under fixed exchange rates.

Adjustment through direct expenditure rather than relative price channels
In the small open economy, money stock adjustment takes place through a direct spending mechanism rather than through a relative price, or price-specie-flow, mechanism. David Hume posited the latter mechanism in 1752 when he argued that home country prices must rise relative to foreign prices to render exports dear and imports cheap and so, by discouraging exports and encouraging imports, produce the trade balance deficit that rids the home country of an excess money stock. Conversely, in the case of a shortage of money, Hume thought that home prices must fall relative to foreign prices so as to produce the trade surplus financed by an inflow of reserves that ends the shortage. But the monetary approach, by contrast, rules out this Humean relative price mechanism on the grounds that commodity arbitrage renders the price of traded goods everywhere the same so that (assuming all goods are traded) domestic prices cannot rise or fall relative to foreign prices. With divergent price movements ruled out, adjustment of actual to desired money balances must occur entirely through changes in spending. Therefore an excess money supply, because it must be spent away, leads to a rise in expenditure that, because consumers are already buying all the output the economy is capable of producing, spills over into the balance of payments in the form of an increased demand for imports. The resulting trade balance deficit, financed by outflows of foreign reserves, shrinks the money supply into equality with money demand.

Neutrality of money
Changes in the nominal money stock and its components have no lasting effect on real variables such as output, real money stocks, or the balance of payments.

Embodying the foregoing propositions, the monetary approach yields its hallmark conclusion that traditional monetary and balance of payments policies are unnecessary and useless. They are unnecessary because the international adjustment mechanism works automatically to correct monetary disequilibria and to provide each country with sufficient money to accommodate full capacity levels of output. They are useless because the domestic authorities cannot, except perhaps temporarily, control the real money supply or the balance of payments, both of which are exogenous variables determined by the public's demand for money.

Let the authorities try to improve the country's balance of payments by devaluing the currency; that is; by engineering a one-time increase in the pegged, or fixed, exchange rate e. The devaluation has no permanent impact on the balance of payments. Instead, the home price level P rises identically with the exchange rate as it must to preserve the law of one price $P = eP^*$. The domestic price increase in turn raises the public's demand for cash balances. With the money stock initially given, the result is to generate an excess demand for money leading to a reduction in domestic expenditure on importable and exportable goods (thereby freeing the latter to be sold abroad). The consequent fall in imports and rise in exports manifest themselves in a temporary trade balance surplus accompanied by an inflow of reserves that eventually closes the gap between actual and desired cash balances. At this point, adjustment ceases, domestic spending again equals production, and the trade surplus vanishes. No real variables including the real money stock and the balance of payments are affected. The sole long-run effect of the devaluation is on the price level, which rises, in exact proportion to the money stock and exchange rate.

Exactly the same result occurs when the authorities try to improve the balance of payments by levying a tariff on goods imported from abroad. The tariff, imposed at gross rate $(1 + t)$ on the foreign price of imports eP^* raises the home price level by exactly that same amount as indicated by the expression $P = eP^*(1 + t)$. The rise in domestic prices in turn raises the demand for money relative to the money stock. To eliminate the resulting excess money demand, there occur a temporary trade balance surplus and accompanying reserve inflow until the excess vanishes. In the final analysis, the real money stock and balance of payments remain unchanged. The sole result is an equiproportional rise in the nominal money stock and the price level. Once again, the authorities are powerless to exercise permanent control over the balance of payments.

The approach described here pertains to fixed exchange rate regimes. But the approach also has a dual or counterpart, called the *monetary approach to exchange rates*, that extends to floating rate regimes. In this latter case, it is not the balance of payments (which now is kept in continuous equilibrium by the floating rate), but rather the exchange rate itself that adjusts to achieve money-supply-and-demand equilibrium across nations. Since monetary equilibrium between any two countries requires that the purchasing power of their currencies be everywhere the same, and since this purchasing power parity condition implies equality between the exchange rate and the ratio of national price levels as determined by relative national money supplies and real money demands, it therefore follows that the floating exchange rate itself is determined by those same relative money supplies and demands according to the expression

$$e = P/P^* = (M/kY)/(M^*/k^*Y^*) = [M/M^*][k^*Y^*/kY], \qquad (7)$$

where asterisks distinguish foreign country variables from home country ones and the notation is otherwise the same as before. This expression predicts that the exchange rate will depreciate (that is, rise) when domestic monetary expansion and output growth, respectively, exceed and fall short of their foreign counterparts. Conversely, slower money growth and faster output growth at home than abroad will strengthen the home currency relative to the foreign one and cause the exchange rate to appreciate. Here is the notion that exchange rate movements may signal the occurrence of either monetary laxity or real stagnation (or both) in one country relative to others.

These factors, however, are not the only ones moving exchange rates. Inflationary expectations operating through the nominal interest rate variables of money demand functions – variables omitted up to this point – also play a role. Incorporating these variables into the money demand functions of equation (7) yields the interest rate-augmented expression

$$e = [M/M^*][k^*Y^*/kY][i^*/i]^a, \qquad (8)$$

where i and i^* denote nominal interest rates at home and abroad and a is the interest rate elasticity of domestic and foreign money demand functions, this elasticity taken to be the same for both countries.

One additional step is necessary to show how expectations affect exchange rates through interest rates. That step is to define the nominal interest rate i as the sum of the real rate of interest r (assumed to be equalized globally by free flows of capital across integrated world capital markets) and the expected rate of price inflation I resulting in the expression

$$e = [k^*/k][(M/Y)/(M^*/Y^*)][(r+I^*)/(r+I)]^a. \qquad (9)$$

This expression says that, with the real rate of interest r equalized across nations, differential expected rates of inflation I and I^* (reflecting differential rates of expected future money and income growth) affect the exchange rate. The implication is that divergent national monetary policies can influence exchange rates both directly through divergent national money stocks per unit of real income $(M/Y)/(M^*/Y^*)$ and indirectly through the creation of divergent inflationary expectations I and I^*. Monetary policies, actual and expected, drive exchange rates.

Finally, equation (9) teaches that floating rate regimes do what fixed rate regimes cannot. They permit national monetary authorities to control their own money stocks and domestic price levels. In other words, they restore money-to-price causality in the small open economy.

THOMAS M. HUMPHREY

See also:

Exchange Rate Determination: Monetary Approach; Fixed Exchange Rate System; Flexible Exchange Rate System; Purchasing Power Parity Theory; Quantity Theory of Money.

Bibliography

Frenkel, J.A. and H.G. Johnson (eds) (1976), *The Monetary Approach to the Balance of Payments*, London: Allen & Unwin.

Humphrey, T.M. (1981), 'Adam Smith and the Monetary Approach to the Balance of Payments', *Federal Reserve Bank of Richmond Economic Review*, **67**, November/December, pp. 3–10.

Humphrey, T.M. and R.E. Keleher (1982), *The Monetary Approach to the Balance of Payments, Exchange Rates, and World Inflation*, New York: Praeger.

International Monetary Fund (1977), *The Monetary Approach to the Balance of Payments*, Washington, DC: International Monetary Fund.

Kreinin, M. and L. Officer (1978), *The Monetary Approach to the Balance of Payments: A Survey*, Princeton Studies in International Finance, no. 43. Princeton: Princeton University Press.

Balanced Budget Multiplier

The Keynesian Revolution transformed the status of fiscal policy. Hitherto, there was virtually no role for macro-oriented fiscal intervention. Indeed, the Treasury View cautioned against public sector expenditure programmes as a means of creating employment on the grounds that they would draw resources from the private sector to the detriment of employment within that sector. This view, a precursor to the crowding out debate, effectively denied a role for countercyclical fiscal policy. It was then but a short step to the advocacy of the view that fiscal prudence demanded an annually balanced budget.

In stark contrast, the economics of the *General Theory* sanctioned deficit finance in the attempt to control the level of aggregate demand. Once that fundamental step had been taken, it was inevitable that greater attention would be paid to the implications of both government expenditure and taxation policies for the macro economy. In the process, the doctrine of the balanced budget multiplier evolved. Although it was not until 1941 that the balanced budget multiplier theorem finally emerged in published form (Gelting, 1941) the thesis was already implicit in the elementary Keynesian analysis.

Stated simply, the balanced budget multiplier theorem asserts that an increase in government spending financed by a simultaneous increase in taxation, so that the overall position of the budget deficit or surplus remains unchanged, will not be neutral upon the level of national income. More precisely, an increase in government spending upon goods and services financed by a simultaneous increase in tax revenues will generate an expansion of income *exactly equal* to the increase in government spending. As stated, the doctrine is endowed with great conceptual appeal suggesting, as it does, a degree of precision normally absent from conventional macro-economic analysis.

The rationale for this non-neutral multiplier is simplicity itself. An increase in government spending upon goods and services adds directly to demand whereas the imposition of equal taxes deflates demand by the amount of the tax multiplied by the marginal propensity to consume (MPC). Providing the MPC is less than one there will be some net addition to the level of aggregate demand in the economy. The resulting expansion of income is then simply this net increase in aggregate demand multiplied by the conventional Keynesian multiplier.

Formally, it is convenient to demonstrate the logic of the balanced budget multiplier by invoking a lump-sum tax, although the argument applies regardless of the form of taxation. Let us assume the following simple closed economy model:

$$Y = C + I + G$$

$$C = a + bYd,$$

where Yd is disposable income and equal to $Y - L$, and L is a lump-sum tax. If investment and government spending are autonomously determined then we have;

$$Y = \frac{a - bL + I + G}{(1 - b)}$$

and the balanced budget multiplier is obtained from the total differential:

$$dY = \frac{\partial Y}{\partial G} \cdot dG + \frac{\partial Y}{\partial L} \cdot dL = \frac{(1)}{1 - b} \cdot dG + \frac{(-b)}{1 - b} \cdot dL.$$

Since $dG = dL$ by assumption this reduces to;

$$\frac{(1 - b)}{(1 - b)} \cdot dG = dG.$$

Moreover, it will be noted that this result is quite independent of the value of the marginal propensity to consume providing the latter is less than one. This follows from the fact that the increase in aggregate demand is given by

$$\Delta D = \Delta G - \Delta L(MPC).$$

But since $\Delta G = \Delta L$, this may be written as

$$\Delta D = \Delta G(1 - MPC).$$

The resulting expansion of income is this increase in demand multiplied by the multiplier which in this elementary model is simply $1/1 - MPC$. Hence

$$\Delta Y = \Delta G(1 - MPC) \cdot \frac{1}{(1 - MPC)}$$

and accordingly the value of the marginal propensity to consume is irrelevant to the outcome.

Of course, the example of a unity multiplier is very much a special case. More complex models and more real-world situations will depart from this conceptually appealing result. In the context of an open economy model, for example, it is perfectly possible to obtain a negative balanced budget multiplier. This might arise in a situation where marginal propensities to import differ significantly between the public and private sector. Particularly in third world economies, where governments often combine seemingly insatiable demands for imported military equipment with extremely high duties on imported consumption goods to protect the overall balance of payments, this is a likely outcome. Again, more sophisticated models might allow for the higher rate of taxation exerting adverse effects upon the supply side of the economy, suggesting possible limits to the extent to which the positive multiplier may be invoked. Equally, it is crucial to the general tenor of the balanced budget multiplier that the increased government expenditures should not be competitive with private sector investment. Alternatively, of course, it might be argued that the government's expenditure programme raises business confidence in the future level of aggregate demand, thus stimulating private sector investment even further. This is one scenario consistent with a balanced budget multiplier in excess of unity.

Other difficulties present themselves. If the increase in government expenditures were to take the form of transfer payments, for example, the resulting impact upon the level of income would be precisely nil providing taxpayers and transfer recipients enjoyed the same marginal propensity to consume. Normally, one might assume that the latter possess the higher marginal propensity, suggesting that the multiplier would still be positive. A more complex case arises if the government raises taxation to purchase goods and services which it then gives free of charge as payments in kind to deserving recipients. This scenario is illustrated by the American example of providing food vouchers for the poor and the unemployed. Taxpayers, it is argued, are more willing to sanction such payments as opposed to providing equal-costing cash transfers. If the recipients experience an income gain in consequence and their marginal saving propensity is positive they will increase their saving. Since it is virtually impossible to increase saving out of payments in kind, this will lead to increased saving out of alternative income streams. In consequence, part of the overall expansionary impetus of the balanced budget multiplier will be eliminated. Indeed, in the extreme case, where the payment in kind is valued at cost – by the recipient – and where marginal consumption propensities are identical between the recipient and the taxpayer, the entire impact of the balanced budget multiplier will be negated.

Clearly, the range of potential outcomes is almost unlimited depending upon the assumptions incorporated into the model analysis. In particular, the textbook example of the unit multiplier must be treated with extreme caution as a practical guide to fiscal policy. Baumol and Peston (1955) detail many of the essential reservations and caveats surrounding this result. Nonetheless, the balanced budget multiplier remains an integral feature of fiscally oriented macro models. It reminds us that, normally, government expenditure changes are more high powered than equivalent tax changes and that this should be fully allowed for in the design of macroeconomic strategies. Too great a concentration on the sheer size of the public sector borrowing requirement, without regard to its composition, can be seriously misleading.

Secondly, the balanced budget multiplier theorem provides a theoretical justification for the dismissal of the Treasury View. It may well be that government public works expenditure programmes of necessity withdraw resources from the private sector but nonetheless the overall demand impact remains positive, with beneficial results for employment and national income. Previous attempts to refute the Treasury View had relied upon the rather dubious assertion that public works programmes would be inherently more labour-intensive. The balanced budget multiplier theorem provided a more convincing reason for believing that the government could effectively spend its way out of recession.

The balanced budget multiplier also provides a classic example of a *novel fact* in the Lakatosian sense of a theoretically and empirically progressive scientific research agenda. It pointed to outcomes which were not part of the formal model analysis and which were not even suspected when the initial Keynesian research programme began. In this sense it revealed 'excess empirical content' when compared to competing theories, which doubtless contributed to its acceptance into mainstream Keynesian economics. Finally, and paradoxically, it provides a Keynesian justification for the annually balanced budget. Stated simply, it implies that a deficit is no longer needed to raise aggregate demand as long as the government is willing to enlarge the budget (both expenditures and taxes) sufficiently.

G.K. SHAW

See also:

Consumption Function; Crowding Out; Keynesian Economics; Multiplier.

Bibliography

Baumol, W.J. and M.H. Peston (1955), 'More on the Multiplier Effects of a Balanced Budget', *American Economic Review*, **45**, March, pp. 140–48.
Gelting, J. (1941), 'Nogle Bemaerkninger om Finansieringen af offentlig Virksomhed', *Nationalokonomisk Tidsskrift*, **79**(5), pp. 293–9.
Haavelmo, T. (1945), 'Multiplier Effects of a Balanced Budget', *Econometrica*, **13**, October, pp. 311–18.
Peston, M.H. (1987), 'Balanced Budget Multiplier' in J. Eatwell, M.Milgate and P. Newman (eds), *The New Palgrave: A Dictionary of Economics*, London: Macmillan Press, pp. 176–7.

Barro, Robert J.

Robert Barro (b.1944, New York City, New York, USA) obtained his BS (Physics) from the California Institute of Technology in 1965 and his PhD from Harvard University in 1970. His main past posts have included the following: Assistant Professor (1968–72) and Associate Professor (1972–3) at Brown University; Associate Professor (1973–5) and Professor of Economics at the University of Chicago (1982–4); and Professor of Economics at the University of Rochester, 1975–82 and 1984–7. Since 1987 he has been the Robert C. Waggoner Professor of Economics at Harvard University. He was editor of the *Journal of Political Economy* in 1973–5 and 1983–5 and since 1978 has been a Research Associate at the National Bureau of Economic Research. He is best known for his work on Ricardian equivalence; empirical studies of the effects of unanticipated monetary growth on output and employment; the application of rules, discretion and reputation to monetary policy; and more recently, theories and empirical determinants of economic growth and convergence. Among his best known books are *Money, Employment and Inflation* (co-authored with H. Grossman) (Cambridge University Press, 1976); *Modern Business Cycle*

Theory (ed.) (Harvard University Press, 1979); *Economic Growth* (co-authored with X. Sala-i-Martin) (McGraw-Hill, 1995); *Determinants of Economic Growth: A Cross-Country Empirical Study* (MIT Press, 1997); and *Macroeconomics*, 5th edn (MIT Press, 1998). His most widely read articles include 'Are Government Bonds Net Wealth?' (*Journal of Political Economy*, **82**, November–December 1974); 'Unanticipated Money Growth and Unemployment in the United States' (*American Economic Review*, **67**, March 1977); 'Rules, Discretion and Reputation in a Model of Monetary Policy' (co-authored with D.B. Gordon) (*Journal of Monetary Economics*, **12**, July 1983); 'Economic Growth in a Cross Section of Countries' (*Quarterly Journal of Economics*, **106**, May 1991); and 'Inequality and Growth in a Panel of Countries' (*Journal of Economic Growth*, **5**, March 2000).

See also:

Business Cycles: New Classical Approach; Convergence; Credibility and Reputation; National Bureau of Economic Research; Policy Ineffectiveness Proposition; Ricardian Equivalence; Rules versus Discretion.

Bastard Keynesianism

A term coined by the Cambridge University economist Joan Robinson (1903–83) to describe the neoclassical synthesis version of Keynesianism which spread from North America across the world after World War II.

See also:

Hydraulic Keynesianism; Keynes's *General Theory*; Keynesian Economics; Neoclassical Synthesis; Robinson, Joan.

Blanchard, Olivier J.

Olivier Blanchard (b.1948, France) obtained his DES (Econ.) in France, 1972 and his PhD from Massachusetts Institute of Technology (MIT) in 1977. His main past posts have included Assistant Professor (1977–81) and Associate Professor (1981–3) at Harvard University; Associate Professor (1983–5) and since 1985 Professor at MIT. He is currently Class of 1941 Professor of Economics at MIT. He is best known for his work on nominal rigidities, high unemployment in Western Europe and economic problems associated with transition in Eastern Europe. Among his best known books are *Lectures in Macroeconomics* (co-authored with S. Fischer) (MIT Press, 1989); *The Economics of Transition* (Oxford University Press, 1997);

and *Macroeconomics*, 2nd edn (Prentice Hall, 2000). His most widely read articles include 'The Monetary Mechanism in the Light of Rational Expectations' in S. Fischer (ed.), *Rational Expectations and Economic Policy* (University of Chicago Press, 1980); 'Hysteresis and European Unemployment' (co-authored with L. Summers) (*NBER Macroeconomics Annual*, 1986); 'Monopolistic Competition and the Effects of Aggregate Demand' (co-authored with N. Kiyotaki) (*American Economic Review*, 77, September 1987); 'The Dynamic Effects of Aggregate Demand and Supply Shocks' (co-authored with D. Quah) (*American Economic Review*, **79**, September 1989); and 'What Do We Know About Macroeconomics That Fisher and Wicksell Did Not?' (*Quarterly Journal of Economics*, **115**, November 2000).

Blaug, Mark

Mark Blaug (b.1927, The Hague, Netherlands) obtained his BA from Queen's College, New York in 1950 and his MA (1952) and PhD (1955) from Columbia University. His main past posts have included the following: statistician at the US Department of Labor, New York, 1952–3; Assistant Professor at Yale University, 1954–62; Senior Lecturer (1963–5), Reader (1965–9) and Professor of the Economics of Education (1969–84) at the University of London Institute of Education; and Consultant Professor of Economics at the University of Buckingham, 1984–91. Since 1991 he has been Professor, Emeritus, at the University of London and the University of Buckingham; Visiting Professor at Exeter University; and since 2000 Visiting Professor at the University of Amsterdam. He is best known for his work on the economics of education; methodology; biographies of leading economists; and the history of economic thought. Among his best known books are *The Methodology of Economics: Or How Economists Explain*, 2nd edn (Cambridge University Press, 1992); *Economic Theory in Retrospect*, 5th edn (Cambridge University Press, 1997); *Great Economists Before Keynes*, 2nd edn (Edward Elgar, 1997); *Great Economists Since Keynes*, 2nd edn (Edward Elgar, 1998); and *Who's Who in Economics*, 3rd edn (Edward Elgar, 1999).

Blinder, Alan S.

Alan Blinder (b.1945, New York City, New York, USA) obtained his BA from Princeton University in 1967, a MSc from the London School of Economics in 1968 and his PhD from Massachusetts Institute of

Technology (MIT) in 1971. His main past posts have included Assistant Professor (1971–6), Associate Professor (1976–9) and Professor of Economics (1979–82) at Princeton University. Since 1982 he has been the Gordon S. Rentschler Memorial Professor of Economics at Princeton University. Between 1993 and 1994 he was a Member of the Council of Economic Advisers and from 1994 to 1996 Vice-Chair of the Board of Governors of the Federal Reserve System. He is best known for his work on fiscal policy, inventories, central banking and his staunch defence of Keynesian economics. Among his best known books are *Economic Policy and the Great Stagflation* (Academic Press, 1979); *Hard Heads, Soft Hearts: Tough-Minded Economics for a Just Society* (Addison-Wesley, 1987); and *Central Banking in Theory and Practice* (MIT Press, 1998). His most widely read articles include: 'Does Fiscal Policy Matter?' (co-authored with R.M. Solow) (*Journal of Public Economics*, **2**, November 1973); 'Inventories, Rational Expectations and the Business Cycle' (co-authored with S. Fischer) (*Journal of Monetary Economics*, **8**, November 1981); 'The Fall and Rise of Keynesian Economics' (*Economic Record*, **64**, December 1988); and 'What Central Bankers Can Learn from Academics and Vice Versa' (*Journal of Economic Perspectives*, **11**, Spring 1997).

See also:

Council of Economic Advisers; Federal Reserve System; Keynesian Economics.

Boom

The period of rapid expansion before the movement of output from trend begins to flatten out near the top of the business cycle.

See also:

Business Cycle.

Bretton Woods

The 1944 Bretton Woods Agreement established the framework which governed the international payments system in the first 25 years after World War II, and set up the two key international financial institutions, the International Monetary Fund and World Bank, which are still with us today. The United Nations Monetary and Financial Conference, as it was officially called, was held at the disused Mount Washington hotel at Bretton Woods, New Hampshire for three weeks in July 1944.

Background

The final Agreement was the culmination of many months of preparatory discussions between British and American officials led by John Maynard Keynes and Harry White, respectively. Keynes had been anxious to devise a new postwar regime for international payments which would obviate the crises and deflationary pressures leading to the unemployment of the inter-war years. The experience of these years had demonstrated the problem of trying to operate a fixed rate system, such as the gold standard, without any provision for dealing with foreign exchange crises or the orderly adjustment of exchange rates. It was also evident that every crisis tended to invoke a deflationary response, in the form either of higher interest rates or of efforts to reduce a budget deficit, with consequent increases in unemployment. There was an increasing realization of the need to devise some orderly system of international payments which would minimize the deflationary tendencies of any payments difficulties.

In 1941, Keynes, working in the British Treasury, had produced proposals for an 'International Currency Union' (Keynes, 1980). The two key elements were to establish (a) a multilateral clearing system for international payments, and (b) arrangements for dealing with creditors and debtors in such a way as to minimize the impact on employment. His proposals were revolutionary in a number of respects. They would have set up an International Central Bank (ICB) managing a world currency, with each national currency having a fixed value in terms of the world currency, 'bancor'. There were provisions for changing exchange rates where countries were out of balance, but these took much of the power to vary rates out of the hands of individual countries and put it into the hands of the new central bank. Statutory provisions were made to force creditors as well as debtors to get back into balance.

Writing at a time when trade and payments were tightly controlled, Keynes was concerned to establish that, after the necessary period of postwar adjustment, there would be a dismantling of wartime controls and other obstacles to *current* trade and payments. But Keynes consistently maintained the need to maintain control over *capital* movements in order to deal with speculative movements of funds. (To make this possible all foreign exchange transactions would need to continue to be controlled in order to be able to rule out unlicensed capital transactions.) This had been a constant theme of Keynes before the war, but the practicality of doing so was enhanced by the existence of wartime currency restrictions and the probable need to maintain them for some years.

The official UK Proposals for an International Clearing Union, eventually published in 1943 as a White Paper, were somewhat less radical than Keynes's original proposals. They reflected discussions not only in

Whitehall but also with the American government. The published proposals did, however, emphasize the concept of an international central bank with an international currency whose volume was 'capable of deliberate expansion and contraction to offset deflationary or inflationary tendencies in effective world demand'. The proposed new bank would relend credit balances to other countries as a domestic bank could relend to another customer. But these loans would only be introduced to give time for adjustment rather than to perpetuate existing imbalances.

At the same time as the British proposals were published in April 1943, the Americans published their own plan, originating from Harry White in the US Treasury. Since both the original Keynes plan and the original White plan had been discussed between British and American officials, the two sets of proposals had come closer together. White envisaged both a stabilization fund (to become the International Monetary Fund) and a bank (later to become the International Bank for Reconstruction and Development). Like the Clearing Union, the stabilization fund would have quotas for each country and an international currency, in this case called the 'unitas'. Exchange rates would be fixed and could only be varied with the agreement of three-quarters of the members' votes, but with more elastic provisions for an initial three years' postwar transition period.

The most radical feature of the US plan was the treatment of creditors whose currency became scarce. The fund would report on the reasons for the scarcity and make recommendations. In addition, the fund would 'apportion its sales of such currency' which meant that other countries could be free to restrict their imports from the scarce currency country. As the most likely target of any such action was the United States, and in view of their anxiety to reduce discriminatory restrictions, as soon as possible, this was a remarkable proposal. Although it was eventually embodied in the Scarce Currency clause, it was in the event never used.

The agreement
Although the resulting agreement was not as revolutionary as Keynes's original proposals, it reflected a wide-ranging vision of how the postwar economic system might work, including a liberal regime for trade and tariffs, and measures to stabilize commodity prices. It established for the first time a formal framework of rules governing exchange rates and international payments, designed to overcome the problems experienced in the inter-war period. The rules were intended first to encourage a speedy, but orderly, dismantling of wartime restrictions on imports, and movement to currency convertibility, and then to establish, as a permanent regime, a liberal system of trade and payments and fixed exchange rates which would

be compatible with the pursuit of full employment. The operation of the international payment system was to be supervised by the International Monetary Fund controlled by the leading Allied Powers with a system of weighted voting ensuring a dominant voice for the United States.

As set out in Article I, the purposes of the International Monetary Fund were to promote international monetary cooperation; facilitate the expansion of international trade and 'contribute thereby to the promotion and maintenance of high levels of employment'; promote exchange rate stability; assist in establishing a system of multilateral trade and eliminating foreign exchange restrictions; facilitate correction of balance of payments maladjustments without destroying national or international prosperity; and minimize international balance of payments disequilibrium.

It was a fixed, but adjustable, exchange system in which members could not change the par value of their currencies except to correct a 'fundamental disequilibrium'. There was no provision for the Fund (formally) proposing changes in exchange rates, but members could only change rates after consultation with the Fund (which would make no objections to changes of less than 10 per cent).

Countries in balance of payments difficulties could borrow from the Fund by drawing on their 'quotas', which were fixed in the Agreement. There was explicit provision for the continued control of capital movements (Article VI.3) but current transactions were to be unrestricted. The Scarce Currency clause (Article VII) enabled members to take restrictive measures against the currency of a persistent credit.

The Conference also set up the International Bank for Reconstruction and Development (now known as the 'World Bank'). Although its principal function came to be that of making long-term development loans out of its own resources (including money borrowed on world capital markets), its original terms of reference were rather wider. They included the promotion of private foreign investment by means of guarantees, or participation, to be supplemented by loans from the Bank's own resources when private capital was not available on reasonable terms. With inter-war problems in mind the Bank was also 'to promote the long-range balanced growth of international trade and the maintenance of equilibrium in balance of payments by encouraging international investment . . . [and] to conduct its operation with due regard to the effect of international investment on business conditions'.

Bretton Woods itself did not deal with the issues of tariffs and trade, or commodities; these took longer to resolve. But eventually the foundations of a liberal international economic regime were completed in 1948, with the General Agreement on Tariffs and Trade providing for the gradual reduction of tariffs by international negotiation.

The outcome

The IMF and the World Bank remain in operation, but the fixed exchange rate regime which was the key feature of the Bretton Woods payments system broke down in the early 1970s. In the early postwar years the exchange controls inherited from wartime limited the scope for speculative runs on currencies – although, when countries such as the UK were in obvious balance of payments difficulties, there was still sufficient room for delays in payments and so on to cause a run on the pound. As exchange controls, both capital and current, were progressively eased, the scope for speculative movements increased. The inability of the fixed rate system to provide for adjustments in exchange rates before crises developed then became acute. Such adjustments nearly always took place in conditions of economic and political crisis, after repeated government statements that no devaluation was contemplated, as with, for example, the UK in 1967.

Fundamental changes in the US balance of payments position also affected the picture. At the end of World War II, the United States was running a large balance of payments surplus and there was a worldwide dollar shortage. The dollar, with a firm link to gold, was thus the basic reserve currency in the world system. However, American aid (such as the Marshall Plan to aid European recovery) and foreign investment provided sufficient dollars to enable the rest of the world to rebuild and expand. But by the end of the 1960s, the United States was in balance of payments deficit and the dollar had weakened. In August 1971, the United States abandoned the convertibility of the dollar into gold at a fixed rate. This heralded the start of a new era with an increasing resort to floating exchange rates as the continued liberalization of capital movements made fixed rates harder to maintain. With the development of global capital markets, floating rates have become the norm, with only a small number of countries pegging their rates to a currency such as the dollar.

JOHN GRIEVE SMITH

See also:

Devaluation; Fixed Exchange Rate System; Flexible Exchange Rate System; General Agreement on Tariffs and Trade; Gold Standard; International Monetary Fund; World Bank.

Bibliography
Eichengreen, B. (1992), *Golden Fetters: The Gold Standard and the Great Depression, 1919–1939*, Oxford: Oxford University Press.
Gardner, R. (1980), *Sterling–Dollar Diplomacy in Current Perspective*, New York: Columbia University Press.
Keynes, J.M. (1980), *Collected Writings, Volumes XXV and XXVI*, London and Cambridge: Macmillan and Cambridge University Press.
Kindleberger, C. (1973), *The World in Depression, 1929–39*, London: Allen Lane.
Moggridge, D.E. (1992), *Maynard Keynes: An Economist's Biography*, London: Routledge.

Panic, M. (1988), *The National Management of the International Economy*, London: Macmillan.
Panic, M. (1995), *The Bretton Woods System in Managing the Global Economy*, ed. J. Michie and J. Grieve Smith, Oxford: Oxford University Press.
Skidelsky, R. (2000), *John Maynard Keynes: Fighting for Britain 1937–1946*, London: Macmillan.
Solomon, R. (1982), *The International Financial System 1945–81*, New York: Harper & Row.
Tew, B. (1988), *The Evolution of the International Monetary System*, London: Hutchinson.
US Department of State (1948), *Proceedings and Documents of United Nations Monetary and Financial Conference, Bretton Woods, New Hampshire, July 1–22, 1944*, Washington, DC: US Government Printing Office.
Van Dormael, A. (1978), *Bretton Woods: Birth of a Monetary System*, London: Macmillan.

Brookings Institution

The Brookings Institution was founded in 1927, following the consolidation of the Institute for Government Research, the Institute of Economics and the Robert Brookings Graduate School. Named in honour of Robert Somers Brookings (1850–1932), a St Louis businessman, it is based in Washington, DC. In addition to its educational activities the institution conducts research into economic, foreign policy and government studies. Among its publications are the prestigious *Brookings Papers on Economic Activity* (first published in 1970). The research institute is also renowned for its forecasting model which, when first constructed in the early 1960s, was the largest econometric model of the US economy. For more information the reader is referred to the official website of the Brookings Institution (*http://www.brook.edu/*).

See also:
Forecasting; Macroeconometric Models.

Brunner, Karl (1916–89)

Karl Brunner (b.1916, Zurich, Switzerland) obtained his doctorate from the University of Zurich in 1943. His main past posts included Assistant Professor (1951–7), Associate Professor (1957–62) and Professor (1962–6) at the University of California, Los Angeles; Professor at Ohio State University, 1966–71; and Professor of Economics at the University of Rochester, 1971–89. He was editor of the *Journal of Money, Credit and Banking* from 1969 to 1974, and the *Journal of Monetary Economics* between 1974 and 1984. He is best known for his contributions to monetarism (a term he coined), including influential work on the transmission mechanism for, and indicators of, monetary policy and monetary growth rules. Among his best known books are *The Great Depression Revisited* (ed.) (Martinus Nijhoff, 1981) and *Money and the Economy: Issues in Monetary Analysis* (co-authored with A.H. Meltzer) (Cambridge University Press, 1993). His most widely read articles include: 'The Role of Money and Monetary Policy' (*Federal Reserve Bank of St. Louis Monthly Review*, **50**, July 1968); 'The Monetarist Revolution in Monetary Theory, (*Weltwirtschaftliches Archiv*, **105**, March 1970); 'The Uses of Money: Money in the Theory of an Exchange Economy' (co-authored with A.H. Meltzer) (*American Economic Review*, **61**, December 1971); and 'Money, Debt and Economic Activity' (co-authored with A.H. Meltzer) (*Journal of Political Economy*, **80**, September–October 1972).

See also:

Monetarism; Monetary Policy: Role of.

Budget Balance

The difference between government expenditure and tax revenue. A balanced budget arises where government expenditure and tax revenue are equal, while a budget deficit (surplus) occurs where tax revenue is less than (greater than) expenditure. The actual size of the budget deficit/surplus depends in part on the level of economic activity; that is, the budget position is endogenous to the level of income. The budget balance is an unreliable guide to the direction of fiscal policy as a given change in the actual budget deficit/surplus over time may be the result of (a) planned or discretionary policy changes (such as a planned increase in government expenditure) and/or (b) unplanned, automatic or non-discretionary changes due to changes in the level of economic activity (such as increased tax receipts due to an increase in income).

See also:

Automatic Stabilizers; Balanced Budget Multiplier; Budget Deficits: Cyclical and Structural.

Budget Deficits: Cyclical and Structural

Public sector deficits arouse much passionate debate and have done so for many years. Both Adam Smith and David Ricardo were critical of deficits, viewing them as a means through which monarchs avoided parliamentary approval of increased spending. Today's commentators criticize public sector deficits from a variety of perspectives. Libertarians, who advocate a minimalist state, see deficits as a device for today's generation to enjoy the benefits of public spending while imposing payment burdens on future generations. Others draw attention to the adverse impacts of the financing of public sector deficits on interest rates, exchange rates, private sector savings and investment, and economic growth.

Taken together, those who see the costs of public sector deficits tend to be strong advocates of some form of constitutionally based balanced budget or other product fiscal rule. In 1992, for example, the European Union Maastricht Treaty defined sound public financing in terms of a public sector borrowing requirement (PSBR)-to-GDP ratio of 3 per cent and a 60 per cent limit to the public sector debt-to-GDP ratio.

Public sector deficits are, however, fraught with definitional and measurement difficulties (see, for example, Blejer and Cheasty, 1991). This poses a challenge to those who seek to measure the impact of deficits upon the economic system or who wish to regulate the activities of the public sector through fiscal rules. Which measure of the deficit is relevant for these purposes?

The figures which represent the public sector deficit are the result of complex financial flows. Which flows are, therefore, to be counted? First, there is a need to define the boundaries of the public sector. What is in and what is out? Some countries, for example the United States and Germany, separate out deficits (and hence public sector debt) which originate in the social security budget. In recent years creative public sector accounting has resulted in increases in off-budget items. Without international agreements on public sector accounting standards, inter-country comparisons of public deficits will be meaningless. For example, the sale of an asset can be counted as revenue, negative expenditure or an offset against debt. Another important consideration which is often ignored, especially when making international comparisons, is which level of government the deficit refers to: is it the total public sector, the federal (central) level of government, state government or local government?

Public sector deficits of the major OECD countries have increased the levels of public sector debt since 1970, with one notable exception which is that of the UK, whose accumulated public sector debt as a percentage of GDP has fallen, owing, in part, to a series of prudent fiscal policies and the revenue proceeds of a series of major privatizations.

The introduction of the Euro has significantly changed the fiscal environment for EU member states. Previously, it was an individual country which confronted the costs of a fiscal policy financed through large deficits – these costs are increases in inflation and a weakening of the exchange rate. In a monetary union it is not the single member state which faces these costs. Instead, it is all member states. The fiscal policy of one member state can have significant externalities for all others. It is this problem which the Maastricht Treaty sought to deal with through establishing a set of fiscal rules. These rules, however, require unambiguous definitions of deficits and debt for their effective implementation.

Any measure of the fiscal deficit needs to pay regard to the boundaries of the public sector, the activities which result in the deficit and the time period over which the deficit arises. A frequently used measure is the PSBR. This is a measure of a government's use of new financial resources net of repayment of debt. Public expenditure (use of new financial resources) encompasses cash outlays including debt repayments. Depreciation is not included because it does not affect cash flow. Within the scope of this definition above-the-line items (that is, revenues or expenditures) are those transactions that do not create or extinguish a liability. The repayment of principal is, therefore, a below-the-line item. It therefore follows that net public spending above the line has a potential impact upon aggregate demand in the economy, whereas the repayment of debt, which is in effect an income transfer, does not have an impact upon aggregate demand. If some items of public expenditure result in the repayment of private sector debt then technically that should be regarded as a below-the-line item.

A cash deficit (the PSBR is calculated on a cash basis) means that only cash outlays and cash revenues during a 365-day period are counted. An accruals deficit is the result of accounting for government resource use irrespective of whether or not the transactions have actually been paid for. For example, depreciation will be included in an accruals accounting system whereas a cash flow system will exclude depreciation. The System of National Accounts (SNA) uses an accruals accounting system.

In practice, actual systems are a mixture of cash and accruals accounting, which means that actual recorded deficits are a mixture of cash and accruals deficits. For example, when calculating the PSBR, interest payments are usually accounted for when they accrue, not when they are actually paid, whereas depreciation is ignored. This means that recorded deficits can be sensitive to judgments about when expenditures are actually recorded.

Deficits measure the difference between public sector investment and saving. The current deficit excludes public sector investment spending and capital revenues, such as the proceeds from the sale of assets (as in privatization). In essence, the current deficit refers to current spending which is not covered by current period taxation. It is the current deficit which indicates the burden placed upon future generations. This definition of the current deficit is not without its problems because some items of current expenditure are on capital items: for example, if a capital item is leased rather than purchased outright. Also current expenditure on human capital items (as in education and health) does not strictly place a 'burden' on future generations.

The public sector deficit is undoubtedly influenced by the business cycle (see Blinder and Solow, 1974). Automatic stabilizers are built into an economy. As money incomes fall (*ceteris paribus*) over the cycle, so too do tax revenues, especially those associated directly with incomes. Thus, in a downturn, the public sector deficit will automatically increase, provided that public spending remains constant. Many subsidies are related to income. Thus, as incomes fall, tax revenues decline and certain subsidies and welfare payments (public spending) increase.

The structural deficit is the public sector's discretionary deficit; that is, it is the outcome of deliberate decisions and choices made by the government. Thus the structural deficit represents the government's fiscal stance (see Brown, 1956). It indicates whether or not the government's intention is to use the budget to expand or to dampen economic activity. The structural deficit measures what the deficit (or surplus) would be at the natural rate of unemployment, that is, that level of unemployment which is consistent with a Walrasian general equilibrium and at which the inflation rate is not accelerating. Any changes in the structural deficit reflect discretionary government decisions about tax rates, tax bases and other public expenditure items.

Some authors use the 'full employment budget surplus' to measure a government's fiscal stance. This concept, which originates in the 1947 report of the US Committee for Economic Development, has been used, since 1962, by the Council of Economic Advisers to the President in its annual reports.

In a recession the actual deficit will be greater than the structural deficit because the actual level of unemployment will exceed the natural rate of unemployment. Moreover, the automatic stabilizers will kick in.

The cyclical deficit represents the difference between the actual and the structural deficit. In a boom the level of unemployment will be lower than the natural rate. Inflation rates will increase; money incomes will chase inflation and money tax revenues will increase, whilst welfare-related public expenditures will fall. The actual deficit will be less than the structural deficit in that case. The opposite will clearly be the case for a recession. In this case the business cycle affects inflation and inflation affects the budget through 'fiscal drag', that is, the impact of inflation upon tax revenues and index linked transfer payments. The issue which arises is whether the cyclical deficit should be adjusted for inflation.

Why are fiscal economists interested in calculating the cyclically adjusted budget deficit? It is a means of calculating the structural deficit or the government's fiscal stance. Once the cyclical element is eliminated from the actual deficit, what remains is the deficit originating in deliberate government policy. In other words, to obtain a meaningful measure of a government's fiscal performance, it is necessary to filter out the cyclical element from the actual deficit. This measure of the government's performance indicates its control over public spending.

Clearly, the measurement of the performance of government as indicated by the structural budget deficit depends crucially upon the reliability of the estimate of the cyclical deficit. This in turn depends upon having a reliable macro model of the economy which will enable the potential (full employment) trend in GDP to be estimated. Some commentators use the trend (peak to peak) GDP rather than potential GDP – the two measures are not the same (see Giorno *et.al.*, 1995; Haliassos and Tobin, 1990). History is not necessarily a good predictor.

Given the many problems of measuring the cyclical deficit, the structural deficit need not be a reliable measure of a government's fiscal stance or overall fiscal performance. Moreover, is the long-run full employment growth path of the economy independent of current fiscal policies? The traditional measures of the cyclical adjusted deficit assume that current policies do not affect the long-run rate of growth of the economy. If the long-run level of output is affected by discretionary fiscal policy then the structural deficit becomes meaningless (see Solow, 1988).

PETER M. JACKSON

See also

Automatic Stabilisers; Balanced Budget Multiplier; Fiscal Policy: Role of.

Bibliography

Blejer, M. and A. Cheasty (1991), 'The Measurement of Fiscal Deficits: Analytical and Methodological Issues', *Journal of Economic Literature*, **29**, December, pp. 1644–78.
Blinder, A.S. and R.M. Solow (1974), 'Analytical Foundations of Fiscal Policy', in A.S. Blinder, *et.al., The Economics of Public Finance*, Washington, DC: Brookings Institution.
Brown, E.C. (1956), 'Fiscal Policy in the Thirties: A Reappraisal', *American Economic Review*, **46**, December, pp. 857–79.
Giorno, D., P. Richardson, D. Roseveare and P. Van den Noord (1995), 'Potential Output, Output Gaps and Structural Budget Balances', *OECD Economic Studies*, no. 24, pp. 167–212.
Haliassos, M. and J. Tobin (1990), 'The Macroeconomics of Government Finance', in B.M. Friedman and F.H. Hahn (eds), *Handbook of Monetary Economics*, Amsterdam: North-Holland.
Solow, R.M. (1988), 'Growth Theory and After', *American Economic Review*, **78**, June, pp. 307–17.

Built-in Stabilizers

See also:

Automatic Stabilizers.

Burns, Arthur F. (1904–87)

Arthur Burns (b.1904, Stanislau, Austro-Hungary) obtained his BA (1925), MA (1925) and PhD (1934) from Columbia University. His main past posts included Assistant Professor (1930–33), Associate Professor (1933–43) and Professor of Economics (1943–58) at Rutgers University; John Bates Clark Professor of Economics at Columbia University, 1959–69; Director of Research (1945–53) and President (1957–67) of the National Bureau of Economic Research (NBER); Chairman of the Council of Economic Advisers, 1953–6; Chairman of the Board of Governors of the Federal Reserve System, 1970–78; and member of the President's Economic Advisory Board, 1981–7. He is best known for his influential studies of economic growth; business cycles; forecasting; and economic policies for the management of prosperity. Among his best known books are *Measuring Business Cycles* (co-authored with W.C.Mitchell) (NBER, 1946); *Prosperity without Inflation* (Fordham University Press, 1957); *The Management of Prosperity* (Columbia University Press, 1966); and *Reflections of an Economic Policy Maker* (American Enterprise Institute, 1978).

See also:

Council of Economic Advisers; Federal Reserve System; Mitchell, Wesley C.; National Bureau of Economic Research.

Business Cycle

Periodic, but irregular, fluctuations in the pattern of aggregate economic activity. Usually defined as deviations of output (real GDP) from its secular or long-term trend.

Business Cycles: Austrian Approach

Originally conceived by Ludwig von Mises (1953) early last century and developed most notably by Friedrich A. von Hayek (1967) before and during the Great Depression, the Austrian theory of the business cycle is a theory of the unsustainable boom. Its logic is firmly anchored in the notion that the price system is a communications network. A miscommunication in the form of an interest rate held below its market, or 'natural', level by central bank policy sets the economy off on a growth path that is inherently unsustainable. Given actual consumer preferences and resource availabilities, such a policy-induced boom contains the seeds of its own undoing. The temporal pattern of resource allocation is inconsistent with the preferred pattern of consumption. In time, this inconsistency precipitates a bust.

The uniqueness of the Austrian theory lies in the extra-market origins of the boom (central bank policy) and in the self-reversing market process that turns boom into bust. Complications in the form of a possible spiralling downward of the economy into deep depression are only tangential to the Austrian theory. Similarly, the duration of the depression phase of the cycle, especially in the case of the Great Depression, depends upon many considerations (including the perversities of depression-born regulations on trade, industry and labour) that are not integral to the Austrian theory of the unsustainable boom.

The interest rate is a price. It is the price that strikes a balance between people's eagerness to consume now and their willingness to save for the future. Preferences relevant to this trade-off are dubbed 'time preferences' in the Austrian literature. And like preferences generally, time preferences can change: people may become more future-oriented, for instance, because of increased life expectancy or out of concern for the future well-being of their children. An increase in saving (a decrease in time preferences) has two mutually reinforcing effects: (1) it lowers the rate of interest, signalling to the business community that more and longer-term projects are now profitable, and (2) it frees resources (that before were committed to producing consumer goods) for carrying these projects through to completion. In this way, changes in intertemporal consumption preferences get translated into changes in intertemporal production plans.

The market process that guides the intertemporal allocation of resources is inherently complex owing to the radical heterogeneity of capital goods, a point emphasized by Ludwig Lachmann (1978). But, for analytical tractability, Hayek (1967) assumed away many of the complexities and depicted the economy's structure of production as a right triangle: one leg represents the time dimension of the production process; the other leg represents the value of the consumable output. The time dimension of this Hayekian triangle is divided into a number of 'stages of production', the output of one stage serving as the input to the next. A single 'project' that converts (early-stage) raw materials into (final-stage) consumables involves the plans of many different producers – plans that are mutually coordinated by the price system, including (importantly) the rate of interest. A decrease in the interest rate, for example, causes resources to be transferred from the late and final stages to the early stages. The modified structure of production, depicted by a triangle with a longer time-dimension leg and an (initially) shorter consumable-output leg, causes the time profile of consumption to be skewed towards the future.

An artificial boom is an instance in which the change in the interest-rate signal and the change in resource availabilities are at odds with one another. If the central bank pads the supply of loanable funds with newly created money, the interest rate is lowered just as it is with an increase in saving. But in the absence of an actual change in time preferences, no additional resources for sustaining the policy-induced boom are freed. In fact, facing a lower interest rate, people will save less and spend more on current consumables. The central bank's credit expansion, then, results in an incompatible mix of market forces.

Increased investment in longer-term projects is consistent with the underlying economic realities in a genuine saving-induced boom, but not in a policy-induced artificial boom. The artificial boom is characterized by 'malinvestment and overconsumption', a phrase used repeatedly by Mises (1966). With seemingly favourable credit conditions, long-term investment projects are being initiated at the same time that the resources needed to see them through to completion are being consumed. As the market guides these projects into their intermediate and late stages, the underlying economic realities become increasingly clear: not all of the investment undertakings can be profitably completed. On the eve of the bust, distress borrowing allows some producers to finish their projects and minimize their losses. In this phase, the high interest rates bolstered by distress borrowing cause people to curtail their consumption and to save instead. The resources thus freed constitute an explicit form of 'forced saving' – a term used more broadly by Hayek to characterize all the boom-related commitments of resources that are at odds with consumers' time preferences. With scope for sustaining the boom on the basis of forced saving severely limited, the economy is forced to adjust to a slower growth path.

The liquidation of some incomplete projects frees resources to help complete others. The period of liquidation involves higher-than-normal levels of unemployment. While unemployment beyond that associated with inherent frictions in the market is conventionally separated into 'structural' and 'cyclical' components, the unemployment that accompanies the initial downturn in the Austrian theory is actually a special category of structural unemployment, namely, the unemployment associated with a discoordinated capital structure.

The sequence of malinvestment and overconsumption followed by forced saving and then liquidation and unemployment characterizes the intertemporal disequilibrium that is summarily described as a business cycle. The Austrian theory of the business cycle is consistent with the more broadly conceived Austrian vision of the market as a process and the price system as a communications network (Hayek, 1945). The theory allows for expectations to affect the course of the cycle and to cause each cyclical episode to differ in its particulars from the preceding ones. However, the assumption of 'rational expectations', as that term has come to be used in modern macroeconomics, would be inconsistent with the Austrian theory. That assumption would collapse the market process into its ultimate outcome on the basis of a supposed knowledge on the part of market participants of the structure of the economy.

Unlike alternative treatments of the consequences of credit expansion, the Austrian theory focuses on the interest rate movements and intertemporal resource allocation and only secondarily on changes in the general level of prices. In fact, the most straightforward application of the Austrian theory involves a price level that is not changing, because the increase in the money supply and the increase in real output have offsetting effects. The inter-war episode of boom and bust in the United States is a prime example in which the economy did actually experience real growth while unduly favourable credit conditions caused the growth path to be unsustainably high. There was no significant price inflation during the 1920s, but the intertemporal misallocation of resources eventually brought the boom to an end.

With no actual or expected change in the price level, the more common accounts of boom and bust, such as those that hinge on labour market dynamics associated with the short-run and long-run Phillips curves or those that feature monetary misperception in a more direct way, are simply not applicable to the 1920s. Instead, the near-constant price level during that decade is seen as a hallmark of macroeconomic stability, and the troubles that began in the late 1920s are taken to be independent of the preceding boom. An extended contrast featuring Phillips curves and Hayekian triangles is provided by Bellante and Garrison (1988).

In the Austrian view, a credit expansion strong enough to cause an actual price inflation does complicate the course of the cycle. Diverse judgments about the magnitude of the inflation premium that attaches to the interest rate can have discoordinating effects that compound the underlying intertemporal discoordination. And, as Hayek (1978) notes, a possible lag of expectations behind actuality can allow the central bank to postpone the inevitable downturn. But the point of Hayek's discussion of accelerating inflation is that there is no simple monetary fix for an economy that finds itself in the final throes of an artificial boom.

Lionel Robbins (1934) made the case that Austrian theory fits the inter-war experience well, though he later repudiated his Austrianism in favour of Keynesianism. Murray Rothbard (1963) drew on the Austrian theory in chronicling America's inter-war experience. Both Hayek and Rothbard (in Mises *et al.*, 1996) suggest that the theory has application to the postwar behaviour of the macro economy, while contemporary proponents see clear application of the theory in the twenty-first century.

Recent developments in the Austrian theory of the business cycle include new interpretations of the theory (Skousen, 1990) and reassessments of old debates (Cochran and Glahe, 1999) as well as renewed attention to the theory's micro foundations (Horwitz, 2000) and a generalization of the business cycle theory into a more comprehensive capital-based macroeconomics (Garrison, 2001).

ROGER W. GARRISON

See also:
Great Depression; Hayek, Friedrich A. von.

Bibliography
Bellante, D. and R. Garrison (1988), 'Phillips Curves and Hayekian Triangles: Two Perspectives on Monetary Dynamics', *History of Political Economy*, **20**, Summer, pp. 207–34.
Cochran, J. and F. Glahe (1999), *The Hayek–Keynes Debate: Lessons for Current Business Cycle Research*, Lampeter, Wales: Edwin Mellen.
Garrison, R. (2001), *Time and Money: The Macroeconomics of Capital Structure*, London: Routledge.
Hayek, F.A. ([1935] 1967), *Prices and Production*, 2nd edn, New York: Augustus M. Kelley.
Hayek, F.A. (1945), 'The Use of Knowledge in Society', *American Economic Review*, **35**, September, pp. 519–30.
Hayek, F.A. ([1969] 1978), 'Three Elucidations of the Ricardo Effect', *New Studies in Philosophy, Politics, Economics and the History of Ideas*, Chicago: University of Chicago Press, pp. 165–78.
Horwitz, S. (2000), *Microfoundations and Macroeconomics: An Austrian Perspective*, London: Routledge.
Lachmann, L. ([1956] 1978), *Capital and Its Structure*, Kansas City: Sheed, Andrews and McMeel.
Mises, L. ([1912] 1953), *The Theory of Money and Credit*, New Haven, CT: Yale University Press.
Mises, L. (1966), *Human Action: A Treatise on Economics*, 3rd rev. edn, Chicago: Henry Regnery.
Mises L., G. Haberler, M. Rothbard and F. Hayek ([1978] 1996), *The Austrian Theory of the Trade Cycle and Other Essays*, Auburn, AL: Ludwig von Mises Institute.
Robbins, L. ([1934] 1971), *The Great Depression*, Freeport, NY: Books for Libraries Press.
Rothbard, M. ([1963] 2000), *America's Great Depression*, 5th edn, Auburn, AL: Ludwig von Mises Institute.
Skousen, M. (1990), *The Structure of Production*, New York: New York University Press.

Business Cycles: Keynesian Approach

It has been observed that choosing amongst the various possible causes of business cycle fluctuations is somewhat akin to solving the Murder on the Orient Express: all suspects turn out to be guilty. For economists engaged in data analysis there are a host of economic variables that fluctuate within the business cycle with different time lags and varying degrees of amplitude. In Keynesian economics, however, there is a strong theoretical argument for choosing investment as the driving force of the business cycle.

Keynes developed his *General Theory* (1936) as a rebuttal to Say's Law, the classical proposition that supply creates its own demand. Key to this proposition is a process by which savings are automatically channelled into investment, with changes in the rate of interest acting to ensure equality between the two. Under Say's Law this induced investment fills the gap provided by insufficient demand. From this classical perspective it is as if the economy saves a proportion of its corn produced in a particular year, and invests this surplus as seed corn in the production of the next period's output.

For Keynes, however, capitalism is a monetary production economy in which savings take the form of money. If savings increase, investors may for various reasons, relating to the uncertainty of future events, choose to hold money balances instead of carrying out investment expenditures. Moreover, the ability to hold money balances means that investors can freely decide at different points in time to switch between money balances and investment. Using this analysis of money as a starting point, Keynes argued that investment expenditure is susceptible to wide and sudden fluctuations. Investment decisions are vulnerable to tides of irrational optimism and pessimism, causing large swings in the state of business confidence. According to Keynes (1937, p. 121), expectations of the future profitability of investment are far more important than the rate of interest in linking the future with the present: since 'given the psychology of the public, the level of output and employment as a whole depends on the amount of investment' and it is those factors 'which determine the rate of investment which are most unreliable, since it is they which are influenced by our views of the future about which we know so little'.

Although the factors that determine investment are difficult to capture in a succinct economic model, Keynes developed a clear analysis of the way in which investment, as the key economic variable, generates economic activity. Investment determines income and employment via the multiplier process. Each injection of investment generates employment in the production of investment goods, and these workers buy consumption goods produced by workers in the consumption goods sector. The level of income, and the volume of savings forthcoming from that income, are determined by the volume of investment in the economy. Keynes never developed a complete framework for modelling the business cycle, but subsequent to the *General Theory* the multiplier has provided the foundation for the development of a Keynesian theory of the business cycle.

In the most widely known Keynesian model of the business cycle, Samuelson (1939) combined the multiplier process with an investment accelerator. This concept captures the notion that the rate of change in output is the main factor that influences the level of investment in the economy. From this perspective firms increase their capital stock (net investment) because there is an increase in demand for their products. The greater the change in output the greater the investment in capital stock that is required to meet this demand.

The two building blocks of the multiplier-accelerator model take the form:

1.   change in output = multiplier × change in investment;
2.   net investment = accelerator × change in output.

In a typical boom the multiplier and accelerator mechanisms feed off each other. Increases in output induce firms to increase their capital stock – via the accelerator there is positive net investment. Through the multiplier, increases in investment result in an expansion of output, that feeds back further into more investment via the accelerator. Similarly, in a downturn, reductions in investment lead to reductions in output (via the multiplier) which feed back to lower investment (via the accelerator).

The key question is why each boom or downturn should come to an end. Why are there turning points in the business cycle? The reason is provided by the way in which investment is defined in the multiplier and accelerator processes. In the multiplier process a change in output is driven by the *change* in investment. The same level of investment will generate no change in output via the multiplier. Only new investment will change output. In the accelerator process, however, the *absolute level* of net investment is driven by the change in output. This means that the feedback loop between investment and changes in output is incomplete. In a boom, changes in investment will generate increases in output (via the multiplier), but these are insufficient to sustain further changes in investment – only absolute volumes of net investment are required to meet these changes (via the accelerator). The problem with investment is that it is useful. It generates changes in demand via the multiplier but cannot provide sufficient demand to require investment to expand indefinitely.

For Hicks (1950) the Keynesian approach requires the addition of 'ceilings' and 'floors' to account for turning points in the cycle. During an expansionary phase of growth, as the economy approaches its full employment or potential output 'ceiling' the rate at which output increases will slow down because of resource constraints. The slowdown in output reduces investment, through the operation of the accelerator, which in turn leads to a fall in output through the multiplier process. The cycle now passes into its contractionary phase as it moves from an upper turning point to a lower turning point. The contractionary phase of the cycle will be reversed when the economy hits a 'floor'. Sooner or later, as the existing capital equipment wears out, it will fall to a level where it needs replacing in order to produce current production of output. New investment for replacement orders will, through the interaction of the multiplier and accelerator, start the expansionary phase of the cycle again.

There has been some dispute about the extent to which this multiplier–accelerator model provides an accurate portrayal of the business cycle conditions. Michal Kalecki, who, it is claimed by some, discovered the substance of the *General Theory* prior to Keynes, argued that the accelerator fails to take into account the high degree of excess capacity that is prevalent throughout the business cycle of most capitalist countries: 'It is well known that large reserve capacities exist, at least throughout a considerable part of the cycle, and that output may therefore increase without an actual increase in existing capacities' (Kalecki, 1954, p. 285). Kalecki argues, using data from the US economy, that there is 'no appreciable time lag' between investment and output during the course of the business cycle (ibid., p. 286).

Kalecki suggests a different accelerator mechanism in which the rate of profit (instead of output) provides the main driver of investment (see Trigg, 1994). This relates to Keynes's own attempts to explain investment in terms of profitability in the *General Theory* (Keynes uses the concept of the marginal efficiency of capital, which broadly refers to the profitability of capital). Kalecki's approach also has a Marxian flavour, the rate of profit providing the key variable in Marx's economics, although Marx never used the rate of profit directly to explain investment.

Other writers in the Keynesian tradition have concentrated on the multiplier process, and in particular upon the role of finance. Asimakopulos (1983) argues that Keynes and Kalecki wrongly assume that capitalists can finance investment from their own resources. The crux of this problem concerns the so-called 'widow's cruse' or 'Kalecki principle' that capitalists earn what they spend. Capitalists decide how much to invest and, as shown above, this generates a new level of income via the multiplier process. Capitalists do not react to the amount of resources available (as in a corn economy), but rather generate these resources through their own spending. For Keynes, finance is 'revolving fund'; for Kalecki, the 'circle [of finance] will close itself' (Asimakopulos, 1983, p. 222).

The key problem is that the multiplier process takes time to work itself out. Capitalist investment generates an initial volume of income in the first instance, but the impact of subsequent rounds, in which newly employed workers consume goods produced by other workers, takes time to work through the economy. In the meantime, capitalists must borrow money from the financial markets in order to fund their investment activities. Since investment is the main driving force of the business cycle, the role of the financial markets takes centre stage in the Keynesian approach.

Hyman Minsky provides the most developed theoretical discussion of the role of finance in the business cycle. His financial instability hypothesis provides a devastating critique of the financial system, and its role in the determination of investment. This hypothesis is founded upon an institutional analysis of the way in which firms use the financial markets. Investment projects are funded in three main ways: 'hedge', 'speculative' and 'Ponzi' finance. Under hedge finance, debt repayments are smaller than profits expected during each period. Such projects are not subject to the vagaries of the financial markets, so long as cash flows from sales of goods and services are forthcoming.

Under speculative finance, firms are unable in each period to pay off all of their debts out of proceeds of production. Either cash reserves are required or debts are rolled over into the next period. The solvency of these firms is vulnerable to changes in the interest rate. With Ponzi finance – named after Charles Ponzi, an Italian immigrant who swindled poor and respectable investors in Boston in 1919 and 1920 with a pyramid banking scheme – firms are the most exposed to the financial markets. Debt cannot be fully paid off until the end of the investment project. The Channel Tunnel link between Britain and France, for example, did not start to pay off its debtors until the end of the investment project. Many of the Dot Com investments in Internet start-ups, during the economic boom of the late 1990s, involved a period of investment without any immediate prospect of a reward in terms of profits. This means that even repayment of interest requires further debt. There is a pyramid of finance, with debt financing debt (Nasica, 2000).

For Minsky, a typical boom phase in the business cycle involves a shift from hedge to more speculative and Ponzi finance. 'Over a period in which the economy does well, views about acceptable debt structure change. In the deal-making that goes on between banks, investment bankers, and businessmen, the acceptable amount of debt to use in financing various types of activity and positions increases' (Minsky, 1982, p.65–6). As the stock market booms, each firm is compelled to finance more and more expansion of investment to ensure that the price of its own shares does not fall behind.

From the point of view of each firm, Dymski and Pollin (1992, p.44) argue: 'the lesson of history may be that their financial posture was reasonable, but that a onetime shock, for which they bore no responsibility, brought the system, and themselves, to a crisis'. The possibility of firms applying rational expectations to ensure that they do not take on too much debt is excluded in this approach. In the absence of Keynesian intervention to regulate the financial markets, the business cycle is likely to overheat, its fragility exposed by particular historical events and circumstances.

ANDREW B. TRIGG

See also:

Financial Instability; Investment: Accelerator Theory of; Kalecki, Michal; Keynes's *General Theory*; Minsky, Hyman P.; Multiplier; Rational Expectations; Say's Law.

Bibliography

Asimakopulos, A. (1983), 'Kalecki and Keynes on Finance, Investment and Saving', *Cambridge Journal of Economics,* **7**, September–December, pp. 221–33.

Dymski, G. and R. Pollin (1992), 'Hymen Minksy as Hedgehog: The Power of the Wall Street Paradigm', in S. Fazzari and D. Papadimitiou (eds), *Financial Conditions and Economic Performance: Essays in Honor of Hyman Minsky,* Armonk, New York: M.E. Sharpe.

Hicks, J.R. (1950), *A Contribution to the Theory of the Trade Cycle,* Oxford: Oxford University Press.

Kalecki, M. ([1954] 1991), 'The Theory of Economic Dynamics', in J. Osiatynski (ed.), *Collected Works of Michal Kalecki, Vol. 2. Capitalism: Economic Dynamics,* Oxford: Clarendon Press, pp. 207–338.

Keynes, J.M. (1936), *The General Theory of Employment, Interest and Money,* New York: Harcourt Brace.

Keynes, J.M. (1937), 'The General Theory of Employment', *Quarterly Journal of Economics,* **51**, February, pp. 209–33.

Minsky, H.P. (1982), *Can 'It' Happen Again?,* Armonk, New York: M.E. Sharpe.

Nasica, E. (2000), *Finance, Investment and Economic Fluctuations: An Analysis in the Tradition of Hyman P. Minsky,* Cheltenham, UK and Northampton, MA, USA: Edward Elgar.

Samuelson, P. (1939), 'Interaction Between the Multiplier Analysis and the Principle of Acceleration', *Review of Economics and Statistics,* **21**, May, pp. 75–8.

Trigg, A.B. (1994), 'On the Relationship Between Kalecki and the Kaleckians', *Journal of Post Keynesian Economics,* **17**, Fall, pp. 91–109.

Business Cycles: Marxian Approach

Marxian economics sees the capitalist system as driven by the accumulation of capital – the latter's generator being the production for profit through the exploitation of labour. Accumulation of capital is the process of appending profits to the initial capital size. Capital in process is necessarily both monetary and physical without prejudice to either. Although, from a static point of view, capital may appear as something either monetary or physical, such a one-sided view is an illusion. In fact, any actual 'stasis' of capital means an interruption of the capital circuit and thus bears the germ of an economic crisis. Hence 'accumulation of capital' implies expansion of the circuit of capital. Although, as just indicated, the capitalist system is driven by this expansive accumulation of capital, we see in practice its recurrent negation, that is, phases of expansion alternating with phases of contraction.

Because the explanation of this alternation has always been a core of Marxian economics, it should not be surprising that over its one hundred years' tradition several strands have developed. Before specifying differences in the second half of this entry, I first indicate the similarities of these strands.

Their *first* and most important common characteristic is that cyclical development is seen to be endemic to the capitalist system – later on we will see why. The *impetus* to cycles is *endogenous* to the system and not something coming accidentally from the outside as a 'shock'.

Second, endogeneity applies also to the *propagating* processes – the dynamic repercussions – however much these also depend on the structural–institutional development *of* the capitalist system. Together these generate recurrent cycles, though not inherently regular in either length (top to top) or amplitude (top to trough). Since 'cycle' often implies such regularity, Marxist economists only reluctantly use the term 'cycle', referring instead to 'waves' or to one phase of the cycle, crisis, that is, the turn from expansion to contraction. Accordingly, much of Marxian cycle theory bears the heading of 'theory of crisis'.

A *third* common characteristic, developed by Marx early on in *Capital Vol. 1*, is that the general *possibility* of economic crisis is seen to lie in the elementary form of money-mediated market exchange. Money is not just a convenient medium of exchange. Money is primarily the incarnation of value. This is conditioned by its being a fiduciary store of value. Therefore money can, for various reasons, in principle be withdrawn from circulation, hence interrupt the exchange process, and so interrupt the circuit of capital alluded to in the opening paragraph above. This is the elementary basis for Marx's, and the current Marxian, rejection of Say's Law.

As preamble to the fourth point it needs to be stressed that Marxian economists make a sharp distinction between profit and interest (and the profit rate versus the interest rate). Structurally (the rate of) profit is larger than (the rate of) interest. Interest is a share of profits distributed to debtors (various forms of loan capital such as bonds or bank loans). Bearing this in mind – and notwithstanding the fact that accumulation is largely financed by retained profits – the *fourth* common view is that the accumulation of capital is necessarily accompanied by an expansion of (particularly) bank credit. To put it more strongly: accumulation of capital without any accommodating credit expansion is impossible (profits 'produced' cannot be realized without credit). In phases of expansion, credit accommodates profit increase and accumulation of capital, and indeed boosts them; at that time the interest payment is no problem. However, the counterpart is that in phases of contraction – when profits may be nullified – interest operates as a strangling burden and can only be settled by capital devaluation (amplified upon below).

Although the accommodating role of credit is played out in different degrees by the different strands within Marxian economics, it is always seen as core to the propagation of the cycle's impetus and hence to the cycle itself.

Fifth, all strands see the development of the profit rate (profits over capital invested) as the crucial constituent for the cyclical unfolding of capitalist economies. The rate of profit is, as explained below, 'a concentration of many determinants' and its (current) development is the key measure for the (current) state of the economy; as such its development is also the key prospect determinant for the accumulation of capital and its finance (both internal through retained profits and external through, especially, bank credit). A decreasing rate of profit is seen as the principal determinant of decreasing investment by firms near to the upper turning point of the cycle and eventually the move to economic crisis and contraction.

Of course, the cardinal question then becomes the explanation of changes in the rate of profit (see below). For example, why is it that the rate of profit starts decreasing halfway through the expansion phase of the business cycle, as is the case with recent cycles in major capitalist economies? Note that this involves controversial theoretical and empirical–statistical measurement issues: for example, the periodization and the stage/pattern of cycles, or the measurement of profits and capital themselves. Similar problems, of course, apply to any approach in economics and in science generally.

A final, *sixth*, common view, although stressed to a different degree, is that 'restructuring of capital' in the crisis and recession phases of the cycle is seen to lay the foundation for a renewed expansion. This restructuring involves a destruction of segments of capital through bankruptcies, closure of plants as well as other reorganizations within companies; it also involves the selling of parts of the company as well as takeovers. Thus restructuring in this stage of the cycle contributes to the general concentration and centralization of capital (oligopolization) – the latter not restricted to this cycle stage. This restructuring along with a general devaluation (writing off) of capital restores the rate of profit and so initiates a renewed expansion phase.

Note that – returning to point five – there is not much difference of opinion as to which are the 'many determinants' of the profit rate:

1. the power of labour in production (or the 'intensity' of work) in relation to the state of technology (the technological trajectory);

2.   the wage rate and the capital–labour distribution of income (the so-called 'rate of exploitation of labour' is shorthand for this and the previous factor taken together);
3.   the 'realization ratio' which is a measure for overproduction and/or overcapacity in relation to macroeconomic expenditures (with disagreement over the 'and/or');
4.   relating to (1), tranche-wise steps within a technological trajectory (or, in the long run, change of the trajectory itself) and, in relation to that, structural change of the power of labour (shorthand for this is the change in the so-called 'organic composition of capital').

Of course, these factors are complex and interrelated. All of them are (at least potential) variables over the course of the cycle. Differences between Marxian strands concern the key impetus(es) to the cyclical changes in rate of profit and their propagation.

We now come to these differences. Within the confines of this entry I will make no distinction between 'long' and 'short' cycles, because this requires detailed theoretical and measurement discussions (for some researchers a recession, as defined by two quarters of contraction, is simply not the object of enquiry). The same limitation requires a rather schematic account, doing some injustice to those authors referred to, as well as to authors not referred to. (See Clarke, 1994, ch. 2 for a concise historical overview of theories; he also describes how in the course of the twentieth century all the theories below have been applied, by different authors, to long and short cycles. For an introductory treatment see Laibman, 1997, chs 8–10.)

Labour reserve profit squeeze
This comparatively recent approach – at least within Marxian economics – originates from work done by Glyn and Sutcliffe, and Boddy and Crotty in the early 1970s (a precursor at an abstract theoretical level is the work of Uno in the 1950s; cf. Glyn, 1997). A sophisticated recent account is that of Goldstein (1996, 1999) on which my summary statement draws in part.

In short, this theory holds that the capital broadening aspect of accumulation within a technological trajectory leads to a reduction in the reserve army of unemployed and the relative strength of labour. This results in both increases in the rate of growth of wages (distribution) and decreases in the rate of growth of productivity (labour's power in production), especially in the second half of the expansion phase. The concomitant increase in unit labour costs cannot be fully passed on in prices – because of competitive demand constraints along with a rise in capacity utilization – whence the rate of profit declines. With some lag this leads to investment decline and the turn to contraction. Restructuring of capital and lay-offs, along with contraction, restore the reserve of unemployed, so weakening labour's position in the labour market and at the point of production (the reverse of the initial process) and so on. Thus economic crisis and recession/depression disciplines workers.

Overproduction
Several varieties of this approach developed over the twentieth century. There are two main variants of the overproduction impetus to a profit squeeze. In the first (sometimes called 'underconsumption'), profits are squeezed by limited demand. Briefly, it is argued that, in the first segments of the expansion phase, the distribution of income (measured as the macro profit share in income) develops in favour of profits. This reduces the ratio of consumption to income, eventually generating a decline in capacity utilization, and so a decrease in the rate of profit. In the last segment of the expansion, costs rise faster than output, so squeezing profits. Wage increases in this segment of the expansion come too late. In the phase of crisis and contraction, profits decrease and capacity is cut through restructuring of capital. With the rate of profit restored via the analogous devaluation of capital the foundation is laid for a new expansion. Note that the initial condition only holds with a reserve of labour such that wage increases lag behind productivity increases. Therefore this type of theory is mostly combined with a variant of the labour reserve profit squeeze (above), as in Sherman (1991; 1997) and Sherman and Kolk (1996).

In the second variant, the overproduction impetus results in a profit squeeze via 'disproportionality' (imbalance between branches or sectors of production). It is inherent to capitalism that the 'forces of production' are perpetually developed in order to appropriate profits. Capitalist firms do not respond to fluctuations in demand by mere quantity adaptation, but by introducing more productive methods of production, in order to reduce costs below those of competitors. Production is expanded in anticipation of undercutting competitors. This impetus cannot be checked by competition because, as Clarke (1994, pp. 281–3) puts it, 'Competition presupposes overproduction, since capitalists only experience competitive pressure when the product is greater than the amount that can be sold at a price corresponding to the price of production. Competition is simply the form in which overproduction is experienced.' Whereas in the long run this process develops in every branch of production, the opportunities for the introduction of new methods of production 'are unevenly developed between the various branches . . . which therefore would tend to expand at different rates'. When overproduction in a (major) branch comes to the fore in the market, it soon spirals down into other branches; in this way, a fall in the rate of profit multiplies around the economy. In the wake of the crisis, over-production is removed through destruction of productive capacity, redundancy of labour and devaluation of capital.

Rising organic composition of capital
Until about 1970, a third Marxian approach was exclusively applied to long-term secular development. Via, amongst others, the work of Mattick, Yaffe, Fine and Harris, Shaikh and Weeks, cyclical approaches have since been developed. Whereas the first theory's focus is on the capital broadening aspect of capital accumulation within a technological trajectory, this third theory focuses on the so-called 'rising organic composition of capital' (capital deepening) – either its moderate tranche-wise development within a trajectory, or that from one trajectory to another. Both of the latter stem from the continuous force to revolutionize the methods of production in order to extract more profits – the expression of which comes to a temporary halt in the early contraction phase.

Consider the rate of profit $r = R/K$, the ratio of profits and capital invested in means of production. Dividing by the sum of wages, wL, we have $r = (R/wL)/(K/wL)$. The numerator measures the macroeconomic distribution of income and the denominator can be taken as a measure of the technique together with the productivity or intensity of labour. (A more sophisticated presentation would have K/L together with a more complicated numerator; a rise in K/L means that labour works up an increasing mass of means of production). In this theory it is argued that K/wL rises throughout the expansion phase. Then, of course, with a constant distribution of income the rate of profit would decline. Instead, though, R/wL tends to increase in the first half of expansion, with a downward pressure developing in the second half, owing to increasing labour strength. Nevertheless, on average the rise in K/wL is greater than the rise in R/wL. The ensuing decrease in the rate of profit, especially in the upper segment of the expansion, leads, with some lag, to decline in investment and the turn to contraction. In this theory much stress is laid on the restructuring of capital in the contraction phase (see above, sixth common view) which through devaluation of capital restores the rate of profit, so laying the foundation for a new expansion.

Although the analytic part of this theory seems simple, it is really the most complicated theory in terms both of its micro foundations and of its empirical measurement difficulties. For the micro foundations – grounded in a disequilibrium framework – the reader is referred to Laibman (1997) and Reuten (1991); the latter also uses this framework to set out the endogenous turn from contraction to expansion. As for measurement problems, a first observation is that the conventional measurement of K in National

Account statistics is based on static equilibrium estimates that are difficult to adapt to notions of 'devaluation of capital'. Second, some researchers within this approach differentiate between investments that are strictly capacity increasing and others ('unproductive') that have to do with the realization of output (for example, Moseley, 1991; 1997).

Synthetic approaches

Already from this schematic summary it can be inferred that there is ample room for synthetic approaches (in fact there is a long-standing Marxian tradition of multicausal approaches, going back to Bauer and Kautsky early in the twentieth century). In brief, there are two variants of these. A first variant stresses the continuous 'tendential' interaction of all three components (for example, Reuten and Williams, 1989, chs 3–5). A second variant sees different factors as actual in different historical periods, the institutional conditions of which have been variously theorized, especially from the mid-1970s onwards, as 'phases', 'regimes' and 'social structures' of accumulation. Albritton *et al.* (2001) provide a useful collection of all the latter approaches, with further references.

To complete this review it may finally be noted that non-linear dynamic and chaotic models are an area of concern among a number of Marxian economists (see Freeman and Carchedi, 1996).

In sum, it has been indicated that amongst Marxian economists there are six major points of common ground about the cyclical development of capitalist economies. There is disagreement about what should count – if so – as the key factor setting in motion the recurrent decline in the rate of profit. On the other hand, since the various approaches do not seem to be inconsistent, there is room for integrating these into a general theory.

GEERT REUTEN

See also:

Marxian Macroeconomics: an Overview; Marxian Macroeconomics: Some Key Relationships; Say's Law.

Bibliography

Albritton, R., M. Itoh, R. Westra and A. Zuege (eds) (2001), *Phases of Capitalist Development: Booms, Crises and Globalizations*, Basingstoke and New York: Palgrave.
Clarke, S. (1994), *Marx's Theory of Crisis*, London and New York: Macmillan/St Martin's Press.
Duménil, G. and D. Lévy (1993), *The Economics of the Profit Rate: Competition, Crises and Historical Tendencies in Capitalism*, Aldershot, UK and Brookfield, US: Edward Elgar.
Freeman, A. and G. Carchedi (1996), *Marx and Non-Equilibrium Economics*, Aldershot, UK and Brookfield, US: Edward Elgar.
Glyn, A. (1997), 'Does Aggregate Profitability *Really* Matter?', *Cambridge Journal of Economics*, **21**, pp. 593–619.

Goldstein, J. (1996), 'The Empirical Relevance of the Cyclical Profit Squeeze: A Reassertion', *Review of Radical Political Economics*, **28**, pp. 55–92.
Goldstein, J. (1999), 'The Simple Analytics and Empirics of the Cyclical Profit Squeeze and Cyclical Underconsumption Theories: Clearing the Air', *Review of Radical Political Economics*, **31**, pp. 74–88.
Laibman, D. (1997), *Capitalist Macrodynamics: A Systematic Introduction*, London: Macmillan.
Moseley, F. (1991), *The Falling Rate of Profit in the Postwar United States Economy*, London: Macmillan.
Moseley, F. (1997), 'The Rate of Profit and the Future of Capitalism', *Review of Radical Political Economics*, **29**, pp. 23–41.
Reuten, G. (1991), 'Accumulation of Capital and the Foundation of the Tendency of the Rate of Profit to Fall', *Cambridge Journal of Economics*, **15**, pp. 79–93.
Reuten, G. and M. Williams (1989), *Value-form and the State: The Tendencies of Accumulation and the Determination of Economic Policy in Capitalist Society*, London and New York: Routledge.
Sherman, H.J. (1991), *The Business Cycle: Growth and Crisis under Capitalism*, Princeton, NJ: Princeton University Press.
Sherman, H.J. (1997), 'Theories of Cyclical Profit Squeeze', *Review of Radical Political Economics*, **29**, pp. 139–47.
Sherman, H.J. and D. Kolk (1996), *Business Cycles and Forecasting*, New York: Harper-Collins.

Business Cycles: Monetarist Approach

The monetarist approach to the study of business cycles is associated primarily, though not exclusively, with Milton Friedman and Anna J. Schwartz's 'money in business cycles' project for the National Bureau of Economic Research and with work by Friedman's students in the University of Chicago Workshop in Money and Banking. This approach is distinguished both by the methods employed and by the conclusions about business cycles derived therefrom. Friedman learned how to analyse business cycles from Wesley Mitchell as a graduate student at Columbia University. Mitchell put his methods to use in *Business Cycles* (1913), then institutionalized them in the research programme of the National Bureau. Mitchell's other major publications on business cycles included *Business Cycles: The Problem and its Setting* (1927) and, with Arthur Burns, *Measuring Business Cycles* (1946). When Milton Friedman and Anna J. Schwartz embarked on their monetary factors in business cycles project for the National Bureau in 1948, they brought to the task the same methods Mitchell used (see Hammond, 1996).

The term 'monetarist' as applied to Friedman and Schwartz's analysis came later, in response to their conclusions about money, income and the price level. These conclusions are found in numerous monographs, articles and reports, including 'Money and Business Cycles' (1963a), *A Monetary History of the United States, 1867–1960* (1963b) and *Monetary Trends in the United States and the United Kingdom: Their Relation to Income, Prices, and Interest Rates 1867–1975* (1982).

Friedman and Schwartz's methods place heavy emphasis on observation and measurement, developing theories in response to patterns observed in data. Wesley Mitchell referred to his use of this approach as 'analytical description'. Friedman and Schwartz wrote in another of their books, *Monetary Statistics*:

> To put the matter differently, the economic theory accepted at any time is in part a systematic summary of the empirical generalizations that have been arrived at by students of economic phenomena. This theory implicitly contains a specification of the empirical counterparts to the concepts in terms of which it is expressed – otherwise it would be pure mathematics (1970, p. 91)

Following Mitchell's practice, Friedman and Schwartz developed numerous detailed time series of monetary data. From these they extracted cycles and trends, and then compared the amplitude, duration and variability of monetary cycles with the same measures for 'reference cycles'. Reference cycles are the National Bureau's measures of the general business cycle.

It should be emphasized that Friedman and Schwartz made a massive effort, both in time and creative energy, producing monetary evidential data, regarding this as an important research product in its own right. For approximately seven years from their start in 1948 the overwhelming part of their work, and of Friedman's students' in the Workshop, was in building a record of historical data. Not until the mid-1950s did the balance of their work shift from producing evidence to analysing the evidence. One of the three monographs from their project is *Monetary Statistics* (1970), a volume of statistical data, not of statistical (econometric) theory or analysis. This allocation of scholarly resources fitted perfectly into the National Bureau vision of research, but ran counter to the postwar 'Keynesian' emphasis on formal general equilibrium theory. Outside the National Bureau and the University of Chicago, the overwhelming concern was to get the theory 'right' by formal abstract standards. A year before Friedman and Schwartz began their project, Arthur Burns and Wesley Mitchell were tarred with the 'measurement without theory' brush. This was the title of Tjalling Koopmans's review article (1947) of Burns and Mitchell's *Measuring Business Cycles* (1946). Friedman and Schwartz's critics used the same brush throughout their collaboration, charging that their conclusions derived from factual evidence were not supported by adequate theory.

Monetarism is a label coined by fellow monetarist Karl Brunner (1968) for assertions about money, income and prices that challenged Keynesian views. Part of the intellectual background against which Friedman and Schwartz conducted their studies was the belief that fiscal policy was more powerful and effective than monetary policy. Keynesians diagnosed business cycles as being caused by instability of private investment expenditure and prescribed countercyclical fiscal policy as the remedy. They thought monetary policy's effectiveness faltered at two points: weak linkages between changes in the money supply and interest rates (the liquidity trap) and between interest rates and an investment function dominated by 'animal spirits'. The Great Depression in the United States (1929–33) was generally viewed as having occurred despite the Federal Reserve's best efforts to brake it. Friedman and Schwartz's study of monetary data and banking history led them to conclude that inept policy responses by the Federal Reserve converted an ordinary recession into the Great Depression. The Fed could have expanded the money supply to lessen and shorten the recession of 1929. Instead, they stood by, allowing the money supply to shrink by one-third.

Friedman shared the view of Wesley Mitchell that lags in adjustment are essential features of business cycles. His eye for dynamic patterns in time series was a natural outgrowth of National Bureau cycle analysis, but put Friedman at odds with Keynesians who framed macroeconomic problems in general equilibrium modelling. From himself and others, Friedman sought empirically tested theory of business cycles. He believed that economists' understanding of business cycles was rudimentary relative to the knowledge needed for active countercyclical policy. He also believed that theoretical analysis was not alone sufficient for expansion of knowledge. Friedman's emphasis on observation and measurement is clearly on display in a remark from his dialogue with Walter W. Heller on monetary and fiscal policy: 'The fascinating thing to me is that the widespread faith in the potency of fiscal policy . . . rests on no evidence whatsoever. It's based on pure assumption. It's based on *a priori* reasoning' (1969, pp. 52–3).

Friedman provides a general summary of monetarist conclusions from business cycle analysis in the 1964 annual report of the National Bureau:

> Money does matter and matters very much. Changes in the quantity of money have important, and broadly predictable, economic effects. Long-period changes in the quantity of money relative to output determine the secular behavior of prices. Substantial expansions in the quantity of money over short periods have been a major proximate source of the accompanying inflation in prices. Substantial contractions in the quantity of money over short periods have been a major factor in producing severe economic contractions. And cyclical variations in the quantity of money may well be an important element in the ordinary mild business cycle. (1964, p. 277)

J. Daniel Hammond

See also:

Brunner, Karl; Burns, Arthur, F.; Business Cycles: Keynesian Approach; Friedman, Milton; Great Depression; Liquidity Trap; Mitchell, Wesley C.; Monetarism; National Bureau of Economic Research; Quantity Theory of Money; Schwartz, Anna J.; Theory and Measurement in Macroeconomics: Role of.

Bibliography

Brunner, K. (1968), 'The Role of Money and Monetary Policy', *Federal Reserve Bank of St. Louis Review*, **50**, July, pp. 9–24.

Burns, A.F. and W.C. Mitchell (1946), *Measuring Business Cycles*, New York: National Bureau of Economic Research.

Friedman, M. (1964), 'The Monetary Studies of the National Bureau', *The National Bureau Enters its 45th Year*, 44th Annual Report, New York: National Bureau of Economic Research; reprinted in M. Friedman (1969), *The Optimum Quantity of Money*, Chicago: Aldine.

Friedman, M. and W.W. Heller (1969), *Monetary vs. Fiscal Policy*, New York: W.W. Norton & Company.

Friedman, M. and A.J. Schwartz (1963a), 'Money and Business Cycles', *Review of Economics and Statistics*, **45**, February, pp. 32–64; reprinted in M. Friedman (1969), *The Optimum Quantity of Money*, Chicago: Aldine.

Friedman, M. and A.J. Schwartz (1963b), *A Monetary History of the United States, 1867–1960*, Princeton, NJ: Princeton University Press for the National Bureau of Economic Research.

Friedman, M. and A.J. Schwartz (1970), *Monetary Statistics of the United States: Estimates, Sources, and Methods*, New York: Columbia University Press for the National Bureau of Economic Research.

Friedman, M. and A.J. Schwartz (1982), *Monetary Trends in the United States and the United Kingdom: Their Relation to Income, Prices and Interest Rates 1867–1975*, Chicago: University of Chicago Press.

Hammond, J.D. (1996), *Theory and Measurement: Causality Issues in Milton Friedman's Monetary Economics*, Cambridge: Cambridge University Press.

Koopmans, T.C. (1947), 'Measurement Without Theory', *Review of Economics and Statistics*, **29**, August, pp. 161–72.

Mitchell, W.C. (1913), *Business Cycles*, Berkeley, CA: University of California Press.

Mitchell, W.C. (1927), *Business Cycles: The Problem and Its Setting*, New York: National Bureau of Economic Research.

Business Cycles: New Classical Approach

'There seems to be no way to determine how business cycles are to be dealt with short of understanding what they are and how they occur' (Lucas, 1977).

In the post World War II period up to the 1970s, the main approach to the analysis of business cycles within mainstream macroeconomics was provided by Keynesians and monetarists (see Mullineux, 1984; the approach to business cycle analysis prior to Keynes is surveyed by Haberler, 1946). During the 1970s a new approach to the study of aggregate fluctuations was initiated by Robert E. Lucas Jr, who advocated an *equilibrium* approach to business cycle modelling. Lucas's equilibrium theory was a significant departure from Keynesian business cycle analysis where fluctuations of GDP were viewed as *disequilibrium* phenomena. Keynesian macroeconomic models are typically characterized by various rigidities and frictions that inhibit wage and price flexibility. Consequently, in the short run, markets fail to clear and GDP can depart significantly from its potential for extended periods of time. Milton Friedman was highly critical of Keynesian models for their failure to recognize the importance of monetary disturbances as a major source of aggregate instability. Friedman and Schwartz's (1963) study proved to be highly influential on a whole generation of economists. In particular, Friedman and Schwartz argued that the Great Depression was 'a tragic testimonial to the importance of monetary factors'. While Lucas was very much influenced by Friedman's monetarist ideas, he preferred to utilize a Walrasian research methodology rather than build on Friedman's Marshallian approach when analysing business cycles (see Hoover, 1984; Lucas, 1996, 1999).

Lucas (1975) defines business cycles as the serially correlated movements about trend of real output that 'are not explainable by movements in the availability of factors of production'. Associated with fluctuations in GDP are co-movements among different aggregative time series, such as prices, consumption, business profits, investment, monetary aggregates, productivity and interest rates (for an excellent discussion of this subject, see Abel and Bernanke, 2001). Such are the regularities that Lucas (1977) declares that 'with respect to the qualitative behaviour of co-movements among series, *business cycles are all alike*' (the Great Depression being an exception). To Lucas, the 'recurrent character of business cycles is of central importance'. As Lucas (1977) explains:

> Insofar as business cycles can be viewed as repeated instances of essentially similar events, it will be reasonable to treat agents as reacting to cyclical changes as 'risk', or to assume their expectations are *rational*, that they have fairly stable arrangements for collecting and processing information, and that they utilise this information in forecasting the future in a stable way, free of systematic and easily correctable biases.

Building on his path-breaking 1972 and 1973 papers, Lucas (1975, 1977) provides a 'new classical' monetarist explanation of the business cycle as an equilibrium phenomenon. As Kevin Hoover (1988) observes, 'To explain the related movements of macroeconomic aggregates and prices without recourse to the notion of disequilibrium is the *desideratum* of new classical research on the theory of business cycles'. As Lucas (1975) wrote, 'the central problem in macroeconomics' is to find a theoretical framework where monetary disturbances can cause real output fluctuations which, at the same time, does not imply 'the existence of persistent, recurrent, unexploited profit opportunities' such as those that occur in Keynesian models characterized by price rigidities and non-rational expectations. Although initially Lucas claimed some affinity, via the notion of equilibrium theorizing, with the work of Hayek on business cycles, it is now clear that new classical and Austrian theories of the business cycle are very different (see Lucas, 1977; Hoover, 1984, 1988; Zijp, 1993)

Lucas's monetary equilibrium business cycle theory (MEBCT) incorporates Muth's (1961) rational expectations hypothesis, Friedman's (1968) natural rate hypothesis and Walrasian general equilibrium methodology. With continuous market clearing due to complete wage and price flexibility, the fluctuations in MEBCT are described as competitive equilibria. But how can monetary disturbances create fluctuations in such a world? In the stylized classical model where agents have perfect information, changes in the money supply should be strictly neutral: that is, have no impact on real variables such as real GDP and employment. However, the leading and pro-cyclical behaviour of money observed empirically by researchers such as Friedman and Schwartz (1963), and more recently by Romer and Romer (1989), suggests that money is non-neutral (ignoring the possibility of reverse causation). The intellectual challenge facing Lucas was to account for the non-neutrality of money in a world inhabited by rational profit-maximizing agents and where all markets continuously clear. His main innovation was to extend the classical model so as to allow agents to have *imperfect information*. As a result, Lucas's MEBCT has come to be popularly known as the *misperceptions theory*, although the idea of instability being the result of monetary-induced misperceptions is also a major feature of Friedman's (1968) analysis of the Phillips curve (see Abel and Bernanke, 2001). In Lucas's (1975) pioneering attempt to build a MEBCT, his model was characterized by prices and quantities determined in competitive equilibrium; agents with rational expectations; and imperfect information, 'not only in the sense that the future is unknown, but also in the sense that no agent is perfectly informed as to the current state of the economy'.

In neoclassical microeconomic theory, the supply curve of an individual producer in a competitive market slopes upwards, indicating that the supplier will produce more in response to a rise in price. However, this profit-maximizing response is a reaction of producers to a rise in the *relative price* of the goods being supplied. Therefore individual suppliers need to know what is happening to the general price level in order to make a rational calculation of whether it is profitable to expand production in response to an increase in the nominal price of the good they supply. If all prices are rising because of inflation, suppliers should not increase production in response to a rise in price of their goods because it does not represent a relative (real) price increase. And yet the data reveal that aggregate output increases as the *general* price level increases, that is, the short-run aggregate supply curve slopes upwards in *P-Y* space. This must mean that the aggregate response of thousands of individual suppliers to an inflation of the general price level is positive and yet profit-maximizing individuals should not be reacting in this way. How can that be? Rational agents should only respond to real variables and their behaviour should be invariant to nominal variables.

The answer provided by Lucas relates to agents (workers, households, firms) having imperfect information about their relative prices (Lucas, 1972). If agents have been used to a world of price stability they will tend to interpret an increase in the supply price of the good (or service) they produce as a relative price increase and produce more in response (agents and households will engage in intertemporal labour substitution: see Lucas and Rapping, 1969; Lucas, 1977). Therefore an unexpected or *unanticipated* increase in the price level will *surprise* agents and they will misinterpret the information they observe with respect to the rise in price of their good and produce more. Agents have what Lucas (1977) refers to as a 'signal processing problem' and if all agents make the same error we will observe an aggregate increase in output correlated with an increase in the general price level. Since Lucas's model is 'monetarist', the increase in the general price level is caused by a prior increase in the money supply and we therefore observe a positive money to output correlation; that is, the non-neutrality of money. MEBCT emphasizes monetary shocks as the main cause of aggregate instability and the whole story is based on a confusion on the part of agents between relative and general price movements (Dore, 1993). In MEBCT, the supply of output at any given time (Y_t) has both a permanent (secular) component (Yn_t) and a cyclical component (Yc_t) as shown in equation (1):

$$Y_t = Yn_t + Yc_t \qquad (1)$$

The permanent component of GDP reflects the underlying growth of the economy and follows the trend line given by (2):

$$Yn_t = \lambda + \phi_t \qquad (2)$$

The cyclical component is dependent on the price surprise together with the previous period's deviation of output from its natural rate, as shown in equation (3):

$$Yc_t = \alpha[P_t - E(P_t|\Omega_{-1})] + \beta\,(Y_{t-1} - Yn_{t-1}) \qquad (3)$$

where P_t is the actual price level; $E(P_t|\Omega_{t-1})$ is the rational expectation of the price level subject to the information available up to the previous period

(Ω_{t-1}). The lagged output term in (3) is to recognize that deviations in output from the trend will be more than transitory and the coefficient $\beta >$ 0 determines the speed with which output returns to its natural rate after a shock. Several *propagation mechanisms* in Lucas's model (such as information lags and investment accelerator effects) give rise to persistence or serial correlation. Combining (1) and (3) we get the Lucas aggregate supply relationship given by equation (4):

$$Y_t = Yn_t + \alpha[P_t - E(P_t|\Omega_{-1})] + \beta(Y_{t-1} - Yn_{t-1}) + \varepsilon_t, \qquad (4)$$

where ε_t is a random error process.

Although the actions of agents in Lucas's model turn out *ex post* to be non optimal, they are in a rational expectations equilibrium doing the best they can, given the (imperfect or incomplete) information they have acquired. As Lucas (1973) demonstrated, this implies that monetary disturbances (random shocks) are likely to have a much bigger impact on real variables in countries where price stability has been the norm. In countries,where agents are used to inflation, monetary disturbances are unlikely to have an impact in any significant way on real variables. Let θ represent the fraction of total individual price variance due to relative price variation. Thus the larger is θ, the more any observed variability in prices is attributed by economic agents to a real shock (that is, a change in relative price) and the less it is attributed to purely inflationary (nominal) movements of the general price level. We can therefore modify equation (4) and present the Lucas aggregate supply curve as it appeared in his 1973 paper, 'Some International Evidence on Output–Inflation Tradeoffs'.

$$Y_t = Yn_t + \theta\alpha[P_t - E(P_t|\Omega_{-1})] + \beta(Y_{t-1} - Yn_{t-1}) + \varepsilon_t. \qquad (5)$$

According to (5) an *unanticipated* monetary disturbance that takes place in a country where agents are expecting price stability will lead to a significant real output disturbance.

A major policy implication of MEBCT is that a benign monetary policy would eliminate a large source of aggregate instability. Thus new classical economists come down on the side of rules in the rules versus discretion debate over the conduct of stabilization policy.

The business cycle research of Lucas during the 1970s had an enormous methodological impact on the way macroeconomists conducted research and looked at the world (Lucas, 1980, 1981; Hoover, 1992, 1999). However, by 1982 the monetary version of new classical equilibrium models had reached both a theoretical and an empirical impasse. For example, on the theoretical front the implausibility of the assumption relating to information confusion was widely recognized (Okun, 1980; Tobin, 1980). With sticky prices ruled out on methodological grounds, new classical models were left without an acceptable explanation of business cycles involving money-to-output causality. Furthermore, the doubts cast by Sims (1980) on the causal role of money in money–output correlations raised question marks with respect to monetary explanations of the business cycle. On the empirical front, despite some early success, the evidence in support of the proposition that anticipated money was neutral did not prove to be robust (see Barro, 1977, 1978, 1989; Snowdon *et al.*, 1994). As a consequence of these twin difficulties, the monetary surprise model has come to be widely regarded as inappropriate for modern information-rich industrial economies and has been replaced since the early 1980s by new classical real business cycle models emphasizing technological shocks (Stadler, 1994), new Keynesian models emphasizing monetary disturbances (Gordon, 1990) and new neoclassical synthesis models combining insights from both approaches (see Lucas, 1987; Goodfriend and King, 1998; Blanchard, 2000).

BRIAN SNOWDON
HOWARD R. VANE

See also:

Business Cycles: Austrian Approach; Business Cycles: Keynesian Approach; Business Cycles: Monetarist Approach; Business Cycles: Stylized Facts; Great Depression; Intertemporal Substitution of Labour; Lucas, Robert E. Jr; Lucas 'Surprise' Supply Function; Natural Rate of Unemployment; Rational Expectations; Rules versus Discretion.

Bibliography

Abel, A.B. and B.S. Bernanke (2001), *Macroeconomics*, 4th edn, New York: Addison Wesley.
Barro, R.J. (1977), 'Unanticipated Money Growth and Unemployment in the United States', *American Economic Review*, **67**, March, pp. 101–15.
Barro, R.J. (1978), 'Unanticipated Money, Output and the Price Level in the United States', *Journal of Political Economy*, **86**, August, pp. 549–81.
Barro, R.J. (1989), 'New Classicals and Keynesians, Or the Good Guys and the Bad Guys', *Schweiz Zeitschrift für Volkswirtschaft und Statistik*.
Blanchard, O. (2000), 'What Do We Know About Macroeconomics that Fisher and Wicksell Did Not?', *Quarterly Journal of Economics*, **115**, November, pp. 1375–409.
Dore, M. (1993), *The Macrodynamics of Business Cycles*, Oxford: Blackwell.
Friedman, M. (1968), 'The Role of Monetary Policy', *American Economic Review*, **59**, March, pp. 1–17.
Friedman, M. and A.J. Schwartz (1963), *A Monetary History of the United States, 1867–1960*, Princeton, NJ: Princeton University Press.
Goodfriend, M. and R.G. King (1998), 'The New Neoclassical Synthesis and the Role of Monetary Policy', *National Bureau of Economic Research Macroeconomics Annual*, pp. 231–95.
Gordon, R.J. (1990), 'What is New-Keynesian Economics?', *Journal of Economic Literature*, **28**, September, pp. 1115–71.
Haberler, G. (1946), *Prosperity and Depression*, New York: United Nations.
Hoover, K.D. (1984), 'Two Types of Monetarism', *Journal of Economic Literature*, **22**, March, pp. 58–76.

Hoover, K.D. (1988), *The New Classical Macroeconomics: A Sceptical Inquiry*, Oxford: Basil Blackwell.

Hoover, K.D. (ed.) (1992), *The New Classical Macroeconomics*, Aldershot, UK and Brookfield, US: Edward Elgar.

Hoover, K.D. (ed.) (1999), *The Legacy of Robert Lucas Jr*, Cheltenham, UK and Northampton, MA, USA: Edward Elgar.

Lucas, R.E. Jr (1972), 'Expectations and the Neutrality of Money', *Journal of Economic Theory*, **4**, April, pp. 103–24.

Lucas, R.E. Jr (1973), 'Some International Evidence on Output–Inflation Tradeoffs', *American Economic Review*, **63**, June, pp. 326–34.

Lucas, R.E. Jr (1975), 'An Equilibrium Model of the Business Cycle', *Journal of Political Economy*, **83**, December, pp. 1113–44.

Lucas, R.E. Jr (1977), 'Understanding Business Cycles', in K. Brunner and A.H. Meltzer (eds), *Stabilization of the Domestic and International Economy*, Carnegie Rochester Conference Series in Public Policy, Amsterdam: North-Holland.

Lucas, R.E. Jr (1980), 'Methods and Problems in Business Cycle Theory', *Journal of Money, Credit and Banking*, **12**, November, pp. 696–715.

Lucas, R.E. Jr (1981), *Studies in Business Cycle Theory*, Oxford: Basil Blackwell.

Lucas, R.E. Jr (1987), *Models of Business Cycles*, Oxford: Basil Blackwell.

Lucas, R.E. Jr (1996), 'Nobel Lecture: Monetary Neutrality', *Journal of Political Economy*, **104**, August, pp. 661–82.

Lucas, R.E. Jr (1999), 'Interview with Robert Lucas', in B. Snowdon and H.R. Vane, *Conversations With Leading Economists: Interpreting Modern Macroeconomics*, Cheltenham, UK and Northampton, MA, USA: Edward Elgar.

Lucas, R.E.Jr and L.A. Rapping (1969), 'Real Wages, Employment and Inflation', *Journal of Political Economy*, **77**, September/October, pp. 721–54.

Mullineux, A.W. (1984), *The Business Cycle After Keynes: A Contemporary Analysis*, Brighton: Harvester Wheatsheaf.

Muth, J.F. (1961), 'Rational Expectations and the Theory of Price Movements', *Econometrica*, **29**, July, pp. 315–35.

Okun, A. (1980), 'Rational Expectations-With-Misperceptions as a Theory of the Business Cycle', *Journal of Money, Credit and Banking*, **12**, November, pp. 817–25.

Romer, C.D. and D.H. Romer (1989), 'Does Monetary Policy Matter? A New Test in the Spirit of Friedman and Schwartz', *National Bureau of Economic Research Macroeconomics Annual*, pp. 121–83.

Sims, C. (1980), 'Comparison of Inter-war and Post-war Business Cycles: Monetarism Revisited', *American Economic Review*, **70**, March, pp. 250–59.

Snowdon, B., H.R. Vane and P. Wynarczyk (1994), *A Modern Guide to Macroeconomics: An Introduction to Competing Schools of Thought*, Aldershot, UK and Brookfield, US: Edward Elgar.

Stadler, G. (1994), 'Real Business Cycle Theory: A Survey', *Journal of Economic Literature*, **32**, December, pp. 1750–83.

Tobin, J. (1980), 'Are the New Classical Models Plausible Enough to Guide Policy', *Journal of Money, Credit and Banking*, **12**, November, pp. 788–99.

Zijp, R. (1993), *Austrian and New Classical Business Cycle Theories: A Comparative Study Through the Method of Rational Reconstruction*, Aldershot, UK and Brookfield, US: Edward Elgar.

Business Cycles: Political Business Cycle Approach

From the perspective of the political business cycle approach (PBC), macroeconomic fluctuations are generated or reinforced by the political system. Governments intervene in the economy to improve their chances of re-election and/or to pursue ideological goals. Governments thereby create business cycles, instead of pursuing a socially optimal stabilization policy. Political actors are not seen as benevolent, but rather as self-interested individuals, as is generally assumed in economics for other individuals acting in the economy.

The PBC approach builds on systematic interactions between the economy and the polity. A wealth of empirical evidence shows that macroeconomic conditions have important influences on voter attitudes and on election outcomes (Nannestad and Paldam, 1994). 'Vote and popularity functions' link a government's popularity (measured by representative surveys) or election outcomes to the state of the economy, as reflected in the rate of unemployment, inflation or real income. In turn, governments have an incentive to influence these macroeconomic variables by using fiscal and monetary policy instruments ('policy functions').

PBC models can be grouped into four types, which differ along the lines of two main theoretical building blocks. The first block refers to the preferences of policymakers: the government's actions can be assumed to be driven either by electoral considerations ('vote maximizing' or 'opportunistic' models) or by ideological considerations ('partisan' models). The second building block refers to the real impact of government policy: the individuals in the economy can be assumed to have either adaptive or rational expectations.

Although there are some forerunners (Kalecki, 1943; Åkerman, 1947; Frey and Lau, 1968), research on PBCs started with the seminal paper by Nordhaus (1975) entitled 'The Political Business Cycle'. It is the best known of the vote-maximizing models, which assume that the government's goal is to muster the largest possible popular support at election time, subject to the constraints imposed by the economic system. Nordhaus derives a political business cycle for a vote-maximizing government confronted with an exploitable Phillips curve, that is, one based on inflationary expectations adjusting over time. This allows the government to manipulate the economy in such a way that unemployment and inflation are low before an election, while the negative consequences (a rise in inflation and unemployment) appear only after the citizens' vote.

Vote-maximizing models have been criticized on various grounds. First, rational voters can be expected to react to the regular occurrence of electoral cycles produced by the government. Rational expectation approaches to PBCs have captured some of this aspect. Rogoff and Siebert (1988) show that PBCs are possible even when voters have rational expectations, especially when (at least temporary) information asymmetries exist between government and voters. Second, empirical studies, which tested for systematic Nordhaus-type business fluctuations coinciding with election periods in the major industrial countries, have found at best mixed results (see Alesina *et al.*, 1997). Third, governments can be assumed not to be simply vote maximizers (just getting votes does not yield much utility), but to have other goals, in particular putting their ideological ideas into practice.

A second central type of approach, known as 'partisan models', addresses how business cycles are influenced by various types of government ideologies. Hibbs (1977) shows for 12 West European and North American countries that governments pursue macroeconomic policies broadly in accordance with the subjective preferences of their class-defined core political constituencies. 'Left-wing' administrations tend to drive down the unemployment rate, and 'right-wing' governments increase it, at the same time lowering inflation. While Hibbs's analysis is based on an adaptive expectations framework, Alesina (1987) and co-researchers have developed partisan models further, and have succeeded in integrating this variant of political economy fully into modern macroeconomics by basing it on rational expectations. In these models, partisan politics does not result in permanent effects on the economy, but only in transitory post-election effects on output and unemployment. These emerge because it is to some degree uncertain which party will win the election and, as a consequence, which partisan policy is implemented. Given sluggishness in wage adjustments, changes in the inflation rate associated with changes in government then create a temporary business cycle, until agents have fully adjusted. In a study of OECD economies, Alesina and Roubini (1992) find evidence for this type of business cycle: there are temporary partisan differences in output and employment and long-run partisan differences in the inflation rate, but virtually no permanent partisan differences in output and employment.

Vote-maximizing models, as well as partisan models, produce rather mechanistic cycles, usually regular upswings and downswings around election dates. Frey and Schneider (1978a, 1978b), following the earlier model by Frey and Lau (1968), integrate the two types of models and therewith arrive at a less mechanistic view of government behaviour: when the government is confident of winning the next election, there is no need to produce a PBC – it would only do so if it would otherwise win too few votes. These vote-cum-partisan models combine the features that governments pursue ideological goals (ideology is an argument in the politicians' utility function) and that governments need electoral victories in order to stay in power (re-election is taken as a constraint). The resulting cycles are no longer regular. Econometric estimates of such a model for various industrial countries have produced evidence for more complex PBC patterns than predicted by less integrative approaches.

The PBC approach has been extended in various ways. First, the central bank has been analysed as an important additional actor. One possibility for governments to produce a PBC is to influence monetary policy. Several studies have shown that even formally independent central banks, such as the German Bundesbank or the United States Federal Reserve, are influenced by the political process, and electoral considerations have played a significant role in their policy decisions (Frey and Schneider, 1981; Grier, 1987; Mayer, 1990). It remains an open question, however, whether this aspect of the PBC phenomenon is time-dependent; that is, that changes in central bank independence and policies during the 1990s have altered the picture. As in most democracies elections take place only every four years, data limitations leave this question to future research. Second, political systems beyond representative democracies have been analysed. Differences in institutional settings matter as they shape the government's possibilities to produce a PBC. Politico-economic cycles have been studied and identified for direct democracies (Schneider *et al.*, 1981), for East European communist countries (Lafay, 1981) and also for developing countries (Schuknecht, 1996).

The literature on PBCs has recently been surveyed in Paldam (1997). More theoretically oriented accounts are given in Drazen (2000, ch. 7), Persson and Tabellini (2000, ch. 16) and Gärtner (2000). The most influential papers in the field have been collected in Frey (1997).

Bruno S. Frey
Matthias Benz

See also:

Adaptive Expectations; Central Bank Independence; Phillips Curve; Rational Expectations.

Bibliography

Åkerman, J. (1947), 'Political Economic Cycles', *Kyklos*, **1**, February, pp. 107–17.
Alesina, A. (1987), 'Macroeconomic Policy in a Two-Party System, as a Repeated Game', *Quarterly Journal of Economics*, **102**, August, pp. 651–78.
Alesina, A. and N. Roubini (1992), 'Political Cycles in OECD Economies', *Review of Economic Studies*, **59**, October, pp. 663–88.
Alesina, A. and N. Roubini, with G.D. Cohen (1997), *Political Cycles and the Macroeconomy: Theory and Evidence*, Cambridge, MA: MIT Press.
Drazen, A. (2000), *Political Economy in Macroeconomics*, Princeton: Princeton University Press.
Frey, B.S. (ed.) (1997), *Political Business Cycles*, The International Library of Critical Writings in Economics, **79**, Cheltenham, UK and Lyme, US: Edward Elgar.
Frey, B.S. and L. Lau (1968), 'Towards a Mathematical Model of Government Behaviour', *Zeitschrift für Nationalökonomie*, **28**, June, pp. 355–80.
Frey, B.S. and F. Schneider (1978a), 'An Empirical Study of Politico-Economic Interaction in the United States', *Review of Economics and Statistics*, **60**, May, pp. 174–83.
Frey, B.S. and F. Schneider (1978b), 'A Politico-Economic Model of the United Kingdom', *Economic Journal*, **88**, June, pp. 243–53.

Frey, B.S. and F. Schneider (1981), 'Central Bank Behaviour: A Positive Empirical Analysis', *Journal of Monetary Economics*, **7**, May, pp. 291–315.

Gärtner, M. (2000), 'Political Macroeconomics: A Survey of Recent Developments', *Journal of Economic Surveys*, **14**, December, pp. 527–61.

Grier, K. (1987), 'Presidential Elections and Federal Reserve Policy: An Empirical Test', *Southern Economic Journal*, **54**, October, pp. 475–86.

Hibbs, D. (1977), 'Political Parties and Macroeconomic Policy', *American Political Science Review*, **71**, December, pp. 1467–87.

Kalecki, M. (1943), 'Political Aspects of Full Employment', *Political Quarterly*, **14**, October/December, pp. 322–31.

Lafay, J.D. (1981), 'Empirical Analysis of Politico-economic Interaction in East European Countries', *Soviet Studies*, **33**, July, pp. 386-400.

Mayer, T. (1990), *The Political Economy of American Monetary Policy*, Aldershot, UK and Brookfield, US: Edward Elgar.

Nannestad, P. and M. Paldam (1994), 'The VP-Function. A Survey of the Literature on Vote and Popularity Functions After 25 Years', *Public Choice*, **79**, June, pp. 213–45.

Nordhaus, W. (1975), 'The Political Business Cycle', *Review of Economic Studies*, **42**, April, pp. 169–90.

Paldam, M. (1997), 'Political Business Cycles' in D. Mueller (ed.), *Perspectives on Public Choice: A Handbook*, Cambridge: Cambridge University Press.

Persson, T. and G. Tabellini (2000), *Political Economics: Explaining Economic Policy*, Cambridge, MA: MIT Press.

Rogoff, K. and A. Siebert (1988), 'Elections and Macroeconomic Policy Cycles', *Review of Economic Studies*, **55**, January, pp. 1–16.

Schneider, F., W. Pommerehne and B.S. Frey (1981), 'Politico-Economic Interdependence in a Direct Democracy: The Case of Switzerland' in D. Hibbs and H. Fassbender (eds), *Contemporary Political Economy*, Amsterdam: North Holland.

Schuknecht, L. (1996), 'Political Business Cycles and Fiscal Policies in Developing Countries', *Kyklos*, **49**, May, pp. 155–70.

Business Cycles: Real Business Cycle Approach

For many years economists have struggled to understand economic fluctuations in the hope that this would enable them to eliminate the unpalatable effects of recessions and booms, such as unemployment or house price inflation. Under this view of the macro economy there existed a desirable level of full (or natural level) employment output which could be attained save for the vagaries of demand fluctuations. These fluctuations, according to Keynes, depended on the 'animal spirits' of consumers and investors. Alternatively, according to monetarists, they depended on expectation errors or rigidities caused by monetary fluctuations. Thus it was believed that governments, by undertaking economic research and judicious use of fiscal or monetary policy, could control the worst excesses of the business cycle.

One of the difficulties with the models used by policy makers to understand the effect of their policy actions was that the parameters (such as the marginal propensity to consume) employed in traditional models might change as government economic policy changed. If this were the case then the policy predictions based on these models would be useless. This was the so-called 'Lucas critique'. Lucas instead suggested that models ought to be based on primary elements of microeconomic behaviour such as utility and production functions. In attempting to formulate such a model, Kydland and Prescott (1982) founded what we now call real business cycle theory.

Essentially, the model they built led them to the conclusion, surprising at the time, that most fluctuations were caused not by demand variations due to changing expectations or 'animal spirits' but rather by agents' reactions to shocks to the production function or in other words, 'real' shocks, hence the title 'real business cycle theory' (see Long and Plosser, 1983).

This 'discovery' came about as a result of the methods Kydland and Prescott used to build and test their model. Since the model was not based on reduced-form equations (such as the IS or LM curves we usually estimate) it could not be tested econometrically and instead they used a technique known as computer simulation. Computer simulation is sometimes derogatorily referred to as doing econometrics with one observation! In practice, the original research took data from a particular base year and, using parameters from previous econometric studies for the consumption, production and other functions, fitted (or calibrated) the model to the base year data. The intertemporal utility and production functions were simple Cobb–Douglas-type functions, with production being subject to shocks. These shocks were derived by first calculating the level of economic growth that could be attributed to changes in labour and capital in any period. The difference between the predicted change and the actual change (Solow residuals) was attributed to random economic shocks. The model, which has been calibrated to the base year, is then run through the computer with a different shock for each year and the resulting choices of consumption, employment, production and investment are noted and compared with the actual data for the economy.

Kydland and Prescott found that, when the computer simulation of their model was compared with actual US data, the fluctuations in the model economy looked very like those in the real data. Thus, they concluded, the new model, where fluctuations in economic variables only arise as a result of shocks to the production function, provided a good fit of the 'stylized facts'. This was seen as a dramatic result at that time, since, as was noted above, it was believed up to that point that production (or supply-side) shocks only accounted for a very small percentage of the real fluctuations, and that either demand or monetary shocks were the more important determinants. This new theory called the traditional view into question.

The policy implications of this were enormous. Instead of the business cycle and the associated fluctuations in employment, consumption and investment being caused by some demand-side market failure which the government needed to eliminate, this research suggested that the fluctuations we observe are optimal responses on the part of individual consumers, producers and investors to real economic shocks (such as weather, natural events, strikes, political upheaval and new inventions). It follows that any attempt on the part of government to smooth out these variations must cause consumers to deviate from their freely chosen, optimal actions and hence make them worse off.

To put it another way, the Keynesian ideal of striving to attain some target level of full-employment equilibrium is misplaced. What is actually happening is that equilibrium output is constantly moving about over time, in response to 'real' shocks. Furthermore, proponents of the real business cycle approach prefer to think of these shocks, not as some predetermined cyclical process, but as random shocks along the long-run growth path of the economy.

The result also had another profound implication and, along with other research questioning the efficacy of short-run interventionist policy, has had a significant influence on many modern western governments. The theory suggested that the object of fiscal policy was not short-term counter-cyclical intervention, but rather to design tax and expenditure policies particularly as regards the provision of public goods and education which maximize the growth rate of the economy. Furthermore, monetary policy has no role in this framework as its distortionary effects on prices and expectations can only interfere with optimal consumer choices. Sometimes this policy prescription is referred to as 'supply-side economics' as it is concerned with devising policies that maximize the supply of output in the long run. In summary, real business cycle theory suggests that governments ought to be concerned with achieving the best long-run trend of GNP, rather than being concerned with the fluctuations around it. Needless to say, this view provoked considerable controversy on a variety of fronts, both because its interpretation of the process generating the stylized facts we observe was so radically different from our previous understanding, and because it was seen to diminish the role of government and was thus seen as a right-wing agenda-setting theory (though defenders would argue that the emphasis on designing optimal fiscal policies rather than on discretionary monetary policy is strongly in the Keynesian tradition). The theory was thus attacked on a number of levels.

Economists first tackled the claim that the model fitted the data well. It was suggested that the Cobb–Douglas forms of the utility and production functions employed by researchers were too convenient, that their choice of parameters for these functions based on past empirical work was arbitrary and, unlike econometric studies, the claim that the results of the simulated model were 'close' to the real data was purely subjective and unverifiable.

Subsequent refinements of the simulation technique (which had been employed in international trade and tax policy studies for decades) helped to address some of these problems. An advanced econometric technique, known as the Generalized Method of Moments, allows the data to tell the researcher what the appropriate functional form and parameters of the functions should be and removes some of the subjective choices a researcher must make when setting up the model. Similarly, sensitivity tests can be conducted to see just how much the results of the model vary as the parameters of the functions vary. Finally, it was noted that the stylized facts we are measuring the model against are not rigid observations but, rather, they are derived by sampling real economic data, and we can measure the sampling variability. Thus it is possible to ask if a given set of simulated observations is likely to have come from the underlying population, given the real data at our disposal. Despite these refinements to the simulation method, there are many economists who remain sceptical about this type of approach, advocating instead the refinement and improvement of econometrics-based macroeconomic modelling.

The second key development was to marry some of the improvements in the methodology, as outlined above, with refinements to the model to tackle areas where the simulation results did not perform well in matching the real data. The key deficiency was the performance of the model with respect to the labour market. Firstly, the original simulated model could only gener-ate about half the fluctuations actually observed in the employment market; secondly the model failed the famous 'Dunlop–Tarshis' test. This is the stylized fact, established as long ago as the 1930s, that there was a near-zero correlation between hours worked and real wages over the cycle.

One line of research tried to improve the model's ability to match labour market variations by allowing for, amongst others, such phenomena as the effect of a minimum 40-hour week on the employment/unemploy-ment/overtime/rest decision and the effect of household opportunities (doing your own housework/maintenance/decorating versus working and paying someone else). These sorts of refinements all succeeded in substan-tially improving the performance of the model.

The second line of research tackled the 'Dunlop–Tarshis' problem that there should not be any relationship between wages and hours. The real business cycle model implies a positive correlation because the demand curve for labour moves up and down the labour supply curve as shocks hit the production function. By contrast, the older Keynesian/monetarist approach saw the labour supply curve as moving up and down the labour demand curve (for example, owing to employees' misperceptions of the real wage or sticky wage contracts) and thus predicts a negative correlation. Thus what was necessary was a model that would generate movements in both the labour demand and supply curves. This was addressed by, for example, allowing for the influence of cyclical government spending on labour supply decisions and by extending the model to incorporate Keynesian-type labour market failures.

More recently, research in this field has concentrated on trying to extend the model to explain nominal and monetary stylized facts rather than the real issues. In these models either money or a banking sector is incorporated into the model and then the influence of either real production or nominal money supply-side shocks are considered. To date, these models have enjoyed mixed success in explaining the monetary stylized facts and much work remains to be done in this area.

CILLIAN RYAN

See also:

Business Cycle: Stylized Facts; Calibration; Lucas Critique; Supply-Side Economics.

Bibliography

Christiano, L.J. and M. Eichenbaum (1992), 'Current, Real Business Cycle Theories and Aggregate Labour Market Fluctuations', *American Economic Review*, **82**, June, pp. 430–50.
Danthine, J.P. and J.B. Donaldson (1990), 'Efficiency Wages and the Business Cycle Puzzle', *European Economic Review*, **34**, November, pp. 1275–1301.
Hartley, J.E., K.D. Hoover and K.D.Salyer (eds) (1998), *Real Business Cycles: A Reader*, London: Routledge.
Kydland, F.E. and E.C. Prescott (1982), 'Time to Build and Aggregate Fluctuations', *Econometrica*, **50**, November, pp. 1345–69.
Long, J.B. and C.I. Plosser (1983), 'Real Business Cycles', *Journal of Political Economy*, **91**, February, pp. 39–69.
Ryan, C. and A.W. Mullineux (1997), 'The Ups and Downs of Modern Business Cycle Theory', in B. Snowdon and H.R. Vane (eds), *Reflections on the Development of Modern Macroeconomics*, Cheltenham, UK and Lyme, US: Edward Elgar.

Business Cycles: Stylized Facts

When economists want to explain an economic phenomenon, we typically start by trying to characterize it by describing the 'stylized facts'. The 'stylized facts' are a set of observations about some real world variables relevant to the problem at hand. Usually, these facts are uncontroversial in themselves and the controversial element arises when we try to model the explanation of the process which generates these facts.

We may say 'usually' because, in the case of business cycles, neither the facts themselves nor the process that generates them is uncontroversial. The various theories concerning the processes which might generate these facts are covered in other entries in this volume. However, in this entry we are concerned exclusively with the facts themselves.

GDP over the last century has been rising steadily in most western economies. However, as Figures 1 and 2 show, this process has been far from
smooth, and there have been substantial fluctuations up and down in both the
level of output and the rate of growth during this period. Some fluctuations
in GDP are short-lived owing to seasonal factors, such as harvests or major
festivals, but others are clearly of much longer duration. These medium-term
fluctuations of 3–36 months are the subject of some controversy. We can view
these variations either as medium-term fluctuations around some deterministic long-run growth trend or as random shocks to the long-run growth
process itself. Up to the 1980s, economists tended to the former view and saw
these medium-term 'business cycle' fluctuations as something distinct from
growth. More recently, however, economists have tended to think of fluctuations and growth as being intimately related. The latter view is most strongly
associated with real business cycle theory which, despite its name, focuses on
dynamic responses to the shocks to the growth processes rather than on some
intrinsic business cycle process. Thus, in their view, there is no business cycle
as such, merely fluctuations around the long-run trend.

Figure 1   UK GDP, quarterly, 1963–2001, and its long-run trend

However, whichever school of thought one subscribes to, there is a need
to dissect these fluctuations, and the co-movement of other variables, if
macroeconomists are successfully to understand and explain the apparent
cyclical elements of economic progress. From now on we will refer to these

fluctuations as 'the business cycle', with the caveat that the distinction between trend and fluctuation is a statistical distinction, and there is no reason to conclude that the economics forces which determine trend or fluctuation are necessarily different.

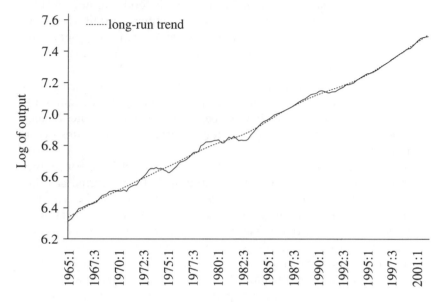

Figure 2 US GDP, quarterly, 1965–2001, and its long-run trend

In order to establish the stylized facts of the business cycle (the statistics we think a good model ought to be able to replicate), we have to extract these medium-term fluctuations from the raw data. If we had an extremely accurate model of the short-term seasonal fluctuations and long-term investment and growth, we could predict output at each date and attribute the residual to the business cycle. Fairly obviously, this is not an easy task and any business cycle series derived from a model of long-run growth will only be as good as the model that underlies it.

In order to avoid dependence on theory in trying to analyse the facts we usually generate business cycle data by using what we call a 'frequency filter'. This eliminates the long-run trend in the data (which we attribute to the long-run growth process) and regular short-term fluctuations (which we attribute to seasonal factors). The remaining medium-term fluctuations are thus the 'observed business cycles'. There are a variety of such filters available and which one we use can be important. It matters because precisely how the long-run trend is fitted will influence where the trend line cuts through the data, and hence determine the beginning and end of each cycle.

As a consequence, the fitting of the trend line could give rise to different facts, though thankfully most seem fairly robust no matter which filter we use. In Figures 1 and 2 we use the popular Hodrick–Prescott filter to derive the trend line.

However, to explain what is going on over the cycle we need a much richer set of observations than simply the fluctuations in GDP. Thus, if we are trying to develop a theoretical model of the economy, we would like it to explain what is happening to prices, interest rates, unemployment, investment, consumption and so on over the cycle. So we need to know what the data tell us about a whole variety of other variables. For example, we might like to know whether prices fluctuate proportionally more than GDP, whether they are likely to be above or below their long-run trend during a boom and whether they peak (or bottom out) before or after the level of GDP has done so.

To discuss these issues in more detail, the 'stylized facts' (generated using the Hodrick–Prescott filter) for the UK and the US are reported in Tables 1 and 2, respectively. The first issue above, whether a variable varies proportionally more or less than output, is captured by the standard deviation of the variable around its trend. This figure is reported in column 1 in both tables. For example, in the UK we see that consumption of non-durable goods such as food, clothing and so on tends to vary less than output, whereas investment and consumption of durable goods (such as cars and fridges) vary more. The US data display a similar pattern, though the consumption figure aggregates both durable and non-durable consumption.

The second issue, whether a variable is rising or falling on average as output is rising, is captured by the correlation coefficient of the two variables. The sixth column of each table, headed $X(t)$, tells us the correlation between output and the variable in each row. If two variables tend to move up and down together then the correlation is positive and close to 1. Thus, in Table 1, the correlation coefficient of 0.79 for non-durable consumption and output suggests that they move up and down quite closely together. Thus we say that non-durable consumption is positively correlated with output or that non-durable consumption is *procyclical*. By contrast, the coefficient for unemployment (row 7) is −0.59. A negative number tells us that unemployment tends to fall when output rises and the closer this number is to −1, the stronger is this negative relationship. So we say that unemployment is negatively correlated or *countercyclical*. Finally, if a variable displays a zero correlation then either there is no relationship between the two variables or the pattern is so random that we cannot identify a relationship. For example, the fifth row, sixth column of Table 2 tells us that there is a very low positive correlation between the US real interest rate and output in the same period. This may be because the interest rate rises in

Table 1 Cyclical behaviour in the UK: deviations from trend of key variables, 1963:3–2001:1

Variable (X)	Standard deviation (per cent)	Correlation of output with:								
		X(t+4)	X(t+3)	X(t+2)	X(t+1)	X(t)	X(t-1)	X(t-2)	X(t-3)	X(t-4)
1. Output	1.54	0.31	0.50	0.65	0.80	1.00	0.80	0.65	0.50	0.30
2. Non-durable consumption	1.42	0.19	0.36	0.50	0.64	0.79	0.67	0.59	0.49	0.36
3. Durable consumption	7.00	0.32	0.50	0.52	0.54	0.60	0.34	0.27	0.19	-0.01
4. Investment	3.63	0.19	0.32	0.42	0.53	0.66	0.63	0.56	0.50	0.36
5. Prices	2.13	-0.42	-0.54	-0.61	-0.62	-0.61	-0.51	-0.41	-0.26	-0.12
6. Real interest rates	2.44	0.21	0.34	0.41	0.41	0.40	0.28	0.20	0.07	-0.07
7. Unemployment	14.51	0.23	0.04	-0.17	-0.38	-0.59	-0.74	-0.81	-0.79	-0.69
8. Wages	2.24	-0.48	-0.54	-0.59	-0.55	-0.49	-0.44	-0.36	-0.26	-0.10

Table 2 *Cyclical behaviour in the US: deviations from trend of key variables, 1965:1–2001:1*

Variable (X)	Standard deviation (per cent)	Correlation of output with:								
		X(t+4)	X(t+3)	X(t+2)	X(t+1)	X(t)	X(t−1)	X(t−2)	X(t−3)	X(t−4)
1. Output	1.62	0.25	0.47	0.68	0.87	1.00	0.87	0.67	0.45	0.22
2. Consumption	1.67	0.58	0.72	0.83	0.87	0.80	0.61	0.40	0.17	−0.04
3. Investment	7.27	0.26	0.44	0.61	0.77	0.90	0.78	0.56	0.31	0.07
4. Prices	1.45	−0.70	−0.76	−0.77	−0.71	−0.58	−0.42	−0.25	−0.07	0.11
5. Real interest rates	1.20	−0.07	0.00	0.08	0.21	0.26	0.17	0.03	−0.12	−0.21
6. Unemployment	11.12	−0.05	−0.27	−0.49	−0.72	−0.87	−0.89	−0.81	−0.65	−0.45
7. Wages	1.84	0.31	0.48	0.67	0.82	0.89	0.83	0.71	0.53	0.30

some booms and falls in others, and on average this results in only a weak positive pattern between output and the interest rate in the same period. In this case, rather than saying that the interest rate was acyclical we might say that it was weakly procyclical.

The third issue, highlighted above, is when a series peaks, relative to output. For example, the second row, fifth column of Table 2 tells us that the correlation coefficient between consumption in the previous period and output today is 0.87. As this is higher than in the current period (0.80), it suggests that consumption reaches its maximum before the high point of GDP. Thus we say that consumption is procyclical and *leading*. By contrast, the greatest response in unemployment appears to come one period later in the case of the US and two periods later in the case of the UK, so we say that it is negatively correlated and *lagging*. Surprisingly, both Tables 1 and 2 seem to suggest that prices are countercyclical and leading; that is, they reach their lowest point before output reaches its peak.

A number of features of the summary above are worthy of further comment. Our finding in Tables 1 and 2 that prices are countercyclical was first identified by Kydland and Prescott (1990). Their claim caused a considerable stir in the profession, as it was previously believed that prices were procyclical. This view arose because of the strong positive correlation between the price level and output during the Great Depression and subsequent recovery. However, postwar data for most countries suggest the opposite, that prices are countercyclical. Thus the 'stylized facts' may be sensitive to special time-dependent factors (such as the Great Depression) and may not be universally true for all time. Similarly, the 'facts' may not be invariant across countries. Although most measures for real variables display considerable uniformity at least in direction if not precise magnitude, monetary facts seem much more variable. Employment variability is another exception. Employment and unemployment in most mainland European countries typically display much smaller standard deviations compared with US or UK data. This international variability may suggest that there are country-specific, labour market, stylized facts that any theoretical model of an economy must address.

Finally, note that the stylized facts are simply statistical correlations and there may be more complex stories underlying the facts than we might first suspect. For example, we noted above that prices are countercyclical and lead the cycle. This means that they bottom out before output reaches its peak. However, this implies that while prices are below trend in a boom, inflation is rising, as is conventionally believed. However, the rudimentary stylized facts suggest to us that the subsequent peak in the price level is more closely correlated to the following recession than to this boom. While real business cycle theorists offer an explanation of this apparent countercyclicality of prices based on the quantity theory of money (output up implies prices must fall for a given fixed money stock), we cannot rule out some complex story which might explain why a boom is inflationary but the effect on price data takes considerable time to manifest itself.

Theory must always be tested by relating it to real data and the stylized facts of any economic problem are merely a simple way of characterizing the problem that theory is seeking to address. That the stylized facts of the business cycle turn out to be more complex than we might have first considered should be no surprise, given the complexity of the economies we are trying to describe. However, these facts offer us a simple framework in which we can discuss competing theories before we confront them with more complex statistical analysis.

CILLIAN RYAN

See also:

Business Cycles: Austrian Approach; Business Cycles: Keynesian Approach; Business Cycles: Marxian Approach; Business Cycles: New Classical Approach; Business Cycles: Political Business Cycle Approach; Business Cycles: Real Business Cycle Approach.

Bibliography

Blackburn, K. and M.O. Ravn (1992), 'Business Cycles in the United Kingdom: Facts and Fiction', *Economica*, **59**, November, pp. 383–402.

Kydland, F.E. and E.C. Prescott (1990), 'Business Cycles: Real Facts and a Monetary Myth', *Federal Reserve Bank of Minneapolis Quarterly Review*, **14**, Spring, pp. 3–18.

Ryan, C. and A.W. Mullineux (1997), 'The Ups and Downs of Modern Business Cycle Theory', in B. Snowdon and H.R. Vane (eds), *Reflections on the Development of Modern Macroeconomics*, Cheltenham, UK and Lyme, US: Edward Elgar.

Cagan, Philip D.

Philip Cagan (b.1927, Seattle, Washington, USA) obtained his BA from the University of California, Los Angeles in 1948 and his MA (1951) and PhD (1954) from the University of Chicago. His main past posts have included the following: Assistant Professor at the University of Chicago, 1955–8; Associate Professor (1959–61) and Professor (1962–4) at Brown University; and Professor of Economics, Emeritus, at Columbia University, 1966–95. He is best known for his work on hyperinflations and the determinants and effects of changes in the US money stock. Among his best known books are *Determinants and Effects of Changes in the Stock of Money 1875–1960* (NBER, 1965) and *Persistent Inflation* (Columbia University Press, 1979). His most widely read articles include 'The Monetary Dynamics of Hyperinflations', in M. Friedman (ed.), *Studies in the Quantity Theory of Money* (University of Chicago Press, 1956); 'Has the Growth of Money Substitutes Hindered Monetary Policy?' (co-authored with A.J. Schwartz) (*Journal of Money, Credit and Banking*, **7**, May 1975); and 'Docs Endogeneity of the Money Supply Disprove Monetary Effects on Economic Activity?' (*Journal of Macroeconomics*, **15**, Summer 1993).

Calibration

Calibration was introduced to macroeconomics by Kydland and Prescott (1982) as a means of reducing the free parameters of their paradigm, a new-classical equilibrium, real business cycle model. Of course there are fore-runners (for example, Johansen, 1960; Shoven and Walley, 1972), but they did not label their method of parameterization as calibration. Kydland and Prescott characterized calibration in two different ways. First, as 'specifica-tions of preferences and technology . . . close to those used in many applied studies' and secondly as 'the selection of parameter values for which the model steady-states values are near average values for the American economy during the period being explained' (Kydland and Prescott, 1982, p.1360). But the purpose of the parameterization was not sufficiently clear, allowing for three different interpretations: estimation, testing and stan-dardization.

Generally, calibration is seen as method of estimation (Dawkins *et al.*, 2001; Pagan, 1994): 'simulating a model with ranges of parameters and selecting elements from these ranges which best match properties of the simulated data with those of historical data' (Gregory and Smith, 1990, p.57; Gregory and Smith, 1993). In other words, calibration is a simulation-based estimation method, 'the operation of fitting model-parameters to observational data obtained from the real system (within a specified experimental frame)' (Elzas, 1984, p.51). Simulation-based methods may be useful in parameterizing models in which there are unobservable variables or simply analytical intractabilities. An often used calibration criterion is to measure the difference between some empirical moments computed on the observed variable and its simulated counterpart. The estimator derived by calibrating some empirical moments based on observations and simulations is the so-called 'Method of Simulated Moments' (MSM) estimator (Gouriéroux and Monfort, 1996).

An alternative but more criticized interpretation is that calibration is a method to test a model. If there are no free parameters, the comparison of a model's population moments (or perhaps some other population measure) with those of historical time series can be thought of as a test of the model, namely a specific type of 'characteristics testing' (Kim *et al.*, 1995). If the correspondence between some aspect of the model and the historical record is deemed to be reasonably close, the model is viewed as satisfactory. If the distance between population and historical moments is viewed as too great, the model is rejected (Gregory and Smith, 1991). A drawback of this procedure is that, unlike the case of estimation, the method itself does not supply a metric that can judge closeness. However, Watson (1993) provides measures of fit for the calibrated models, based on the size of the stochastic error needed to match the second moments of the actual data exactly.

Both views of calibration are based on strategies in which models are considered as simulation devices and (often historical) data are available with which the simulated data can be compared for estimation or testing purposes. But if one considers models as a means to provide 'quantitative answers', or in other words as a measuring instrument, a third interpretation of calibration is needed – the one used in metrology. In metrology, calibration is the 'set of operations that establish, under specified conditions, the relationship between values of quantities indicated by a measuring instrument or measuring system, or values represented by a material measure or a reference material, and the corresponding values realized by standards' (VIM, 1993, 6.11). A standard is the 'material measure, measuring instrument, reference material or measuring system intended to define, realize, conserve or reproduce a unit or one or more values of a quantity to serve as a reference' (ibid., 6.1). The general philosophy adopted for the creation of standards is that they should be based upon some principle that is known to be as invariant as possible. Standards are entirely of man's choice, nothing about the natural world defines them, but they are often based upon naturally occurring phenomena when these possess the required degree of definition.

Calibration in metrology is a way of checking the accuracy of the measuring instrument. Besides this problem of reliability, measuring instruments or other observation instruments are validated by verifying whether
the result of the measurement or observation is a fact of the observed phenomenon or an artifact created by the instrument. Franklin (1986) discusses nine epistemological strategies to distinguish between a valid
observation and an artifact. One of these strategies is calibration, 'the use
of a surrogate signal to standardize an instrument. If an apparatus repro-
duces known phenomena, then we legitimately strengthen our belief that
the apparatus is working properly and that the experimental results produced with that apparatus are reliable' (Franklin, 1997, p. 31).

The ambiguity surrounding calibration methods in economics has led to
a substantial controversy captured by the heading, Calibration versus
Estimation, in which both labels not only refer to specific methods but more
broadly to opposing methodologies, each claiming sound scientific practice. Quah (1995, p. 1594) characterises both as 'research styles' that are 'disrespectful of econometrics' and 'disrespectful of economic theory'. Hoover
(1995) stylizes calibration as an 'adaptive strategy' and estimation as a
'competitive strategy'. Under the latter strategy, 'theory proposes, estimation and testing disposes' (ibid., p. 29). But the aim of the adaptive strategy
is never to test, let alone to reject, a theory, 'but to construct models that
reproduce the economy more and more closely within the strict limits of the
basic theory' (ibid.).

Whether there is a difference between estimation and calibration, big or
small (Hansen and Heckman, 1996; Kim and Pagan, 1995), in the discussions so far there is no mention of the interpretation Kydland and Prescott
themselves ultimately have given to calibration, namely standardization. In
a special symposium, 'Computational Experiments in Macroeconomics' in
the *Journal of Economic Perspectives* (1996), Kydland and Prescott expli-
cated the 'tool' they used in their (1982) 'Time to Build' paper. Any economic computational experiment involves five major steps: 'pose a
question; use a well-tested theory; construct a model economy; calibrate
the model economy; and run the experiment' (Kydland and Prescott, 1996,
p. 70; Kydland and Prescott, 1991, p. 169). Discussing business cycle
research, Prescott explicitly specified a model as 'a measurement instrument used to deduce the implication of theory' (1998, p. 2). Borrowing from
Lucas, he defined a theory as 'an implicit set of instructions for constructing a model economy for the purpose of answering a question' (ibid.), so
that the 'quantitative answer to the question is deduced from the model
economy' (ibid., p. 3). Comparing economic models with measuring instruments, Kydland and Prescott arrive at an interpretation of calibration –
referring to the graduation of measuring instruments, like a thermometer

– that comes very close to the one given by Franklin above: 'Generally, some economic questions have known answers, and the model should give an approximately correct answer to them if we are to have any confidence in the answer given to the question with unknown answer' (Kydland and Prescott, 1996, p. 74; Smith, 1995, p. 201). The question with unknown answer was 'What is the quantitative nature of fluctuations induced by technology shocks?' (Kydland and Prescott, 1996, p. 71). And the answer to this question was that 'the model economy displays business cycle fluctuations 70 percent as large as did the U.S. economy' (Kydland and Prescott, 1996, p. 74). In other words, the answer is supposed to be the measurement result carried out with a calibrated instrument.

But what are the economic questions for which we have known answers? Or what are the facts with which the model is calibrated? The answer is most explicitly given by Cooley and Prescott. They described calibration as choosing parameters for the model economy 'so that it mimics the actual economy on dimensions associated with long term growth' by setting parameter values equal to certain 'more or less constant' ratios. These ratios were the so-called 'stylized facts' of economic growth, 'striking empirical regularities both over time and across countries', the 'benchmarks of the theory of economic growth' (Cooley and Prescott, 1995, p. 3). Originally, they were Kaldor's (1958) 'stylized facts' of growth, but the ones that were used in the real business cycle literature are those characterized by Solow (1970).

Although we have seen that equilibrium business cycle modellers aim to model from invariants (see Hoover, 1995), the choice to take these stylized facts as empirical facts of growth is dubious. Solow has already remarked that 'There is no doubt that they are stylized, though it is possible to question whether they are facts' (1970, p. 2). Hacche (1979) provided an account of the British–US evidence relating to Kaldor's six stylized facts and showed inconsistencies between economic history and Kaldor's stylized facts.

As the second source for facts to calibrate their models, Kydland and Prescott referred to 'relevant micro observations' (1982, p. 1359), but they never provided any coherent framework for extracting macro parameters from microeconomic data. Besides the problem whether microeconomic data can be used to fill macroeconomic models, it is not clear whether there is a 'filing cabinet full of robust micro estimates ready to use in calibrating dynamic stochastic general equilibrium models' (Hansen and Heckman, 1996, p. 90).

MARCEL BOUMANS

Bibliography

Cooley, T.F. and E.C. Prescott (1995), 'Economic Growth and Business Cycles', in T.F. Cooley (ed.), *Frontiers of Business Cycle Research*, Princeton: Princeton University Press.

Dawkins, C., T.N. Srinivasan and J. Whalley (2001), 'Calibration', in J.J. Heckman and E.E. Leamer (eds), *Handbook of Econometrics, vol. 5*, Amsterdam: North-Holland.

Elzas, M.S. (1984), 'System Paradigms as Reality Mappings' in T.l. Ören, B.P. Zeigler and M.S. Elzas (eds), *Simulation and Model-Based Methodologies: An Integrative View*, Berlin: Springer-Verlag.

Franklin, A. (1986), *The Neglect of Experiment*, Cambridge: Cambridge University Press.

Franklin, A. (1997), 'Calibration', *Perspectives on Science*, **5**, pp. 31-80.

Gouriéroux, C. and A. Monfort (1996), *Simulation-Based Econometric Methods*, Oxford: Oxford University Press.

Gregory, A.W. and G.W. Smith (1990), 'Calibration as Estimation', *Econometric Reviews*, **9**, pp. 57–89.

Gregory, A.W. and G.W. Smith (1991), 'Calibration as Testing: Inference in Simulated Macroeconomic Models', *Journal of Business and Economic Statistics*, **9**, July, pp. 297–303.

Gregory, A.W. and G.W. Smith (1993), 'Statistical Aspects of Calibration in Macroeconomics', in G.S. Maddala, C.R. Rao and H.D. Vinod (eds), *Handbook of Statistics, vol. 11*, Amsterdam: North-Holland.

Hacche, G. (1979), *The Theory of Economic Growth: An Introduction*, London: Macmillan Press.

Hansen. L.P. and J.J. Heckman (1996), 'The Empirical Foundations of Calibration', *Journal of Economic Perspectives*, **10**, Winter, pp. 87–104.

Hoover, K.D. (1995), 'Facts and Artifacts: Calibration and the Empirical Assessment of Real-Business-Cycle Models', *Oxford Economic Papers*, **47**, pp. 24–44.

Johansen, L. (1960), *A Multi-Sectoral Study of Economic Growth*, Amsterdam: North-Holland.

Kaldor, N. (1958), 'Capital Accumulation and Economic Growth', reprinted in N. Kaldor (1978), *Further Essays on Economic Theory*, London: Duckworth.

Kim, J., N. De Marchi and M.S. Morgan (1995), 'Empirical Model Particularities and Belief in the Natural Rate Hypothesis', *Journal of Econometrics*, **67**, May, pp. 81–102.

Kim, K. and A.R. Pagan (1995), 'The Econometric Analysis of Calibrated Macroeconomic Models', in M.H. Pesaran and M.R. Wickens (eds), *Handbook of Applied Econometrics*, Oxford: Blackwell.

Kydland, F.E. and E.C. Prescott (1982), 'Time to Build and Aggregate Fluctuations', *Econometrica*, **50**, November, pp. 1345–70.

Kydland, F.E. and E.C. Prescott (1991), 'The Econometrics of the General Equilibrium Approach to Business Cycles', *Scandinavian Journal of Economics*, **93**, pp. 161–78.

Kydland, F.E. and E.C. Prescott (1996), 'The Computational Experiment: An Econometric Tool', *Journal of Economic Perspectives*, **10**, Winter, pp. 69–85.

Pagan, A. (1994), 'Introduction: Calibration and Econometric Research: An Overview', *Journal of Applied Econometrics*, **9**, pp. S1–S10.

Prescott, E.C. (1998), 'Business Cycle Research: Methods and Problems', working paper, Federal Reserve Bank of Minneapolis.

Quah, D.T. (1995), 'Controversy; Business Cycle Empirics: Calibration and Estimation', *Economic Journal*, **105**, November, pp. 1594–6.

Shoven, J.B. and J. Whalley (1972), 'A General Equilibrium Calculation of the Effects of Differential Taxation of Income from Capital in the U.S.', *Journal of Public Economics*, **1**, November, pp. 281–321.

Smith, G.W. (1995), 'Commentary on "The Econometrics of the General Equilibrium Approach to Business Cycles"', in K.D. Hoover (ed), *Macroeconometrics: Developments, Tensions, and Prospects*, Boston: Kluwer.

Solow, R.M. (1970), *Growth Theory: An Exposition*, Oxford: Clarendon Press.

VIM (1993), *International Vocabulary of Basic and General Terms in Metrology*, Geneva: ISO.

Watson, M.W. (1993), 'Measures of Fit for Calibrated Models', *Journal of Political Economy*, **101**, December, pp. 1011–41.

Capital Account

A record of a country's international transactions in capital assets (both real and financial) with the rest of the world over a given period (such as, a year). The capital account will be in deficit when outflows of capital (for example, to finance overseas investment) are greater than inflows of capital, resulting in a net capital outflow. In contrast the capital account will be in surplus when inflows of capital are greater than outflows of capital, resulting in a net capital inflow.

Capital–Labour Ratio

The ratio of the quantity of capital inputs to the number of workers; the amount of capital input per worker.

See also:
Neoclassical Growth Model.

Capital–Output Ratio

The ratio of the amount of capital to the amount of output produced by it. The capital–output ratio is central to the accelerator principle.

See also:
Harrod-Domar Growth Model; Investment: Accelerator Theory of.

Capital-stock Adjustment Principle

The principle that net investment is some proportion of the difference between the actual capital stock and the desired capital stock. A number of approaches dealing with the speed at which adjustment takes place have been developed, including those that stress factors internal to capital-using-firms and those that emphasize factors determined by the firms supplying capital goods.

See also:
Investment: Accelerator Theory of; Investment: Neoclassical Theories of.

Catching Up and Convergence

The catching up hypothesis is customarily traced back to Gerschenkron's (1962) observation that economies industrializing late appear to have an advantage; they experience higher growth rates of output and productivity than early starters, leading to convergence of productivity and per capita income levels. The catch-up idea provides an endogenous explanation of growth rate differentials among countries that is consistent with several theoretical models. For example, Barro (1997) uses a neoclassical production function growth model, Cornwall (1977) adopts a Keynesian approach, Verspagen (1992) takes an evolutionary stance, and Perez and Soete (1988) develop an institutional analysis.

In its simplest form, neoclassical theory predicts convergence of per capita income as the consequence of declining marginal product of capital as the capital–labour ratio rises. Barro (1997, pp. 2–3) defines two types of convergence. *Absolute convergence* applies when two or more economies are identical except for their initial capital intensities. Then per capita incomes grow faster in poor countries (where capital–labour ratios are low) than in rich ones. This is a concept of limited interest, since it does not consider changing technologies, and per capita income growth ceases in the steady state. *Conditional convergence* applies when economies differ, for example in their savings ratios, educational levels and access to modern technologies. These and other variables define the long-run steady state per capita income of an economy; growth is more rapid the further is actual per capita income from its steady state level. In this case, continued long-run growth depends on technological progress, which is exogenous. These 'extended' neoclassical models have generated a large volume of empirical work. Early 'new' (or endogenous) growth theory attempted to overcome this exogeneity, but the resulting growth models did not predict convergence. Recent extensions have concentrated on restoring the convergence property, (for example, Barro and Sala-i-Martin, 1997, which includes a diffusion mechanism). Empirical tests using this type of model have not supported their claimed applicability to convergence (Aghion and Howitt, 1998).

In contrast to endogenous growth theory, which has tended to view technological progress as a public good, other interpretations of catching up have recognized the existence of property rights; they have stressed direct foreign investment in new plant, the importation of new capital goods or the acquisition of licences as common mechanisms for the transfer of technology from advanced to less developed economies. The gap between an economy's technology and best practice technology is a measure of its opportunity to catch up. Then, *ceteris paribus*, an economy's growth rate is predicted to be inversely related to the size of its technology gap. This has been the basis for empirical studies of the relationship between an initial level of per capita income (to approximate the state of technology) and the labour productivity growth rate in the ensuing period. Thus Baumol (1986) considers 16 currently advanced economies over the period 1870–1979, and finds the inverse relation between initial income levels and productivity growth rates, and convergence of income levels. He finds similar results for a group of currently industrializing countries and another of centrally planned economies, but no evidence of these trends for the poorest countries or for the entire sample. Abramovitz (1986) finds strong evidence of convergence for 15 advanced economies to be confined to the post-World War II period; the earlier years include changes in the rank of countries as well as some incidences of income divergence.

Some of these variations of experience are explained by examining the preconditions for successful technological borrowing. Cornwall (1977) notes that the first requirement is to have open channels for international diffusion of technology. There must be no restrictions on the export of capital equipment or patents, or barriers to its importation caused by culture or vested interests in the potential borrowing economy. Second, the capacity to exploit the advanced technology requires the borrower to have adequately skilled labour and entrepreneurs, both to use the technology and to effect the innovations needed for local markets. Baumol *et al.* (1989) find that, when educational levels are considered, conditional convergence is observed for a group of 59 countries; others, such as, Fagerberg (1988), have shown R & D activity to be necessary for successful borrowing. Third, the appropriate infrastructure for the financing, distribution and marketing of the new production should be in place Fourth, social institutions that foster orderly transition as the pace of modernization increases will encourage investment and continuation of the process.

Even when all these conditions are met, the pattern of productivity growth rates that leads to convergence of income levels is not assured. Actual productivity growth in any economy is still conditional on economic conditions, particularly on the state of aggregate demand. In the absence of strong aggregate demand, and the expectation that it will continue to be strong, firms will not undertake the large-scale investment needed for modernization. A prolonged period of sluggish or unstable aggregate demand will reduce the rate of adoption of new technology, and is a potential cause of changed rankings among economies.

In assessing the strong evidence for catching up and convergence among advanced economies in the postwar period, three further factors should be considered. First, the 'technology borrowers' in Baumol's sample faced a massive task of reconstruction in the early part of the period, creating the imperative rather than simply the opportunity to modernize. The resulting political will, combined with their high levels of labour skills and well-developed social, economic and political institutions, created a uniquely favourable set of circumstances; studies of economies with less favourable initial conditions would provide a better test of the prerequisites for catching up. Second, the rapid and large expansion of trade in the period allowed even small economies to modernize, since external demand justified the large-scale production the new technologies required. This suggests that trade expansion is yet another precondition for successful technology borrowing. Sachs and Warner (1995) provide evidence that openness accelerates convergence. Abramovitz (1994) stresses international economic institutions such as the Bretton Woods exchange rate system, Marshall Aid and European integration, all of which enhanced trade, as key contributors to the postwar 'convergence boom'.

The third point concerns the increasing share of output and employment of the service sector as per capita incomes rise. Because this sector has typically displayed lower productivity levels and growth than other sectors, this reallocation of labour acts to slow the economy's average growth of productivity. This slowing growth creates the same relationship as catching up; that is, higher per capita incomes (and the larger service sectors that accompany them) are associated with slower productivity growth. This reallocation has been especially marked in the postwar era, and has contributed to the strength of convergence observed by Abramovitz. Estimates of the sources of productivity growth that consider the shift toward services show it to have made a significant contribution to slowing growth in high-income countries (McCombie, 1991; Cornwall and Cornwall, 2001, ch. 10).

Although catching up and convergence have not been universally experienced, the data provide strong evidence of their existence within particular groups of countries, notably the advanced capitalist economies and the newly industrializing economies of South East Asia. Besides encouraging theoretical explanation, these observations have generated a large body of empirical work; a useful survey is included in Fagerberg (1994). Refinements of both are needed for greater understanding of the conditions that foster catching up, and of the processes that sustain it. Such understanding is relevant, not only to developing and advanced economies, but also to countries not currently enjoying the benefits of catching up.

JOHN CORNWALL
WENDY CORNWALL

See also:
Endogenous Growth Theory; Neoclassical Growth Model; Steady State Growth.

Bibliography

Abramovitz, M. (1986), 'Catching Up, Forging Ahead, and Falling Behind', *Journal of Economic History*, **45**, June, pp. 385–406.
Abramovitz, M. (1994), 'Catch-Up and Convergence in the Postwar Growth Boom and After', in W.J. Baumol, R.R. Nelson and E.N. Wolff (eds.), *Convergence of Productivity*, Oxford: Oxford University Press.
Aghion, P. and P. Howitt (1998), *Endogenous Growth Theory*, Cambridge, MA: MIT Press.
Barro, R. (1997), *Determinants of Economic Growth*, Cambridge, MA: MIT Press.
Barro, R. and X. Sala-i-Martin (1997), 'Technological Diffusion, Convergence, and Growth', *Journal of Economic Growth*, **2**, March, pp. 1–27.
Baumol, W.J. (1986), 'Productivity Growth, Convergence, and Welfare: What the Long-Run Data Show', *American Economic Review*, **76**, December, pp. 1072–85.
Baumol, W.J., S.A.B. Blackman and E.N. Wolff (1989), *Productivity and American Leadership*, Cambridge, MA: MIT Press.
Cornwall, J. (1977), *Modern Capitalism, Its Growth and Transformation*, Oxford: Martin Robertson.
Cornwall, J. and W. Cornwall (2001), *Capitalist Development in the Twentieth Century*, Cambridge, UK: Cambridge University Press.
Fagerberg, J. (1988), 'International Competitiveness', *Economic Journal*, **98**, June, pp. 355–74.
Fagerberg, J. (1994), 'Technology and International Differences in Growth Rates', *Journal of Economic Literature*, **32**, September, pp. 1147–75.
Gerschenkron, A. (1962), *Economic Backwardness in Historical Perspective*, Cambridge, MA: Belknap Press.
McCombie, J. (1991), 'The Productivity Growth Slowdown of the Advanced Countries and Intersectoral Reallocation of Labour', *Australian Economic Papers*, **30**, June, pp. 70–85.
Perez, C. and L. Soete (1988), 'Catching Up in Technology: Entry Barriers and Windows of Opportunity', in G. Dosi, C. Freeman, R. Nelson, G. Silverberg and L. Soete (eds), *Technical Change and Economic Theory*, London and New York: Pinter Publishers.
Sachs, J.D. and A. Warner (1995), 'Economic Reform and the Process of Global Integration', *Brookings Papers on Economic Activity*, **1**, pp. 1–118.
Verspagen, B. (1992), 'An Evolutionary Approach to Why Growth Rates Differ', in W. Blaas and J. Foster (eds), *The Mixed Economies in Europe*, Aldershot, UK and Brookfield, US: Edward Elgar.

Central Bank

The institution responsible for the conduct of monetary policy, such as the Federal Reserve System in the United States, the Bank of Japan in Japan and the Bank of England in the United Kingdom. In exercising its control over the banking and financial system a central bank may use a number of instruments, including undertaking open market operations, setting reserve requirements and issuing directives to banks and other financial institutions.

See also:

Central Bank Accountability and Transparency; Central Bank Independence; Federal Reserve System; Monetary Policy: Role of.

Central Bank Accountability and Transparency

In contrast to the concept of central bank independence, there is no consensus in the literature about the concept of central bank accountability. Various authors have different views on the definition and crucial elements of democratic accountability. In a general sense, we define *accountability* as meaning that policy makers can and will be held to account for economic performance of the targets in their care. In other words, policy makers will be held responsible for how close indicators for the economic performance come to the target values set. In a democratic society, parliament represents the views of the electorate. Therefore it is crucial that the central bank is directly accountable either to parliament or to government, which in turn is, of course, accountable *vis-à-vis* parliament. In the latter case, government should have instruments to influence the central bank (for example, the possibility to override policy decisions of the central bank). Some authors are not convinced of the democratic accountability of independent central banks because they represent narrower financial interests rather than other groups in society (for example, Stiglitz, 1998).

The concept of central bank accountability has three main features: (1) decisions about the *ultimate objectives* of monetary policy; (2) *transparency* of actual monetary policy; (3) *final responsibility* with respect to monetary policy (see also De Haan *et al.*, 1999). Decisions about the *ultimate objective(s)* of monetary policy should be taken by parliament and not be left to the central bank. So the central bank law – as enacted by parliament – should provide the ultimate objective(s) of monetary policy. The less a central bank is bound to specific objectives, the more difficult it becomes to evaluate the bank's performance, since a suitable yardstick is missing. As the evaluation of the performance of the central bank is the crucial element of accountability, a clearly stated objective is essential.

It is also important that the objective(s) be clearly defined. The quantification of policy objectives (such as, a maximum inflation rate) may enhance accountability. A good example is the Reserve Bank of New Zealand, which has price stability as its primary objective. The governor of the Reserve Bank of New Zealand has to agree with the government a tight target range for inflation. In this so-called 'Policy Target Agreement' (PTA) a target for the inflation rate is provided.

Finally, in the case of various objectives, a clear prioritization should be provided, since otherwise it is left to the central bank to decide which of the statutory objectives is given priority at any given time.

In the past, the statutes of most European central banks were rather vague in terms of final objectives, or contained various (possibly conflicting) objectives without giving indications as to their prioritisation. For instance, the primary objective of the German Bundesbank was the defence of the value of the currency. Even more vague was the objective of the Dutch Central Bank, which was to regulate the value of the guilder in a welfare-enhancing way.

Transparency forms one of the central elements of democratic account-ability. Information concerning the behaviour of the central bank is crucial for the evaluation of its performance. Without this information a sound decision on whether the bank has fulfilled its tasks will be impossible.

It is fairly straightforward to analyse transparency in terms of Rogoff's (1985) model of a 'conservative' and independent central banker. Suppose that there is uncertainty about the preferences of the central banker: for example, how inflation-averse is the central banker? An easy way to model this is to assume that there are preference shocks, leading to a higher or lower level of conservativeness. The central banker has private information about the realization of the uniformly distributed preference shock on the interval $[-h, h]$. The loss function of the central bank now becomes (instead of equation (4) in the entry, 'Central Bank Independence'):

$$L^{cb} = \frac{1 + \varepsilon - x}{2} \pi_t^2 + \frac{\chi}{2} (y_t - y_t^*)^2 \text{ with } x \sim U[-h, h] \text{ and } h < \varepsilon. \quad (1)$$

Inflation will be higher in comparison to equation (6) in 'Central Bank Independence', if it is not clear how conservative the central bank is. A posi-tive preference shock makes the central bank less conservative, leading to higher (expected) inflation and a stronger reaction to supply shocks. A neg-ative preference shock $(-h)$ has an opposite effect. However, the effect on inflation of a positive preference shock is larger than the effect of a nega-tive one. Because of this asymmetry, a lower variance of preference shocks (more transparency) decreases (expected) inflation and reduces the credibil-ity problem (see Eijffinger and Hoeberichts, 2001).

Transparency can be accomplished in various ways. A central bank could, for instance, be required to publish monetary policy reports regu-larly in addition to the annual central bank report. These reports should include details on its past performance and future plans for monetary policy in accordance with the primary objective. This is even more impor-tant where a clear objective is missing because then the central bank can only be judged on the basis of its own statements. On the basis of these reports (or other information), the central bank should be required to explain publicly to what extent it has been able to reach its objectives. According to some observers, transparency is enhanced by a requirement to publish the minutes of meetings and/or the (reasoned) decisions of the governing board of the bank. The new Bank of England Act 1998, for instance, prescribes publication of the minutes of the Monetary Policy Committee.

Proponents of an accountable central bank argue that ultimately democratically elected politicians should bear the *final responsibility* for monetary policy. Two issues may be considered crucial: the relationship with parliament and the existence of some kind of override mechanism.

The relationship between the central bank and parliament has to play a major role in any evaluation of the democratic accountability of the central bank itself. Indeed, while the transparent conduct of monetary policy supports parliament in its decision-making process regarding the performance of the bank, institutionalized contacts support the overall transparency of monetary policy. Parliament has the opportunity to review the performance of the central bank with regard to monetary policy on a regular basis, while the central bank at the same time can explain and justify its conduct. These contacts should be provided for in the legal basis of the central bank because informal and, thus, non-binding arrangements in this respect put the central banker in a much stronger position *vis-à-vis* parliament. It may be argued that parliament always holds the ultimate responsibility for monetary policy since it can change the legal basis of the bank. Parliament's legislative power can function as a mechanism of *ex ante* control whereby parliament sets the rules with which the central bank must comply. Moreover, it can function as a mechanism of *ex post* accountability because parliament may decide to change the legal basis of the bank in reaction to actual policy.

Proponents of a monetary policy, that is performed independently of government generally reject override mechanisms. Nevertheless, such a mechanism may be one way to enhance accountability, especially if the central bank is not directly accountable to parliament. Coming back to our model of a 'conservative' and independent central banker, an override mechanism could be modelled as follows (see Lohmann, 1992):

$$L^G = \frac{1}{2} \pi_t^2 + \frac{\chi}{2} (y_t - y_t^*)^2 + \delta c, \tag{2}$$

where c ($c > 0$) denotes the cost of overriding decisions of the central bank and $\delta = 0$ (no overriding) or $\delta = 1$ (overriding) It is intuitively clear that, owing to the possibility of overriding the central bank, the inflationary bias will increase ($\pi^G > \pi^{cb}$). When there is no overriding, inflation will be $\pi^{cb} = y_t^* + \pi_t^e + u_t/2 + \varepsilon$; with overriding, inflation will be $\pi^G = y_t^* + \pi_t^e + u_t/2$. In other words, the credibility problem of government will increase if it has the possibility to put decisions by the central bank aside.

Government should explain to parliament why it has (not) used the override and parliament in turn can decide whether it agrees with government. So, eventually parliament decides about monetary policy. The question that arises in this context is whether an override mechanism is *per se* an infringement of the independent position of the central bank. The key to the answer is that, in examining override mechanisms, attention has to be paid to the type of override mechanism and the procedure for its application. Generally, three types of override mechanisms can be distinguished, including (in descending order) the right to issue instructions, the right to approve, suspend, annul or defer decisions, and the right to censor decisions on legal grounds. The first one especially may enhance accountability. For instance, until recently, under the Dutch Bank Act 1948, the Minister of Finance had the right to give the Dutch central bank certain instructions concerning the conduct of monetary policy. Whether he really used this right – which indeed he did not – is of limited importance. By not applying it, the minister and thus the government thereby implicitly approved of actual policy and was to this extent accountable *vis-à-vis* parliament. Similarly, the Reserve Bank Act 1989 gives the New Zealand Minister of Finance the right to override the objective of price stability. The central bank remains in charge of monetary policy but should aim for the objective as specified by the government. This type of override mechanism is of a very different nature than, for example, the right that the German government had to suspend a decision of the governing council of the Deutsche Bundesbank, since only the first gives the government the power to really change monetary policy. It is important to realize that the simple fact that government can override the central bank does not necessarily add to the democratic accountability of monetary policy. Indeed, it may, as opponents of such mechanisms emphasize, only open a floodgate for political influence on monetary policy. Therefore the conditions under which an override mechanism could be applied have to be laid down in detail *ex ante*. The procedure for the application for the override mechanism also needs to be transparent. The decision to apply the override mechanism should be made public. Furthermore, the procedure to apply an override should provide for some kind of review, such as a possibility for the central bank to appeal, in order to ensure that the override is being used carefully.

Although the legal basis of the European Central Bank (ECB) defines an explicit *primary objective*, it is up to the Governing Council of the ECB to quantify price stability In October 1998, the Council defined price stability as an annual increase in the Harmonised Index of Consumer Prices (HICP) for the Euro area of less than 2 per cent. The Council explicitly announced that price stability is to be maintained over the medium term. As far as *transparency* is concerned, the legal basis of the ECB foresees the publication of reports on the activities of the ECB on at least a quarterly basis. In addition, the ECB has decided to publish a Monthly Bulletin. Furthermore, the Governing Council of the ECB has decided that it will regularly inform the public about its monetary policy decisions. The Council will meet every fortnight. The first meeting in every month will be followed by a press conference. When policy decisions are made, the reasoning behind specific decisions will be communicated to the public immediately after the meeting at which they have been taken. Minutes of the meetings will not be published. However, the idea behind presenting the reasoning of the Governing Council is, of course, exactly the same as the idea of those who are in favour of publishing minutes: providing the explanation for the decisions taken. The only difference is that minutes could also reveal voting patterns in the Governing Council. As the Council has a clear collective responsibility the usefulness of making voting behaviour public seems limited.

With respect to the *final responsibility for monetary policy*, it should be noted that the relationship between the ECB and the European Parliament (EP) cannot be easily compared with that between a national parliament and a national central bank. First of all, the EP is not a true legislative. Although in various cases it decides together with the Council, in a number of important areas the EP only plays a consultative role. The EP clearly has not the power to change the legal basis of the ECB. Apart from some minor amendments, a change of the institutional structure of the ECB would require an amendment of the Maastricht Treaty. Neither the Maastricht Treaty nor the ECB statute contains any provisions that would enable the Council or any other Community institution to override the ECB with regard to monetary policy. The reason for this is apparent as every effort was put into insulating the ECB from any political influence from either Community institutions or member states (see De Haan and Eijffinger, 2000).

SYLVESTER C.W. EIJFFINGER

See also:

Central Bank Independence; Inflation Targeting; Monetary Policy: Role of.

Bibliography

De Haan, J. and S.C.W. Eijffinger (2000), 'The Democratic Accountability of the European Central Bank: A Comment on Two Fairy-tales', *Journal of Common Market Studies*, **38**, September, pp. 393–407.

De Haan, J., F. Amtenbrink and S.C.W. Eijffinger (1999), 'Accountability of Central Banks: Aspects and Quantification, *Banca Nazionale del Lavoro Quarterly Review*, **52**, June, pp. 169–93.

Eijffinger, S.C.W. and M.M. Hoeberichts (2001), 'Central Bank Accountability and Transparency: Theory and Some Evidence', Discussion Paper 6/00, Economic Research Centre of the Deutsche Bundesbank, Frankfurt-am-Main.

Lohmann, S. (1992), 'Optimal Commitment in Monetary Policy: Credibility versus Flexibility', *American Economic Review*, **82**, March, pp. 273–86.
Rogoff, K. (1985), 'The Optimal Degree of Commitment to an Intermediate Monetary Target', *Quarterly Journal of Economics*, **100**, November, pp. 1169–90.
Stiglitz, J (1998), 'Central Banking in a Democratic Society', *De Economist*, **146**, July, pp. 199–226.

Central Bank Independence

Before we discuss the arguments put forward in favour of an independent central bank, we first have to be clear what central bank independence really means. Central bank independence refers to three areas in which the influence of government must be excluded or drastically curtailed (Eijffinger and De Haan, 1996): independence in personnel matters, financial autonomy and policy independence.

In practice, it is not feasible to exclude government influence completely when appointments are made to such important public institutions as central banks. So *personnel independence* refers to the influence that government has in appointment procedures. Various criteria are relevant here, like governmental representation in the governing body of the central bank, appointment procedures, terms of office and procedures governing dismissal of the board of the bank.

It is clear that politicians can influence central bank policy if the government is able to finance its expenditure either directly or indirectly via central bank credits. In that case there is *no financial independence*. Direct access to central bank credits implies that monetary policy is subordinated to fiscal policy. Indirect access may result if the central bank is cashier of the government or if it handles the management of government debt. In these cases restrictions may be necessary to prevent government interference with monetary policy.

Policy independence is related to the room for manoeuvre given to the central bank in the formulation and execution of monetary policy. As has been pointed out by Debelle and Fischer (1995), it may be useful to distinguish between goal independence and instrument independence. A central bank has goal independence if it can decide on the formulation of its ultimate objective(s). In practice, most central bank laws formulate one or more objectives. However, if the central bank has been trusted with various (possibly conflicting) goals – such as achieving low inflation and low unemployment – it has some scope in deciding about its priorities. In that case the central bank has considerable *goal independence*, since it is relatively free to set the final goals of monetary policy. It could, for instance, decide that price stability is less important than output stability, and act accordingly.

Finally, a central bank must wield effective instruments in order to defend its objective(s). A bank that has *instrument independence* is free to choose the means by which it seeks to achieve its goals. Clearly, if government approval is required of the central bank's use of policy instruments, no instrument independence exists.

Why would central bank independence, *ceteris paribus*, yield lower rates of inflation? The theoretical reasoning in this field stresses the *time inconsistency problem* (Kydland and Prescott, 1977; Barro and Gordon, 1983). The basic idea behind this problem can be explained as follows. Suppose that the policy maker announces a certain inflation rate that (s)he considers optimal. If private sector agents take this announced inflation rate into account in their behaviour, it becomes at that time optimal for the government to renege and to create a higher than announced inflation rate. The reason for this is that a burst of unexpected inflation yields certain benefits. For instance, unexpected inflation reduces real wages, thereby increasing employment. Of course, this is only part of the story. The next step is to add rational expectations. Under rational expectations economic agents know government's incentive to create unexpected inflation and take this into account in forming their expectations. Government has no other choice than to vindicate these. It is clear that the inflation rate will be higher than under the situation in which government would stick to its promise. No matter which factors exactly cause the dynamic inconsistency problem, in all cases the resulting rate of inflation is suboptimal. So in the literature devices have been suggested to reduce this so-called *inflationary bias*.

Rogoff (1985) has proposed delegating monetary policy to an independent and 'conservative' central banker. 'Conservative' means that the central banker is more averse to inflation than the government, in the sense that (s)he places a greater weight on price stability than the government does. Why would a central banker be more inflation-averse than the government? Two main differences have been pointed out in the literature between preferences of the government and those of the central bank (Cukierman, 1992). One relates to possible differences in the time preference of political authorities and that of central banks. For various reasons, central banks tend to take a longer view of the policy process than do politicians. The other difference concerns the subjective weights in the objective function of the central bank and that of government officials. It is often assumed that central bankers are relatively more concerned about inflation than about other policy goals such as achieving high employment levels and adequate government revenues.

If monetary policy is set at the discretion of a 'conservative' and independent central banker, a lower average time-consistent inflation rate will result. The central insights of this literature can be explained as follows. It is assumed that policy makers seek to minimize the following loss function (*L*), which represents the preferences of the society:

$$L^G = \frac{1}{2}\pi_t^2 + \frac{\chi}{2}(y_t - y_t^*)^2,$$ (1)

where y_t is output, y^* denotes desired output and χ is government's weight on output stabilization ($\chi > 0$). Output is driven by a simplified Lucas supply function (the natural rate of output is normalized and the slope is set at one):

$$y_t = (\pi_t - \pi_t^e) + u_t,$$ (2)

where π is actual inflation, π^e is expected inflation and u_t is a random shock. Policy makers minimize (1) on a period-by-period basis, taking the inflation expectations as given. With rational expectations, inflation turns out to be

$$\pi_t = \chi y_t^* - \frac{\chi}{\chi + 1} u_t.$$ (3)

The first term on the right-hand side of equation (3) is the inflationary bias. A country with a high inflationary bias has a credibility problem, as economic subjects realize government's incentives for surprise inflation. The second term in equation (3) reflects the degree to which stabilization of output shocks influence inflation.

Suppose now that a 'conservative' central banker is put in charge of monetary policy. 'Conservative' means that the central banker is more inflation-averse than government. The loss function of the central banker can therefore be written as

$$L^{cb} = \frac{1 + \varepsilon}{2}\pi_t^2 + \frac{\chi}{2}(y_t - y_t^*)^2,$$ (4)

where ε denotes the additional inflation aversion of the central banker. The preferences of the central banker do not matter, unless (s)he is able to determine monetary policy. In other words, the central bank should be able to pursue monetary policy without (much) government interference. This can simply be modelled as follows (Eijffinger and Hoeberichts, 1998):

$$M_t = \gamma L^{cb} + (1 - \gamma)L^G,$$ (5)

where γ denotes the degree of *central bank independence*, that is, the extent to which the central banker's loss function affects monetary policy making.

If $\gamma = 1$, the central bank fully determines monetary policy M. With rational expectations, and minimizing government's loss function, inflation will be

$$\pi_t = \frac{\chi}{1 + \gamma\varepsilon}y_t^* - \frac{\chi}{1 + \gamma\varepsilon + \chi}u_t. \qquad (6)$$

Comparing equations (3) and (6), one can immediately see that the inflationary bias (the first term on the right-hand side of the equations) is lower for positive values of γ and ε. In other words, delegating monetary policy to an independent and 'conservative' central bank will yield a lower level of inflation. There is an optimal level of independence cum conservativeness $(\gamma\varepsilon^*)$. *Optimal* means that the loss function of the society (equation 1) is minimized. This optimum is not necessarily one with zero inflation, as it also depends on output stabilization.

It also follows from equation (6) that both independence and the inflation aversion of the central bank matter. If the central banker has the same inflation aversion as government (that is, $\varepsilon = 0$), the independence does not matter. And similarly, if the central bank is fully under the spell of government ($\gamma = 0$), the conservativeness of the central bank does not matter. There are various combinations of γ and ε that may yield the same outcome, including the optimal one.

From a practical point of view, however, the concept of a 'conservative' central banker seems void, if only since the preferences of possible candidates for positions on the governing board of a central bank are generally not very easy to identify and may change after they have been appointed. So it is hard to find some real-world example of a 'conservative' central banker. Still, one could argue that the statute of the central bank could be relevant here, especially with respect to the question of whether or not it defines price stability as the primary goal of monetary policy. Whether or not the statute of a central bank defines price stability as the primary policy goal can be considered as a proxy for the 'conservative bias' of the central bank as embodied in the law (Cukierman, 1992).

The *legislative approach* to create by law an independent central bank and to mandate it to direct its policies towards achieving price stability has mainly been followed with respect to the European Central Bank. Other mechanisms have been suggested to overcome the incentive problems of monetary policy as well. The so-called *contracting approach* regards the design of monetary institutions as one that involves the structuring of a contract between the central bank (the agent) and the government (the principal). The nature of the contract will affect the incentives facing the bank and will, thereby, affect monetary policy (Persson and Tabellini, 1993). Walsh (1995) has pointed out that the government could set the central banker's rewards contingent upon realized inflation. The Walsh solution takes the form of a contract between the government and the central bank. The contract is structured in such a way that a linear tax is imposed upon the central bank for any inflation in excess of the inflation target. In all other respects, the central bank is given complete discretion when setting policy. It turns out that an inflation contract can be designed so as to eliminate the inflation bias, while ensuring that the central banker's stabilization of the real economy is at the optimal level

So from a theoretical point of view it can be argued that an independent central bank may reduce the inflationary bias of monetary policy making. What about the empirical evidence? A substantial amount of empirical research supports the inverse relationship between central bank independence and the level of inflation (see Eijffinger and De Haan, 1996; Berger *et al.*, 2001). This evidence generally consists of cross-section regressions in which average inflation over a certain period is 'explained' *inter alia* by some measure of central bank independence.

The negative relationship between indicators of central bank independence and inflation in OECD countries is quite robust also, if various control variables are included in the regression. Still, it should be noted that a negative correlation does not necessarily imply causation. The correlation between both variables could be explained by a third factor, such as the culture and tradition of monetary stability in a country.

SYLVESTER C.W. EIJFFINGER

See also:

Central Bank Accountability and Transparency; Monetary Policy: Role of; Rational Expectations; Time Inconsistency.

Bibliography

Barro, R.J. and D.B. Gordon (1983), 'Rules, Discretion, and Reputation in a Positive Model of Monetary Policy', *Journal of Monetary Economics*, **12**, July, pp. 101–21.
Berger, H., J. de Haan and S.C.W. Eijffinger (2001), 'Central Bank Independence: An Update of Theory and Evidence', *Journal of Economic Surveys*, **15**, February, pp. 3–40.
Cukierman, A. (1992), *Central Bank Strategy, Credibility and Independence*, Cambridge, MA: MIT Press.
Debelle, G. and S. Fischer (1995), 'How Independent Should a Central Bank Be?', in J.C. Fuhrer (ed.), *Goals, Guidelines and Constraints Facing Monetary Policymakers*, Federal Reserve Bank of Boston, Conference Series no. 38, Boston.
Eijffinger, S.C.W. and J. de Haan (1996), 'The Political Economy of Central-Bank Independence', *Princeton Special Papers in International Economics*, no. 19.
Eijffinger, S.C.W. and M. Hoeberichts (1998), 'The Trade-off Between Central Bank Independence and Conservativeness', *Oxford Economic Papers*, **50**, July, pp. 397–411.
Kydland, F.W. and E.C. Prescott (1977), 'Rules Rather than Discretion: The Inconsistency of Optimal Plans', *Journal of Political Economy*, **85**, June, pp. 473–91.
Persson, T. and G. Tabellini (1993), 'Designing Institutions for Monetary Stability', *Carnegie-Rochester Conference Series on Public Policy*, **39**, December, pp. 53–84.

Rogoff, K. (1985), 'The Optimal Degree of Commitment to an Intermediate Monetary Target', *Quarterly Journal of Economics*, **100**, November, pp. 1169–90.
Walsh, C.E. (1995), 'Optimal Contracts for Central Bankers', *American Economic Review*, **85**, March, pp. 150–67.

Central Parity

The centre of a target zone or band for the exchange rate under a fixed exchange rate system.

See also:
Fixed Exchange Rate System.

Classical Dichotomy

The classical dichotomy refers to a conceptual division of the economy into two sectors: the real and the monetary. In the former were determined real phenomena such as output, employment, relative prices and interest rates; in the latter were determined monetary phenomena such as nominal prices and (if not institutionally fixed) nominal exchange rates. This dichotomy, which was a durable feature of classical and neoclassical economics, was intimately linked to the quantity theory of money and implied the neutrality of money.

It is important to recall here the extent to which classical economists focused on long-term horizons. They did not ignore short-term problems (indeed, they often argued about them) but their theories were mainly directed to explaining situations of long-term equilibrium after all short-term adjustments had been completed. Hence, when the classical economists dichotomized the economy, what they were arguing was that, in situations of long-term equilibrium, real forces (such as the amount and productivity of capital and of labour) would determine real outcomes and monetary forces would determine monetary outcomes. Put another way, changes in the quantity of money would tend to have an effect only on prices: money was (approximately) neutral, or at least would be so if one could ignore the distribution of income. And explicit references to distributional issues are found at least as far back as Cantillon (1755).

The classical dichotomy was one of outcome or of effects: it did not mean that real and monetary forces could, in practice, be separated or that both were not jointly responsible for most day-to-day outcomes. This was made clear in the classic essay 'Of Money' by David Hume (1752). In the long term, according to Hume: 'it is evident that the greater or less plenty of

money is of no consequence; since the prices of commodities are always pro-
portioned to the plenty of money'. But in the short term it is a different story:

> alterations in the quantity of money . . . are not immediately attended with pro-
> portionable alterations in the price of commodities. There is always an interval
> before matters be adjusted to their new situation; and this interval is as perni-
> cious to industry, when gold and silver are diminishing, as it is advantageous
> when these metals are increasing.

Not only does Hume make it clear that changes in the quantity of money
are of importance for output and employment in the 'interval' between
changes in money and changes in prices, he also makes it clear that the
interval can last for many years. Nevertheless, ultimately changes in the
quantity of money affect only the general price level, while real things such
as output and employment depend upon real forces.

The crucial distinction between the short term and the long term was re-
emphasized in the early nineteenth century both by Thornton (1802) and
by Ricardo (1810, 1821). Writing at the time of the Napoleonic wars when
convertibility of Bank of England notes into gold had been suspended,
they had to deal with the theory of an inconvertible paper money. This
meant that they had to deal explicitly with the way money was created.

Given the then-existing structure of the banking system in Great Britain,
the supply of inconvertible paper money, it was argued, would depend upon
the volume of loans made by the Bank of England. The demand for these
loans would, in turn, depend upon the gap between the rate of interest
charged by the Bank of England and the rate of return on capital employed
in commodity markets. If the former were below the latter there would be
gains to be made with borrowed funds, the demand for loans would be high
and, in consequence, the money supply would expand rapidly, demand for
goods would be high and prices would rise. Equilibrium in commodity
markets could only be restored when the Bank of England curbed its
lending (or was forced to do so by the restoration of convertibility) and
when market interest rates rose to their equilibrium level.

The theoretical approach of Thornton, which was followed by Ricardo
and subsequently by John Stuart Mill (1871), clearly anticipates the work,
nearly a century later, of Wicksell (1898) wherein the distinction between
market and natural rates of interest is central to explaining the growth of
the money supply and inflation. It is important to stress that the approach
provides not only a clear transmission mechanism to explain *how* changes
in the quantity of money affect the economy but also makes plain that the
effects are, in the first instance, on real magnitudes: rates of interest, investment, output.

But the long-term effects were still seen as falling mainly on prices. Once the money supply ceased to grow there would be no cause of excess demand for commodities and no reason for output and employment to continue to deviate from the equilibria determined by real forces. Prices would cease to rise but would remain at a level which reflected the higher stock of money. It was all in accordance with the classical dichotomy: a dichotomy of outcomes.

Convertibility was restored after the end of the Napoleonic wars and gold again resumed a role in determining the money supply in the UK as it (or silver) did elsewhere. Although both Mill and Marshall (1887) were careful to point out that imported gold would enter the money supply via the money markets and the banking system, not all writers were so careful. Some presented the dichotomy between real and monetary forces as if there were an actual (as opposed to conceptual) division between two halves of the economy. This, according to Patinkin (1965), was notable of the early exponents of general-equilibrium analysis, Walras (1926), Fisher (1911) and Cassel (1925). Statements were made to the effect that all real economic decisions depended upon incomes and relative prices and were unaffected by the absolute level of prices. Versions of Say's Law or, alternatively, the homogeneity postulate were advanced to claim that real outcomes were not only independent of monetary forces in the long run but were, apparently, detached from them in the short run as well.

This was clearly invalid and one can only assume that a preoccupation with developing new analytical techniques led some writers to be careless as to the words they used to describe their ideas. Be that as it may, the issue of the classical dichotomy provoked a spirited controversy in the 1940s and 1950s before Patinkin, in a work of great scholarship, once again showed how real and monetary sectors were inevitably integrated: there was one economy, not two, and only outcomes could be dichotomized. Patinkin argued that decisions to spend would depend, *inter alia*, on economic agents' money holdings. There was an important but poorly recognized real balance effect: if agents found their money balances deficient they would tend to reduce expenditures; if they found their money balances excessive they would tend to increase expenditures. This real balance effect was an important part of any explanation of the dynamics of the response of the economy to changes in the quantity of money. It was also crucial in explaining the stability of the price level.

In this way Patinkin showed that all commodity demand functions could be expected to depend, *inter alia*, on holdings of money. There was no partitioned economy, both real and monetary forces influenced all economic decisions. Furthermore, the homogeneity postulate was not only not necessary to any analysis of classical monetary theory, it was contradictory to it and only had relevance for a barter economy. Similarly, Say's

Law, if presumed to apply in the short term (an interpretation now often referred to as Say's Identity), also implied a barter economy. Any explanation of the determination of relative prices as if it occurs divorced from the determination of money prices is quite simply wrong and is, moreover, a misrepresentation of the traditional views of classical economists.

The only theoretically valid dichotomy is of outcomes. Real and monetary forces interact to determine jointly day-to-day outcomes but, notwithstanding this and all other things equal, in the long term the principal effect of changes in the quantity of money will be on prices, not on output or employment.

But whether this theoretically tenable position would be acceptable today as an explanation of reality would be hotly contested. It is contested, but the focus of the debate now concerns the issue of whether the long-term Phillips curve is or is not vertical. The substance of the debate remains: whether or not changes in demand have long-term effects beyond changes in the price level.

RICHARD L. HARRINGTON

See also:

Classical Economics; Neutrality of Money; Phillips Curve; Quantity Theory of Money; Real Balance Effect; Say's Law.

Bibliography

Cantillon, R. (1755), *Essai sur la Nature du Commerce en Général*, reprinted in H. Higgs (trans. & ed.) (1931), *Essay on the Nature of Trade*, London: Macmillan.

Cassel, G. (1925), *Fundamental Thoughts in Economics*, London: Fisher Unwin.

Fisher, I. (1911), *The Purchasing Power of Money*, New York: Macmillan.

Hume, D. (1752), *Essays, Moral, Political and Literary*, Edinburgh. Hume's essays have been reprinted many times, for example in E. Rotwein (ed.) (1955), *David Hume: Writings on Economics*, London: Nelson.

Marshall, A. (1887), 'Evidence to the Royal Commission on the Values of Gold and Silver', reproduced in J.M. Keynes (ed.) (1926), *Official Papers of Alfred Marshall*, London: Macmillan.

Mill, J.S. (1871), *Principles of Political Economy*, 7th edn, London; reprinted in J.M. Robson (ed.) (1965), Toronto: University of Toronto Press.

Patinkin, D. (1965), *Money, Interest and Prices*, 2nd edn, New York: Harper & Row.

Ricardo, D. (1810), *The High Price of Bullion*, London; reprinted in P. Sraffa (1951–2), *The Works of David Ricardo*, Cambridge: Cambridge University Press.

Ricardo, D. (1821), *The Principles of Political Economy and Taxation*, 3rd edn, London; reprinted in P. Sraffa (1951–2), *The Works of David Ricardo*, Cambridge: Cambridge University Press.

Thornton, H. (1802), *An Inquiry into the Nature and Effect of the Paper Credit of Great Britain*, London; reprinted with introduction by F. Von Hayek (1939), London: George Allen & Unwin.

Walras, L. (1926), *Eléments d'Economie Politique Pure*, definitive edn; trans. W. Jaffé (1954), *Elements of Pure Economics*, Homewood IL: R. Irwin.

Wicksell, W. (1898), *Geldzins und Gütepreise*, trans. R.F. Kahn (1936), *Interest and Prices*, London: MacMillan & Co.

Classical Economics

The macroeconomic analysis in classical economics stems, like so much else in the classical literature, from the work of David Hume (1752) and Adam Smith (1776), though it is possible that Hume had seen Richard Cantillon's *Essai* (1730) (circulated, but not published until 1755).

The basic building block provided by Hume was the theory of a self-correcting balance of payments under a metallic currency regime, which became known as the price-specie-flow mechanism in later commentary. If the money supply in one country resulted in a price level which was too high for balance of payments equilibrium (and Hume is quite explicit about the role of the price level) then a reduction in the money supply would result from a balance of payments deficit settled in precious metal, and the price level would fall until the balance of payments deficit was eliminated. Conversely, too small a money supply, and consequently too low a price level, would result in a balance of payments surplus and a rise in the money supply.

Smith avoided explicit presentation of this mechanism in *The Wealth of Nations*, leaving the equilibration mechanism unclear. He also argued that the supply of metal substitutes, in the form of paper money, would remain consistent with international equilibrium, as notes would only be issued in accordance with the 'needs of trade', if the method of issue were confined to the discounting of bills originating in transactions in goods and services, a belief which became known as the Real Bills doctrine.

There was thus a fundamental tension between the views of Hume and Smith, with the former holding that the price level depended on the money supply and the latter taking the price level as fixed by the price of gold – which was correct as a long-run proposition but of little help when issues of short-run monetary control had to be faced. For Smith, the money supply depended on the (exogenous) price level and the level of transactions.

These theoretical foundations were developed during three defining eras in classical monetary theory: the Bullion Controversy, the Currency and Banking Controversy, and Bank Charter debates.

In 1797, the convertibility of British bank notes into gold was suspended, owing to wartime conditions. There followed the development of the theory of an inconvertible paper currency. There were essentially three theoretical positions articulated during the suspension period, which lasted until 1819. Firstly there were those, of whom the most prominent (though not the most original) was Ricardo, who applied the logic of Hume's analysis without regard either to time lags or to modifying circumstances. Their position may be summarized in the Ricardian definition of excess; if the price of gold (in terms of paper currency) was above its official Mint parity, and the exchange rate was depressed, then, *by definition*, the Bank of England had issued too many notes and inflated the money supply, *whatever* extraneous factors (such as harvest failure to depress the exchange, or a need for gold to pay for military operations abroad) were also present.

Opposed to these rigid Bullionists were the Anti-Bullionists, who really took their cue from Adam Smith. In their view, overissue of bank notes was impossible, so long as the bank adhered to discounting real bills (of course in practice it did not) and the direction of causality was from the price level to the money supply. Symptoms such as a depressed exchange were simply due to exogenous shocks; they did not have monetary causes.

The most subtle and profound contribution to the debate came, however, from a group of moderate Bullionists of whom the most important was Henry Thornton. They accepted the importance of the exchange rate and the price of bullion as long-run tests of excess additions to the money supply, but argued that the short-term importance of other factors made it necessary to avoid contracting the money supply whenever these symptoms appeared. Indeed, inappropriate contraction could produce financial disaster. One of this group, William Blake, distinguished two underlying components of the observed ('computed') exchange: the real and the nominal exchange. The first of these was, in the long run, self-correcting; a depressed real exchange would increase exports and reduce imports. The second, which reflected the depreciation of paper currencies, was not self-correcting. Thus a depressed exchange over a long period indicated overissue.

For this group, as for the more rigid Bullionists, causality definitely ran from the money supply to the price level. Thornton provided the fundamental critique of the Real Bills doctrine, as failing to distinguish between the marginal rate of profit and the bank lending rate. If the latter were lower than the former, there would be an indefinitely large demand for loans in the form of discounts of bills, and the money supply would go on increasing, raising the price level, and maintaining profit margins. He also pointed out that the real (that is, deflated) rate of interest would be less than the nominal bank lending rate in inflation, thus producing profit. Restricting the supply of new notes to the discounting of real bills, even had it been possible, provided no safeguard against excessive increases in the money supply.

With the resumption of convertibility in 1819, the general assumption was that monetary stability would be reimposed. This proved not to be the case; convertibility was not its own safeguard. There emerged in the mid-1820s a new approach, the doctrine of *metallic fluctuation*. This idea, which was put forward more or less simultaneously by a group of writers, was essentially a deduction from the Ricardian definition of excess. It proposed that a mixed currency of metal and paper should fluctuate in amount *exactly as an identically circumstanced metallic one would.* Thus a gold outflow, consequent on a balance of payments deficit, should result in an equal reduction in the stock of bank notes. The idea, deriving ultimately from Hume, was that this would produce exactly the reduction in the price level required to correct the balance of payments; the gold outflow would cease, and the reserves would not be exhausted.

Though this idea was supported by one of the Bank of England directors, George Warde Norman, it did not appeal immediately to the bank, which favoured discretion rather than rules. The bank instead had resort to a balance sheet device called the 'Palmer Rule' (after the governor of the Bank, Horsley Palmer). This allowed a drain of gold, on the asset side of the balance sheet, to fall on the *combined* liabilities of notes and deposits. It thus allowed the bank to choose how far notes were contracted, and since deposits were likely to be withdrawn to obtain gold, there might be no reduction in the note issue. If the notes were the key part of the high-powered money base, as the bank's critics believed, this was a serious mistake. In addition, the bank used its discretion quite freely, to the extent of ignoring the Palmer Rule when convenient.

This led, in the 1830s, to the development of a critique of the bank's behaviour, based on a distinction between the *Currency Principle* and the *Banking Principle*. The first of these, following from the principle of metallic fluctuation, was designed to be countercyclical. Samuel Jones Lloyd, later Lord Overstone, advanced the idea of an endogenous trade cycle, which could be magnified or damped by monetary control. In the upswing, the balance of payments moved into deficit, and gold flowed out. If the money supply were contracted, in conformity with the principle of metallic fluctuation, the upswing would be damped. Conversely, the severity of the downswing would be reduced by allowing inflowing gold to increase the money supply. This was the Currency Principle. The Banking Principle was to allow the money supply to expand and contract passively in response to the needs of trade; and increasing the money supply, just when prices and incomes were rising, would magnify the amplitude of the cycle.

The common assumption of almost all parties was that the money supply depended on the supply of Bank of England notes. In this they were almost certainly mistaken, as Thomas Joplin was to argue; the note issues of the country banks, which were not really controlled by those of the Bank of England, were the critical ones for transactions, and thus for the cycle.

The views of the Currency School were embodied in the Bank Charter Act of 1844, despite strong opposition from the Banking School, whose members included Thomas Tooke and John Fullarton. Tooke in particular argued that causality ran from the price level to the money supply. The price level itself was determined by the price of gold. Though this was undoubtedly true in long-run equilibrium, it provided no information about the correct policy of monetary control. Tooke attempted to bridge the gap by explaining the price level in terms of aggregate demand and supply; but it turned out that his aggregate demand schedule and his aggregate supply schedule were identical – the total of money incomes – so there was no determinate equilibrium price level. But the Banking School also denied the connection between the balance of payments and the money supply, maintaining that gold flows abroad came from 'hoards'. The Real Bills doctrine was resurrected as the doctrine of Reflux, according to which any issue of notes in excess of the needs of trade would be returned to the issuer to avoid the interest cost. Since the needs of trade were in part determined by the price level, there was a hole in the Banking School position

With the Act in place, rules had replaced discretion, the monetary base was the control instrument, and the bank was free to use its discount rate (Bank Rate) as it saw fit. Unfortunately, it failed to use it to protect its reserve, or even to acknowledge its role as lender of last resort, and liquidity crises ensued in 1847 and 1857, as fears developed that the bank could not fulfil this role – as indeed it could not, if its reserve were low, as the Act prevented it from printing extra notes not backed by gold. In both crises the Act had to be suspended by the government, and the Currency School reluctantly accepted the Bank's last resort role, though logically it was not only inconsistent with the 1844 Act but posed a problem of moral hazard: the market might not observe its own liquidity precautions if it were confident of extra notes being forthcoming in a crisis, and thus the counter-cyclical nature of the Act would be undermined. The Act had indeed provided for weekly publication of the state of the Bank's reserve, precisely to encourage the financial sector to increase reserves when monetary contraction threatened.

Unfortunately, as Walter Bagehot pointed out, both in the *Economist* (which he edited), and in his classic *Lombard Street* (1873), there was no reserve *except* that in the Banking Department of the bank itself. Thus the bank was forced to be the lender of last resort, and from 1857 onwards it systematically used Bank Rate to protect its reserve. The last crisis engendered by the monetary system itself was that of 1857 (there was one more in 1866, but that was due to special City circumstances) and the monetary system, and the theory which lay behind it, both modified by experience and confrontation with the data, lasted until 1914.

The outcome was an enduring body of theory. When Alfred Marshall set out to reconstruct economics after the Marginal Revolution of the 1870s, the macroeconomic theory of classical economics was quietly incorporated into the new theoretical system.

D.P. O'BRIEN

See also:

Hume, David.

Bibliography

Bagehot W. (1873), *Lombard Street*; reprinted (1996), Düsseldorf: Verlagsgruppe. Handelsblatt.
Cantillon, R. (1755), *Essai sur la Nature du Commerce en Général*, ed. and trans. H. Higgs; reprinted (1964) New York: A.M. Kelley.
Clapham, J.H. (1944), *The Bank of England*, Cambridge: Cambridge University Press.
Hume, D. (1752), 'Of Money' and 'Of the Balance of Trade', reprinted in E. Rotwein (ed.) (1955), *David Hume, Writings on Economics*, Edinburgh: Nelson.
Humphrey, T.M. (1993), *Money, Banking and Inflation*, Aldershot, UK and Brookfield, US: Edward Elgar.
O'Brien, D.P. (1975), *The Classical Economists*, Oxford: Clarendon.
O'Brien, D.P. (1993), *Thomas Joplin and Classical Macroeconomics*, Aldershot, UK and Brookfield, US: Edward Elgar.
O'Brien, D.P. (1995), 'Long-run Equilibrium and Cyclical Disturbances: the Currency and Banking Controversy over Monetary Control', in M. Blaug, W. Eltis, D.P. O'Brien, D. Patinkin, R. Skidelsky and G.Wood, *The Quantity Theory of Money*, Aldershot, UK and Brookfield, US: Edward Elgar.
Smith, A. (1776), *An Inquiry into the Nature and Causes of the Wealth of Nations*, reprinted in R.H. Campbell, A.S. Skinner and W. B. Todd (eds) (1981), Indianapolis: Liberty Press.
Viner, J. (1937), *Studies in the Theory of International Trade*, London: Allen & Unwin.

Classical Model

A stylized pre-Keynesian model used to portray the general tenor of views held by classical economists writing from around the mid-eighteenth century through to the 1930s. Given the critical assumption that wages and prices adjust to clear markets, the level of output is that produced by a fully employed labour force. Say's Law rules out the possibility of any deficiency of aggregate demand ensuring that the full employment level of output finds a market. The average price of final output is itself determined solely by the supply of money, in line with the quantity theory of money. Within the classical model, monetary policy has no influence on any of the real variables in the long run.

See also:

Classical Dichotomy; Keynesian Economics; Neutrality of Money; Quantity Theory of Money; Say's Law.

Clean Float

An exchange rate regime where the exchange rate is determined by the market forces of demand and supply without any intervention by the central monetary authorities.

See also:
Dirty Float; Flexible Exchange Rate System.

Clower, Robert W.

Robert Clower (b.1926, Pullman, Washington, USA) obtained his BA (1948) and MA (1949) from Washington State University, and his BLitt (1952) and DLitt (1978) from Oxford University. His main past posts have included Assistant Professor at Washington State University, 1952–6; Associate Professor (1957–62) and Professor of Economics (1963–71) at Northwestern University; and Professor of Economics at the University of California, Los Angeles, 1972–86. Since 1986, he has been the Hugh C. Lane Professor of Economic Theory at the University of South Carolina. He was managing editor of *Economic Inquiry* between 1973 and 1979 and the *American Economic Review* from 1980 to 1985. He is best known for his influential contributions to monetary theory and macroeconomics, and in particular for his seminal contribution to the disequilibrium approach in Keynesian macroeconomics. Among his best known books are *Monetary Theory: Selected Readings* (ed.) (Penguin, 1969); *Money and Markets: Selected Essays of R. W. Clower*, ed. by D.A. Walker (Cambridge University Press, 1984); and *Economic Doctrine and Method: Selected Papers of R. W. Clower* (Edward Elgar, 1995). His most widely read articles include 'The Keynesian Counter-Revolution: A Theoretical Appraisal', in F.H. Hahn and F.P.R. Breckling (eds), *The Theory of Interest Rates* (Macmillan, 1965); 'A Reconsideration of the Microfoundations of Monetary Theory' (*Western Economic Journal*, **6**, December 1967); and 'The Coordination of Economic Activities: A Keynesian Perspective' (co-authored with A. Leijonhufvud) (*American Economic Review*, **65**, May 1975).

See also:
Dual Decision Hypothesis; Keynesian Economics: Reappraisals of.

Coddington, Alan (1941–82)

Alan Coddington (b.1941, Doncaster, England) obtained his BSc from the University of Leeds in 1963 and his DPhil from the University of York in 1966. His main past posts included Assistant Lecturer in Economics (1966–7) and Lecturer in Economics (1967–75) at the University of Manchester; and Senior Lecturer in Economics (1975–7), Reader in

Economics (1977–9) and Professor of Economics (1980–82) at Queen Mary College, University of London. He is best known for his contributions to methodology and to the analytical foundations of Keynesian economics. Among his best known books are *Theories of the Bargaining Process* (George Allen & Unwin, 1968); and *Keynesian Economics: The Search for First Principles* (George Allen & Unwin, 1983). His most widely read articles include 'Keynesian Economics: The Search for First Principles' (*Journal of Economic Literature*, **14**, December 1976); and 'Deficient Foresight: A Troublesome Theme in Keynesian Economics' (*American Economic Review*, **72**, June 1982).

See also:
Hydraulic Keynesianism.

Cold Turkey

A rapid and permanent reduction in the rate of monetary growth aimed at reducing the rate of inflation.

See also:
Gradualism; Gradualism versus Cold Turkey; Inflation: Costs of Reducing; Sacrifice Ratio.

Comparative Advantage

The determinants of the pattern of international trade (which goods and services a country imports and which it exports), was one of the earliest issues ever investigated by economists and continues to receive attention to this day. The theory of comparative advantage is the outcome of these investigations. When examined in a fully general equilibrium context, the pattern of trade only emerges once a set of relative prices that clears world markets has been found. Each country will then export those goods in which it has an excess supply, and import those goods in which it has an excess demand, at these prices. In turn, these excess demands and supplies depend on three important country characteristics: the preferences of the country's residents over the various goods and services; the country's resource endowments; and the technologies to which its producers have access. The world trading equilibrium then reflects the interaction of these characteristics across all countries. The explanation of the trade pattern, and the sources of comparative advantage, therefore lie in inter-country differences in preferences, resource endowments and technologies.

Unfortunately, tracing the exact channels through which these character-istics determine the trade pattern proves difficult in a general equilibrium context. Traditionally, trade economists have therefore fallen back on rela-tively simple models which they hope will capture the essential features of the problem but allow important principles to be illustrated. Thus the early analyses of comparative advantage employed a simple competitive model, with two countries, two goods, constant returns to scale in production and free intersectoral mobility of factors within each country, but complete immobility of factors among countries. Ricardo's original demonstration of the principle of comparative advantage (Ricardo, 1817), concentrated on factor productivity differences as a source of trade, and showed that it was comparisons of relative productivity differences across sectors, rather than absolute productivity, that determined the pattern of trade (and the potential gains from trade). These results can be illustrated quite simply. Suppose the two goods (1 and 2) are produced using a single factor input (labour), with a_j (a_j^*) units of labour required to produce one unit of output j ($j=1,2$) in the home country (rest-of-the-world). Then competition will ensure that the relative prices of good 2 in terms of good 1 in autarky are a_2/a_1, and a_2^*/a_1^* in the home country and rest-of-the-world, respectively. Each relative price represents the opportunity cost of producing a unit of good 2 (which requires respectively a_2 or a_2^* units of labour) in terms of the number of units of good 1 that are forgone (since each worker can produce $1/a_1$ or $1/a_1^*$ units, respectively, of good 1). The home country is said to have a *comparative advantage* in the production of good 2 if its opportunity cost of producing that good is lower than that in the rest-of-the-world's when in their respective autarky equilibria; that is, $a_2/a_1 < a_2^*/a_1^*$. It follows that the rest-of-the-world has the comparative advantage in good 1. This is consis-tent with any pattern of productivity differences, except that where the home country has the superior productivity (*absolute advantage*) in good 1, and the rest-of-the-world has the absolute advantage in good 2. The home comparative advantage in good 2 is translated into a lower relative price of good 2 in autarky and hence exports of good 2 once trade becomes pos-sible. In this model, resource endowment differences across countries are removed as a potential determinant of the pattern of trade by assuming a single factor and constant returns to scale in production. Similarly, prefer-ence differences have limited impact because fixed opportunity costs lead to a linear production possibility frontier so that technology determines autarky-relative prices (unless there is specialization even in autarky).

Ricardo's result has been extended to a world of many goods (some non-traded) by Dornbusch *et al.* (1977). Goods can be ordered by decreasing strength of home comparative advantage (that is, the home country has a stronger comparative advantage in good j than in good k if $a_j/a_j^* < a_k/a_k^*$)

and in the trading equilibrium the home country will export those goods in which it has the strongest comparative advantage. Preferences and relative country sizes determine the equilibrium trading margin, but if the home country exports (imports) good k it will also export (import) those goods in which it has a stronger (weaker) comparative advantage than in good k.

Before accepting this as the fundamental explanation of the trade pattern, it is only natural to wonder why labour productivity should differ internationally. One explanation is different technologies, but an alternative is different availability of other required inputs. The role of differences in resource endowments as a source of comparative advantage was explored by Heckscher (1919) and Ohlin (1933), whose work has been developed into the Heckscher–Ohlin model. Here technologies are assumed to be the same across countries, but to differ across goods, and production requires the services of two inputs (labour and land, say). These assumptions yield a 'bowed out' production possibility frontier, so that opportunity costs are no longer constant, and autarky-relative prices depend on preferences. If we assume that production of good 1 is always relatively labour-intensive (that is, the cost-minimizing production of good 1 employs a higher labour-to-land ratio than the production of good 2, at any common factor price ratio) and that the home country is relatively labour-abundant (there are more workers per unit of land in the home country than in the rest-of-the-world), then we can establish the Heckscher–Ohlin theorem: the relatively labour-abundant country will export (import) the relatively labour (land)-intensive good in the trading equilibrium. Assuming identical homothetic preferences (and thereby eliminating tastes as a determinant of the pattern of trade), the production equilibrium in the relatively labour-abundant country will involve a relatively higher output of the relatively labour-intensive good at any common product price ratio (the Rybczynski theorem). The relatively labour-abundant country will then have the lower relative price of the labour-intensive good in autarky. Relative product prices reflect relative opportunity costs, hence the relatively labour-abundant country has the comparative advantage in the labour-intensive good. Thus relative factor endowment differences are also a source of comparative advantage.

Subsequent work has extended these models (Jones and Neary, 1984) and tested their predictions (Deardorff, 1984). In practice, it may be difficult to distinguish among them empirically. Theory suggests that trade flows and labour productivity differences are likely to be positively related even in factor endowment-based models (Falvey, 1981). Consideration of technology differences in the Heckscher–Ohlin model yields Ricardian predictions of comparative advantage if technology differences are product-augmenting, and Heckscher–Ohlin predictions of comparative advantage if technology differences are factor-augmenting. As noted at the outset, once we move in the direction of including many goods and factors in the model, it becomes difficult to establish definitive results. While concepts such as factor intensity can be generalized in principle, it is less obvious how these generalizations can be linked to the available data. One problem is that differences in autarky-relative prices, and hence the differences in the underlying determinants of the pattern of trade that they reflect, cease to be reliable predictors of the trade pattern at the level of the individual product when there are many goods. A positive correlation between autarky price differences and trade flows can be established, however, so that the former can be used to predict the latter 'on average'.

The preceding discussion has primarily related to inter-industry trade – the international exchange of products that are the outputs of separate industries – where it is reasonable to assume that different goods are produced using different technologies or combinations of factor inputs. However, much international trade, particularly among developed countries, is intra-industry trade – the exchange of outputs from the same industries. Over the last 30 years a substantial effort has been devoted to explaining this phenomenon. While one can apply the type of trade models discussed above, the more popular approach is to model industries as producing differentiated products using identical technologies for which economies of scale are important. Firms then specialize in a single product, and trade is the exchange of these products, but there is no comparative advantage, and hence no predictable pattern of trade, within the industry.

Finally, while this discussion has concentrated on applying the principle of comparative advantage to the pattern of international trade, where it has seen its greatest use, the principle itself has much wider application to the division of labour between individuals, firms and countries.

ROD FALVEY

See also:

Heckscher–Ohlin Approach to International Trade.

Bibliography

Deardorff, A.V. (1984), 'Testing Trade Theories and Predicting Trade Flows', in R.W. Jones and P.B. Kenen (eds), *Handbook of International Economics*, vol. 1. Amsterdam: North-Holland.

Dornbusch, R., S. Fischer and P.A. Samuelson (1977), 'Comparative Advantage, Trade, and Payments in a Ricardian Model with a Continuum of Goods', *American Economic Review*, **67**, December, pp. 823–39.

Falvey, R.E. (1981), 'Comparative Advantage in a Multi-Factor World', *International Economic Review*, **22**, May, pp. 401–13.

Heckscher, E. (1919), 'The Effects of Foreign Trade on the Distribution of Income', in H.S. Ellis and L.A. Metzler (eds), *Readings in the Theory of International Trade*, Philadelphia: Blackston, 1949.

Jones, R.W. and J.P. Neary (1984), 'The Positive Theory of International Trade', in R.W. Jones and P.B. Kenen (eds) *Handbook of International Economics*, vol. 1, Amsterdam: North-Holland.

Ohlin, B. (1933), *Inter-Regional and International Trade*, Cambridge: Cambridge University Press.

Ricardo, D. (1951), *The Works and Correspondence of David Ricardo*, ed. P. Sraffa, Cambridge: Cambridge University Press.

Consumption Function

The relationship between aggregate consumption and income. As consumption is the largest component of aggregate expenditure, the functional relationship between consumption and income is central to the theory of income determination developed by Keynes in the *General Theory*. Keynes's view that consumption increases as income increases, but not by as much as the increase in income, has come to be known as the absolute income hypothesis. Keynes suggested that: consumption is a stable function of income; the marginal propensity to consume (MPC) is positive and less than unity; and the marginal propensity to consume is less than the average propensity to consume (APC) so that the APC declines as income increases. While early empirical studies (both budget studies of a cross-section of the population and short-run aggregate time series studies) of the consumption–income relationship supported Keynes's theory, empirical work undertaken by Simon Kuznets, which was published in 1946, revealed that the APC had not in fact changed significantly since 1869. Kuznet's findings contradicted Keynes's views, suggesting that in the long run the consumption–income relationship is best represented by a straight line through the origin with a slope of approximately 0.9 (that is, MPC = APC). Subsequent attempts to reconcile the conflicting evidence from various types of study, in terms of a unified theory, have included the relative income, permanent income and life cycle hypotheses.

See also:

Absolute Income Hypothesis; Average Propensity to Consume; Keynes's *General Theory*; Keynesian Cross; Kuznets, Simon S.; Life Cycle Hypothesis; Marginal Propensity to Consume; Permanent Income Hypothesis; Relative Income Hypothesis.

Contractionary Phase

The period in the business cycle between a peak or upper turning point and a successive trough or lower turning point.

See also:
Business Cycle; Peak; Trough.

Convergence

The tendency for income per capita (standards of living) in different countries to converge over time. One of the key predictions of the neoclassical growth model is absolute or unconditional convergence for economies with identical rates of savings and population growth, and unlimited access to the same technology. Such an outcome is only likely to be observed across a group of countries or regions that share similar characteristics. For economies with different rates of savings or population growth, conditional convergence is predicted.

See also:
Barro, Robert J.; Catching Up and Convergence; Neoclassical Growth Model.

Coordination Failures

During a depression economic activities are badly coordinated. Firms allow plant and equipment to fall idle despite increasing numbers of able-bodied people willing to operate it in exchange for less than the value of their marginal product. Savers continue as before to make provision for extra future consumption while production of the new capital needed to produce more consumer goods is reduced. Stocks of consumer goods pile up unsold even though the desire to consume them is, if anything, intensified by rising poverty. Farmers are forced off their land while others go hungry.

Many economists therefore think of depression as being a state of coordination failure; a state in which market forces have failed to coordinate the millions of transactors that interact daily through a web of interconnected markets. What Smith called the 'invisible hand', or Mummery and Hobson (disparagingly) called the 'automatic machinery of commerce', has not guided them to a state in which markets clear. Instead, people are somehow led to act at cross-purposes, failing collectively to take full advantage of potential gains from trade. As Keynes put it, the system is not 'self-adjusting'.

The first step in understanding how a mechanism can fail is to understand how it works. Although modern economic theory is rather vague on how market forces work, the beginning student is left in little doubt that they operate mainly through the adjustment of prices. According to all undergraduate textbooks, a free market will quickly reach a coordinated (market-clearing) state, because prices rise when there is an excess demand and fall when there is an excess supply. Analytical accounts of coordination failure therefore focus on why something might go wrong with the process of price adjustment.

The classical tradition from Thornton to Marshall was to blame prolonged unemployment on impediments to price adjustment, particularly impediments to adjusting the price of labour. This was also the approach of mainstream Keynesianism which, from Modigliani to Fischer, was based on the assumption of sticky wages. But Keynes himself believed that coordination failure had a deeper reason, namely that wage and price adjustment, which classical theory pictured as corrective forces, are actually destabilizing. If given full rein they would lead an economy even further into depression, because a general decrease in wages and prices would produce 'debt deflation' (to use Fisher's term, which Keynes did not), destabilizing expectations of further price decreases, and adverse distributional effects.

Patinkin (1948) elaborated on Keynes's account of coordination failure by portraying the process of wage and price adjustment as a dynamic system that fails to converge to its (full-employment) equilibrium. Clower (1965) pointed out another possible reason for non-convergence, namely that transactors will respond not just to the price signals of classical theory but also to quantity signals they receive when their attempts to trade are frustrated by existing imbalances between supply and demand. Thus excess supply in one market can lead frustrated sellers to curtail their demands in other markets, causing the excess supply to spread. As Leijonhufvud (1968) later elaborated, the cumulative decline in effective demand resulting from this process will tend to amplify deviations from full employment equilibrium rather than dampening them.

The approach taken by these writers, of analysing coordination failure in terms of disequilibrium price adjustment, gained support from the demonstration by Scarf (1960) that price adjustment in a Walrasian general equilibrium setting does not always converge to a general equilibrium; in effect, adjustments in one market may be continually thwarted by independent adjustments in other related markets. However, work on disequilibrium dynamics fell out of fashion in the 1970s, largely because its proponents offered no conceptually coherent account of the many logistical problems that arise when expectations are mutually inconsistent and markets are not clearing, or of the institutions (firms, shops, money, markets and so on) that deal with these logistical problems in real life. The final blow was dealt by Lucas (1972), who showed that one can provide a conceptually coherent account of at least transitory coordination problems within a framework of rational expectations with clearly specified informational imperfections, a framework in which none of the awkward problems of disequilibrium theory are visible.

After a decade of relative neglect, the theory of coordination failure re-emerged in the 1980s, when various authors found a way to model it using the rational expectations equilibrium approach which by that time had become *de rigueur* in macroeconomic theory. Since then, the term 'coordination failure' has taken on a different meaning, with no reference to disequilibrium dynamics. Specifically, as elaborated by Cooper and John (1988) and later by Cooper (1999), it now means the existence of multiple equilibria, often Pareto-ranked, of the kind that exist in games with strategic complementarity.

Suppose, for example, that there is a strategic complementarity that works through 'thin-market externalities' in the process of search and matching (see Diamond, 1982; Howitt, 1985). That is, when people on one side of a market put more effort into the matching process, this makes it more worthwhile for those on the other side to do the same thing, because it makes transacting less costly for them. Then the general expectation on the part of firms that it will be difficult to find customers can be self-fulfilling. It leads firms to cut back their hiring effort, which leads to a fall in job vacancies, which makes it harder for unemployed workers to find jobs. As a result unemployment rises, and the consequent fall in incomes makes people generally less willing to buy goods. This completes the vicious circle by confirming the original expectation that it will be harder for firms to find customers.

On the other hand, the same chain of reasoning can often be applied to show that the expectation that customers will be *easy* to find would also be self-fulfilling. Thus there are multiple equilibria, some with optimistic expectations, high income and low unemployment, and others with pessimistic expectations, low income and high unemployment. The latter might be interpreted as depressions. They persist because they are *non-Walrasian* equilibria in which people are interacting not just through prices but also through such non-price variables as the difficulty of finding customers, or the difficulty of finding a vacancy in the labour market. In a low-level equilibrium it would be pointless for firms to try lowering their prices since their problem is not that they have overpriced their goods but that the cost of marketing products is too high; similarly, it would be pointless for workers to offer to work for lower wages since their problem is not that they are asking too much but that they cannot find a potential employer with an opening.

Such low-level equilibria imply a coordination failure, in the sense that, if only everyone would get together and raise their expectations in coordinated fashion, they could potentially reach a high-level equilibrium where everyone is better off. They remain in a depression because no mechanism exists for bringing about such a coordinated change in beliefs. Thus, according to this approach, the process of price adjustment fails to coordinate activities because it fails to deal with the root problem, namely that of pessimistic expectations with respect to non-price variables.

The contemporary notion of coordination failure as multiple non-Walrasian equilibrium thus shows the need to go beyond wage and price adjustment if we are to achieve a deeper understanding of depressions. There are, however, two important related problems with this notion. The first is that although, as explained above, multiple-equilibrium models do illustrate a kind of coordination failure, they evade the task of analysing the coordination process. A rational expectations equilibrium is by definition a highly coordinated state of affairs, in which each transactor has managed somehow to anticipate, as fully as possible given informational constraints, the actions of others. By focusing exclusively on such equilibria, the modern coordination failure literature thus presumes that coordination is managed costlessly by some unspecified mechanism. This begs the question of how people can achieve such precise coordination and yet fail in the seemingly simpler task of agreeing that the equilibrium they coordinate on should be a good one.

The second problem is that any model of multiple equilibrium without some mechanism for describing which, if any, equilibrium the economy will be led to lacks empirical content. Indeed, the problem is greater than it might seem at first glance, because the model will have not just a high-level equilibrium and a low-level equilibrium but also a large number of other equilibria, in which people randomize between the high-level and low-level equilibrium in correlated fashion, according to the realization of some extraneous random variable. Because of this second problem, standard comparative-statics analysis applied to the model cannot predict, even qualitatively, how the economy will respond to variations in exogenous variables or policy instruments that impinge on the economy, because the system might respond by changing from one equilibrium to another.

In short, the rational expectations equilibrium theory of coordination failures is incomplete without an account of the disequilibrium dynamics that the older literature sought to provide. For it is only by studying what happens out of equilibrium that one can understand which equilibrium will be arrived at, if any, by what route, and with what time delays. Howitt and McAfee (1992) show how one might add such an account in a highly stylized example, in which Bayesian learning can lead people to oscillate between a high-level and low-level equilibrium on the basis of an extraneous random variable that they interpret as 'animal spirits'.

Finally, none of the above-mentioned contributions attempts to identify and analyse the agents that perform the role of coordinating markets in actual economies. A tradition going back at least to J.B. Say identifies them as commercial enterprises – retailers, wholesalers, brokers, jobbers and so on. These 'shops' are the visible counterparts of Smith's invisible hand. Howitt and Clower (2000) show how a coherent network of shops can emerge from competitive evolution. In their analysis no one has any understanding of the whole economy, yet the adaptive adjustments made by shops seeking to profit by serving their individual markets often combine to guide the whole system to a fully coordinated state. Current theoretical research into the dynamics of such a self-organizing network may provide further clues as to how coordination normally works in a decentralized free-market economy, and why it occasionally fails.

PETER HOWITT

See also:

Clower, Robert W.; Leijonhufvud, Axel; Lucas, Robert E. Jr; Patinkin, Don; Rational Expectations.

Bibliography

Clower, R. (1965), 'The Keynesian Counter-revolution: A Theoretical Appraisal' in F. Hahn and F. Brechling (eds), *The Theory of Interest Rates*, London: Macmillan.
Cooper, R. (1999), *Coordination Games: Complementarities and Macroeconomics*, New York: Cambridge University Press.
Cooper, R. and A. John (1988), 'Coordinating Coordination Failures in Keynesian Models', *Quarterly Journal of Economics*, **103**, August, pp. 441–63.
Diamond, P. (1982), 'Aggregate Demand Management in Search Equilibrium', *Journal of Political Economy*, **90**, October, pp. 881–94.
Howitt, P. (1985), 'Transaction Costs in the Theory of Unemployment', *American Economic Review*, **75**, March, pp. 88–100.
Howitt, P. and R. Clower (2000), 'The Emergence of Economic Organization', *Journal of Economic Behaviour and Organization*, **41**, January, pp. 55–84.
Howitt, P. and P. McAfee (1992), 'Animal Spirits', *American Economic Review*, **82**, June, pp. 493–507.
Leijonhufvud, A. (1968), *On Keynesian Economics and the Economics of Keynes: A Study in Monetary Theory*, New York: Oxford University Press.
Lucas, R.E. Jr (1972), 'Expectations and the Neutrality of Money', *Journal of Economic Theory*, **4**, April, pp. 103–24.
Patinkin, D. (1948), 'Price Flexibility and Full Employment', *American Economic Review*, **38**, September, pp. 543–64.
Scarf, H. (1960), 'Some Examples of Global Instability of the Competitive Equilibrium', *International Economic Review*, **1**, September, pp. 157–72.

Cost-push Inflation

Inflation caused by cost increases even though there are no shortages of goods and services and the economy is below full employment.

See also:
Full Employment; Inflation; Inflation: Alternative Theories of.

Council of Economic Advisers

The CEA was set up under the Employment Act of 1946 to provide economic advice to the US president on such matters as stabilization policy, economic regulation and international economic policy. The Council, which consists of a small team of three economists, is supported by a professional staff of about 10 senior staff economists (usually professors on leave of duty from their universities), 10 junior staff economists (usually advanced graduate students) and four permanent economic statisticians. One of the main tasks of the Council is to help the president prepare his annual Economic Report to Congress. Previous Chairmen of the Council have included Arthur F. Burns (19 March 1953 – 1 December 1956); Arthur M. Okun (15 February 1968 – 20 January 1969); Alan Greenspan (4 September 1974 – 20 January 1977); Martin Feldstein (14 October 1982 – 10 July 1984); and Joseph E. Stiglitz (28 June 1995 – 10 February 1997). For more information on the CEA the reader is referred to Martin Feldstein's article, 'The Council of Economic Advisers and Economic Advising in the United States' (*Economic Journal*, **102**, September 1992) and the official website of the CEA (*http://www.whitehouse. gov/cea/*).

See also:
Employment Act of 1946.

Countercyclical Policy

Government fiscal and monetary policy which attempts to counter shocks or disturbances to the economy in order to reduce cyclical fluctuations and help stabilize the economy.

See also:
Activism; Discretionary Policy; Fine Tuning; Rough Tuning.

Countercyclical Variable

A variable that tends to move in the opposite direction to aggregate economic activity over the business cycle. For example, unemployment tends to fall with positive deviations of output (real GDP) from its trend.

See also:

Business Cycle: Stylized Facts.

Cowles Commission

The Cowles Commission for Research in Economics was founded in 1932 by the economist and businessman Alfred Cowles. Initially located in Colorado Springs, it subsequently moved, in 1939, to the University of Chicago and again, in 1955, to its present home at Yale University. Its motto, 'Science is Measurement', expresses its dedication to linking economic theory with mathematics and statistics. The Commission is best known for its pioneering work in the fields of general equilibrium theory and econometrics. For more information the reader is referred to the website (*http://cepa.newschool.edu/het/schools/cowles.htm*).

Crawling Peg

A method of adjusting exchange rates where the par value of an exchange rate is changed by small amounts gradually over time; also known as a sliding peg.

See also:

Fixed Exchange Rate System.

Credibility and Reputation

The theory of policy 'credibility', and the associated need to build 'reputation', has grown out of the literature on the 'rational expectations hypothesis' (REH) and the subsequent work on 'time inconsistency' pioneered by Kydland and Prescott (1977). Using a rational expectations model, in which private agents are assumed to understand both the structure of the economy and the objectives of the monetary policy maker, Kydland and Prescott argued that the private sector would use this knowledge to form their inflationary expectations. They demonstrated that, if the policy maker seeks to maximize a representative social welfare function – in which social welfare is increased, *ceteris paribus*, by lower inflation and higher output – then, when the long-run (natural) rate of output is determined wholly by supply-side factors, the optimal monetary policy is to pursue zero inflation. This is, of course, the standard New Classical prescription for monetary policy.

By assuming that, on a period-by-period basis, private sector agents agree wages (on the basis of expected inflation in the next time period) *before* the monetary policy maker chooses his/her policy stance, Kydland and Prescott showed that the optimal policy would change over time (that is, it is 'time inconsistent'). For example, if private sector agents believe the policy maker to be pursuing the optimal zero inflation policy, they will set wages on the basis that prices in the following time period will be stable. Once wage bargains have been concluded, however, optimal control theory would lead the policy maker to raise social welfare by using 'surprise inflation' to depress real wages and so increase output. This led Kydland and Prescott to conclude that, since the private sector knows how the policy maker will respond to any given set of economic circumstances, expectations of zero inflation cannot be rational. In fact, the only rational expectation is a unique, positive rate of inflation (the 'inflation bias'). At this equilibrium rate, the policy maker's best response is to validate this rate of inflation precisely, since a higher or lower inflation rate (and, respectively, a lower or higher rate of output) will reduce social welfare.

In this way, the time inconsistency problem leads to an example of the 'prisoner's dilemma', in which the rational, welfare-maximizing behaviour of the monetary policy maker (who shares a common social welfare function with the private sector) and private sector agents leads to an outcome which is socially suboptimal, namely, a sustained, positive inflation bias at the natural rate of output. Kydland and Prescott concluded that, since an optimal control ('discretionary') approach to monetary policy making, which optimizes social welfare on a period-by-period basis, gives rise to the time inconsistency problem and an inflation bias, the best solution is for the policy maker to follow a strict, zero inflation 'monetary rule'. The private sector will understand this policy rule and price stability at the natural rate of output can be achieved.

Barro and Gordon (1983) challenged this solution to the time inconsistency problem. They argued that, although the policy maker could switch to a monetary rule, the underlying social welfare function would not have changed. If the announcement of a monetary rule were to succeed in bringing down inflationary expectations, the paradox is that the policy maker would then have an incentive to return to optimal control and increase inflation (and social welfare). But since the private sector is fully aware of the temptations the monetary policy maker faces, it should rationally ignore any declaration of a monetary policy rule and continue to base its inflation expectations on the assumption that the policy maker is using an optimal control approach. In other words, a monetary rule is simply not 'credible' and cannot provide a solution to the problem of time inconsistency.

The flaw in Kydland and Prescott's solution is that, when the policy maker adopts the monetary rule, the private sector has no guarantee that the policy regime will not return to optimal control when it is in the policy maker's interests to do so. Within the literature, there have been two broad responses to the credibility problem, both of which have greatly influenced the design of monetary institutions and the conduct of real-world monetary policy.

The first response, often referred to as 'tying one's hands', is to commit oneself to the long-run optimal policy in such as way as to make the costs of reneging on the commitment outweigh the benefits. If this can be achieved, the policy maker can effectively signal to the private sector its change of policy and this will be believed. An early example of commitment from military history was the Roman practice of burning their landing boats once they had disembarked their invading army. This clearly signalled to the waiting defenders that, whereas spirited resistance might otherwise have changed the Romans' optimal policy from invasion to retreat, the Romans were committed to victory or death. This action, in turn, was calculated to influence the defenders' expectations of the outcome of the battle and encourage flight rather than fight.

In the monetary policy arena, commitment may take the form of setting monetary, exchange rate or inflation targets. At first sight, these targets appear to be nothing more than a variation on Kydland and Prescott's monetary rule theme and suffer from the same credibility problem. However, if the targets are given great public prominence by the policy maker, so that missing the targets would cause damaging embarrassment to the policy maker (so that the achievement of the target becomes part of the policy maker's welfare function), the private sector may be persuaded of the policy maker's commitment. Exchange rate targets, particularly as part of a wider apparatus of international cooperation such as the European exchange rate mechanism, have a particular appeal in this regard, since the costs of reneging on the exchange rate target are high and visible. Walsh (1995) has suggested reinforcing targets by using contracts which financially (or otherwise) penalize policy makers for deviating from their commitment.

More influentially, Rogoff (1985) is widely attributed with introducing the idea that the government can commit itself to a zero inflation policy by delegating the conduct of monetary policy to a politically independent central bank. For this solution to work, the central bank must have – and must be known by the private sector to have – a welfare function which gives a higher weight to minimizing inflation, and a lower weight to maximizing output, than the social welfare function. Rogoff suggested that the instinctive 'conservatism' of central bankers would provide the extra required inflation aversion. The issue of independence is important insofar as operational autonomy is necessary to allow the central bank to adopt a more conservative attitude to inflation without incurring political censure from the government – which, by definition, attributes greater importance to output.

The Rogoff solution mitigates, but does not eliminate, the time inconsistency problem unless the central bank has a particularly extreme welfare function which gives absolute weight to minimizing inflation and zero weight to output. Some architects of monetary policy institutions have taken this logic at face value and created independent central banks (for example, the European Central Bank) with a statutory obligation to make price stability their primary objective. In fact, Rogoff pointed out that commitment to low inflation may prevent the policy maker from being able to respond optimally to exogenous economic shocks. In other words, the solutions to the time inconsistency and stabilization problems are in conflict. Rogoff concluded that the optimal degree of 'conservatism' (that is, the weight assigned to minimizing inflation) was reached when the marginal benefits of further reducing the inflation bias were matched by the marginal costs of limiting stabilization policy.

The second response to the problem of policy credibility is for the policy maker to stick rigidly to its declared monetary rule, despite the obvious temptations to switch policy over time, and thereby steadily build a reputation for pursing a zero inflation stance. In other words, by consistently following a monetary rule, even though this is suboptimal on a period-by period basis, the policy maker may be able to convince the private sector that it is no longer operating optimal control and thereby influence the expectations formation process. This approach was pioneered by Backus and Driffill (1985) using a game-theoretic framework. They argued that, initially, the private sector does not know the policy maker's welfare function and so wage bargains are set on the basis of its best guess. The policy subsequently chosen in response to this wage setting provides a clearer guide to the private sector about the policy maker's relative attitudes to inflation and output. If the policy maker chooses a low inflation response, then, in the next time period, the private sector will take this into account and revise downwards its inflation expectations. Provided that the policy

150 *Credibility and reputation*

maker sticks to a zero inflation policy, its anti-inflation reputation builds up over time until the inflation bias is eliminated.

Backus and Driffill explored the dynamics of this policy 'game', which are complicated by that fact that the policy maker understands the process by which reputation is built and may, under certain circumstances, pretend to be inflation-averse in order to build a reputation which can later be exploited by returning to optimal control. In general, however, the basic hypothesis that the behaviour of the policy maker in response to any particular set of economic circumstances will influence the credibility of its subsequent policy announcements (that is, the extent to which announcements are incorporated into the private sector's inflation expectations) accords with both common sense and real world experience. The fabled 'boy who cried wolf' suffered a rapid and ultimately fatal loss of reputation, while central bank governors and finance ministers demonstrably take great pains to construct public personae as hawkish, hard-nosed guardians of stable prices and strong public finances.

While the theory of policy credibility – and the related theory of reputation which it has spawned – have been extremely influential in policy-making circles, some economists have questioned its theoretical and practical significance. Goodhart and Huang (1998), for example, question the importance of credibility in circumstances where the monetary policy lag (the lag between the policy maker's actions and the consequent effect on inflation) exceeds the length of wage contracts. In such circumstances, surprise inflation cannot exist, since the private sector can renegotiate wage contracts once the actions of the policy maker are known – and long before the inflationary impact is felt. More generally, if any of the key assumptions underpinning the New Classical model are relaxed, time inconsistency and credibility do not exist as meaningful concepts. For instance, if wage bargainers negotiate on the basis of historic inflation over the *last* time period, rather than expected inflation over the *next* time period, there is no relationship between the policy maker's expected behaviour in the future and today's wage-setting behaviour. McCallum (1995) and Blinder (1997) have argued that, compared with the practical difficulties of making monetary policy in the face of external shocks and shifting economic relationships, policy credibility has little practical significance, with Blinder also noting that, despite the academic influence of the concept, it appears to have little currency amongst practising policy makers.

Useful surveys of issues relating to credibility and reputation can be found in Blackburn and Christensen (1989), Fischer (1990), Goodhart (1994) and Blinder (1998).

NIGEL M. HEALEY

See also:

Central Bank Accountability and Transparency; Central Bank Independence; New Classical Economics; Rational Expectations; Rules Versus Discretion; Time Inconsistency.

Bibliography

Backus, D. and J. Driffill (1985), 'Inflation and Reputation', *American Economic Review*, **75**, June, pp. 530–38.

Barro, R.J. and D.B. Gordon (1983), 'Rules, Discretion and Reputation in a Positive Model of Monetary Policy', *Journal of Monetary Economics*, **12**, July, pp. 101–21.

Blackburn, K. and M. Christensen (1989), 'Monetary Policy and Policy Credibility: Theories and Evidence', *Journal of Economic Literature*, **27**, March, pp. 1–45.

Blinder, A. (1997), 'What Central Bankers Can Learn from Academics – and Vice Versa', *Journal of Economic Perspectives*, **11**, Spring, pp. 3–19.

Blinder, A. (1998), *Central Banking in Theory and Practice*, Cambridge, MA: MIT Press.

Fischer, S. (1990), 'Rules Versus Discretion in Monetary Policy', in B.M. Friedman and F.H. Hahn (eds), *Handbook of Monetary Economics*, Amsterdam: North-Holland.

Goodhart, C. (1994), 'Game Theory for Central Bankers: A Report to the Governor of the Bank of England', *Journal of Economic Literature*, **32**, March, pp. 101–14.

Goodhart, C. and H. Huang (1998), 'Time Inconsistency in a Model with Lags, Persistence and Overlapping Wage Contracts', *Oxford Economic Papers*, **50**, pp. 378–96.

Kydland, F.E. and E.C. Prescott (1977), 'Rules Rather than Discretion: The Inconsistency of Optimal Plans', *Journal of Political Economy*, **85**, June, pp. 473–91.

McCallum, B. (1995), 'Two Fallacies Concerning Central Bank Independence', *American Economic Review: Proceedings*, **85**, May, pp. 207–11.

Rogoff, K. (1985), 'The Optimal Degree of Commitment to an Intermediate Monetary Target', *Quarterly Journal of Economics*, **100**, November, pp. 1169–90.

Walsh, C.E. (1995), 'Optimal Contracts for Central Bankers', *American Economic Review*, **85**, March, pp. 150–67.

Credit Channels

The *Modigliani–Miller theorem* asserts that a firm cannot increase its value by changing the composition of its liabilities. As such, credit should not matter for real activity. Modigliani and Miller (1958) view marginal invest-ment decisions as dependent only upon the expected rate of return on the project relative to some 'constant' average cost and not on the source of finance. There should be no preference between internal and external finance, or between intermediated (bank) finance and direct finance (bonds and equity). In reality, however, preferences do exist and the Modigliani–Miller theorem only holds when capital markets are perfect.

Myers and Majluf (1984) indicate that, in a less perfect world, firms may have a preference ordering over alternative sources of finance which ranks internal sources, based on retained earnings, above external sources, such as trade credit, bank borrowing and non-bank finance. The reasons for this *hierarchy of finance* are additional costs associated with external sources of finance that can be pecuniary or non-pecuniary, that is, non-price terms and conditions, which external providers of finance attach to credit provision. These give rise to an *external finance premium* and preferences towards internal rather than external finance and bank rather than non-bank finance.

Attempts to justify the external finance premium have focused on the distortions introduced by taxation and transaction costs, but the majority have focused on *agency costs* associated with information asymmetry. Under imperfect information, borrowers have a better idea of their likelihood of defaulting on a loan than do lenders, and this creates agency costs and the possibility of *adverse selection* and *moral hazard*, (see Jaffee and Russell, 1976; Stiglitz and Weiss, 1981). Adverse selection arises from the unobservable risks of lending that occur because higher costs of borrowing can only be paid by those investors with high returns and the associated high risks. Moral hazard arises from the unobservable objectives of the firm and the incentives that asymmetric information creates for firms to conceal their true performance.

To counter the adverse effects of asymmetric information, banks have developed as specialist institutions with the capability to overcome adverse selection and moral hazard problems through their ongoing depositor–lender relationships with firms (see Espezel and Mizen, 2000). They can match their liability structure to the term to maturity of loans and gather information on the financial background of companies (see Leland and Pyle, 1977; Fama, 1985; Himmelberg and Morgan, 1995). This reduces their exposure to costs incurred through adverse selection (see Diamond, 1984). Banks are potentially able to use these advantages to offer more favourable rates to borrowers than they can obtain from other forms of external finance.

The implications of agency costs are illustrated in Figure 1. The firm has a demand for credit, DD, to fund its investment, I. The firm faces a credit supply function, SS_0 which is flat up to point A because the firm has internal finance up to this point at a constant cost r_1, which equals the risk-free rate plus firm-specific risk. After point A, the firm faces an increasing cost of finance reflecting the external finance premium. Owing to asymmetric information, the premium rises in proportion to the total amount of externally raised finance because higher gearing and limited liability create incentives for firms to take higher risks and become more prone to default. The premium also rises in proportion to the risk-free rate because this reduces the present discounted value of collateral and reduces cash flow. The rising premium implies an upward-sloping supply schedule SS_0 after point A, which is steeper the greater the agency costs. A rising interest rate shifts SS_0 upwards from SS_0 to SS_1 and increases its slope beyond point A.

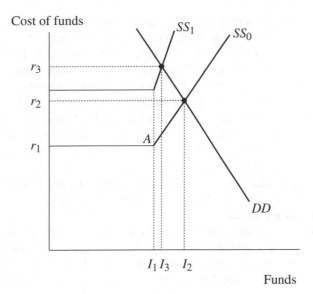

Figure 1   The marginal cost of finance

These imperfections give rise to the *credit channel*. Whilst the monetary transmission mechanism has traditionally focused on money, the *liabilities* side of the banking sector's balance sheet, the credit channel operates through the *asset* side. The credit view is supported by the twin-pillars of the *balance-sheet channel* and the *bank-lending channel*.

The balance-sheet channel argues that business cycles may be propagated to the extent that the state of firms' balance sheets affects their ability to borrow and to spend from all external sources. The crucial link is between the availability of funds and a borrower's net worth. The true worth of a firm is not known under imperfect information and therefore indicators of creditworthiness such as cash flow, profitability and previous loan history become measures of financial health. Monetary policy changes can be propagated and amplified through this part of the credit channel as the reduction in cash flow, and the present discounted value of assets for collateral, reduce access to funds for future investment. Endogenous credit cycles and accelerator effects generate cycles in real variables as a result of credit market imperfections (see Kiyotaki and Moore, 1997; and Bernanke *et al.*, 1998).

The bank-lending channel focuses upon one component of external finance as the primary source of loanable funds, bank loans. The effects of a monetary contraction are magnified by the reduction in loans supplied by banks (see Gertler and Gilchrist, 1994; Kashyap *et al.*, 1994) which amplifies the demand-side effects on expenditure decisions of the private sector. The extent to which the bank-lending channel is important depends on the substitutability between internal and external sources of funds and between bank lending and other forms of external finance. Under certain circumstances, firms may be forced to borrow from banks (even at a higher rate) if they cannot obtain funds elsewhere. Small and medium-sized firms may be unable to gain access to other markets for funds and therefore have a certain dependence on banks for external sources of funds (see Kashyap and Stein, 1994; Gertler and Gilchrist, 1994; Bernanke and Gertler, 1995). The absence of available substitutes gives rise to dependence on sources of funds from banks and imparts a particular leverage from bank lending to real activity. Hence the bank-lending channel is an extension of the argument that banks are special.

The empirical evidence for the credit channel is difficult to assess. Measures of financial health and the tightness of the credit market have demand side- as well as supply-side effects. Nevertheless, the evidence is supportive of credit effects. For the balance sheet channel, links between loan supply and financial health have been confirmed for the United States by Berger and Udell (1990) and for the United Kingdom by Brigden and Mizen (1999). Panels that differentiate (using size, evidence of low dividend payments and cash flow as proxies) between financially constrained firms and others confirm that financially unhealthy firms do face credit constraints (see Carpenter *et al.*, 1994; 1998 for the USA; Devereux and Schianterelli, 1990 for the UK). While measures of financial health may help differentiate between credit constrained and unconstrained firms, they may also categorize firms by the quality of their investment projects, and could be responsible for the positive association.

Researchers have also used aggregate and segmented firm-level panels to determine the importance of the bank-lending channel. The evidence is drawn from the actual stock of bank lending or its ratio to total bank lending, and the interest-rate spread between lending and other forms of finance, such as equity. In the first category, aggregate data from the USA used by Bernanke and Blinder (1992) and Kashyap *et al.* (1993) confirm that bank lending to firms contracts after a lag at times of monetary policy tightening, a result confirmed on UK data by Espezel and Mizen (2000). However, segmentation of firms into credit-constrained and unconstrained by Oliner and Rudebusch (1996) overturned the US result. The results from firm-level panels show that small firms are more bank-dependent than large firms, which have alternative sources of funds to substitute for bank lending when credit supply contracts (see Gertler and Gilchrist, 1994). The evidence from spreads implies that loan rates are sticky (Berger and Udell, 1992) but respond one-for-one in the long run (Cotarelli and Kouralis,

1994). Spreads are difficult to interpret because they are unlikely to capture fully the shadow price of loans, which include many non-price factors, and may reflect other bank-specific influences such as the banks' portfolio considerations.

The credit channel is an accepted channel of monetary transmission that arises from the imperfections in credit markets due to information asymmetry. Agency costs give rise to an external finance premium that ensures that firms prefer internal to external sources of funds and bank to non-bank finance. The amplification of monetary policy through balance-sheet and bank-lending channels creates cycles in real variables but empirical evidence suggests that small and medium-sized firms may be affected more than larger firms that have access to alternative sources of finance.

PAUL MIZEN

See also:

Credit Views in Macroeconomic Theory; Monetary Policy: Role of.

Bibliography

Berger, A. and G. Udell (1990), 'Collateral, Loan Quality and Bank Risk', *Journal of Monetary Economics*, **25**, January, pp. 21–42.

Berger, A. and G. Udell (1992), 'Some Evidence on the Empirical Significance of Credit Rationing', *Journal of Political Economy*, **100**, October, pp. 1047–77.

Bernanke, B. and A. Blinder (1992), 'The Federal Funds Rate and the Channels of Monetary Transmission', *American Economic Review*, **82**, September, pp. 901–21.

Bernanke, B. and M. Gertler (1995), 'Inside the Black Box: The Credit Channel of Monetary Policy Transmission', *Journal of Economic Perspectives*, **9**, Fall, pp. 27–48.

Bernanke B., M. Gertler and S. Gilchrist (1998), 'The Financial Accelerator and the Flight to Quality', *NBER Working Paper*, no. 4789.

Brigden, A. and P.D. Mizen (1999), 'Money, Credit and Investment in the UK Corporate Sector', *Bank of England Discussion Paper*, no. 100.

Carpenter, R., S. Fazzari and B. Peterson (1994), 'Inventory Investment, Internal Finance Fluctuations and the Business Cycle', *Brookings Papers on Economic Activity*, pp. 75–138.

Carpenter, R., S. Fazzari and B. Peterson (1998), 'Financing Constraints and Inventory Investment: A Comparative Study with High Frequency Panel Data', *Review of Economics and Statistics*, **80**, November, pp. 513–19.

Cotarelli, C. and A. Kouralis (1994), 'Financial Structure, Bank Lending Rates and the Transmission Mechanism of Monetary Policy', *IMF Working Paper*, no. WP/94/39.

Devereux, M. and F. Schianterelli (1990), 'Investment, Financial Factors and Cash Flow: Evidence from UK Panel Data', in G. Hubbard (ed.), *Asymmetric Information, Capital Markets and Investment*, Chicago: University of Chicago Press.

Diamond, D. (1984), 'Financial Intermediation and Delegated Monitoring', *Review of Economic Studies*, **51**, July, pp. 393–414.

Espezel, C. and P.D. Mizen (2000), 'The Credit Channel and Firms' Choices Regarding the External Financing Mix', *Experian Centre for Economic Modelling Discussion Paper*, no. 4, University of Nottingham, UK.

Fama, E. (1985), 'What's Different About Banks?', *Journal of Monetary Economics*, **15**, January, pp. 29–40.

Gertler, M. and S. Gilchrist (1994), 'Monetary Policy, Business Cycles and the Behaviour of Small Manufacturing Firms', *Quarterly Journal of Economics*, **109**, May, pp. 309–40.

Himmelberg, C.P. and D.P. Morgan (1995), 'Is Bank Lending Special?', in J. Peek and E.S. Rosengren (eds), *Is Bank Lending Important for the Transmission Mechanism of Monetary Policy?*, Federal Reserve Bank of Boston Conference Series, no 39, June.

Jaffee, D. and T. Russell (1976), 'Imperfect Information, Uncertainty and Credit Rationing', *Quarterly Journal of Economics*, **90**, November, pp. 651–66.

Kashyap, A.K. and J.C. Stein (1994), 'Monetary Policy and Bank Lending,' in N.G. Mankiw (ed.), *Monetary Policy*, Chicago: University of Chicago Press for NBER. pp. 221–56.

Kashyap, A.K. and J.C. Stein (1997), 'The Role of Banks in Monetary Policy', *Economic Perspectives, Federal Reserve Bank of Chicago*, **XXI**, September/October, pp. 2–18.

Kashyap, A.K. and O. Lamont (1994), 'Credit Conditions and the Cyclical Behaviour of Inventories', *Quarterly Journal of Economics*, **109**, August, pp. 565–92.

Kashyap, A.K., J.C. Stein and D.W. Wilcox (1993), 'Monetary Policy and Credit Conditions: Evidence from the Composition of External Finance', *American Economic Review*, **83**, March, pp. 78–98.

Kiyotaki, N. and J. Moore (1997), 'Credit Cycles', *Journal of Political Economy*, **105**, April, pp. 211–48.

Leland, H. and D. Pyle (1977), 'Information Asymmetries, Financial Structures and Financial Intermediaries', *Journal of Finance*, **32**, May, pp. 371–87.

Modigliani, F. and M.H. Miller (1958), 'The Cost of Capital, Corporation Finance and the Theory of Investment', *American Economic Review*, **48**, June, pp. 261–97.

Myers, S. and N. Majluf (1984), 'Corporate Financing and Investment Decisions When Firms Have Information That Investors Do Not Have', *Journal of Financial Economics*, **13**, June, pp. 187–221.

Oliner, S. and G. Rudebusch (1996), 'Monetary Policy and Credit Conditions: Evidence from the Composition of External Finance: Comment', *American Economic Review*, **86**, March, pp. 300–309.

Stiglitz, J. and A. Weiss (1981), 'Credit Rationing in Markets with Imperfect Information', *American Economic Review*, **71**, June, pp. 393–410.

Credit Views in Macroeconomic Theory

Macroeconomic models are typically set in the framework of a supply and demand for *money to hold*. The volume of money is conceptualized as part of the real balances or the asset holdings of the representative agent(s). In modern economies, about 90 per cent of those assets consist of deposits, which are liabilities of commercial banks. The banks create a large fraction of these deposits by way of their lending to the non-bank sector (firms, households and public institutions). Yet bank lending does not receive much attention in standard macroeconomic analysis, since the supply of deposits is taken to be a stable function of the politically determined supply of base money – a function that is usually expressed in terms of money multipliers. The interaction of loans and deposits in the banks' balance sheets implies nevertheless that, underlying the supply and demand for money to hold, there is a supply and demand for *money to spend*. *Credit views* is a common label for macroeconomic theories in which transactions in this bank-intermediated credit market exert a considerable influence on the levels and structures of prices and production.

There have been numerous credit views since the days of Henry

Thornton's *Paper Credit* (1802) and the classical currency-banking controversy in the nineteenth century (Schwartz, 1987). Only a few of them can be discussed here, and it is useful to distinguish between three different approaches in modern macroeconomics: the *loanable funds* views of the early twentieth century, the *new view* of the 1960s, and the *credit view* of monetary policy transmission which has recently grown out of the literature on imperfect and asymmetric information. The three approaches differ mainly in their views on how bank lending affects the macroeconomic finance constraints of real activity.

Loanable-funds theories played an important role in the development of modern macroeconomics. The list of key contributions comprises prominent names such as Wicksell (1898), Schumpeter (1912), Hawtrey (1919), Robertson (1926, 1937), Hayek (1929, 1931), Keynes (1930, 1937) and the Stockholm School (Lindahl, 1930; Myrdal, 1931; Ohlin, 1937a and 1937b; Lundberg, 1937). The defining characteristic of this early modern credit view is the emphasis placed on the banks' systemic potential to expand credit and aggregate demand beyond prior planned saving. This potential arises from the capacity of banks to create '*credit money*' in the sense that cashless payments from deposits are accepted as substitutes for base money. The flow supplies and demands for capital and money are inextricably linked in the market for loanable funds. Banks are central institutions in this market, not only because they help to transfer funds from surplus to deficit units, but also because they create credit money by making additional supplies of loanable funds.

Inter-bank clearing does not set any binding constraint on the funding of investment projects, as long as banks expand their lending business in step. According to the writers on the early credit view, this tends to happen whenever the expected rate of return on real investment, the so-called '*capital rate of interest*', exceeds the loan rate in the market. Loan demand will rise and banks will adjust their supply (secured by collaterals), as they intend to make profits. The market for loanable funds will continue to clear, but there will be excess demands for goods and labour. These disequilibria give rise to cumulative changes in prices, if not to changes in the structure and level of production. Thus, when the rates of return on real and financial capital are out of balance, prices and quantities in *other* markets have to adjust in order to return the economy to an equilibrium position. Sooner or later those changes will feed back on one of the interest rates, or both, and make them converge. This emphasis on the interdependence of markets makes the early modern credit view a truly macroeconomic approach to intertemporal price theory.

The typical loanable-funds story is illustrated in Figure 1 (see Leijonhufvud, 1981; Trautwein, 2000). The initial equilibrium A at the

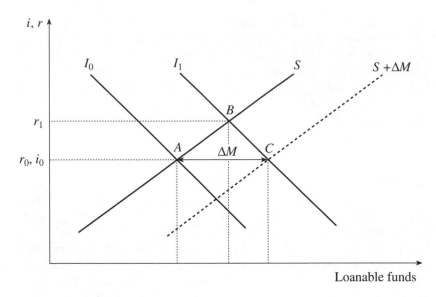

Figure 1

intersection of investment (I_0) and saving (S) can be interpreted as a classical capital market equilibrium, which is solely determined by the forces of
productivity and thrift. The loan rate (i_0) equals the capital rate of interest
(r_0), so the banks do not create additional credit money ($\Delta M = 0$). Suppose
an increase in productivity raises the expected rate of return on real investment to r_1, shifting investment to I_1. Loan demand will increase at the going
interest rate (i_0). The preservation of macroeconomic equilibrium (at B)
requires an instantaneous adjustment of i to r_1. If, however, the banks
accommodate demand at the original loan rate, continuous clearing of the
credit market (at C) implies an excess of aggregate demand over aggregate
supply, which induces changes of prices and/or quantities in other markets.
The $S+\Delta M$ curve is drawn as a broken line, since the sustainability of C as
a new equilibrium position – with the implication of adjustments of saving
to investment *ex post* (hence of r to i_0) – was one of the issues at stake in
the early modern credit view. It is here that we find the origins of modern
controversies about the long-run neutrality of money.

Wicksell (1898) set his focus on cumulative processes of inflation and,
ignored changes in output and employment. In Schumpeter's theory of
economic development (1912), bank credit is a driving force of cyclical
growth; but Schumpeter differed from the standard loanable-funds
approach (and does not quite fit into the framework of Figure 1), insofar
as he derived the existence of interest rates from temporary monopoly rents

on innovations, a disequilibrium phenomenon. Hawtrey (1919), Hayek (1929, 1931) and Keynes (1930) developed monetary theories of the business cycle, but only Hayek insisted on the classical proposition that money is neutral in the long run. Robertson (1926) and the Stockholm School constructed sequences of credit expansion and contraction in which money can affect the growth path of the economy under certain conditions. The early modern credit view helped to form the common opinion that central banks could and should control the supply of credit money by way of base reserve requirements and interest-rate policy. Yet it remained a matter of dispute whether monetary policy alone was capable of stabilizing aggregate demand.

In the so-called '*New View*' of the 1960s, Tobin (1963) rejected the idea that banks can endlessly create money out of nothing. Gurley and Shaw (1960), Brainard and Tobin (1963) and Tobin (1969) certainly stressed the relevance of financial intermediaries for an efficient expansion of the financial capacity of the economy, and hence of aggregate demand. Yet, contrary to the macroeconomic orthodoxy of their time, the exponents of the New View argued that the conventional multipliers in the money supply functions are neither stable nor necessary levers for political control of the volume of money. They claimed that the authorities need not discriminately bind bank lending with reserve requirements, for fear of an inflationary creation of money out of nothing. Market forces would limit the loan supply of banks, just as they (seem to) limit it in the case of other financial intermediaries.

In recent years, another new '*Credit View*' has developed from theories of finance under imperfect and asymmetric information. Most of this new credit literature is focused on identifying credit channels of policy transmission. At least three different lines of analysis can be discerned. The first is the perspective of *credit rationing* models in which the market does not clear because of asymmetrical information about risks and returns to loan-financed projects (Stiglitz and Weiss, 1981, 1992). The second line stresses the effects of variations in *external finance premia* that arise from the imperfect substitutability of bank loans and securities, both in the banks' portfolios and in the availability of finance for a large class of borrowers (Calomiris and Hubbard, 1990; Bernanke and Blinder, 1992; Kashyap, Stein and Wilcox, 1993; Friedman and Kuttner, 1993). Along the third line the emphasis is on the *financial accelerator* which captures changes in borrowers' net worth (liquid assets plus marketable collaterals) that result from shocks and feed back to interest rates and the creditworthiness of firms and households (Greenwald and Stiglitz, 1993; Kiyotaki and Moore, 1997; Bernanke et al., 1999). The three perspectives have been combined in various ways.

Many of the contributions to this latest credit view subscribe to the research programme of New Keynesian economics, aiming at the reproduction of Keynesian results by a more rigorous adaptation of micro- to macroeconomic theory and its stylized facts. Standard Keynesian analysis had based the explanation of underemployment equilibria on binding finance constraints that arise from the interest elasticity of money *demand* implicit in the liquidity preference of wealth holders. The new credit view has, like the pre-Keynesian loanable-funds theories, set the focus on the interaction of the money *supply* and loan demand. Yet, contrary to that older credit view, it emphasizes the existence of binding finance constraints of macroeconomic activity below full-employment equilibrium. Its microeconomic arguments about the consequences of imperfect and asymmetric information are intuitively and analytically appealing, but they should not obscure the view of the potential for relaxing the macroeconomic finance constraint that is inherent in the banking *system*. Further extensions of financial accelerator modelling could provide the analytical framework to make the early and the latest modern credit views compatible with each other (see Trautwein, 2000).

HANS-MICHAEL TRAUTWEIN

See also:

Credit Channels; Neutrality of Money; New Keynesian Economics.

Bibliography

Bernanke, B. and A. Blinder (1992), 'The Federal Funds Rate and the Channels of Monetary Transmission', *American Economic Review*, **82**, September, pp. 901–21.

Bernanke, B., M. Gertler and S. Gilchrist (1999), 'The Financial Accelerator in a Quantitative Business Cycle Framework', in J.B. Taylor and M. Woodford (eds), *Handbook of Macroeconomics*, vol. 1C, Amsterdam: North-Holland.

Brainard, W. and J. Tobin (1963), 'Financial Intermediation and the Effectiveness of Monetary Controls', *American Economic Review*, **53**, May, pp. 383–400.

Calomiris, C. and G. Hubbard (1990), 'Firm Heterogeneity, Internal Finance, and "Credit Rationing"', *Economic Journal*, **100**, March, pp. 90–104.

Friedman, B. and K. Kuttner (1993), 'Economic Activity and the Short-Term Credit Markets: An Analysis of Prices and Quantities', *Brookings Papers on Economic Activity*, **24**, pp. 193–283.

Greenwald, B. and J. Stiglitz (1993), 'Financial Market Imperfections and Business Cycles', *Quarterly Journal of Economics*, **108**, February, pp. 77–114.

Gurley, J. and E. Shaw (1960), *Money in a Theory of Finance*, Washington, DC: Brookings Institution.

Hawtrey, R. (1919), *Currency and Credit*, London: Longmans, Green.

Hayek, F.A. (1929), *Geldtheorie und Konjunkturtheorie*, Vienna: Julius Springer; tr.: *Monetary Theory and the Trade Cycle*, 1933.

Hayek, F.A. (1931), *Prices and Production*, London: Routledge & Kegan Paul.

Kashyap, A., J. Stein and D. Wilcox (1993), 'Monetary Policy and Credit Conditions: Evidence from the Composition of External Finance', *American Economic Review*, **83**, March, pp. 78–98.

Keynes, J.M. (1930), *A Treatise on Money*, vol. 1: *The Pure Theory of Money*, New York: Harcourt, Brace & Co.

Keynes, J.M. (1937), 'The *Ex-Ante* Theory of the Rate of Interest', *Economic Journal*, **47**, December, pp. 663–9.

Kiyotaki, N. and J. Moore (1997), 'Credit Cycles', *Journal of Political Economy*, **105**, April, pp. 211–48.

Leijonhufvud, A. (1981), 'The Wicksell Connection: Variations on a Theme', *Information and Coordination: Essays in Macroeconomic Theory*, New York: Oxford University Press.

Lindahl, E. (1930), *Penningpolitikens Medel*, Lund: Gleerup; tr.: *Studies in the Theory of Money and Capital*, part 11, 1939.

Lundberg, E. (1937), *Studies in the Theory of Economic Expansion*, London: P.S. King.

Myrdal, G. (1931), 'Om penningteoretisk jämvikt', *Ekonomisk tidskrift*, **33**, pp. 191–302 tr.: *Monetary Equilibrium*, 1939.

Ohlin, B. (1937a), 'Some Notes on the Stockholm Theory of Savings and Investment', *Economic Journal*, **47**, March, part I: pp. 53–69, June, part II: pp. 221–40.

Ohlin, B. (1937b), 'Alternative Theories of the Rate of Interest', *Economic Journal*, **47**, September, pp. 423–7.

Robertson, D. (1926), *Banking Policy and the Price Level: An Essay in the Theory of the Trade Cycle*, London: P.S. King.

Robertson, D. (1937), 'Alternative Theories of the Rate of Interest', *Economic Journal*, **47**, September, pp. 428–36.

Schumpeter, J.A. (1912), *Theorie der wirtschaftlichen Entwicklung*, Berlin: Duncker & Humblot, tr.: *The Theory of Economic Development*, 1934.

Schwartz, A.J. (1987), 'Banking School, Currency School, Free Banking School', in J. Eatwell *et al.* (eds), *The New Palgrave*, vol. I, London: Macmillan.

Stiglitz, J. and A. Weiss (1981), 'Credit Rationing in Markets with Imperfect Information', *American Economic Review*, **71**, June, pp. 393–410.

Stiglitz, J. and A. Weiss (1992), 'Asymmetric Information in Credit Markets and its Implications for Macro-Economics', *Oxford Economic Papers*, **44**, October, pp. 694–724.

Tobin, J. (1963), 'Commercial Banks as Creators of "Money"', reprinted 1987 in *Essays in Economics I: Macroeconomics*, Cambridge, MA: Harvard University Press.

Tobin, J. (1969), 'A General Equilibrium Approach to Monetary Theory', *Journal of Money, Credit and Banking*, **1**, February, pp. 15–29.

Trautwein, H.-M. (2000), 'The Credit View, Old and New', *Journal of Economic Surveys*, **14**, April, pp. 155–89.

Wicksell, K. (1898), *Geldzins und Güterpreise*, Jena: Gustav Fischer (tr.: *Interest and Prices*, 1936).

Crowding Out

If final output if fixed at its (say) capacity level, any increase in one form of demand, whichever sector it comes from, must lead to a decrease in some other form of demand. Thus, if public sector current expenditure on goods and services rises, private or public capital expenditure or private consumption expenditure must fall. That, of course, is a matter of arithmetic: any component of a fixed sum can rise only at the expense of another component.

The economics comes in when an attempt is made to set out the process by which this happens. At fixed capacity, if government expenditure rises, what determines whether it is investment or consumption that falls? This question is deceptively simple. Firstly, final output and its components are usually expressed in constant prices. But the initial effect of an increase in government expenditure is to raise aggregate demand relative to aggregate supply, which will in turn tend to raise the price level. The path to equilibrium will then involve some degree of monetary adjustment. Secondly, there is the problem of saying in what sense capacity output is fixed. In economics terms, capacity may be defined as the largest level of output it is profitable to produce. This will be less than the largest physically possible output. In recent theory it is asserted that, possibly as a result of misperceptions on the part of the firm, actual output, paradoxically enough, may for a while exceed capacity output. The adjustment process must then involve ways in which the misperceptions are corrected. Thirdly, while in elementary economics the focus is on a closed economy, more sophisticated economics, attempting to get closer to the real world, so to speak, requires an emphasis on an open, trading economy. The rest of the world provides an additional source of demand and supply. At full capacity some overseas demand may crowd out domestic demand. Equally, an increase in domestic demand may be met by foreign supply. Attention must be paid to the current account, and for how long excess demand for foreign goods and services can be sustained. Fourthly, the emphasis so far has been on an increase in one component crowding out another. What about the opposite case, when one component falls? Do we then get what might be called 'crowding in'? Obviously, if capacity output is to be purchased, a fall in consumer expenditure must lead to a rise in investment expenditure, for example. From Keynes onwards, however, this consideration has led economists along another track, namely to predict that in such circumstances actual output will fall below capacity output. Indeed, they have gone further. If consumption falls, private investment will for a while appear to be less profitable, and it too will fall, causing output to fall further. In other words there is no symmetry here. There will be no crowding in unless and until a recovery occurs. The analysis of the recovery process, including whether it exists at all in an automatic form, is central to debate in modern macroeconomics.

This takes us on to the question of crowding out as it originally emerged in modern economics. This was especially intriguing, for it referred to what might happen at less than full capacity. The simple formulation of Keynes's (1936) *General Theory* was static. The components of demand were determined *inter alia* by gross domestic product, which simultaneously was determined by the sum of those components. The equilibrium output arrived at could well be below full capacity (or what was usually termed full employment). In many versions of the theory it would certainly be below full capacity. Moreover, either no automatic recovery process was examined, or possible processes were thought to be so slow that they could be ignored. A return to full capacity would then require positive policy intervention in either a fiscal or a monetary guise. In simple terms, the former meant a rise in government expenditure or a cut in taxes, while the latter meant an increase in the stock of money and a fall in the rate of interest.

Within this theoretical framework, usually set out in the so-called 'IS–LM model', some further possibilities of crowding out occur (see, for example, Carlson and Spencer, 1975). This is so even though the economy is at less than full employment. Three important assumptions are made. One is that private investment varies inversely with the rate of interest. The second is that the demand for money varies inversely with the rate of interest and directly with GDP (or income). Thirdly, the stock of money is fixed.

Consider now the consequences of an increase in public expenditure. Adding to aggregate demand will, at less than full capacity, lead to higher supply or GDP. Higher GDP will lead to an increase in the demand for money. With a fixed money stock the rate of interest will rise. The result will be some fall in private investment; that is, some crowding out occurs because of the higher rate of interest. It is worth mentioning that this result also applies to an autonomous increase in private consumption, which would crowd out private investment in the same way. Furthermore, an increase in investment itself will raise the interest rate and may crowd out some other private investment which was just profitable at the initial rate of interest.

These results have an intellectual interest, but it was quickly pointed out that they all depended on taking the money supply as given. If instead monetary policy were one of monetary accommodation, it would aim at keeping the interest rate constant by varying the money supply in line with GDP. No crowding out would then occur. (In IS–LM terms, the *LM* curve would be horizontal.)

More recent work on the effects of (say) an increase in public expenditure have paid explicit attention to the way it is to be financed (see Blinder and Solow, 1973). With taxes given, increased government spending will, starting from a balanced budget, cause a budget deficit. This will mean either an increase in long-terms bonds issued by the government or, effectively, an increase in the money supply. The increase in private sector wealth may lead to a rise in the propensity to consume and a further rightward shift in the *IS* curve. The wealth effect will also lead to a rise in the demand for both money and bonds. The *LM* curve will shift to the left or right, depending on whether the supply of money is increased by more or less than the demand. Yet again the so-called 'government budget constraint' does not mean that inevitably there will be crowding out of private expenditure by public.

This leads to the conclusion that the crowding out phenomenon at less than full employment is little more than a curiosum. It is a good test of whether students understand the theory, but no more than that. It must be remarked, however, that the idea persists in macroeconomics for a number of reasons. One is that, in the real world, the question of crowding out is often raised as part of the debate on the role of public expenditure. This is political or ideological, but the fact that economic problems have such connotations does not detract from their interest or significance.

Thus, to revert to the earlier discussion, if policy intervention is required, a choice will still have to be made between interventions which raise public expenditure and those which raise private expenditure. If there are limits to the speed at which demand can rise to get back to full capacity, the public expenditure route could then crowd out the private expenditure one, and vice versa. In addition, if the path itself affects the final outcome, the public sector route may lead to 'too little' private expenditure once full capacity is reached. This will require further fiscal and monetary adjustment at that point.

The limit to the speed of adjustment is very important. If it did not exist, the economy could always be made to jump to full employment, and be kept there except for very short periods of time. It would then be the case that our original remarks relating to the fixed capacity model would be all that was relevant and would dominate the discussion. The real world economy does adjust slowly. It follows that, if crowding out is interpreted in rather broad terms, involving the mix between current and capital expenditure and also that between public and private expenditure, it is relevant at all stages of the economic cycle.

There is one other comment to be made. In modern theory, expectations and market psychology play an important part. (We say 'modern theory' although both these phenomena are given a prominent role in Keynes's (1936) *General Theory*.) Such theorizing, while often *ad hoc*, adds a different slant to the crowding out question. It is stated both as a theoretical possibility and as a practical reality that concerns about 'excessive' government borrowing may create fears about future interest and tax rates and cause people to spend less on consumption and investment.

A particular variant of this is what has come to be called the Ricardian equivalence theorem (see Buchanan, 1976). An increase in government expenditure financed by an increase in bond sales may lead to an expectation of future tax increases to finance their interest payments and eventual redemption. Households and firms will reduce present spending, current and capital, in order to meet these future tax liabilities. In essence they will treat the increased public expenditure as if it were tax-financed. Such a quasi-balanced budget increase in public expenditure would still be expansionary, but less than if future liabilities were not taken into account. In addition, the wealth effect referred to above would not occur, and the *IS* curve would shift to the right but to a lesser degree than would occur if people did not anticipate the future in this way. To say the least, this is an area of considerable controversy, and acceptance of Ricardian equivalence is certainly a minority taste among economists.

Finally, it is worth mentioning that many attempts have been made to ascertain the scale of crowding out in practice. This has often been based on simulations of policy changes using large-scale econometric models. The usual difficulties arise, namely that (a) the models themselves often reflect the *a priori* beliefs of the model builders, and (b) very large models are so complicated that at best only their authors understand them. Worst of all, the policy simulations depend on the detailed properties of the models themselves. Furthermore, the cynical might say that the models are built to ensure that certain results follow, which makes their conclusions in this area worthless. The debate on the extent of crowding is not over. It would be foolhardy, however, to come to an extreme conclusion, either that crowding out never happens, or always occurs to a 100 per cent extent.

MAURICE PESTON

See also:

Balanced Budget Multiplier; Fiscal Policy: Role of; IS–LM Model: Closed Economy; Macroeconometric Models; Ricardian Equivalence.

Bibliography

Blinder, A.S. and R.M. Solow (1973), 'Does Fiscal policy Matter?', *Journal of Public Economics*, **2**, November, pp. 319–37.
Buchanan, J.M. (1976), 'Barro on the Ricardian Equivalence Theorem', *Journal of Political Economy*, **84**, April, pp. 337–42.
Carlson, K.M. and R.M. Spencer (1975), 'Crowding Out and Its Critics', *Federal Reserve Bank of St. Louis Review*, December, pp. 1–17.
Keynes, J.M. (1936), *The General Theory of Employment, Interest and Money*. London: Macmillan.

Current Account

A record of a country's international transactions in goods and services with the rest of the world over a given period (such as a year). The current account of the balance of payments will be in deficit when the total value of imported goods and services is greater than the total value of goods and services exported, and vice versa; also known as the trade deficit and surplus.

See also:

Trade Balance.

Cyclical Unemployment

See:
Demand-deficient Unemployment.

Cyclically Adjusted Budget Balance

See:
Full Employment Budget Balance.

Davidson, Paul

Paul Davidson (b.1930, New York City, USA) obtained his BS from Brooklyn College, New York in 1950, his MBA from the City University, New York in 1955 and his PhD from the University of Pennsylvania in 1959. His main past posts have included Assistant Professor at Rutgers University, 1958–60; Assistant Professor (1961–3) and Associate Professor (1963–6) at the University of Pennsylvania; and Professor of Economics at Rutgers University, 1966–86. Since 1986 he has held the J.F. Holly Chair of Excellence in Political Economy at the University of Tennessee. He has edited the *Journal of Post Keynesian Economics* since it was founded in 1978. He is best known for his important contributions to Post Keynesian economics, including influential work on money and real economic activity, and international financial relationships. Among his best known books are *Money and the Real World* (Macmillan, 1972); *International Money and the Real World* (Macmillan, 1982); and *Post Keynesian Macroeconomic Theory: A Foundation for Successful Economic Policies for the Twenty-First Century* (Edward Elgar, 1994). His most widely read articles include 'Keynes's Finance Motive' (*Oxford Economic Papers*, **17**, March 1965); 'Money as Cause and Effect' (co-authored with S. Weintraub) (*Economic Journal*, **83**, December 1973); 'Rational Expectations: A Fallacious Foundation for Studying Crucial Decision-Making Processes' (*Journal of Post Keynesian Economics*, **5**, Winter 1982–3); and 'Post Keynesian Employment Analysis and the Macroeconomics of OECD Unemployment' (*Economic Journal*, **108**, May 1998).

See also:

Post Keynesian Economics.

Deflation

A situation in which the overall or general level of prices falls over time; for example, during the twentieth century deflation occurred in both the UK and US economies in the early 1920s and 1930, and more recently in Japan in the late 1990s.

Demand for Money: Buffer Stocks

In a far-sighted comment on Goldfeld's (1976) paper which exposed the breakdown of the demand for money function in the United States,

Brainard (1976) suggested an explanation that 'money balances serve as a buffer stock, or a temporary abode of purchasing power, and one would expect the transitory income to be absorbed passively in money holdings in the short run' (p. 735). If we recognize that there can be departures from equilibrium in the money market based on commonly accepted microeconomic principles then money may act as a buffer stock. There are four main models that treat money as a buffer stock, and we will focus on three of them. The fourth is a separate group of models based on different microeconomic foundations to determine *optimal inventory management*, for which the reader is referred to Mizen (1994).

First, *flow disequilibrium models* question the direction of causality between money and other variables reversing the money demand relationship to make money balances exogenous and some other variables, such as prices, income or interest rates, endogenous (see Artis and Lewis, 1976; Laidler, 1982). The general procedure was to invert the money demand function by isolating the dependent variable and taking the remaining variables to the other side of the equation. The chosen variable was then supposed to adjust slowly according to a partial adjustment approach to give a correctly specified short-run money demand function.

Artis and Lewis (1976), for example, use a model in which the dependent variable is the interest rate. The money demand function is inverted to derive the long-run interest rate so that for a given money demand function:

$$R_t^* = \frac{1}{\gamma}\{(m-p)_t - \phi - \beta y_t^p\}, \tag{1}$$

where p_t is the logarithm of prices, y_t^p is the logarithm of permanent income and R_t is the interest rate. Interest rates follow a partial adjustment process to adjust to the equilibrium rate R_t^* and by substituting the long-run equation for R_t^* into this adjustment model gives:

$$R_t = \frac{\theta}{\gamma}\left((m-p)_t - \phi - \beta y_t^p\right) - (1-\theta)\, R_{t-1}. \tag{2}$$

A similar format has been used by Laidler (1982) with prices as the dependent variable. These equations have been estimated using narrow and broad measures of the money stock, M1 and M2, for the period 1953(1) to 1973(4), for the United Kingdom and the United States (see Laidler, 1980; Wren-Lewis, 1984). These models typically suffer from autocorrelation and simultaneous equations bias; this is because other variables later evolve in response to the money supply shock, in addition to the evolution of the chosen dependent variable, to bring the money market to equilibrium. This means that they cannot be treated as exogenous variables except in the very short run. Attempts to incorporate these insights into larger models with many endogenous variables can be found in Jonson and Trevor (1979) for Australia, Spinelli (1979) for Italy, Laidler and O'Shea (1980) for the UK, and Laidler and Bentley (1983) for Canada.

When 'reverse causation' was initially broached, there was the belief that it implied overshooting of the arguments of the demand function in response to an exogenous money supply shock, with a short-run interest elasticity greater than the long-run elasticity. The problem with this interpretation was that there was no observable evidence to suggest that overshooting of the long-run value occurred in practice. Nor is it clear that there should be. Starleaf (1970) has argued that the standard partial adjustment model cannot be applied to situations where the money stock is exogenous, and overshooting in any case relies on the money market always clearing.

Second, *shock absorber models* introduce expectations into the analysis and allow unexpected and anticipated events to affect the money demand function differentially (see Carr and Darby, 1981). An unexpected money supply shock would not be neutral, and would differ in its effect on money demand from anticipated supply shocks. Empirical research seemed to confirm that an unexpected shock to the money stock had very little impact on prices. Accordingly, a quantity effect, operating through real money balances, must take up the shock.

The 'surprise term' was introduced in two ways. Firstly, the term, $(m - m^a)_t$, was added to the partial adjustment model to reflect unexpected nominal money supply shocks, where m_t^a is the anticipated money supply, and m_t is the actual money supply; and secondly, transitory income, y_t^T, was included since money was suggested to be the temporary abode of any unexpected variations to income. The result was an equation which allowed for positive and negative variations to money balances in response to unexpected events in the short run:

$$m_t = (1 - \lambda)m_{t-1} + \lambda m^*_t + p_t + by_t^T + f(m_t - m_t^a) + u_t. \qquad (3)$$

Carr and Darby (1981) and Carr *et al.* (1985) tested the model, using a two-stage least squares simultaneous equation method over the sample period 1957(1) to 1976(4) for the UK, USA, Canada, France, West Germany and the Netherlands. The results supported the hypothesis that unexpected money supply shocks have an impact on the demand for money, suggesting that the real money stock is a shock absorber, but rejected the hypothesis that transitory income is held in money balances. Cuthbertson and Taylor (1987c) retested the Carr and Darby method for a narrow definition of money in the UK. The anticipated money supply series, m^a, was generated using the one-step-ahead predictions from a Kalman filter process and the unanticipated money supply shocks, m^u, were extracted as the difference between this series and the actual money stock. In general, the results supported the Carr and Darby model as an acceptable model.

The third group of models extended the shock absorber principle to an infinite horizon of future events creating *forward-looking buffer stock models* (see Cuthbertson and Taylor, 1987a, 1987b, 1992; Mizen, 1994). Central to this kind of framework is the notion that it may be in the individual's interest not to make instantaneous adjustments to money balances because of the time required for search (Kanniainen and Tarkka, 1986), or because of high costs of adjustment in the short run (Cuthbertson and Taylor, 1987a).

The cost function of (Cuthbertson and Taylor, 1987a) is

$$C = E_{t+i-1} \sum_{i=1}^{\infty} D^i \big[a_1 (m_{t+i} - m_{t+i}^*)^2 + a_2 (m_{t+i} - m_{t+i-1})^2 \big], \qquad (4)$$

which states that adjustment is based on the squared deviation from desired money balances, m_t^*, (the cost of being out of equilibrium) and the squared deviation from last period's money balances (the cost of actually adjusting balances). Money holdings, m_t, are made up of planned components, m_t^p, based on the minimization of an intertemporal cost function, (4), unplanned parts, m_t^u, and unanticipated shocks, e_t.

$$m_t = m_t^p + m_t^u + e_t \qquad (5)$$

and the 'desired' level of money holdings is given by the long-run demand for money function. The short-run demand for money equation is

$$m_t = \lambda m_{t-1} + (1-\lambda)(1-\lambda D) \sum_{i=1}^{\infty} (\lambda D)^i E_{t-1} m_{t+i}^* + m_t^u + e_t, \qquad (6)$$

where λ is equal to (a_1/a_2), D is a discount factor set at 0.97 for empirical work and unexpected shocks to money balances, m_t^u, are explicitly modelled as part of the equation. The second term reflects anticipated future changes to the desired level of the demand for money which will affect current money balances in such a way that the adjustment takes place slowly, minimizing the cost function, in advance of the expected change. The shock terms affect money balances immediately, with the effect decaying over time as the individual moves back to long-run equilibrium by a slow real balance effect.

Cuthbertson and Taylor (1987a) estimated this model for M1 in the UK using quarterly data 1963(1) to 1983(3) and three-stage least squares. The coefficients were found to be significant and correctly signed. The coefficient λ gives an estimate of a_1/a_2, which is an indication of the ratio of the relative weights placed on the deviation from 'desired' money balances and on adjustment in the multi-period cost function. They showed that the adjustment costs are 'something like thirty times more important than deviations of the actual from desired holdings in the loss function' (p. 73). In determining the optimal buffer aggregate, Mizen (1992) showed that buffer stock theorists should be 'broad rather than narrow minded'. These findings were supported for further disaggregations of monetary aggregates by sector in Mizen (1994).

Money is by definition the most liquid asset, and therefore the least costly to adjust, so portfolio reallocation and expenditure patterns should be more sluggish than changes to money balances. Smoothing of adjustments is used to overcome the costs that would otherwise be incurred when alterations are required to less liquid balances and expenditures. The interpretation as a buffer stock has some very useful features. Success comes from its ability to 'mop up' the excesses and deficiencies in liquidity observed over short periods in a more flexible way than other models were able to do. The important point to note is that adjustment of money balances is determined according to an optimal rule derived from a cost minimization exercise; it is not a mistake or an error but a sanctioned and rational cost-minimizing option chosen by the individual. Buffer stock models have worked particularly well in the countries that experienced significant instability in the money demand function owing to unexpected shocks.

PAUL MIZEN

Bibliography

Artis, M.J. and M.K. Lewis (1976), 'The Demand for Money in the UK: 1963–73', *Manchester School*, **44**, June, pp. 147–81.
Brainard, W. (1976), 'Comments and Discussion on Goldfield, 1976', *Brookings Papers on Economic Activity*, **3**, pp. 732–6.
Carr, J. and M.R. Darby (1981), 'The Role of Money Supply Shocks in the Short-Run Demand for Money', *Journal of Monetary Economics*, **8**, September, pp. 183–99.
Carr, J., M.R. Darby, and D.L. Thornton (1985), 'Monetary Anticipations and the Demand for Money: Reply', *Journal of Monetary Economics*, **16**, September, pp. 251–7.
Cuthbertson, K. and M.P. Taylor (1987a), 'Buffer Stock Money: An Appraisal', in D.A. Currie, C.A.E. Goodhart, and D.T. Llewellyn (eds), *The Operation and Regulation of Financial Markets*, London: Macmillan.
Cuthbertson, K. and M.P. Taylor (1987b), 'The Demand for Money: A Dynamic Rational Expectations Model', *Economic Journal* (Supplement), **97**, pp. 65–76.
Cuthbertson, K. and M.P. Taylor (1987c), 'Monetary Anticipations and the Demand for Money: Some Evidence for the UK', *Weltwirtschaftliches Archiv*, **123**, pp. 509–20.
Cuthbertson, K. and M.P. Taylor (1992), 'A Comparison of the Rational Expectations and General-to-Specific Approaches to Modelling the Demand for M1', *Manchester School*, **60**, March, pp. 1–22.

Goldfeld, S.M. (1976), 'The Case of the Missing Money', *Brooking Papers on Economic Activity*, **3**, pp. 683–739.
Jonson, P.D. and R. Trevor (1979), 'Monetary Rules: A Preliminary Analysis', *Reserve Bank of Australia*, Discussion Paper 7903.
Kanniainen, V. and J. Tarkka (1986), 'On the Shock-Absorption View of Money: International Evidence from the 1960s and 1970s', *Applied Economics*, **18**, October, pp. 1085–1101.
Laidler, D.E.W. (1980), 'The Demand for Money in the US – Yet Again', in K. Brunner and A.H. Meltzer (eds), *On the State of Macroeconomics*, Amsterdam: North-Holland.
Laidler, D.E.W. (1982), *Monetarist Perspectives*, Oxford: Philip Allan.
Laidler, D.E.W. and B. Bentley (1983), 'A Small Macro-Model of the Post-War United States', *Manchester School*, **51**, December, pp. 317–40.
Laidler, D.E.W. and P. O'Shea (1980), 'An Empirical Macro-Model of an Open Economy Under Fixed Exchange Rates: The UK 1954–70', *Economica*, **47**, May, pp. 141–58.
Mizen, P.D. (1992), 'Should Buffer Stock Theorists be Broad or Narrow-Minded? Some Answers from Aggregate UK Data 1966–89', *Manchester School*, **60**, December, pp. 403–18.
Mizen, P.D. (1994), *Buffer Stock Models of the Demand for Money in the UK*, Basingstoke: Macmillan.
Spinelli, F. (1979), 'Fixed Exchange Rates and Monetarism: The Italian Case', University of Western Ontario, mimeo.
Starleaf, D.R. (1970), 'The Specification of Money Demand–Supply Models Which Involve the Use of Distributed Lags', *Journal of Finance*, **25**, June, pp. 743–60.
Wren-Lewis, S. (1984), 'Omitted Variables in Equations Relating to Prices and Money', *Applied Economics*, **16**, August, pp. 483–96.

Demand for Money: Friedman's Approach

Friedman's theory of the demand for money was developed in the context of the Quantity Theory of Money (Friedman, 1956) and formed the central element of that theory. The supply of money – a *nominal* variable – was determined by institutional factors, with major disturbances caused by events such as wars or sustained government deficit spending. The demand for money, in contrast, was a demand for purchasing power – that is, it was a *real* variable – and was a reasonably stable function of a limited number of factors, including wealth and a set of opportunity cost variables, which were largely independent of the factors governing supply. If supply and demand for money were out of kilter, it was changes in the price level that restored equilibrium by bringing the *nominal* demand back into line with the supply. According to Friedman, since changes in demand generally occurred only slowly and gradually, 'substantial changes in prices or nominal incomes are almost invariably the result of changes in the nominal supply of money' (Friedman, 1968, p. 434).

Though Friedman (1956) claimed that his approach to the Quantity Theory was in tune with a written and oral tradition that had been developed by his predecessors at the University of Chicago, analysis of the writings and lectures of those authors does not support his contention (see

Patinkin, 1972). In fact, when the earlier Chicago economists had discussed money in the context of wealth portfolios, they had referred to the work of English economists, notably Keynes (1936), who had stressed the demand for money as an asset, and Hicks (1935), who had discussed in general terms all the variables specified more precisely in Friedman's model. The structure of Friedman's theoretical approach followed this English tradition.

However, Friedman departed from both the English and the Chicago traditions in postulating that the demand function was *stable*, in focusing on the roles of *prices* and *rates of inflation*, and in his denial of the *liquidity trap* phenomenon, that is, conditions in which the interest elasticity of the demand for money was effectively infinite. His policy conclusions also conflicted with those of Keynesian economists: for Friedman, the stability of the demand function meant that monetary targets could, and should, play a central role in the conduct of macroeconomic policy, and led him to advocate a fixed monetary growth rate rule, whereas for Keynesians generally fiscal policy held centre stage. Noted Cambridge (England) Keynesians dismissed the notion that the demand for money was stable, stating that 'it cannot be emphasised too strongly that there is no relationship between the amount of money in circulation . . . and the amount of money spent on goods and services' (Kaldor, 1960) and 'it is the behaviour of interest rates which matters . . . not the behaviour of the quantity of money' (Kahn, 1960).

Friedman's theory is couched in the theory of consumer choice: people choose how they will allocate their wealth between the available alternatives, and their decisions depend on their preferences and on the returns, and other properties, of the different forms of wealth holding. For expository purposes the array of possible assets is simplified into four categories: money, which has a fixed nominal value and provides an implicit return derived from its convenience in making payments, security and so on; bonds, which are claims to income streams fixed in nominal terms (but whose capital value is uncertain); equities, comprising claims to income streams which, though even less certain than those of bonds, can be expected to move in line with the general price level; and physical capital, which provides a yield in the form of services and whose value also moves with the general price level. The wealth to be allocated is measured indirectly from the expected flow of income, including income-in-kind, discounted at an appropriate rate of interest; and account is taken of the fact that future labour income is not generally as readily convertible into other assets as income from other forms of wealth. Finally, Friedman recognizes that wealth-holders' preferences for money will depend on the degree of uncertainty surrounding their lives, which can, however, be represented by objective indexes. Thus his key equation reduces to

$$M/P = f\left[r_b, r_e, (1/P)dP/dt;\ w;\ Y/P;\ u\right]$$

(Friedman, 1956, p.11, equation 11), where

M = nominal money balances,
r_b = expected rate of return on bonds,
r_e = expected rate of return on equities,
P = price level,
w = ratio of non-human to human wealth,
Y = expected nominal income from all kinds of wealth,
u = variables affecting tastes and preferences.

The first three right-hand side variables reflect the opportunity cost of holding money rather than bonds, equities or physical assets; the last three reflect the wealth constraint (w and Y/P) and all other factors (u); and the price level enters in a way that ensures that the demand for money is a demand for real balances.

In fact, for Friedman, prices rather than nominal interest rates were the key elements in the demand function, with expected inflation being a particularly important opportunity cost element during periods of high inflation. As noted above, the notions that money demand was 'a will-o'-the-wisp, shifting erratically and unpredictably with every rumor and expectation' (ibid., p.16), or that there might be a liquidity trap, were resisted. And while uncertainty about both bond yields and general economic conditions enters implicitly through the variable u, there is no explicit analysis of the effects of changing uncertainty on the demand for money. (C.f. Keynes's analysis of the speculative demand for money – Keynes, 1936 – and Tobin's analysis of liquidity preference – Tobin, 1958).

The key elements in Friedman's approach have become standard in empirical studies of the demand for money. The constraint variable, in conceptual terms, is generally wealth, though it is often proxied by some long-run concept of income; long-run (though not necessarily short-run) proportionality with prices is imposed; and there is a selection of opportunity cost variables. By focusing on the demand for money as a whole, Friedman also helped to divert the economics profession from the practice of allocating money holdings conceptually against the transactions, precautionary and speculative motives – a valuable theoretical distinction, but a blind alley as regards empirical work.

However, while at first empirical studies (see Laidler, 1993) appeared to confirm the existence of stable demand functions for money, these had an inconvenient habit of breaking down subsequently. Contributory factors included the growth of financial instruments that act as close substitutes for those previously classified as money, accelerating change in payments technology and practices, central banking behaviour rendering money endogenous in the economic system, and even the re-emergence (in Japan in the 1990s – see Krugman, 1998) of conditions akin to those that had led Keynes to propose his liquidity trap hypothesis. Thus the stability, on which Friedman's fixed monetary growth rate rule depended, has not been found in practice, and other aspects of the demand for money (such as buffer stocks) have proved important in the conduct of monetary policy.

ANDREW D. BAIN

See also:

Demand for Money: Buffer Stocks; Demand for Money: Keynesian Approach; Friedman, Milton; Liquidity Trap; Monetarism; Quantity Theory of Money.

Bibliography

Friedman, M. (1956), 'The Quantity Theory of Money – a Restatement', in M. Friedman (ed.), *Studies in the Quantity Theory of Money*, Chicago: University of Chicago Press.
Friedman, M. (1968), 'Money: Quantity Theory', in D.L. Sills (ed.), *International Encyclopedia of the Social Sciences*, vol. 10, New York: Free Press.
Hicks, J.R. (1935), 'A Suggestion for Simplifying the Theory of Money', *Economica*, **2**, February, pp. 1–19, reprinted in F.A. Lutz and W.L. Mints (eds) (1951), *Readings in Monetary Theory*, Homewood, IL: Irwin.
Kahn, R.F. (1960), 'Memorandum 19', in *Committee on the Working of the Monetary System (The Radcliffe Committee), Memoranda and Minutes of Evidence, Vol. 3*, Cmnd 827, London: Her Majesty's Stationery Office.
Kaldor, N. (1960), 'Memorandum 20', in *Committee on the Working of the Monetary System (The Radcliffe Committee), Memoranda and Minutes of Evidence, Vol. 3*, Cmnd 827, London: Her Majesty's Stationery Office.
Keynes, J.M. (1936), *The General Theory of Employment. Interest and Money*, London: Macmillan.
Krugman, P. (1998), 'It's Baaack! Japan's Slump and the Return of the Liquidity Trap', *Brookings Papers on Economic Activity*, pp. 137–205.
Laidler, D.E.W. (1993), *The Demand for Money: Theories, Evidence and Problems*, 4th edn, New York: Harper Collins.
Patinkin, D. (1972), *Studies in Monetary Economics*, New York: Harper & Row.
Tobin, J. (1958), 'Liquidity Preference as Behaviour towards Risk', *Review of Economic Studies*, **25**, February, pp. 65–86.

Demand for Money: Keynesian Approach

The word 'Keynesian' in this entry will be used in the mainstream sense of the term; the interpretations of Keynes given by 'Post-Keynesians' or by those who distinguish between 'Keynes and the Keynesian' will be noted only in the last paragraph.

The main characteristic of the Keynesian demand for money is that it is a function of the rate of interest. This is asserted or assumed not only by the Keynesians; even the well-known monetarists accept this as one of the defining characteristics of Keynes's contribution. Thus Harry Johnson (1965), commenting on Friedman's work, writes, 'to admit interest rates in the demand function for money is to accept the Keynesian Revolution', an assessment that retains its force in spite of Friedman's objections (1966, p. 152; also see below). This demand function when confronted with a given supply or supply function of money determines the rate of interest.

This is not to claim that Keynes's was the first presentation of a monetary theory of interest. Keynes (1936) himself attributes this to the Mercantilists, and he must have been aware of Wicksell's distinction between the 'market' (essentially, monetary) and 'real' rates of interest ([1898] 1965). But the mainstream economists, from Hume to Marshall and Pigou, designated 'classical economists' by Keynes, did not allow the demand for money to have any significant role in the determination of the rate of interest, and even the others who did gave no explanation of the basis of the assumed functional relationship between the demand for money and the rate of interest. Keynes set out to provide just that.

He began by distinguishing between several motives for holding money, including the precautionary motive (discussed, among others, by Miller and Orr, 1966) and the business motive, but later he merged these with the *transactions motive*. He then went on to distinguish this composite concept from the *speculative motive*, now commonly designated as the 'asset motive'. Although in his detailed discussion he allowed the money held for transaction purposes to be a function of the rate of interest (Keynes, 1936, p. 196) beside that of the 'value of the current output', in his formal presentation he allowed it to be a function of only the latter. The money held for speculative purposes, on the other hand, was treated exclusively as the function of the rate of interest. He thus wrote (ibid., 1936 p. 199):

$$M = M_1 + M_2 = L_1(Y) + L_2(r). \tag{1}$$

The symbols need no explanation, except perhaps a reminder that M_1 and M_2 here should not be confused with the same symbols used in the *supply* of money in more recent discussions.

As Hicks (1967) tells us, these two motives distinguished by Keynes can be related to the much older concepts of the functions of money as a 'medium of exchange' and the 'store of value' – a distinction that can be traced back at least as far as Aristotle – a very solid 'classical' foundation indeed! More recently, Milton Friedman (1956, clause 14) seems to object to making such a distinction, perhaps on the basis of Keynes's (1936, p. 195) throwaway point that the same money can be used for either of these two purposes. The upshot of Friedman's objection can be illustrated by the argument that, since the same apple provides vitamin C as well as carbohydrate, one does not need one apple for providing one and another for providing the other. The weakness of this argument lies in ignoring the property of exclusiveness in the use of money – that once it has been used for a transactions purpose, the owner cannot use the same money for asset purposes as well. The appropriate analogy would be with an urchin's use of apples for hitting the passers-by: once he has used one apple to hit one person, he does not have it available to hit another. Hence, unlike Friedman, he would have to add the demand for the two purposes in the Keynesian fashion.

In the later development of the study of demand for money along Keynesian lines, the demand for transactions purposes has, in line with Keynes's informal (rather than formal) statement, been also related to the rate of interest. The well known formulation of this idea is due to Baumol (1952), who traces it back to the inventory theories of the 1920s. Baumol's results are based on a scenario in which the objective is to minimize the total cost of holding money, which is the sum of the lost interest on money held, on the one hand, and the cost of conversion between bonds and money, on the other. In symbols, if M is the average quantity of money held (the average of $2M$ initial money withdrawn and the zero amount left just before the next withdrawal), b the cost of conversion between bonds and money each time, Y the income per period received in bonds and spent during the same period in $2M$ instalments, and r the rate of interest per period, the total cost adds up to $bY/2M + rM$, which, when derived with respect to M, has its minimum with

$$M = (bY/2r)^{1/2}.$$ (2)

This implies the economy of scale in the use of money, since a doubling of M can transact more than double the amount of Y. More directly relevant to the main issue, equation (2) also shows that even the transactions demand for money is inversely related to the rate of interest. Both these characteristics were absent in the traditional quantity theory which formed the background of Keynes's work. (Friedman's (1956) 'Quantity Theory' formula has little to do with transactions demand for money because its y representing permanent income has little relation to current transactions. His equation is essentially related to the theory of 'portfolio selection', discussed below, but without the sophistication of risk or uncertainty being a part of the analysis.) Baumol extends his analysis to the case where Y is received in money rather than in bonds, and shows that there is no qualitative change in the results. Attempts to bring this analysis back into the quantity theory fold (for instance by Brunner and Meltzer, 1967) were not successful, and in fact in relation to the rate of interest led to just the opposite result (Ahmad, 1977).

For Keynes the primary characteristic of the asset (speculative) demand for money is its sensitivity to the rate of interest. Its basis is the difference between the actual rate of interest and the individual's expected (subjectively, and hence differently by different individuals) rate. If the former is lower than the latter, the individual holds all his/her financial assets in the form of money; if higher, all in the form of bonds. Since people's expectations are different, the asset demand for money is negatively inclined; the lower the actual rate, the more individuals have their expected rates higher than the actual, hence more of them hold money as an asset. If the actual interest is so low that everybody's expected rate is higher than the actual, everybody holds their financial assets in the form of money – the economy will then be in the famous 'liquidity trap'.

There were at least two criticisms of Keynes's approach to the asset demand for money by those who would be later considered 'Keynesians': one, that, contrary to experience, this does not allow an individual to hold simultaneously both money and bonds as assets; the other, that the assumed expectation is absolute and not in the form of the usual probability distribution. The theory of 'portfolio selection', due to Markowitz (1952, 1959) and Tobin (1958) (related to the earlier work by Hicks, 1935) was intended to overcome these 'shortcomings'. Their theory is based on Bernoulli's ([1738] 1954) hypothesis of the diminishing marginal utility of an asset (which can also apply to income). The well known result of his paper is that, with the same mean value of such a variable, the utility obtained diminishes as the deviation from the mean becomes larger. Markowitz and Tobin used standard deviation (or variance) as the measure of deviation, and obtained 'indifference curves' between the mean and the standard deviation of the *rate of return* (we assess the merit of the choice of this variable below). Since the increase in its mean is assumed to increase utility, and an increase in its standard deviation to decrease it, for maintaining the utility constant the increase in one has to be accompanied by an increase in the other. Hence the indifference curves between the two are positively inclined.

Turning now to the corresponding budget line for the rate of return on the *portfolio* consisting of money and bonds, we assume that the rate of return from money is always zero; hence both the mean and the standard deviation of this rate are also zero. On the other hand, both the mean of the rate of return on bonds (equated to the rate of interest) and its standard deviation are positive. Hence the larger the proportion of bonds in a given portfolio, the larger will be both the mean and the standard deviation of the rate of return; the budget line (or curve, see Hicks, 1967, but only 'line' in what follows) will be positively inclined, starting from zero where the portfolio consists entirely of money and ending at the point where it consists entirely of bonds. The tangency of this budget line with a positively inclined indifference curve determines the proportional division of the individual's asset between money and bonds. (Note that he/she can now hold both these simultaneously.) A change in the rate of interest would change the budget line and provide a new equilibrium proportion of money and bond holdings. This is how Tobin relates the demand for money held as an asset to the rate of interest. However, since the mechanism is similar to the substitution and income effects which can work against each other, this relationship is not always negative. It is somewhat ironical that, while the extension of Keynes's transaction motive (Baumol's) leads to an unambiguously negative, or at least non-positive, relation between the rate of interest and the demand for money, the (Tobin) extension of Keynes's asset (speculative) motive, a motive that was purposely intended by Keynes to establish such a negative relationship, fails to do so in an unambiguous fashion.

The criticisms and modification of this theory can be divided between the 'internal', that is those made within the framework of the probability approach used by Tobin, and 'external', those which are critical of the approach itself. Here we can only touch upon a few main criticisms. Taking the internal ones first, we have the criticism of the choice of the variable on which utility is defined. The argument is that utility in the current context can be meaningfully defined over asset, as Bernoulli does, or over income. Tobin, however, does neither; instead, he defines it over the *rate* of return, which leaves the matter hanging in the air, so to speak. This criticism and the attempts to modify the approach by defining utility over a more suitable variable – income or asset – can be found in, among others, Hicks (1967) and Laidler ([1969] 1993). The other internal criticism is that all the relevant probability distributions cannot be represented just by its mean and standard deviation; hence Tobin's treatment cannot be generally applied (Borch, 1969; but also see Tsiang, 1972, 1974, for some softening of this criticism).

The 'external', criticisms, those made against the use of the probability approach itself for such problems are also at least twofold: one is that this can lead to choices that are extremely improbable, approaching the absurd (Rabin, 2000; Rabin and Thaler, 2001); the other, and the more fundamental, is that the whole approach misses the point about the nature of uncertainty. 'Uncertainty', according to this view, is not amenable to treatment through the usual, almost mechanical, probability distribution approach. This argument can be traced back at least to Keynes (1921), Knight (1921), to Keynes (1936, 1937) and Shackle (1938, 1949) as well as to the more recent 'Post-Keynesian' writings on money. Turning from 'Post-Keynesian' to 'Keynes and Keynesians', we may note that, *from the point of view of the demand for money alone*, the writings of those who distinguish between 'Keynes' and 'Keynesian' (Clower, 1965; Leijonhufvud, 1968) are formally based on the 'cash-in-advance' approach – you need money before you can buy anything – not very different in this respect from Baumol's, although their overall objectives are of course very different from his. However, we can only note these issues here, as we can the views of those who claim that the existence of innumerable types of 'near-money' makes the sharp distinction between money and bonds used in the above 'Keynesian' approaches too artificial to be helpful in practice.

SYED AHMAD

See also:

Demand for Money: Friedman's Approach; Liquidity Trap; Quantity Theory of Money.

Bibliography
Ahmad, S. (1977), 'Transactions Demand for Money and the Quantity Theory', *Quarterly Journal of Economics*, **91**, May, pp. 327–35.
Baumol, J. (1952), 'The Transactions Demand for Cash: An Inventory Theoretic Approach', *Quarterly Journal of Economics*, **66**, November, pp. 545–56.
Bernoulli, D. ([1738] 1954), 'Exposition of a New Theory of the Measure of Risk', *Econometrica*, **22**, January, pp. 23–36.
Borch, K. (1969), 'A Note on Uncertainty and Indifference Curves', *Review of Economic Studies*, **36**, January, pp. 1–4.
Brunner, K. and A. Meltzer (1967), 'Economies of Scale in Cash Balances Reconsidered', *Quarterly Journal of Economics*, **LXXXI**, August, pp. 422–36.
Clower, R. (1965), 'The Keynesian Counter-Revolution: A Theoretical Appraisal', in F. Hahn and F. Brechling (eds), *Theory of Interest Rates*, London: Macmillan.
Friedman, M. ([1956] 1969), 'The Quantity Theory of Money: A Restatement', reprinted in the *Optimum Quantity of Money*, London: Macmillan, pp. 51–67.
Friedman, M. ([1966] 1969), 'Interest Rate and the Demand for Money', reprinted in the *Optimum Quantity of Money*, London: Macmillan, pp. 141–56.
Hicks, J.R. (1935), 'A Suggestion for Simplifying the Theory of Money', *Economica*, **2**, February, pp. 1–19.
Hicks, J.R. (1967), *Critical Essays in Monetary Theory*, London: Clarendon Press.
Johnson, H. (1965), 'A Quantity Theorist's Monetary History of the United States', *Economic Journal*, **LXXV**, June, pp. 388–96.
Keynes, J.M. (1921), *A Treatise on Probability*, London: Macmillan.
Keynes J.M. (1936), *The General Theory of Employment, Interest, and Money*, London: Macmillan.
Keynes, J.M. (1937), 'The General Theory of Employment', *Quarterly Journal of Economics*, **51**, February, pp. 209–23.
Knight, F. ([1921] 1933), *Risk, Uncertainty and Profit*, London: London School of Economics.
Laidler, D. ([1969] 1993), *Demand for Money: Theories, Evidence and Problems*, New York: Harper Collins.

Leijonhufvud, A. (1968), *On Keynesian Economics and the Economics of Keynes*, London: Oxford University Press.

Markowitz, H. (1952), 'Portfolio Selection', *Journal of Finance*, **7**, March, pp. 77–91.

Markowitz, H. (1959), *Portfolio Selection: Efficient Diversification of Investment*, New York: J. Wiley and Sons.

Miller, M. and D. Orr (1966), 'A Model of Demand for Money by Firms', *Quarterly Journal of Economics*, **79**, November, pp. 413–35.

Rabin, M. (2000), 'Risk Aversion and the Expected Utility Theory: A Calibration Theorem', *Econometrica*, **68**, September, pp. 1281–92.

Rabin, M. and R. Thaler (2001), 'Anomalies: Risk Aversion', *Journal of Economic Perspectives*, **15**, Winter, pp. 219–32.

Shackle, G.L.S. (1938), *Expectations, Investment and Income*, London: Oxford University Press.

Shackle, G.L.S. (1949), *Expectations in Economics*, London: Oxford University Press.

Tobin, J. (1958), 'Liquidity Preference as Behaviour Towards Risk', *Review of Economic Studies*, **25**, February, pp. 65–86.

Tsiang, S.C. (1972), 'Rationale of the Mean-Standard Deviation Analysis, Skewness Preference and the Demand for Money', *American Economic Review*, **62**, June, pp. 354–71.

Tsiang, S.C. (1974), 'Rationale of the Mean-Standard Deviation Analysis: Reply and Errata for the Original Article', *American Economic Review*, **64**, June, pp. 442–50.

Wicksell, K. ([1898] 1965), *Interest and Prices*, New York: Kelly.

Demand Management

See:
Aggregate Demand Management.

Demand-deficient Unemployment

Unemployment that results because aggregate demand is insufficient to provide employment for everyone who wants to work at the prevailing real wage; also known as cyclical unemployment.

See also:
Involuntary Unemployment in Keynesian Economics.

Demand-pull Inflation

Inflation caused by an excess demand for goods and services when the economy is at, or above, full employment.

See also:
Full Employment; Inflation; Inflation: Alternative Theories of.

Denison, Edward F. (1915–92)

Edward Denison (b.1915, Omaha, Nebraska, USA) obtained his BA from Oberlin College in 1936, and his MA (1938) and PhD (1941) from Brown University. His main posts included Economist and Associate Director (from 1949) at the Office of Business Economics, US Department of Commerce, 1941–56; Associate Director of the Committee for Economic Development, 1956–62; Senior Fellow of the Brookings Institution, 1962–78; Associate Director for National Economic Accounts of the Bureau of Economic Analysis, US Department of Commerce, 1979–82; and Senior Fellow, Emeritus, Brookings Institution, 1978–92. He is best known for his pioneering work on growth accounting or sources of growth analysis and its application to the study of growth in the United States, Japan and eight European countries. His most famous books include *The Sources of Economic Growth in the United States and the Alternatives Before Us* (Committee for Economic Development, 1962); *Why Growth Rates Differ: Postwar Experience in Nine Western Countries* (Brookings Institution, 1967); *Accounting for United States Economic Growth, 1929–1969* (Brookings Institution, 1974); *How Japan's Economy Grew so Fast: The Sources of Postwar Expansion* (co-authored with W.K. Chung) (Brookings Institution, 1976); *Accounting for Slower Economic Growth: The United States in the 1970s* (Brookings Institution, 1979); and *Trends in American Economic Growth, 1929–82* (Brookings Institution, 1985).

See also:

Brookings Institution; Growth Accounting.

Depreciation (Nominal) of a Currency

A decrease in the price of one currency in terms of other currencies in a flexible exchange rate system; a decrease in the nominal exchange rate in a flexible exchange rate system.

See also:

Flexible Exchange Rate System; Nominal Exchange Rate.

Depression

A very severe and prolonged recession.

See also:

Great Depression; Recession.

Devaluation

A devaluation of a currency involves a deliberate decrease in the value of one currency in terms of other currencies when the currency in question is part of a fixed exchange rate system. Devaluation which, *ceteris paribus*, increases the home currency price of imports and lowers the foreign currency price of exports, has on occasions been used in an attempt to remedy a deficit on the current account of the balance of payments. Whether or not devaluation succeeds in improving the current account of the balance of payments critically depends on the elasticity of demand and supply. A necessary condition is that the sum of the elasticities of demand for imports and exports is greater than unity (known as the Marshall–Lerner condition). However, devaluation on its own will not be sufficient unless there are resources available to meet the increased demand for exports and domestically produced import substitutes. At full employment, for example, there is a need to combine the expenditure switching policy of devaluation with an expenditure reducing policy.

See also:

Absorption Approach to the Balance of Payments; Balance of Payments; Elasticities Approach to the Balance of Payments; Expenditure Reducing Policy; Expenditure Switching Policy; Fixed Exchange Rate System; Marshall–Lerner Condition.

Dirty Float

An exchange rate regime where the exchange rate is influenced by intervention by governments and central banks in the foreign exchange market; also known as a managed float. Intervention may be limited to preventing excessive fluctuations in the exchange rate, in which case the position will more closely approximate a flexible exchange rate system. On the other hand, where there is heavy intervention by the central monetary authorities to manage the exchange rate, the position will more closely approximate a fixed exchange rate system.

See also:

Clean Float; Fixed Exchange Rate System; Flexible Exchange Rate System.

Discount Rate

The interest rate the central bank (for example, the Fed) charges when it lends reserves to banks.

See also:
Federal Reserve System.

Discretionary Policy

A situation in which the authorities are free to vary the strength of fiscal and/or monetary policy, in any way they see fit, in order to achieve their desired objectives.

See also:
Fine Tuning; Rough Tuning; Rules versus Discretion.

Disinflation

A decrease in the rate of inflation.

See also:
Inflation.

Disposable Income

Income that households have at their disposal after the payment of tax on their income.

Domar, Evsey D. (1914–98)

Evsey Domar (b.1914, Lodz, Russia – now Poland) obtained his BA from the University of California, Los Angeles in 1939, his MA in mathematics from the University of Michigan in 1941, and his MA (1943) and PhD (1947) from Harvard University. His main past posts included the following: Economist for the Board of Governors of the Federal Reserve System, 1943–6; Assistant Professor at the Carnegie Institute of Technology, 1946–7; Assistant Professor at the University of Chicago, 1947–8;

Associate Professor (1948–55) and Professor of Political Economy (1955–8) at Johns Hopkins University; Professor of Economics (1958–72) and Ford International Professor of Economics, (1972–84) at Massachusetts Institute of Technology (MIT); and Ford International Professor of Economics, Emeritus, MIT, 1984–98. He is best known for his work on: growth theory and models, and in particular the Harrod–Domar growth model. His books include *Essays in the Theory of Economic Growth* (Oxford University Press, 1957). His most widely read articles include 'Capital Expansion, Rate of Growth, and Employment' (*Econometrica*, **14**, April 1946); and 'Expansion and Employment' (*American Economic Review*, **37**, March 1947).

See also:
Federal Reserve System; Harrod–Domar Growth Model.

Dornbusch, Rudiger

Rudiger Dornbusch (b.1942, Krefeld, West Germany) obtained his Licence de Sciences Politiques from the University of Geneva in 1966 and his MA (1969) and PhD (1971) from the University of Chicago. His main past posts have included Assistant Professor at the University of Rochester, 1972–3; and Associate Professor at the University of Chicago, 1974–8. Since 1978, he has been Professor of Economics and International Management at MIT. He is best known for his work on open economy macroeconomics and exchange rates. Among his best known books are *International Economic Policy* (co-edited with J. Frenkel) (Johns Hopkins University Press, 1979); *Dollars, Debts and Deficits* (MIT Press, 1986); and *Keys to Prosperity: Free Markets, Sound Money and a Bit of Luck* (MIT Press, 2000). His most widely read articles include 'Devaluation, Money and Non-Traded Goods' (*American Economic Review*, **63**, December 1973); 'Expectations and Exchange Rate Dynamics' (*Journal of Political Economy*, **84**, December 1976); and 'Comparative Advantage, Trade and Payments in a Ricardian Model with a Continuum of Goods' (co-authored with S. Fischer and P.A. Samuelson) (*American Economic Review*, **67**, December 1977).

Dual Decision Hypothesis

Conceived by Robert W. Clower, the dual decision hypothesis first appeared (in English) in Clower's 1965 seminal paper 'The Keynesian Counter-Revolution: A Theoretical Appraisal'. The essence of the hypothesis is the distinction between notional and effective demand in a monetary economy, in that the offer of labour services by unemployed workers does not constitute an ability to buy goods as it is not backed by the wherewithal to pay for the goods. Market signals will only be transmitted if they are backed by the ability to pay with money.

See also:

Clower, Robert W.; Keynesian Economics: Reappraisals of.

Duesenberry, James S.

James Duesenberry (b.1918) obtained his BA (1939), MA (1941) and PhD (1948) from the University of Michigan. His main past posts have included Assistant Professor (1948–53) and Associate Professor (1953–7) at Harvard University. Since 1957, he has been Professor of Economics at Harvard University. Between 1966 and 1968, he was a member of the US President's Council of Economic Advisers and between 1969 and 1974 he was Chairman of the Board of Directors of the Federal Reserve Bank of Boston. He is best known for his pioneering work on the consumption–income relationship. His best known books include *Income, Saving and the Theory of Consumer Behavior* (Harvard University Press, 1949). His most widely read articles include 'Income–Consumption Relations and Their Implications', in L. Metzler (ed.) *Income, Employment and Public Policy: Essays in Honor of Alvin H. Hansen* (W.W. Norton, 1948).

See also:

Council of Economic Advisers; Relative Income Hypothesis.

Ecological Macroeconomics

Ecological macroeconomics situates the aggregate economy in the physical world, acknowledging the reality of physical limits to economic growth. From an ecological perspective, orthodox macroeconomics is based upon an unrealistic model of the economy. To model the economy as a circular flow of income is to model it as an isolated and self-sufficient system, factors of production being endlessly recycled into goods and services and back again. Ecological macroeconomics puts the economy back into the physical world from which the conventional circular flow model had abstracted it. There is still a circular flow but this time it is energy, that is drawn from the physical environment, used in production and consumption and returned to the physical environment as waste.

This debate has its roots in an interchange that occurred in the early 1970s, between the 'Club of Rome' and economists studying the use of natural resources. The way in which most economists had traditionally looked at the economy implied that the physical world did not impose any limits on growth. The intuition behind this approach is that, if one natural resource runs out, it is always possible to replace it with another that will maintain the rate of economic growth. The argument presented by the 'Club of Rome' in *The Limits to Growth* (Meadows *et al.*, 1972) challenged this traditional approach. The ecological argument was that development could not be sustained indefinitely because the world's supply of non-renewable resources such as oil, gas and metals is finite, and the ultimate exhaustion of these resources implies a physical limit to economic growth. This pessimistic vision of the future led to a flurry of research intended to reassess the human plight, which was given further stimulus in 1973 by the fourfold increase in the international price of oil.

The significance of this way of thinking about the economy is its demonstration that the foundation of ecological macroeconomics lies in the natural sciences and ultimately in physics. On this view economics is based on the second law of thermodynamics and the concept of entropy (see Georgescu-Roegen, 1971, 1986; Faber *et al.*, 1996; Beard and Lozada, 2000). Physics tells us that matter and energy are governed by the laws of thermodynamics, the 'science of energy'. The first law of thermodynamics states that matter and energy can neither be created nor destroyed. The second law of thermodynamics, which is also known as the law of entropy, goes on to say that in a thermodynamic system the unchanging quantity of energy undergoes a qualitative change from available or low-entropy energy to unavailable or dissipated or high-entropy energy. For example, oil is found in the Earth's crust in a state of low entropy, it is turned into fuel and emits CO_2, which is dissipated throughout the atmosphere in a state of high entropy. The second law of thermodynamics stands on solid experimental ground; it has withstood experiments designed to falsify it.

Ecological macroeconomics rejects economic growth as a policy objective, replacing it with sustainable development. The most commonly cited public definition of sustainable development emanated from the World Commission on Environment and Development WCED (or the 'Brundtland Commission') in 1987. Sustainable development is development that 'meets the needs of the present without compromising the ability of future generations to meet their own needs' (WCED, 1987, p. 8). So sustainable development is development that generates current human welfare without imposing significant costs on the future. For the Brundtland Commission, significant costs are translated into the inability to meet future development needs.

Sustainable development implies that development should be evenly distributed across generations. The way in which the current generation is using the environment may represent one way in which potentially large costs are being passed on to the future. The suggestion that this is not an acceptable trade-off raises philosophical issues concerning fairness or justice that are not easy to resolve and highlights the normative foundations of ecological macroeconomics (see Daly, 1996; Joseph, 1991, pp. 77–9; Hirsch, 1976).

The measurement of sustainable development is a major issue for ecological macroeconomics (Atkinson *et al.*, 1997). A simple rule for sustainable development is that capital should be left intact; that is, productive capacity should not be eroded. This might be achieved via capital bequests: the current generation must pass on a capital stock that in terms of its productive capacity is at least as large as it inherited. This 'constant capital rule' implies that one particular capital asset does not matter insofar as its services can be provided by a substitute asset. For example, increases in machinery and plant, in human capital (the stock of knowledge and skills) and in social capital (relationships such as trust and institutions) can compensate for the depletion of natural capital (natural resources). Hamilton (2000) develops Pearce and Atkinson's (1993) estimate of sustainability defined in these terms and finds that the EU is 'sustainable', albeit only in the sense that increasing environmental degradation is justified by increases in the other forms of capital (see Pearce, 2001). The legitimacy of development based on replacing environmental or natural capital with 'produced' capital is a contentious issue, for some natural resources are regarded as unique and irreplaceable.

A commitment to sustainable development entails the obsolescence of the standard approach to national income accounting. The use of gross national product (GNP) as a measure of social welfare reflects the assumption that any goods or services that are exchanged for money increase the value of national income. There is nothing unique and irreplaceable about any particular component of GNP and no adjustments are made for environmental damage caused by components of GNP. In an attempt to resolve the deficiencies of GNP, Daly and Cobb (1994) constructed and estimated an index of sustainable economic welfare (SEW). The amendments made by Daly and Cobb are not purely ecological, in that they include adjusting for inequality in the distribution of income and for unpaid domestic labour. A number of deductions are made to reflect environmental degradation, including the costs of pollution, defensive health expenditures and loss of biodiversity. The main results of the exercise are that, in the United States during the period 1950 to 1990, SEW was found to have increased at a lower rate than GNP and that in the 1980s SEW actually declined while GNP rose.

To the extent that macroeconomic policy is guided by SEW rather than GNP, it will reflect a targeting of fiscal measures towards environmentally sensitive activities, taxing environmentally damaging or entropy-inducing activities and subsidizing 'green' production such as renewable energy sources. Ecological macroeconomics reinforces a trend towards a convergence of microeconomic and macroeconomic policy measures. This is seen elsewhere, for example in the justification of competition policy, traditionally an area of microeconomic policy, in terms of macroeconomic objectives such as productivity growth and, ironically, economic growth (see Stelzer, 2001).

The implications of the ecological approach to macroeconomics are particularly acute for the question of economic growth and the 'new economy' that allegedly fuelled the long US boom of the 1990s. Some proponents of the absolute newness of the 'new economy' claimed that it would overthrow the physical limits to growth. On this view, the knowledge base of the new economy was 'anti-entropic' and would transcend the thermodynamic world economy, in which economic activity turns natural resources into entropy (see Gilder, 1989).

However, at a theoretical level, an early statement of the ecological point of view had already anticipated claims of this kind: 'But we can be fairly certain that no new technology will abolish absolute scarcity because the laws of thermodynamics apply to all possible technologies' (Daly, 1974, p.19). In more practical terms, ecological macroeconomics continues to insist on placing the economic system in the context of physical limits to growth, pointing out, for example, that it is still necessary to mine materials for PCs and other physical manifestations of the new economy and to use energy in manufacturing them and shipping them all over the world (Lutz, 1999, p.231).

Finally it should be pointed out that despite the environmentalist concerns raised in the ecological approach to macroeconomics many mainstream economists are sceptical that there are definitive physical limits to economic growth (see, for example, Nordhaus, 1992; Romer, 1999, pp. 310–11; Jones, 2001, ch. 9; Beckerman, 2001).

GRAHAM DAWSON

Bibliography

Atkinson, G., R. Dubourg, K. Hamilton, M. Munasinghe, D.W. Pearce and C. Young (1997), *Measuring Sustainable Development: Macroeconomics and the Environment*, Cheltenham, UK and Lyme, US: Edward Elgar.
Ayres, R.U. (1998), *Turning Point: The End of the Growth Paradigm*, London: Earthscan.
Beard, T.R. and G.A. Lozada (2000), *Economics, Entropy and the Environment*, Cheltenham, UK and Northampton, MA, USA: Edward Elgar.
Beckerman, W. (2001), 'Economists and Sustainable Development', *World Economics*, **2**, October–December, pp. 1–17.
Daly, H.E. (1974), *Towards a Steady-State Economy*, San Francisco: W.H. Freeman.
Daly, H.E. (1996), *Beyond Growth: The Economics of Sustainable Development*, Boston: Beacon Press.
Daly, H.E. and J.B. Cobb (1994), *For the Common Good*, Boston: Beacon Press.
Faber, M., R. Manstetten and J. Proops (1996), *Ecological Economics: Concepts and Methods*, Cheltenham, UK and Brookfield, US: Edward Elgar.
Georgescu-Roegen, N. (1971), *The Entropy Law and the Economic Process*, Cambridge, MA: Harvard University Press.
Georgescu-Roegen, N. (1986), 'The Entropy Law and the Economic Process in Retrospect', *Eastern Economic Journal*, **12**, pp. 3–23.
Gilder, G. (1989), *Microcosm: The Quantum Revolution in Economics and Technology*, New York: Simon and Schuster.
Hamilton, K. (2000), *Sustaining Economic Welfare: Estimating Changes in Wealth per Capita*, Washington, DC: Environment Department, World Bank (*www.econ.nyu.edu/dept/iariw*).
Hirsch, F. (1976), *The Social Limits to Growth*, Cambridge, MA: Harvard University Press.
Jones C.I. (2001), *An Introduction to Economic Growth*, 2nd edn, New York: W.W. Norton.
Joseph, M. (1991), *The Green Economy*, London: Pluto Press.
Lutz, M.A. (1999), *Economics for the Common Good: Two Centuries of Social Economic Thought in the Humanistic Tradition*, London: Routledge.
Meadows, D.H., D.L. Meadows, J. Randers and W. Behrens (the 'Club of Rome') (1972), *The Limits to Growth*, London: Earth Island.
Nordhaus, W. (1992), 'Lethal Model 2: The Limits to Growth Revisited', *Brookings Papers on Economic Activity*, no. 2, pp. 1–59.
Pearce, D.W. (2001), 'Environmental Policy', in M. Artis and F. Nixson (eds), *The Economics of the European Union*, Oxford: Oxford University Press.
Pearce, D.W. and G. Atkinson (1993), 'Capital Theory and the Measurement of Sustainable Development', *Ecological Economics*, **8**, pp. 103–8.
Romer, P.M. (1999), 'Interview with Paul Romer', in B. Snowdon and H.R. Vane *Conversations with Leading Economists: Interpreting Modern Macroeconomics*, Cheltenham, UK and Northampton, MA, USA: Edward Elgar.
Stelzer, I.M. (2001), 'Competition Policy and Superior Macroeconomic Performance: You Can't Have One Without the Other', *Lectures on Regulatory and Competition Policy*, London: Institute of Economic Affairs.
WCED (1987), *Our Common Future*, Oxford: Oxford University Press.

Econometric Society

The Econometric Society was founded in 1930 by Irving Fisher (who became its first president) and the Norwegian economist Ragnar Frisch. The main purpose of the society is 'to promote studies that aim at a unification of the theoretical–quantitative and empirical–quantitative approach to economic problems and that are penetrated by constructive and rigorous thinking similar to that which has come to dominate in the natural sciences'. Its main activities include organizing meetings in six regions (North America, Europe and Other Areas, Latin America, Australasia, Far East and India–Southeast Asia) and every five years a World Congress; the publication of a monograph series; and the publication of the prestigious journal *Econometrica* (first published in 1933). *Econometrica*, which since the 1970s has been published six times a year, is widely acknowledged as one of the leading journals in economics. For more information, the reader is referred to the website (*http://gemini.econ.yale.edu/es*).

See also:

Fisher, Irving; Frisch, Ragnar A.K.

Economic Growth

An increase in real GDP over time which reflects an increase in the economy's capacity to produce goods and services.

See also:

Economic Growth and the Role of Institutions; Endogenous Growth Theory; Harrod–Domar Growth Model; Neoclassical Growth Model.

Economic Growth and the Role of Institutions

In the analysis of economic growth it is useful to begin by distinguishing between *proximate* and *fundamental* causes of growth. The proximate causes relate to the accumulation of factor inputs such as capital and labour, and also to variables which influence the productivity of these inputs, such as scale economies and technological change. The research of growth accountants such as Denison (1985) and Maddison (1995) has produced a useful taxonomy of the various proximate sources of growth and neo-Keynesian, neoclassical and endogenous growth theories tend to concentrate on modelling these proximate variables. In his historical survey of economic growth analysis, Rostow (1990) put forward a central proposition that 'from the eighteenth century to the present, growth theories have been based on one formulation or another of a universal equation or production function'. As formulated by Adelman (1961), this can be expressed as equation (1):

$$Y_t = f(K_t, N_t, L_t, A_t, S_t), \tag{1}$$

where K_t, N_t and L_t represents the services flowing from the capital stock, natural resources and labour resources, respectively, A_t denotes an economy's stock of applied knowledge, and S_t represents what Abramovitz (1986) has called 'social capability', within which the economy functions. According to Rostow, the universal equation encompasses both proximate and fundamental causes of economic growth. Clearly, S_t contains the influence of non-economic as well as economic variables which can influence the growth potential and performance of an economy, including the incentives, rules and regulations that determine the allocation of entrepreneurial talent (Baumol, 1990). Hence in recent years economists' research into determinants of growth have led some to stress the importance of institutions and incentive structures (North, 1990; Olson, 2000).

The fundamental sources of growth relate to those variables which have an important influence on a country's ability and capacity to accumulate factors of production and invest in the production of knowledge. Moving from the proximate to the fundamental causes of growth shifts the focus of attention to the institutional framework of an economy, to its 'social capability' (Abramovitz, 1986) or 'social infrastructure' (Hall and Jones, 1999). There is now widespread acceptance of the idea that 'good' institutions and incentive structures are an important precondition for successful growth and development (North, 1990; Abramovitz and David, 1996; Barro, 1997; Dawson, 1998; World Bank, 2002).

Economic history is essentially about the performance of economies over long periods of time and it has a very important contribution to make in helping growth theorists improve their ability to develop a better analytical framework for understanding long-run economic change (North and Thomas, 1973; North, 1989, 1994). The story that emerges from economic history is one which shows that the unsuccessful economies, in terms of achieving sustained growth of living standards, are those that fail to produce a set of enforceable economic rules of the game that promote economic progress. As Douglass North (1991) argues, the 'central issue of economic history and of economic development is to account for the evolution of political and economic institutions that create an economic environment that induces increasing productivity'.

North (1991) defines institutions as 'the humanly devised constraints that structure political, economic and social interaction'. The constraining institutions may be *informal* (customs, traditions, taboos, conventions, self-imposed codes of conduct involving guilt and shame) and/or *formal* (laws, contract enforcement, rules, constitutions, property rights). In an ideal world the informal and formal institutions will complement each other. These institutions provide a structure within which repeated human inter-action can take place, they support market transactions, they help to trans-mit information between economic agents and they give people the incentives necessary to engage in productive activities. History is 'largely a story of institutional evolution' and effective institutions 'raise the benefit of co-operative solutions or the costs of defection' (ibid.).

According to the World Bank (2002), there is a growing body of evidence linking the quality of institutional development to economic growth and efficiency across both time and space. If property rights are the key to reducing transaction costs and the promotion of specialization and trade, then it should be no surprise to observe that 'almost all of the countries that have enjoyed good economic performance across generations are countries that have stable democratic governments' (Olson, 2000; Rodrik, 2000). Whereas good governance and economic prosperity are good bedfellows, autocrats, who are also invariably kleptomaniacs, are a high-risk form of investment. As Easterly (2001a) notes, 'governments can kill growth'.

For most of human history the vast majority of the peoples of the world have been governed by what Mancur Olson (1993, 2000) calls 'roving bandits' and 'stationary bandits'. History provides incontrovertible evi-dence that benevolent despots are a rare breed. Roving bandits (warlords) have little interest in promoting the well-being of the people living within their domain. A territory dominated by competing roving bandits repre-sents a situation of pure anarchy and any form of sustainable economic development is impossible. With no secure property rights there is little incentive for people to produce any more than is necessary for their survi-val, since any surplus will be expropriated by force. Stationary bandits, however, can extract more tax revenue from the territory they dominate if a stable and productive economy can be encouraged and maintained. In this situation despots have an incentive to provide key public goods such as law and order. But property rights can never be fully secure under auto-cratic forms of governance. History shows that absolutist princes always find it difficult to establish stable dynasties, and this uncertainty relating to succession prevents autocrats from taking a longer-term view of the economy. For example, the monarchy in England between the rule of William the Conqueror (1066) and the 'Glorious Revolution' (1688) was plagued by repeated crises of succession (such as the 'Wars of the Roses').

Only in a secure democracy, where representative government is account-able and respectful of individual rights, can we expect to observe an envi-ronment created that is conducive to lasting property rights (Fukuyama, 1989, 1992).

The general thesis advocated by North and Olson is confirmed by DeLong and Shleifer (1993) who show that those cities in medieval Europe that were under more democratic forms of government were much more productive than those under the autocratic rule of 'princes'. The incompat-ibility of despotism with sustainable economic development arises because of the insecurity of property rights in environments where there are no con-stitutional restrictions on an autocratic ruler. DeLong and Shleifer assume that the size of urban populations is a useful proxy for commercial pros-perity and 'use the number and sizes of large pre-industrial cities as an index of economic activity, and changes in the number of cities and the sizes of urban population as indicators of economic growth'. Their city data show how, between the years 1000 and 1500, the centre of economic gravity in Europe moved steadily northward. Although in the year 1000 Western Europe was a 'backwater' in terms of urban development, by 1800 it was established as the most prosperous and economically advanced region of the world. While London was ranked as the twenty-fifth largest European city at the beginning of the thirteenth century, by 1650 it had risen to second place (after Paris), and by 1800 London was first. DeLong and Shleifer argue that security of property can be thought of as a form of lower taxation, with the difference between absolutist and non-absolutist governments showing up as different tax rates on private property. It has also been argued by Douglass North that the establishment of a credible and sustainable commitment to the security of property rights in England required the establishment of parliamentary supremacy over the crown. This was achieved following the 'Glorious Revolution' of 1688 which facili-tated the gradual establishment of economic institutions conducive to increasing security in property rights (North and Weingast, 1989; North, 1990). The contrasting economic fortunes of the North and South American continents also bear testimony to the consequences of divergent institutional paths for political and economic performance (Sokoloff and Engerman, 2000; Khan and Sokoloff, 2001).

A further example, demonstrating the importance of institutions for sus-tained economic growth, is provided by the post-World War II reconstruc-tion of Europe. In the immediate aftermath of the war, memories of the Great Depression, and consequent distrust of capitalism and markets as institutions, persuaded a significant number of people in Western Europe that what was needed for economic recovery was a continuation of wartime regulations, controls and perhaps even Soviet-style economic planning.

Partly in response to such ideas, between 1948 and 1951 the Marshall Plan provided for the transfer of some $13 billion of aid from the United States to Western Europe. Although these transfers alleviated some immediate resource shortages they were certainly not sufficient to accelerate economic growth significantly. However, as DeLong and Eichengreen (1993) argue, 'the Marshall Plan significantly sped western European growth by altering the environment in which economic policy was made' and by providing support to a recovery strategy based on the restoration of a market-based economic system, together with the necessary supporting institutions. In retrospect we now know that the period 1950–73 turned out to be a 'Golden Age' of economic growth in the 'mixed' economies of Western Europe and DeLong and Eichengreen conclude that the Marshall Plan was 'history's most successful structural adjustment programme'. Eichengreen (1996) also extends the institution-based explanation of why Europe was able to enjoy a 'Golden Age' of economic growth in the 25-year period following the implementation of the Marshall Plan. European economic growth during this quarter-century was faster than at any period either before or since (Maddison, 2001). According to Eichengreen, the foundation for this 'Golden Age' was a set of *domestic* (the social market economy) and *international* institutions (GATT, the development of free intra-European trade, the Bretton Woods institutions) that 'solved problems of commitment and co-operation that would have otherwise hindered the resumption of growth'.

For individuals living in a typical rich OECD economy in the twenty-first century, it is easy to take most of these market-based institutions for granted because they have evolved over such a long historical period. But the 'trials of transition' witnessed in the former communist economies remind us just how difficult it is to make market economies operate effectively without having the necessary institutional infrastructure in place (see the Stiglitz interview in Snowdon, 2001; World Bank, 2002). Furthermore, transition strategies which do not take account of the history of an economy are unlikely to succeed. Any development policy or transition strategy appropriate for a particular society must take a society's institutions and their resilience into account.

One very important source of divergence in per capita incomes emphasized by DeLong (2001, forthcoming) has arisen because of political developments which have influenced the choice of economic system and policies. Those countries which attempted to 'develop' behind the 'Iron Curtain' now have much lower income per capita than countries which had a comparable income per capita in 1950 and followed the capitalist path. 'The fact that a large part of the globe was under communist rule in the twentieth century is one major reason for the world's divergence . . . depending on how you count and how unlucky you are, 40 to 94 per cent of the potential material prosperity of a country was annihilated if it happened to fall under communist rule in the twentieth century' (DeLong, 2001). The most obvious examples involve the comparative development experiences of East and West Germany, North and South Korea, and China with Taiwan/Singapore/Hong Kong. But comparisons between other neighbouring countries seems reasonable: for example, comparisons between Russia and Finland, Hungary and Austria, Greece and Bulgaria, Slovenia and Italy, Cambodia and Thailand reveal significant differences in living standards. These *'natural experiments'* show that, where national borders also mark the boundaries of public policies and institutions, easily observable differentials in economic performance emerge (Fukuyama, 1992; Olson, 1996). In DeLong's (1992) view, 'Over the course of the twentieth century communism has been a major factor making for divergence: making nations that were relatively poor poorer even as rich industrial economies have grown richer.'

Given that capital and technology can migrate across political boundaries, the persistence of significant differences in the level of output per worker suggests the presence of persistent barriers to growth and development (Parente and Prescott, 2000). An obvious deterrent to the free flow of capital from rich to poor countries arises from the greater risk involved in investing in countries characterized by macroeconomic instability, inadequate infrastructure, poor education, ethnic diversity, widespread corruption, political instability and frequent policy reversals. While the presence of technological backwardness and income per capita gaps creates the potential for catch-up and convergence, Moses Abramovitz (1986) has highlighted the importance of 'social capability' without which countries will not be able to realize their potential. Social capability refers to the various institutional arrangements which set the framework for the conduct of productive economic activities and without which market economies cannot function efficiently. In order to foster high levels of output per worker, social institutions must be developed which protect the output of individual productive units from diversion. Countries with perverse infrastructure, such as a corrupt bureaucracy, generate rent-seeking activities devoted to the *diversion* of resources rather than productive activities such as capital accumulation, skills acquisition and the development of new goods and production techniques (Murphy *et al.*, 1993; Mauro, 1995). In an environment of weak law and contract enforcement, poor protection of property rights, confiscatory taxation and widespread corruption, unproductive profit (rent)-seeking activities will become endemic and cause immense damage to innovation and other growth-enhancing activities (Tanzi, 1998).

Trust between economic agents is a crucial determinant of the cost of transactions. This idea has a long pedigree (Fukuyama, 1995). For example, John Stuart Mill (1848) noted that there are counties in Europe 'where the most serious impediment to conducting business concerns on a large scale, is the rarity of persons who are supposed fit to be trusted with the receipt and expenditure of large sums of money . . . The advantage to mankind of being able to trust one another, penetrates into every crevice and cranny of human life: the economical is perhaps the smallest part of it, yet even this is incalculable'.

In a recent paper, Zak and Knack (2001) have taken up this insight and show that the extent of trust in an economy 'significantly' influences growth rates, and that 'high trust societies produce more output than low trust societies'. In economies where there is a high level of trust between transactors the rate of investment and economic growth is likely to be higher than in low-trust environments. This finding supports the earlier empirical research of Knack and Keefer (1995; 1997a, 1997b), who find a positive relationship between trust and growth for a sample of 29 market economies. Zak and Knack argue that *trust is lower* in countries where (1) there is an absence of formal (laws, contract enforcement) and informal (ostracism, guilt, loss of reputation) mechanisms and institutions which deter and punish cheaters and constrain opportunistic behaviour; (2) where population heterogeneity (ethnic diversity) is greater; (3) and where inequalities are more pervasive. Easterly and Levine (1997) find that ethnic diversity in Africa reduces the rate of economic growth since diverse groups find it more difficult to reach cooperative solutions and scarce resources are wasted because of continuous distributional struggles, of which civil war, 'ethnic cleansing' and genocide are the most extreme manifestations (Bosnia, Rwanda, Kosovo, Afghanistan). Collier's (2001) research suggests that ethnically diverse societies are 'peculiarly ill suited to dictatorship' and that, providing there is not 'ethnic dominance' in the political system, democratic institutions can greatly reduce the potential adverse economic impact of ethnic diversity and the wars of attrition that can take place between competing groups. Easterly (2001b) argues that formal institutions that protect minorities and guarantee freedom from expropriation and contract repudiation can 'constrain the amount of damage that one ethnic group could do to another'. Easterly's research findings show that ethnic diversity does not lower growth or result in worse economic policies, providing that good institutions are in place. Good institutions also 'lower the risk of wars and genocides that might otherwise result from ethnic fractionalisation'.

To understand why some countries have performed so much better than others with respect to growth it is therefore necessary to go beyond the *proximate* causes of growth and delve into the wider *fundamental* determinants.

This implies that we cannot hope to find the magic bullet by using economic analysis alone. To explain growth 'miracles' and 'disasters' requires an understanding of the way policy choices are made in an environment involving political struggle within an institutional structure.

While poor countries have enormous *potential* for catch-up and convergence, these advantages will fail to generate positive results on growth in countries with an inadequate political, legal and regulatory framework (Dawson, 1998). The notion that institutions profoundly influence the wealth of nations is an idea first eloquently expressed by Adam Smith in 1776. In recent years the 'politicisation of growth theory' (Hibbs, 2001) has led to a burgeoning of research into the impact on economic growth of politics, policy and institutional arrangements.

BRIAN SNOWDON
HOWARD R. VANE

See also:
Endogenous Growth Theory; Neoclassical Growth Model.

Bibliography
Abramovitz, M. (1986), 'Catching Up, Forging Ahead, and Falling Behind', *Journal of Economic History*, **46**, June, pp. 385–406.
Abramovitz, M. and P. David (1996), 'Convergence and Deferred Catch-Up: Productivity Leadership and the Waning of American Exceptionalism', in R. Landau, T. Taylor and G. Wright (eds), *The Mosaic of Economic Growth*, Stanford: Stanford University Press.
Adelman, I. (1961), *Theories of Economic Growth and Development*, Stanford: Stanford University Press.
Barro, R.J. (1997), *Determinants of Economic Growth*, Cambridge, MA: MIT Press.
Barro, R.J. (1999), 'Determinants of Democracy', *Journal of Political Economy*, **107**, December, pp. 158–83.
Baumol, W.J. (1990), 'Entrepreneurship: Productive, Unproductive and Destructive', *Journal of Political Economy*, **98**, October, pp. 893–921.
Collier, P. (2001), 'Implications of Ethnic Diversity', *Economic Policy*, **16**, April, pp. 129–66.
Dawson, J.W. (1998), 'Institutions, Investment, and Growth: New Cross-Country and Panel Data Evidence', *Economic Inquiry*, **36**, pp. 603–19.
DeLong, J.B. (1992), 'Growth in the World Economy, ca. 1870–1990', in H. Siebert (ed.), *Economic Growth in the World Economy*, Tübingen: Mohr/Siebeck.
DeLong, J.B. (2001), *Macroeconomics*, Burr Ridge: McGraw-Hill.
DeLong, J.B. (forthcoming), *The History of the Twentieth Century: Slouching Towards Utopia?*, Cambridge: Cambridge University Press.
DeLong, J.B. and B. Eichengreen (1993), 'The Marshall Plan: History's Most Successful Structural Adjustment Programme', in R. Dornbusch, W. Nolling and R. Layard (eds), *Post-War Reconstruction and Lessons for the East Today*, Cambridge, MA: MIT Press.
DeLong, J.B. and A. Shleifer (1993), 'Princes and Merchants: City Growth Before the Industrial Revolution', *Journal of Law and Economics*, **36**, October, pp. 671–702.
Denison, E.F. (1985), *Trends in American Economic Growth 1929–1982*, Washington, DC: Brookings Institution.
Easterly, W. (2001a), *The Elusive Quest for Growth*, Cambridge, MA: MIT Press.
Easterly, W. (2001b), 'Can Institutions Resolve Ethnic Conflict?', *Economic Development and Cultural Change*, July, pp. 687–706.

Easterly, W. and R. Levine (1997), 'Africa's Growth Tragedy: Policies and Ethnic Divisions', *Quarterly Journal of Economics*, **112**, November, pp. 1203–50.
Eichengreen, B. (1996), 'Institutions and Economic Growth: Europe After World War II', in N.C.R. Crafts and G. Toniolo (eds), *Economic Growth in Europe Since 1945*, Cambridge: Cambridge University Press.
Fukuyama, F. (1989), 'The End of History', *National Interest*, pp. 3–18.
Fukuyama, F. (1992), *The End of History and the Last Man*, New York: The Free Press.
Fukuyama, F. (1995), *Trust: The Social Virtues and the Creation of Prosperity*, New York: The Free Press.
Hall, R.E. and C.I. Jones (1999), Why do Some Countries Produce so Much More Output Per Worker Than Others?', *Quarterly Journal of Economics*, **114**, February, pp. 83–116.
Hibbs, D.A. (2001), 'The Politicisation of Growth Theory', *Kyklos*, **54**, pp. 265–86.
Khan, B.Z. and K.L. Sokoloff (2001), 'The Early Development of Intellectual Property Institutions in the United States', *Journal of Economic Perspectives*, **15**, Summer, pp. 233–46.
Knack, S. and P. Keefer (1995), 'Institutions and Economic Performance: Cross Country Tests Using Alternative Institutional Measures', *Economics and Politics*, **7**, November, pp. 207–27.
Knack, S. and P. Keefer (1997a), 'Why Don't Poor Countries Catch Up? A Cross-National Test of an Institutional Explanation', *Economic Inquiry*, **35**, July, pp. 590–602.
Knack, S. and P. Keefer (1997b), 'Does Social Capital Have an Economic Payoff?: A Cross Country Investigation', *Quarterly Journal of Economics*, **112**, November, pp. 1251–88.
Maddison, A. (1995), *Explaining the Economic Performance of Nations*, Aldershot, UK and Brookfield, US: Edward Elgar.
Maddison, A. (2001), *The World Economy: A Millennium Perspective*, Paris: OECD.
Mauro, P. (1995), 'Corruption and Growth', *Quarterly Journal of Economics*, **110**, August, pp. 681–712.
Mill, J.S. (1848), *Principles of Political Economy*, edited by D. Winch (1970), Harmondsworth: Penguin.
Murphy, K.M., A. Shleifer and R.W. Vishny (1993), 'Why is Rent Seeking so Costly for Growth?', *American Economic Review*, **83**, May, pp. 409–14.
North, D.C. (1981), *Structure and Change in Economic History*, New York: W.W. Norton.
North, D.C. (1989), 'Institutions and Economic Growth: An Historical Approach', *World Development*, **17**, September, pp. 1319–32.
North, D.C. (1990), *Institutions, Institutional Change and Economic Performance*, Cambridge: Cambridge University Press.
North, D.C. (1991), 'Institutions', *Journal of Economic Perspectives*, **5**, Winter, pp. 97–112.
North, D.C. (1994), 'Economic Performance Through Time', *American Economic Review*, **84**, June, pp. 359–68.
North, D.C. and R. Thomas (1973), *The Rise of the Western World: A New Economic History*, Cambridge: Cambridge University Press.
North, D.C. and B.R. Weingast (1989), 'Constitutions and Commitment: The Evolution of Institutions Governing Public Choice in Seventeenth-Century England', *Journal of Economic History*, **49**, December, pp. 803–32.
Olson, M. (1993), 'Dictatorship, Democracy and Development', *American Political Science Review*, **87**, September.
Olson, M. (1996), 'Distinguished Lecture on Economics in Government: Big Bills Left on the Sidewalk: Why Some Nations are Rich, and Others Poor', *Journal of Economic Perspectives*, **10**, Spring, pp. 3–24.
Olson, M. (2000), *Power and Prosperity: Outgrowing Communist and Capitalist Dictatorships*, New York: Basic Books.
Parente, S.L. and E.C. Prescott (2000), *Barriers to Riches*, Cambridge, MA: MIT Press.
Rodrik, D. (2000), 'Participatory Politics, Social Co-operation, and Economic Stability', *American Economic Review*, **190**, May, pp. 140–44.
Rostow, W.W. (1990), *Theories of Economic Growth from David Hume to the Present*, Oxford: Oxford University Press.

Snowdon, B. (2001), 'Redefining the Role of the State: Joseph Stiglitz on Building a Post-Washington Consensus', *World Economics*, **2**, July–September, pp. 45–86.

Sokoloff, K. and S. Engerman (2000), 'Institutions, Factor Endowments, and Paths of Development in the New World', *Journal of Economic Perspectives*, **14**, Summer, pp. 217–32.

Tanzi, V. (1998), 'Corruption Around the World: Causes, Consequences, Scope and Cures', *IMF Staff Papers*, **45**, December, pp. 559–94.

World Bank (2002), *Building Institutions for Markets*, Oxford: Oxford University Press.

Zak, P.J. and S. Knack (2001), 'Trust and Growth', *Economic Journal,* **111**, April, pp. 295–321.

Efficiency Wage

The real wage that maximizes worker productivity or effort per pound (dollar) of real wages.

Efficiency Wage Theory

An integral element of the new Keynesian explanation of real wage rigidity in the labour market, efficiency wage theory seeks to explain why an 'equilibrium' real wage rate can emerge, that is above the market-clearing real wage rate. Such theory is therefore capable of generating involuntary unemployment in long-run equilibrium.

The essence of efficiency wage theory is that the productivity (effort or efficiency) of workers depends positively on the real wage that workers are paid. In consequence, it is both profitable and rational for firms to pay a so-called 'efficiency wage' that is above the market-clearing real wage rate. Efficiency wage theory suggests that even in the face of an excess supply of labour it will not be in firms' interests to lower the real wage rate, as to do so would lower productivity and raise costs.

Four versions of efficiency wage theory can be found in the literature. First, the *labour turnover model* suggests that quit rates are a decreasing function of the real wage paid to workers. In consequence, firms have an incentive to pay an efficiency wage in order to deter workers from quitting and reduce costly labour turnover. At the same time, the existence of involuntary unemployment that results from the payment of an efficiency wage above the market-clearing real wage rate acts as a disincentive to workers to quit their job. Second, the *adverse selection model* suggests that workers' abilities and reservation or minimum wage, which would induce them to take a job, are closely connected. In consequence, by paying an efficiency wage, firms will not only attract the best or most productive applicants but will also deter the most productive workers from quitting. Third, the *shirking model* suggests that in many jobs workers can exercise considerable discretion with respect to how well they perform their job and that there is a real possibility that some workers will shirk their work effort. By paying an efficiency wage above the market-clearing real wage rate firms will discourage shirking and raise worker productivity. In addition to an efficiency wage acting as a disciplinary device, it also allows firms to reduce costs in monitoring workers' performance. Finally, the *fairness model* suggests that workers' productivity is closely connected to their morale, which is in turn linked to the notion of being treated fairly with respect to pay. In consequence, if an efficiency wage above the market-clearing real wage rate is paid, the morale and loyalty of workers will increase and workers will respond by working harder, increasing their productivity. For a fuller discussion of efficiency wage theory, the reader is referred to G.A. Akerlof and J.L. Yellen (eds), *Efficiency Wage Models of the Labour Market* (Cambridge University Press, 1986).

See also:

Adverse Selection Model; Efficiency Wage; Involuntary Unemployment in Keynesian Economics; New Keynesian Economics; Real Rigidity; Shirking Model.

Elasticities Approach to the Balance of Payments

An approach which examines the conditions under which devaluation will be successful in remedying a balance of payments deficit on the current account. The approach concentrates on the response of exports and imports to relative price changes following devaluation. A necessary condition (known as the Marshall–Lerner condition) for devaluation to improve the current account of the balance of payments is that the sum of the elasticities of demand for imports and exports should exceed unity.

See also:

Balance of Payments; Devaluation; Marshall–Lerner Condition.

Employment Act of 1946

The Employment Act of 1946 charged the Federal Government of the United States with the responsibility of achieving three main macroeconomic goals, namely: 'maximum employment, production and purchasing power'. Two groups were established under the Act, the Council of Economic Advisers (CEA) and the Joint Economic Committee of the Congress. One of the main tasks of the three-member CEA is to help the president prepare his annual Economic Report to Congress, assessing current events and policy in the United States. The 11-member Joint Economic Committee of the Congress has the responsibility of evaluating the Economic Report of the President.

See also:
Council of Economic Advisers.

Endogenous Growth Theory

Setting the stage

We begin with the distinction between 'development economics', and 'growth theory' (Brinkman, 1965). What is 'the nature and causes of the wealth of nations'?, Adam Smith asked over two centuries ago and the answer to that question is the subject of development economics. Why is India poor and America rich? asks the modern development economist, and the answer is bound to include such things as the security of property rights, the efficiency of the judiciary system, the size of the public sector, the liberality of the trade regime and so on. But growth theory asks a smaller and much more precise question: what is the balanced, steady-state, long-run equilibrium growth path of an economy, balanced in the sense that all the critical variables in the growth model – output, capital, labour, saving and investment – change at a constant exponential rate into the indefinite future? Alas, actual economies do not grow in balanced steady states even for quite short time-spans; instead they undergo almost continual structural changes in their sectoral and industrial composition of output. The dynamics of those inherently volatile out-of-steady states are difficult to model and perhaps do not lend themselves to many useful generalizations. But whatever the reasons, economists almost never build growth models which do not possess steady-state solutions. This inherent limitation of all growth theories, their preoccupation with what must necessarily be an idealized representation of actual economic growth, must be kept in mind in everything that follows.

The old and the new growth theory

Growth theory begins with the Harrod–Domar model of the 1940s and moves forward with a jolt in the 1950s to the work of Robert Solow, who endogenized the capital–labour ratio which had been assumed as given by technology in the Harrod–Domar model. After furious activity in the 1960s, growth theory stagnated and was brought back in a new form by Paul Romer and Robert Lucas in the 1980s. The Solow (1956) model invoked an aggregate Cobb–Douglas production function with constant returns to scale, but diminishing returns to each input. Since past growth has always been characterized by a steady rise in the capital–labour ratio, this implies a steady state, long-run equilibrium rate of zero per capita income growth (because of diminishing returns to capital) unless offset by a sufficient amount of exogenous technical progress, the A in Solow's equation:

$$Y = Af(K, L).$$

From this model grew the Denison studies (for example, Denison, 1967) in growth accounting of the 1960s and 1970s. The new Lucas–Romer growth theory suggested that capital-deepening may not encounter diminishing returns owing to various inter-firm externalities, permitting the aggregate production function to exhibit increasing rather than constant returns to scale. But increasing returns to scale are incompatible with perfect competition and so, in Romer's second growth model, he adopted the theory of imperfect competition but, as before, he endogenizes A, which is why it was soon labelled 'endogenous growth theory' (EGT) in contrast to exogenous growth theory *à la* Solow.

Why exogenous or endogenous? The term 'exogenous' in economics usually means that the variable so described is not itself accounted for in the theory, as for example the money supply in the quantity theory of money or the pattern of demand in the theory of consumer behaviour. The old growth theory is called exogenous growth theory because technical progress or A is not itself explained in the theory: neither what it is, nor how much there is of it; it is a 'measure of our ignorance' as Moses Abramovitz (1956) once said because it is everything that accounts for increases in total factor productivity that we cannot explain in the theory.

What do we mean by endogenous growth theory (EGT) as a label for the new growth theory? Presumably that growth is explained in the theory as a product of growth itself and, moreover, as the intended or unintended consequence of the profit-driven activity of private firms (that is precisely what makes it *neoclassical* endogenous growth theory).

Is EGT an improvement on the old growth theory? Consider first that some technical progress is the result of deliberate profit-motivated R&D activities by individual firms and these are endogenized in the new growth theory, whereas there was no room for such activities in the old growth theory. On the other hand, there is government-subsidized applied R&D in military research institutes and pure basic research in universities, which are motivated by non-pecuniary considerations, and these remain exogenous in the new as in the old growth theory. In addition, there is Arrow's learning-by-doing, which is the unintentional by-product of past investment plus experience and this will always be at least partially exogenous because it is not fully predictable. In short, economic growth and particularly the growth of technical knowledge is necessarily exogenous at least in some part and this is so even before we take account of the radical Knightian uncertainty that surrounds the innovative process, which is by definition exogenous because it is unpredictable. To sum up, a totally endogenous growth theory is realistically impossible. On the other hand, a totally exogenous growth theory, besides being methodologically embarrassing for leaving too much of importance unexplained, is also realistically impossible because too many companies are investing heavily in R&D, some of which will pay off in generating new techniques and new products. It follows that we really cannot choose between the old and the new growth theory on grounds of realism or descriptive accuracy (Valdés, 1999, pp. 171–2). It also turns out (more on this below) that the two theories are observationally equivalent and even their growth-oriented policy implications are virtually identical. Clearly, if we must choose between them, we will have to base our choice on modelling grounds: the simplicity, elegance and tractability of one model over another.

Three channels of endogenous growth
Within the analytical constraints of the problematic addressed by EGT – how to introduce profit-inspired technical progress in a model of perfect competition and constant returns of scale – there are three avenues by which constant steady-state growth theory might proceed. We cannot entertain increasing or decreasing returns to scale because the former would soon destroy perfect competition and the latter is of course denied by steady-state growth itself. However, endogenous growth might result despite linearly homogeneous aggregate production functions from 'learning-by-doing' (Arrow, 1962): unit costs decline in all or most production processes as time passes simply because firms acquire experience in making the product in question. Although this effect is well documented in a number of industries, it strains credulity to believe that this could account, not just for a once-and-for-all increase in the level of output, but also for a *constant* rate of increase in total factor productivity year in and year out.

The second and third avenues to steady-state growth both employ the notion of externalities, the first being associated with the writings of Paul Romer, the second with those of Robert Lucas. In Romer (1986), the production function of each individual firm exhibits diminishing marginal productivity to its own capital input, as in the Solow model, but it now also depends on the capital of other firms. More capital in one firm increases productivity in other firms because the knowledge that is generated by investment embodied in R&D in one firm can never be entirely appropriated by the innovating firm in question but spills over to other firms; new knowledge thus partakes of the nature of 'public goods' being non-rivalrous and in large part non-excludable. Lucas (1988) applies the same notion to a firm's decision to provide on-the-job training to its workforce and even to its decision to hire more formally educated workers. Putting the two arguments together, constant returns to scale to any accumulable factor of production, be it physical or human capital, will now generate endogenous growth in a perfectly competitive economy via external effects on other firms, industries and even countries.

Constant returns to scale plus positive externalities is not unlike what Kaldor (1967) analysed years ago as dynamically increasing returns to scale in which output growth itself has a positive feedback effect on productivity growth. The notion that economies of scale are fundamental to the explanation of long-run growth is of course as old as Adam Smith's story of the pin factory, but the difficulty with increasing returns is that its introduction threatens the assumption of perfect competition which lies at the heart of standard microeconomics. Perhaps in recognition of that fact, later papers by Romer (1990) marry the non-convexity inherent in a non-rival and only partially excludable public good like knowledge to the assumption of monopolistic competition in order to obtain an even more persuasive account of endogenous growth. He supplements the traditional production-function model by assuming that a number of intermediate inputs are produced from physical capital with increasing returns to scale and because of monopolistic competition in the supply of inputs, each input provider generates an externality for the others; as the number of intermediate inputs expands, the productivity of further investment is enhanced by the increasing degree of specialization. He calls this 'Growth Based on Increasing Returns Due to Specialization' (Romer, 1987), thus coupling increasing returns to monopolistic competition and incomplete appropriability as the three essential building blocks of his version of EGT.

The difference between Romer$_1$ (1986) and Romer$_2$ (1990) is worth underlining. Romer$_1$, which truly launched EGT, is not properly speaking an endogenous growth theory at all. In this first version of EGT, profit-maximizing firms in a regime of perfect competition decide to invest in a certain quantity of physical capital and this leads, through a process of learning-by-doing and unintentional spillovers, to instantaneous and cost-less diffusion of new technical knowledge from one firm to another. What happens, however, to firms who invest in R&D deliberately in order to produce new technical knowledge? The next step is obviously to take account of them: but firms that invest in R&D expect to be compensated for it. Under perfect competition, however, there is no revenue available to any firm to finance R&D activity because the firm's proceeds are exactly exhausted by payments to all the contributory inputs in accordance with their marginal value products; since the firm's output requires the use of labour and capital, competitive factor payments will ensure that there is no output left to reward a 'third' factor like R&D. But, surely, R&D is itself decomposable into capital and labour applied to doing research? No, not entirely, because what is produced in R&D is new knowledge with the aid of the previous knowledge and experience of the research team, and so new knowledge is produced by capital, labour and old knowledge. Neither old nor new knowledge is divisible, homogenous factors of production with well-specified marginal product. We are left with the previous conclusion that there is no output available under perfect competition to pay for R&D. This is the famous product-exhaustion theorem, which is almost as old as neoclassical economics itself (Blaug, 1997, pp. 422–35). So, if we are serious about the introduction of R&D into our picture of firm behaviour in a theory of endogenous growth, we must abandon the assumption of perfect competition and the associated assumption of constant returns to scale. Romer$_2$ is thus a final capitulation of neoclassical theory to almost 60 years of criticism of the postulate of perfect competition.

The origins of EGT
So far, all this is simply a good story well told. But what is the evidence that should lead us to believe that it is also a true story? Before trying to answer that fundamental question, let us consider what evidence led Romer and Lucas to invent EGT in the first place. The old Solow-type growth theory suggested that all national economies with access to the same (exogenous) world-wide technology should have converging per capital income growth rates, at least after a lapse of time to allow for different initial conditions. This is the so-called 'convergence hypothesis' according to which poor countries should grow more quickly but rich countries should grow more slowly than average. However, it was widely believed in the 1980s that there had been divergence rather than convergence, at least on a global level (see Grossman, 1996, pp. xi–xii; Pritchett, 1997; Lucas, 2000), and Solow (1991, p. 398) was convinced that the failure to see any sign of worldwide convergence was 'the observation that motivated Romer and Lucas to the theoretical extensions that underlie the new growth theory'. If there is not convergence, then the growth rate itself should somehow be endogenous (that is, capable of differing from country to country). But Romer (1994, p. 11) himself scoffed at the idea that the convergence controversy had much to do with the origin of EGT: 'My original work in growth was motivated primarily by the observation that in the broad sweep of history, classical economists like Malthus and Ricardo came to the conclusions that were completely wrong about prospects for growth. Over time, growth rates have been increasing, not decreasing.'

Let us take a moment to note that the classical economists did have much in common with endogenous growth theorists: they did conceive of economic growth as a self-generating cumulative process but it is nevertheless profoundly misleading to suggest, as some have done (Kurz, 1997), that EGT is just old wine in new bottles. First of all, classical growth theory was, in modern language, development economics and not growth theory. Secondly, classical development economics and particularly Ricardian development economics was pessimistic in that it expected growth to exhaust itself despite technical progress because of irremedial natural resource scarcities; it believed, not just in diminishing returns to single inputs, not just in diminishing returns to scale, but in what Schumpeter called 'historically diminishing returns', so that even technical progress itself was expected to slow down and eventually peter out (Blaug, 1997, pp. 68,76). Thirdly, while Smith, John Stuart Mill and particularly Karl Marx recognized all the essential components of economic growth, they did not take serious account of human capital, inter-firm externalities and R&D, the principal components of the EGT of Romer and Lucas. If we must look for forerunners of EGT, the true progenitors were not the classical economists but Allyn Young, Laughlin Currie and Nicholas Kaldor, who espoused the cumulative, self-propelling approach to growth theory as early as the 1920s (Palley, 1996; Sandilands, 2000) .

The theory–evidence ratio for EGT

Putting the origins of EGT to one side, let us now ask: what is the empirical evidence that corroborates EGT? The answer to that question confronts us immediately with an *embarras de richesses*. Since the take-off of EGT with Romer and Lucas in the late 1980s, the subject has spawned three fat textbooks (Grossman and Helpman, 1991; Barro and Sala-i-Martin, 1995; and Aghion and Howitt, 1998) and literally thousands of articles. The typical paper begins with an aggregate production function defined on capital and labour, or capital alone composed of standard capital and human capital – the so-called 'AK models' – displaying increasing returns to scale via R&D expenditure or inter-firm externalities, although constant returns to scale continues to rule at the level of the individual firm. Productivity increases are thus generated endogenously by a variety of mechanisms but, whatever the mechanism – firms investing in R&D, workers opting for education and training, consumers saving by giving up current income – they all have the characteristic that they derive from choices made autonomously by individuals. These individuals do not differ significantly from one another and so the aggregation problem is usually solved by assuming the existence of 'representative agents'. Likewise, all the difficult dynamics of out-of-steady states are usually evaded by collapsing the long run into the short run: the 'Ricardian Vice', as Schumpeter dubbed it because Ricardo was fatally attracted to it. Putting these two features together, what we have is standard microeconomics interpreted unapologetically as macroeconomics, and long-run macroeconomics at that (Fine, 2000). The scope for fancy modelling opened up by these developments is enormous and so is the scope for empirical verification.

The alleged motivation for the research programme of EGT is to explain why growth rates differ, and so with per capita growth per country as the left-hand dependent variable and the right-hand independent variables as the proxies for any of the factors cited in the theoretical literature, an almost endless number of papers have examined an ever larger number of countries for an ever greater variety of different time-periods, paying little attention to the precise mechanics by which the various elements enter into the theoretical model. In the end, it is far from clear in many of these regression studies how the coefficients on the right-hand side still tell us anything about their causal influence on the left-hand side.

The pointlessness of much of this econometric research can be traced back to the attitudes of the fathers of EGT, Romer and Lucas, who were clearly more interested in straightening out the theory than in gathering convincing evidence for it. Romer's approach to the theory–evidence relationship is to emphasize stylized facts about growth and to show that the implications of EGT are in conformity with these facts. But the stylized facts in question are so innocuous – knowledge is non-rivalrous not totally excludable; technical advance comes not from things but from what people do; firms have market power and earn monopoly rents on discoveries; and so on and so forth (Romer, 1994, pp. 12–13) – that a wide variety of growth theories would endorse them. If we ask, not for stylized facts that verify EGT, but for statistical data that are compatible and only compatible with EGT, the brutal truth is that there is no such evidence. Lucas, for example, builds an elegant model of growth in which human capital formation is endogenized, but when it comes to quantifying 'the elasticity of US output with respect to the external effects of human capital on production', he candidly admits that there is no evidence from which to guesstimate the value of that elasticity (Lucas, 1988, pp. 317–18). He likens the problem to the agglomeration effects of cities as expressed in land rents and notes that, analogously, the externalities of human capital formation should be measured by schooling-induced earnings differentials – at which point he leaves the subject. But even the most upbeat assessment by an enthusiast of EGT (Gemmel, 1997) fails to find any difference in social rates of return to higher education (in the United Kingdom) calculated so as to allow for external effects and private rates of return calculated from micro-wage-based estimates that exclude externalities. Similarly, Nancy Stokey (1991) builds a model in which growth is due to the externalities generated by improvements in the quality of schooling but admits that she has no idea how these might be measured.

The old and the new growth theory seem to agree that any satisfactory theory of growth must imply four well-established empirical regularities of long-run economic growth or 'stylized facts' that Kaldor laid down 40 years ago (Valdés, 1999, pp. 10–12): (1) increasing per capita income growth; (2) a trendless, indeed constant, capital–output ratio; (3) a trendless rate of profit or rate of return to physical capital; and (4) substantial and persistent differences in per capita income growth rates across countries. Alas, both the old Solow exogenous growth theory and the new Romer–Lucas EGT imply all four of these stylized facts; if they are the criteria, the two theories are observationally equivalent. Even worse, their growth-oriented policy implications are virtually identical despite the fact the old growth theory implies that such policies have once-and-for-all level effects, whereas the new growth theory implies that they have cumulative, rate-of-growth effects. Here is a brief list of them: economic integration but not necessarily free trade; anti-populationist policies; encouragements to private saving and private investment in education; and subsidies to R&D in publicly-funded research centres (Valdés, 1999, pp. 169–70). So here too, there is not really much to choose between the old and the new growth theories. But in that case, why there is so much fuss about EGT? The answer is that it seems to explain what was previously left in the dark but, more importantly, it features a brand of theorizing that is at times analytically elegant and at all times analytically demanding. Indeed, much of the literature of the new growth theory is so exclusively preoccupied with the modelling requirements of neoclassical theorizing (can we get a competitive equilibrium when there are increasing returns to scale and externalities?; if innovations require the existence of monopoly profits, how can equilibria be Pareto-optimal?; and so forth) that there is little space left for the consideration of empirical evidence. Analogies with other neoclassical models of consumer-demand-for-variety and Becker-type household production models are proudly displayed at the expense of even a sketchy explanation of how final equilibrium is actually achieved in real world markets. The modelling itself is frequently ingenious but it simply reeks of *ad hoc* assumptions that sound plausible and may even be true, but we are given no hints of how to discover whether they are in fact true. In the words of one who is entitled to be called the 'father' of modern growth theory, namely, Robert Solow (1991, p. 412):

> If the goal of growth theory is the elaboration of a preferred complete model ready for formal econometric application to observed time series, as many economists seem to believe, then the new growth theory falls well short. One is struck

by the proliferation of special assumptions about technology, about the nature of research activity, about the formation and use of human capital, about market structure, about family structure and about intertemporal preferences. Most of these particular assumptions have been chosen for convenience, because they make a difficult analytical problem more transparent. There is no reason to assume that they are descriptively valid, or that their implications have significant robustness against equally plausible variations in assumptions.

There is reason to believe that growth theorists have been looking in the wrong place for evidence, when they have looked at all, and that the best source of empirical material is not the alleged precision of time-series data but the admittedly fuzzy insights of historical case studies. We learn more about the role of technology in growth from the writings of an economic historian like Nathan Rosenberg (1982, 1994) than we do from reading Romer and Lucas. To quote Solow (1994, p.53) once again: 'the best candidate for a research agenda right now would be an attempt to extract a few workable hypotheses from the variegated mass of case studies, business histories, interviews, expert testimony, anything that might throw light on good ways to model the flow of productivity-increasing innovations and improvements'. Modelling first and looking for evidence afterwards, the approved orthodox formula for tackling economic problems, may be doing economics exactly the wrong way round! Ludwig Wittgenstein once said that 'Philosophy only solves problems created by philosophers.' It sometimes seems that growth theory only solves problems posed by growth theorists.

This grim conclusion should not really surprise us because EGT is scarred by the same defects as the old exogenous growth theory. A theory of an economy in constant exponential growth, not just in the aggregate but in all its essential components, can only be a mathematical toy, incapable in its very construction of bearing any resemblance to an actual economy. Frank Hahn (1984, p.138) once said of general equilibrium theory: 'It cannot be denied that there is something scandalous in the spectacle of so many people refining the analyses of economic states which they give no reason to suppose will ever, or have ever come about.' Substituting modern growth theory for general equilibrium theory (easy enough, for one is an offshoot of the other), these words say it all.

MARK BLAUG

See also:

Aggregate Production Function; Catching Up and Convergence, Harrod–Domar Growth Model; Lucas, Jr, Robert E.; Neoclassical Growth Theory; Romer, Paul M.; Solow, Robert M.

Bibliography

Abramovitz, M. (1956), 'Resource and Output Trends in the United States Since 1870', *American Economic Review*, **46**, May, pp. 5–23.

Aghion, P. and P. Howitt (1998), *Endogenous Growth Theory*, Cambridge, MA: MIT Press.

Arrow, K.J. (1962), 'Economic Implications of Learning by Doing', *Review of Economic Studies*, **29**, June, pp. 155–73, reprinted in Becker and Burmeister (1991), I, pp. 399–418.

Barro, R.J. and X. Sala-i-Martin (1995), *Economic Growth*, New York: McGraw-Hill.

Becker, R. and E. Burmeister (eds) (1991), 2 vols, *Growth Theory*, Aldershot, UK and Brookfield, US: Edward Elgar.

Blaug, M. (1997), *Economic Theory in Retrospect*, 5th edn, Cambridge: Cambridge University Press.

Brinkman, R. (1965), 'Economic Growth versus Economic Development', *Journal of Economic Issues*, **29**, pp. 1171–81.

Denison, E.F. (1967), *Why Growth Rates Differ*, Washington, DC: Brookings Institution.

Fine, B. (2000), 'Endogenous Growth Theory: A Critical Survey', *Cambridge Journal of Economics*, **29**, pp. 245–65.

Gemmell, N. (1997), 'Externalities to Higher Education: A Review of the New Growth Literature', in the National Committee of Enquiry into Higher Education, *Higher Education in the Learning Society*, London: Crown, Report 8, pp. 109–50.

Grossman, G. M. (ed) (1996), 2 vols, *Economic Growth: Theory and Evidence*, Cheltenham, UK and Brookfield, US: Edward Elgar.

Grossman, G.M. and E. Helpman (1991), *Innovation and Growth in a Global Economy*, Cambridge, MA: MIT Press.

Hahn, F.H. (1984), *Equilibrium and Economics*, Oxford: Basil Blackwell.

Kaldor, N. (1967), *Strategic Factors in Economic Development*, Ithaca, NY: Cornell University Press.

Kurz, H. (1997), 'What Could the "New" Growth Theory Teach Smith or Ricardo?', *Journal of Economic Issues*, **2**, pt. 2, pp. 1–20.

Lucas, R.E. Jr (1988), 'On the Mechanics of Economic Development', *Journal of Monetary Economics*, **22**, July, pp. 3–42, reprinted in Grossman (1996), I, pp. 284–323.

Lucas, R.E. Jr (2000), 'Some Macroeconomics for the 21st Century', *Journal of Economic Perspectives*, **14**, Winter, pp. 159–68.

Palley, T. (1996), 'Growth Theory in a Keynesian Mode: Some Keynesian Foundations for New Endogenous Growth Theory', *Journal of Post-Keynesian Economics*, **19**, Fall, pp. 113–35.

Pritchett, L. (1997), 'Divergence, Big Time', *Journal of Economic Perspectives*, **11**, Summer, pp. 3–18.

Romer, P. (1986), 'Increasing Returns and Long-Run Growth', *Journal of Political Economy*, **94**, October, pp. 1002–37, reprinted in Grossman (1966), I, pp. 241–76.

Romer, P. (1987), 'Growth Based on Increasing Returns Due to Specialization', *American Economic Review*, **77**, March, pp. 56–62; reprinted in Grossman (1996), I, pp. 277–83.

Romer, P. (1990), 'Endogenous Technical Change', *Journal of Political Economy*, **98**, October, pp. S71–S102, reprinted in Grossman (1996), I, pp. 426–57.

Romer, P. (1994), 'The Origins of Endogenous Growth', *Journal of Economic Perspectives*, **8**, Winter, pp. 3–22.

Rosenberg, N. (1982), *Inside the Black Box: Technology and Economics*, Cambridge: Cambridge University Press.

Rosenberg, N. (1994), *Exploring the Black Box: Technology, Economies and History*, Cambridge: Cambridge University Press.

Sandilands, R.J. (2000), 'Perspectives on Allyn Young in Theories of Endogenous Growth', *Journal of the History of Economic Thought*, **22**, Fall, pp. 309–28.

Solow, R. (1956), 'A Contribution to the Theory of Economic Growth', *Quarterly Journal of Economics*, **70**, February, pp. 65–94, reprinted in Becker and Burmeister (1991), I, pp. 3–32.

Solow, R. (1970), *Growth Theory: An Exposition*, Oxford: Oxford University Press.

Solow, R. (1991), 'Growth Theory', in D. Greenaway, M. Bleaney and I. Stewart (eds), *Companion to Contemporary Economic Thought*, London: Routledge, pp. 393–412.
Solow, R. (1994), 'Perspectives on Growth Theory', *Journal of Economic Perspectives*, **8**, Winter, pp. 45–54.
Stokey, N.L. (1991), 'Human Capital, Product Quality and Growth', *Quarterly Journal of Economics*, **56**, May, pp. 58–61, reprinted in Grossman (1996), I, pp. 324–53.
Valdés, B. (1999), *Economic Growth: Theory, Empirics and Policy*, Cheltenham, UK and Northampton, MA, USA: Edward Elgar.

Endogenous Variable

A variable that is explained within a particular model; its value depends on the value of other variables in the model.

Equation of Exchange

An algebraic expression associated with Irving Fisher's transactions version of the quantity theory of money. In the expression, $MV = PT$, the quantity of money (M) times the transactions velocity of circulation (V) *must equal* the average price of all transactions (P) times the number of transactions that take place (T).

See also:

Fisher, Irving; Quantity Theory of Money; Velocity of Circulation.

Euro

The Euro is the name given to the single common currency that replaced the national currencies of 12 of the 15 European Union (EU) countries in the year 2002. The 12 countries concerned are Austria, Belgium, Finland, France, Germany, Greece, Ireland, Italy, Luxembourg, Netherlands, Portugal and Spain. Of the remaining three countries, Sweden and the United Kingdom may join at some time in the future, while Denmark voted against adopting the Euro in a referendum held at the end of September 2000. The timetable for full conversion involved Euro coins and bank notes being introduced on 1 January 2002, when they started to circulate alongside national currencies. National currencies were subsequently taken out of circulation and from 1 July 2002 the Euro became the only currency in circulation in the 12 participating EU countries.

See also:

European Monetary Union; Optimum Currency Area.

European Central Bank

Located in Frankfurt, the European Central Bank (ECB), which replaced a number of European national central banks, is responsible for determining monetary policy in the Euro zone. Its main duty is to ensure price stability within the Euro zone. For more information the reader is referred to the website (*http:/www.ecb. intl*).

European Currency Unit

See:
European Monetary System.

European Monetary System

The European Monetary System (EMS), which determined exchange rate movements within the European Union (EU) between 1979 and 1998, came into being in March 1979 when members of the European Community (EC) set out to create a zone of exchange rate stability among its members. Central to the EMS was the establishment of the exchange rate mechanism (ERM) and the introduction of the European Currency Unit (ECU). The ERM required full members of the EMS to maintain their exchange rates within specified bands around an agreed central rate for member currencies and the ECU. The ECU was a composite basket of the currencies of all EMS member states. The value of the ECU was calculated by summing specified amounts of various European currencies which were based on the importance of each economy. As such the ECU was a weighted average of the currencies of all EMS member states. Although the amounts of each currency were originally subject to periodic revision, they were formally fixed in 1994, when the Deutschmark comprised roughly 30 per cent, the French franc roughly 19 per cent, the pound sterling roughly 13 per cent, and the Italian lira and Dutch guilder roughly 10 per cent each of the basket. The ECU acted as the official unit of account in the EU, a means of settlement between central banks within the account in the EU, a means of settlement between central banks within the EU and a denominator for the ERM. Inside the ERM each currency was valued in terms of the ECU, establishing a parity grid for participating member currencies. The system provided for fixed exchange rates between members of the ERM with compulsory intervention points according to the bands set around the central parity. Central banks were also expected to intervene when particular currencies moved out of line, even though they may not have been near to the edge of their bands. While the ERM met with some measure of success in reducing fluctuations in member countries' exchange rates between 1979 and 1998, it came under varying degrees of pressure on a number of occasions. In particular, prior to 1987 and after 1992, several realignments took place. Despite these pressures progress towards full European monetary union (EMU) ensued following the Maastricht Treaty (1991) with the creation of a single common currency, the Euro, in January 1999.

See also:

Euro; European Monetary Union; European Union; Optimum Currency Area; Fixed Exchange Rate System.

European Monetary Union

The long road towards the final establishment of EMU began in April 1951 with the formation of the European Coal and Steel Community (the ECSC was a 'common market' in the production and trade of coal, iron and steel). The success of this venture led to the Treaty of Rome (1957) and the formation of the European Economic Community (EEC) in 1958. This 'customs union' became popularly, but incorrectly, known as the 'Common Market'. Only after the completion of the 'Single Market' in 1992 did the European Union (EU) take on the characteristics of a Common Market, a form of economic integration that requires free labour and capital mobility, as well as free trade among members, and a common external tariff. The initial membership of the EEC consisted of six countries: France, Germany, Italy, Luxembourg, Belgium and the Netherlands. In 1967, the ECSC, EEC and European Atomic Energy Community merged to form the European Community (EC) and, following the ratification of the Maastricht Treaty in 1992, the EC became the European Union (EU). Since the early 1970s, membership of the EC/EU has expanded to include the UK, Ireland and Denmark (1973), Greece (1981), Spain and Portugal (1986) and Sweden, Austria and Finland (1995).

The Treaty of Rome made no mention of monetary union and the issue of EMU was first seriously placed on the European agenda in 1969 at the Hague summit. While the German and Dutch representatives preferred a gradualist approach to EMU, the European Commission, together with the French and Belgian representatives, were more inclined towards a shock therapy approach. *The Werner Plan* (1970) represented a compromise to these conflicting views and advocated the completion of EMU by 1980 (the turbulent economic conditions of the 1970s put an end to this possibility). This compromise initially led to the 'snake in the tunnel' system of fixed exchange rates prior to the establishment of the European Monetary System (EMS) in 1979. The EMS had two main features, the European Currency Unit (ECU) and the Exchange Rate Mechanism (ERM).

However, probably the most crucial step towards EMU occurred with the *Delors Report* in 1989. This envisaged the establishment of EMU in 'three stages'. Stage I, beginning in July 1990, consisted of the completion of the single market; increased economic cooperation and coordination of policies, especially in the monetary field; a continuation and strengthening of the EMS; and a larger role for the Committee of Central Bank Governors. In December 1991, the *Maastricht Treaty*, which amended the Treaty of Rome, set out the 'convergence criteria' that countries wishing to participate in EMU would need to meet and also provided for the establishment of the European System of Central Banks (ESCB) with the European Central Bank (ECB) as the pinnacle of the system. The overriding objective of the ESCB–ECB was the achievement of price stability. Also established at Maastricht was the European Monetary Institute (EMI). The role of the EMI was to monitor the convergence of those countries wishing to participate in EMU and to prepare the way for the ECB.

Although the ERM crises of 1992–3, German reunification and economic recession in Europe almost derailed progress, Stage II of the Delors Plan, involving the above elements, began in January 1994. The third and final stage of the Delors Plan began in January 1999, when the 11 EU member states satisfying the Maastricht criteria and wishing to participate in EMU commenced the irrevocable fixing of their exchange rates. From January 1999, these 11 countries also entered into a monetary policy regime conducted by the ECB whose primary objective is to maintain price stability (see *http://www.ecb.int/*). Sweden, Denmark and the UK chose, at this particular point, not to participate and Greece failed to meet the Maastricht criteria. However, Greece entered the third stage of EMU in January 2001 and the Euro currency was finally launched into circulation in January 2002. Table 1 provides population, GDP and GDP per capita data for 14 EU countries, the United States, Japan, China and India. If Sweden, Denmark and the UK eventually join EMU, it will form the second largest currency union in the world in terms of total GDP, after the USA, and the third largest in terms of population, after China and India.

The current UK Government's policy towards EMU was set out by Chancellor Gordon Brown in October 1997. The official policy is that the Government is in favour of membership 'in principle', providing that the 'economic conditions are right'. The Chancellor's 'five tests' for UK membership require consideration of the UK's 'sustainable convergence' with

Table 1   GDP, GDP per capita and population: USA, the EU and Japan, 1998

Country	Population (thousands)	GDP (1990, PPP $mill)	GDP per capita (1990, PPP$)
Austria	8078	152712	18905
Belgium	10197	198249	19442
Denmark	5303	117319	22123
Finland	5153	94421	18324
France	58805	1150080	19558
Germany	82029	1460069	17799
Greece	10511	118433	11268
Ireland	3705	67368	18183
Italy	57592	1022776	17759
Netherlands	15700	317517	20224
Portugal	9968	128877	12929
Spain	39371	560138	14227
Sweden	8851	165385	18685
United Kingdom	59237	1108568	18714
European Union*	374500	6661912	17724
United States	270561	7394598	27331
Japan	126486	2581576	20410
China	1242700	3873352	3117
India	975000	1702712	1746

Note: *Excluding Luxembourg.

Source: Adapted from A. Maddison (2001), *The World Economy: A Millennium Perspective*, Paris: OECD.

the existing EMU countries; the likely impact of EMU on investment in the UK; the evidence that there is sufficient flexibility in the UK economy to cope with the economic changes that EMU will bring; the impact of EMU on the UK financial services industry; and the impact of EMU on employment. If an assessment by the Treasury of the five tests is favourable to UK membership of EMU, the government intend to put their recommendation to Parliament and then to conduct a referendum. (See M. Artis and F. Nixon (eds), *The Economics of the European Union: Policy and Analysis*, 3rd edn, Oxford: Oxford University Press, 2001).

See also:

Euro; European Currency Unit; European Monetary System; European Union; Exchange Rate Mechanism; Fixed Exchange Rate System; Optimum Currency Area.

European Union

The name given since 1992 to the economic and political union of 15 European countries (formerly known as the European Community) which in 2002 comprised Austria, Belgium, Denmark, Finland, France, Germany, Greece, Ireland, Italy, Luxembourg, Netherlands, Portugal, Spain, Sweden and the United Kingdom.

Eurosclerosis

A term used to describe the belief that Europe suffers from excessive rigidities, most notably in the labour market. In the latter case it is suggested that labour market rigidities have led to the *sclerosis* (a term applied to describe a hardening of the tissues) of the economic system in Europe and resulted in high unemployment.

Evolutionary Macroeconomics

To most economists outside the evolutionary stream, it is fair to say that evolutionary macroeconomics is thought of simply as any study of the dynamics of capitalism that encompasses structural change as well as growth. This is acceptable as far as it goes, as it points to one important difference between the evolutionary and the mainstream approach to macro dynamics. This is the latter's focus on economic growth and lack of interest in structural change. However, a more insightful and precise characterization is that evolutionary macroeconomics models economic processes as the long-run outcome of endogenously generated change.

To see more clearly the implications of this statement, consider the structure of mainstream growth theory. Mainstream macro dynamics today comprises two forms of production function growth theory, neoclassical and new growth theory. From the vantage point of evolutionary theorists, the differences between these two forms are less important than their similarities. Both theories assume continuous full employment, balanced growth and virtually ignore institutions and, in modelling the dynamics of an economic system, both emphasize a distinction between structural and economic variables. The structural variables, tastes and technologies represent phenomena subject to change but usually in some long-run sense. They determine the values of the endogenous economic variables, but are themselves exogenous; that is, their behaviour is given from outside the system and not explained within it.

Furthermore, the long-run equilibrium performance of the economy depends only upon exogenous variables (the rate of growth of the labour force in the neoclassical models and the preferences of the representative agent in new growth theory). As a result, changes in the long-run equilibrium growth path of the system are determined by unexplained changes in exogenous variables. The assumption of exogeneity of the structural variables rules out any possibility of long-run outcomes being generated within the model. This suggests how critical is the treatment of the structural variables in distinguishing evolutionary from non-evolutionary processes or systems. To be evolutionary, changes in the structural variables must be influenced by the performance of the system itself; that is, they must be endogenously determined. And since the structural variables affect the performance of the economy (otherwise they would not be part of its structure) in evolutionary systems there will exist interactions between economic structure and performance. Long-run changes in economic structure and performance are generated endogenously as part of the same evolutionary process.

The emphasis on endogeneity of the structural variables is a generally accepted defining feature used by theoretical evolutionary economists (Witt, 1992; 1993), including those macro theorists who treat evolutionary economics as part of the broader fields of non-linear dynamics (Goodwin, 1990; 1991) and complexity theory (Rosser, 1995). This is not the case in the applied work in evolutionary macroeconomics, where there has been a strong tendency of the practitioners to describe their work as evolutionary as long as structural change, especially in technology but also in institutions, is included as an integral part of economic development. An unfortunate result is that, in applied work, several types of theories, differing in their treatment of technological and institutional change, have been improperly designated evolutionary.

The applied studies fall into three groups. The first group includes various versions of long-cycle theory. The driving force explaining the alleged historical long-run swings in GDP is investment, initiated by technical changes, which is treated as exogenous (Dosi *et al.*, 1988; Kondratiev,1925; Schumpeter, 1934; Van Duijn, 1983). Unlike the other two groups, there is little interest in institutions in this literature, other than to treat them as exogenous. The second group of theories includes institutions as part of the changing structure of the system, with exogenous technology the key determinant of both institutions and performance. Included in this group are the 'old' institutional economics school (Ayres, 1962; Commons, 1950; Veblen, 1899), the Regulation School (Aglietta, 1979; Boyer, 1988) and the Social Structure of Accumulation School (Bowles and Edwards, 1985; Gordon, 1980). In effect, rather than assume institutions are exogenous, these theories simply introduce an alternative exogenous structural force to explain institutional change and performance. Neither of these two groups of theories is evolutionary. Both groups lack a mechanism that allows the performance of the economy to alter the system's institutions or technology, thereby providing the interaction between the structural framework and performance that defines evolutionary systems.

The third group comprises theories that incorporate such interactions and are therefore evolutionary theories. It includes the later work of Schumpeter (1942). In *Capitalism, Socialism and Democracy*, Schumpeter argued that the very process of sustained growth and rising living standards during the period of capitalism's industrialization would sow the seeds of its destruction. This would result from induced institutional changes such as worker discontent, the atrophy of entrepreneurship and eventually tend to socialism. Thus the trajectory of capitalism would start from a mature capitalist institutional framework and a period of successful performance and in the long run a negative feedback would induce radical changes in institutions and performance. This pessimistic scenario is one in which structural change and performance are generated endogenously within the system.

Setterfield's study (1997) develops in detail a theoretical evolutionary model of an advanced capitalist economy, allowing the performance of the economy to alter both institutions and technology. He then shows that the model provides a convincing explanation of some key 'stylized facts' of the historical development of the British economy since 1780. In particular, he finds that, while in the nineteenth century Britain had been a relatively rapid growing economy, it 'failed to undergo the type of structural transformation . . . necessary to maintain . . . its position of relative economic dominance.'

The recent study by Cornwall and Cornwall (2001) is another example. It models the macroeconomic performance of developed capitalist economies over the twentieth century as the result of an interaction of economic performance variables with the economic structure, generating endogenous changes in both. While Schumpeter's evolutionary process led to socialism, in this study the interaction between performance and technology leads to the Great Depression. Then the post-World War II era of alternating periods of poor and superior macroeconomic performance is modelled as the outcome of interactions between performance and institutions. More specifically, the institutional framework emerging from World War II provided the institutions required to generate a 'golden age' of capitalism. Unfortunately, the quarter of a century of superior performance induced institutional changes leading to an equally long period of mass unemployment accompanied by a shift in power to capital.

This entry has concentrated on evolutionary macroeconomics. A much larger body of literature covering both theoretical and applied evolutionary microeconomics has also developed and shows signs of growing acceptance (Nelson, 1995). These studies focus on a sector of an economy, say firms in some industry undergoing continual changes in technology, and emphasize selection processes that determine the success or failure of the firms to adapt to structural change. Evolutionary macroeconomics until now has never offered a serious challenge to the dominant position of mainstream macrodynamics. However, a continuing inability of mainstream economics to provide a general framework capable of explaining the historical development of modern capitalism provides an opportunity for a wider acceptance of alternatives to equilibrium analysis. Indeed, Nobel Prize laureate Kenneth Arrow (1995) cites the 'steady erosion' of belief in the foundations of mainstream equilibrium analysis, with 'a more appropriate paradigm' for economics emerging. Equilibrium theory rooted in mechanics will be displaced by evolutionary theory as the new foundation for economic analysis.

JOHN CORNWALL

See also:

Endogenous Growth Theory; Neoclassical Growth Model; Schumpeter, Joseph A.

Bibliography
Aglietta, M. (1979), *The Theory of Capitalist Regulation*, London: New Left Review.
Arrow, K. (1995), 'Viewpoint: the Future', *Science*, **267**, March, pp. 1617–18.
Ayres, C. (1962), *The Theory of Economic Progress*, New York: Schocken Books.
Bowles, S. and R. Edwards (1985), *Understanding Capitalism: Competition, Command and Change in the U.S. Economy*, New York: Harper & Row.
Boyer, R. (1988), 'Technical Change and the Theory of Regulation', in G. Dosi, C. Freeman, R. Nelson, G. Silverberg and L. Soete (eds), *Technical Change and Economic Theory*, London and New York: Pinter Publishers.
Commons, J.R. (1950), *The Economics of Collective Action*, Madison: University of Wisconsin Press.
Cornwall, J. and W. Cornwall (2001), *Capitalist Development in the Twentieth Century: An Evolutionary–Keynesian Analysis*, Cambridge: Cambridge University Press.
Dosi, G. *et al.* (1988), *Technical Change and Economic Theory*, London: Pinter.
Goodwin, R. (1990), *Chaotic Economic Systems*, Oxford: Oxford University Press.
Goodwin, R. (1991), 'Schumpeter, Keynes and the Theory of Economic Evolution', *Journal of Evolutionary Economics*, **1**, pp. 29–48.
Gordon, D. (1980), 'Stages of Accumulation and Long Economic Cycles' in T. Hopkins and I. Wallerstein (eds), *Processes of the World System*, Beverly Hills, CA: Sage Publications.
Kondratiev, N. (1925), Translation in 'The Long Wave in Economic Life', *Review of Economic Statistics*, **17**, November, 1935, pp. 105–15.
Nelson, R. (1995), 'Recent Economic Theorizing about Economic Change', *Journal of Economic Literature*, **33**, March, pp. 48–90.
Rosser, B. (1995), 'On the Complexities of Complex Economic Dynamics', *Journal of Economic Perspectives*, **9**, Fall, pp. 169–92.
Schumpeter, J. (1934), *The Theory of Economic Development*, Cambridge, MA: Harvard University Press.

Schumpeter, J. (1942), *Capitalism, Socialism and Democracy*, New York: Harper and Brothers.
Setterfield, M. (1997), *Rapid Growth and Economic Decline*, London: Macmillan.
Van Duijn, J. (1983), *The Long Cycle in Economic Life*, London: Allen & Unwin.
Veblen, T. (1899), *The Theory of the Leisure Class*, New York: Macmillan.
Witt, U. (1992), 'Evolutionary Concepts in Economics', *Eastern Economic Journal*, **18**, Fall, pp. 405–19.
Witt, U. (1993), 'Emergence and Dissemination of Innovations: Some Principles of Evolutionary Economics', in R. Day and P. Chen (eds), *Non Linear Dynamics and Evolutionary Economics*, Oxford: Oxford University Press.

Ex Ante, Ex Post

A distinction, coined by the Swedish economist and 1974 Nobel Laureate Gunner Myrdal (1898–1987), between what is planned, desired or intended (*ex ante*) and what is realized or actually happens (*ex post*). *Ex post* and *ex ante* will not be the same when plans are not realized.

Ex Post

See:
Ex Ante, Ex Post.

Exchange Rate Determination: Monetary Approach

This is one of the main explanations of what determines a floating exchange rate. Between 1945 and 1973 the world was more or less on fixed exchange rates and, with the rise of monetarism, there was a need to have a monetary explanation of the balance of payments. The early literature looked at trade flows and considered items above the line on the balance of payments; these represented autonomous flows. Monetarism, on the other hand, considered the situation from below the line in terms of the change in reserves. The fundamental distinction was that models of the balance of payments above the line were flow models while monetarist models were stock–flow models. In other words, they added a stock dimension to the analysis that was absent in the pure flow models. With the advent of floating exchange rates in the early 1970s, there was a clear need to model exchange rate determination. Since floating was thrust onto the world by circumstances, little in the way of modelling of exchange rates had been undertaken at the time floating began. Economists soon developed various models to explain the determination of the exchange rate, some of these being monetarist in conception.

The usual starting point for explaining the exchange rate is the demand and supply of foreign currency. In this entry we define the exchange rate as the price of foreign currency in terms of domestic currency. The demand and supply of foreign currency determine the equilibrium level of the exchange rate. Any disequilibrium represents either a deficit or a surplus on the balance of payments, which under floating can be eliminated by either a depreciation or an appreciation. The demand and supply of foreign currency arise from imports and exports of goods and services and from the flows of short-term capital. Such a conception of the determination of the exchange rate, however, considers the issue from the point of view of above-the-line transactions, and represents a flow explanation.

The monetary approach, and there is more than one, emphasizes money as a main determinant of the explanation, and considers the issue from below the line. Accordingly, it takes a stock–flow approach to exchange rate determination. More significantly, it views the exchange rate as simply a relative asset price, of which expectations play an important part.

There are two core elements to the monetary approach: purchasing power parity, and interest rate parity. Absolute purchasing power parity (PPP) asserts that the exchange rate is the ratio of the domestic price level to that of the foreign price level, often explained in terms of the *law of one price*. Utilizing the 'law', $P = SP^*$, where P is the domestic price level, P^* the foreign price level and S the price of foreign currency per unit of domestic currency. It follows, therefore, that $S = P/P^*$. The model assumes perfectly flexible prices at home and abroad. Relative PPP considers only percentage changes. If $\hat{S}$ denotes the percentage change in the exchange rate and π and π^* denote the percentage change in prices (inflation) at home and abroad, then $\hat{S} = \pi - \pi^*$. In the naïve monetarist model of exchange rate determination, real money demand (equal to money supply) is determined by real income (held constant at the natural level). Utilizing the quantity theory of money, $M = kPy_n$, where M denotes nominal money balances, k the reciprocal of the income velocity of circulation of money and y_n the natural level of income – assumed constant in the long run. Exactly the same relationship is assumed to hold abroad, with the same terms, except with an asterisk. Taking percentage changes and substituting into the relative PPP, we derive the expression $\hat{S} = \hat{M} - \hat{M}^*$. The *long-run* explanation of the exchange rate, therefore, is the differential growth rates of money in the two countries. If the growth of the domestic money supply exceeds that abroad, then the domestic currency is depreciating (S is rising). This is a naïve long-run explanation.

Of course, the demand for money in each country is inversely related to the nominal rate of interest. Let i and i^* denote nominal interest rates at home and abroad, respectively. In a world of capital mobility, investors can choose where to invest their funds. Investing at home will lead to a return of $(1+i)$, while investing abroad will lead to an expected return in domestic currency of $(S^e/S)(1+i^*)$, where S^e denotes the expected exchange rate. Uncovered interest rate parity asserts that funds will flow until these are equalized. If $\hat{S}^e = (S^e - S)/S$, then this condition approximates to $\hat{S}^e = i - i^*$.

The monetarist model incorporating interest rate parity is modelled in terms of logarithms. Hence the demand for money (equal to the supply of money) at home is $m = p + \eta y - \sigma i$. Abroad, we have a similar relationship, namely $m^* = p^* + \eta y^* - \sigma i^*$, where for simplicity we assume the coefficients of income and interest rates at home and abroad are identical. Utilizing absolute PPP, then in logarithms (and using lower-case letters to denote the logarithms), then $s = p - p^*$ holds continuously. Substituting the demand for money equations into this gives an expression for the exchange rate. Since monetarists also believe domestic and foreign bonds are perfect substitutes, uncovered interest parity holds. In this monetarist model, therefore, we have two results:

$$s = (m - m^*) - \eta(y - y^*) + \sigma(i - i^*),$$

$$s^e = i - i^*.$$

Additional expectations can be included in monetarist models if real interest rates are considered. The real interest rate, r, is equal to $r = i - \pi^e$, and abroad $r^* = i^* - \pi^{e*}$ Assuming, as monetarists do, that real interest rates are equalized in the two countries, then

$$s = (m - m^*) - \eta(y - y^*) + \sigma(\pi^e - \pi^{e*}),$$

$$s^e = \pi^e - \pi^{e*}.$$

What these results direct attention to is that countries with high money growth tend to have high rates of expected inflation, leading to an actual depreciation of the domestic currency and an expected depreciation also. These influences can be partially offset by high-income growth at home relative to that abroad.

A small-country monetarist model of exchange rate determination is that provided by Dornbusch (1976). This has been a fairly influential model because of its emphasis on price stickiness and overshooting of exchange rates. Its most essential feature, besides being monetarist in conception, is that of asymmetric adjustment in the goods and asset markets. Goods markets adjust slowly while asset markets adjust quickly. It is this characteristic which leads to an explanation of exchange rate overshooting. (In the presence of imperfect capital mobility, there can arise undershooting.) An essential assumption of this model too is that absolute PPP holds in long-run equilibrium. Frankel (1979) provides a general monetarist model that includes the flexible price model outlined above and as a special case the sticky-price model of Dornbusch. There has also been some empirical testing of the various monetary models of exchange rate determination, such as Bilson (1978), Choudhry and Lawler (1997) and Abbot and De Vita (2001). Different monetarist theories give different predictions about the way exogenous variables influence the exchange rate. Regression results are generally poor, with exogenous variables being insignificant or even having the opposite sign from what theory predicts. Monetarist models of exchange rate determination are not alone in this. It suggests that exchange rates depend on a complex set of factors and not just on monetary stance, and that predicting exchange rate movements is very difficult.

RON SHONE

See also:

Balance of Payments: Monetary Approach; Fixed Exchange Rate System; Floating Exchange Rate System; Monetarism; Purchasing Power Parity Theory.

Bibliography

Abbot, A.J. and G. De Vita (2001), 'A Reassessment of the Long-run Validity of the Flexible Price Monetary Exchange Rate Model', *Economic Issues*, **6**, March, pp. 47–57.

Bilson, J.F.O. (1978), 'The Monetary Approach to the Exchange Rate: Some Empirical Evidence', *IMF Staff Papers*, **25**, March, pp. 48–75.

Bilson, J.F.O. (1979), 'Recent Developments in Monetary Models of Exchange Rate Determination', *IMF Staff Papers*, **26**, June, pp. 201–23.

Choudhry, T. and P. Lawler (1997), 'The Monetary Model of Exchange Rates: Evidence from the Canadian Float of the 1950s', *Journal of Macroeconomics*, **19**, Spring, pp. 349–62.

Dornbusch, R. (1976), 'Expectations and Exchange Rate Dynamics', *Journal of Political Economy*, **84**, December, pp. 1161–76.

Dornbusch, R. (1990), 'Real Exchange Rates and Macroeconomics: A Selective Survey', in S. Honkapohja (ed.), *The State of Macroeconomics*, Oxford: Basil Blackwell.

Frankel, J.A. (1979), 'On the Mark: A Theory of Floating Exchange Rates Based on Real Interest Differentials', *American Economic Review*, **69**, September, pp. 610–22.

MacDonald, R. and M.P. Taylor (1989), 'Economic Analysis of Foreign Exchange Markets: An Expository Survey', in R. MacDonald and M.P. Taylor (eds), *Exchange Rates and Open Economy Macroeconomics*, Oxford: Basil Blackwell.

Exchange Rate Mechanism

A central element of the European Monetary System (EMS), the exchange rate mechanism (ERM) required full members of the EMS to maintain their exchange rates within specified bands around an agreed central rate for member currencies and the European Currency Unit (ECU). The ERM was subsumed by the creation of the Euro in January 1999, when 11 out of the 15 European Union (EU) countries irrevocably fixed the parity of their currencies to the Euro.

See also:
Euro; European Monetary System; European Union.

Exogenous Variable

A variable, that is not explained within a particular model; its value is taken as given.

Expansionary Phase

The period in the business cycle between a trough or lower turning point and a successive peak or upper turning point.

See also:
Business Cycle; Peak; Trough.

Expectations-augmented Phillips Curve

The natural-rate expectations-augmented Phillips curve, developed by Milton Friedman (1966, 1968) and Edmund Phelps (1967, 1968, 1970), became the dominant framework of macroeconomic analysis as a result of the monetarist counter-revolution. It undermined the policy of using macroeconomic stimulation to close the 'Okun Gap' (between actual and potential output) and of using price and wage guidelines, or controls, to eliminate any inflationary pressure that might emerge in the process. Friedman (1968, p. 8), who opposed wage and price controls, argued that inflationary expectations placed a binding constraint on the ability of policy makers to choose a combination of Phillips curve inflation–unemployment outcomes at any position other than the natural rate of unemployment. The natural-rate expectations-augmented Phillips curve thus contributed to the process by which Keynesianism (and faith in government intervention) was replaced by monetarism (and faith in market outcomes).

The model can be described using the $ diagram (Figure 1), with the upper half representing inflationary macroeconomic policy and the lower

half representing disinflationary macroeconomic policy. The original theoretical Phillips curve described the relationship between the rate of change
of prices and the level of production; the original empirical Phillips curve
documented the historical process by which wage inflation fluctuated
during the pendulum swings of the business cycle (Phillips, 2000 [1954],
p. 151, Fig. 16.11; [1958], p. 245, Fig. 25. 1). One interpretation of Phillips's
sophisticated analysis appeared to imply that the locus BAD offered a sustainable menu of policy choice. The pursuit of high levels of economic
activity might push the economy towards point *B*, but the associated pressure on the price level and the exchange rate would require continued
government monitoring and intervention.

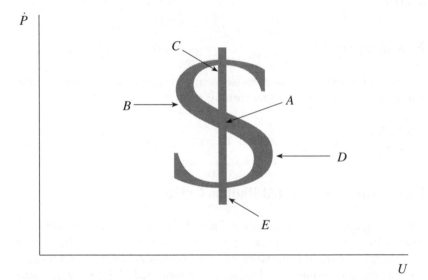

Figure 1

However, in several countries policy makers were exhausted by the per-
ennial problems of avoiding devaluation and preserving wage and price
guidelines. To these problems Friedman added another. Using neoclassical price theory he argued that *BAD* was one of a family of short-run
Phillips curves (along which inflationary expectations were constant). The
economy was in disequilibrium at all points along *BAD* other than *A*
(where inflationary expectations were equal to actual inflation). Using
macroeconomic stimulation to reduce unemployment below the natural
rate would generate expectational disequilibrium. As agents realized that
actual inflation was greater than expected inflation they would alter their
labour supply behaviour and the economy would return to equilibrium at

the natural rate. As inflationary expectations were corrected the short-run Phillips Curve would shift upwards and the economy would trace out the points *BC*. While policy makers were attempting (in Phillips curve space) to pull the economy downwards (to achieve lower inflationary outcomes for a given rate of unemployment) Friedman described the gravitational forces which were pushing the economy in the opposite direction. Unemployment, therefore, could not be permanently reduced through macroeconomic stimulation: the natural rate of unemployment (points *E*, *A* or *C*) was the best that could be achieved in the long run. To reduce the natural rate required microeconomic reform, not macroeconomic stimulation.

Measured unemployment (*U*) became, by definition, identically equal to the natural rate of unemployment (U^N), plus any unnatural increment (U^{UN}). This unnatural component of unemployment was perceived to be a function of a delusion variable: the discrepancy between actual inflation ($\dot{P}$) and expected inflation ($\dot{P}^e$). Unemployment would return to its natural level as soon as this delusion was overcome, and wage contracts ceased to be based on unrealistic calculations of future inflation. Formally:

$$U = U^N + U^{UN}, \text{ and } U^{UN} = f[\forall(\dot{P}^e - \dot{P})],$$

where $\forall$ = the speed of adjustment of incorrect inflationary expectations, often measured using the adaptive expectations formula popularized by Philip Cagan (1956) and Mark Nerlove (1958).

From the late 1960s, Friedman's theoretical gravitational forces became empirically observable. Western economies began to shift from *B* to *C*: inflation and unemployment increased simultaneously (stagflation). Since predictive success was the judge and jury of Friedman's (1953) methodology of positive economics this gave his macroeconomic model a large degree of scientific respectability. As a consequence, monetarist economists recommended a disinflation strategy designed to push the economy out from *A* to *D* in the hope that the model was symmetric and that the equilibrating forces of dissipating expectational delusion would take the economy rapidly from *D* to *E*.

In both the United States and the United Kingdom the journey from *A* to *D* was rapid. In the USA the journey from *D* to *E* was also quite rapid (beginning in late 1982). But since this experience was complicated by the simultaneous macroeconomic stimulation caused by the large government deficits of the 1980s, it is difficult to infer that the USA provided compelling evidence about the symmetry of the natural rate model. In the UK, point *D* was much further out than anticipated and the journey from *D* to *E* more prolonged than expected.

Economists increasingly questioned the symmetry assertion: the 'hysteresis' argument suggested that U^N might be gravitationally attracted to U, rather than the other way round. The economy's stock of human and physical capital clearly deteriorates as factories close and unemployment increases (A to D). Since this capital stock presumably underpins the quantity of the natural rate of output it is possible that the natural rate (the vertical line CAE) shifts outwards towards D in addition to (or instead of) the actual rate of unemployment shifting inwards towards a fixed natural rate.

Three further aspects of this intellectual counter-revolution deserve mention. First, Phillips's (2000 [1954], pp.153–6) original curve did not need to be augmented by expectations since expectations were one of the forces driving his system. The final and most crucial sub-sections of the theoretical Phillips curve were 'Inherent Regulations of the System' and 'Stabilization of the System': 'Some examples will be given below to illustrate the stability of this system under different conditions of price flexibility *and with different expectations concerning future price changes*' (emphasis added). The theoretical Phillips curve was then tested against a variety of scenarios, inflationary expectations being a crucial factor in determining whether the system has satisfactory outcomes or not:

> Demand is also likely to be influenced by the rate at which prices are changing, or have been changing in the recent past, as distinct from the amount by which they have changed, this influence on demand being greater, the greater the rate of change of prices . . . The direction of this change in demand will depend on expectations about future price. If changing prices induce expectations of further changes in the same direction, as will probably be the case after fairly rapid and prolonged movements, demand will change in the same direction as the changing prices . . . there will be a positive feed-back tending to intensify the error, the response of demand to changing prices thus acting as a perverse or destabilising mechanism of the proportional type.

Secondly, the natural rate model was an assault on the high-inflation Phillips curve. But Phillips argued that 'One of the important policy problems of our time is that of maintaining a high level of economic activity and employment *while avoiding a continual rise in prices*' (emphasis added). Phillips explained that there was 'fairly general agreement' that the prevailing rate of 3.7 per cent inflation was 'undesirable. It has undoubtedly been a major cause of the general weakness of the balance of payments and the foreign reserves, and if continued it would almost certainly make the present rate of exchange untenable'. Phillips did not devote much attention to 'unthinkable' levels of unemployment or 'undesirable' rates of inflation; he stated that he was only 'interested' in the low-inflation 'compromise solution' where the trade-off operated (2000 [1959], p.261; [1962], p.208; [1961], p.201; [1962], p.218; [1958], p.259).

Inflation had more serious consequences in Phillips's analysis than in Friedman's. For Friedman, the purely internal imbalance corrected itself through utility-maximizing labour supply adjustments, as inflation ceased to be incorrectly anticipated. Only a temporary boom would result, and would soon be eroded by real wage resistance. But in Phillips's model, external imbalance (driven by only minor inflation differentials) could be addressed by exchange rate adjustment, but the internal imbalance (an adverse inflation differential) would be in need of still greater attention after devaluation. In addition, the role Friedman allocated to inflationary expectation was benign, whereas for Phillips (2000 [1954], pp. 153–5) inflationary expectations were destabilizing, which denied the possibility of a stable target in the presence of such expectations. For Phillips the expectation of further inflation

> tend[s] to introduce fluctuations . . . The strength of the integral regulating mechanisms increases with the increasing degree of price flexibility, while the total strength of the proportional regulating mechanisms decreases as demand responds perversely to the more rapid rate of change of prices, and both these effects tend to introduce fluctuations when price flexibility is increased beyond a certain point. When price expectations operate in this way, therefore, the system . . . becomes unstable.

The third noteworthy aspect of this episode of intellectual and policy counter-revolution is that leading Chicago economists had despaired of the project of modelling an empirically valid expectations variable with a reliable empirical counterpart (Stigler, 1941, pp. 358–9; Friedman, 1953 [1946], pp. 277–300). In the 1950s, Phillips's contribution to the analysis of inflationary expectations was common knowledge (see, for example, Phelps Brown and Weber, 1953, p. 279). In May 1952, during a visit to the London School of Economics, Friedman asked Phillips 'how to approximate expectations about future inflation' (cited by Leeson, 1997). Phillips then wrote down the adaptive inflationary expectations equation, which via Cagan (1956) transformed the general analysis of inflation, and which, via Friedman, transformed high-inflation Phillips curve analysis. Thus what Cagan (2000) calls 'Phillips's Adaptive Expectations Formula' was used to undermine a somewhat crude version of Phillips's original curve.

ROBERT LEESON

See also:

Adaptive Expectations; Hysteresis; Inflation: Costs of Reducing; Keynesian Economics; Monetarism; Natural Rate of Unemployment; Phillips Curve.

Bibliography
Cagan, P. (1956), 'The Monetary Dynamics of Hyperinflation', in M. Friedman (ed), *Studies in the Quantity Theory of Money*, Chicago: University of Chicago Press.
Cagan, P. (2000), 'Phillips' Adaptive Expectations Formula', in R. Leeson (ed.), *A.W.H. Phillips: Collected Works in Contemporary Perspective*, Cambridge: Cambridge University Press.
Friedman, M. (1953), *Essays in Positive Economics*, Chicago: University of Chicago Press.
Friedman, M (ed) (1956), *Studies in the Quantity Theory of Money*, Chicago: University of Chicago Press.
Friedman, M. (1966), 'Comments', in G. Shultz and R.Z. Aliber (eds), *Guidelines, Informal Controls and the Market Place*, Chicago: University of Chicago Press.
Friedman, M. (1968), 'The Role of Monetary Policy', *American Economic Review*, **58**, March, pp.1–17.
Leeson, R. (1997), 'The Trade-Off Interpretation of Phillips' Dynamic Stabilization Exercise', *Economica*, **65**, February, pp.155–73.
Nerlove, M. (1958), 'Adaptive Expectations and the Cobweb Phenomena', *Quarterly Journal of Economics*, **72**, May, pp.227–40.
Phelps, E.S. (1967), 'Phillips Curves, Expectations of Inflation and Optimal Unemployment over Time', *Economica*, **XXXIV**, August, pp.254–81.
Phelps, E.S. (1968), 'Money Wage Dynamics and Labour Market Equilibrium', *Journal of Political Economy*, **76**, July-August, pp.638–711.
Phelps, E.S. (ed) (1970), *Microeconomic Foundations of Employment and Inflation Theory*, London: Norton.
Phelps Brown, E.H. and B. Weber (1953), 'Accumulation, Productivity and Distribution in the British Economy 1870–1938', *Economic Journal*, **63**, June, pp.263–88.
Phillips, A.W.H. (2000), *A.W.H. Phillips: Collected Works in Contemporary Perspective*, (ed.) R. Leeson, Cambridge: Cambridge University Press.
Shultz, G. and R.Z. Aliber (eds) (1966), *Guidelines, Informal Controls, and the Market Place*, Chicago: University of Chicago Press.
Stigler, G. (1941), 'Review of Hart's *Anticipations, Uncertainty and Dynamic Planning*', *American Economic Review*, **31**, June, pp.358–9.

Expenditure Reducing Policy

Expenditure reducing policy – a term coined by Harry Johnson (Johnson, 1961) – refers to an attempt by the authorities to damp down the level of aggregate demand in an economy in order to effect an improvement in the balance of payments on current account.

Expenditure reducing policy should only be necessary in the presence of a *fixed* or managed exchange rate. In theory, as Friedman (1953) has argued, a *flexible* exchange rate provides for the automatic adjustment of the balance of payments. When the exchange rate is market-determined, any emergent deficit (surplus), because it is associated with an excess supply (excess demand) of the domestic currency on the foreign exchange market, will be quickly and painlessly corrected by an appropriate currency depreciation (appreciation). Thus, in a flexible exchange rate environment the balance of payments 'disappears' as a potential policy problem.

But why, in a fixed or managed exchange rate environment, is the balance of payments on current account a matter that requires a policy response from the authorities? A current account deficit entails a net monetary liability on the part of domestic residents with the rest of the world. Note that this liability is expressed in foreign currencies. A deficit country is – in general terms – importing more than it is exporting, and therefore its foreign currency income from exports is insufficient to meet its foreign currency expenditure on imports. A deficit country's net monetary liability can be discharged or financed (the conventional term) in one of two ways. Either it can draw on the reserves of foreign currencies held by its central bank, or it can borrow the foreign currencies it needs from abroad. The difficulty the deficit country must face is that neither of these financing possibilities can be continued indefinitely. Unless replenished, the central bank's reserves of foreign currency will run out; and the patience of lenders will at some stage be exhausted by an economy that is seemingly content to pile up indebtedness to fuel current consumption. The implication is that a *persistent* current account deficit must eventually prompt some kind of policy response by the authorities.

Expenditure reduction policy is one such response. Using contractionary fiscal or monetary policy or both, the authorities can reduce the rate of growth of the domestic economy which in turn should effect a reduction in the demand for imported goods and services. Because the demand for exports is largely unaffected by expenditure reduction policy, the balance of payments on current account should improve. Export demand is determined by factors such as foreign incomes and the relative prices of domestic and foreign goods and services. It is worth noting that, although foreign incomes will not be influenced by expenditure reduction policy, the relative prices of domestic and foreign goods and services may be, but in a way that reinforces the positive effect of expenditure reduction on the current account. Insofar as expenditure reduction moderates the domestic rate of inflation it will also improve the international price competitiveness of exports and import substitutes and provide a secondary fillip to current account recovery.

However, while expenditure reduction may be used to confront persistent external deficits, the policy is not costless: it has unwelcome implications for output and employment in the domestic economy. To put it crudely, expenditure reduction means sacrificing certain internal objectives of macroeconomic policy for an external one. The reduction in aggregate demand implied by contractionary fiscal and/or monetary policy will almost inevitably translate into lost output and higher unemployment.

This tension between an external policy objective and internal objectives is revealing in that it indicates a broader construction that may be placed upon the balance of payments. The objective of policy in respect of the balance of payments on current account is *balance*. Deficit is a problem for reasons already outlined, but surplus too may be considered regrettable if, for example, it is achieved simply by running the domestic economy at a consistently low pressure of demand. Here, surplus would hardly be any kind of achievement – it would simply be the external reflection of the stagnation of the domestic economy under the strictures of expenditure reduction. For completeness we may also note that current account surpluses arising from dynamic export performance – rather than internal deflation – may also be undesirable. Surplus is necessarily associated with an excess of foreign currency earnings over foreign currency expenditure and therefore represents a missed opportunity for consumption. At the same time, because, in balance of payments terms, the world economy is a zero sum game – one country's surplus is another's deficit – current account imbalances may give rise to the spread of protectionist sentiment with attendant negative implications for the prospects for world trade and growth.

Although correcting current account deficit is the explicit target of expenditure reduction policy, in the event of persistent current account surplus that the authorities wish to adjust the policy may be reversed to useful effect. Because it raises the level of aggregate demand, expansionary fiscal and/or monetary policy will increase the domestic demand for imports and erode the surplus. Again, however, there may be an internal cost associated with this externally oriented expenditure *changing* policy. If the domestic economy is operating at or near full employment, an expansionary fiscal and/or monetary stance is likely to be associated with a higher domestic inflation rate.

An early overview of the *range* of tensions between external and internal balance was provided by Meade (1951). Meade's conclusion was that, in the 'major' countries at least, the authorities must operate domestic policies for internal balance. This was necessary to prevent significant deflations in the international economy which themselves might promote cumulative balance of payments problems if affected countries responded with inappropriate policies such as direct controls on trade. An implication of Meade's work was that the simultaneous achievement of the twin objectives of external and internal balance actually required the implementation of two distinct policies; there are limits to what expenditure reduction policy can achieve on its own.

CHRIS MULHEARN

See also:

Balance of Payments; Expenditure Switching Policy; Fixed Exchange Rate System; Flexible Exchange Rate System.

Bibliography

Friedman, M. (1953), 'The Case for Flexible Exchange Rates', *Essays in Positive Economics*, Chicago: University of Chicago Press.

Johnson, H. (1961), *International Trade and Economic Growth: Studies in Pure Theory*, Cambridge, MA: Harvard University Press.

Meade, J.E. (1951), *The Theory of International Economic Policy, Vol. 1, The Balance of Payments*, Oxford: Oxford University Press.

Expenditure Switching Policy

Expenditure switching policy – a term credited to Harry Johnson (Johnson, 1961) – refers to attempts by the authorities to redirect domestic and/or foreign expenditure towards the exports and/or import substitutes of the domestic economy and away from goods and services produced by competitor economies. The ultimate purpose of expenditure switching policy is to improve the balance of payments on current account. Expenditure switching policy may be implemented in conduction with expenditure reducing policy when the economy is at or close to full employment.

Expenditure switching policy should only be necessary in the presence of a *fixed* or managed exchange rate. In theory, as Friedman (1953) has argued, a *flexible* exchange rate provides for the automatic adjustment of the balance of payments. When the exchange rate is market-determined, any emergent deficit (surplus), because it is associated with an excess supply (excess demand) of the domestic currency on the foreign exchange market, will be quickly and painlessly corrected by an appropriate currency depreciation (appreciation). Thus, in a flexible exchange rate environment, the balance of payments 'disappears' as a potential policy problem.

But why, in a fixed or managed exchange rate environment, is the balance of payments on current account a matter that requires a policy response from the authorities? A current account deficit entails a net monetary liability on the part of domestic residents with the rest of the world. Note that this liability is expressed in foreign currencies. A deficit country is – in general terms – importing more than it is exporting, and therefore its foreign currency income from exports is insufficient to meet its foreign currency expenditure on imports. A deficit country's net monetary liability can be discharged or financed (the conventional term) in one of two ways. Either it can draw on the reserves of foreign currencies held by its central bank, or it can borrow the foreign currencies it needs from abroad. The difficulty the deficit country must face is that neither of these financing possibilities can be continued indefinitely. Unless replenished, the central bank's reserves of foreign currency will run out; and the patience of lenders will at some stage be exhausted by an economy that is seemingly content to pile up indebtedness to fuel current consumption. The implication is that a *persistent* current account deficit must eventually prompt some kind of policy response by the authorities.

Expenditure switching policy is one such response. It can take a range of forms. Most obviously, *devaluation* of the domestic currency, because it reduces the foreign currency price of exports and raises the home currency price of imports, may prompt the redirection of domestic and foreign expenditure towards exports and import substitutes, thus improving the balance of trade, the major component of the current account. Other measures intended to promote the demand for exports and/or import substitutes may have similar expenditure switching effects. For example, forms of *protectionist trade policy*, such as the use of a tariff, will raise the price of an import and may encourage domestic demand to shift in favour of import substitutes. However, note that trade policy measures are not usually implemented for balance of payments reasons. Their common purpose tends to be to enhance the prospects of particular branches of domestic industry, perhaps in response to adverse shifts in comparative advantage, or perceptions of predatory trading practice by competitor nations, such as dumping. Moreover, the regulation of international trade by supranational bodies like the World Trade Organization (WTO) and the proliferation of open regional trading arrangements – for example, the North American Free Trade Agreement (NAFTA) – make the systematic use of trade policy as an instrument for external balance highly unlikely. A third and relatively minor form of expenditure switching policy may arise when the authorities simply seek to *exhort* domestic residents to purchase domestic goods and services rather than imports.

Because the interests of particular industries tend to be the main focus of trade policy, and government campaigns intended to promote domestic goods and services are not usually a major component of macroeconomic management, expenditure switching policy is most often taken to entail devaluation of the domestic currency. As noted above, devaluation provides a fillip to the current account because it lowers the foreign currency price of exports and increases the domestic currency price of imports. For devaluation to improve the trade balance two criteria must be satisfied. The first, known as the Marshall–Lerner condition, concerns the nature of price elasticity of demand for exports and imports. Clearly, if a devaluation is to be effective, the price changes it invokes must themselves have an impact in appropriate ways upon the demand for traded goods and services. The Marshall–Lerner condition states that the sum of the absolute values of the price elasticities of demand for exports and imports must be greater than unity. If the condition is fulfilled then the combined elasticities will be sufficiently high for demand to shift in the required way and the trade balance of the devaluing country will improve. The Marshall–Lerner condition was formalized by Lerner (1944) using Marshall's work on elasticity. The second criterion for an effective devaluation concerns the capacity of export and import-substituting industries in the domestic economy to respond to the new demands placed upon them. At best a devaluation will serve little purpose if the domestic economy is already operating close to full capacity and there is little or no scope for additional resources to be devoted to raising the output of exports or import substitutes. Thus for a devaluation to work the domestic economy must not be operating at full capacity.

It should be noted that, even where both of these criteria are satisfied, the current account may be likely to deteriorate at first before improving later. This eventuality is known as the 'J' curve effect. The initial worsening of the current account happens because, although devaluation shifts the prices of exports and import substitutes immediately, demand patterns usually take some time to adjust to the change in prices. This means that the same volume of exports is initially sold in foreign markets but at lower foreign currency prices, and an unchanged volume of imports is initially demanded in the domestic market at higher prices. The net effect – as overseas revenues from exports fall and payments overseas for imports increase – is to worsen the current account. Eventually, as demand adjusts to reflect the changes in foreign and domestic prices, the effect is reversed and the current account rebounds past its starting position at the time of the devaluation. The 'J' curve is so called because the path of the current account balance resembles the letter J.

Let us reflect a little further on the criterion that there should be spare capacity in the domestic economy if devaluation is to improve the current account. Prior to the period of full employment which began after 1945, this was not a serious consideration for policy makers. The general absence of full employment conditions meant that the effect of currency devaluations upon the external balances of devaluing nations would not be impeded by capacity constraints. However, in the 1950s and 1960s, when full employment conditions became widespread, devaluation was much more likely to be compromised as an effective policy instrument. An insight into balance of payments policy in these circumstances was provided by Alexander (1952) in his *absorption approach* to the balance of payments.

Alexander's analysis proceeded from the simple equation for the current balance:

$$B = Y - A, \tag{1}$$

where B is the current balance, Y is national income or output and A is total expenditure or absorption. From equation (1) it can be seen that any deficit on *B* arises from an excess of total expenditure over domestic output. One way in which *B* might be restored to balance involves increasing *Y* relative to *A* using devaluation. There are a number of possible difficulties with this option, most obviously the question of what effect the devaluation has on absorption, both directly and indirectly through changes in income. If increases in income are matched or outweighed by increases in absorption, the current balance stays the same or worsens. Moreover, the case against using devaluation *on its own* is clearly strengthened at full employment when *Y* cannot increase by definition. It is possible that absorption might be dampened directly by devaluation, through, for example, the impact of rising prices on consumption in the light of a real balance effect; but the major implication of Alexander's work, as highlighted by Johnson (1961), is that, at or near conditions of full employment, expenditure switching policy (devaluation) needs to be accompanied by expenditure reducing policy if the current balance is to be improved. Expenditure reducing policy creates the 'room' for the devaluation to work by making available resources to be allocated to export and import substituting industries. In terms of equation (1), expenditure reducing policy constrains absorption, while devaluation raises output, thus improving the current balance.

The reader is referred to Krugman and Obstfeld (2000) for further discussion of issues raised in this entry.

CHRIS MULHEARN

See also:

Absorption Approach to the Balance of Payments; Balance of Payments; Expenditure Reducing Policy; Fixed Exchange Rate System; Flexible Exchange Rate System; Marshall–Lerner Condition.

Bibliography

Alexander, S.S. (1952), 'The Effects of a Devaluation on a Trade Balance', in *IMF Staff Papers*, pp. 359–73.

Friedman, M. (1953), 'The Case for Flexible Exchange Rates', *Essays in Positive Economics*, Chicago: University of Chicago Press.

Johnson, H. (1961), *International Trade and Economic Growth: Studies in Pure Theory*, Cambridge, MA: Harvard University Press.

Krugman, P.R. and M. Obstfeld (2000), *International Economics: Theory and Policy*, 5th edn, Reading, MA: Addison-Wesley Longman.

Lerner, A.P. (1944), *The Economics of Control: Principles of Welfare Economics*, New York: Macmillan.

Federal Funds Rate

The interest rate charged on reserves lent by one bank to another. The rate is determined in the federal funds market where those banks with excess reserves lend them to banks with inadequate reserves.

Federal Open Market Committee

See:
Federal Reserve System.

Federal Reserve System

Established by Congress in 1913, the Federal Reserve System, or Fed as it is more frequently referred to, undertakes the functions of a central bank for the United States. Its present-day mandate, defined in the 1978 Humphrey–Hawkins Act of Congress, is to 'maintain long-run growth of the monetary and credit aggregates commensurate with the economy's long-run potential to increase production, so as to promote effectively the goals of maximum employment, stable prices, and moderate long-term interest rates'. In short, the Fed is charged with the responsibility of sta-bilizing output and keeping inflation low in the United States. The system is headed by the Federal Reserve Board of Governors, responsible for the design of monetary policy. The Board is also responsible (in conjunction with the US Treasury) for US exchange rate policy. The board, which is based in Washington, has seven governors, including the chair of the Fed. Appointed by the US president, with Senate approval, governors serve for a non-renewable term of 14 years, while the chair serves for a renewable term of four years. The board oversees the operations of 12 Federal Reserve District Banks whose principal functions are to supervise banking and financial activities within their Districts and manage cheque clearing. The Federal Open Market Committee (FOMC), which is also based in Washington, has 12 voting members comprising seven board governors plus five of the presidents of the Federal Reserve District Banks (voting responsibilities on the FOMC among the other presidents are rotated). The chair of the Federal Reserve Board of Governors (cur-rently Alan Greenspan) serves as chair of the FOMC and the president of the Federal Reserve Bank of New York serves as vice-chair. The FOMC meets regularly (about every six weeks) to discuss and set mone-tary policy. The main instrument of monetary policy in the United States is open market operations. Through its open market operations, in which it buys and sells government bonds, the Fed is able to change the stance of monetary policy.

See also:

Central Bank Accountability and Transparency; Central Bank Independence; Greenspan, Alan; Inflation Targeting; Monetary Policy: Role of.

Feedback Rule

See:

Activist Policy Rule.

Feldstein, Martin

Martin Feldstein (b.1939, New York City, New York, USA) obtained his BA from Harvard University in 1961 and his BLitt (1963), MA (1964) and DPhil (1967) from Oxford University. His main past posts have included Fellow at Nuffield College, Oxford, 1965–7. Since 1967, he has been Professor of Economics at Harvard University and he has also been president, since 1977, of the National Bureau of Economic Research. In 1977 he was awarded the John Bates Clark Medal of the American Economic Association. Between 1982 and 1984 he was chairman of the US President's Council of Economic Advisers. He is best known for his work on various aspects of public sector economics, in particular the effects of tax, transfer and spending programmes on private sector capital formation and employment. Among his best known books are *The Effects of Taxation on Capital Accumulation* (University of Chicago Press, 1987); *Taxes and Capital Formation* (University of Chicago Press, 1987); and *The Costs and Benefits of Price Stability* (ed.) (University of Chicago Press, 1999). His most widely read articles include 'Supply-Side Economics: Old Truths and New Claims' (*American Economic Review*, **76**, May 1986); 'The Council of Economic Advisers and Economic Advising in the United States' (*Economic Journal*, **102**, September 1992); and 'The Political Economy of the European Economic and Monetary Union: Political Sources of an Economic Liability' (*Journal of Economic Perspectives*, **11**, Fall 1997).

See also:

Council of Economic Advisers; John Bates Clark Medal; National Bureau of Economic Research.

Financial Instability

Economists have long been concerned with the economic fluctuations that occur more or less regularly in all capitalist economies (Sherman, 1991; Wolfson, 1994). To be sure, there are different kinds of economic fluctuations, ranging from the Kitchin cycle (tied to inventory swings and lasting on average 39 months) to the Juglar cycle (lasting about seven or eight years and linked to investment in plant and equipment) to the Kuznets cycle of 20 years (associated with demographic changes) and finally to the Kondratieff long-wave cycles attributed to major innovations (electrification, the motor car) (Kindleberger, 1989). Financial factors might play only a small role in some of these fluctuations. Generally, economists studying financial instability have tended to focus on periodic financial crises that frequently coincide with the peak of the common business cycle, although financial crises (especially in recent years) can occur at other times during the cycle. Furthermore, an economy might be financially unstable but manage to avoid a financial crisis. It is best to think of financial instability as a tendency rather than as a specific event, although the typical financial crisis might be the result of unstable financial processes generated over the course of a business cycle expansion. In this entry, we will be concerned primarily with economic instability that has at its roots a financial cause, with less interest in either economic fluctuation that is largely independent of finance or in isolated financial crises that do not spill over to the economy as a whole.

A variety of explanations of the causes of financial instability have been offered. One possible cause could be a speculative 'mania' in which a large number of investors develop unrealistic expectations of profits to be made, borrowing heavily to finance purchases of assets and driving their prices to absurd levels. Eventually, the mania ends, prices collapse and bankruptcies follow (Kindleberger, 1989). The tulip mania of 1634, the South Sea bubble in 1719, or the Dot-com boom of the late 1990s might be cited as examples of speculative manias. Speculative booms often develop, and are fuelled by, fraudulent schemes. Recent examples of financial crises in which fraud played a large role include the collapse of the Albanian national pension system (1990s), as well as the American Savings and Loan fiasco (1980s) (Mayer, 1990).

Other explanations have tended to focus on a sudden interruption of the supply of money or credit that prevents borrowing and forces spending to decline, precipitating a cyclical downturn. The modern monetarist approach attributes financial instability and crises to policy errors by central banks. According to monetarist doctrine, when the central bank supplies too many reserves, the money supply expands too quickly, fuelling a spending boom. If the central bank then overreacts to the inflation this is believed to generate, it reduces the money supply and causes spending to collapse (Friedman, 1982). Others advance a 'credit crunch' thesis according to which lenders (mostly banks) suddenly reduce the supply of loans to borrowers, either because the lenders reach some sort of institutional constraint or because the central bank adopts restrictive monetary policy (as in the monetarist story) (Wojnilower, 1980; Wolfson, 1994). Finally, one could add exchange rate instability and foreign indebtedness as a precipitating cause of economic instability, especially in developing nations since the break-up of the Bretton Woods system (Huerta, 1998).

Other analyses have identified processes inherent to the operation of capitalist economies (Magdoff and Sweezy, 1987). In other words, rather than looking to fundamentally irrational manias or to 'exogenous shocks' emanating from monetary authorities, these approaches attribute causation to internal or endogenous factors. Karl Marx had claimed that the 'anarchy of production', that is an inevitable characteristic of an unplanned economy in which decisions are made by numerous individuals in pursuit of profit is subject to 'disproportionalities' of production such that some of the produced goods cannot be sold at a price high enough to realize expected profits. Key to his explanation was the recognition that production always begins with money, some of which is borrowed, used to purchase labour and the instruments of production in order to produce commodities for sale. If, however, some of the commodities cannot be sold at a sufficiently high price, loans cannot be repaid and bankruptcies occur. Creditors then may also be forced into bankruptcy when their debtors default because the creditors, themselves, will have outstanding debts they cannot service. In this way, a snowball of defaults spreads throughout the economy generating a panic as holders of financial assets begin to worry about the soundness of their investments. Rather than waiting for debtors to default, holders of financial assets attempt to 'liquidate' (sell) assets to obtain cash and other safer assets. This high demand for 'liquidity' (cash and marketable assets expected to hold nominal value) causes prices of all less liquid assets to collapse, and at the same time generates reluctance to spend as all try to hoard money. Thus the financial crisis occurs in conjunction with a collapse of aggregate demand (Sherman, 1991; Marx, 1990, 1991, 1992).

Some of the elements of Marx's analysis were adopted by Irving Fisher in his 'debt deflation' theory of the Great Depression, as well as by John Maynard Keynes in his *General Theory*. While Fisher devised a theory of special conditions in which markets would not be equilibrating, in Keynes's theory these were general conditions operating in monetary economies. Briefly, Fisher attributed the severity of the Great Depression to the collapse of asset prices and the ensuing financial crisis that resulted from an avalanche of defaults (Fisher, 1933; also Galbraith, 1972). Adopting Marx's notion that capitalist production begins with money on the expectation of ending with more money later, Keynes developed a general theory of the determination of equilibrium output and employment that explicitly incorporated expectations (Keynes, 1964). He concluded that there are no automatic, self-righting forces operating in capitalist economies that would move them towards full employment of resources. Indeed, he described destabilizing 'whirlwinds' of optimism and pessimism, in striking contrast to the Smithian notion of an 'invisible hand' that would guide markets towards stable equilibrium. Also, like Marx, Keynes identified what he called the 'fetish' for liquidity as a primary destabilizing force that erects barriers to the achievement of full employment. Most relevantly, rising liquidity preference lowers the demand for capital assets, which leads to lower production of investment goods and thus falling income and employment through the multiplier effect.

Hyman Minsky, arguably the foremost twentieth-century theorist on the topic of financial instability, extended Keynes's analysis with two primary contributions (Minsky, 1975, 1986). First, Minsky developed what he labelled 'a financial theory of investment and an investment theory of the cycle', attempting to join the approaches of those who emphasized financial factors and those who emphasized real factors as causes of the cycle by noting that the two are joined in a firm's balance sheet (Papadimitriou and Wray, 1998). As in Keynes's approach, fluctuations of investment drive the business cycle. However, Minsky explicitly examined investment finance in a modern capitalist economy, arguing that each economic unit takes positions in assets (including, but not restricted to, real physical assets) that are expected to generate income flows by issuing liabilities that commit the unit to debt service payment flows.

Because the future income flows cannot be known with certainty (while the schedule of debt payments is more or less known), each economic unit operates with margins of safety, collateral, net worth and a portfolio of safe, liquid assets to be drawn upon if the future should turn out to be worse than expected. The margins of safety, in turn, are established by custom, experience and rough rules of thumb. If things go at least as well as expected, these margins of safety will prove in retrospect to have been larger than what was required, leading to revisions of operating rules. Thus a 'run of good times' in which income flows are more than ample to meet contracted payment commitments will lead to reductions of margins of safety. Minsky developed a classification scheme for balance sheet positions that adopted increasingly smaller margins of safety: hedge (expected income flows sufficient to meet principal and interest payments), speculative (near-term expected income flows only sufficient to pay interest) and Ponzi (expected income flows not even sufficient to pay interest, hence funds would have to be borrowed merely to pay interest).

This leads directly to Minsky's second contribution, the financial instability hypothesis. Over time, the economy naturally evolves from one with a 'robust' financial structure in which hedge positions dominate, towards, a 'fragile' financial structure dominated by speculative and even Ponzi positions. This transition occurs over the course of an expansion as increasingly risky positions are validated by the booming economy that renders the built-in margins of error superfluous – encouraging adoption of riskier positions. Eventually, either financing costs rise or income comes in below expectations, leading to defaults on payment commitments. As in the Marx–Fisher analyses, bankruptcies snowball through the economy. This reduces spending and raises planned margins of safety. The recession proceeds until balance sheets are 'simplified' through defaults and conservative financial practices that reduce debt leverage ratios.

Central to Minsky's exposition is his recognition that development of the 'big bank' (central bank) and the 'big government' (government spending large relative to GDP) helps to moderate cyclical fluctuation. The central bank helps to attenuate defaults and bankruptcies by acting as a lender of last resort; countercyclical budget deficits and surpluses help to stabilize income flows. The problem, according to Minsky, is that successful stabilization through the big bank and the big government creates moral hazard problems because economic units will build into their expectations the supposition that intervention will prevent 'it' (another Great Depression) from happening again. Thus, risk taking is rewarded and systemic fragility grows through time, increasing the frequency and severity of financial crises even as depression is avoided. While there may be no ultimate solution, Minsky believed that informed and evolving regulation and supervision of financial markets is a necessary complement to big bank and big government intervention. Like Keynes, Minsky dismissed the belief that reliance upon an invisible hand would eliminate financial instability; indeed, he was convinced that an unregulated, small government capitalist economy would be prone to great depressions and the sort of debt deflation process analysed by Irving Fisher.

L. RANDALL WRAY

See also:

Business Cycles: Keynesian Approach; Business Cycles: Marxian Approach; Business Cycles: Monetarist Approach; Great Depression; Minsky, Hyman P.; Speculative Bubbles.

Bibliography

Fisher, I. (1933), 'The Debt-Deflation Theory of Great Depressions', *Econometrica*, **1**, October, pp. 337–57.

Friedman, M. (1982), *Capitalism and Freedom*, Chicago and London: University of Chicago Press.

Galbraith, J.K. (1972), *The Great Crash*, Boston: Houghton-Mifflin.

Huerta, A. (1998), *La Globalizacion, Causa de la Crisis Asiatica Y Mexicana*, Mexico: Editorial Diana.

Keynes, J.M. (1964), *The General Theory of Employment, Interest, and Money*, New York and London: Harcourt Brace Jovanovich.

Kindleberger, C. (1989), *Manias, Panics and Crashes: A History of Financial Crises*, New York: Basic Books.

Magdoff, H. and P. Sweezy (1987), *Stagnation and the Financial Explosion*, New York: Monthly Review Press.

Marx, K. (1990), *Capital: Volume 1*, London: Penguin Classics.

Marx, K. (1991), *Capital: Volume 2*, London: Penguin Classics.

Marx, K. (1992), *Capital: Volume 3*, London: Penguin Classics.

Mayer, M. (1990), *The Greatest-Ever Bank Robbery: The Collapse of the Savings and Loan Industry*, New York: Charles Scribner's Sons.

Minsky, H. (1975), *John Maynard Keynes*, New York: Columbia University Press.

Minsky, H. (1986), *Stabilizing an Unstable Economy*, New Haven and London: Yale University Press.

Papadimitriou, D. and L.R. Wray (1998), 'The Economic Contributions of Hyman Minsky: Varieties of Capitalism and Institutional Reform', *Review of Political Economy*, **10**, pp. 199–225.

Sherman, H. (1991), *The Business Cycle: Growth and Crisis under Capitalism*, Princeton, NJ: Princeton University Press.

Wojnilower, A. (1980), 'The Central Role of Credit Crunches in Recent Financial History', *Brookings Papers on Economic Activity*, pp. 277–326.

Wolfson, M. (1994), *Financial Crises: Understanding the Postwar U.S. Experience*, Armonk, NY and London: M.E. Sharpe.

Fine Tuning

A term used to describe the frequent use of fiscal and monetary policy in an attempt to maintain output and employment at, or near, their full employment or natural levels.

See also:

Aggregate Demand Management; Discretionary Policy; Rough Tuning.

Fiscal Policy: Role of

In the early post-World War II era, fiscal policy was conceived largely in Keynesian terms. Changes in taxes and government spending were viewed primarily for their affects on aggregate demand. Abba Lerner (1951) perhaps best characterized this view with his notion of functional finance.

Governments should incur budget deficits, through increased spending or reduced taxation, until inflation emerges in the economy. 'Only tax to prevent inflation' was the dictum.

During the 1960s and early 1970s, the debate shifted to the relative efficacy of fiscal versus monetary policy in influencing the course of nominal income. This debate is nicely reviewed in Blinder and Solow (1974). In the early phases of the debate, proponents of monetary versus fiscal policy put forth a variety of single-equation econometric studies, which initially suggested that monetary policy was more potent than fiscal policy. However, the econometric issues, particularly the endogeneity of traditional measures of monetary and fiscal policy, raised severe questions about the usefulness of these studies.

Blinder and Solow (1974) also put forth a theoretical argument that debt-financed government expenditure needed to be stronger than monetary policy if the economy was stable. Their argument was that, as a consequence of debt-financed government expenditure, the stock of government debt would increase in the long run. Required debt service would thus also increase in the long run. If the budget was to be balanced in the long run, fiscal policy must increase nominal income to increase taxes sufficiently, not just to close the initial deficit caused by the increase in government expenditure, but also to service the increased government debt. Critics of this approach, however, questioned its reliance on the supposition of a long-run stability analysis not based on economic theory.

As a practical matter, by the mid-1970s discussions of fiscal policy in the United States were more affected by concerns about long-run deficit than by those about stabilization issues. Debates about the size and role of federal government made it difficult for major activist stabilization policies to emerge from the US Congress. Since monetary policy can be used for stabilization policy without engaging in these debates, monetary policy increasingly began to assume centre stage for stabilization policy, whereas long-run concerns became the focus of fiscal policy. The one exception was automatic stabilization through the tax system, which does not require explicit legislation.

In contrast to these discussions, most recent thinking on fiscal policy has taken a more neoclassical turn and uses models based on intertemporal maximizing behaviour. From a neoclassical point of view, the key issues can be decomposed into two parts. First, what are the effects of changes in government spending? Second, holding the path of government spending constant, what are the effects, if any, of changing the time path for taxes?

One of the first issues involved in analysing government spending is the extent to which it substitutes directly for private consumption. For example, if the government spends more money on swimming pools or health care, to what extent does the private sector reduce its purchases of these goods? David Aschauer (1985) provides some macroeconometric evidence on this point, finding that, for every dollar of government expenditure, there was a decrease in private consumption spending of approximately 30 cents.

The time path of government spending can also have important effects on the economy. Robert Barro (1989) provides a convenient treatment of this topic. To analyse this issue, consider a neoclassical growth model with a representative agent who maximizes discounted intertemporal utility. In the steady state of this model, the capital–labour ratio will be the level dictated by the modified golden rule. A permanent increase in government spending will reduce consumption by an equal amount and the capital stock will remain constant. However, a temporary increase in government spending will have a different effect. In order to smooth intertemporal consumption, the economy will initially decrease the stock of capital to prevent consumption from falling by the full amount of the increase in government spending. The economy will later reaccumulate capital in such a way as to maintain the consumption profile over time. Thus temporary and permanent changes in government spending will have different effects on the path of capital accumulation in an economy.

In intertemporal models of fiscal policy, the government faces an intertemporal budget constraint. That means that, holding spending constant, decreases in taxes today will mean increases in taxes tomorrow to satisfy the intertemporal budget constraint. Under a strong set of assumptions, including infinitely lived households (or dynasties) and lump-sum taxation, a change in taxation will have no effect on household consumption choices and no effects on capital accumulation. This result, known as Ricardian equivalence, implies that deficits *per se* do not matter. Since the government must balance its budget intertemporally, a deficit today must be met with a surplus tomorrow. In present value terms, the household's intertemporal budget constraint has not changed. A cut in taxes, therefore, will be saved in order to meet a higher tax bill in the future.

Critics of Ricardian equivalence have developed several rigorous models in which this result does not hold. Peter Diamond (1965) uses an overlapping generations model to demonstrate that government deficits do affect the path of capital accumulation. Olivier Blanchard (1985) develops a model in which agents face an exogenous and constant probability of death each period. They choose consumption and savings optimally, given their economic environment. A temporary tax cut to be financed by higher taxes in later periods will result in increased consumption because, in consideration of their own mortality, rational agents will partially discount future taxes. Blanchard's model reduces to a pure neoclassical model, exhibiting Ricardian equivalence, when the probability of death reaches zero.

Several other objections have also been raised against Ricardian equivalence. Both myopia and liquidity constraints can overturn Ricardian equivalence in standard models. It can also fail in models in which taxes are not lump-sum. Actually testing for Ricardian equivalence is quite difficult. Most changes in taxation occur for a reason – either to meet changes in spending or as the result of underlying changes in the economy. Thus successful tests must control for these factors and pose challenging econometric problems.

If Ricardian equivalence does not hold then deficits will impose costs on an economy. Using a life-cycle model, Franco Modigliani (1961) showed that government bonds held in the portfolio of savers will displace private capital. Thus the cost of deficits is ultimately a lower capital stock in the future.

The burden of debt can also vary by generation and is not necessarily reflected in traditional measures. Auerbach *et al.* (1993) emphasize that the true burden of the debt may not be measured by the current fiscal deficit. Promises of higher social insurance benefits for the elderly have similar effects as current deficits, but do not show up anywhere in traditional fiscal accounting. These authors develop a new approach to measuring the stance of fiscal policy – generational accounting – which explicitly calculates these transfers and measures their burden over different generations.

The intertemporal approach to fiscal policy also has implications for monetary policy and inflation. A government's intertemporal budget constraint can be satisfied either through taxation or through seigniorage from money creation. If government do not raise taxes sufficiently to finance spending, they will have to resort to money creation and use the inflation tax to satisfy their budget constraint. In the extreme case, this could lead to hyperinflation. Sargent and Wallace (1981) show that, when the interest rate exceeds the growth rate of an economy, a policy of tight money today can lead to higher inflation in the future. The logic of their argument is that tight money today requires more debt issuance. With interest rates higher than the growth rate, the debt-to-GDP ratio will increase. Ultimately, there will be a need for increased seigniorage both to finance spending and to maintain the higher debt-to-GDP ratio. Higher seigniorage, however, requires higher inflation.

Economists have also studied various political economy aspects of fiscal policy. As examples, Alesina and Perotti (1995) provide a comprehensive overview of the political economy of government debt and deficits with a view to assessing the empirical import of different theories, while Alesina and Drazen (1991) use related political economy reasoning to explain why stabilization policies are often delayed. As a concrete example of this approach, some economists have theorized that ideological divisions and divided government can lead to larger fiscal deficits through political paralysis. Based in part, perhaps, on the experience in the United States in the 1980s, the work of other economists has explored the notion that large budget deficits can be used to constrain the spending of future governments. This can be important if there are likely to be changes in the political orientation of ruling parties. Hoover and Sheffrin (1992) examine the popular view that restricting the tax revenues available to politicians can control government spending. They show that traditional time-series methods, such as Granger-causality or timing evidence, cannot address this issue in an intertemporal perspective. They develop an approach that can address this issue, based on exogenous interventions in the time-series processes governing taxes and spending.

In the last decade there has been a resurgence of interest in the determinants of economic growth. Fiscal policy has figured prominently in this debate. Myles (2000) provides a review of the different channels through which fiscal policy can affect economic growth. While the theoretical models provide for a wide range of effects, the actual empirical evidence is not conclusive at the present time. This work on fiscal policy and economic growth is representative of modern work in fiscal policy that takes an intertemporal perspective to the issues.

STEVEN M. SHEFFRIN

See also:

Automatic Stabilizers; Functional Finance; Government Budget Constraint; Life Cycle Hypothesis; Neoclassical Growth Model; Representative Agent Model; Ricardian Equivalence.

Bibliography

Alesina, A. and A. Drazen (1991), 'Why Are Stabilizations Delayed?', *American Economic Review*, **82**, pp. 1170–88.
Alesina, A. and R. Perotti (1995), 'Political Economy of Budget Deficits', *International Monetary Fund Staff Papers*, **42**, pp. 1–31.
Aschauer, D.A. (1985), 'Fiscal Policy and Aggregate Demand', *American Economic Review*, **75**, March, pp. 117–27.
Auerbach, A.J., J. Gokhale and L.J. Kotlikoff (1993), 'Generational Accounts and Lifetime Tax Rates, 1900–1991', *Federal Reserve Bank of Cleveland Economic Review*, **29**, pp. 2–13.
Barro, R.J. (1989), 'Modern Business Cycle Theory', in R.J. Barro (ed.), *The Neoclassical Approach to Fiscal Policy*, Cambridge, MA: Harvard University Press, pp. 178–235.
Blanchard, O.J. (1985), 'Debt, Deficits and Finite Horizons', *Journal of Political Economy*, **93**, April, pp. 223–47.
Blinder, A.S. and R.M. Solow (1974), 'Analytical Foundations of Fiscal Policy', *The Economics of Public Finance*, Washington, DC: The Brookings Institution, pp. 3–115.
Diamond, P.A. (1965), 'National Debt in a Neoclassical Growth Model', *American Economic Review*, **55**, December, pp. 1126–50.

Hoover, K.D. and S.M. Sheffrin (1992), 'Causation, Spending and Taxes: Sand in the Sandbox or Tax Collector for the Welfare State?', *American Economic Review*, **82**, March, pp. 225–48.

Lerner, A.P. (1951), *Economics of Employment*, New York: McGraw-Hill.

Modigliani, F. (1961), 'Long-Run Implications of Alternative Fiscal Policies and the Burden of the National Debt', *Economic Journal*, **LXXI**, December, pp. 130–55.

Myles, G. (2000), 'Taxation and Economic Growth', *Fiscal Studies*, **21**, pp. 141–68.

Sargent, T.J. and N. Wallace (1981), 'Some Unpleasant Monetarist Arithmetic', *Federal Reserve Bank of Minneapolis Quarterly Review*, **5**, Fall, pp. 1–17.

Fischer, Stanley

Stanley Fischer (b.1943, Lusaka, Zambia) obtained his BSc (1965) and MSc (1966) from the London School of Economics and his PhD from Massachusetts Institute of Technology (MIT) in 1969. His main past posts have included Assistant Professor at the University of Chicago, 1969–73; Associate Professor at MIT, 1973–7; Visiting Scholar at the Hoover Institution, Stanford University, 1981–2; and Vice-President, Development Economics and Chief Economist at the World Bank, 1988–90. Since 1977, he has been Professor of Economics at MIT, and from September 1994 to August 2001 he was First Deputy Managing Director at the IMF. Between 1986 and 1994 he was the editor of the *NBER Macroeconomics Annual*. He is best known for his work on the role of policy in stabilizing the economy, in particular in terms of developing a macro model with rational expectations and price-stickiness; the effects of indexation of wages; and the effects and costs of inflation. Among his best known books are *Rational Expectations and Economic Policy* (ed.) (University of Chicago Press, 1980); *Indexing, Inflation and Economic Policy* (MIT Press, 1986); *Lectures in Macroeconomics* (co-authored with O. Blanchard) (MIT Press, 1989); and *Macroeconomics* (co-authored with R. Dornbusch and R. Startz) (7th edn, McGraw-Hill, 1998). His most widely read articles include: 'Long-Term Contracts, Rational Expectations and the Optimal Money Supply Rule' (*Journal of Political Economy*, **85**, February 1977); 'Towards an Understanding of the Real Effects and Costs of Inflation' (co-authored with F. Modigliani) (*Weltwirtschaftliches Archiv*, **114**, 1978); 'Recent Developments in Macroeconomics' (*Economic Journal*, **98**, June 1988); and 'Exchange Rate Regimes: Is the Bi-Polar View Correct?' (*Journal of Economic Perspectives*, **15**, 2001).

Fisher Effect

The one-for-one effect of expected inflation on the nominal interest rate, leaving the expected real interest rate unaffected. The Fisher equation states that the nominal interest rate is equal to the sum of expected inflation and the expected real interest rate.

See also:
Real Interest Rate.

Fisher, Irving (1867–1947)

Irving Fisher (b.1867, Saugerties, New York, USA) obtained his BA (1888) and PhD (1891) from Yale University. His main past posts included Professor of Economics at Yale University, 1892–1935. In 1930, he helped to found, and was the first president of, the Econometric Society. He is best known for his work on capital theory; monetary theory, in particular how money affects interest rates, prices and economic activity; and economic statistics. Among his best known books are *The Nature of Capital and Income* (Macmillan, 1906); *The Rate of Interest* (Macmillan, 1907); *The Purchasing Power of Money* (Macmillan, 1911); *The Making of Index Numbers* (Houghton Mifflin, 1922); *The Money Illusion* (Adelphi, 1928); and *The Theory of Interest* (Macmillan, 1930).

See also:
Econometric Society; Equation of Exchange; Quantity Theory of Money.

Fixed Exchange Rate System

The international monetary system has, at different times in the past, been based on a system of fixed exchange rates. The Gold Standard, under which individual countries fixed the price of gold in terms of domestic currency, was essentially a fixed exchange rate system, with its heyday between 1870 and 1914. There was a temporary return to a variant of the Gold Standard (the Gold Exchange Standard) for a time between the two world wars. This was followed by the Bretton Woods system of fixed exchange rates from 1947 to 1971 (where the US dollar supplanted gold as the centrepiece of the system). Following the breakdown of Bretton Woods, all countries have been free to go their own way in what John Williamson has called 'the non-system', whereby countries have complete unilateral freedom of choice regarding their exchange rate arrangements. In this new context, there is no longer a global fixed exchange rate system, but groups of countries (most notably the Euro-zone within the EU) have opted to operate a fixed exchange rate system among themselves, and many individual countries continue to fix their exchange rate with respect to another currency (often the dollar) or a composite currency (often a trade-weighted basket of currencies). The remainder operate variants of floating exchange rate regimes.

In this entry, and the entry, *Flexible Exchange Rate System*, we shall use the following taxonomy. Within fixed rates, we distinguish between 'hard' pegs, where the exchange rate is not intended to be adjusted and where institutional arrangements are designed to ensure as far as possible that the exchange rate will not succumb to speculative attack, and 'conventional pegs', where such institutional arrangements do not exist and where the exchange rate may be adjustable, either as an act of policy or as an involuntary response to market pressure. (These are referred to as 'other conventional fixed peg arrangements' in the IMF classification.) Arrangements which fall between hard pegs and floating exchange rates (both managed and independent floating) are referred to as 'soft pegs'. These intermediate regimes comprise both conventional pegs (including pegs within bands) and crawling pegs of various kinds. Crawling pegs are discussed in greater detail under *Flexible Exchange Rate System*, in this volume.

Hard pegs comprise common currency arrangements and currency boards. In recent years, there has been a trend towards bipolarity in exchange rate regimes, with countries opting either for hard pegs or for some form of floating, with fewer countries opting for the intermediate arrangements of soft pegs. However, it has been argued by some (see, for example, Calvo and Reinhart, 2000) that to some extent this trend has been more apparent than real, with many nominal floating regimes still involving substantial intervention by the authorities in practice.

Fixed exchange rates and macroeconomic policy
A textbook description of the operation of a fixed exchange rate regime is usually one in which the authorities systematically intervene in the foreign exchange market, selling domestic currency and buying foreign exchange when there is excess demand for domestic currency on the foreign exchange market, and vice versa. The extent of foreign exchange intervention is generally taken as the measure of the balance of payments surplus or deficit. Thus in the case where there is excess demand for a currency, this leads to the purchase of foreign exchange, and the increase in the country's foreign exchange reserves measures the size of the balance of payments surplus.

Other things remaining equal, foreign exchange intervention will have implications for the domestic money supply. Purchase of foreign exchange by the central bank has the effect of increasing the domestic money supply and vice versa. However, the authorities may attempt to sterilize the currency flow and thus sever the link between the balance of payments and the money supply. In the case of a surplus, this would involve open-market sales of government bonds. Successful sterilization policies would enable the authorities to target the exchange rate solely by means of intervention, leaving monetary policy free to pursue domestic objectives. However, such sterilized intervention has become increasingly difficult in the postwar period, as world capital markets have developed, facilitated both by the extensive dismantling of postwar direct controls on international capital movements and by the development of more efficient markets incorporating IT innovations. Under conditions of capital mobility, any attempt to sterilize, say, a currency inflow by open-market bond sales puts upward pressure on domestic interest rates, attracts a capital inflow and therefore places renewed upward pressure on the exchange rate, requiring further foreign exchange intervention. If perfect capital mobility is assumed (where domestic interest rates cannot diverge from world rates) sterilization policies are deemed to be ineffective.

Another way of making the same point is to note that, under fixed exchange rates and high capital mobility, the authorities lose independent control of the interest rate. The uncovered interest parity condition (UIP) states that, under perfect capital mobility, the domestic interest rate can only diverge from the foreign interest rate if the exchange rate is expected to change. More precisely, UIP ensures that the domestic interest rate will be above (below) the foreign interest rate by an amount equal to the expected depreciation (appreciation) of the domestic exchange rate (assuming no risk premium). This ensures that the expected return from holding assets in each currency is equalized. Under successfully fixed exchange rates, the expected change in the exchange rate must be zero, thus tying the domestic interest to the foreign interest rate. Similarly, if the exchange rate is under speculative attack and is therefore expected to depreciate, if they were to defend the exchange rate, the authorities would have to increase interest rates. The likely ineffectiveness of sterilization policies means that the exchange rate must be targeted by domestic monetary policy, leaving only fiscal policy to pursue domestic objectives. Under conditions of high capital mobility, the central bank can target the exchange rate or the money supply, but not both. Independent monetary policy, a fixed exchange rate and an absence of capital controls are sometimes described as the impossible trinity.

Given the assignment of monetary policy to targeting the exchange rate, fiscal policy assumes central importance in the pursuit of domestic objectives. The Mundell–Fleming model implies that fiscal policy is a powerful alternative. The argument is that, under fixed exchange rates, fiscal expansion, for example, increases the demand for money and domestic interest rates, generating a capital inflow, a balance of payments surplus and therefore an increase in the supply of money which accommodates the fiscal expansion, rendering it more effective. However, the effectiveness of fiscal policy under fixed rates has not gone unquestioned (laying to one side issues of Ricardian equivalence and intertemporal fiscal burden). For example, under the law of one price, as in the monetary approach to the balance of payments, the aggregate demand curve is horizontal at the world price level. Under such circumstances, fiscal policy cannot affect total aggregate demand, but only domestic absorption, and therefore the trade balance. (Note, however, that there is now a considerable weight of evidence against the law of one price in international markets – see Obstfeld, 2001). Moreover, under fixed rates, fiscal expansion is likely to push the current account towards deficit. While under perfect capital mobility a current account deficit can be financed indefinitely by borrowing from abroad, in practice this is unlikely to be the case without denting confidence and therefore placing pressure on the exchange rate to depreciate, leading to a fall in the domestic money stock. Moreover, a current account deficit constitutes a foreign drain on domestic wealth holdings, with possible implications for consumption expenditure in the longer run. (Similar conclusions may be reached from the New Open Economy Macroeconomics about the current account consequences of fiscal expansion.) However, we may finally note in passing that flexible price models have suggested a longer-run effectiveness for fiscal policy under fixed rates, by focusing on the effects of relative import costs on the wedge between the real product wage and the real consumption wage. As fiscal expansion pushes up domestic prices, this reduces the real cost of imports. For a given real consumption wage, this enables the real product wage to fall, increasing employment, and therefore output. Note, however, that this conclusion depends on the pricing strategies of foreign exporters. For example, under pricing to market (where import prices may be expected to follow domestic prices), this effect would not be present. Rather, exporters' profit margins would increase and real import prices would remain unchanged.

Advantages of fixed exchange rates
We may divide the perceived advantages of fixed exchange rates into microeconomic and macroeconomic arguments. The microeconomic arguments relate to the removal of exchange risk from international trade. Under flexible exchange rates, exchange rate risk is borne by the trader in whose currency the contract is not denominated. Thus, for example, if a contract is invoiced in the exporter's currency, the exchange risk is borne by the importer. The economic cost of this risk is the disincentives that it presents to trade, so that a fixed exchange rate should reduce trading costs. (However, the argument, and the associated empirical evidence, needs to be treated with care; see the entry, *Flexible Exchange Rate System* in this

volume). For an individual country to reap significant benefits under this heading, it is necessary for its trade to be concentrated with a single country, or with a group of countries which have already formed a fixed exchange rate bloc, and for much of its trade to be invoiced in a foreign currency.

The macroeconomic arguments for fixed exchange rates generally focus on their implications for the effectiveness of anti-inflation policies, but they may be extended to macroeconomic economic stabilization generally.

The anti-inflation arguments focus on the role of the exchange rate as a nominal anchor for monetary policy. Under capital mobility, the exchange rate may be preferred to the money supply as a nominal anchor on the grounds that the exchange rate anchor enhances the credibility of monetary policy. By using monetary policy to peg the exchange rate, the authorities essentially tie their monetary policy to that of their exchange rate partners, and thereby benefit from their anti-inflation credentials and credibility. This argument was frequently rehearsed during the late 1980s in the UK during the period of the 'shadowing of the Deutschmark', and then during UK membership of the ERM. By the same token, an exchange rate anchor is frequently part of the package whereby a country attempts to stabilize from very high inflation. Successful recent examples are afforded by Argentina (1991), Estonia (1992), Lithuania (1994) and Bulgaria (1997) (all of which operated currency boards), while in the cases of Mexico (1994), Russia (1998) and Brazil (1999) the exchange rate eventually crashed. The problem with a nominal anchor in this context is the real appreciation which inevitably occurs while the inflation rate is still high. If the peg is maintained, not only does the rate of inflation have to fall, it needs to fall (temporarily) below international levels to enable the real appreciation of the transition period to be reversed. This can give rise to slower (or even negative) growth and increased unemployment, which then lead markets to question the credibility and therefore the sustainability of the peg. The use of an exchange rate anchor as a disinflation and credibility-enhancing device is more likely to succeed in the context of a hard, rather than a soft, peg.

There is also a more general argument as to whether economies will tend to be more stable under fixed rather than flexible exchange rates (see Artis and Currie, 1981). Much depends on the origin of any stochastic shocks to which the economy might be subjected. For example, if the demand for money is unstable, an exchange rate target is likely to be more stabilizing than a money supply target, and therefore the authorities should target the exchange rate, surrendering control of the money supply. For other disturbances, however, flexible rates are often held to be more stabilizing. For example, it is generally argued that flexible exchange rates insulate the economy from world inflation (though this may not be advantageous for an inflation-prone economy, where the nominal anchor argument set out above may be more relevant) and, for an economy with unstable real demand, flexible exchange rates may be stabilizing. The picture on the international transmission of aggregate demand shocks under alternative exchange rate regimes is less clear, and depends on the nature of the shocks and the precise specification of the model. However, it is frequently argued that, where an economy under fixed exchange rates is subjected to a competitiveness shock, the adjustment of the current account back to equilibrium requires adjustment to domestic wages and prices with associated output and employment costs.

It is also important that an appropriate foreign currency is selected for the peg. The emerging European economies (such as Estonia, Bulgaria and Lithuania) selected the Deutschmark, while Caribbean and Latin American countries peg to the dollar. It has been suggested that the fact that the East Asian economies pegged to the dollar rather than to a basket of currencies (which would have been more in line with their structure of trade) may have contributed to the instability of these economies after 1995 (see, for example, Williamson, 1998.)

In terms of general macroeconomic stability and performance, there is no clear empirical evidence that one regime is preferable to any other (see Caramazza and Aziz, 1998; Eichengreen, 1994; Quirk, 1996). While earlier studies (for example, Baxter and Stockman, 1989) find evidence of a move from fixed to flexible exchange rates to be associated with increased real output volatility, these results are not confirmed in Eichengreen (1994) or Bordo (1993).

The sustainability of fixed exchange rate arrangements
Recent history suggests that a fixed exchange rate is difficult to sustain, at least for countries facing high international capital mobility, unless the regime is that of a hard peg. These difficulties are reflected in recent trends away from intermediate soft peg regimes (comprising conventional pegs and crawling pegs of various kinds) towards hard pegs on the one hand, or some form of free floating on the other – see the entry under *Flexible Exchange Rate System* for a discussion of crawling pegs.

A hard peg is operated where the institutional arrangements carry sufficient inherent credibility that the exchange rate cannot be altered by speculative capital flows. The first general example of a hard peg is where the country has no separate legal tender. There are currently 39 countries in this category. The most prominent example is the creation and adoption of the Euro by 12 economies currently in the Euro-zone but a further example is afforded by the CFA franc zone comprising 13 countries in Africa. For the most part, the remainder are small economies, mostly in Latin America, which have implemented a policy of 'dollarization', that is, they have simply adopted the US dollar as their domestic currency. Ecuador and El Salvador are two recent examples of dollarization.

A common currency arrangement is clearly the hardest peg, effectively removing the possibility of any speculation between member countries. The economic advantages of such a system will be greater, the more integrated are the member economies. More specifically, a high degree of intra-area trade and labour mobility, the existence of a system of inter-country fiscal policy and the absence of asymmetric shocks will all contribute to the success of such an arrangement. Unilateral 'dollarization' by an individual economy is unlikely to be accompanied by these conditions, and an economy adopting such a regime has to weigh the advantages of lower interest rates and lower inflation against the possible unemployment and real income costs of adjustment to asymmetric shocks.

The other form of hard peg involves the setting up of a currency board, and there are currently eight economies in this category, the most prominent of which are Hong Kong, Estonia, Lithuania, Bulgaria and Argentina. Under a currency board, the monetary authorities are committed to exchange domestic currency for a key foreign currency (either the US dollar or, for the European emerging economies, the Euro) at a fixed rate, and the supply of domestic currency is fully backed by foreign exchange reserves. This arrangement not only ties the hands of the central bank, but it also removes from the central bank certain key functions such as lender of last resort. It is essentially an explicitly institutionalized commitment to abide by the rules of the game of the modern equivalent of the gold standard (especially a commitment not to sterilize). This can make the transition from high to low inflation under a currency board quite painful. However, it carries enhanced credibility due to the explicit legal and institutional framework whereby hands are tied, and the perceived costs of dismantling such an arrangement. However, a currency board is more likely to be successful when it is backed up by fiscal policies which are unlikely to impose additional strains either on domestic inflation or on the current account. The advantages and disadvantages of such an arrangement are similar to those of dollarization, but with the additional disadvantage that there is always the possibility that the currency board might be dismantled. This possibility may introduce a risk premium into domestic interest rates and under certain circumstances might ignite a speculative attack, triggering significant increases in domestic interest rates (which can be a problem in the absence of a lender of last resort facility) as occurred in Hong Kong in 1998.

Such arrangements are to be contrasted with conventional pegs, where exchange rates are the target of a combination of intervention and discretionary policy actions by the authorities. Under such arrangements, no matter what the authorities may declare, there is always the possibility that the exchange rate may be adjusted. As *de facto* 'adjustable pegs', such exchange rates are always potentially open to speculative attack. There are 44 economies which adhere to such conventional peg arrangements (within parity bands of plus or minus 1 per cent). Of these, 31 economies peg with respect to a single currency – often the dollar – and the remainder peg with respect to a composite – usually a trade-weighted basket of currencies. For the most part, these are small developing countries. In many cases they are highly dependent on the economies to which they have pegged (for example, Caribbean countries to the US dollar and southern African countries to the rand). Finally, there are six countries which operate a fixed peg, but within broader bands (for example, Denmark as the remaining vestigial member of the ERM).

In recent years, there has been a marked movement away from conventional soft pegs to hard pegs or floating (see Fischer, 2001; Caramazza and Aziz, 1998; Obstfeld and Rogoff, 1995). For example, the number of countries operating hard pegs increased from 25 to 47 between 1991 and 2001, while the number of soft pegs (including crawling pegs) fell from 99 to 59 over the same period (although we should again note the caveat of Calvo and Reinhart, 2000, that some nominally floating regimes may be akin to adjustable pegs). Within this group, there are only nine emerging market economies, and Denmark is the only developed market economy operating a soft peg (following its decision not to join EMU).

This reflects the growing view that only hard pegs are viable as an alternative to floating within a world of highly mobile capital. The collapse of the ERM in 1992–3 provided dramatic evidence of the problems faced by countries trying to adhere to a soft peg. More recent examples are provided by the subsequent currency crises in Mexico, Thailand, Indonesia, Korea, Russia and Brazil. Such exchange rate collapses can inflict significant costs on the domestic economy. For example, during the life of a peg, there may be considerable liability dollarization; that is, domestic firms, banks or governments may borrow in dollars rather than in domestic currency. A collapse in the exchange rate then greatly increases the domestic currency value of this debt, with adverse real consequences.

The central problem for soft pegs is that, in a world of perfect capital mobility, intervention is unlikely to be sufficient to peg the exchange rate in the face of adverse market sentiment. In theory, so long as a central bank has sufficient foreign exchange reserves to buy back all of its monetary base, it has the ability to peg its exchange rate (see Obstfeld and Rogoff, 1995). However, in practice, this can imply domestic interest rate levels which would clearly conflict with other economic objectives. When this is perceived to compromise the resolve of the domestic authorities, the currency is open to speculative attack. It is now customary to distinguish between first and second generation models of speculative attacks. In first generation models, the source of the crisis lies in inappropriate domestic policies, often unsustainable fiscal expansion. As inflation proceeds, the authorities attempt to protect the exchange rate by engaging in intervention, but the inevitability of foreign exchange reserve depletion triggers the crisis well before that point is reached. The blame with such crises lies firmly with the domestic authorities rather than the speculators. The key element of second generation models is the belief of the market as to whether or not a peg will be vigorously defended by the authorities. If a currency begins to weaken, speculators will only attack once they are convinced that the authorities have more to lose by defending the peg than by letting it go. UIP implies that, once market sentiment has moved against a currency, the required increase in interest rates can be very large indeed. More particularly, the exchange rate can only be defended by an interest rate differential which is large enough to balance the annualized expected rate of depreciation of the currency. This explains the massive short-term increases in Swedish interest rates in 1992, which still failed to defend the exchange rate successfully.

Conventional pegs are generally set within parity limits of plus or minus 1 per cent (as under Bretton Woods), but there have been systems of broader bands, most notably within the ERM, where the parity bands were set at plus or minus 2.25 per cent (with plus or minus 6 per cent for Italy, Spain and the UK). However, the success of such a system depends critically on its credibility, especially if the system allows an adjustable peg. If the system is indeed credible, an exchange rate will tend to be stabilized automatically within the bands. If, for example, a currency falls to near the floor of its parity limits, then, under a credible system, the market will expect successful intervention by the authorities to return the exchange rate towards the centre of its band. These expectations will therefore make the system a stable one. However, if the system lacks credibility, then, as the currency nears the floor of the band, speculators will face an asymmetric bet, where the currency will either be realigned or remain at the floor, with little chance of rising back up from the floor of the bands. The narrower are the bands, the more this will approach a one-way bet for speculators. This was a typical situation in 1992–3, when the ERM virtually broke down. Similar episodes also punctuated the later years of the Bretton Woods system.

Much of the difficulty in operating a pegged exchange rate arises out of the degree of capital mobility. It is notable that the Bretton Woods system operated with pervasive international capital controls and that the ERM crisis came in 1992, only after capital controls in the EU had been dismantled. In view of the spate of currency crises in the 1990s, it is not surprising that capital controls have reappeared on the agenda for discussion (see Rodrik, 1998). The arguments against capital controls focus on misallocation of resources and lack of discipline on domestic governments. The arguments in favour of such controls are that they would return a degree of monetary sovereignty to governments even under fixed exchange rates and that they would remove some of the instability from international currency markets. An early proponent of such controls was James Tobin (1978), who proposed a flat rate tax on all foreign exchange transactions to 'throw some sand in the wheels' of international capital movements. In recent currency crises, China and Malaysia imposed controls on outflows, while Chile and Colombia have in the past employed controls on capital inflows.

ANDREW STEVENSON

See also:

Balance of Payments: Keynesian Approach; Balance of Payments: Monetary Approach; Bretton Woods; Euro; European Monetary System; European Monetary Union; Exchange Rate Determination: Monetary Approach; Exchange Rate Mechanism; Flexible Exchange Rate System; Gold Standard; IS–LM Model: Open Economy.

Bibliography

Artis, M, and D. Currie (1981), 'Monetary Targets and the Exchange Rate: A Case for Conditional Targets', in W.A Eltis and P.J.N. Sinclair (eds), *The Money Supply and the Exchange Rate*, Oxford: Oxford University Press.
Baxter, M. and A. Stockman (1989), 'Business Cycles and the Exchange Rate Regime: Some International Evidence', *Journal of Monetary Economics*, **23**, May, pp. 377–400.
Bordo, M. (1993), 'The Bretton Woods International Monetary System: An Historical Overview', in M. Bordo and B. Eichengreen (eds), *A Retrospective on the Bretton Woods System*, Chicago: University of Chicago Press.
Burda, M. and C. Wyplosz (2001), *Macroeconomics*, 3rd edn, Oxford: Oxford University Press.
Calvo, G. and C. Reinhart (2000), 'Fear of Floating', *NBER Working Paper*, no. 7993.
Caramazza, F. and J. Aziz (1998), 'Fixed or Flexible? Getting the Exchange Rate Right in the 1990's', *IMF Economic Issues*, April.
Eichengreen, B. (1994), 'History of the International Monetary System: Implications for Research in International Macroeconomics and Finance', in F. Van Der Ploeg (ed.), *The Handbook of International Macroeconomics*, Oxford: Blackwell.
Fischer, S. (2001), 'Exchange Rate Regimes: Is the Bipolar View Correct?', *Journal of Economic Perspectives*, **15**, Spring, pp. 3–24.
Krugman, P. (1989), 'The Case for Stabilizing Exchange Rates', *Oxford Review of Economic Policy*, **5**, Autumn, pp. 61–72.
Miles, D. and A. Scott (2002), *Macroeconomics*, New York: Wiley.
Obstfeld, M. (2001), 'International Macroeconomics: Beyond the Mundell–Fleming Model', *NBER Working Paper*, no. 8369.
Obstfeld, M. and K. Rogoff (1995), 'The Mirage of Fixed Exchange Rates', *Journal of Economic Perspectives*, **9**, Autumn, pp. 73–96.

Quirk, P. (1996), 'Exchange Rate Regimes as Inflation Anchors', *Finance and Development*, Washington: The World Bank.

Rodrik, D. (1998), 'Who Needs Capital Account Convertibility?', in P. Kenen (ed.), *Should the IMF Pursue Capital Account Convertibility?*, Princeton, NJ: Princeton University Press.

Tobin, J. (1978), 'A Proposal for International Monetary Reform', *Eastern Economic Journal*, **4**, July–October, pp. 153–9.

Williamson, J. (1998), 'Crawling Bands or Monitoring Bands: How to Manage Exchange Rates in a World of Capital Mobility', *International Finance*, **1**, October, pp. 59–79.

Flexible Exchange Rate System

Under a system of flexible exchange rates, the authorities do not intervene in the foreign exchange market to peg the exchange rate, as they would under fixed exchange rates. Under pure flexible exchange rates, supply and demand in the foreign exchange market determines the exchange rate. Since there is no intervention by the authorities, the pure flexible exchange rate regime affords the monetary authorities complete sovereignty in monetary policy. However, pure floating is not common, and there is a range of possible floating regimes, each implying different degrees of intervention in the market.

At one extreme, there is independent floating, where, as defined by the IMF, intervention is limited to 'moderating the rate of change and preventing undue fluctuations in the exchange rate'. Such a regime may involve merely smoothing out more extreme day-to-day fluctuations in the exchange rate in order to provide a more stable environment for international trade. According to the IMF, as at 31 March 2001, there were 47 countries in this category, including all the major developed economies except the members of the Euro-zone and Denmark. There were a further 33 countries (mainly developing countries and transition economies) where the authorities operated a more active, managed float, aimed at influencing 'the movement of the exchange rate through active intervention in the foreign exchange market without specifying, or pre-committing to, a predetermined path for the exchange rate'. As noted below, it has been argued that, within this group, there is evidence that intervention and monetary policy is akin to operating an adjustable peg regime (see Calvo and Reinhart, 2000).

Lying between these 80 countries which operate a form of floating exchange rate and those countries operating hard pegs (discussed under *Fixed Exchange Rate System* in this volume) are the so-called 'intermediate exchange rate regimes', comprising conventional pegs (also discussed under *Fixed Exchange Rate System*) and crawling pegs, which we discuss here. Under such arrangements, the exchange rate is adjusted in small discrete steps, often as an automatic response to some policy indicator. The most common crawling peg arrangement is to adjust the nominal exchange rate in line with inflation differentials, thus keeping the real exchange rate fixed. This policy rule may be seen as an intention to allow a domestic economy to 'live with' inflation, or alternatively to insulate itself from foreign inflation. However, the peg could also crawl in line with alternative indicators such as foreign exchange reserves. Like other pegging arrangements, a crawling peg has to be specified with respect to a particular currency or set of currencies. For economies with highly concentrated trading patterns, the adoption of a single currency would be appropriate (for example, the dollar for Colombia) but for more diversified trade structures (for example, Israel and Chile) a trade-weighted basket is adopted. As at 31 March 2001, only four countries were officially operating a crawling peg. A slightly looser arrangement is to adopt a crawling peg, but within bands (of between 5 and 15 per cent) and there are five countries currently operating this system. These arrangements tie the hands of the monetary authorities to a much greater extent than the managed floating regimes outlined above, with a consequent loss of monetary sovereignty for the domestic authorities. In recent years there has been a significant movement out of the intermediate soft peg regimes into either hard pegs or floating. For example, following the failure of their respective soft peg arrangements, Chile, Russia, Brazil, Mexico, Korea, Indonesia, Colombia and Thailand have all recently joined the ranks of those countries independently floating their exchange rates.

Monetary sovereignty, inflation and the exchange rate
It is usually argued that a regime of flexible exchange rates affords greater monetary sovereignty to the domestic authorities, since monetary policy is no longer committed to pegging the exchange rate. In terms of the uncovered interest parity condition (UIP) (see *Fixed Exchange Rate System*), under flexible exchange rates, the expected change in the exchange rate is no longer zero, enabling domestic interest rates to diverge from foreign interest rates. Thus, under flexible exchange rates, the authorities may increase domestic interest rates, generating a capital inflow and appreciation until the spot exchange rate is such as to generate expectations of a future depreciation to match the home–foreign interest differential. Moreover, in most macroeconomic models, the effectiveness of monetary policy is actually enhanced by flexible exchange rates, as the exchange rate response to domestic monetary policy affects competitiveness and net exports. In this context, monetary policy is described as a 'beggar-thy-neighbour' policy, since it generates negative spillovers to trading partners. A similar short-run result is generated in the Dornbusch (1976) 'overshooting' model. Once flexible prices are assumed, effects on real income

are, at best, confined to the short run, but, in such a context, monetary policy then emerges as a strong anti-inflation weapon. Monetary contraction and exchange rate appreciation not only reduce aggregate demand through competitiveness effects on net exports, they also result in lower import prices and therefore lower domestic costs. Again, this is a beggar-thy-neighbour policy, in that it also serves to export inflationary pressures to trading partners. (Note, however, that these effects will be weakened if there is significant 'pricing to market' in international trade – see below.)

Increased monetary sovereignty may not be an advantage to an inflation-prone economy, unless the domestic institutional framework is such as to ensure the credibility of anti-inflation policy. Hence, of the 80 floating economies, 15 have in place an inflation targeting framework, frequently including an independent and accountable central bank and policy transparency. Under flexible rates and weak anti-inflation credibility, higher inflation expectations will tend to be factored into wage and price behaviour, making the removal of inflation more costly in terms of lost output and employment. In these circumstances, an inflation-prone economy which is unable to implement a credible domestic inflation targeting regime may not wish to be insulated from (lower) world inflation, as would tend to be the case under flexible rates.

Flexible exchange rates and external balance
In a strict sense, floating exchange rates remove the balance of payments as a policy issue, in that, since there is no official intervention in the foreign exchange market, the balance of payments is always zero. However, it may be that fundamental balance of payments equilibrium is more properly to be expressed in terms of the current account. It might be argued that, in the long run, the real exchange rate must tend towards that which clears the current account. Indeed, models of exchange rate determination frequently cite the current account as the long-run anchor. Under fixed exchange rates, movement to the equilibrium (current account clearing) real exchange rate must come through domestic wage and price adjustment, and this might be seen as a slow and potentially painful process. Advocates of flexible exchange rates would argue that nominal exchange rate adjustment could speed up this process, although it should be noted that, by whatever mechanism the real exchange rate adjustment comes, it must involve a fall in real wages. (The criteria for optimum currency areas reflect the same concerns – see the entry in this volume, *Fixed Exchange Rate System*.)

However, there are some caveats to this argument. The adjustment of the current account to exchange rate changes is not rapid, for a number of reasons. First, besides the obvious lags in trade flows adjusting to relative price changes, the Marshall–Lerner conditions need to be satisfied for, say, a depreciation to improve the current account. These conditions relate to supply and demand elasticities for both imports and exports. If the supply of both imports and exports are assumed to be perfectly elastic, these conditions reduce to the requirement that the sum of the price elasticities of demand for imports and exports must exceed unity. If these elasticities are low, there is the possibility that depreciation will push the current account further into deficit. Second, the outcome of an exchange rate change for net exports depends on the pricing behaviour of exporting firms. There is increasing evidence of 'pricing to market' in international trade, whereby, following a depreciation, for example, exporters continue to charge the same foreign currency price, with no immediate effect on export demand (see Obstfeld, 2001).

Similarly, there may be hysteresis effects in export markets following exchange rate changes. 'Beach-head effects' refer to markets where exporters choose to incur sunk costs at a time when large but temporary exchange rate changes allow these costs to be absorbed, given temporarily favourable margins. This enables exporters to gain a foothold in overseas markets. When the exchange rate change is reversed, the exporters do not lose market share, having already incurred and covered the sunk costs. This was thought to be an important element in Japanese penetration of US markets during and after the temporary real appreciation of the dollar in the 1980s. Again, this will blur the effect of exchange rate changes on trade flows, and therefore the current account.

Finally, the response of exchange rates to current account developments, and therefore their role in current account adjustment, is dominated in the short run by capital flow effects, and it is the potential instability associated with such effects that constitutes one of the major arguments against flexible exchange rates.

Exchange rate instability

As an early proponent of flexible exchange rates, Milton Friedman (1953) argued that speculation was unlikely to generate increased instability in foreign exchange markets. The argument was simply that speculators who tried to move the exchange rate away from equilibrium would lose money and vice versa. Thus speculation would tend to be equilibrating rather than destabilizing. However, this argument stands in contrast to the empirical experience of floating rates since 1971. Not surprisingly, nominal exchange rate instability has increased dramatically. For example, taking the Deutschmark/dollar rate, the standard deviation increased from 2.4 per cent in the 1960s to somewhat above 10 per cent in the three decades since then. In addition, there is every indication that real exchange rates have frequently moved away from levels consistent with 'fundamentals', and for significant periods of time. The most spectacular example is afforded by the real appreciation of the dollar in the 1980s. Such casual empirical observations can be accompanied by more formal econometric evidence. Most notably, there is no convincing evidence that the forward exchange rate is an unbiased predictor of the future spot rate, casting severe doubt on the view that the foreign exchange market is 'efficient' (in the sense of making optimal use of all relevant information). There is evidence that, in the long run, the exchange rate may tend to adjust to an equilibrium which reflects economic fundamentals, but only after a considerable period. For example, there is evidence that in the long run floating rates revert to some form of purchasing power parity (PPP) equilibrium, but the process is a slow one, estimated to be half-completed in five years (Rogoff, 1996).

There are a number of potential explanations for this observed instability, particularly in the short run. Some exchange rate models, notably the Dornbusch model, predict overshooting in the exchange rate following a disturbance. If the exchange rate is considered to embody all information relevant to the future course of exchange rates, the arrival of new information ('news'), which happens continuously, can be expected to have an impact upon the current exchange rate. Additional instability may, however, be attributable to the presence of relatively small numbers of 'noise traders' in the market – traders who either are misinformed, have incomplete information, or are irrational. It has been demonstrated that the presence of a relatively small number of noise traders can cause disproportionate disturbances to exchange rates. Finally, there is the possibility of speculative bubbles. In theory, these can be supported by quite rational behaviour, as speculators with relatively short time horizons 'ride the bubble', in the knowledge that the exchange rate will return towards its long-run equilibrium at some point in the future, but the prospect of short-term gain dominates.

Part of the case against flexible exchange rates rests on the view that such instability can be harmful. To the extent that observed instability is simply a response of the exchange rate to relevant fundamentals (for example, differential inflation rates) it could be argued that fixed exchange rates would not eliminate this instability, but would merely redirect it in some way. However, if foreign exchange markets exhibit instability that is not rooted in the behaviour of fundamentals, floating exchange rates will carry additional economic costs. The obvious direct cost is simply that unstable exchange rates may translate into instability in domestic price levels, competitiveness and, hence, real income and unemployment. This argument is sometimes extended to claim that unstable exchange rates might generate increased inflation on the grounds that the increase in wages and prices which might accompany a depreciation might not be mirrored by movements in the opposite direction when the currency appreciates. This latter view is, however, largely unsupported by empirical evidence.

A key argument against flexible exchange rates (and in favour of fixed rates) is that unstable exchange rates generate risk and uncertainty. Notwithstanding the availability of forward markets as a means of hedging this risk (though this is effectively limited to periods of a year or less) and the fact that some traders may be risk-neutral, it is argued that this instability imposes costs on international traders and therefore inhibits trade. However, again empirical evidence does not suggest that these effects have been very large (see Moreno, 2000). For example, Frankel and Wei (1993) estimate that doubling exchange rate instability in Europe would reduce European trade by less than 1 per cent, while Gagnon (1993) estimates that post-Bretton Woods instability reduced trade by between 1 and 3 per cent. However, these results need to be interpreted with some care. *Ex post* instability may not be a complete measure of uncertainty. Pegged exchange rates may also carry uncertainty, given their short average life, for example in Latin America. More generally, studies need to provide a measure of expected exchange rate volatility, and ideally such studies should focus on firm-level behaviour and instability in bilateral exchange rates. Also it should be noted that there is evidence that trade is encouraged by membership of a currency union, in which exchange rate uncertainty is completely eliminated.

Finally, we should note the argument that volatility in exchange rates is more likely to affect investment decisions than international trade volumes (see Krugman,1989; Dixit, 1989). Under exchange rate uncertainty, the costs of installing capital ahead of an adverse exchange rate movement are greater than the costs of delaying investment ahead of a favourable exchange rate movement. This asymmetry, it is argued, delays the process of allocating resources in response to changing comparative advantage. A related argument is that exchange rate uncertainty might induce multinational companies to operate with excess capacity in order to respond quickly to changing exchange rates.

It has been argued that the costs of flexible exchange rates are such that there is evidence of 'fear of floating' among countries that have nominally flexible exchange rate regimes. Work by Calvo and Reinhart (2000) suggests that many countries operate flexible exchange rates in name only. Many of these countries, which are probably subject to greater real shocks owing to their export dependence on primary products, have significantly more stable exchange rates than 'true' floaters such as the United States, Australia and Japan. By the same token, they have exhibited greater fluctuations in both interest rates and foreign exchange reserves, which is indicative of a degree of informal pegging.

Crawling pegs and bands

Set against the costs of exchange rate instability and alongside the gains in terms of monetary sovereignty, a key argument in favour of floating is simply that it avoids the need to peg the exchange rate. If a country is not closely integrated with its trading partners and is subject to asymmetric shocks, the costs of adjustment to real shocks under fixed exchange rates can be large. Of itself, this can reduce the credibility of the peg, unless it is a hard peg. The country is then subject to the costs of adjustment when the peg fails. The exchange rate adjustment can be large once the peg is broken, and it may be that, during the life of the peg, both the government and the private sector have built up foreign currency liabilities. The large exchange rate adjustment then inflicts severe real dislocation and bankruptcies as the domestic currency value of debt soars.

The fact that both fixed and flexible regimes carry costs has prompted some to look for 'intermediate solutions' for the choice of exchange rate regime (see Williamson, 1998). Variants of the crawling peg have been proposed, perhaps the most interesting of which is the 'crawling band'. Under this arrangement, the central bank uses foreign exchange intervention and interest rate policy to keep the exchange rate within bands around a central parity, which is, in turn, gradually adjusted over time. In practice these bands have been between 5 and 15 per cent either side of the central parity. The central parity is adjusted, generally in line with inflation differentials, against the selected currency or basket. This implies a target real exchange rate which may be specified as the Fundamental Equilibrium Exchange Rate (FEER), which is generally defined as the real exchange rate consistent with medium-term current account equilibrium, which is, in turn, adjusted to take account of medium-term equilibrium capital flows.

What are the advantages of such a regime? If the regime is credible (and the central bank must publicly announce the central parity, the rate of crawl and the band width) then speculation will tend to be stabilizing. As the exchange rate nears the edge of the band, speculators will expect intervention or interest rate changes to return the exchange rate to the centre of the band, and speculate accordingly, stabilizing the rate. However, if the regime is not credible, then, as the rate approaches the edge of the band, speculators will interpret this as providing the opportunity of at least an asymmetric (and, in extreme cases, a one-way) bet. Speculation would then be destabilizing. The width of the band allows limited flexibility in the exchange rate, partly as a recognition that FEERs cannot be estimated with pinpoint accuracy and partly to accommodate short-term cyclical macro-economic policy. It also dilutes the extent to which the system might present speculators with a one-way bet at the edge of the bands. Finally, since the adjustment of the exchange rate is in small steps, this reduces the scope for speculation about expected large exchange rate changes. Several countries (for example, Colombia, Chile, Ecuador, Russia, Israel and Indonesia) have employed variants of this regime in recent years.

ANDREW STEVENSON

See also:

Bretton Woods; Central Bank Accountability and Transparency; Fixed Exchange Rate System; Hysteresis; Inflation Targeting; Marshall–Lerner Condition; Purchasing Power Parity Theory; Speculative Bubbles.

Bibliography

Begg, D. (1989), 'Flexible Exchange Rates in Theory and Practice', *Oxford Review of Economic Policy*, **5**, Autumn, pp. 24–39.
Burda, M. and C. Wyplosz (2001), *Macroeconomics*, 3rd edn, Oxford: Oxford University Press.
Calvo, G. and C. Reinhart (2000), 'Fear of Floating', *NBER Working Paper*, no. 7993.
Dixit, A. (1989), 'Entry and Exit Decisions Under Uncertainty, *Journal of Political Economy*, **97**, June, pp. 620–38.
Dornbusch, R. (1976), 'Expectations and Exchange Rate Dynamics', *Journal of Political Economy*, **84**, December, pp. 1161–76.
Frankel, J. and S-J. Wei (1993), 'Trade Blocs and Currency Blocs', *NBER Working Paper*, no. 4335.
Friedman, M. (1953), 'The Case for Flexible Exchange Rates', *Essays in Positive Economics*, Chicago: University of Chicago Press.
Gagnon, J. (1993), 'Exchange Rate Variability and the Level of International Trade', *Journal of International Economics*, **34**, May, pp. 269–87.
Krugman, P. (1989), 'The Case for Stabilising Exchange Rates', *Oxford Review of Economic Policy*, **5**, Autumn, pp. 61–72.
Miles, D. and A. Scott (2002), *Macroeconomics*, New York: Wiley.
Moreno, R. (2000), 'Does Pegging Increase International Trade?', *Federal Reserve Bank of San Francisco: Economic Letter*, 29 September.
Obstfeld, M. (2001), 'International Macroeconomics: Beyond the Mundell–Fleming Model?', *NBER Working Paper*, no. 8369.
Obstfeld, M. and K. Rogoff (1995), 'The Mirage of Fixed Exchange Rates', *Journal of Economic Perspectives*, **9**, Autumn, pp. 73–96.
Rogoff, K. (1996), 'The Purchasing Power Parity Puzzle', *Journal of Economic Literature*, **34**, June, pp. 647–68.
Williamson, J. (1998), 'Crawling Bands or Monitoring Bands: How to Manage Exchange Rates in a World of Capital Mobility', *International Finance*, **1**, October, pp. 59–79.

Floating Exchange Rate System

See:

Flexible Exchange Rate System.

Forecasting

The methods used in economic forecasting depend on the time horizon over which the forecasts are made. For very short-term forecasts (over the next hour or day with hourly or daily data), statistical methods, such as those of Box and Jenkins (1970) are adopted. These forecasts are based on recent values of the series being forecast and, where available, data on related series. For short to medium-term forecasts (over the next month to two to three years ahead, with monthly or quarterly data) econometric models are used. For long-term forecasts (beyond three years ahead) scenario analysis is preferred whereby the effects of alternative futures are considered (for example, scenario 1: the United Kingdom leaves the EU in 2004 and links closely with the United States, there is high growth outside Europe to 2006, and financial markets in the Far East collapse in 2005; scenario 2: the EU economies expand slowly to 2010, the USA has a major depression in 2007 and does not recover until 2010, other international growth is negligible to 2010).

This entry considers medium-term economic forecasts which are usually based on predictions from econometric models. The other types of forecasting are discussed in Holden *et al.* (1990). The process of econometric modelling results in a set of equations from which conditional forecasts can be made. These forecasts are conditional on assumptions about future values of the variables. For those variables which are exogenous, it may be possible to obtain forecasts using the methods of Box and Jenkins (1970). For policy variables, it is necessary to make suitable assumptions about their future values. One of the valuable properties of econometric models is the fact that the effects of different assumptions about policy variables can be evaluated as a guide to what policies are desirable.

Assessing forecast accuracy

While it may seem obvious that an accurate forecast is one that is correct, a simple classification of forecasts as being right or wrong is not helpful. Instead there are basically four ways of analysing the accuracy of forecasts which are used in the literature. These are (i) checking for unbiasedness and efficiency, (ii) calculating measures such as the root mean square error and inequality coefficients, (iii) examining forecasts for a particular epoch, and (iv) decomposing the forecast error into its components.

The first of these is concerned with the use of information and is related to the concept of rational expectations. An optimal forecast can be defined as one which is the best that can be made in the particular circumstances. It is the prediction from economic theory using all the relevant information that is available at the time the forecast is made, and is referred to as the rational expectation of the variable. Assuming a quadratic cost function, the rational expectation will be unbiased and efficient. Unbiasedness requires an expected forecast error of zero. Efficiency means that the available information has been fully exploited and so the forecast errors are uncorrelated with this information. Holden and Peel (1990) suggest using a simple *t*-test on the mean forecast error as a test for unbiasedness. The method of testing for efficiency is to define the 'relevant' information set and then see if the forecast errors are correlated with it. In Holden and Peel (1985) the information set chosen was to be the four most recently observed actual values of the variables, while McNees (1978) uses the latest known forecast errors.

The second method of assessing forecast accuracy involves calculating a numerical measure of the accuracy. The simple measures, such as the mean error and mean absolute error, are generally not used, since a quadratic cost function is assumed which gives a higher weight to larger errors. Instead, the mean square error (MSE) and its square root, the root mean square error (RMSE) are preferred. The MSE can be expanded to be the sum of the variance of the forecast error plus the square of the mean error, and so increases as either of these increase.

Theil (1966) has suggested an inequality coefficient which takes the value zero for perfect forecasts, one if all the forecasts are zero (which is a no-change forecast if the forecasts are rates of change variables) and is greater than one if the forecasts are worse than the no-change forecasts.

The third way of analysing forecast accuracy is to examine in detail how accurate the forecasts were during a particular period. Examples of this for the United Kingdom are given by Artis (1982), who examines forecasts published late in 1981, Barker (1985), who considers the forecasts made in 1979 and 1980 for the period when the Thatcher government first took office, and Wallis (1989), who looks at forecasts for the recessions of 1974–5 and 1979–81. Such studies allow a detailed examination of the timing of turning points, the depth of a recession and the way in which forecasts are revised as new information becomes available. They tend to consider periods when the economy is changing rapidly, so that forecasting is difficult.

The final way of examining forecast accuracy is to recognize that the observed forecast error can be allocated to particular types of error. That is, the forecast errors from a model can be split into components corresponding to (i) the error due to the model, (ii) the error due to the incorrect projection of the exogenous and policy variables, and (iii) the errors resulting from judgmental and residual adjustments. In order to be able to examine these sources of error in detail, the analyst requires cooperation from the modelling organization since access to the econometric model and the data set used to make the forecasts is needed. Artis (1982) and Wallis *et al.* (1986) report such studies for UK forecasts and they conclude that the forecaster's judgmental adjustments made to the predictions from their models were important, compensating for errors in the models and errors in the exogenous assumptions.

Combining forecasts
It is well known that, when forecasts from a number of economic models are compared, they are generally found to be different. Also, there is empirical evidence (see, for example, Holden and Peel, 1983, or compare McNees, 1979, and McNees, 1988) that the best forecaster for a particular variable over a particular period is likely to be dominated by another forecaster in a different period. The question then is whether forecasts from one particular forecaster should be selected or some form of average of those available should be taken. If the agent is convinced that one particular model is correct then it will be appropriate to ignore the other forecasts. However, in the absence of such a conviction, it is sensible to take account of forecasts from other models.

Granger and Ramanathan (1984), following Bates and Granger (1969), demonstrate that the optimal combination of two forecasts can be found by regressing the outcome series on the two series of forecasts. One assumption, that is important in using this method for combining forecasts is that the variances and covariances between the forecasts are constant. If this is not true the weights will be unstable and a better combined forecast might be obtained by taking the mean of the available forecasts. This has some attractions since each forecaster might be expected to know their own track record and so should be able to correct for any past biases. Thus, *ex ante*, any forecast from an economic modelling organization should be unbiased and can therefore be written as the true value plus a random error (which has a mean of zero). The average of a number of such forecasts will also have a mean equal to the true value.

The picture that emerges from the survey by Clemen (1989) is that the best overall forecasts come from taking forecasts based on different methods, having discarded any known to be consistently bad, and forming either the optimal linear combination or the simple average of them.

KEN HOLDEN

See also:
Macroeconometric Models; Rational Expectations.

Bibliography
Artis, M.J. 1982), 'Why do Forecasts Differ?', Paper presented to the Panel of Academic Consultants, no.17, London: Bank of England.

Barker, T. (1985), 'Forecasting the Economic Recession in the UK 1979–82: A Comparison of Model-Based *Ex Ante* Forecasts', *Journal of Forecasting*, **4**, April-June, pp. 133–51.

Bates, J.M. and C.W.J. Granger (1969), 'The Combination of Forecasts', *Operational Research Quarterly*, **20**, December, pp. 451–68.

Box, G.E.P. and G.M. Jenkins (1970), *Time-Series Analysis: Forecasting and Control*, San Francisco: Holden-Day.

Clemen, R.T. (1989), 'Combining Forecasts: A Review and Annotated Bibliography', *International Journal of Forecasting*, **5**, pp. 559–84.

Granger, C.W.J. and R. Ramanathan (1984), 'Improved Methods of Combining Forecasts', *Journal of Forecasting*, **3**, April-June, pp. 197–204.

Holden, K. and D.A. Peel (1983), 'Forecasts and Expectations: Some Evidence from the UK', *Journal of Forecasting*, **2**, January-March, pp. 51–8.

Holden, K. and D.A. Peel (1985), 'An Evaluation of Quarterly National Institute Forecasts', *Journal of Forecasting*, **4**, April-June, pp. 227–34.

Holden, K. and D.A. Peel (1990), 'On Testing for Unbiasedness and Efficiency of Forecasts', *The Manchester School*, **58**, June, pp. 120–27.

Holden, K., D.A. Peel and J.L. Thompson (1990), *Economic Forecasting: An Introduction*, Cambridge: Cambridge University Press.

McNees, S.K. (1978), 'The Rationality of Economic Forecasts', *American Economic Review*, **68**, May, pp. 301–5.

McNees, S.K. (1979), 'The Forecasting Record for the 1970s', *New England Economic Review*, September/October, pp. 33–53.

McNees, S.K. (1988), 'How Accurate are Macroeconomic Forecasts?' *New England Economic Review*, July/August, pp. 15–36.

Theil, H. (1966), *Applied Economic Forecasting*, Amsterdam: North-Holland.

Wallis, K.F. (1989), 'Macroeconomic Forecasting – A Survey', *Economic Journal*, **99**, March, pp. 28–61.

Wallis, K.F., M.J. Andrews, P.G. Fisher, G.A. Longbottom and J.D. Whitley (1986), *Models of the UK Economy: A Third Review*, Oxford: Oxford University Press.

Foreign Exchange Reserves

Stocks of foreign currencies held by the central bank.

Foreign Trade Multiplier

The ratio of the change in income to a change in exports. The foreign trade multiplier plays a crucial role in explanations of both the adjustment to correct balance of payments disequilibria and the international transmission of cyclical fluctuations.

See also:

Balance of Payments; Multiplier.

Frictional Unemployment

Unemployment that results because it takes time for workers to search for suitable jobs; also known as search unemployment.

Friedman, Milton (b.1912)

Milton Friedman developed a distinctive, markets-oriented attitude towards work, promotion, and pay quite early in his life. Upon entering Rutgers University just after his sixteenth birthday in 1928, he worked in a men's clothing store, and initially envisioned a career as an actuary. At Rutgers, he became interested in mathematics and took some economics with instructors Arthur F. Burns (who had Columbia ties to Wesley C. Mitchell) and Homer Jones. Through Jones's influence and ties to Chicago, Friedman entered the University of Chicago as a graduate student in economics in the school year 1932–3. In that year his first important ties were to Henry Schultz (in statistics) and Frank H. Knight (an economist, philosopher and ethicist). The influence of Schultz was important primarily because he urged Friedman to transfer to Columbia University to study statistics under Harold Hotelling. Via Hotelling, financial support was provided to study at Columbia.

At Columbia, Friedman found additional interest in Wesley Mitchell's course in business cycles, which cemented Friedman's ties to Burns, Mitchell and the Mitchell-founded National Bureau of Economic Research (NBER). The use of data in testing hypotheses derived from bodies of economics and observations themselves was gaining importance there. Around this time, Simon Kuznets's contribution to GNP accounting and the study of economic growth emerged at the NBER, as did the measurement of business cycles (first so called by Mitchell). Coinciding with much of this were Friedman's early connections to Kuznets, the NBER and the Hotelling-connected, US government, wartime Statistical Research Group (Frazer, 1988).

In the school year 1946–7, Friedman was back at Chicago as an Associate Professor. By 1948, his career, and the major money-oriented, National Bureau publications that defined it, were on track. By 1951, Friedman was reacting critically, from his mathematical-statistics background, to what became the fashionable econometric models, and in 1953 his collection of papers entitled *Essays in Positive Economics* was published, with an added lead essay which he entitled at the last minute 'The Methodology of Positive Economics'. Though essentially a philosophical tract, it connects to Friedman's uses of statistical methods which became a hallmark of his work and his place as the theorist of the Mitchell–Burns era at the NBER. In the crucial consumption function and liquidity preference areas, we turn to theories that derive from observations rather than from existing bodies of economics. Moreover, for Friedman, economic theories are arguments for social reform. Supporting statistical results are supposed to persuade others and eliminate disagreements about the needed reforms.

The 1953 essay, which I shall call Friedman's 'famous essay', foretold of much to come when seen with hindsight. Many have written and commented on it and Bruce Caldwell (1982) called it 'probably the best known piece of methodological writing in economics' (see also Frazer and Boland, 1983; Frazer, 1997; Snowdon and Vane, 1997). If an essay of this sort ever has a 'limited shelf life' it surely extended over four decades.

Going back to 1946, Friedman would have very much rejected the work of Henry Schultz at Chicago on the measurement of demand, saying '*he [Schultz] always tried to wrench the data into a pre-existing theoretical scheme, no matter how much wrench was required*' (Stigler, 1994). Further, by the date of the 'famous essay', Friedman had turned 180-degrees from Frank Knight's distinction between risk and uncertainty, and Knight's view that economics could not become an empirical science.

The distinction Knight made between risk as actuarial (or classical) probability (what Friedman called 'objective' probability in Snowdon and Vane, 1997), on the one hand, and uncertainty as incomplete information, on the other hand, became a part of Robert Lucas's New Classical School (NCS), in contradiction to Friedman's work. For Friedman, uncertainty as regards incomplete information and probability is a part of probability itself, while for the NCS incomplete information is the main source of the business cycle (Frazer, 1997). In other words, there is inconsistency between Friedman's work and the NCS's view of the business cycle. The NCS's view also lacks the motion, the dynamics and the statistical orientation found in Friedman's theories and their connections to what is shown in Figure 1.

To be sure, and by contrast to Knight, Friedman embraces personalistic probability in the spirit of Leonard Savage where probability is the language of uncertainty (Frazer, 1997). By contrast, the NCS goes back to Knight's distinction and adopts John Muth's 1961 definition of rationality, even as it embraces Friedman's NBER-connected distinction between a cycle (or transitory) component and a trend (long-run or more permanent) component in a time series such as is illustrated in Figure 1 for income (Y). As shown, the transitory component is $|Y - Y_p|$ and the permanent component is Y_p. Friedman obtains the trend through a method of averaging data points from peak to trough, and trough to peak, and by the use of three points so obtained to get the trend via regression methods.

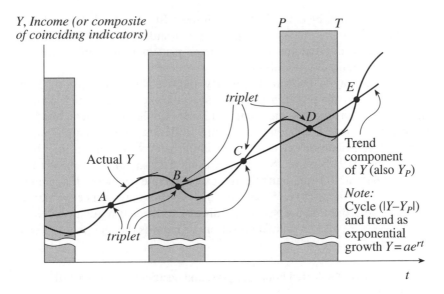

Figure 1 The cycle and trend components in the time series

Much mischief has been done by the failure to recognize the foregoing probability distinctions. In Paul Krugman's (1994) case, the failure leads him to place Friedman and Lucas incorrectly in the same Chicago School camp. As pointed out by Krugman (1994), Lucas's long run is where the economic actors and players understand 'the economic situation', meaning that they do not understand the transitory state $|Y - Y_p|$ even though such understanding may be perfectly rational in personal probability terms. The Lucas view of long-run rationality cannot accommodate the Friedman–Schwartz announced change in the structure underlying the formation of inflationary expectations, to which we turn below.

Going back to 1948, the National Bureau, and Friedman's 1950 piece entitled 'Wesley C. Mitchell as an Economic Theorist', Friedman's most famous works on the money stock and monetary theory were anticipated. They include *Studies in the Quantity Theory of Money* (1956), the Friedman–Schwartz (FS) *Monetary History* (1963), and the FS *Monetary Trends* (1982). Viewing the use of statistical methods found in FS's *Monetary Trends* in its most developed form, we may also go back and note Friedman's NBER imprinted *Theory of the Consumption Function* (1957), where consumption is a variable proportion of permanent income (that is, a variable proportion of the trend path illustrated in Figure 1).

The fact that Friedman also wrote on political-economy matters (and embraced the market economy in particular) is not distinct from the monetary research he embarked upon at the NBER. Indeed, Marx, Lenin and the socialist we place on the political left had little use for the monetary arrangements that are crucial to the proper functioning of the market economy Friedman writes about.

Along the way in Friedman's journey many papers were spun off from the main line of the research and other special topics were treated. Among these, as emphasized by Snowdon and Vane (1997), and others, are 'The Case for Flexible Exchange Rates' and 'Inflation and Unemployment' which ties to Friedman's critique of the Phillips curve, so called after Alban W. Phillips's (1958) paper. So we turn to an assessment of each of these main books and to Friedman's flexible exchange rate paper and his encounters with the Phillips curve. Since Friedman adopts a preference for market solutions to economic problems over direct government regulations, as we will see, we turn also to political positions as regards the alignment of economic ideas.

An assessment of selected books, papers, and positions identified with Friedman

When assessing Friedman's contributions, three possibly interrelated approaches arise. One is holistic and looks at Friedman's works as a total body of interrelated parts. A second, and possibly overlapping, approach is Friedman's own long-run (or 50-year) standard whereby the effects of the body of works ending in 1982 are still to be judged (Frazer, 1988; Snowdon and Vane, 1997). And the third, found in Hatzel (1997), Snowdon and Vane (1997) and Krugman (1994), reduces to an assessment of Friedman's impacts within the community of economists (about the mid-1970s). This comes about largely by way of judgments about an interplay of *a priori* arguments, counterarguments and content found in dated economics textbooks and rarely found by way of a treatment of empirical-science/real-world-policy study.

The first approach recognizes an empirical-science/real-world/policy orientation on Friedman's part. For his work that means the following: appearances before legislative committees; the presence of positive, money-stock/inflation-rate arguments found in the transcripts of television news programmes as well as in the print media of New York, Washington and London; television appearances on the part of Reagan administration appointees; the appearance and content of counteralignments among highly visible, political economists of the early Thatcher years in the publications of Her Majesty's Stationery Office; the early, pre-publication of positions that only later appear in FS's *Monetary Trends* (1982); pamphlets produced in London by Lord Harris's Institute for Economic Affairs; Friedman's direct and indirect connections to Margaret Thatcher (including those to Sir Keith Joseph) and to Ronald Reagan; and the appearance of the bestseller *Free to Choose* (Friedman and Friedman, 1980), as well as television presentations based on it (Frazer, 1988).

The second standard gains visibility on the occasion of Friedman's first learning, through media contacts, that he had received the Nobel Prize in economics for 1976 (Frazer, 1988), although he was no stranger to professional recognition (having received the American Economic Association's John Bates Clark medal in 1951 and having been president of the AEA in 1967). Upon first learning that he was to receive the Nobel Prize, and no doubt hoping for the acceptance of his work in a more permanent long run, Friedman said, with characteristic candour, 'I would not want a professional judgement of my scientific work to be by those . . . people who selected me for the award.'

No doubt reflecting the common understanding of Friedman's work in the mid-1970s, the Nobel committee's official citation read, 'for his achievements in the field of consumption analysis, monetary history and theory, and for his demonstration of the complexity of stabilization policy'.

Studies in the Quantity Theory of Money (1956)
The first chapter of this book contains the rudiments of Friedman's money demand relation (Frazer, 1988, 1994, 1997, 2000) which gets its clearest statement 26 years later in *Monetary Trends* (FS, 1982). Largely a collection of essays drawn from the early dissertations written under Friedman, the volume reflects the topics Friedman introduced much earlier in his paper on Wesley Mitchell as an economic theorist (Frazer, 1988, 1997; Friedman, 1950).

Monetary History (1963) and Monetary Trends (1982)
Monetary History was the first of the NBER planned books. Its main impact was to dramatically alter the explanation for the Great Depression in the United States (Frazer and Yohe, 1966; Frazer, 1988; FS, 1963, ch. 7) and to introduce evidence regarding business conditions and a leading time rate of change in the money stock. This was to require more explanation and elaboration and gain reinforcement with *Monetary Trends* which was in fact about both business cycles (or transitory states $|Y - Y_p|$) and trends, as illustrated in Figure 1. By the 1982 date of *Monetary Trends*, the cycle state as a transitory one was more clearly dealt with and the trend state as a more permanent state was dealt with along far more explicitly dynamic lines than previously.

Although the leading time rate of change in the money stock was still present, three of the numerous features of this newer work may be stated. First, the theoretical arguments behind it were more explicit and graphically based, as was the money demand relation from the much earlier, Friedman-directed, 1956 volume. Second, FS (1982) were able to reject previous NBER and other works on production trends and long swings in business conditions, saying their authors had stayed in 'well-worn ruts' and holding that Hamlet, the Prince of Denmark, had been left out of the long-swing drama (Frazer, 1994; FS, 1982). Third, FS acknowledged the structural change underlying the formation of inflationary expectations in the 1960s (FS, 1982).

This structural change was such that the time lags in the impacts of accelerated and decelerated growth in the money stock started to appear in a shorter amount of time. At stake was a part of FS's statement of the liquidity preference demand for money balances with overshooting (Frazer, 1994; 2000; FS, 1982), as well as other prior research where time lags appeared. In adjusting for the time lag found in the liquidity preference block, I turn to bond traders who begin to process information bearing on the prospects for inflation/deflation more rapidly (Frazer, 1997, ch. 6; Frazer, 2000). This is such that nominal interest rates respond more rapidly to information as the traders form inflationary/deflationary expectations $(+/- \Delta \dot{P}^e)$. This shortened lag time may be attributed in part to the publication of the *Monetary History* in 1963 and to the early, pre-publication circulation of the manuscript for *Monetary Trends*. The latter included early statements of the lagged relation between the money stock and interest rates and it was here that Yohe and Karnosky (1969) made a contribution that caused FS to place added emphasis on the change in the structure underlying the formation of inflationary expectations $(+ \Delta \dot{P}^e)$.

Theory of the Consumption Function (1957)
In confronting cross-section and time series data (which showed support for Keynes's consumption function in the first instance and that indicated permanence of a sort in the saving-to-income ratio over time) Friedman reformulated the consumption function so as to render it compatible with both sets of data. With hindsight, the methodology underlying this work bears similarity to that found in *Monetary Trends*, where permanent income is simply a trend state (also expected income and all as in Figure 1) and consumption is a variable proportion of the permanent income component shown there.

The policy implications of Keynes's simple function (with declining marginal prosperity to consume) and Friedman's redirection of that function *à la* permanent income consumption function (as in Frazer, 1988, 1994, 2000) are at odds with one another as regards tax policy in particular. Keynes's function suggests that income tax rates may be used to obtain an increase in household spending by transferring income from high- to lower-income households where the marginal propensity to consume is higher. Moreover, such analysis parallels another that Friedman encountered early on when he reviewed Abba Lerner's *The Economics of Control* (and reprinted the review in *Essays in Positive Economics*, 1953). It is there that we encounter Lerner's justification for income redistribution (Lerner, 1944). Though Friedman connects his 1953 emphasis on the term 'positive [how-the-world-works] economics' to John Neville Keynes (1891), it was his review of Lerner's book that called attention to 'normative [how-the-world-ought-to-work] economics', as distinct from 'positive'.

In contrast, the hypothesis connecting consumption to permanent income treats consumption as a variable proportion of the permanent income component illustrated in Figure 1. In the first instance, a neutral income tax cut (or tax increase) becomes for Friedman a flat-rate tax. The analysis surrounding it excludes low-income households, to be sure, and arguments for this tax lay behind the radical reductions in the ceilings on the marginal income tax rate in both the UK with Margaret Thatcher and in the USA with Ronald Reagan in the early 1980s and George W. Bush in 2001. Moreover, the arguments are reinforced by Friedman's link to freedom as a goal and its connection to voluntary association in markets, where the flat tax interferes least with that association.

In the second instance, economic growth may be shown to depend on the saving-to-income ratio (Frazer, 1988, 1994). In terms of Figure 1, tax changes that favour more saving rotate the trend line upward and thus increase expenditures on consumption when made in combination with monetary policy. This combination occurs in a world where we encounter an element of so-called 'supply-side economics': the tax policy sets the rate of economic growth in a US-style economy, while monetary policy stabilizes the economy (including by the elimination of inflation from household and business decisions *à la* Alan Greenspan, as in Frazer, 2000). Furthermore, in a global context, such as appears in Frazer (2000), the flow of saving into investment is not simply dependent on domestic-side saving. To be sure, in the global economy some societies and/or cultures may serve as predominantly consumer societies, as in the case of the USA at the close of the twentieth century, while others such as Japan are providing a sizable part of the saving that flows into capital expenditures.

Flexible exchange rates
While a consultant to a Marshall Plan agency in 1950, Friedman wrote a memorandum he first reprinted in *Essays in Positive Economics* (1953) under the title 'The Case for Flexible Exchange Rates' (also reprinted in Leube, 1987). Over the years he made a great deal out of such rates in inter-related contexts. Most notably, in a gold flows (or inflation rate-targeting)

world, trade (or current account) adjustments to imbalances between countries could occur through price-average/purchasing-power means, while in a Keynesian (or Phillips curve) world inflation became the fashionable/domestic-side way to reduce (or maintain) unemployment rates. The inconsistency in these two worlds gained resolution for Friedman by way of his economic freedom goal.

With respect to this goal, countries were free to pursue their own domestic-side policies, which they could do under a system of floating (or 'flexible') exchange rates, even as Friedman himself advocated a domestic-side/market economy ethic where freedom meant voluntary association in markets. There parties to exchanges in markets paid, on the demand side, and received payments, on the supply side. The payments are according to the value of the marginal products of labour and capital.

In a later power and ideas context, where there is the confluence of a problem (such as inflation and a currency tied to a fixed price for gold) and an idea (such as floating exchange rates), Friedman saw his floating rates advocacy as simply an idea President Nixon and his advisors adopted when they had to confront the US inflation and the inability of the USA to continue support of the dollar with gold at a fixed/dollar price in a high-inflation context (Friedman, 1993). The later conflict that arises, as the world becomes more interdependent in trade and financial terms (as in Frazer, 2000), is that countries should not be encouraged via the use of US-supported aid to pursue policies that are potentially destabilizing for the larger, global economy world (Frazer, 2000). A key term is 'moral hazard' whereby some countries may be encouraged to take unacceptable risks in the management of their economies because they are assured of being bailed out by a US-supported aid package. The aid packages favour their doing so.

Friedman's critique of the Phillips Curve

In recognition of Phillips's 1958 piece, the idea of an inverse relation between the unemployment rate and the inflation rate gained ascendancy. To be sure, as Snowdon and Vane (SV) (1997) conclude, the curve came to serve as a significant appendage to the Keynesian investment saving/liquidity money (IS–LM) model. SV argue that the IS–LM and Phillips curve synthesis dominated macroeconomics textbooks in the era in and around 1968.

However, SV say that by 1972 the old consensus was in disarray, and that Friedman by way of the AEA address (Friedman, 1968) 'demonstrated the flaws inherent in the original Keynesian analysis of the Phillips curve'. They say further, in developments surrounding the Phillips curve, that 1976 – the year Friedman received the Nobel Prize in economics – 'marked the pinnacle of Friedman's influence in academia'. They also argue that this is true 'even if monetarism had yet to rise (and fall) in the policy-making arena'. They do this despite the fact that Alan Greenspan's success with the US economy after the July 1990 to March 1991 recession followed from his efforts to eliminate the anticipation of inflation ($\dot{P}^e$) from business and household decisions, by way of Friedman's monetarist work (Frazer, 2000, ch. 6). Incorrectly, SV associated the initiation of the rise with Paul Volcker who, in a flurry of activity on and about 6 October 1979, simply initiated a change in announcing a policy rather than a change in policy towards the containment of inflation (Frazer, 1988, 2000).

Although much has been written on the Phillips curve, we simply note that, in Friedman's last research on it (with Schwartz, 1982), he translated the argument and offered a radically different conclusion for the 1867–1975 period with negative correlation between the price index (P) and the ratio of output to capacity output rather than the positive correlation called for by the Phillips curve argument (Frazer, 1988; 1994; FS, 1982). In the translated Phillips relation, the price index is supposed to be positively related to the ratio of output to capacity output (or $|Q-Q_P|$ in terms analogous to $|Y-Y_P|$ in Figure 1). The transitory component for the production series is $|Q-Q_P|$, while Q_P is the trend.

The transitory component for production is also linked by Friedman (1976) to a firm in a competitive market with overshooting that is analogous to the liquidity preference demand for money with overshooting (Frazer, 1994, chs 3 and 7). At the firm level, the transitory component of production may be stated as $|q-q_P|$. As far back as his 1949 paper, 'The Marshallian Demand Curve' (reprinted in Friedman, 1953), Friedman linked the ordinary and compensated, demand-curve distinctions to a price index (P).

Contrary to the FS restatement of the Phillips relation in *Monetary Trends*, FS reported statistical results in *Monetary Trends* that show the price index (P) to be negatively related to the ratio (Q/Q_P, or alternatively $|Q-Q_P|$). Said differently, the results suggest an analogy to Marshall's downward-sloping demand curve, only now a decline in the price index calls forth increases in production and employment.

Looking simply at trends in the unemployment and inflation rates data series for the USA in the 1960s and 1970s, in one instance, and the 1980s and 1990s, in another, we observe parallel movements upward in the respective data/trend series in the first instance and downward in the second. And of course a declining trend in the inflation rate ($-\Delta\dot{P}$) eventually becomes a decline in the price level ($-\Delta P$), if the trend continues (or is projected) into the future. In this context, and via liquidity preference with overshooting, in any case, we come to the prospect of declining inflation and unemployment rates by way of the relation between the long-bond's nominal interest rate (i_L) and the sum of the 'natural' rate of interest and the probability-weighted expected inflation rate $(Pb[\dot{P}^e]\dot{P}^e)$.

A political alignment of ideas and economics

As Friedman's positions on taxes, the market economy, the dispersement of economic power, Keynesian topics, the failures of the Federal Reserve and the US inflation in the 1960s and 1970s suggest, there is a political–ideological element to Friedman's work. It led him to consider during his career 'Why Government is the Problem' (Friedman, 1993).

The interplay of government and economics in Friedman's work, the professional reactions to it and the impact of Friedman's ideas on the world, and his reactions to the economics he inherited and confronted during much of his career lead to what I have called 'Hotelling's line' (Frazer, 1988, 1994, 1997, 2000). The label comes from a piece by Friedman's statistics professor (Hotelling, 1929) where the professor deals with the positioning of voters on a line viewed as a street and the way centrist politicians may go about positioning themselves to get the most votes. What I add is fourfold: the classification of ideas from economics, as to political left, centre, or right; a concrete treatment of ideas from the mid-nineteenth century to the twentieth century; probability distributions with means and consequently other measures of central tendency to deal with the positioning of voters, politicians and the ideas; and the shifting of mean values, as where Margaret Thatcher asked the voters to join her rather than vice versa, as she sought to redirect Britain and control inflation (Frazer, 1988, chs 14 and 15).

The lines with probability distributions, mean values and all (Frazer, 2000) appear as the vertical lines in Figure 2, with time along a horizontal line. The ideas regarding collectivist-command economics (Marx and the socialists mainly) appear on the left of the line, while on the right of the line we encounter ideas regarding 'the managed market economy' (to use a reference for the positions associated with Friedman). There freedom is a goal, power is dispersed, associations in markets are voluntary, and price averages are controlled indirectly through monetary means rather than via direct, detailed intervention in the economic system. To be sure, on the right of the vertical lines is monetary discipline over prices (the elimination of inflation as a factor in bond trading, business and household decisions). The ideas of the Keynesians' scheme of things are shown in the middle of the vertical lines in Figure 2.

An overview of Friedman's contributions and alignments

As Friedman progressed on his 'empirical science' track to become the NBER's cycle trend, turning points theorist, he did not hesitate to change

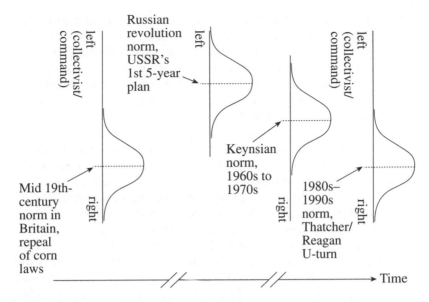

Figure 2 Hotelling's line, with time and shifting norms

his position on hypotheses and the search for a stable statistical relationship when the statistical results went against them. By the time of *Monetary Trends* (FS, 1982) he was attacking parts of Arthur Burns's work that he himself once admired (Frazer, 1997). Another example is Friedman's switch from an income elasticity for the money stock of 1.8 in the *Monetary History* to one of approximately 1 in *Monetary Trends*, as reported in Frazer (1988). And still another example appears in the disappointment FS expressed when they confronted change in the structure underlying the formation of inflationary expectations in the mid 1960s (FS, 1982).

This structural change gains importance principally because the previously emphasized lags in the effect of monetary policy changes occur in a much shorter period of time where agents (and the crucial bond traders we point to) gather information and process it more rapidly. The processing and the short lag time regarding the effects of policy are such that transitory components in key data series are hardly explained by incomplete information and irrationality in the NCS sense.

Following from the concept of the 'bond trader' (Frazer, 1997, 2000), the traders move more towards keeping an eye on Federal Reserve actions and inactions regarding inflation as well as the prospects of future actions. They adjust positions rapidly and rationally in the sense of 'personalistic probability' as opposed to so-called 'objective probability'.

Although central banks encountered difficulties in hitting the range for announced money-growth rates *à la* Milton Friedman (Frazer, 2000), the ultimate goal for Friedman-linked central banking gained ascendancy in another form, namely, that of targeting inflation rates (Frazer, 2000). The Fed's Alan Greenspan adopts both the notion of a sustainable growth path (as in Figure 1) and the notions of structural change and price-level stability. The latter exists when the prospect of inflation is no longer a consideration in household and business decisions (Frazer, 2000).

In Friedman's sojourn his work was approached in its influence on the world in the twentieth century only by that of J.M. Keynes. While embracing Keynes's definition of money and his most basic building blocks known as liquidity preference and the consumption function, Friedman gave them new direction. He set the more static Keynesian constructions in motion to generate verifiable conclusions and on other occasions he proceeded indirectly to relate static constructions such as Marshall's demand curve to measurable variables such as the price level (Frazer, 1994, 2002).

The visibility of Friedman's work and its ultimate impact on the world were advanced by the USA's, the UK's, and the world's policy-induced inflations of the 1960s and 1970s (Frazer, 1988, 2000; and Krugman, 1994). Of course, Friedman's influence did not just happen as a result of his ideas, rising inflation and unemployment rates and the productivity slowdowns.

Although he offended many in his attacks, Friedman was a masterful pedlar of ideas. His arguments were simple and persuasive. Perhaps at times the arguments were too simple and thus subject to much misunderstanding. An outsider as to conventional economics, Friedman drew on his special background and offered originality. He sought acceptability, as he feigned orthodoxy in doing so (Frazer, 1988, 1997).

In his zeal for markets and the dispersement of power, Friedman made a great deal out of his case for flexible exchange rates which appears as a freedom issue for him in the Keynesian era of the 1960s and 1970s. That is, according to it, countries should be free to follow their own respective policies without having to adjust domestic-side economic policies to an internationally fixed exchange rate system (Frazer, 2000). In a later power and ideas context, Friedman saw the 'flexible-rate' case as simply an idea President Nixon and his advisors adopted when they had to confront the problem whereby the dollar could no longer be supported with gold (Friedman, 1993). The conflict that arises as regards Friedman's early advocacy of floating rates is that countries are seen as being more interdependent. This is such that, under the circumstances prevailing at the outset of the twenty-first century, one country should not be encouraged via the use of international aid to pursue policies that are destabilizing for the aid-granting countries and the larger global units (Frazer, 2000).

Friedman's case for markets turns on the freedom issue. The power that may otherwise reside in a government bureau is dispersed by markets operating under a satisfactorily functioning monetary umbrella (the elimination of anticipated inflation and so on). Government becomes the problem when it intervenes via the control of details (such as via direct price, interest rate, and exchange rate controls).

In the mid-1970s, Friedman argued for his positions with increasing aggressiveness, even to the extent of calling for the indexation of wages in labour contracts and placing the Federal Reserve under the US Treasury (Frazer, 1988). Against the backdrop of these times – and before the turn away from the economic and political conditions of the 1970s in the UK and the USA – Friedman could not have envisioned the extent to which changes later occurred in the USA (including those associated with Alan Greenspan and Bill Clinton). Turning to the global scene of the later 1990s, he would not have envisioned in his wildest dreams the emphasis placed on 'moral hazard' and the positive leadership roles of US Treasury Secretary Robert Rubin, his understudy Larry Summers and the International Monetary Fund during the Asian, Russian and other crises of the late 1990s (Frazer, 2000).

WILLIAM FRAZER

See also:

American Economic Association; Business Cycles: Monetarist Approach; Consumption Function; Demand for Money: Friedman's Approach; Expectations-augmented Phillips Curve; Flexible Exchange Rate System; Great Depression; John Bates Clark Medal; Kuznets, Simon S.; Mitchell, Wesley C.; Monetarism; National Bureau of Economic Research; Natural Rate of Unemployment; New Classical Economics; Nobel Prize in Economics; Permanent Income Hypothesis; Phillips Curve; Supply-side Economics.

Bibliography

Caldwell, B. (1982), *Beyond Positivism: Economic Methodology in the Twentieth Century*, London: George Allen & Urwin.
Frazer, W. (1973), *Crisis in Economic Theory*, Gainesville, FL: University of Florida Press.
Frazer, W. (1988), *Power and Ideas: Milton Friedman and the Big U-Turn*, 2 vols, Gainesviile, FL: Gulf Atlantic Publishing Company.
Frazer, W. (1994), *Legacy of Keynes and Friedman*, Westport, CT: Praeger Publishers.
Frazer, W. (1997), *The Friedman System: Economic Analysis of Time Series*, Westport, CT: Praeger Publishers.
Frazer, W. (2000), *Central Banking, Crises, and Global Economy*, Westport, CT: Praeger Publishers.
Frazer, W. and L. Boland (1983), 'An Essay on the Foundations of Friedman's Methodology', *American Economic Review*, **73**, March, pp. 129–44.
Frazer, W. and W. Yohe (1966), *Analytics and Institutions of Money and Banking*, Princeton, NJ: D. Van Norstrand Company.
Friedman, M. (1950), 'Wesley C. Mitchell as an Economic Theorist', *Journal of Political Economy*, **58**, December, pp. 463–95.
Friedman, M. (1953), 'The Methodology of Positive Economics', *Essays in Positive Economics*, Chicago: University of Chicago Press, pp. 3–43.

Friedman, M. (1956), *Studies in the Quantity Theory of Money*, Chicago: University of Chicago Press.

Friedman, M. (1957), *A Theory of the Consumption Function*, Princeton, NJ: Princeton University Press.

Friedman, M. (1968), 'The Role of Monetary Policy', *American Economic Review*, **58**, March, pp. 1–17.

Friedman, M. (1976), *Price Theory*, Chicago: Aldine.

Friedman, M. (1977), 'Inflation and Unemployment', the 1976 Nobel Lecture; reprinted in K.R. Leube (ed.) (1987), *The Essence of Friedman*, Stanford, CA: Hoover Institution Press, pp. 347–69.

Friedman, M. (1993), 'Why Government is the Problem', *Essays in Public Policy*, Stanford, CA: Hoover Institution Press.

Friedman, M. and R. Friedman (1980), *Free to Choose*, New York: Harcourt Brace Jovanovich.

Friedman, M. and A.J. Schwartz (1963), *A Monetary History of the United States, 1867–1960*, Princeton, NJ: Princeton University Press for the National Bureau of Economic Research.

Friedman, M. and A.J. Schwartz (1982), *Monetary Trends in the United States and the United Kingdom: Their Relation to Income, Prices and Interest Rates, 1867–1975*, Chicago: University of Chicago Press for the National Bureau of Economic Research.

Hatzel, R.L. (1997), 'Friedman, Milton', in T. Cate (ed.), *An Encyclopaedia of Keynesian Economics*, Cheltenham, UK and Lyme, US: Edward Elgar.

Hotelling, H. (1929), 'Stability and Competition', *Economic Journal*, **39**, Spring, pp. 541–7.

Keynes, J.N. (1891), *The Scope and Method of Political Economy*, London: Macmillan & Co.

Krugman, P. (1994), *Peddling Prosperity*, New York: W.W. Norton.

Lerner, A. (1944), *The Economics of Control: Principles of Welfare Economics*, New York: Macmillan & Co.

Leube, K.R. (ed.) (1987), *The Essence of Friedman*, Stanford, CA: Hoover Institution Press.

Muth, J.F. (1961), 'Rational Expectations and the Theory of Price Movements', *Econometrica*, **29**, July, pp. 315–35.

Phillips, A.W. (1958), 'The Relation Between Unemployment and the Rate of Change in Money Wage Rates in the United Kingdom, 1861–1957', *Economica*, **25**, November, pp. 283–99.

Snowdon, B. and H.R. Vane (1997), 'Modern Macroeconomics and Its Evolution from a Monetarist Perspective: An Interview with Professor Milton Friedman', *Journal of Economic Studies*, **24**, pp. 192–222.

Stigler, S.M. (1994), 'Some Correspondence on Methodology Between Milton Friedman and Edwin B. Wilson', *Journal of Economic Literature*, **32**, September, pp. 1197–203.

Yohe, W.P., and D.S. Karnosky (1969), 'Interest Rates and Price Level Changes', *Federal Reserve Bank of St. Louis Review*, **51**, December, pp. 19–36.

Frisch, Ragnar A.K. (1895–1973)

Ragnar Frisch (b.1895, Oslo, Norway) obtained his BA (1919) and PhD (1926) from the University of Oslo. His main posts included lecturer at the University of Oslo, 1928–9; Visiting Professor at Yale University, 1930–31 and Professor at the University of Oslo, 1931–65. In 1930 he helped to found the Econometric Society (a term he coined in 1926) and was editor of the society's journal *Econometrica* from 1935 to 1955. In 1969 he was awarded (together with Jan Tinbergen) the first Nobel Prize in Economics 'for having developed and applied dynamic models for the analysis of economic processes'. He is best known for his work on the application of mathematical and statistical methods to the development of dynamic models of the macroeconomy, in particular dynamic models explaining business cycles. Among his best known books are *Statistical Confluence by Means of Complete Regression Systems* (Oslo University Institute of Economics, 1934); and *Economic Planning Studies: A Collection of Essays* (ed. by F. Long) (D. Reidel, 1976). His most widely read articles include 'Propogation Problems and Impulse Problems in Dynamic Economics', in *Economic Essays in Honour of Gustav Cassel* (Allen and Unwin, 1933).

See also:
Econometric Society; Nobel Prize in Economics.

Full Employment

A situation in which all unemployment is frictional and structural, and cannot be permanently reduced by increasing aggregate demand; alternatively, a situation where the labour market clears and unemployment is at its natural rate.

See also:
Aggregate Demand; Frictional Unemployment; Natural Rate of Unemployment; Structural Unemployment.

Full Employment Budget Balance

Given a particular fiscal programme (current tax and spending policies), the full employment budget balance measures the difference between what government tax revenue and expenditure would be *if* the economy were at full employment; also known as the cyclically adjusted budget balance or the structural budget balance. As such it attempts to distinguish the influence of the budget on the economy (due to discretionary policy changes) from that of the economy on the budget (due to automatic changes). The full employment budget deficit/surplus indicates whether fiscal policy is stimulative/restrictive, while its size indicates the degree of stimulus/restraint being exerted on the economy. Compared to the budget balance, the full employment budget balance gives a more reliable guide to the stance of fiscal policy.

See also:
Budget Balance; Budget Deficits: Cyclical and Structural.

Full Employment Output

See:
Potential Output.

Functional Finance

The idea of functional finance runs counter to the idea of 'sound finance' or 'balanced budgets'. In the case of a balanced budget rule a government would be forced to reduce its expenditures and/or increase taxes during a recession (since tax receipts fall as GDP declines) and increase government expenditures and/or decrease taxes during a boom (since tax receipts rise during a boom). From a Keynesian perspective these actions would destabilize even more an already unstable economy; that is, stabilizing a government's finances destabilizes the economy. The principle of functional finance suggests that governments should balance their budgets over the cycle; that is, run deficits during recessions and surpluses during booms. By doing so the government will help to reduce the severity of aggregate fluctuations. The principle of functional finance was promoted in particular by Abba Lerner, in his *The Economics of Control* (New York: Macmillan, 1944).

See also:
Keynesian Economics; Lerner, Abba P.

GDP Deflator

The ratio of nominal GDP to real GDP; a measure of the overall price level which shows the cost of final goods and services currently produced in a country relative to the cost of the same goods and services in a particular base year.

See also:
Gross Domestic Product (GDP); Nominal GDP; Real GDP.

GDP in Current Prices

See:
Nominal GDP.

GDP in Real Prices

See:
Real GDP.

General Agreement on Tariffs and Trade

A multinational trade agreement initially signed by 23 signatory countries, or so-called 'contracting parties', at the Geneva Conference in 1947. The agreement set out rules of conduct for international trade relations and provided a forum for the refinement of the rules and codes that GATT contracting parties agreed would govern trading relations between them. During the life of GATT eight trade negotiations or rounds took place which, between them, reduced both tariff and other barriers to trade, and helped to liberalize trade relations. The most notable rounds included the Kennedy Round (1964–7) which significantly reduced tariffs on whole groups of goods; the Tokyo Round (1973–9) which dealt with both tariff and non-tariff measures; and the Uruguay Round (1986–94) which dealt with, among other issues, the problem of agricultural protection and support, trade in services and the trade-related aspects of intellectual property rights. The Uruguay Round led to the creation of the World Trade Organization, which was established in 1995.

See also:
World Trade Organization.

General Theory

See:
Keynes's *General Theory*.

Globalization

Although globalization is a relatively new concept, it has already provoked all kinds of analyses and discussions, and has given rise to a rich mosaic of theories and diagnoses. Academics from different disciplines, policy makers and non-governmental organizations (NGOs) continue to study and debate, sometimes passionately, the extent to which globalization really exists and is or is not something new. Innumerable books, research papers and articles have been written about globalization's causes, dynamics, consequences and future. And all over the world conferences and seminars are being organized to study and debate the impact and effects of globalization, the need for and conceivability of regulation, and/or the rationales for resistance to globalization's outcomes. All this reflects the fact that, since the end of the 1970s, important changes have taken place in the functioning and organization of the world economy (see Rodrik *et al.*, 1998).

Globalization has not left economic science untouched. There is a continuing debate among economists, especially among trade and labour market specialists, about the extent to which increased inequality in developed countries, and between developed and developing countries, can be explained by economic globalization (see O'Rourke, 2001; Lindert and Williamson, 2001). Economists have debated whether we should talk about *regionalization* or *triadization* rather than globalization, if we look at actual developments in the world economy. The question whether the nation-state is (virtually) dead as an instrument of economic policy has been taken up by many economists (for example, Rodrik, 2000; Prakash, 2001; see also Weiss, 1998). And economists have studied the question to what extent big companies have become 'footloose' (for example, Doremus *et al.*, 1998; Van Tulder *et al.*, 2001). But economists' most important contributions on globalization have been made in debates about just how new current global economic integration is. In this discussion, which has been rather important especially during the 1990s, one can – a bit schematically – distinguish three currents of opinion. Economists, such as former US Secretary of Labour Reich (1992) and Japanese business guru Ohmae (1995), have argued that globalization is a definite trend, that is changing everything, and against which nation-states or trade unions can do very little or even nothing. Partly in reaction to these claims, economists such as Hirst and

Thompson (1996) and Ruigrok and Van Tulder (1995) have strongly questioned the importance, novelty and effects of globalization. Among other things, these authors have argued that the world economy was at least as internationalized at the end of the nineteenth century as it is today (for a discussion of this issue, see Bordo *et al.*, 1999; O'Rourke and Williamson, 2000). Finally, economists such as Altvater and Mahnkopf (1996) and Boyer and Drache (1996) have defended a third position, which can be summed up in the proposition that globalization is an exaggeration. These economists have argued that the world economy is changing significantly, with important implications for the organization and functioning of the world economy, but that we are (still) far from a truly globalized economy, and that many of the claims of globalization ideologues are untenable.

From this last perspective, four developments stand out as especially important. First is an increase in the number of really integrated global markets for goods and services, and especially for finance. This implies that the calculations behind economic decision making must take global conditions and prices into account. Since the 1980s, international trade in goods and services has on average increased twice as fast each year as world output; and, as far as trade orientation is concerned, the world economy has never been as open as it is today. But financial markets are doubtless the most globalized markets, and financial globalization and the corresponding increase in speculation have been spectacular (see Mishkin *et al.*, 1999; Summers, 1990, 2000). Deregulation and financial innovations – in 1980, financial futures, swaps and options still hardly existed – have significantly increased the economic weight of financial markets. Bond markets, stock markets and currency markets are connected – and mutually dependent – worldwide to an extent that has never been seen before in history. While it was still possible in the early 1970s to speak of national financial markets, this is no longer the case.

Second, the role and weight of multinationals in the world economy has increased immensely. Companies prefer to plan and organize the conception, production and distribution of their products and services not only regionally or biregionally but globally, with major consequences for their structures. Thanks to new information technology, production is increasingly being organized on an international scale. The number of enterprises operating internationally is growing immensely. In 1999, according to UNCTAD (2000, p.xv), there were 63 000 such companies with at least 690 000 foreign affiliates.

Third, there has been a far-reaching globalization of a certain type of macroeconomic policies. This can be seen from the fact that variants of the same policy prescriptions are being followed – or pushed through, with the help of international organizations and the discipline imposed by 'the financial markets' – in all parts of the world. Creditor countries seized upon the 1980s debt crisis, for example, to end import-substitution strategies in the south and open southern markets to trade and investment. Key elements of economic policies in the east, west, north and south are (a combination of) export-oriented growth, fewer governmental social policies, reduction of the public sector, deregulation, flexibilization, privatization and priority to price stability. This policy package is sometimes referred to as the 'Washington consensus' (see Williamson, 1990).

Fourth, there is a trend towards more regional and global economic cooperation among countries. One expression of this trend is the increased role and weight of supranational organizations, such as the G7, IMF, WFO, BIS and OECD. Another is the multiplication of regional agreements and blocs, such as the EU, NAFTA and MERCOSUR. Many analysts and observers expect such international bodies and forms of cooperation to gain steadily in importance and to coordinate and take over functions previously performed by national states. More international cooperation seems a logical step for governments increasingly losing control over their own territories as a result of the internationalization of markets for goods, services and finance, companies and economic policies.

Using an analytical tool originating from Marx (1884), the 'circuit of social capital', which can analytically be decomposed into the three separate but indivisible circuits of money capital, commodity capital and production capital, it is possible to differentiate degrees of internationalization. If we look at the current global economy from this perspective, there are three important observations to be made. First, and most important, we can observe for the first time in history a combined internationalization of trade, finance *and* production. In the decades before World War I, which are often compared with modern globalization, trade, finance – and, much more than today, also migration of labour (see, for example, Sutcliffe, 1998) – were strongly internationalized. While the combination of international trade and international capital flows is therefore not new, the accelerated internationalization of production capital since the early 1980s adds a new dimension to current globalization, one that is without precedent.

Second, by contrast with capitalism's golden years (1945–74), finance capital is now dominant, and financial norms, promoting shareholder value, affect companies' mode of functioning and the distribution of income and wealth. Moreover, the ascendancy of finance has major consequences for nation-states' room for manoeuvre. As a result of financial deregulation after the break-up of the Bretton Woods agreement, most transactions in exchange markets are now speculative, and exchange rates depend on capital flows rather than trade flows. Chesnais (1997, p. 297) therefore speaks about a 'globalized regime of accumulation with financial predominance', which is definitely more constraining for states and more homogenizing than the post-World War II 'Fordist accumulation regime'. Consequently, the space for different modalities of countries' participation in the international system has been gradually reduced. The opening up of national financial markets since the mid-1970s, which meant a radical break with the postwar regime, was of course a precondition for these changes. Thirdly, and also as a caveat in the face of (too) schematic inter-pretations, it must be stressed that there are no firewalls between the three types of capital, which are in reality often intermingled.

For a full understanding of how momentous the current international-ization of the three circuits of capital is, another dimension must finally be taken into account. Not only is capital extending capitalist social relations to more and more people and more and more aspects of people's lives, so as to be able to accumulate, but this process also entails an expansion of the scale of production through the growth of individual capitals (concentra-tion of capital) and the extension of command over capital via agglomer-ation of existing capitals, that is by way of mergers and acquisitions (centralization of capital).

Although nobody denies that technological developments play an important enabling role in processes of globalization, at the beginning of the twenty-first century very few modern analysts or observers would still claim that globalization is brought about by natural or technological phe-nomena (see, for example, Went, 2000). In an editorial that was published in the week of the protests that were organized in Prague in September 2000 against the IMF, the British weekly *The Economist* (2000) noted, for example: 'If technological progress were the only driver of global integra-tion, the anti-capitalist threat would be less worrying. (. . .) [T]he protestors are absolutely right: governments are not powerless.' In reaction to mobil-izations by international social movements against (the consequences of) globalization, such as in Seattle (1999), Prague (2000) and Genoa (2001), policy makers, economists and the business press have expressed their fears for what they call a 'backlash against globalization'. Such statements would be senseless if globalization was to be understood as the automatic outcome of exogenous technological processes, since that would imply that globalization is irrevocable. But as Frankel (2000) argues: 'There is a ten-dency to see globalization as irreversible. But the political forces that frag-mented the world for 30 years (1914–1944) were evidently far more powerful than the accretion of technological progress in transport that went on during that period. The lesson is that there is nothing inevitable about the process of globalization.'

ROBERT WENT

Bibliography

Altvater, E and B Mahnkopf (1996), *Grenzen der Globalisierung*, Münster: Westfälisches Dampfboot.

Bordo, M.D., B. Eichengreen and D.A. Irwin (1999), 'Is Globalization Today Really Different than Globalization a Hundred Years Ago?', *National Bureau of Economic Research Working Paper*, no. 7195, June, pp. 1–73.

Boyer, R. and D. Drache (eds) (1996), *States Against Markets: The Limits of Globalization*, London and New York: Routledge.

Chesnais, F. (1997), *La Mondialisation du Capital*, new expanded edn, Paris: Syros.

Doremus, P., W. Keller, L Pauly and S. Reich (1998), *The Myth of the Global Corporation*, Princeton: Princeton University Press.

Economist (2000), 'Editorial: The Case for Globalization', 23 September, pp. 17–18.

Frankel, J. (2000), 'Globalization of the Economy', *National Bureau of Economic Research Working Paper*, no. 7858, August, pp 1–41.

Hirst, P. and G. Thompson (1996), *Globalization in Question*, Cambridge: Polity Press.

Lindert, P.H. and J.G. Williamson (2001), 'Does Globalization Make the World More Unequal?', *National Bureau of Economic Research Working*, Paper, no. 8228, April, pp 1–43.

Marx, K. ([1884] 1978), *Capital*, vol. II, Harmondsworth: Penguin.

Mishkin, F.S. *et al.* (1999), 'Symposium on Global Financial Instability', *Journal of Economic Perspectives*, **13**, Fall, pp. 3–84.

Ohmae, K (1995), *The End of the Nation State: The Rise of Regional Economies*, New York. Free Press

O'Rourke, K.H. (2001), 'Globalization and Inequality: Historical Trends', World Bank Website (*www.worldbank.org*), April, pp. 1–38.

O'Rourke, K.H. and J.G. Williamson (2000), 'When Did Globalization Begin?', *National Bureau of Economic Research Working Paper*, no. 7632, March, pp. 1–33.

Prakash, A. (2001), 'Grappling with Globalization: Challenge for Economic Governance', *The World Economy*, **24**, April, pp. 543–65.

Reich, R. (1992), *The Work of Nations: Preparing Ourselves for 21st Century Capitalism*, New York: Vintage Books.

Rodrik, D. (2000), 'How Far Will International Economic Integration Go?', *Journal of Economic Perspectives*, **14**, Winter, pp. 177–86.

Rodrik, D. *et al.* (1998), 'Symposium on Globalization in Perspective', *Journal of Economic Perspectives*, **12**, Fall, pp. 3–72.

Ruigrok, W. and R. Van Tulder (1995), *The Logic of International Restructuring*, London: Routledge.

Summers, L.H. (1999), 'Reflections on Managed Global Integration', *Journal of Economic Perspectives*, **13**, Spring, pp. 3–18.

Summers, L.H. (2000), 'International Financial Crises: Causes, Prevention and Cures', *American Economic Review*, **94**, May, pp. 1–16.

Sutcliffe, B. (1998), 'Freedom to Move in the Age of Globalization', in D. Baker, G. Epstein and R. Pollin (eds), *Globalization and Progressive Economic Policy*, Cambridge: Cambridge University Press.

United Nations Conference on Trade and Development (UNCTAD) (2000), *World Investment Report 1999. Cross-border Mergers and Acquisitions and Development*, New York and Geneva: UNCTAD.

Van Tulder, R., D. Van den Berghe and A. Muller (2001), *The World's Largest Firms and Internationalization*, Rotterdam: Rotterdam School of Management/Erasmus University.

Weiss, L. (1998), *The Myth of the Powerless State*, Ithaca: Cornell University Press.

Went, R. (2000), *Globalization: Neoliberal Challenge, Radical Responses*, London: Pluto Press.

Williamson, J.G. (1990), 'What Washington Means by Policy Reform', in J.G. Williamson (ed.), *Latin American Adjustment: How Much Has Happened?*, Washington, DC: Institute of International Economics.

Gold Standard

A gold standard is a monetary regime in which the value of the unit of account is tied to the value of a unit of gold. Typically, though not necessarily, a gold standard involves a regime in which a central bank or currency board buys and sells its currency on demand for a fixed amount of gold, or for assets whose value is tied to that of a fixed amount of gold. A gold standard is the best known form of commodity-based monetary system. As Niehans pointed out,

> from a practical point of view, commodity money is the only type of money that, at the present time, can be said to have passed the test of history in market economies. Except for short interludes of war, revolution and financial crisis, Western economies have been on commodity money systems from the dawn of their history almost up to the present time. More precisely, it is only since 1973 that the absence of any link to the commodity world is claimed to be a normal feature of the monetary system. (Niehans, 1978, pp. 140–41)

The gold standard grew out of the earlier bimetallic coinage systems that had been in use in one form or another since classical times. However, the direct origins of the gold standard go back to 1717, when Sir Isaac Newton, as Master of the UK Mint, reformed the coinage in a way that left gold overvalued relative to silver, even though the country was still legally bimetallic. This reform put Britain on a *de facto* gold standard, and over the course of the eighteenth century the convertibility of Bank of England notes into gold became the linchpin of the British monetary system. However, in 1797, the fiscal pressures of the French Revolutionary War led the government to suspend the convertibility of Bank of England currency into gold and Britain went onto a fiat or inconvertible paper standard. The suspension of convertibility was only a temporary measure, and only intended as such, and the gold standard was restored – this time *de jure* and not just *de facto* – at the old parity in 1819. Britain then remained continuously on the gold standard until 1914. For much of the nineteenth century most other countries remained on bimetallic standards, but from the early 1870s onwards there was a move away from bimetallic standards to the gold standard, with major countries such as France, Germany and the United States all on the gold standard by 1880. By then, bimetallism had been abandoned, although fierce debate on the subject continued for a long time in countries such as the USA. The period from 1880 to 1914 was later to be seen as the heyday of the 'classical' international gold standard. Most countries then suspended convertibility into gold on the outbreak of World War I in 1914.

After the war ended, there were various attempts to 'return to gold' in the

1920s (for example, by Britain in 1925), but the inter-war gold standard was a more limited and more fragile affair than its predecessor, and also involved much more management (that is, control) by the major central banks involved. The financial crisis of September 1931 then saw most countries again driven off the gold standard, and the world economy went into depression. The connection between the gold standard and the speed of recovery from the Depression is a highly controversial subject, but most scholars believe that abandoning the gold standard helped the recovery process: see, for example, Temin (1989) or Eichengreen (1992), although Rothbard (1962) offers a contrary view.

A new gold standard – the Bretton Woods system – was only established after World War II. This new standard was a gold standard in theory rather than in practice: participating countries tied their currencies to the US dollar, and the dollar was tied to gold. It was therefore in effect a dollar standard, but the inflationary policies of the Federal Reserve in the 1960s eventually made it impossible for the Fed to maintain the fixed price of gold: the price of gold was then allowed to float, and what was left of the gold standard was abandoned. Thereafter, for the first time in world monetary history, the major countries of the world were on an inconvertible paper standard, not just as a temporary measure to deal with a war or other crisis, but permanently, with no serious intent to restore any commodity standard. The world has been on this fiat monetary standard ever since.

In a gold standard, the central bank or currency board fixes the price of gold in terms of its own currency by offering a (more or less) perfectly elastic supply of currency at the fixed gold price. We can then think of the price level under the gold standard as determined by supply and demand in the gold market. If the demand for gold rises, other things being equal, the relative price of gold – the price of gold against goods and services in general – must rise and, since the nominal price of gold is fixed, the relative price of gold can only rise if the price level falls: a rise in the demand for gold therefore tends to produce a fall in the price level. Conversely, a rise in the supply of gold leads, other things again being equal, to a fall in the relative price of gold, and the relative price of gold can only fall if the price level rises: so a rise in the supply of gold tends to lead to a rise in the price level. Generally speaking, we might also expect the price level under a gold standard to fall with economic progress, because such progress leads to a rising demand for gold (that is, economic progress under a gold standard tends to be deflationary), and we might expect the gold standard price level to rise with improvements in gold extraction technology, because of the resulting increase in the supply of gold. One other theoretical feature of the gold standard is the Gibson paradox – a positive correlation between the interest rate and the price level – which was noted by Keynes (1930,

p. 198). The Gibson paradox arises because of the durability of gold: a higher interest rate reduces the demand to hold durable goods, and hence reduces the demand to hold gold. The relative price of gold must therefore fall to equilibrate the market for it, and the relative price of gold can only fall if the price level rises (see, for example, Barsky and Summers, 1988). Hence, a rise in interest rates leads to a rise in the price level.

Perhaps the most striking stylized fact about the historical gold standard is its very considerable degree of long-run price stability: for example, the UK price level in 1914 was roughly the same as it had been when the UK first went onto a *de facto* gold standard two centuries earlier, and other gold standard countries experienced broadly similar long-run price stability. However, the gold standard price level was much less stable over shorter periods: prices rose significantly following the Californian and Australian gold discoveries of the late 1850s; they then began to fall again in the late 1860s, and continued to fall until the mid-1890s; technical advances in gold processing and further gold discoveries then led to rising prices until the outbreak of World War I. The short-run price level was thus heavily influenced by developments in the gold market. There is also some evidence to support the theoretical predictions that economic progress under the gold standard can be deflationary, and to support the Gibson paradox associating increases in interest rate with higher prices.

There is much controversy over the monetary policy implications of a gold standard, and the most controversial issue relates to the extent to which a gold standard constrains a central bank from pursuing its own independent discretionary monetary policy. Under a gold standard, a central bank has little, if any, monetary policy discretion: interest rates, prices and so on are largely beyond its control. But whether one regards the absence of any substantial degree of monetary policy discretion as good or bad boils down to one's views about the usefulness or otherwise of monetary policy discretion in the first place: those who agree with the 'rules' side of the 'rules versus discretion' debate will approve of this particular feature of the gold standard, even if the gold standard is not their preferred rule; and those of a Keynesian disposition who support discretion will regard this feature as a drawback. That said, a gold standard can still leave room for some monetary policy discretion, as the experience of the 'managed' (or rather, mismanaged) gold standard of the 1920s amply demonstrates.

Another controversial issue relates to so-called 'resource costs' of the gold standard. A standard (*sic*) argument made by opponents is that a gold standard involves high resources costs (high costs of mining and storing gold for monetary policy purposes) but there is no necessary reason why a gold standard should involve a large amount of monetary gold: it is quite possible for a central bank or currency board to operate on a gold standard using relatively small amounts of monetary gold. In any case, we should not presume that the resource costs of a monetary standard are a social waste that could be eliminated without costly side-effects. Irredeemable currencies also involve 'resource costs' even though the issuers have no need to keep reserves: these costs include the costs of inflation made possible by central bank freedom from the constraints of a gold standard. These costs appear to be very large indeed, and include the costs incurred as agents use up resources trying to protect themselves against the inflationary and asset-price instability associated with irredeemable currencies, as well as the broader social costs of inflation. In the words of Milton Friedman,

> In earlier discussions, other monetary economists and I took it for granted that the real resource cost of producing irredeemable paper money was negligible. Experience under a universal irredeemable paper money standard makes it crystal clear that such an assumption, while it may be correct with respect to the direct cost to the government of issuing fiat outside money, is false for society as a whole. (Friedman, 1986, p. 643)

All in all, the gold standard has a respectable historical record and in terms of the most important criterion, price-level stability, it compares very well to the fiat monetary regime that succeeded it. It also goes to show that in monetary issues, 'progress' – in this case, the replacement of the gold standard by inconvertible fiat money – does not necessarily lead to better outcomes.

KEVIN DOWD

See also:
Bretton Woods; Great Depression; Rules versus Discretion.

Bibliography
Barsky, R.B. and L.H. Summers (1988), 'Gibson's Paradox and the Gold Standard', *Journal of Political Economy*, **96**, June, pp. 1161–76.
Eichengreen, B. (1992), *Golden Fetters: The Gold Standard and the Great Depression, 1919–1939*, New York: Oxford University Press.
Friedman, M. (1986), 'The Resource Cost of Irredeemable Paper Money', *Journal of Political Economy*, **94**, June, pp. 642–7.
Keynes, J.M. (1930), *A Treatise on Money, Volume Two*, London: Macmillan.
Niehans, J. (1978), *The Theory of Money*, Baltimore and London: Johns Hopkins University Press.
Rothbard, M.N. (1962), *Man, Economy and State: A Treatise on Economic Principles*, Princeton, NJ: D. Van Nostrand.
Temin, P. (1989), *Lessons from the Great Depression*, Cambridge, MA: MIT Press.

Golden Age Growth

During the period 1950–73 the world economy witnessed unparalleled rates of growth of per capita GDP. Table 1 contains Angus Maddison's (2001) most recent calculations for per capita growth of GDP for the period 1820–1998 and, as is clearly evident, the 1950–73 era stands out in comparison to all other periods either before or since.

Table 1   Growth of per capita GDP, world and major regions, 1820–1998 (annual average compound growth rates)

Region	1820–70	1870–1913	1913–50	1950–73	1973–98
Western Europe	0.95	1.32	0.76	4.08	1.78
Western offshoots*	1.42	1.81	1.55	2.44	1.94
Japan	0.19	1.48	0.89	8.05	2.34
Asia (excluding Japan)	−0.11	0.38	−0.02	2.92	3.54
Latin America	0.10	1.81	1.42	2.52	0.99
Eastern Europe and former USSR	0.64	1.15	1.50	3.49	−1.10
Africa	0.12	0.64	1.02	2.07	0.01
World	0.53	1.30	0.91	2.93	1.33

Note: *The 'Western offshoots' are the USA, Canada, Australia and New Zealand.

Source: Angus Maddison (2001), *The World Economy: A Millennial Perspective*, Paris: OECD, Table 3-1a.

In particular, the growth achievements witnessed in the postwar Western European economy are so impressive that this period has been referred to as the 'Golden Age' (see N.C.R. Crafts, 'The Golden Age of Economic Growth in Western Europe', *Economic History Review*, **48**, August, 1995; N.C.R. Crafts and G. Toniolo (eds) (1996), *Economic Growth in Europe Since 1945*, Cambridge University Press, 1996; A. Maddison, 'The Nature and Functioning of European Capitalism: A Historical and Comparative Perspective, *Banca Nazionale Del Lavoro Quarterly Review*, December 1997; G. Toniolo, 'Europe's Golden Age, 1950–73: Speculations from a Long-Run Perspective', *Economic History Review*, **51**, May, 1998). Although Crafts and Toniolo (1996) view the 'Golden Age' as a 'distinctly European phenomenon', it should be noted that the growth miracle also extended to the centrally planned economies, Latin America, Asia and Africa. During this same period Japan's growth performance was nothing less than exceptional.

Several factors contributed to the 'Golden Age' in the capitalist economies, including (1) increasing liberalization of international transactions;

(2) the active promotion of buoyant domestic demand by Keynesian-inspired governments; (3) an investment boom; (4) a backlog of technological developments that had not been fully exploited during 20 years of depression and war; (5) the beneficial foundations for growth established by the Marshall Plan; (6) the adoption of American-style mass production techniques; and (7) the establishment of political and economic institutions that were conducive to high investment and wage moderation. All of these factors contributed to the growth miracle and, as a result, during the 'Golden Age', many OECD countries experienced a significant degree of 'catch-up' and 'convergence' on US levels of economic performance (in keeping with the predictions of the Solow growth model). From a growth accounting perspective, much of the acceleration of total factor productivity growth during the 'Golden Age' was due to scale effects, improvements in resource allocation as well as catch-up influences (see N.C.R. Crafts, 'Globalisation and Growth in the Twentieth Century', *IMF Working Paper*, WP/00/44, 2000, *http://www.imf.org/*).

After 1973, there was a marked slowdown in growth, with the major OECD economies returning to growth rates more in line with the longer-run trend. If the quarter century following the implementation of the Marshall Plan in 1948 was a period where conditions were conducive to catch-up and convergence, the period after the first OPEC oil shock was one characterized by a 'productivity slowdown' and increased cyclical volatility.

See also:

Catching Up and Convergence; Growth Accounting; Neoclassical Growth Model; Productivity Slowdown.

Gordon, Robert J.

Robert Gordon (b.1940, Boston, Massachusetts, USA) obtained his BA from Harvard University in 1962 and his PhD from Massachusetts Institute of Technology in 1967. His main past posts have included Assistant Professor at Harvard University, 1967–8; and Assistant Professor at the University of Chicago, 1968–73. Since 1978, he has been a Research Associate at the National Bureau of Economic Research and since 1983 a Research Fellow at the Centre for Economic Policy Research. He is currently the Stanley G. Harris Professor in the Social Sciences at Northwestern University. He is best known for his work on demonstrating the importance of supply shocks and demand pressure to inflation; and price inertia in the postwar period in the Unites States. Among his best known books are *Milton Friedman's Monetary Framework: A Debate with his Critics* (ed.) (University of Chicago Press, 1974); and *Macroeconomics* (8th edn, Addison-Wesley, 2000). His most widely read articles include 'Output Fluctuations and Gradual Price Adjustment' (*Journal of Economic Literature*, **19**, June 1981); 'Price Inertia and Policy Ineffectiveness in the United States, 1890–1980' (*Journal of Political Economy*, **90**, December 1982); 'What is New-Keynesian Economics?' (*Journal of Economic Literature*, **28**, September 1990); 'The Time-Varying NAIRU and its implications for Economic Policy' (*Journal of Economic Perspectives*, **11**, Winter 1997); and 'Does the New Economy Measure Up to the Great Inventions of the Past?' (*Journal of Economic Perspectives*, **14**, Fall, 2000).

See also:

National Bureau of Economic Research.

Government Budget Constraint

The budget constraint faced by the government. Assuming a closed economy for simplification purposes (so that there is no need to take into account finance via balance of payments flows), if a government wishes to increase its expenditure, the increase must be financed by tax revenue; borrowing from the private sector, through issuing bonds; and/or borrowing from the central bank, through the creation of high-powered money.

See also:

High-Powered Money.

Gradualism

A slow and gradual reduction in the rate of monetary growth aimed at reducing the rate of inflation.

See also:

Cold Turkey; Gradualism versus Cold Turkey; Inflation: Costs of Reducing; Sacrifice Ratio.

Gradualism versus Cold Turkey

Gradualism versus cold turkey involves the debate about how quickly, and by how much, the authorities should reduce the rate of monetary growth in order to reduce the rate of inflation.

Those economists who advocate cold turkey (for example, New Classical economists), involving a rapid and permanent reduction in the rate of monetary growth, do so arguing that the output/employment costs of disinflation will be negligible provided policy is credible. The New Classical approach implies that, if the authorities announce a reduction in the rate of monetary growth and the policy announcement is believed to be credible, rational economic agents will rapidly revise their expectations of inflation downwards in line with the anticipated effects of monetary contraction on the rate of inflation, enabling disinflation to be achieved with little increase in unemployment and loss of output, that is, with a low sacrifice ratio.

In contrast, those economists who advocate gradualism (for example, orthodox Keynesians and monetarists), involving a slow and gradual reduction in the rate of monetary growth, do so in order to minimize the output/employment costs of disinflation, fearing that cold turkey would cause substantial and prolonged unemployment. In new Keynesian models the gradual adjustment of prices (for example, owing to menu costs) and wages (for example, owing to wage contracts) implies that any policy of monetary disinflation, even if credible and anticipated by rational economic agents, will lead to a significant increase in unemployment and a substantial reduction in output, that is, a high sacrifice ratio. Furthermore, if following monetary disinflation the economy experiences a prolonged recession, the natural rate of unemployment, or NAIRU, will tend to increase owing to hysteresis effects.

See also:

Credibility and Reputation; Hysteresis; Inflation: Costs of Reducing; Menu Costs; Monetarism; New Classical Economics; New Keynesian Economics; Sacrifice Ratio.

Great Depression

Peter Lindert (1981, p. 125) has written that 'explaining the onset, the severity, and the duration of the Great Depression is almost as central a task to macroeconomics as is the study of viral epidemics to medicine'. The traumatic decade of the 1930s spawned refinements of several schools of thought on the nature of the market system and fluctuations in its secular progress. The so-called 'Keynesian Revolution' was one such outcome, though Laidler (1999) has shown that Keynes's achievement in his *General Theory* (1936) lay mainly in his new configuration of established ideas on savings, investment, interest and money. His income–expenditure theory suggested an economy could not only lapse into an ordinary recession but, absent a more activist fiscal role for government, could be stuck there for an inordinate time, as in the 1930s, even if prices and wages responded flexibly to the vagaries of aggregate demand. The *General Theory* was quickly followed by the IS–LM synthesis that was to transform macroeconomics and show that monetary as well as fiscal policy plays a central role in stabilization, partly depending on whether the authorities are dealing with normal cycles or abnormal slumps.

Peter Temin (1976) later presented one of the most influential Keynesian diagnoses of the Great Depression in the United States. (The proper focus of attention is the USA: it was by far the most important economy in the 1930s, was the country where depression started earliest, ended latest, struck most deeply, and transmitted the greatest worldwide shock waves; see Romer, 1993.) Temin suggested that excess capacity had developed in key industries in the 'booming' 1920s, causing a sharp downturn in investment (notably in construction, which peaked in 1928), exacerbated by the stock market crash of October 1929 that caused consumer confidence and spending to slump, a point also highlighted by Romer (1990). There were then multiplier effects on output and employment.

According to Temin, a period of easy money ensued, as evidenced by falling interest rates and a rise in the real money supply as prices fell faster than the nominal money supply. The latter had fallen in passive response to the fall in expenditures and demand for bank credit. The behaviour of money was therefore a symptom rather than the cause of the problem, and fiscal rather than monetary policy the vital missing cure. However, Temin's 'monetary theory' critics (see below) point out that falling nominal interest rates could be due to falling loan demands caused by a downturn in activity created by prior monetary contraction. In the early 1930s, when nominal rates were falling, real rates were rising sharply. Likewise, rising real money stocks may be the result of price-level deflation generated by tight, not easy, monetary policy. Bernanke (1983) also noted that bank failures and a shift into cash caused surviving banks to make only the safest, high-quality, short-term investments. So the average interest rate was lower but volume smaller. Higher-rate lending to households, farmers and small businesses was sharply curtailed.

The 1930s also saw refinements of Austrian theories of capital and the business cycle that built on the insights of Carl Merger, Eugen Böhm-Bawerk and Ludwig von Mises. Most prominent was the work of Friedrich von Hayek and Lionel Robbins at the London School of Economics, and Gottfried Haberler and Joseph Schumpeter at Harvard. They worried about the power of banks not only to intermediate between savers and investors but also to create new fiat money. This enables them to lend to investors at interest rates below the 'natural' rate, so that resources are misallocated between consumer and investment goods, creating an unhealthy, unsustainable boom and distortion of relative prices. The more the authorities try to stave off the inevitable crisis by pumping yet more money or credit into the system, the more trouble they brew. These writers (and their modern exponents such as Garrison, 1999, 2001) deduced that the severity of the slump of 1929–33 in the USA must have been largely due to exceptionally irresponsible credit expansion in the preceding years, creating distortions that could only be purged by a salutary liquidation of poor investments. They were policy nihilists in the sense that, apart from recommending measures to promote greater downward price and wage flexibility (the opposite of what Roosevelt's New Deal offered), they argued that expansionist fiscal or monetary measure would only deepen the depression.

The Austrian view suggests that a major slump must have been preceded by a major boom. In fact the average annual real growth rate in the United States, 1920–29, was only 3.4 per cent (1.6 per cent in per capita terms, with population growing at about 1.8 per cent a year) – roughly in line with the long-term trend – and the index of wholesale prices actually fell slightly between 1925 and the peak of GNP in August 1929. (In the United Kingdom, struggling to maintain her return to the gold standard in 1925 at the pre-war parity, prices were falling sharply over the same period. Recovery soon followed after she left the gold standard in September 1931.) See Eichengreen (1992) and Temin (1989) on the importance of the gold standard in transmitting depression from one country to another and in constraining expansionist policies. For the Austrians, however, their 'neutral money' theory asserted that credit has been dangerously inflationary if the price level, overall and in each sector, has not fallen fully in line with cost reductions associated with technical change.

A related view held by the Federal Reserve Board in 1923–9 was that the rapid rise in stock prices was also symptomatic of excessively easy credit. Thus they pursued a tightening of policy through this period, culminating in a sharp increase in the discount rate in August 1929, just as the real economy was turning down. Their focus was on the quality of bank assets, and they became increasingly anxious as 'unproductive' loans for speculative stock market investments rose faster than productive commercial loans that 'accommodate the needs of trade.' This was in tune with the real bills doctrine, or the commercial loan theory of prudent monetary policy.

This doctrine was called into question first by Lauchlin Currie (1931, 1934) at Harvard (influenced by Allyn Young, Ralph Hawtrey and the early Keynes) and, more famously, in the later magisterial work of Milton Friedman and Anna J. Schwartz (1963), who showed that, while broad 'credit' grew rapidly in the late 1920s, the money supply itself was growing more slowly than national income, and commercial banks were becoming increasingly indebted to the reserve banks.

When the stock market crashed on 29 October, the initial response of the powerful Federal Reserve Bank of New York was to engage in substantial open-market purchases but, believing that falling interest rates signalled that the Fed had done all it could to stave off depression, these purchases were not sustained. Confidence was badly shaken and reduced spending on investment and consumer goods meant that the velocity of money declined sharply to accentuate the 2.6 per cent fall in the money stock during August 1929 to October 1930. Nominal national income thus declined by about 15 per cent in this period, or by about 11 per cent in real terms (Friedman and Schwartz, 1963, p. 301). In 1930–31, real income fell by 9 per cent; in 1931–2 by 18 per cent; and in 1932–3 by a further 3 per cent. Unemployment rose from about 3 per cent of the workforce to nearly 25 per cent, with many more put on short-time working.

From 1933 there followed nearly four years of strong recovery from a very low base. But in April 1937 there was another very sharp recession. Over the next 15 months real national income fell by about 18 per cent. Only with the build-up of preparations for war in 1939–41 would the US economy firmly recover its 1929 level of output, and only with war itself would full employment be restored.

'Monetary' interpretations of the Great Contraction, 1929–33, emphasize the failure of the Federal Reserve Board to engage in adequately expansionist policies. The banks used new reserves mainly to reduce their indebtedness to the Fed rather than to increase lending. Had the Fed provided a net increase in reserves the banks, at that time fully loaned up, with very few excess reserves, would certainly have increased their assets and liabilities. That way the circular flow of national income would have been maintained at a higher level and the downturn would not have evolved into prolonged collapse. In October 1930, the downturn produced a spate of bank failures that caused panic moves into currency for the first time. Distress spread throughout the land as small farmers and businesses lost their customary access to working capital from their local unit banks. The banks' loss of reserves was met with only minor and temporary Federal Reserve credit. In the face of system-wide liquidations, the Fed failed to provide the lender-of-last-resort facilities that had been the classic Bagehotian response to such crises in the past. This story was repeated in the face of a second banking crisis in March 1931, and again after Britain left the gold standard in September 1931. As gold flowed out of the USA, the Fed responded passively instead of attempting to sterilize these flows (see Wheelock, 1992). Perversely, the tendency was to sterilize gold inflows but not gold outflows.

By this time the depression had shaken confidence so badly that private demand for loanable funds may have made open-market operations relatively ineffective on their own. In January 1932, the Harris Foundation sponsored a conference at the University of Chicago on 'Gold and Monetary Stabilization' (Wright, 1932) that convened the country's most distinguished economists. Twenty-four of them, including 12 from Chicago, cabled a list of recommendations to President Herbert Hoover, urging him to support vigorous open-market operations combined with public works. These recommendations, along with Jacob Viner's contribution to the conference, are the earliest of the sources cited by Milton Friedman (1974) as epitomizing the economics of the 'Chicago Tradition' of the 1930s from which, he claimed, his own work drew its inspiration. For a heavily depressed economy they endorsed budget deficits as the means whereby, in conjunction with open-market operations, money could most effectively be put into circulation and spent.

These ideas had been even more forcefully expressed a little earlier by three young Harvard instructors, Lauchlin Currie, Paul Theodore Ellsworth and Harry Dexter White (Laidler and Sandilands, 2002). They urged a relaxation of the gold reserve constraint on fiscal and monetary expansion, plus a reduction of the 1930 Smoot–Hawley tariffs and relief of reparations and inter-allied debts that were depressing world demand with adverse feedbacks upon the USA. Their 'fiscal inflationist' views were well represented at the Chicago conference by Harvard's John H. Williams, who played a key role in drafting the cable to President Hoover. Among those who did not sign were Gottfried Haberler (visiting Harvard from Vienna), the real-bills advocate Henry Parker Willis (Columbia) and Paul H. Douglas (Chicago) who espoused alternative 'underconsumptionist' ideas.

Shortly afterwards, in April 1932, the Federal Reserve banks did engage in more positive open-market purchases but these were again short-lived. They also coincided with an outflow of gold (mostly to France), and then came a package of tax increases in June as part of Hoover's budget-balancing programme. The latter was thought necessary 'to restore confidence' and because tax revenues had naturally declined with the decline in national income. Thus a fiscal squeeze reinforced the consequences of the monetary squeeze.

Finally, there came the calamitous banking crisis of March 1933. The newly installed President Franklin Roosevelt, who in his inaugural speech had declared that 'the only thing we have to fear is . . . fear itself', now declared a week-long banking holiday. Over 2000 banks never reopened, and so yet more of the nation's money supply was wiped out.

Though the pragmatic Roosevelt had, like Hoover, run on a budget-balance ticket in the presidential campaign, on assuming office he launched his wide-ranging New Deal. A host of regulatory measures, including price and wage supports, galvanized him politically while not necessarily helping the economy (Brinkley, 1995; Cole and Ohanion, 1999). More helpful was the policy of lowering the gold content of the dollar in 1933 to 1934, plus major spending programmes and banking reforms supervised by a new Federal Reserve Board governor, Marriner Eccles, an expansionist who over the next few years battled for influence with the president against the more cautious Treasury Secretary, Henry Morgenthau, Jr. Gold inflows from a nervous Europe also played a major part in expanding the money supply, though the banks were now building up large excess reserves.

The net effect was strong recovery from 1933 to early 1937. As a precautionary measure, the Fed took steps in late 1936 and early 1937 to mop up a portion of the banks' excess reserves. The fear was that, as recovery proceeded and the velocity of existing money recovered its more normal value (that is, as desired holdings of money as a fraction of income declined), monetary spending might recover far faster than the real economy, with potentially serious inflationary consequences. The existence of excess bank reserves could then frustrate the Fed's ability to control the situation.

Nevertheless, in view of the still substantial spare capacity that existed in 1936, fear of inflation has puzzled students of the period. Yet in early 1936 even the leading Chicago economist Henry C. Simons (1936, p.17) spoke of the 'drastic measures for debt retirement that may soon become imperatively necessary to prevent a disastrous inflationary boom'. (This presumably meant that he was calling for inflation control via a fiscal surplus to pay off debt without increasing the money supply.) In fact, shortly afterwards the economy suffered a serious reverse – even sharper, though much shorter, than the 1929–33 contraction. Most economists (such as Steindl, 1995) support Friedman and Schwartz in blaming the increased reserve requirements, though much of that effect was offset by continuing gold inflows from Europe. Excess reserves remained at around $2 billion, interest rates remained very low, and the money supply continued to increase through to the end of March 1937. The decline in the economy thus *coincided* with the fall in the money supply (though its rate of growth had been slowing for some time), rather than with the usual six-month (or so) lag that theory predicted.

An alternative diagnosis focused on the sharp fiscal contraction in 1937, and on how fears relating to the 1935 Wagner Act had led to large inventory accumulations in 1936 in anticipation of labour market strife that did indeed occur in 1937, when stockpiling ceased. In the crucial period March to September 1937 the net government contribution to spending fell to only $60 million a month compared with an average of $335 million a month in 1936 (for details see Sandilands, 1990, pp.87–92). The banks accordingly lost an important outlet for safe lending (purchase of new government securities) and needed time to find alternative borrowers. The fiscal downturn and related fall in aggregate demand must also have discouraged private demand for bank loans. Thus, in 1936 and 1937 the trajectory of money (M) and monetary expenditures (M times its periodic income velocity) was itself partly dependent on fiscal policy. For in conditions of abnormally severe depression net public spending is an important way to add (1936) or subtract (1937) money from the circular flow, directly or indirectly. With monetary and fiscal variables thus intertwined, attempts to estimate the separate effects of monetary and fiscal stimuli during this period (for example, Romer, 1992) can be misleading.

In any event, in 1937 the Keynesians and their allies (notably Lauchlin Currie, a pre-Keynesian 'fiscal inflationist' now a senior adviser at the Fed) on the one hand, and the budget balancers on the other, became locked in a furious 'struggle for the soul of FDR' (Stein, 1969). Roosevelt initially sided with Morgenthau, and disaster followed. Not until April 1938, after the worst period of his long tenure in the White House, and after a strong letter from Keynes in February, did Roosevelt at last ask Congress for more than $3 billion of spending or lending in the immediate future for relief, public works, housing and assistance to state and local governments (Barber, 1996, p.114). In 1939 the net federal contribution to spending nearly doubled to around $3.6 billion and the build-up to war afforded more relief. However, the final battle against the Great Depression would be won only after Pearl Harbor.

ROGER J. SANDILANDS

See also:

Business Cycles: Austrian Approach; Federal Reserve System; Gold Standard; Keynesian Economics.

Bibliography

Barber, W.J. (1996), *Designs within Disorder: Franklin D. Roosevelt, the Economists and the Shaping of American Economic Policy, 1933–1945*, Cambridge: Cambridge University Press.
Bernanke, B.S. (1983), 'Nonmonetary Effects of the Financial Crisis in the Propagation of the Great Depression', *American Economic Review*, **73**, June, pp.257–76.
Brinkley, A. (1995), *The End of Reform: New Deal Liberalism in Recession and War*, New York: Vintage Books.
Cole, D.C. and L.E. Ohanion (1999), 'The Great Depression in the United States from a Neoclassical Perspective', *Federal Reserve Bank of Minneapolis Quarterly Review*, **23**, Winter, pp.25–31.
Currie, L. (1931), 'The Decline of the Commercial Loan', *Quarterly Journal of Economics*, **45**, August, pp.698–709.
Currie, L. (1934), *The Supply and Control of Money in the United States*, Cambridge, MA: Harvard University Press.

Eichengreen, B. (1992), *Golden Fetters: The Gold Standard and the Great Depression, 1919–39*, Oxford and New York: Oxford University Press.

Friedman, M. (1974), 'Comments on the Critics', in R.J. Gordon (ed.), *Milton Friedman's Monetary Framework*, Chicago: University of Chicago Press.

Friedman, M. and A.J. Schwartz (1963), *A Monetary History of the United States, 1867–1960*, Princeton: Princeton University Press.

Garrison, R.W. (1999), 'The Great Depression Revisited', *The Independent Review*, **III**, Spring, pp. 595–603.

Garrison, R.W. (2001), *Time and Money: The Macroeconomics of Capital Structure*, London and New York: Routledge

Keynes, J.M. (1936), *The General Theory of Employment, Interest and Money*, London: Macmillan.

Laidler, D. (1999), *Fabricating the Keynesian Revolution: Studies of the Inter-war Literature on Money, the Cycle and Unemployment*, Cambridge: Cambridge University Press.

Laidler, D. and R.J. Sandilands (2002), 'An Early Harvard *Memorandum* on anti-Depression Policies', *History of Political Economy*, **34**, Fall, 515–52.

Lindert, P.H. (1981), 'Comments on "Understanding 1929–32"', in K. Brunner (ed.), *The Great Depression Revisited*, Boston: Martinus Nijhoff Publishing.

Romer, C.D. (1990), 'The Great Crash and the Onset of the Great Depression', *Quarterly Journal of Economics*, **105**, August, pp. 597–624.

Romer, C.D. (1992), 'What Ended the Great Depression?' *Journal of Economic History*, **52**, December, pp. 757–84.

Romer, C.D. (1993), 'The Nation in Depression', *Journal of Economic Perspectives*, **7**, Spring, pp. 19–39.

Sandilands, R.J. (1990), *The Life and Political Economy of Lauchlin Currie: New Dealer, Presidential Adviser and Development Economist*, Durham, NC and London: Duke University Press.

Simons, H.C. (1936), 'Rules versus Authorities in Monetary Policy', *Journal of Political Economy*, **44**, February, pp. 1–30.

Stein, H. (1969), *The Fiscal Revolution in America*, Chicago: University of Chicago Press.

Steindl, F.G. (1995), *Monetary Interpretations of the Great Depression*, Ann Arbor: University of Michigan Press.

Temin, P. (1976), *Did Monetary Forces Cause the Depression?*, New York: W.W Norton.

Temin, P. (1989), *Lessons from the Great Depression*, Cambridge, MA and London: MIT Press.

Wheelock, D.C. (1992), 'Monetary Policy in the Great Depression: What the Fed Did, and Why', *The Federal Reserve Bank of St. Louis Review*, **74**, pp. 2–28.

Wright, Q. (ed.) (1932), *Gold and Monetary Stabilization*, Chicago: University of Chicago Press.

Great Inflation

The 'Great Inflation' is the name given by John Taylor to the prolonged period of relatively high inflation experienced in the major OECD countries, beginning in the mid-1960s and lasting throughout the 1970s and finally declining sharply in the early 1980s (see J.B. Taylor, 'The Great Inflation, the Great Disinflation, and Policies for Future Price Stability', in A. Blundell-Wignall (ed.), *Inflation, Disinflation and Monetary Policy*, Ambassador Press, 1992). Bradford DeLong argues that the '1970s are America's only peacetime outburst of inflation', although that view ignores the inflationary consequences of America's heavy involvement in the

Vietnam war after 1965 (see J.B. DeLong, 'America's Only Peacetime Inflation: The 1970s', in C. Romer and D. Romer (eds), *Reducing Inflation: Motivation and Strategy*, University of Chicago Press, 1997).

See also:
Stagflation.

Greenspan, Alan

Alan Greenspan (b.1926, New York City, USA) obtained his BA in economics (summa cum laude) in 1948, an MA in economics in 1950, and a PhD in economics in 1977, all from New York University. His main past posts have included chairmanship (1954–74) and presidency (1977–87) of Townsend-Greenspan & Co. Inc., a major economic consulting firm. Between 1974 and 1977 he served as chairman of President Ford's Council of Economic Advisers. Dr Greenspan has also been a consultant to the Brookings Panel on Economic Activity, Chairman of the National Commission on Social Security Reform, a member of President Reagan's Economic Policy Advisory Board, and a consultant to the Congressional Budget Office. In August 1987 he succeeded Paul Volcker as Chairman of the Federal Reserve Board, the Washington, DC-located head office of the United States central bank. In this position Alan Greenspan is, arguably, the most powerful economic policy maker not only in the USA, but also in the world. He has been appointed and reappointed by Presidents Ronald Reagan, George Bush, Sr and Bill Clinton, and in 2000 he began his fourth four-year term as Chairman of the Federal Reserve (see L. Kahaner, *The Quotations of Chairman Greenspan: Words from the Man Who Can Shake the World*, Adams Media, 2000; B. Woodward, *Maestro:Greenspan's Fed and the American Boom*, Pocket Books, 2001).

See also:
Council of Economic Advisers; Federal Reserve System.

Gross Domestic Product (GDP)

The total value of goods and services produced in a country by the factors of production located in that country, regardless of who owns them.

Gross National Product (GNP)

The value of final goods and services produced by domestically owned factors of production; GDP plus net property income from abroad.

Group of Five (G5)

A group of five main industrial economies (France, Germany, Japan, the United Kingdom and the United States) whose economic ministers meet periodically to discuss international monetary relations.

Group of Seven (G7)

A group of seven main industrial economies (Canada, France, Germany, Italy, Japan, the United Kingdom and the United States) whose heads of government or economic ministers meet periodically to discuss international monetary relations.

Growth Accounting

Economists not only need a theoretical framework for understanding the causes of growth, they also require a simple method of calculating the relative importance of capital, labour and technology in the growth experience of actual economies. The established framework, following Solow's (1957) seminal contribution, is called *growth accounting* (see Abel and Bernanke, 2000; DeLong, 2001).

The Solow (1956) growth model is built around the neoclassical aggregate production function (1) and focuses on the *proximate* causes of growth:

$$Y = A(t) \, F(K, L), \tag{1}$$

where Y is real output, K is capital, L is the labour input and $A(t)$ is a measure of technology (that is, the way that inputs to the production function can be transformed into output) which is exogenous and taken simply to depend on time. Sometimes $A(t)$ is called *total factor productivity* (TFP). The aggregate production function in equation (1) shows that output (Y) is dependent on the inputs of capital (K), labour (L) and the currently available technology [$A(t)$]. One specific type of production function frequently used in empirical studies relating to growth accounting is the Cobb–Douglas production function shown by equation (2):

$$Y = A(t) \, K^{\alpha} \, L^{1-\alpha}, \tag{2}$$

where α and $1-\alpha$ are weights reflecting the share of capital and labour in the national income. As far as the proximate causes of growth are concerned we can see by referring to equation (2) that increases in total GDP (Y) come from the combined weighted impact of changes in capital, labour and technological progress. Economists can measure changes in the amount of capital and labour that occur in an economy over time, but changes in technology (total factor productivity) are not directly observable. However, it is possible to measure changes in TFP as a 'residual' after taking into account the contributions to growth made by changes in the capital and labour inputs. Solow's (1957) technique was to define technological change as changes in aggregate output minus the sum of the weighted contributions of the labour and capital inputs.

In short, under the neoclassical assumptions of competitive factor markets and input exhaustion, the 'Solow residual' (TFP) measures that part of a change in aggregate output which cannot be explained by changes in the measurable quantities of capital and labour inputs. The derivation of the Solow residual can be shown as follows. Output will change if A, K or L change. In equation (2) the exponent on the capital shock (α) measures the *elasticity of output* with respect to capital and the exponent on the labour input ($1-\alpha$) measures the *elasticity of output* with respect to labour. The weights α and $1-\alpha$ are estimated from national income statistics and reflect the income shares of capital and labour, respectively (see Abel and Bernanke, 2000; Mankiw, 2000). Since these weights sum to unity this indicates that equation (2) is a constant returns to scale production function. Hence an equal percentage increase in both factor inputs (K and L) will increase Y by the same percentage. Since the growth rate of the product of the inputs will be the growth rate of A plus the growth rate of K^{α} plus the growth rate of $L^{1-\alpha}$, equation (2) can be rewritten as (3), which is the basic growth accounting equation used in numerous empirical studies of the sources of economic growth (see Kendrick, 1961; Denison, 1967, 1974, 1985; Maddison, 1987; Jorgenson, 2001).

$$\Delta Y / Y = \Delta A / A + \alpha \, \Delta K / K + (1-\alpha) \, \Delta L / L. \tag{3}$$

Equation (3) is simply the Cobb–Douglas production function written in a form representing rates of change. It shows that the growth of aggregate output ($\Delta Y / Y$) depends on the contribution of changes in total factor productivity ($\Delta A/A$), changes in the weighted contribution of capital ($\alpha\Delta K/K$) and changes in the weighted contribution of labour [$(1-\alpha)\Delta L/L$]. By rearranging equation (2) we can represent the productivity index (TFP) which we need to measure as equation (4):

$$TFP = A = Y/K^{\alpha}L^{1-\alpha} \tag{4}$$

As already noted, because there is no direct way of measuring TFP it has to be estimated as a *residual*. By writing down equation (4) in terms of rates of change or by rearranging equation (3), which amounts to the same thing, we can obtain an equation from which the growth of TFP (technological change) can be estimated as a residual. This is shown in equation (5):

$$\Delta A/A = \Delta Y/Y - [\alpha\Delta K/K + (1-\alpha)\,\Delta L/L]. \tag{5}$$

Data relating to output and the capital and labour inputs are available. Estimates of α and hence $1-\alpha$ can be acquired from historical national income data. For example, in Solow's original paper covering the US economy for the period 1909–49, he estimated that the rate of growth of total output ($\Delta Y/Y$) had averaged 2.9 per cent per year, of which 0.32 percentage points could be attributed to capital ($\alpha\Delta K/K$) and 1.09 percentage points could be attributed to labour [$(1-\alpha)\,\Delta L/L$], leaving a 'Solow residual' ($\Delta A/A$) of 1.49 percentage points. In other words, almost half of the growth experienced in the USA during this period was due to unexplained technological progress! In Denison's (1985) later work he found that, for the period 1929–82, $\Delta Y/Y = 2.92$ per cent, of which 1.02 percentage points could be attributed to $\Delta A/A$. Recent controversial research by Alwyn Young (1992, 1995) on the sources of growth in the East Asian Tiger economies suggested estimates of $\Delta A/A$ for Taiwan of 2.6, for South Korea of 1.7, for Hong Kong of 1.7 and for Singapore a meagre 0.2. So, although these economies have experienced unprecedented growth rates of GDP since the early 1960s, Young's controversial research suggests that these economies are examples of miracles of accumulation. According to Young, once we account for the growth of labour and physical and human capital there is little left to explain, especially in the case of Singapore (see Krugman, 1994; Collins and Bosworth, 1996; Hsieh, 1999; Bhagwati, 2000, Snowdon, 2001).

Going further back in history, Nick Crafts (1994, 1995) has provided estimates of the sources of growth for the British economy during the period 1760–1913. These estimates are reproduced in Table 1. From these data we can see the growth acceleration of the British economy between the middle of the eighteenth and nineteenth centuries and the later growth slowdown during the Victorian–Edwardian period. It is also clear that 'by twentieth century standards both the output growth rates and the TFP rates are quite modest' (Crafts, 1995).

Table 1   The British economy, 1760–1913

	$\Delta Y/Y\%$	$\alpha\Delta K/K$	$(1-\alpha)\Delta L/L$	$\Delta A/A$
1760–1780	0.6	0.25	0.35	0.00
1780–1831	1.7	0.60	0.80	0.30
1831–1873	2.4	0.90	0.75	0.75
1873–1899	2.1	0.80	0.55	0.75
1899–1913	1.4	0.80	0.55	0.05

Source: Crafts (1995).

An alternative method of calculating the Solow residual is to decompose the growth of output per worker (labour productivity) into that which is due to capital deepening (an increase in the capital labour ratio, K/L) and that which comes from the contribution of TFP, as shown in equation (6):

$$\Delta Y/Y - \Delta L/L = \alpha[\Delta K/K - \Delta L/L] + \Delta A/A. \tag{6}$$

We can illustrate this approach by referring to Figure 1. Suppose that output per worker ($Y/L = y$) in the US economy grew from $ya(t_0)$ in 1995 to $yc(t_1)$ in 2000; that is, the economy moved from point a to point c in the figure. As illustrated, this increase can be attributed in part to a rise in TFP (technological progress) measured as $yb - ya(t_0)$, and in part to capital deepening, measured by $yc(t_1) - yb$.

Using this framework, DeLong provides estimates of the sources of US growth in the period 1948–2000. These estimates are reproduced as Table 2.

Table 2   The sources of growth in the United States, 1948–2000 ($\alpha = 0.4$)

Period	$\Delta Y/Y$	$\Delta Y/Y - \Delta L/L$	$\alpha[\Delta K/K - \Delta L/L]$	$\Delta A/A$
1948–1973	4.0%	3.0%	1.2%	1.8%
1973–1995	2.7%	0.9%	0.8%	0.1%
1995–2000	4.2%	3.0%	1.1%	1.9%

Source: DeLong's website (*http://www.j-bradford-delong.net/*).

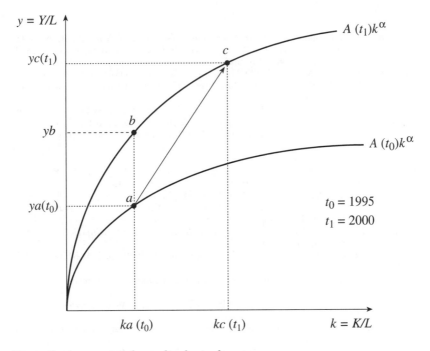

Figure 1 Accounting for technological progress

The most obvious feature of these data is the well known puzzle of the 'productivity slowdown' in the period after 1973. This slowdown has been attributed to many possible causes including the adverse impact on investment and existing capital stocks of the 1970s oil price shocks, a slowdown in the rate of innovation, adverse demographic trends, an increasingly regulatory environment and problems associated with measurement, such as accounting for quality changes (Fischer *et al.*, 1988; Abel and Bernanke, 2000).

  If the neoclassical assumptions underlying Solow's technique fail to hold, the Solow residual will not measure only technical progress. Distortions to the Solow residual may arise from the impact of imperfect competition, cyclical effects, externalities and production spillovers, non-constant returns to scale and reallocation effects (Stiroh, 2001). As early as 1956, Abramovitz was referring to the Solow residual as 'a measure of our ignorance about the causes of growth'. Although some economists remain highly sceptical about the whole methodology and theoretical basis of growth accounting (for example, Nelson, 1973; Scott, 1989), the technique remains an important component of growth analysis.

BRIAN SNOWDON
HOWARD R. VANE

Bibliography

Abel, A.B. and B.S. Bernanke (2000), *Macroeconomics*, 4th edn, New York: Addison-Wesley.

Abramovitz, M. (1956), 'Resource and Output Trends in the United States Since 1870', *American Economic Review*, **46**, May, pp. 5–53.

Bhagwati, J. (2000), 'The Miracle That Did Happen: Understanding East Asia in Comparative Perspective', *The Wind of the Hundred Days: How Washington Mismanaged Globalisation*, Cambridge, MA: MIT Press.

Collins, S.M. and B.P. Bosworth (1996), 'Economic Growth in East Asia: Accumulation Versus Assimilation', *Brookings Papers on Economic Activity*, no. 2, pp. 135–203.

Crafts, N.F.R. (1994), 'The Industrial Revolution', in R. Floud and D. McCloskey (eds), *The Economic History of Britain Since 1700: Volume I*, 2nd edn, Cambridge: Cambridge University Press.

Crafts, N.F.R. (1995), 'Exogenous or Endogenous Growth? The Industrial Revolution Reconsidered', *Journal of Economic History*, **55**, December, pp. 745–72.

DeLong, J.B. (2001), *Macroeconomics*, Burr Ridge: McGraw-Hill.

Denison, E.F. (1967), *Why Growth Rates Differ: Post-War Experience in Nine Western Countries*, Washington, DC: Brookings Institution.

Denison, E.F. (1974), *Accounting for United States Economic Growth, 1929–1969*, Washington, DC: Brookings Institution.

Denison, E.F. (1985), *Trends in American Economic Growth 1929–1982*, Washington, DC: Brookings Institution.

Fischer, S. *et al.* (1988), 'Symposium on the Slowdown in Productivity Growth', *Journal of Economic Perspectives*, **2**, Fall, pp. 3–21.

Hsieh, C. (1999), 'Productivity Growth and Factor Prices in East Asia', *American Economic Review*, **89**, May, pp. 133–8.

Jorgenson, D.W. (2001), 'Information Technology and the US Economy', *American Economic Review*, **91**, March, pp. 1–32.

Kendrick, J.W. (1961), *Productivity Trends in the United States*, Princeton, NJ: Princeton University Press.

Krugman, P. (1994), 'The Myth of Asia's Miracle', *Foreign Affairs*, **73**, November/December, pp. 62–78.

Maddison, A. (1987), 'Growth and Slowdown in Advanced Capitalist Economies: Techniques of Quantitative Assessment', *Journal of Economic Literature*, **25**, June, pp. 649–98.

Mankiw, N.G. (2000), *Macroeconomics*, 4th edn, New York: Worth.

Nelson, R.R. (1973), 'Recent Exercises in Growth Accounting: New Understanding or Dead End?', *American Economic Review*, **63**, June, pp. 462–8.

Scott, M.F.G. (1989), *A New View of Economic Growth*, Oxford: Clarendon Press.

Snowdon, B. (2001), 'Redefining the Role of the State: Joseph Stiglitz on Building a Post-Washington Consensus', *World Economics*, **2**, July–September, pp. 45–86.

Solow, R.M. (1956), 'A Contribution to the Theory of Economic Growth', *Quarterly Journal of Economics*, **70**, February, pp. 65–94.

Solow, R.M. (1957), 'Technical Change and the Aggregate Production Function', *Review of Economics and Statistics*, **39**, August, pp. 312–20.

Stiroh, K.J. (2001), 'What Drives Productivity Growth', *Federal Reserve Bank of New York Economic Policy Review*, **7**, pp. 37–59.

Young, A. (1992), 'A Tale of Two Cities: Factor Accumulation and Technical Change in Hong Kong and Singapore', *National Bureau of Economic Research Macroeconomics Annual*, pp. 13–54.

Young, A. (1995), 'The Tyranny of Numbers: Confronting the Statistical Realities of the East Asian Growth Experience', *Quarterly Journal of Economics*, **110**, August, pp. 641–80.

Hansen, Alvin H. (1887–1975)

Alvin Hansen (b.1887, Viborg, South Dakota, USA) obtained his BA from Yankton College in 1910 and his MA (1915) and PhD (1918) from the University of Wisconsin. His main posts included Professor of Political Economy at Harvard University, 1937–57. In 1938, he was president of the American Economic Association. He is best known for helping to bring Keynesianism to America; using Hicks's IS–LM diagram in his teaching and for what is often referred to as the Hicks–Hansen synthesis between classical and Keynesian economics. His best known books include *Full Recovery or Stagnation?* (W.W. Norton, 1938); *Monetary Theory and Fiscal Policy* (McGraw-Hill, 1949); *Business Cycles and National Income* (W.W. Norton, 1951); and *A Guide to Keynes* (McGraw-Hill, 1953).

See also:

American Economic Association; Hicks, John R.; IS–LM Model: Closed Economy; Keynesian Economics.

Harrod, Roy F. (1900–1978)

Roy Harrod (b.1900, Norfolk, England) obtained his BA from the University of Oxford in 1922. His main posts included Lecturer in Economics at Christ Church College, Oxford, 1922–67. Between 1945 and 1966 he was editor of the *Economic Journal* and from 1962 to 1964 president of the Royal Economic Society. He is best known for his work on growth theory, in particular developing a model where, under certain conditions, growth can be sustained at a steady rate and which has come to be known as the Harrod–Domar growth model; promoting Keynesian economics; and writing the first biography of Keynes. Among his best known books are *The Trade Cycle* (Macmillan, 1936); *Towards a Dynamic Economics* (Macmillan, 1948); *Life of John Maynard Keynes* (Macmillan, 1951); and *Economic Dynamics* (Macmillan, St Martins, 1973). His most widely read articles include 'An Essay in Dynamic Theory' (*Economic Journal*, **49**, March 1939).

See also:

Harrod-Domar Growth Model; Keynes, John Maynard; Keynesian Economics; Royal Economic Society.

Harrod–Domar Growth Model

Evsey Domar (1914–98) and Roy Harrod (1900–1978), on different sides of the Atlantic, were the co-discoverers of a neo-Keynesian approach to modelling economic growth and deserve to be regarded as the co-founders of modern growth theory (Asimakopulos, 1985; Young, 1989). Following their contributions in the period 1939–47, their model became popularly known as the 'Harrod–Domar growth model' even though there were differences in their respective contributions (see Harrod, 1939, 1948; Domar, 1946, 1947). For example, according to Easterly (2001), Domar never intended his 1946–7 contribution to be used as a 'growth model' at all, but was simply intending to make a contribution to the analysis of employment in the business cycle by establishing a link between employment and capital accumulation. Domar was concerned that the early Keynesians, by concentrating too much on the short-run multiplier effects of investment expenditures, were neglecting the impact of investment on the productive capacity of the economy (see Domar, 1957; Easterly, 2001). He later repudiated his model in favour of Solow's (1956) neoclassical growth theory. In contrast to Domar, the explicit objective of Harrod was to dynamize Keynesian theory. However, he was concerned that the Keynesian model needed to be extended to take into account the impact of growth on investment and in doing so produced a theory of the trade cycle which combined the concept of the multiplier and the accelerator (Harrod, 1936). In 1939, Harrod produced his seminal dynamic analysis of the *General Theory*.

The Harrod–Domar model, with exogenously determined technological progress, 'sanctioned the overriding importance of capital accumulation in the quest for enhanced growth' (Shaw, 1992). A major strength of this model is its simplicity. Within the Harrod–Domar framework the growth of real GDP is assumed to be proportional to the share of investment spending (I) in GDP and, for an economy to grow, net additions to the capital stock are required. The relationship between the size of the total capital stock (K) and total GDP (Y) is known as the capital output ratio ($K/Y=v$). If we assume that total new investment is determined by total savings then the essence of the Harrod–Domar model can be set out as follows. Assume that total saving is some proportion (s) of GDP, as shown in equation (1):

$$S=sY. \tag{1}$$

Since investment spending can be defined as a change of the capital stock (assuming, for simplicity, no depreciation) we have equation (2):

$$I=\Delta K. \tag{2}$$

Given that we have defined $v = K/Y$, it also follows that $v = \Delta K/\Delta Y$ (the incremental capital output ratio or ICOR). Since the equality $S = I$ must hold *ex post* we can write equation (3):

$$S = sY = I = \Delta K = v\Delta Y. \tag{3}$$

This simplifies to equation (4):

$$sY = v\Delta Y. \tag{4}$$

Rearranging (4) we have (5):

$$\Delta Y/Y = G = s/v. \tag{5}$$

Here $\Delta Y/Y = Y_t - Y_{t-1}/Y_t$ is the growth rate of GDP. Letting $G = \Delta Y/Y$, we have the famous Harrod–Domar growth equation, $G = s/v$. This simply states that the growth rate (G) of GDP is jointly determined by the savings ratio (s) divided by the capital output ratio (v). The higher the savings ratio and the lower the capital output ratio, the faster will an economy grow. Allowing for depreciation of the capital stock (δ), the equation becomes $G = (s/v) - \delta$.

The Harrod–Domar model, as Bhagwati (Snowdon, 2001) recalls, was tremendously influential in the development economics literature during the third quarter of the twentieth century, and was a key component within the framework of economic planning. The implications of this simple and popular model were dramatic and reassuring. It suggested that the key problem facing developing countries was simply to increase the share of resources devoted to investment. For example, if a developing country desired to achieve a growth rate of per capita income of 2 per cent per annum (that is, with living standards doubling every 35 years), and population was estimated to be growing at 2 per cent, then economic planners would need to set a target rate of GDP growth (G^*) equal to 4 per cent. If $v = 4$, this implies that G^* can only be achieved with a desired savings ratio (s^*) of 0.16, or 16 per cent of GDP. If $s^* > s$, there is a 'savings gap', and planners needed to devise policies for plugging this gap.

Since the rate of growth in the Harrod–Domar model is positively related to the savings ratio, development economists during the 1950s concentrated their research effort on understanding how to raise private savings ratios in order to enable less developed economies to 'take off into 'self-sustained growth' (Lewis, 1954; Rostow, 1960). Reflecting the contemporary development ideas of the 1950s, government fiscal policy was also seen to have a prominent role to play since budgetary surpluses could (in theory) substitute for private domestic savings. If domestic sources of finance were inadequate to achieve the desired growth target then foreign aid could fill the 'savings gap'. Aid requirements (A) would simply be calculated as $s^{*} - s = A$ (Chenery and Strout, 1966; Easterly, 2001). However, a major weakness of the Harrod–Domar approach was the assumption of a fixed capital output ratio. Since the inverse of v ($1/v$) is the productivity of investment (κ), we can rewrite equation (5) as follows:

$$G = s\kappa. \qquad (6)$$

Unfortunately, as Bhagwati (1998) observes, the productivity of investment is not datum but reflects the efficiency of the policy framework and the incentive structures within which investment decisions are taken. The weak growth performance of India reflects, 'not a disappointing savings performance, but rather a disappointing productivity performance' (Bhagwati, 1993). Hence the growth–investment relationship turned out to be 'loose and unstable' owing to the multiple factors that influence growth (Easterly, 2001). Furthermore, economists soon became aware of a second major flaw in the 'aid requirements' or 'financing gap' model. The model assumed that aid inflows would go into investment one to one. But it soon became apparent that inflows of foreign aid, with the objective of closing the savings gap, did not necessarily boost total savings. Aid does not go into investment one to one. Indeed, in many cases inflows of aid led to a reduction of domestic savings, together with a decline in the productivity of investment (White, 1992; Burnside and Dollar, 2000). The research of Boone (1996) confirms that inflows of foreign aid have not raised growth rates in most recipient developing countries.

A further problem is that in many developing countries the 'soft budget constraints' operating within the public sector created a climate for what Bhagwati calls 'goofing off'. It is therefore hardly surprising that public sector enterprises frequently failed to generate profits intended to add to government saving. In short, 'capital fundamentalism' and the 'aid financed investment fetish', which dominated development thinking for much of the period after 1950, led economists up the wrong path in their 'elusive quest for growth' (King and Levine, 1994; Easterly, 2001). Indeed, William Easterly (1999), a well known and highly respected World Bank economist, argues that the Harrod–Domar model is far from dead and still continues to exercise considerable influence on economists working within the major International Financial Institutions even if it died long ago in the academic literature. Easterly shows that economists working at the World Bank, International Monetary Fund, Inter-American Bank, European Bank for Reconstruction and Development, and International Labour

Organisation still frequently employ the Harrod–Domar–Chenery–Strout methodology to calculate the investment and aid requirements needed in order for specific countries to achieve their growth targets. However, as Easterly convincingly demonstrates, the evidence that aid flows into investment on a one-for-one basis, and that there is a fixed linear relationship between growth and investment in the short run, is 'soundly rejected'.

A further weakness of the Harrod–Domar framework is the assumption of zero substitutability between capital and labour (that is, a fixed factor proportions production function). This is a 'crucial' but inappropriate assumption for a model concerned with long-run growth. This assumption of the Harrod–Domar model also leads to the renowned instability property that 'even for the long run an economic system is at best balanced on a knife-edge equilibrium growth' (Solow, 1956). Only in very special circumstances will an economy remain in equilibrium with full employment of both labour and capital. The problem arises from the assumption of a fixed-coefficient production function. This requires that the capital labour ratio (K/L) must remain constant. In a growth setting this means that K and L must always grow at the same rate to maintain equilibrium. However, because the model also assumes a constant capital output ratio (K/Y), K and Y must also grow at the same rate. Therefore, if we assume that the labour force (L) grows at the same rate as the rate of growth of population (n), we can conclude that the only way that equilibrium can be maintained in the model is for $n = G = s/v - \delta$. It would only be by pure coincidence that $n = G$. If $n > G$, the result will be continually rising unemployment. If $G > n$, the capital stock will become increasingly idle and the growth rate of output will slow down to $G = n$. Thus, whenever K and L do not grow at the same rate, the economy falls off its equilibrium 'knife edge' growth path.

However, the evidence is overwhelming that this property does not fit well with the actual experience of growth. As Solow (1999) has commented in reply to a question on the important influences that led to his 1956 paper,

> I was suspicious of the Harrod–Domar model . . . It occurred to me that if the world works in the way suggested by their model then the history of capitalism would have been much more erratic than it has been. If Harrod–Domar was a good macro model for the long run then it is impossible to explain, to my mind, how contained fluctuations have been, how you can draw a trend and look at fluctuations around that trend, and how those fluctuations stay 3–4 per cent either side of trend, except in a few major depressions. I thought there must be a way of modelling growth that does not have the knife-edge property of the Harrod–Domar model.

Roy Harrod spent his whole academic career at Oxford, was a student of Keynes, eventually succeeding him as editor of the *Economic Journal* in 1945, and was a contemporary of committed Keynesians such as Joan

Robinson, James Meade, Nicholas Kaldor and Richard Kahn. Throughout his life he remained a staunch defender of Keynes and Keynesianism. However, following the seminal contributions of Solow (1956, 1957) and Swan (1956), the neoclassical model, which better fits growth experience, became the dominant approach to the analysis of growth, at least within academia. Between 1956 and 1970, economists refined 'old growth theory' better known as the Solow neoclassical model of economic growth (Solow, 2000). Although the Harrod–Domar model was prominent in the 1964 Hahn and Matthews survey of growth theory, in today's modern macroeconomics textbooks the Harrod–Domar model is rarely mentioned. There is no reference at all to either the Harrod or the Domar models in Charles Jones's (1998) popular textbook, *An Introduction to Growth Theory*, and Robert Barro and Xavier Sala-i-Martin (1995) conclude that, although the Harrod–Domar contributions 'triggered a good deal of research at the time, very little of this analysis plays a role in today's thinking'. And yet, as Easterly (1999) discusses, the Harrod–Domar framework still manages to survive in its 'financing gap' guise within the major international financial institutions. Perhaps, that is why the Harrod–Domar model is still usually discussed in development economics textbooks (see Ray, 1998; Todaro, 2000, Perkins *et al.*, 2001).

BRIAN SNOWDON
HOWARD R. VANE

See also:

Domar, Evsey D.; Harrod, Roy F.; Neoclassical Growth Model.

Bibliography

Asimakopulos, A. (1985), 'Harrod on Harrod: The Evolution of a Line of Steady Growth', *History of Political Economy*, **17**, Winter, pp. 619–35.
Barro, R.J. and X. Sala-i-Martin (1995), *Economic Growth*, New York: McGraw-Hill.
Bhagwati, J. (1993), *India in Transition: Freeing the Economy*, Oxford: Clarendon Press.
Bhagwati, J. (1998), *A Stream of Windows: Unsettling Reflections on Trade, Immigration and Democracy*, Cambridge, MA: MIT Press.
Boone, P. (1996), 'Politics and the Effectiveness of Aid', *European Economic Review*, **40**, February, pp. 289–329.
Burnside, C. and D. Dollar (2000), 'Aid, Policies and Growth', *American Economic Review*, **90** September, pp. 847–68.
Chenery, H.B. and A.M. Strout (1966), 'Foreign Assistance and Economic Development', *American Economic Review*, **56**, September, pp. 680–733.
Domar, E.D. (1946), 'Capital Expansion, Rate of Growth, and Employment', *Econometrica*, **14**, April, pp. 137–47.
Domar, E.D. (1947), 'Expansion and Employment', *American Economic Review*, **37**, March, pp. 34–55.
Domar. E.D. (1957), *Essays on the Theory of Economic Growth*, Oxford: Oxford University Press.
Easterly, W. (1999), 'The Ghost of the Financing Gap: Testing the Growth Model Used in

International Financial Institutions', *Journal of Development Economics*, **60**, December, pp. 423–38.

Easterly, W. (2001), *The Elusive Quest for Growth: Economists' Adventures and Misadventures in the Tropics*, Cambridge, MA: MIT Press.

Hahn, F.H. and R.C.O. Matthews (1964), 'The Theory of Economic Growth: A Survey', *Economic Journal*, **74**, December, pp. 779–902.

Harrod, R.F. (1936), *The Trade Cycle*, London: Macmillan.

Harrod, R.F. (1939), 'An Essay in Dynamic Theory', *Economic Journal*, **49**, June, pp. 14–33.

Harrod, R.F. (1948), *Towards a Dynamic Economics: Some Recent Developments of Economic Theory and their Application*, London: Macmillan.

Jones, C. (1998), *An Introduction to Economic Growth*, New York: W.W. Norton.

King, R. and R. Levine (1994), 'Capital Fundamentalism, Economic Development and Economic Growth', *Carnegie-Rochester Conference Series on Public Policy*, **40**, pp. 259–92.

Lewis, W.A. (1954), 'Economic Development with Unlimited Supplies of Labour', *Manchester School of Economic and Social Studies*, **22**, May, pp. 139–91.

Perkins, D.H., S. Radelet, D.R. Snodgrass, M. Gillis and M. Roemer (2001), *Economics of Development*, New York: W.W. Norton.

Ray, D. (1998), *Development Economics*, Princeton, NJ: Princeton University Press.

Rostow, W.W. (1960), *The Stages of Economic Growth*, Cambridge: Cambridge University Press.

Shaw, G.K. (1992), 'Policy Implications of Endogenous Growth Theory', *Economic Journal*, **102**, May, pp. 611–21.

Snowdon, B. (2001), 'Jagdish Bhagwati on Trade, Democracy and Growth: Championing Free Trade in the Second Age of Globalisation', *World Economics*, **2**, October-December, pp. 53–104.

Solow, R.M. (1956), 'A Contribution to the Theory of Economic Growth', *Quarterly Journal of Economics*, **70**, February, pp. 65–94.

Solow, R.M. (1957), 'Technical Change and the Aggregate Production Function', *Review of Economics and Statistics*, **39**, August, pp. 312–20.

Solow, R.M. (1999), 'Interview with Robert Solow', in B. Snowdon and H.R. Vane, *Conversations with Leading Economists: Interpreting Modern Macroeconomics*, Cheltenham, UK and Northampton, MA, USA: Edward Elgar.

Solow, R.M. (2000), *Growth Theory: An Exposition*, 2nd edn, Oxford: Oxford University Press.

Swan, T.W. (1956), 'Economic Growth and Capital Accumulation', *Economic Record*, **32**, November, pp. 334–61.

Todaro, M.P. (2000), *Economic Development*, New York: Addison-Wesley.

White, H. (1992), 'The Macroeconomic Impact of Development Aid: A Critical Survey', *Journal of Development Studies*, **28**, pp. 163–240.

Young, W. (1989), *Harrod and his Trade Cycle Group: The Origins and Development of the Growth Research Programme*, London: Macmillan.

Hayek, Friedrich A. von (1899–1992)

Friedrich von Hayek (b. 1899, Vienna, Austro-Hungary) obtained his doctorate in law (1921) and his doctorate in political science (1923) from the University of Vienna. His main posts included Director of the Austrian Institute for Business Cycle Research, 1927–31; Professor of Economic Science and Statistics at the London School of Economics, 1931–50; Professor of Social and Moral Sciences at the University of Chicago, 1950–62; and Professor of Economic Policy at the University of Freiburg,

1962–8. In 1974, he was awarded (jointly with Gunnar Myrdal) the Nobel Prize in Economics for, among other things, his pioneering work on the theory of money and economic fluctuations. He is best known for his work on the theory of business cycles, in particular integrating monetary theory with the Austrian theory of business cycles; criticizing Keynesian expansionary aggregate demand policies to reduce unemployment; the harmful effects of inflation; and the benefits of free markets. His best known books include *Prices and Production* (George Routledge and Sons, 1931); *Profits, Interest and Investment* (Routledge & Kegan Paul, 1939); *The Pure Theory of Capital* (Routledge & Kegan Paul, 1941); and *The Road to Serfdom* (George Routledge, 1944).

See also:
Business Cycles: Austrian Approach; Nobel Prize in Economics.

Heckscher–Ohlin Approach to International Trade

An approach, named after its Swedish originators Eli Heckscher (1879–1952) and Bertil Ohlin (1899–1979), which explains the composition of international trade in terms of the relative factor endowments of different countries. For example, countries with a relative abundance of labour should specialize in the production and export of labour-intensive goods and, given their relative scarcity of capital, should import capital-intensive goods. The best known empirical test of the approach was undertaken by Wassily Leontief (1906–99) in the early 1950s. Applying input–output techniques to the study of US foreign trade, he surprisingly found that US exports were less capital-intensive and more labour-intensive than US imports. Leontiefs findings contradicted the Heckscher–Ohlin approach which held that the United States, given its relative abundance of capital, should export capital-intensive goods and import labour-intensive goods. The findings subsequently became known as the Leontief paradox.

Hicks, John Richard

J.R. (later Sir John) Hicks (1904–89) shaped modern macroeconomics, interpreting Keynesian economics through the IS–LM diagram, which became as vital a part of the trained intuition of economists as Alfred Marshall's scissors of supply and demand or Irving Fisher's two-period optimal consumption diagram. A Fellow of the British Academy from 1942, knighted in 1964, Hicks shared the Nobel Memorial Prize in

Economic Science with Kenneth Arrow in 1972 for his contributions to general equilibrium and demand theory and welfare economics, notably in *Value and Capital* (although he would rather have won for *A Theory of Economic History*).

Educated at Balliol College, Oxford, Hicks graduated in 1925 in Philosophy, Politics and Economics, in which 'economics was taught by a historian who really did not know economics at all; he had read very little of it' (Hicks, in Klamer, 1989). He then devoted a year to a higher degree at Oxford that he recalled was really in labour history, and, in his first years at the London School of Economics, Hicks lectured primarily on the labour market. Hicks learned economic theory by reading Pareto in Italian (at Hugh Dalton's suggestion) and working through Pareto's mathematical appendix. He read Wicksell and Myrdal in German translations before they were translated into English. Hicks's first book, *The Theory of Wages* (1932), introduced the elasticity of substitution and presented a marginal productivity theory of distribution. Although the book first established Hicks as an economic theorist, he was sufficiently persuaded by Gerald Shove's criticism of the assumed existence and differentiability of an aggregate production function to reprint Shove's review in the 1963 second edition. *Value and Capital* (1939) drew on the continental tradition of Walras's and Pareto's general equilibrium and Pareto's welfare economics (but with the emphasis on indifference curves rather than on utility functions), as well as on Hicks's own contributions to welfare economics and, with R.G.D. Allen, to demand theory. Before *Value and Capital*, Walrasian general equilibrium theory had little influence among English-speaking economists outside the London School of Economics (apart from Irving Fisher's 1891 dissertation and from a sketch of general equilibrium in Notes XIV and XXI of Marshall's mathematical appendix). Beginning with Hicks's book, general equilibrium came to displace Marshallian partial equilibrium analysis in economic theory.

Hicks's 'Suggestion for Simplifying the Theory of Money' (1935) proposed discarding the division between the theory of value and the theory of money, seeking a choice-theoretic formulation of liquidity preference as part of a larger portfolio-choice theory of demand for the whole range of assets. This was a continuing concern for Hicks, extending through his efforts in the 1960s to reconcile the Keynesian triad of motives for holding money (transactions, precautionary, speculative) with the classical triad of functions of money (medium of exchange, unit of account, store of value) to his final, posthumously published book, *A Market Theory of Money* (1989).

In 1935, Hicks was chosen over Joan Robinson for a lectureship at Cambridge, remaining until he moved to the University of Manchester in

1938. From 1942, he taught at Oxford, serving from 1952 to 1965 as Drummond Professor of Political Economy and Fellow of All Souls. In 1936, he was invited by Austin Robinson to review Keynes's *General Theory* (1936) for the *Economic Journal*, as someone outside Keynes's circle who would take the book seriously. Hicks later spoke of this invitation as a greater honour than the Nobel Prize. From this review Hicks went on to write 'Mr. Keynes and the Classics' (1937), the most reprinted article in macroeconomics, in which he constructed a diagram and a system of equations within which to identify the differences between Keynesian economics and what Keynes termed 'classical economics', treating both as special cases of a more general system. David Champernowne, Brian Reddaway, Roy Harrod and James Meade each published similar systems of simultaneous equations in 1936 and 1937 (Harrod and Meade presented theirs to the same Econometric Society session in Oxford at which Hicks presented 'Mr. Keynes and the Classics'). The later labelling of Hicks's curves as IS and LM is due to Alvin Hansen, but it was Hicks who presented the goods market and money market equilibrium conditions in a diagram that eventually came to dominate the teaching of macroeconomics above the introductory level (Young, 1987). After 1948, Paul Samuelson's Keynesian cross model formed the basis for teaching introductory macroeconomics. However, generations of macroeconomists found the IS–LM diagram and the associated simultaneous equations model a flexible and useful framework for teaching, policy analysis and econometric modelling for both closed and open economies (Young and Zilberfarb, 2000).

In later explanations, Hicks freely acknowledged the limitations of a system of simultaneous equations in dealing with such aspects of Keynes's *General Theory* as expectations and uncertainty (stating that IS–LM was less popular with him than with others), but defended IS–LM as capable of expressing the central ideas of the *General Theory* (with greater doubts about how fair it was to the 'Classics'). Unlike the later Post Keynesian school, Hicks had reservations about Keynes's Chapter 12 on long-period expectations. He argued that such expectations should not be taken as data, because, even if affected by irrational elements, expectations were not so irrational as to be completely random and could be shaped by policy.

Hicks's presentation of a system of simultaneous equations, with Keynesian and classical economics as special cases, was not welcomed by either Sir Dennis Robertson, on the classical or loanable funds side of the Cambridge monetary controversies, or by Joan Robinson on the Keynesian or liquidity preference side, as Hicks (1979) noted. The loanable funds theory that the interest rate is determined by thrift and productivity (the propensity to save and the marginal product of capital), that is, that the interest rate equates the supply of loanable funds (the flow of saving) to the demand for loanable funds (the flow of investment) is equivalent to saying the economy is on the *IS* curve (Investment = Saving) in interest and income space. The liquidity preference theory that the interest rate equates liquidity preference (demand for money) to the money supply amounts to saying the economy is on the *LM* curve (Liquidity preference = Money supply). It makes no more sense to argue whether interest is determined by the *IS* curve (goods market equilibrium) or the *LM* curve (money market equilibrium) than to argue whether the price of a good is determined by demand or by supply.

Hicks's other contributions to macroeconomics include Hicks-neutral technical change, the method of temporary equilibrium (taken up later by J.-M. Grandmont), and a model of the trade cycle (1950), the latter being written in the most Keynesian phase of Hicks's career. Hicks (1965, 1974) developed the concepts of flexprice and fixprice markets (which Hicks, 1979, stated correspond to Arthur Okun's distinction between auction markets and customer markets), with the Keynesian multiplier process operating in a fixprice setting. In some of his later writings, Hicks grappled with issues of time and uncertainty raised by Austrian capital theory. Despite this multiplicity of contributions (some of which, such as temporary equilibrium and the distinction between flexprice and fixprice markets, may be of great importance in the future), Hicks's most influential works remain his two 'Suggestions' of 1935 and 1937 (choice-theoretic approach to demand for money as an asset and the IS–LM diagram) and his 1939 introduction of general equilibrium into the mainstream of English-speaking economics.

ROBERT W. DIMAND

See also:

Classical Economics; IS–LM Model: Closed Economy; Keynesian Economics; Neoclassical Synthesis; Nobel Prize in Economics.

Bibliography

Baumol, W.J. (1990), 'Sir John Versus the Hicksians, or Theorist Malgré Lui?', *Journal of Economic Literature*, **28**, December, pp. 1708–15.
Coddington, A. (1979), 'Hicks's Contributions to Keynesian Economics', *Journal of Economic Literature*, **17**, September, pp. 970–88.
Greek Economic Review (1990), **12**, Autumn, Supplement on Hicks.
Hagemann, H., and O.F. Hamouda (eds) (1994), *The Legacy of Hicks: His Contributions to Economic Analysis*, London and New York: Routledge.
Hahn, F. (1990), 'John Hicks the Theorist', *Economic Journal*, **100**, June, pp. 539–49.
Hamouda, O.F. (1993), *John R. Hicks: The Economist's Economist*, Cambridge, MA: Blackwell.
Hicks, J.R. (1932), *The Theory of Wages*, London: Macmillan (expanded edn, including review by G. Shove, London: Macmillan, 1963).
Hicks, J.R. (1935), 'A Suggestion for Simplifying the Theory of Money', *Economica*, **2**, February, pp. 1–19.

Hicks, J.R. (1937), 'Mr. Keynes and the Classics: A Suggested Interpretation', *Econometrica*, **5**, April, pp. 238–53.

Hicks, J.R. (1939), *Value and Capital*, Oxford: Clarendon Press (2nd edn, 1946).

Hicks, J.R. (1950), *A Contribution to the Theory of the Trade Cycle*, Oxford: Clarendon Press.

Hicks, J.R. (1965), *Capital and Growth*, Oxford: Clarendon Press.

Hicks, J.R. (1969), *A Theory of Economic History*, London: Oxford University Press.

Hicks, J.R. (1974), *The Crisis in Keynesian Economics*, with foreword by R.W. Clower, New York: Basic Books.

Hicks, J.R. (1979), 'On Coddington's Interpretation: A Reply', *Journal of Economic Literature*, **17**, September, pp. 989–95.

Hicks, J.R. (1980), 'IS–LM: An Explanation', *Journal of Post Keynesian Economics*, **3**, Winter, pp. 139–54.

Hicks, J.R. (1981–83), *Collected Essays on Economic Theory*, 3 vols, Cambridge, MA: Harvard University Press.

Hicks, J.R. (1989), *A Market Theory of Money*, Oxford: Clarendon Press.

Indian Journal of Applied Economics (1998–9), **8**, October–December, and **9**, January–March and April–June, three special issues in memory of Hicks.

Keynes, J.M. (1936), *The General Theory of Employment, Interest and Money*, London: Macmillan.

Klamer, A. (1989), 'An Accountant Among Economists: Conversations with Sir John R. Hicks', *Journal of Economic Perspectives*, **3**, Fall, pp. 167–80.

Robertson, D.H. (1966), *Essays on Money and Interest*, ed. J.R. Hicks, London: Fontana.

Wood, J.C. and R.N. Woods (eds) (1989), *J.R. Hicks: Critical Assessments*, 4 vols, London and New York: Routledge.

Young, W. (1987), *Interpreting Mr Keynes: The IS–LM Enigma*, Cambridge, UK: Polity Press and Boulder, CO: Westview.

Young, W. and B.Z. Zilberfarb (eds) (2000), *IS–LM and Modern Macroeconomics*, Boston and Dordrecht: Kluwer Academic Publishers.

High-powered Money

The monetary liabilities of the central bank, consisting of currency in circulation and bank reserves; also known as the monetary base.

Human Capital

The knowledge and skills of workers in an economy.

See also:

Endogenous Growth Theory.

Hume, David (1711–76)

Although primarily known as a philosopher, David Hume (b.1711, Edinburgh, Scotland) made a number of important contributions to economics. He is best known for his work on monetary theory, in particular how money affects interest rates, prices and economic activity; and international trade, in particular the specie flow mechanism which ensures balanced trade. See T. Mayer's article 'David Hume and Monetarism' (*Quarterly Journal of Economics*, **95**, August 1980).

See also:

Classical Economics; Quantity Theory of Money.

Hydraulic Keynesianism

The publication in 1936 of John Maynard Keynes's *The General Theory of Employment, Interest and Money* was a landmark in the history of macroeconomics. Indeed, the *General Theory* gave birth to what we now call macroeconomics, since what existed before 1936 consisted of an 'intellectual witches' brew: many ingredients, some of them exotic, many insights, but also a great deal of confusion' (O. Blanchard, 'What Do We Know About Macroeconomics that Fisher and Wicksell Did Not?', *Quarterly Journal of Economics*, **115**, November, 2000). However, Keynes's most important work also gave rise to a variety of 'Keynesian' research programmes, although the demarcation between them was not clearly defined until the 1960s (see D. Patinkin, 'On Different Interpretations of the *General Theory*', *Journal of Monetary Economics*, **26**, October, 1990).

One of the best known classifications of varieties of Keynesianism is that provided by Alan Coddington in his paper, 'Keynesian Economics: The Search for First Principles' (*Journal of Economic Literature*, **14**, December, 1976). Coddington identifies three varieties, namely, 'Fundamentalist Keynesianism' (better known as 'Post Keynesianism'), 'Hydraulic Keynesianism' and 'Reconstituted Reductionism' (better known as 'disequilibrium Keynesianism'). While the 'fundamentalists' offer, in a variety of forms, a radical interpretation of Keynes, emphasizing the macroeconomic impact of uncertainty and ignorance among heterogeneous economic agents, the disequilibrium Keynesians (such as Clower and Leijonhufvud), following the lead given by Patinkin, offer a neo-Walrasian interpretation of Keynes which focuses on the process and implications of disequilibrium trading (this work was further extended by Barro, Grossman and Malinvaud).

In contrast, Coddington's 'Hydraulic Keynesianism' represents the mainstream (or orthodox) interpretation of Keynes as represented by Samuelson's 'Keynesian cross' (or '45–degree') diagram (see K.A. Pearce and K.D. Hoover, 'After the Revolution: Paul Samuelson and the Textbook Keynesian Model', in A.F. Cottrell and M.S. Lawlor (eds), *New*

Perspectives on Keynes, Duke University Press, 1995). At a more advanced level, hydraulic Keynesianism is synonymous with the Hicks–Hansen IS–LM interpretation of Keynes. To a committed fundamentalist such as the late Joan Robinson, all varieties of hydraulic Keynesianism are a 'bastardization' or 'vulgarization' of what she interprets as being the essence of Keynes's *General Theory* (see J. Robinson (ed.), *After Keynes*, Oxford: Basil Blackwell, 1973). However, Patinkin (1990) argues that the mainstream interpretation of Keynes, particularly the IS–LM framework, is one that Keynes himself basically accepted. It is also important to note that, within the mainstream interpretation of Keynes, the Samuelson '45-degree cross' and Hicks–Hansen IS–LM diagrams certainly created a pedagogical revolution, helping to convey to generations of students the essence of 'Keynesian' economics. Remarkably, given the numerous critiques of Keynesianism that have taken place over the last 60 years or so, the vast majority of intermediate macroeconomics textbooks continue to be 'Keynesian' in a broad sense, even if substantially modified following the monetarist and new classical contributions. Moreover, Samuelson's simple hydraulic model continues to form the macroeconomic core of most introductory principles textbooks with Gregory Mankiw's *Principles of Economics* (The Dryden Press, 1998), a notable exception (see D.C. Colander and H. Landreth (eds), *The Coming of Keynesianism to America*, Edward Elgar, 1996; B. Snowdon and H.R. Vane, 'Transforming Macroeconomics: An Interview With Robert E. Lucas Jr', *Journal of Economic Methodology*, **5**, June, 1998).

See also:

IS–LM Model: Closed Economy; Keynesian Cross; Keynesian Economics.

Hyperinflation

A situation in which the rate of inflation is extremely high for a year or more. For example, in the German hyperinflation of 1922–3 the average rate of inflation was 322 per cent per month.

Hysteresis

The term 'hysteresis' means that which comes later, being derived from the Greek verb meaning 'to be behind'. In terms of cause and effect relationships, a hysteresis effect is one that remains after the initial cause is removed.

In the classical physics embedded in Newton's laws, Maxwell's equations and so on, hysteresis effects do not arise. If a cause or disturbing force is applied and then removed the phenomena in question revert to their original state. The systems are governed by the principles of conservation, reversibility and symmetry (see Feynman, 1992). In order to determine the equilibrium or state of rest of such a system it is necessary to know only the contemporary values of the relevant explanatory variables. Cauchy-Lipschitz conditions are used to show that any previous initial conditions are forgotten. History is bunk in the sense that there is no memory of the forces or disturbances that have been applied or have occurred in the past.

Neoclassical economics was built using metaphors drawn from Newtonian mechanics or Maxwellian fields of force (Mirowski, 1989). Irving Fisher's PhD thesis, for example, analyzed the determination of economic equilibrium using a hydrostatic model in which water 'finds its own level' (Fisher, 1892). In this way, the neoclassical economists imported into economic analysis the properties of classical physics. When, from the 1930s onwards, neoclassical economics was reformulated on an axiomatic basis the metaphorical borrowing became less explicit but the mathematical methods employed served to retain the properties originally imported from physics (Ingrao and Israel, 1990). This is apparent, for example, in the use of fixed point theorems in general equilibrium existence proofs.

In microeconomics the influence of the metaphorical borrowing can be seen in the analysis of demand or supply shocks. A backward shift in the supply curve, for example, leads to an increase in price and reduction in quantity. But if the supply shock is temporary the price and quantity will retrace their steps, until the original equilibrium is restored, as the shock is reversed. This means that the plausible possibility that tastes change as people try out other goods during the disturbance is ruled out. Similarly, in macroeconomics, past demand or supply shocks do not influence the natural rate of unemployment. An anti-inflation policy will involve deflationary measures that raise the actual unemployment rate above the natural rate. As the inflation rate falls the real level of demand recovers and unemployment returns to the natural rate (Friedman, 1968). This again rules out several plausible possibilities, such as that the debilitating effects of the long spells of unemployment experienced during recessions raise the equilibrium rate of unemployment. The big question here, of course, is whether economies behave like the phenomena that classical physics purports to explain.

Ewing, Preisach and Krasnosel'skii–Pokrovskii
The term 'hysteresis' was coined by the Dundonian physicist–engineer Ewing in 1881. The context was his experiments on what happened to

twisted iron and steel wires when magnetized. Ewing found that the wires did not revert to their original position after being exposed to a cycle of magnetization and demagnetization. 'To this action . . . the author now gives the name Hysteresis' (Ewing, 1881, p.22). These experimental results did not accord with Maxwell's equations, which implied that electromagnetic fields should return to their original state if exposed to such a cycle of magnetization. Ewing coined the new term because he thought that the effects that he had identified in ferric metals would be relevant to other phenomena. The subsequent identification of hysteretic phenomena in a wide range of instances, from motorbike tyres to labour migration, is testimony to Ewing's prescience. Ewing himself left another important hysteresis effect behind on world history. During the 1914–18 war, he was the head of the 'Room 40' Naval Intelligence group that deciphered the telegram from Zimmerman, the German foreign secretary, to the German minister in Mexico on 16 January 1917. The telegram outlined a scheme for Mexico to join forces with Germany and Japan in return for the cession, in case of victory, of Texas, New Mexico and Arizona to Mexico. This decoded telegram played an important role in prompting the entry of the United States into the war (Glazebrook, 1935).

Ewing's experimental results were conducted at the macro level. A formal model of the physical mechanisms of magnetization at the micro level that could produce the hysteresis observed at the macro level was provided by the Hungarian physicist Preisach (1938). The basic idea here was that the individual molecules that make up a piece of metal have critical values that determine how they respond to a magnetizing force. If the force increases to some value 'a' or higher they switch into an 'up' position. If the force falls to some value 'b' or lower they switch into a 'down' position. This non-linear response to the magnetizing force means that there is a form of hysteresis at the micro level. Call the value of the magnetizing force in period 1 x_1. Let this value be $x_1 < b$, so the molecule is in the 'down' position. If the force rises in period 2 to $b < x_2 < a$, the molecule will remain in the 'down' position. A further increase in the force in period 3 to $x_3 > a$ will switch the molecule into the 'up' position. But a subsequent fall in the force in period 4 to $b < x_4 < a$ will see the molecule remain in the 'up' position. This means that in the range $b < x < a$ the molecule can either be in the 'down' or 'up' position, depending on whether the magnetizing force has been below or above this range in the past. Thus, in order to explain the state of the molecule, it is necessary to know the past history of the magnetizing force as well as its current value. This is the kernel of hysteresis at the micro level.

At the macro level, the hysteretic properties are stronger. To understand the behaviour of a piece of metal it is necessary to aggregate in some way over the behaviour of the individual molecules. The Preisach model supposes that the 'a' and 'b' switching points differ between molecules. In this way the intermittent response of the molecules at the micro level is transformed into a smoother response at the macro level. A given magnetizing force will lead some molecules to switch, but not others.

The next major development was the conversion of the physical properties of the Preisach model into a purely mathematical form. This work was done by a research group led by the Russian mathematician Krasnosel'skii, and served to model hysteresis as a general property that could, in principle, be applied to any system (Krasnosel'skii and Pokrovskii, 1989). Each micro element in the system is characterized by a hysteresis operator F_{ab}, where $a>b$, and the (a,b) values differ between the elements. The elements face an input shock x_t, where t stands for time, and $g(a,b)$ describes the distribution or density function of the elements with particular (a,b) switching values. The output y_t of the system as a whole can then be written as:

$$y_t = \iint_{a>b} g(a,b) \cdot F_{ab} \cdot x_t \cdot da\, db. \tag{1}$$

The key characteristics here are that the elements are *heterogeneous*, and that they respond *non-linearly* to the input shocks. These conditions suffice to generate hysteresis at the aggregate or macro level. Strong implications follow from this set up (see Cross, 1993). One is *remanence*. If an input shock is applied and then removed, the system does not revert to the *status quo ante*. Instead, the equilibrium or steady state of the system is changed. Thus, unlike what happens in the equilibria in mainstream economics, temporary shocks can have permanent effects. Another property is *time irreversibility* in that the system does not, as in mainstream economic analysis, retrace its steps when a temporary shock abates. As in the Old Testament, we pass this way only once when hysteresis is present. Perhaps most interesting is the *selective memory* property. The system, unlike what happens in the neoclassical model of economic behaviour, retains a memory of the shocks to which it has been exposed. The memory is also erasable. Only the extremum values of the shocks are retained in the memory. So, if the output of the system is aggregate unemployment and the input shocks are oil prices, interest rates or fiscal deficits, the equilibrium rate of unemployment will depend only on the maximum and minimum values of oil prices and so on experienced in the past. The memory erasure property is that only the non-dominated extremum values of the shocks are retained in the memory bank. This means that the memory can be long or short, depending on how big the shocks have been in the recent past. Thus a major deflationary monetary shock in recent years would delete the memory of previous, less deflationary, monetary shocks. And so on.

Hysteresis in economics

Although used occasionally since the 1940s, by economists such as Schumpeter, Georgescu-Roegen, Samuelson and Phelps (see Cross and Allan, 1988), the term 'hysteresis' only came into widespread usage in the 1980s. The term, however, refers to a range of effects that have long been thought to be important. Marshall, for example, saw the exclusion of such effects as being a basic weakness of the neoclassical model:

> the theory of stable equilibrium of normal demand and supply in its most abstract form assumes a certain rigidity in the conditions of demand and supply which does not really exist . . . if the normal production of a commodity increases and afterwards again diminishes to its old amount, the demand price and the supply price are not likely to return, as the pure theory assumes that they will, to their old positions for that amount. (Marshall, 1890, pp. 425–6)

Marshall's example was the shock to the cotton market arising from the burning of the cotton fields during the US civil war. On the demand side, 'habits which have grown up around the use of a commodity while its price is low are not quickly abandoned when its price rises again' (ibid, p. 426). On the supply side, 'the schedule of demand prices which holds for the forward movement of the production of a commodity will seldom hold for the return movement, but will in general require to be raised' (ibid.).

Keynes can be seen in a somewhat similar light. He answered his question 'is the economic system self-adjusting?' in the negative (Keynes, 1934). Keynes's *General Theory* shares with hysteretic models the property that a range of unemployment equilibria are consistent with a given set of exogenous conditions (see Summers, 1988). Ewing, who coined the term 'hysteresis', was a professor at Cambridge from 1890 to 1902. After he left to work for the Admiralty and, subsequently, as Principal of Edinburgh University, he retained a fellowship at King's College. Ewing knew Keynes: 'Maynard Keynes provided those at the high table with interesting ideas about the Economic Conference, on which pessimistic views were general' (A.W. Ewing, 1939). But there is no record of Keynes being exposed to the formal concept of hysteresis, which might have helped in his 'struggle to escape' from (neo)classical economics.

The entry of hysteresis into widespread use amongst economists was associated with some major empirical anomalies that appeared in the 1980s. After the oil price shock of 1979, and after the anti-inflation policies of the early 1980s, unemployment rates in Europe rose sharply. Once the shocks abated, however, unemployment remained high and showed no signs of falling back to some natural rate. Several attempts to explain how a rise in actual unemployment could be translated into an increase in equilibrium unemployment invoked hysteresis. In the Blanchard and Summers (1986) model, wages are negotiated with only the interests of the employed 'insiders' being taken into account. Thus shocks that increase unemployment serve to increase the number of 'outsiders' who are disenfranchised from labour markets. Other models were based on the rise in long-term unemployment associated with a rise in total unemployment. Again the idea is that a disenfranchisement process takes place, the long-term unemployed becoming, or being perceived to be, unemployable (see Cross, 1995). The term 'hysteresis' also came to be used in international trade theory to explain how changes in exchange rates could have lasting effects on exports and imports. The rise in the US dollar in the mid-1980s was associated with an increase in import penetration that was not reversed when the dollar fell in the late 1980s. The explanation was that 'foreign firms that entered the US market when the dollar was high do not abandon these sunk cost investments when the dollar falls' (Dixit, 1989, p. 205). The use of the term 'hysteresis' has enhanced interest in the processes to which the term refers: 'for many years I and others have argued that prolonged actual unemployment will become "natural" . . . but no one paid heed until the label 'hysteresis-effect' came into vogue' (Tobin, letter cited in Cross, 1993, p. 68).

Bastard hysteresis
Many of the hysteresis models produced by economists since the 1980s, however, are illegitimate descendants of the hysteresis analysis developed in physics and mathematics. Some economists use the term to refer to a slow process of adjustment to a fixed point equilibrium (Layard *et al.*, 1991). As was shown earlier, however, when hysteresis is present the out-of-equilibrium behaviour changes the equilibrium. Others have used the term to refer to the special case of a zero root in linear differential equations, or a unit root in linear difference equations (Wyplosz 1987, for example). The reduced form for a model of unemployment might be:

$$u_t = \alpha + \beta u_{t-1} + \gamma \mathbf{z}_t + \delta_t, \tag{2}$$

where u is unemployment, $\mathbf{z}$ is a vector of 'structural' variables that determine the natural rate of unemployment, δ is a disturbance term and α, β and γ are fixed parameters, with $0 < \beta \leq 1$. In the standard natural rate model $\beta \neq 1$, and the natural rate of unemployment u^* is gained by setting $u_t = u_{t-1}$:

$$u_t^* = \frac{\alpha + \gamma \mathbf{z}_t}{1 - \beta}, \tag{3}$$

Hysteresis, in its bastard form, is then said to occur when $\beta = 1$:

$$u_T^* = u_0 + \alpha T + \gamma \sum_{i=0} \mathbf{z}_{T-i} + \sum_{i=1} \delta_{T-1}. \qquad (4)$$

This unit-root case arises in linear models with representative agents, whereas hysteresis is actually a process arising when non-linear responses are made by heterogeneous agents. In the unit-root model 'hysteresis' is a special case. The popularity of this model amongst economists reflects the ease with which this special case can be grafted onto standard economic models. It shares with the rest of the unit root literature, in econometrics for example, a gross implausibility, the implication that economic systems have unselective and indefinitely long memories of shocks. Methuselah is alive and kicking. In contrast, hysteresis actually involves a selective, erasable memory where only the non-dominated extremum values of the shocks experienced remain in the memory bank.

Modelling hysteresis in economic systems

Microfoundations for the presence of hysteresis in economic systems can be readily found in the literature on discontinuous adjustment. Most adjustments in economic behaviour are made intermittently, and in large doses, rather than continuously in smallish doses. The basic reason for this is that there are fixed costs of making adjustments that cannot be recovered should the adjustment be reversed. Dixit and Pindyck (1994), for example, provide an analysis of investment and market entry and abandonment decisions that takes account of the irrecoverable nature of sunk costs and the value of waiting to gain more information about the uncertain future. Their analysis produces a clear rationale for the 'up' and 'down' triggers discussed earlier in this entry. In their context 'up' refers to going ahead with an investment project or entering a market, and 'down' refers to abandoning an investment or quitting a market. Sunk costs and the value of waiting differ between firms, and so yield the heterogeneous trigger values and hence heterogeneous responses to shocks required to produce hysteresis at the aggregate or macroeconomic level.

Since the early 1990s several groups of economists have used such microeconomic foundations to apply the Krasnosel'skii and Pokrovskii (1989) methods – see also Mayergoyz (1991) – to the analysis of economic systems. Cross (1991, 1993) analysed how equilibrium unemployment responds to demand or supply shocks; Amable *et al.* (1991, 1995) deal with the way international trade flows respond to exchange rate shocks; and Cross (2000) looks at the way the EMU countries respond to the common monetary policy. Econometric procedures have been devised to test for the existence of hysteresis using time-series techniques (Göcke, 1994, Cross *et al.*, 1998, Piscitelli *et al.*, 2000). A key development is to extend the analysis to allow the 'up' and 'down' triggers to vary over time in response to perturbations in a vector of explanatory variables (Cross *et al.*, 2001).

This work has important implications for the key issue of how macroeconomic policy should be conducted. The current fashion is to assume that macroeconomic policies have no lasting effects on real variables such as unemployment. On the back of this assumption, monetary and fiscal policies have been confined to the task of achieving inflation targets. If hysteresis is present, this assumption is wrong and monetary and fiscal policies do have lasting effects on real variables such as unemployment (see Ball, 1999, for evidence).

ROD CROSS

See also:
Natural Rate of Unemployment; New Keynesian Economics.

Bibliography

Amable, B., J. Henry, F. Lordon and R. Topol (1991), 'Strong Hysteresis: An Application to Foreign Trade', *OFCE Working Paper*, 9103, Paris.
Amable, B., J. Henry, F. Lordon and R. Topol (1995), 'Weak and Strong Hysteresis: An Application to Foreign Trade', *Economic Notes*, **24**, pp. 239–50.
Ball, L. (1999), 'Aggregate Demand and Long-Run Unemployment', *Brookings Papers on Economic Activity*, **2**, pp. 189–251.
Blanchard, O. and L. Summers (1986), 'Hysteresis and the European Unemployment Problem', *NBER Macroeconomics Annual*, pp. 15–77.
Cross, R. (1991), 'The NAIRU: Not An Interesting Rate of Unemployment', mimeo, University of Strathclyde.
Cross, R. (1993), 'On the Foundations of Hysteresis in Economic Systems', *Economics and Philosophy*, **9**, pp. 53–74.
Cross, R. (ed.) (1995), *The Natural Rate of Unemployment*, Cambridge: Cambridge University Press.
Cross, R. (2000), 'Hysteresis and EMU', *Metroeconomica*, **51**, pp. 367–79.
Cross, R. and A. Allan (1988), 'On the History of Hysteresis', in R. Cross (ed.), *Unemployment, Hysteresis and the Natural Rate Hypothesis*, Oxford: Basil Blackwell.
Cross, R., A.M. Krasnosel'skii and A.V. Pokrovskii (2001), 'A Time-Dependent Preisach Model', *Physica B*, **306**, pp. 206–10.
Cross, R., J. Darby, J. Ireland and L. Piscitelli (1998), 'Hysteresis and Unemployment: Some Preliminary Investigations', *CEPR/ESRC Unemployment Dynamics Workshop Paper*, 25 February.
Dixit, A. (1989), 'Hysteresis, Import Penetration and Exchange Rate Pass-Through', *Quarterly Journal of Economics*, **104**, May, pp. 205–28.
Dixit, A. and R. Pindyck (1994), *Investment under Uncertainty*, Princeton, NJ: Princeton University Press.
Ewing, A.W. (1939), *The Man of Room 40: The Life of Sir Alfred Ewing*, London: Hutchinson.
Ewing, J.A. (1881), 'On the Production of Transient Electric Currents in Iron and Steel Conductors by Twisting them when Magnetised or by Magnetizing them when Twisted', *Proceedings of the Royal Society of London*, **33**, pp. 21–3.
Feynman, R.P. (1992), *The Character of Physical Law*, London: Penguin.

Fisher, I. ([1892] 1925), *Mathematical Investigations in the Theory of Value and Prices*, New Haven, CT: Yale University Press.

Friedman, M. (1968), 'The Role of Monetary Policy', *American Economic Review*, **58**, March, pp. 1–17.

Glazebrook, R.T. (1935), 'James Alfred Ewing 1855–1935', *Obituary Notices of the Royal Society of London*, **1**, pp. 475–92.

Göcke, M. (1994), 'An Approximation of the Hysteresis Loop by Linear Partial Functions', mimeo, Westfälische Wilhems-Universität Münster.

Ingrao, B. and G. Israel (1990), *The Invisible Hand: Economic Equilibrium in the History of Science*, Cambridge, MA: MIT Press.

Keynes, J.M. (1934), 'Poverty in Plenty: Is the Economic System Self-Adjusting?', *The Listener*, 21 November.

Krasnosel'skii, M.A. and A.V. Pokrovskii (1989), *Systems with Hysteresis*, Berlin: Springer-Verlag.

Layard, R., S. Nickell and R. Jackman (1991), *Unemployment: Macroeconomic Performance and the Labour Market*, Oxford: Oxford University Press.

Marshall, A. (1890), *The Principles of Economics*, London: Macmillan.

Mayergoyz, I.D. (1991), *Mathematical Models of Hysteresis*, Berlin: Springer-Verlag.

Mirowski, P. (1989), *More Heat than Light*, New York: Cambridge University Press.

Piscitelli, L., R. Cross, M. Grinfeld and H. Lamba (2000), 'A Test for Strong Hysteresis', *Computational Economics*, **15**, pp. 59–78.

Preisach, F. (1938), 'Über die Magnetische Nachwirkung', *Zeitschrift für Physik*, **94**, pp. 277–302.

Summers, L.H. (1988), 'Should Keynesian Economics Dispense with the Phillips Curve?', in R. Cross (ed.), *Unemployment, Hysteresis and the Natural Rate Hypothesis*, Oxford: Basil Blackwell.

Wyplosz, C. (1987), 'Comments', in R. Layard and L. Calmfors (eds), *The Fight Against Unemployment*, Cambridge, MA: MIT Press.

Identity

An equation, such as the equation of exchange, that *must* hold by definition.

See also:
Equation of Exchange.

Implementation Lag

The time lag involved in implementing a decision to consciously change policy; also known as the administration lag.

See also:
Inside Lag.

Incomes Policy

Debates relating to the use of incomes policy to control inflation reached their height during the stagflationary period of the 1970s and early 1980s. While centrally planned economies by definition operate permanent incomes policies, the use of such policies in 'free market' economies proved to be extremely controversial (Trevithick, 1977). The main aim of any incomes policy is to slow down the rate of increase in the general price level by exerting direct or indirect control on the rate of wage (and possibly non-wage income) inflation within the economy. Advocates of incomes policy believe that *cost-push* factors play a significant role in the inflation process and that modern capitalist economies suffer from an *inflationary bias*, that is, excessive involuntary unemployment is required to keep inflation under control (see Cornwall, 1984). The appropriateness of an incomes policy as the most efficient way to achieve this aim will depend upon how the economy is viewed (Artis, 1981). Three different perspectives on incomes policy can be identified, namely the wage theorem view, the Phillips curve view and the expectations-augmented Phillips curve view.

Wage theorem view
This first rationale for incomes policy is based upon a view of the economy where, despite a permanent excess supply of labour, the money wage remains largely unaffected. Wage rates are seen as performing 'certain basic

social and institutional functions'; that is, 'they define relationships between labour and management, between one group of workers and another . . . the place of individuals relative to one another in the work community, in the neighbourhood, and in the family' (Piore, 1979). From this institutional perspective wages are unable to perform a supply and demand-determined equilibrating role and instead define a series of semi-fixed relationships, or wage contours, between jobs. Once wages have been set, prices are determined by a mark-up on wage and material costs. Following Kalecki (1971), average price (P) is determined in relation to the level of unit prime costs (w/q), multiplied by a mark-up (k) which is determined by the 'degree of monopoly' (all variables defined as weighted averages of individual firm variables). This mark-up pricing relationship is represented by equation (1).

$$P = k. \ w/q. \tag{1}$$

Here w is the money wage and q is average labour product. The unit prime cost curves are assumed horizontal over a normal range of output, implying that the main inflationary triggers will arise from the supply side of the economy via changes in either w/q or k. The role of aggregate demand is in determining real output at the point of intersection with the aggregate supply curve which is perfectly elastic below full capacity output. This enables aggregate demand management to be used as a tool for ensuring full employment, but it is a weak instrument with respect to the control of inflation. Modelling inflation within this framework is often done by examining conflicts over the distribution of income (Rowthorn, 1980). The persistent upward pressure on the general level of prices arises because of 'an excess of income claims over the real income available to satisfy these claims' (Burdekin and Burkett, 1996). These conflicts over income distribution suggest three main inflationary triggers: (i) attempts by workers to increase labour's share of national income; (ii) shocks from the external sector (for example, exchange rate depreciation) that reduce the real wage below the target that satisfies workers' aspirations; and (iii) attempts by firms to increase the share of profits in national income.

It can easily be seen from equation (1) how, via their influence on either w/q or k, each of these triggers will have inflationary consequences by initiating a distributional struggle. From this a clear rationale for an incomes policy can be made. If prices are rising too quickly owing to high levels of wage inflation then the government can intervene to control wage increases, which in turn will translate to lower price increases. It should be noted that, in this framework, incomes policy only provides a short-run solution. By controlling wage increases the policy will impinge on the distribution of income but will do nothing to diminish the underlying conflicts. If a significant conflict remains, political and/or industrial unrest becomes increasingly likely as long as the policy remains in place.

Phillips curve view

The pre–1968 view of the Phillips curve (Phillips, 1958; Samuelson and Solow, 1960), is represented by equation (2), where inflation ($\dot{P}$) is determined in relation to the rate of unemployment (U) acting as a proxy for the excess supply of labour (see Lipsey, 1978).

$$\dot{P} = f(U), \text{ and } f' < 0, \tag{2}$$

Within this framework the money wage is now sensitive to an excess supply of labour and endogenous to the model. Assuming a stable long-run trade-off (an idea, that is now defunct), a policy dilemma is created because it provides policy makers with a difficult choice given that the two key policy objectives, low inflation and low unemployment, are incompatible. However, it allows the tool of demand management to be used in order to achieve a desired balance between them.

This insight significantly reduces the power of the 'wage theorem' rationale for an incomes policy. Now that aggregate demand management can be used for controlling inflation, the superiority of an incomes policy for controlling inflation needs to be demonstrated, by comparing the costs and benefits of the alternative policies (Paish, 1968). The main economic costs of an incomes policy include the following. First, by altering the structure of relative wages within an economy, a misallocation of labour will occur, lowering output. Second, attempts to circumvent the policy by using non-wage forms of payment will lead to additional distortions in the labour market since it becomes more difficult to ascertain the rate of return associated with each job. Third, the effects on the distribution of income may cause possible industrial unrest and strikes, again lowering the output of the economy.

Expectations-augmented Phillips curve view

In order to take into account that workers have an interest in real and not nominal wages, the expectations-augmented Phillips curve adds a variable for expectations to equation (2), and also distinguishes between the actual unemployment rate and the natural rate of unemployment (U^*). According to the Friedman–Phelps analysis, each level of inflationary expectations is associated with a new short-run Phillips curve and in the long run there is no trade-off between inflation and unemployment (Friedman, 1968; Phelps, 1968).

$$\dot{P} = -\beta(U - U^*) + \dot{P}^e. \tag{3}$$

This insight, combined with the natural rate of unemployment, provides policy makers with a vertical long-run Phillips curve, indicating that, whenever $U = U^*$ (that is, when the economy is at its natural rate) inflation will stabilize at a level equal to inflationary expectations. This leads to the familiar Friedman–Phelps policy conclusion that the key to lowering inflation is to lower the expectation of inflation (Laidler, 1971). As with the Phillips curve framework, it must now be demonstrated that an incomes policy can lower inflation by imposing smaller costs on the economy than the alternatives available. The key question for policy makers is 'how do we make our anti-inflationary policy credible?' An incomes policy is one possible option and, during the 1970s, the adoption of incomes policy, acting as a complement to demand management policies in order to reduce inflation, received support in the United States from staunch neo-Keynesian economists such as James Tobin (1987) and Arthur Okun (1981). In the United Kingdom, several economists also favoured the use of incomes policy as a method of reducing inflationary expectations (see Trevithick and Stevenson, 1977; Peston, 1980). However, there are several other options, such as creating an independent central bank with an anti-inflationary mandate. This latter option has turned out to be more enduring than incomes policy. Economists of a more free market persuasion (particularly new classical economists) adopt the view that, once anti-inflationary credibility has been established, monetary policy can move the economy down a vertical long-run Phillips curve, allowing lower inflation with no associated loss of output. If an independent central bank can do this without creating market distortions then there is no case for an incomes policy because of the associated welfare losses ('Harberger triangles'). If market imperfections prevent easy movement down the long-run Phillips curve, an incomes policy *may* still be desirable within this framework. It may be the case that in order for a monetary policy regime to gain the required credibility, the economy would necessarily experience a deep recession, having to move a long way down a short-run Phillips curve in order to reduce inflationary expectations. If it can be demonstrated that an incomes policy can lower inflation while having smaller effects on output which more than compensate for the distortionary effects of the policy, then there is a clear rational for a short-run incomes policy (see Tobin, 1987). Once low inflation credibility has been established, the policy could be switched to one that allows a more efficient functioning of the supply side of the economy.

Incomes policy in practice
There are three main types of incomes policy:

1. A temporary policy with fixed maximum rates of increase (or a freeze) in wages, salaries, dividends and possibly prices for a short period. If this fixed-rate type of policy persisted for any length of time, measures would need to be taken to minimize some of the adverse effects of the policy on market efficiency; for example, with income increases capped, any productivity gains above these maximums would accrue to undistributed profits, and controls will also prevent changes in relative prices, which will distort incentives and reduce economic welfare.

2. A longer-term or permanent policy, favoured mainly by 'Post Keynesian' economists such as Paul Davidson (1994) and 'Institutionalists' such as John Kenneth Galbraith (1952, 1973). Such a policy would use a statutory norm for nominal wage increases, with exceptions to allow for items such as increased wages justified by productivity gains. The criticisms applied to the temporary policy apply with even more force in this case.

3. A longer-term or permanent policy using the taxation system to regulate wage increases. This has the advantage of operating by providing incentives to market participants, rather than relying on legislation (Weintraub and Wallich, 1971; Layard, 1982). A tax-based policy would operate by levying a tax on employers in some proportion to any wage increases paid above a statutory norm, and possibly offering a rebate for wage increases below the norm. In presenting a simplified version of Layard's analysis, the imposition of the tax would have the effect of modifying the familiar expectations-augmented Phillips curve given by equation (3) by adding the additional term λT, where T is the tax rate:

$$\dot{P} = -\beta(U - U^*) + \dot{P}^e - \lambda T. \tag{4}$$

This has the effect of shifting each short-run Phillips curve down and to the left. The explanation is as follows: each employer now has an additional incentive to resist any wage claims above the norm, owing to the additional cost of the 'wage-inflation tax'. This will increase the cost to the employer of paying a given wage increase, reducing wage increases for a given level of unemployment thus shifting down the Phillips curve. This will produce a lower level of wage and hence price inflation.

Once the type of incomes policy has been decided upon, there are numerous difficulties in the design and implementation of any such policy. Blackaby (1972) divides these into four broad areas.

1. Problems associated with deciding the norm and the exceptions to it. This will have implications for the redistributive effects of the policy. Blackaby indicates that, upon the basis of past experience, any norm tends to become a minimum and 'most exceptions are above the norm and very few below'. Past experience suggests a list of arguments which are likely to be made for allowing exceptions to the norm, such as higher increases in sectors of the economy with relatively low pay; increases to reflect the productivity of individual industries or firms; increases that reflect the distribution of manpower to allow labour to move towards industries with relatively high marginal revenue products; and so on. Care needs to be taken to ensure that the number of exceptions does not become so large that the effectiveness of the policy is reduced.
2. Problems created by the number of points of decision and the complexity of settlements, for example, decisions need to be taken on how to deal with overlapping wage contracts of differing duration, the setting of piecework rates for new or redefined jobs and so on.
3. Problems created by having to devise the machinery for applying the norm and any exceptions to it. Most countries which have used incomes policies have set up some form of 'Prices and Incomes Policy Board' that operates using either its own criteria or those given to it by government. One of the central issues is the degree of power the 'Board' is allowed to enforce its decisions. A voluntary system is more likely to gain support from employers, employees and unions, but may be weaker as a method of controlling inflation.
4. Problems related to dealing with non-wage incomes. For example, if it is thought that businesses will be able to take advantage of the policy and make excess profits, then a comparable set of rules will be needed to deal with profit incomes.

Whilst incomes policies in a variety of forms have been used in many countries at different times during the last 50 years, and are still enthusiastically advocated by many Post Keynesian economists, the majority of mainstream economists (that is, 'new Keynesians') prefer to place their faith in a monetary policy regime based on inflation targeting combined with a large element of central bank independence.

To free market economists such as Milton Friedman, the use of incomes policies to control inflation is an exercise in King Canute economics. Whilst such policies suppress inflation in the short run at the cost of distorting market efficiency, in the long run they also fail to control inflation, as experience during the 1970s demonstrated. Post Keynesians like Paul Davidson remain convinced that the fundamental cause of inflation is a deep-seated distributional struggle that can only be resolved by some form of permanent incomes policy.

ANDREW HUNT

See also:

Credibility and Reputation; Expectations-augmented Phillips Curve; Inflation: Alternative Theories of; Inflation: Costs of Reducing; Inflation Targeting; Natural Rate of Unemployment; Phillips Curve; Stagflation.

Bibliography

Artis, M.J. (1981), 'Incomes Policies: Some Rationales' in J.L. Fallick and R.F. Elliot (eds), *Incomes Policies, Inflation and Relative Pay*, London: George Allen & Unwin.

Bernanke, B.S., T. Laubach, F.S. Mishkin and A.S. Posen (1999), *Inflation Targeting: Lessons from the International Experience*, Princeton: Princeton University Press.

Blackaby, F. (1972), 'Incomes Policies', in F. Blackaby (ed.), *An Incomes Policy for Britain*, London: Heinemann.

Burdekin, R.C.K. and P. Burkett (1996), *Distributional Conflict and Inflation: Theoretical and Historical Perspectives*, Basingstoke: Macmillan.

Cornwall, J. (ed.) (1984), *After Stagflation: Alternatives to Economic Decline*, Oxford: Basil Blackwell.

Davidson, P. (1994), *Post Keynesian Macroeconomic Theory: A Foundation for Successful Policies for the Twenty-First Century*, Aldershot, UK and Brookfield, US: Edward Elgar.

Friedman, M. (1968), 'The Role of Monetary Policy', *American Economic Review*, **58**, March, pp. 1–17.

Galbraith, J.K. (1952), *A Theory of Price Control*, Cambridge, MA: Harvard University Press.

Galbraith, J.K. (1973), *Economics and the Public Purpose*, Boston, MA: Houghton Mifflin.

Kalecki, M. (1971), *Selected Essays on the Dynamics of the Capitalist Economy, 1933–1970*, Cambridge: Cambridge University Press.

Laidler, D. (1971), 'The Phillips Curve, Expectations and Incomes Policy', in H.G. Johnson and A.R. Nobay (cds), *The Current Inflation*, London: Macmillan.

Layard, R. (1982), 'Is Incomes Policy the Answer to Unemployment?', *Economica*, **49**, August, pp. 219–39.

Lipsey, R.G. (1978), 'The Place of the Phillips Curve in Macroeconomic Models', in A.R. Bergstrom (ed.), *Stability and Inflation*, Chichester: John Wiley.

Okun, A. (1981), *Prices and Quantities: A Macroeconomic Analysis*, Oxford: Basil Blackwell.

Paish, F.W. (1968), 'The Limits of Incomes Policies', in F.W. Paish and J. Hennessy, *Policy for Incomes*, London: Institute of Economic Affairs.

Peston, M. (1980), 'Monetary Policy and Incomes Policy: Complements or Substitutes?', *Applied Economics*, **12**, December, pp. 443–54.

Phelps, E.S. (1968), 'Money Wage Dynamics and Labour Market Equilibrium', *Journal of Political Economy*, **76**, August, pp. 678–711.

Phillips, A.W.H. (1958), 'The Relation between Unemployment and the Rate of Change of Money Wages in the UK, 1861–1957', *Economica*, **25**, November, pp. 283–99.

Piore, M.J. (1979), 'Unemployment and Inflation: An Alternative View', in M.J. Piore (ed.), *Unemployment and Inflation: Institutionalist and Structuralist Views*, New York: M.E. Sharpe.

Rowthorn, B. (1980), *Capitalism, Conflict and Inflation*, London: Lawrence and Wishart.

Samuelson, P. and R. Solow (1960), 'Analytical Aspects of Anti-Inflationary Policy', *American Economic Review*, **50**, May, pp. 177–94.
Snowdon, B. (1983), *Inflation, Unemployment and the Role of Incomes Policy*, Newcastle Upon Tyne: Anforme.
Tobin, J. (1987), *Policies for Prosperity: Essays in a Keynesian Mode*, ed. P.M. Jackson Brighton: Wheatsheaf.
Trevithick, J.A. (1977), *Inflation: A Guide to the Crisis in Economics*, Harmondsworth: Penguin.
Trevithick, J. and A. Stevenson (1977), 'The Complementarity of Monetary Policy and Prices and Incomes Policy', *Scottish Journal of Political Economy*, **24**, February, pp. 19–31.
Weintraub, S. and H. Wallich (1971), 'A Taxed-Based Incomes Policy', *Journal of Economic Issues*, **5**, June, pp. 1–19.

Indexation

A mechanism for adjusting the value of contracts denominated in money terms to bring them in line with movements in prices, thereby maintaining the real value of the contracts concerned. For example, wage contracts may provide for cost of living adjustment (COLA) whereby, periodically, wages are automatically increased in response to increases in a consumer price index. Two main advantages have been put forward in favour of the widespread introduction of indexation. First, indexation has been advocated on the grounds of distributive equity in order to avoid the arbitrary redistribution of income and wealth caused by inflation. Second, some economists have claimed that indexation would lessen the economic costs of reducing the rate of inflation associated with monetary contraction. With indexation, money wage increases would automatically decline as inflation decreased, thereby removing the danger that employers would be committed under existing wage contracts to excessive money wage increases when inflation fell. In other words, with indexation wage increases would be less rapid and unemployment would rise by a smaller amount following a policy of monetary contraction. In a similar manner indexation would also avoid the danger of firms being locked into paying excessively high nominal interest rates on loans as inflation fell. With indexation, contracts for loans would be fixed in real terms and there would be no reason for firms to delay capital investment projects in anticipation of lower nominal rates of interest. Despite such potential advantages, indexation is not without its critics.

See also:

Inflation: Costs of; Inflation: Costs of Reducing.

Inflation

A situation in which the overall or general level of prices rises over time. Debate exists over the cause of, costs of, costs of reducing, and cure for inflation.

See also:

Inflation: Alternative Theories of; Inflation: Costs of; Inflation: Costs of Reducing; Inflation Rate; Inflation Targeting.

Inflation: Alternative Theories of

Inflation is a process of continuing rises in the general price level. In principle, inflation affects the prices of all (or at least most) goods and services, and is therefore distinct from a change in relative prices (when the prices of some commodities rise vis à vis those of others). Some theories of inflation blur this distinction, however, as does the measurement of inflation in terms of changes in a composite price index (such as the Consumer Price Index). The components of such indices seldom, if ever, vary in equal proportion to one another.

The purpose of inflation theory is to explain the causes of rises in the general price level. A number of competing theories of inflation exist. These can be categorized according to whether they are demand-pull or cost-push theories, and according to whether they identify real or monetary factors as being the source of inflation. Demand-pull inflation occurs when an expansion of aggregate demand (AD) is not (or cannot be) wholly accommodated by an increase in output, with the result that prices must rise. Cost-push inflation is initiated by general increases in the costs of production, which are then passed on by producers in the form of higher prices. The quintessential feature of a monetary theory of inflation, meanwhile, is that monetary factors (usually the money supply) are understood to be the direct cause of inflation. Non-monetary theories posit real forces – such as changes in households' or firms' expenditure behaviour, or conflict over the distribution of income – as causing inflation.

Demand-pull theories

A cornerstone of demand-pull inflation theory is the classical quantity theory of money, which states that $M\bar{V} = P\bar{Y}$, where M is the exogenously determined quantity of money in circulation, V is the income velocity of circulation of money, P is the general price level and Y represents the level of output. If V remains constant and Y is determined independently of the other (monetary) variables in the equation (hence the bars above these variables), an increase in the money supply will increase aggregate purchasing power in the presence of a fixed output. This will create an excess demand for goods, bidding up their prices in equal proportion to the original increase in the money supply. The inflation so described may be international rather than domestic. Monetary expansion in one country can create an excess demand for *foreign* goods, and hence inflation abroad, if exchange depreciation (which might otherwise mitigate the initial increase in demand for foreign goods) is precluded by a regime of fixed exchange rates (Johnson, 1972). The quantity theory is a monetary theory of inflation with a straightforward policy implication: growth of the money supply in excess of supply-determined expansions of output should be eliminated/avoided, as its consequences are purely inflationary.

The classical quantity theory has been extensively modified since the 1950s. In particular, changes in the money supply are now believed to affect output (Y), at least in the short run. According to Monetarism and New Classical Macroeconomics (see, for example, Lucas, 1996), this impact is the result of temporary expectational errors. Unanticipated inflations stimulate supply-side responses that affect output and employment, until inflationary expectations adjust. These models are primarily responsible for the increased emphasis on inflationary expectations in discussions of inflation theory and policy since the mid–1970s (see, for example, Laidler and Parkin, 1975, and contrast with Bronfenbrenner and Holzman, 1963). An alternative view, expressed by New Keynesian Economics, is that changes in M cause changes in Y because product prices are rigid in the short run (see, for example, Mankiw and Romer, 1991). But, like monetarists and new classicists, new Keynesians maintain that an increase in the money supply initiates an excess demand for goods that, in the long run, translates wholly into an increase in prices. The quantity theory remains, therefore, the cornerstone of inflation theory in the classical macroeconomic tradition, in which the money supply is exogenous and money is neutral (at least in the long run).

A different demand-pull theory of inflation emerges from the simple Keynesian model. This model assumes that increases in AD translate entirely into increases in output and employment when the economy is below full employment (FE). But once FE is reached, any subsequent increase in AD creates an excess demand for goods beyond the productive capacity of the economy (an 'inflationary gap'), as a result of which prices rise. This provides a demand-pull theory of inflation, but does not presuppose that the source of rising prices is monetary in origin. Keynesian inflationary gap theory (see Keynes, 1940) also gives rise to straightforward policy implications. Policy makers should stimulate AD whenever the economy is below FE, but take care not to stimulate demand beyond this point, as the consequence will be inflation.

Both the quantity theory and inflationary gap theory characterize inflation as resulting from an excess of AD over and above some pre-defined supply constraint, imposed by either the natural rate of unemployment or NAIRU, on one hand, or FE, on the other. But some demand-pull theories posit that inflation begins in response to increases in demand even before the economy encounters an aggregate supply constraint. Inspired by Tobin (1972), Palley (1996, ch. 10) constructs a theory in which localized output bottlenecks combine with AD growth to create inflation in an economy that is operating below FE. AD growth is assumed to be unevenly distributed across different sectors of the economy, each of which begins each period operating below capacity and facing a local supply constraint. The asymmetric impact of AD growth sees excess demand (and hence demand-pull inflation) emerge in some sectors, even as other sectors (and hence the economy as a whole) operate below FE.

In De Vroey (1984), 'extra money' is the proximate source of demand-pull inflation. Extra money is created when firms borrow in order to cover business losses, or when the state monetizes budget deficits. It contributes to AD, and has inflationary consequences whenever this additional demand finds its way into sectors already operating at full capacity (which may, despite the existence of losses, constitute the entire economy). Like Palley's theory, De Vroey's suggests that policy makers may have to accept higher inflation as a consequence of increasing the level of economic activity. Unlike Palley's theory, De Vroey's is a monetary theory of inflation, but, unlike the quantity theory, the money supply is endogenous and money is non-neutral.

Cost-push theories
Central to cost-push theories of inflation is the idea that workers and firms possess market power, consequently influencing wages and prices independently of demand. The primary role of money in these theories is to accommodate rather than cause inflation.

First generation cost-push (FGCP) theory views rising costs in factor markets – and in particular, the labour market – as the source of inflation (see, for example, Cornwall, 1983, ch. 2). Increases in nominal wages vary directly with the relative bargaining power of labour. To the extent that they are not offset by higher productivity, these increases in nominal wages raise the average cost of labour. If firms mark up prices over average labour costs by a constant fraction, θ, so that $P = (1 + \theta) AC_L$ where P is the price level and AC_L the average cost of labour, then increases in nominal wages will result in prices increasing in equal proportion to average labour costs. Inflation results, therefore, from rising costs that are passed on in the form of higher prices.

   This theory seems to suggest that 'excessive' wage claims – and, by extension, workers and trade unions – are the root cause of inflation. But closer inspection reveals this to be false. If firms accommodate nominal wage increases that exceed productivity gains by lowering the mark-up, θ, it is evident from the equation above that prices need not rise at all. However, this will change the distribution of income between wages and profits. Inflation in FGCP theory is therefore the result of firms' unwillingness to accede to workers' implicit claims for a larger share of income. This interpretation highlights the substance of the conflicting-claims theory of inflation. According to this theory, inflation is caused by both workers *and* firms or, more specifically, by the irreconcilable claims on total income that result from their differing conceptions of what constitutes a fair distribution of income. In conflicting claims theory, inflation can be either wage-led (as in FGCP theory) or profit-led. Hence firms can initiate inflation by increasing prices relative to nominal wages (which will increase the profit share of income). But workers may block this attempted redistribution by bidding up nominal wages (a process called real wage resistance), thereby encouraging firms to further increase prices in the hope of achieving their preferred profit share, which will again prompt real wage resistance, and so on. The result is a process of continually rising prices (see Rowthorn, 1977; Burdekin and Burkett, 1996).

   Cost-push theories suggest that inflation can be reduced by deflationary macroeconomic policies, if these reduce the relative bargaining power of labour (in FGCP theory) or defeat the income share aspirations of either workers or firms (in conflicting claims theory). The cost, however, is reduced economic activity. Alternatively, an incomes policy can be formulated, in an effort to reconcile low inflation with high output and employment. Conflicting claims theory suggests that, if it is to succeed, an incomes policy must be founded on a distribution of income that is mutually accepted as fair. If income share aspirations do not endogenously adjust in response to such policies (and they may not), then the need for an incomes policy to reconcile low inflation with high output and employment will be permanent rather than temporary (see Cornwall, 1994).

Inflation theory and the Phillips curve
There are strong links between inflation theory and the shape of the Phillips curve. Several of the inflation theories described above (including both cost-push theories and the sectoral bottleneck and extra money theories) suggest that there is always a trade-off between inflation and the rate of

unemployment. These theories are consistent with a negatively-sloped Phillips curve. The expectations-augmented Phillips curves of Monetarism and New Classical Macroeconomics are, however, vertical in the long run, since, in these theories, changes in aggregate demand ultimately result only in changes in prices (leading unemployment unchanged). Some New Keynesians postulate that the short-run trade-off between unemployment and inflation that is consistent with all modern variants of the classical quantity theory can give rise to hysteresis in the long-run Phillips curve (Blanchard and Summers, 1987). As a result, even in the classical macro-economic tradition, there may be a long-run trade-off between unemployment and inflation.

The political economy of inflation policy
Complications arise in the pursuit of policies that impinge on inflation if government intervention in the economy is advised by the interests of politicians and the groups they represent, rather than the interests of society at large. One possibility is that governments will exploit the Phillips curve trade-off by sacrificing low inflation to the pursuit of low unemployment in the run-up to elections (Nordhaus, 1975; Cukierman and Meltzer, 1986). If this trade-off is permanent rather than temporary, governments of different political persuasions may systematically pursue low inflation (and hence high unemployment) or low unemployment (and hence high inflation) in order to satisfy the preferences of their core constituencies (Hibbs, 1977).

A second complication is that a government may have an incentive to renege on a previously announced inflation policy, in which case the policy is said to be time-inconsistent. This idea was first introduced by Kydland and Prescott (1977), who show that time-inconsistency may result in an inflationary bias in the economy. Because of their potential time-inconsistency, discretionary government policies (which can be changed over time) may suffer a lack of credibility. One way to combat time-inconsistency – and the opportunistic or partisan behaviours described earlier – is to base inflation policy on constitutional rules rather than government discretion. However, such rules may prove too inflexible in the face of unforeseen events. Moreover, some of these political economy problems may be reduced if governments perceive that the present benefits of, for example, reneging on policy commitments are offset by the future costs of such behaviour (such as loss of reputation).

Summary
The preceding discussion furnishes the following typology of inflation theories:

	Monetary	Real
Demand-Pull	Quantity theory of money	Inflationary gap theory
	Extra money theory	Sectoral bottleneck theory
Cost-Push		First generation cost-push theory
		Conflicting claims theory

Some of these theories are mutually exclusive. The quantity theory, for example, insists that the general price level cannot rise independently of a prior increase in the money supply. Hence cost-push inflation is impossible: inflation is always and everywhere a monetary phenomenon, resulting solely from expansions of the money supply that exceed the growth of real output (Friedman, 1970). Other demand-pull theories admit the possibility of cost-push inflation, however. Also demand can influence inflation indirectly in cost-push theories, as, for example, when an increase in AD that increases the capacity utilization rate enhances the ability of either workers or firms to press their distributional claims. Finally, real theories of inflation permit an indirect role for monetary factors, working through the influence of interest rates on either AD or (in conflicting claims theory) firms' desired mark-ups. Moreover, some form of monetary accommodation is always necessary in order for inflation to result from real causes. It is therefore possible in principle to theorize inflation as a complex process resulting from both demand-pull and cost-push influences, and as having real and monetary causes.

MARK SETTERFIELD

See also:

Expectations-augmented Phillips Curve; Hysteresis; Incomes Policy; Keynesian Cross; Monetarism; Natural Rate of Unemployment; New Classical Economics; New Keynesian Economics; Phillips Curve; Quantity Theory of Money; Time Inconsistency.

Bibliography

Blanchard, O.J. and L.H. Summers (1987), 'Hysteresis in Unemployment', *European Economic Review*, **31**, February/March, pp. 288–95.
Bronfenbrenner, M. and F.D. Holzman (1963), 'A Survey of Inflation Theory', *American Economic Review*, **53**, September, pp. 593–661.
Burdekin, R. and P. Burkett (1996), *Distributional Conflict and Inflation: Theoretical and Historical Perspectives*, London: Macmillan.
Cornwall, J. (1983), *The Conditions for Economic Recovery: A Post-Keynesian Analysis*, Oxford: Martin Robertson.
Cornwall, J. (1994), *Economic Breakdown and Recovery: Theory and Policy*, Armonk, NY: M.E. Sharpe.
Cukierman, A. and A. Meltzer (1986), 'A Positive Theory of Discretionary Policy, the Cost of Democratic Government and the Benefits of a Constitution', *Economic Inquiry*, **24**, July, pp. 367–88.
De Vroey, M. (1984), 'Inflation: A Non-Monetarist Monetary Interpretation', *Cambridge Journal of Economics*, **8**, December, pp. 381–99.

Friedman, M. (1970), *The Counter-Revolution in Monetary Theory*, IEA Occasional Paper no. 33, London: Institute of Economic Affairs.

Hibbs, D. (1977) 'Political Parties and Macroeconomic Policy', *American Political Science Review*, **71**, December, pp. 1467–87.

Johnson, H.G. (1972), 'Inflation: A Monetarist View', in H.G. Johnson (ed.), *Further Essays in Monetary Economics*, London: Macmillan.

Keynes, J.M. (1940), *How to Pay For the War*, London: Macmillan.

Kydland, F.E. and E.C.Prescott (1977), 'Rules Rather than Discretion: The Inconsistency of Optimal Plans', *Journal of Political Economy*, **85**, June, pp. 473–91.

Laidler, D.E.W. and M. Parkin (1975), 'Inflation: A Survey', *Economic Journal*, **85**, December, pp. 741–809.

Lucas, R.E. (1996), 'Nobel Lecture: Monetary Neutrality', *Journal of Political Economy*, **104**, August, pp. 661–82.

Mankiw, N.G. and D. Romer (eds) (1991), *New Keynesian Economics*, Cambridge, MA: MIT Press.

Nordhaus, W. (1975), 'The Political Business Cycle', *Review of Economic Studies*, **42**, April, pp. 169–90.

Palley, T.I. (1996), *Post Keynesian Economics: Debt, Distribution and the Macroeconomy*, London: Macmillan.

Rowthorn, R. (1977), 'Conflict, Inflation and Money', *Cambridge Journal of Economics*, **1**, September, pp 215–39.

Tobin, J (1972), 'Inflation and Unemployment', *American Economic Review*, **62**, March, pp. 1–26.

Inflation: Costs of

Inflation is the sustained increase in the general level of prices and at various times in many national economies it has proved deeply unpopular (see Shiller, 1999). The elimination of inflation or the lasting achievement of price stability has been, and in many economies remains, the cardinal objective of macroeconomic policy. During the past ten years central banks throughout the world have adopted long-run price stability as their primary goal and in many cases moved towards a monetary regime based on inflation targeting. However, economic analysis has failed to establish beyond reasonable doubt that inflation imposes such significant costs that society ought to seek its eradication rather than learn to live with it. In recent years empirical studies have tended to confirm that inflation and economic growth are negatively related but this does not entail that inflation causes low growth (see Temple, 2000).

Inflation may be anticipated by defensive behaviour on the part of economic agents, if their expectations about the future rate of inflation are correct and they are not already 'locked into' nominal contracts dating from a pre-inflationary period. There are two theoretical arguments for believing that even perfectly anticipated inflation imposes welfare costs: shoe leather (or monetary) costs and menu costs (see entry on this topic in the present volume). In an inflationary environment agents will economize on cash balances and sight deposits in favour of time deposits so that the interest earned will protect, at least to a degree, the purchasing power of their income. The shoe leather used up in making frequent trips to the bank is a metaphor for all the productive resources consumed in this endeavour, including fuel, and lost output from labour and capital being idle.

Shoe leather costs may have contributed to economic collapse under hyperinflation, for example in Germany during 1922–3. Empirical studies on the shoe leather costs of moderate inflation are highly sensitive to the assumptions made in the theoretical models underlying them. For the United States, Tobin (1972) reported an estimate that 'an extra percentage point of anticipated inflation embodied in nominal interest rates produces in principle a social cost of 2/10 of 1 per cent of GNP per year' (p. 15) For the United Kingdom, Minford and Hilliard (1978) estimated the shoe leather costs of 30 per cent inflation at almost 6 per cent of GDP. This may overestimate the shoe leather costs of moderate inflation under contemporary financial institutions, where new products allow instant access to cash while paying interest on balances. More generally, a survey of theoretical models of shoe leather costs found a variety of outcomes depending mainly on the interest elasticity of the demand for cash and on the definition of money, given that cash (or 'narrow money') is a relatively small proportion of the broader money supply (Orphanides and Solow, 1990).

On balance, a positive rate of inflation may entail monetary benefits rather than costs, by virtue of seigniorage or the 'inflation tax'. This arises out of the non-payment of interest on currency, the holding of which therefore amounts to an interest-free loan from the public to the government, enabling it to increase its command over real resources. The inflation tax may be no more distorting of economic activity than other taxes available to the government (Briault, 1995, p. 34).

The most serious costs of inflation arise when, and perhaps to the degree that, inflation is unanticipated. Unanticipated inflation is thought to impose costs on society in two main ways: through the unplanned and haphazard redistribution of income and wealth, and through the reduction in economic growth from the effects of 'inflationary noise' (see Fischer, 1993; Barro, 1995).

It is the redistributive effects of inflation that are sometimes thought to be responsible not only for its unpopularity but also for much of the real damage that it causes. Baumol and Blinder (1988) exemplify this view: 'Why, then, is the redistribution caused by inflation so widely condemned? Because its victims are selected capriciously. . . . The gainers do not earn their spoils, and the losers do not deserve their fate. This is the fundamental indictment of inflation' (p. 104). There are many ways in which unanticipated inflation may redistribute income and wealth.

Inflation redistributes current incomes within the private sector in three ways, because (i) the prices of various goods and services rise at different rates; (ii) average incomes and the general level of prices rise at different rates; and (iii) the wages earned in various occupations, and the incomes received in other ways, rise at different rates. For the UK, a piece of research by Fry and Pashardes (1985) suggests that there is an inflation bias of significant magnitude against low-income households and against large families (see also Easterly and Fischer, 2001). Fry and Pashardes concluded that 'the major factor governing differences in the effects of inflation between households is their expenditure level, with price indices falling substantially as expenditure rises' (1985, p. 25).

On the other hand Fender (1990) concludes that there is 'evidence . . . that the upper income groups are particularly badly hit by inflation' (p. 75). Members of right-wing political parties tend to be more concerned about inflation than members of left-wing parties (Mueller, 1989, pp. 286–91), perhaps because they own more financial assets whose real value is threatened by inflation (Minford and Peel, 1981; Higham and Tomlinson, 1982, p. 8). The share of the UK's wealth owned by those groups declined sharply during the inflationary years of 1971–6. It appears that the regressive redistributive effect from building society depositors to mortgage holders suggested by Foster (1976) has been overridden.

There are two problems in evaluating the real-world significance of these effects. First, measurement problems make it difficult to approach an overall estimate of the impact of the redistributive effects of inflation on welfare. The hypothesis that wages lag prices illustrates the problem.

> By one selection of beginning and terminal points for an inflation it can be shown real wages fell; by another selection it can be shown that real wages rose. The fall in real wages reported by these observers is a product of the arbitrary way the time period during which inflation occurred was defined. (Alchian and Kessel, 1960, p. 64)

Second, it is difficult to disentangle the impact of inflation from that of the real economic forces of supply and demand, including the supplies of labour and capital, the quality of the labour force and the pattern of final demand for goods and services (and hence the pattern of the derived demands for labour of different kinds). For these forces influence the extent to which a particular social group can reverse the redistributive effect of a price or wage rise which benefited another social group.

It is sometimes claimed that the government is the principal beneficiary of the redistribution of real resources by inflation. However, the government is not the final consumer of goods and services but a channel for the transfer of resources from one part of society to another. The impact of inflation on the distribution of real resources through government activities cannot be estimated until the ultimate beneficiaries are identified and the effective incidence of the inflation tax, relative to that of conventional taxes, ascertained (Dawson, 1992).

The effects of inflation on taxation is sometimes claimed to cause a substantial deadweight welfare loss (Feldstein, 1997, 1999). First, inflation increases the effective tax rate on businesses by reducing the value of depreciation allowances (Feldstein, 1997, p. 129). Second, inflation reduces the real net return to saving by increasing the effective tax rate on nominal capital gains and nominal interest (ibid., p. 125). This distorts the allocation of lifetime consumption by households. Even if saving decisions are unchanged, there is a reduction in future consumption and hence a deadweight loss. On this basis the benefit of moving from 2 per cent inflation to price stability is estimated to be a perpetual welfare gain with a present value of 35 per cent of the initial level of GDP, far exceeding the one-off cost of the disinflation of 5 per cent of GDP (ibid, p. 153). Distributional issues qualify the desirability of disinflation on these grounds, as Feldstein (ibid., p. 154) acknowledges. The welfare gain is distributed across increasingly distant future generations, while the cost is incurred entirely by the present generation and predominantly, through the rise in unemployment, by its worse-off members.

The idea of 'inflationary noise' captures the impact of inflation on the allocation of resources and hence on economic growth. Hayek (1975, 1978) argued that inflation causes a market economy to misallocate resources. Markets are a discovery procedure, bringing together knowledge of resources and knowledge of consumer demands that would otherwise remain locked away inside the heads of many individuals. Inflationary noise obscures the perception of price signals that transmit information about relative scarcities through changes in relative prices. In this way inflation undermines the allocative efficiency of competitive markets. There is a political dimension to Hayek's case against inflation, in that it frustrates the efforts of free individuals to pursue their livelihoods though market activity. Friedman (1977) argues in a broadly similar way that as inflation rises so does its volatility, with the consequence that 'an additional element of uncertainty is, as it were, added to every market arrangement' (p. 466).

The variability of relative prices does increase as inflation accelerates (Fischer and Modigliani, 1978; Clare and Thomas, 1993). A substantial amount of research has sought to test the hypothesis that inflation inhibits growth in this way, and in others (see Kirshner, 2001). Some studies assume a neoclassical growth model, others see technological innovation as endogenous; some models use time-series analysis for a single country, others employ cross-country analysis. The result of most studies is that there is a significant negative correlation between inflation and growth, particularly at higher rates of inflation (Barro, 1995; Fischer, 1993; Temple, 2000).

However, it does not necessarily follow that low growth is a cost or adverse effect of inflation, for the implication that inflation causes growth to be lower than it otherwise would be is questionable on theoretical grounds. Inflation is an endogenous variable in the economy, which raises the possibility that inflation and (low) growth may themselves be determined by other factors. Fischer (1981) concluded from this that 'there is some logical difficulty in discussing the costs of inflation *per se* rather than the costs and benefits of alternative policy choices'. According to Briault (1995), 'the available evidence supports the view that well-run economies with strong and efficient productive structures tend to exhibit both low inflation and high growth' (p. 33).

GRAHAM DAWSON

See also:

Inflation Targeting; Menu Costs.

Bibliography

Alchian, A.A. and R.A. Kessel (1960), 'The Meaning and Validity of the Inflation-Induced Lag of Wages Behind Prices', *American Economic Review*, **50**, March, pp. 43–66.
Barro, R. J. (1995), 'Inflation and Economic Growth', *Bank of England Quarterly Bulletin*, May.
Baumol, W.J. and A.S. Blinder (1988), *Economics: Principles and Policy*, New York: Harcourt Brace Jovanovich.
Briault, C. (1995), 'The Costs of Inflation', *Bank of England Quarterly Bulletin*, February, pp. 33–45.
Clare, A.D. and S.H. Thomas (1993), 'Relative Price Variability and Inflation in an Equilibrium Price Misperceptions Model', *Economic Letters*, **42**, pp. 51–7.
Dawson, G. (1992), *Inflation and Unemployment: Causes, Consequences and Cures*, Aldershot, UK and Brookfield, US: Edward Elgar.
Easterly, W. and S. Fischer (2001), 'Inflation and the Poor', *Journal of Money, Credit and Banking*, **33**, May, pp. 160–78.
Feldstein, M. (1997), 'The Costs and Benefits of Going from Low Inflation to Price Stability', in C.D. Romer and D.H. Romer (eds), *Reducing Inflation: Motivation and Strategy*, Chicago: University of Chicago Press.
Feldstein, M. (ed.) (1999), *The Costs and Benefits of Price Stability*, Chicago: University of Chicago Press.
Fender, J. (1990), *Inflation: A Contemporary Perspective*, London and New York: Harvester Wheatsheaf.
Fischer, S. (1981), 'Relative Shocks, Relative Price Variability, and Inflation', *Brookings Papers on Economic Activity*, **2**, pp. 381–431.
Fischer, S. (1993), 'The Role of Macroeconomic Factors in Growth', *Journal of Monetary Economics*, **32**, December, pp. 485–512.
Fischer, S. and F. Modigliani (1978), 'Towards an Understanding of the Real Effects and Costs of Inflation', *Weltwirtschaftliches Archiv*, **114**, pp. 810–33.
Foster, J. (1976), 'The Redistributive Effect of Inflation on Building Society Shares and Deposits 1961–74', *Bulletin of Economic Research*, **28**, pp. 68–75.

Friedman, M. (1977), 'Nobel Lecture: Inflation and Unemployment', *Journal of Political Economy*, **85**, June, pp. 451–72.
Fry, V. and P. Pashardes (1985), 'Distributional Aspects of Inflation: Who has Suffered Most?', *Fiscal Studies*, **6**, November, pp. 21–9.
Hayek, F.A. (1975), *Full Employment at Any Price?*, IEA Occasional Paper no. 45, London: Institute of Economic Affairs.
Hayek, F.A. (1978), *A Tiger By the Tail: The Keynesian Legacy of Inflation*, 2nd edn, London: Institute of Economic Affairs.
Higham, D. and J. Tomlinson (1982), 'Why do Governments Worry about Inflation?', *National Westminster Bank Quarterly Review*, May, pp. 2–13.
Kirshner, J. (2001), 'The Political Economy of Low Inflation', *Journal of Economic Surveys*, **15**, pp. 41–70.
Minford, A.P.L. and G.W. Hilliard (1978), 'The Costs of Variable Inflation', in M. Artis and A.R. Nobay (eds), *Contemporary Economic Analysis*, London: Croom Helm.
Minford, A.P.L. and D. Peel (1981), 'Is the Government's Economic Strategy on Course?', *Lloyds Bank Review*, April, pp. 1–19.
Mueller, D.C. (1989), *Public Choice II*, Cambridge: Cambridge University Press.
Orphanides, A. and R.M. Solow (1990), 'Money, Inflation and Growth', in B.M. Friedman and F.H. Hahn (eds), *Handbook of Monetary Economics*, vol. 1, Amsterdam: North-Holland.
Shiller, R.J. (1999), 'Why Do People Dislike Inflation?', in M. Feldstein (ed.), *The Costs and Benefits of Price Stability*, Chicago: University of Chicago Press.
Temple, J. (2000), 'Inflation and Growth: Stories Short and Tall', *Journal of Economic Surveys*, **14**, September, pp. 395–426.
Tobin, J. (1972), 'Inflation and Unemployment', *American Economic Review*, **62**, March, pp. 1–18

Inflation: Costs of Reducing

The costs of reducing inflation are the output and employment forgone as a consequence of a disinflationary policy stance. Different theoretical perspectives on the Phillips curve concerning expectations and credibility yield conflicting judgments concerning the probable magnitude of these losses. In the 1960s, for orthodox Keynesians, the costs of reducing inflation were sufficiently large to justify tolerating inflation in order to avoid an increase in unemployment. The monetarist position is that the costs of reducing inflation are transitory and less significant than the benefits of the subsequent price stability (see Friedman, 1968). On a new classical view (assuming an announced and credible disinflation) there are no costs of reducing inflation at all (see Sargent, 1993). New Keynesians draw attention to menu costs and labour market contracts in reaffirming the significance of the costs of disinflation (see Ball, 1997). This theoretical diversity underlies the spread of empirical estimates of the costs of reducing inflation.

The costs of reducing inflation are measured by the *sacrifice ratio*, which is the ratio of the cumulative percentage loss of GDP incurred by the disinflation to the fall in inflation thereby achieved (see Ball, 1994). Considerable uncertainty surrounds empirical estimates of the sacrifice ratio, which vary from 1 to 10 for the United States (Cecchetti and Rich, 1999). Ball (1993) estimated average sacrifice ratios for a number of economies, ranging from 2.92 for Germany and 2.39 for the USA to 0.79 for the United Kingdom and 0.75 for France. Sacrifice ratios for actual disinflationary episodes are of course dispersed around these averages, reflecting different starting rates of inflation and differences in policy choices concerning the speed of adjustment. For that reason the average sacrifice ratios are of limited value as a guide to policy making.

In addition to the initial inflation rate and the speed of adjustment, empirical estimates of sacrifice ratios for particular disinflationary episodes vary according to policy credibility, the expectations of economic agents and the institutional structure of the economy. The standard shape of the short-run Phillips curve, flatter at lower rates of inflation, implies that the output cost of reducing the inflation rate by one percentage point is lower if the inflation rate at the outset is higher. So the cost of each successive percentage point of disinflation increases the more closely price stability is approached. Lucas (1973) reached a similar conclusion by arguing that output and employment adjustments are higher at low inflation rates, because lower inflation variability leads to changes in the general level of prices being mistaken for movements in relative prices.

The problem of the pace of adjustment is usually summarized as the dilemma between gradualism and cold turkey. A model developed by the IMF found that the sacrifice ratio is lower if the policy is phased in gradually (Chadha *et al.*, 1992). However, cold turkey may be the more appropriate approach to ending hyperinflations, because the costs of very high inflations are likely to be greater than the costs of sharp disinflations (Briault, 1995). Chadha *et al.* (1992) also found that the costs of reducing inflation are lower if the policy stance is credible and if expectations of future inflation play a large part in determining wage and price setting. The theoretical issues underlying these results are not easy to resolve.

Within the orthodox Keynesian view, the trade-off between inflation and unemployment, expressed in the short-run Phillips curve, implies that reducing inflation incurs short-run costs. The explanation of the initially observed empirical regularities invokes nominal rigidities in the labour market, such as wage contracts, that inhibit a swift response by economic agents to an unexpected fall in inflation. Political business theory suggests that, rather than persist with a costly reduction in inflation, policy makers will reverse the disinflationary policy measures in time for output and employment to be on an upward trend in the approach to an election.

Monetarists argued that the costs of reducing inflation will be temporary, not because disinflation is rapidly reversed, but because economic agents adjust their behaviour in the light of policy changes. The behavioural assumption that yields this result is adaptive expectations, which implies that after a lag economic agents adjust to a new inflation rate. Reducing inflation incurs costs only during the lag while unemployment is above the natural rate. The length of this lag and hence the duration of the costs of reducing inflation depend on the speed with which agents' expectations adapt to the new inflation rate. For monetarists, therefore, there is no trade-off between inflation and unemployment *in the long run* because unemployment returns to its natural rate and hence there are no long-run costs of reducing inflation.

The effect of introducing adaptive expectations into the analysis of the relationship between unemployment and inflation was to curtail the trade-off to the short run. The rational expectations revolution, and in particular new classical models emphasizing policy credibility and market clearing assumption, implied an optimistic scenario of 'painless disinflation'. There is no trade-off even in the short run and hence no costs of reducing infla-tion. Rational expectations theory asserts that agents can never be sur-prised by systematic macroeconomic policy. They incorporate policy rules not only into their forecasts of future inflation but also into their behav-iour. A contractionary monetary policy to eliminate inflation works without adding to unemployment, provided agents anticipate the downward pres-sure on prices and adjust their expectations and behaviour accordingly.

Policy credibility drives down expected inflation rate and is therefore a necessary condition of painless disinflation, as well as limiting the costs of reducing inflation in the absence of market clearing. Policy makers have credibility to the extent that economic agents believe their announcements of policy rules. In addition to the government's commitment to a system-atic disinflationary policy being unequivocal, disinflation will be painless, or at least 'low-cost', to the extent that there is a consensus in favour of the policy (Sargent, 1993). Conflict models of the inflationary process and par-tisan theories of macroeconomic policy making raise questions about the likelihood of such a consensus. Post Keynesian theories of the inflationary process have been interpreted as a struggle over the distribution of income between workers and capitalists (Rowthorn, 1977). Partisan theories of macroeconomic policy maintain that governments, particularly in two-party representative democracies, pursue policies which redistribute income in favour of their supporting constituencies (Hibbs, 1987).

In the new classical view painless disinflation requires more than the rational expectations hypothesis and policy credibility. The further condi-tion is the assumption that all markets, including the labour market, clear continuously and immediately in response to shocks, or unexpected changes in the conditions of supply and demand. There is therefore no delay in adjusting behaviour to the disinflationary regime. The idea of painless disinflation played some part in policy formulation in the UK and the USA in the early 1980s. In the event, the disinflation of the early 1980s was far from painless. Unemployment in OECD economies rose sharply, remained high for the rest of the decade, and was associated with an increase in long-term unemployment.

New Keynesians explain the high cost of reducing inflation in terms of the economy's institutional structure (that is, as the consequence of menu costs and wage contracts) which challenge the assumptions that prices adjust rapidly to clear markets. Menu costs 'include the time taken to inform customers, the customer annoyance caused by price changes and the effort required even to think about a price change' (Mankiw, 1990, p. 1657). While menu costs seem small at the aggregate level they may be sufficiently large for individual firms to make them reluctant, in monopolistically competitive markets, to lower their prices when the demand for their goods declines as a consequence of disinflationary policies.

The reduction in output and employment caused by disinflation may also have extremely long-lasting, if not permanent, effects if hysteresis effects are important: that is, the economy's short-run path of adjustment affects its long-run equilibrium. During a sustained recession, capacity is reduced and may even be closed down, while innovations may not be made and hence long-term competitiveness may be damaged. Persistently high unemployment brings long-term unemployment, which causes an attrition of the skills and morale of the unemployed. The permanent reduction in sustainable output from these sources adds to the costs of reducing inflation (see Ball, 1999).

The rational expectations hypothesis and the importance of credibility are widely shared among policy makers but few believe that markets clear rapidly, so reducing inflation incurs costs in the short run. Perfectly informed policy makers would weigh these costs against the costs of inflation and might conclude that 'there are advantages in achieving and maintaining price stability' (Briault, 1995, p.42). In fact Haldane and Quah (1999) interpret the 'horizontal' (relative to historical trend) UK Phillips curve since 1980 as the product of policy makers' adhering to a medium-term inflation target. While this policy stance endures, the question of the costs of reducing inflation is placed in abeyance.

GRAHAM DAWSON

See also:

Adaptive Expectations; Business Cycles: Political Business Cycle Approach; Credibility and Reputation; Expectations-augmented Phillips Curve; Gradualism versus Cold Turkey; Hysteresis; Menu Costs; Natural Rate of Unemployment; Nominal Rigidity; Phillips Curve; Rational Expectations.

Inflation rate

Bibliography

Ball, L. (1993), 'How Costly is Disinflation? The Historical Evidence', *Business Review*, Federal Reserve Bank of Philadelphia, November–December.

Ball, L. (1994), 'What Determines the Sacrifice Ratio?', in N.G. Mankiw (ed.), *Monetary Policy*, Chicago: University of Chicago Press.

Ball, L. (1997), 'Disinflation and the NAIRU', in C.D. Romer and D.H. Romer (eds), *Reducing Inflation: Motivation and Strategy*, Chicago: University of Chicago Press.

Ball, L. (1999), 'Aggregate Demand and Long-Run Unemployment', *Brookings Papers on Economic Activity*, no. 2, pp. 189–251.

Blanchard, O.J. and L.H. Summers (1988), 'Hysteresis and the European Unemployment Problem', in R. Cross (ed.), *Unemployment, Hysteresis and the Natural Rate Hypothesis*, Oxford: Basil Blackwell.

Briault, C. (1995), 'The Costs of Inflation', *Bank of England Quarterly Bulletin*, February, pp. 33–45.

Cecchetti, S.G. and R.W. Rich (1999), 'Structural Estimates of the U.S. Sacrifice Ratio', *Federal Reserve Bank of New York Staff Report*, March.

Chadha, B., P.R. Masson and G. Meredith (1992), 'Models of Inflation and the Costs of Disinflation', *IMF Staff Papers*, **39**, pp. 395–431.

Cross, R. (ed.) (1988), *Unemployment, Hysteresis and the Natural Rate Hypothesis*, Oxford: Basil Blackwell.

Friedman, M. (1968), 'The Role of Monetary Policy, *American Economic Review*, **58**, March, pp. 1–17.

Haldane, A. and D. Quah (1999), 'UK Phillips Curves and Monetary Policy' (*http://econ.lse.ac.uk/~dquah/*).

Hibbs, D.A. (1987), *The Political Economy of Industrial Democracies*, Cambridge, MA: Harvard University Press.

Lucas, R.E. Jr (1973), 'Some International Evidence on Output–Inflation Trade-Offs', *American Economic Review*, **63**, June, pp. 326–34.

Mankiw, N.G. (1990), 'A Quick Refresher Course in Macroeconomics', *Journal of Economic Literature*, **28**, December, pp. 1645–60.

Rowthorn, R. (1977), 'Conflict, Inflation and Money', *Cambridge Journal of Economics*, **1**, pp. 215–39.

Sargent, T.J. (1993), *Rational Expectations and Inflation*, 2nd edn, New York: Harper & Row.

Inflation Rate

The rate at which the general level of prices increases; expressed as a percentage on an annual basis. A wide range of price indices may be used to measure inflation. These include, for example, the UK Retail Price Index (which seeks to measure movements in the cost of a 'basket' of goods and services bought by a typical household) and the implicit GDP deflator (which seeks to measure movements in the prices of all goods and services produced by dividing GDP valued at current prices by GDP at constant prices). Once constructed, the rate of inflation is measured by calculating the percentage change in the index from one year to the next.

See also:

Nominal GDP; Real GDP.

Inflation Targeting

Inflation targeting is a recent monetary policy strategy that encompasses five main elements: (1) the public announcement of medium-term numerical targets for inflation; (2) an institutional commitment to price stability as the primary goal of monetary policy, to which other goals are subordinated; (3) an information-inclusive strategy in which many variables, and not just monetary aggregates or the exchange rate, are used for deciding the setting of policy instruments; (4) increased transparency of the monetary policy strategy through communication with the public and the markets about the plans, objectives and decisions of the monetary authorities; and (5) increased accountability of the central bank for attaining its inflation objectives. The list should clarify one crucial point about inflation targeting: it entails *much more* than a public announcement of numerical targets for inflation for the year ahead. This is especially important in emerging market countries because many of these countries routinely reported numerical inflation targets or objectives as part of the government's economic plan for the coming year and yet their monetary policy strategy should not be characterized as inflation targeting, which requires the other four elements for it to be sustainable over the medium term. Since 1990, inflation targeting has been adopted by many industrialized countries (New Zealand, Canada, the United Kingdom, Sweden, Israel, Australia and Switzerland), by several emerging market countries (Chile, Brazil, Korea, Thailand and South Africa) and by several transition countries (Czech Republic, Poland and Hungary).

Inflation targeting requires that a decision be made on what price stability means in practice. Alan Greenspan has provided a widely-cited definition of price stability as a rate of inflation that is sufficiently low for households and businesses not to have to take it into account in making everyday decisions. This definition of price stability is a reasonable one and, operationally, any inflation number between zero and 3 per cent seems to meet this criterion. Although some economists such as Feldstein (1997) argue for a long-run inflation goal of zero, others, such as Akerlof *et al.* (1996), argue that setting inflation at too low a level produces inefficiency and will result in an increase in the natural rate of unemployment. The Akerlof *et al.* argument is, however, highly controversial, and a possible stronger argument against setting the long-run inflation target at zero is that a target of zero would make deflations more likely and deflations can lead to financial instability and sharp economic contractions (see Mishkin, 2001, for further discussion). In practice, all inflation targeters have chosen long-run inflation targets above zero, with point targets or midpoints of target ranges between 1 and 3 per cent. Once inflation has reached low levels, inflation targeters have also made their inflation targets symmetrical, with undershoots of the targets considered to be as costly as overshoots. Indeed, inflation targeters have argued that symmetrical inflation targeting helps central banks to stabilize real output because, in the face of a weak economy, an inflation targeter can ease more aggressively without being worried that the easing will cause inflation expectations to rise.

Inflation targeting has several advantages as a medium-term strategy for monetary policy. In contrast to an exchange rate peg, it enables monetary policy to focus on domestic considerations and to respond to shocks to the domestic economy. In contrast to monetary targeting, another possible monetary policy strategy, inflation targeting has the advantage that a stable relationship between money and inflation is not critical to its success: the strategy does not depend on such a relationship, but instead uses all available information to determine the best settings for the instruments of monetary policy. Inflation targeting also has the key advantage that it is easily understood by the public and is thus highly transparent.

Because an explicit numerical target for inflation increases the accountability of the central bank, inflation targeting has the potential to reduce the likelihood that the central bank will fall into the time-inconsistency trap. Moreover, since the source of time inconsistency is often found in (covert or open) political pressures on the central bank to undertake overly expansionary monetary policy, inflation targeting has the advantage of focusing the political debate on what a central bank can do in the long run (control inflation) rather than what it cannot do (raise output growth, lower unemployment, increase external competitiveness) through monetary policy.

For inflation targeting to deliver these outcomes, there must exist a strong institutional commitment to make price stability the primary goal of the central bank. Inflation-targeting regimes also put great stress on the need to make monetary policy transparent and to maintain regular channels of communication with the public; in fact, these features have been central to the strategy's success in industrialized countries. As illustrated in Mishkin and Posen (1997) and in Bernanke *et al.* (1999), inflation-targeting central banks have frequent communications with the government, and their officials take every opportunity to make public speeches on their monetary policy strategy. Inflation-targeting central banks have taken public outreach a step further: they publish *Inflation Report*-type documents (originated by the Bank of England in February 1993) to present clearly their views about the past and *future* performance of inflation and monetary policy.

Another key feature of inflation-targeting regimes is that the transparency of policy associated with inflation targeting has tended to make the central bank highly accountable to the public. Sustained success in the conduct of monetary policy as measured against a pre-announced and well-defined inflation target can be instrumental in building public support for an independent central bank, even in the absence of a rigidly defined and legalistic standard of performance evaluation and punishment.

Critics of inflation targeting have noted seven major disadvantages of this monetary policy strategy. Four of these disadvantages – that inflation targeting is too rigid, that it allows too much discretion, that it has the potential to increase output instability, and that it will lower economic growth – have been discussed in Mishkin (1999) and in Bernanke *et al.* (1999), and are in reality not serious objections to a properly designed inflation targeting strategy which is best characterized as 'constrained discretion'. The fifth disadvantage, that inflation targeting can only produce weak central bank accountability because inflation is hard to control and because there are long lags from the monetary policy instruments to the inflation outcome, is an especially serious one for emerging market countries. The sixth and seventh disadvantages, that inflation targeting cannot prevent fiscal dominance, and that the exchange rate flexibility required by inflation targeting might cause financial instability, are also very relevant in the emerging market country context.

In contrast to exchange rates and monetary aggregates, the inflation rate cannot be easily controlled by the central bank; furthermore, inflation outcomes that incorporate the effects of changes in instruments settings are revealed only after a substantial lag. This requires that the central bank engage in what Svensson (1997) has described as 'inflation forecast targeting' in which the central bank seeks to make its inflation forecast equal to the inflation target over the relevant policy horizon. The difficulty of controlling inflation creates a particularly severe problem when inflation is being brought down from relatively high levels. In those circumstances, inflation forecast errors are likely to be large, inflation targets will tend to be missed, and it will be difficult for the central bank to gain credibility from an inflation targeting strategy, and for the public to ascertain the reasons for the deviations. This suggests that, as noted by Masson *et al.* (1997), Bernanke *et al.* (1999) and Mishkin and Savastano (2001), inflation targeting is likely to be a more effective strategy if it is phased in only after there has been some successful disinflation.

A sixth shortcoming of inflation targeting is that it may not be sufficient to ensure fiscal discipline or prevent fiscal dominance. Governments can still pursue irresponsible fiscal policy with an inflation targeting regime in place. In the long run, large fiscal deficits will cause an inflation targeting regime to break down: the fiscal deficits will eventually have to be monetized or the public debt eroded by a large devaluation, and high inflation will follow. Absence of outright fiscal dominance is therefore a key prerequisite for inflation targeting, and the setting up of institutions that help keep fiscal policy in check are crucial to the success of the strategy (Masson *et al.*, 1997; Mishkin and Savastano, 2001). Similarly, a sound financial system is another prerequisite for successful inflation targeting because, when financial systems blow up, there is typically a surge in inflation in emerging market countries. However, as pointed out in Mishkin and Savastano (2001), a sound financial system and the absence of fiscal dominance are also crucial to the sustainability and success of any other monetary policy strategy, including a currency board or full dollarization. Indeed, inflation targeting may help constrain fiscal policy to the extent that the government is actively involved in setting the inflation target (including through the coordination of future adjustments to government-controlled prices).

Finally, a high degree of (partial) dollarization may create a potentially serious problem for inflation targeting. In fact, in many emerging market countries the balance sheets of firms, households and banks are substantially dollarized, on both sides, and the bulk of long-term debt is denominated in dollars (Calvo, 1999). Because inflation targeting necessarily requires nominal exchange rate flexibility, exchange rate fluctuations are unavoidable. However, large and abrupt depreciations may increase the burden of dollar-denominated debt, produce a massive deterioration of balance sheets, and increase the risks of a financial crisis along the lines discussed in Mishkin (1996). This suggests that emerging market countries cannot afford to ignore the exchange rate when conducting monetary policy under inflation targeting, but the role they ascribe to it should be clearly subordinated to the inflation objective (see Mishkin and Savastano, 2001, for details on how this can be done).

Inflation targeting has been a success in the countries that have adopted it. The evidence shows that inflation-targeting countries have been able to reduce their long-run inflation below the levels that they would have attained in the absence of inflation targeting, but not below the levels that have been attained by some industrial countries that have adopted other monetary regimes (Bernanke *et al.*, 1999; Corbo and Schmidt-Hebbel, 2000). Central bank independence has also been mutually reinforced with inflation targeting, while monetary policy has been more clearly focused on inflation under inflation targeting and is likely to have been toughened by inflation targeting (Bernanke *et al.*, 1999; Cecchetti and Ehrmann, 2000; Corbo and Schmidt-Hebbel, 2000). Despite inflation targeting's successes, it is no panacea: it requires that basic institutional infrastructure with regard to fiscal policy and the soundness of financial institutions be addressed and improved in order to attain and preserve low and stable inflation.

FREDERIC S. MISHKIN

See also:

Central Bank Accountability and Transparency; Central Bank Independence; Monetary Policy: Role of; Time Inconsistency.

Bibliography

Akerlof, G., W. Dickens and G. Perry (1996), 'The Macroeconomics of Low Inflation', *Brookings Papers on Economic Activity*, **1**, pp. 1–59.

Bernanke, B.S., T. Laubach, F.S. Mishkin and A.S. Posen (1999), *Inflation Targeting: Lessons from the International Experience*, Princeton, NJ: Princeton University Press.

Calvo, G. (1999), 'Capital Markets and the Exchange Rate', mimeo, University of Maryland, October.

Cecchetti, S. and M. Ehrmann (2000), 'Does Inflation Targeting Increase Output Volatility? An International Comparison of Policymakers' Preferences and Outcomes', *Central Bank of Chile Working Papers*, **69**, April.

Corbo, V. and K. Schmidt-Hebbel (2000), 'Inflation Targeting in Latin America', paper presented at the Latin American Conference on Financial and Fiscal Policies, Stanford University, November.

Feldstein, M. (1997), 'Capital Income Taxes and the Benefits of Price Stability', *NBER Working Paper*, no. 6200, September.

Masson, P.R., M.A. Savastano and S. Sharma (1997), 'The Scope for Inflation Targeting in Developing Countries', *IMF Working Paper*, 97/130, October.

Mishkin, F.S. (1996), 'Understanding Financial Crises: A Developing Country Perspective', in M. Bruno and B. Pleskovic (eds) *Annual World Bank Conference on Development Economics*, Washington, DC: World Bank, pp. 29–62.

Mishkin, F.S. (1999), 'International Experiences with Different Monetary Regimes', *Journal of Monetary Economics*, **43**, pp. 579–606.

Mishkin, F S. (2001), 'Issues in Inflation Targeting', in *Price Stability and the Long-Run Target for Monetary Policy*, Ottawa: Bank of Canada.

Mishkin, F.S and A.S. Posen (1997), 'Inflation Targeting: Lessons from Four Countries', *Federal Reserve Bank of New York Economic Policy Review*, August, pp. 9–110.

Mishkin, F.S. and M.A. Savastano (2001), 'Monetary Policy Strategies for Latin America', *Journal of Development Economics*, October.

Svensson, L. (1997), 'Inflation Forecast Targeting: Implementing and Monitoring Inflation Targets', *European Economic Review*, **41**, June, pp. 1111–46.

Inflation Tax

The revenue raised by the government by issuing currency and bank reserves and creating inflation; also known as seigniorage.

Inside Lag

The time lag it takes for an authority to initiate a policy change. The inside lag can be subdivided into a recognition lag, a decision lag and an implementation lag. The recognition or detection lag arises because it takes time to collect, process and analyse data on key economic variables. In consequence there will be a time lag between the time when planned policy changes are needed and when the authorities realize that corrective action is required. The decision lag arises because in analysing data the authorities must decide whether the shock or disturbance affecting the economy is only temporary and relatively minor, or permanent so that corrective policy changes are required to bring the economy back to its target value. Having decided that a policy change is needed, it takes a further lapse in time to actually implement the decision to change policy. The time lag involved will depend on the administrative procedures involved in obtaining approval for a planned policy change. For example, in the United States the implementation lag associated with monetary policy is shorter than that for fiscal policy changes. While monetary policy actions can be initiated fairly rapidly by the Federal Reserve System, most fiscal policy changes require the approval of both Houses of Congress and are much slower to implement.

See also:

Federal Reserve System; Fiscal Policy: Role of; Monetary Policy: Role of.

Inside Money

Money which is based on private sector debt. The primary example of inside money is commercial bank deposits which are matched by a corresponding private sector liability through bank loans to private sector borrowers.

See also:

Outside Money.

Insider–Outsider Theory

The insider–outsider theory of real wage rigidity was originally put forward as an explanation of involuntary unemployment. An integral element of new Keynesian economics, it was developed during the 1980s in a series of joint contributions by Assar Lindbeck and Dennis Snower – see, for example, A. Lindbeck and D.J. Snower (1988), *The Insider–Outsider Theory of Employment and Unemployment*, MIT Press. Within the theory the so-called *insiders* are the incumbent employees and the *outsiders* are the unemployed workers. Insider power arises from labour turnover costs, which include hiring and firing costs (such as those associated with advertizing and severance pay) and also the costs of training new employees. In addition, the power of insiders is reinforced by the fact that, if they feel that their position is threatened by outsiders, they can refuse to cooperate with, or can even harass, new workers coming from the ranks of the outsiders. As a result, insiders can affect the productivity of new employees. Furthermore, by raising the disutility of work, such behaviour causes outsiders' reservation wage to rise, making it less attractive for the firm to employ them. In these circumstances, it is argued that insiders have sufficient bargaining power to raise real wages above the market-clearing rate without the fear of losing their jobs and being undercut by outsiders. In consequence, the insider–outsider theory is able to explain why real wages are set that result in involuntary unemployment.

See also:

Involuntary Unemployment in Keynesian Economics; New Keynesian Economics; Real Rigidity.

International Monetary Fund

In July 1944, at the Bretton Woods Conference held in New Hampshire, USA, 45 governments agreed on a framework of economic cooperation aimed at avoiding a repeat of the catastrophic events and policies that had created the Great Depression of the 1930s. In December 1945, the International Monetary Fund (IMF) officially came into existence when 29 countries signed its Articles of Agreement (Charter). The IMF finally began financial operations on 1 March 1947. Currently, there are 183 member countries out of the world's total of 193 countries. According to Article I of the IMF's Charter, the purposes of the organization are the following:

1. 'to promote international monetary co-operation through a permanent institution which provides the machinery for consultation and collaboration on international monetary problems';
2. 'to facilitate the expansion and balanced growth of world trade, and to contribute thereby to the promotion and maintenance of high employment and real income and to the development of the productive resources of all members as primary objectives of economic policy';
3. 'to promote exchange stability, to maintain orderly exchange arrangements among members, and to avoid competitive devaluations';
4. 'to assist in the establishment of a multilateral system of payments in respect of current transactions between members and in the elimination of foreign exchange restrictions which hamper the growth of world trade';

5. 'to give confidence to members by making the general resources of the Fund temporarily available to them under adequate safeguards, thus providing them with the opportunity to correct maladjustments in their balance of payments without resorting to measures destructive of national or international prosperity';
6. 'in accordance with the above, to shorten the duration and lessen the degree of disequilibrium in the international balance of payments of members'.

In its operations the IMF conducts surveillance, and provides financial and technical assistance for members. Surveillance activities involve the appraisal of members' economic policies. Financial assistance is provided in the form of credits and loans to IMF members who have balance of payments problems and who need to implement policies of reform and adjustment. Technical assistance comes in the form of economic expertise and support from the IMF to members, including advice on institution building, monetary and fiscal policy, the collection and analysis of statistical data and training officials (see *http://www.imf.org*). IMF lending is conditional on the policies adopted by the borrowing country. The IMF's financial resources come from the quota subscriptions of member countries, the size of the quota being in proportion to the size of the member countries' economy. Hence the United States provides some 17.6 per cent of current total quotas. In recent years the acceleration of globalization has created new problems for the IMF to face, in particular those associated with financial crises. A major task facing the IMF in the twenty-first century is to build a stronger global financial architecture that includes greater openness, transparency and accountability. In recent years, the IMF has come under severe criticism from Nobel Laureate Joseph Stiglitz for the way that it has handled several economic crises (see B. Snowdon, 'Redefining the Role of the State: Joseph Stiglitz on Building a Post-Washington Consensus', *World Economics*, **2**, July–September, 2001; see also P. Collier and J. Gunning, 'The IMF's Role in Structural Adjustment', *Economic Journal*, **109**, November, 1999; B. Eichengreen, *Globalising Capital: A History of the International Monetary System*, Princeton University Press, 1998; B. Eichengreen, *Toward a New International Financial Architecture: A Practical Post-Asia Agenda*, Institute for International Economics Press, 1999; S. Fischer, 'Reforming the International Financial System', *Economic Journal*, **109**, November, 1999; and A. Krueger, 'Whither the World Bank and IMF?', *Journal of Economic Literature*, **36**, December, 1998).

See also:

Bretton Woods; Globalization; Great Depression.

Intertemporal Substitution of Labour

According to the intertemporal labour substitution hypothesis, first introduced by Robert Lucas and Leonard Rapping in their article 'Real Wages, Employment and Inflation' (*Journal of Political Economy*, **77**, September/October 1969), households change their supply of labour in response to perceived *temporary* changes in the real wage, being more willing to work when real wages are temporarily high and working fewer hours when real wages are temporarily low. The essence of the approach can be outlined as follows. During any period, workers have to decide how much time to allocate between work and leisure. Workers, it is assumed, have some notion of the normal or expected average real wage. If the current real wage is above the normal real wage, workers will have an incentive to work more (take less leisure time) in the current period in anticipation of taking more leisure (working less) in the future, when the real wage is expected to be lower. Conversely, if the current real wage is below the norm, workers will have an incentive to take more leisure (work less) in the current period in anticipation of working more (taking less leisure) in the future, when the real wage is expected to be higher. In consequence, the supply of labour is postulated to respond to perceived temporary changes in the real wage. This behavioural response of substituting current leisure for future leisure, and vice versa, is referred to as intertemporal substitution.

Investment: Accelerator Theory of

Accelerator theories of fixed asset investment postulate that net investment is a function of past output growth. Simple accelerator theory focuses on output growth in the current period as the key determinant of net investment. This is because net investment is by definition the process of augmenting the means of production, that is, the capital stock. Fixed asset investors will want a larger capital stock if they expect future demand for output to increase. This implies, given a fixed capital–output ratio, v, that the desired capital stock is:

$$K^*_t = v Y^e_t,$$

where K^*_t is the desired capital stock in period t, v is the capital–output ratio and Y^e_t is expected output in period t. Therefore net investment is given by:

$$I_{nt} = \Delta K^*_t = v \Delta Y^e_{t+1},$$

where I_{nt} is net investment in period t.

Assuming that investors form their expectations of future output on the basis of output in the current period, this gives:

$$I_{nt} = v\Delta Y_t.$$

Simple accelerator theory assumes that there is complete adjustment to the desired capital stock within one period and that there are no lags in the investment decision-making process. Flexible accelerator theory adapts this model to allow for the effects of lags:

$$I_{nt} = v\sum_{j=0}^{\infty} \beta_j \Delta Y_{t-j};$$

that is, flexible accelerator models introduce a distributed lag on the output growth term. In this way, flexible accelerator theory allows that the effects of past output growth are spread over time – reflecting decision, financing, ordering, delivery and installation lags. For partial adjustment models of investment based on an adaptive expectations hypothesis, lags will also reflect expectational factors and delays in adjustment to the desired capital stock. In flexible accelerator models, by assuming geometrically declining weights on the distributed lag on output, this lag structure can be captured using a lagged capital stock term (Koyck, 1954).

Although accelerator theories of fixed asset investment tend to be associated with a Keynesian approach to macroeconomics, the basic ideas were first formulated by Clark (1917), who argued that 'the demand for enlarging the means of production . . . varies, not with the volume of demand for the finished product, but rather with the acceleration of that demand, allowance being made for the fact that the equipment cannot be adjusted as rapidly as demand changes' (p. 234). This, at least at first glance, seems inconsistent with Keynes's approach because Keynes did emphasize the role of price factors in his discussion of the marginal efficiency of capital and prospective yield, as outlined in Chapter 11 of his *General Theory of Employment, Interest and Money*. However, in Chapter 12 of the *General Theory,* Keynes showed that forming reliable expectations of the prospective yield of an investment is problematic given widespread uncertainty. Matthews (1959) goes on to explain that fixed asset investors use current demand as a proxy for expected future profits. This is what provides the link between Keynesian theory and accelerator theory: given uncertainty, quantity variables are used as a proxy for expected future profitability.

Since Clark's seminal article in 1917, numerous accelerator models have been estimated. Early accelerator models were estimated by Harrod (1939), Tinbergen (1938) and Chenery (1952). These analyses showed that output and demand variables were important determinants of fixed asset investment activity. However, the empirical literature took a whole new turn when Jorgenson (1963) first outlined his basic neoclassical theory. In their basic construction, the neoclassical and accelerator theories are similar; both are models of desired or optimal capital stock adjustment. However, the key difference between the two sets of theories comes in the role that each credits to relative factor prices. Within neoclassical theory, the capital–labour ratio will respond smoothly to changes in relative factor prices and the elasticity of factor substitution in response to relative factor prices will be equal to one. This assumes that production processes are like 'putty', that is, flexible with respect to the capital–labour ratio. In contrast, in accelerator theory, production processes are 'fixed in clay' and the capital–output ratio is constant because capital and labour are complements and therefore must be used in fixed proportions, as constrained by existing technology. The elasticity of factor substitution in response to relative factor prices is equal to zero within accelerator theory.

Consequently, a large empirical literature burgeoned, assessing the relative empirical performance of the two sets of theories. This empirical literature focused on attempts to estimate the elasticity of substitution within 'putty–clay' models. Most results seemed to suggest that the elasticity of substitution is closer to zero than to one. For this reason, accelerator theory is usually credited with having superior explanatory power. However, this superior explanatory power is not all that it seems. Some of the difficulties with the successful estimation of neoclassical theory revolved around problems with the measurement of the rental cost of capital (the factor price variable included within neoclassical theory). In addition, some of the key criticisms of Jorgenson's neoclassical theory (that in its basic form it incorporates static expectations and that lags in the empirical specifications are introduced in an *ad hoc* manner) apply equally to accelerator theory. In reality, it seems plausible that the capital stock is like putty in the long run but is more like clay in the short run.

The empirical support for accelerator theory can also be criticized as being tautological: given that capital is a key input into the production process, it is not surprising that there should be a correlation between capital accumulation (that is, net investment) and output. Estimations of accelerator theory did not necessarily focus on establishing directions of causality. However, accelerator theory does have the advantage that it is a coherent macroeconomic model, whereas Jorgenson's theory is based upon strict microeconomic foundations and ignores aggregation problems associated with transforming a microeconomic theory into a macroeconomic theory.

Given the empirical problems with accelerator theory (and Jorgenson's neoclassical theory) recent research into fixed asset investment has focused on the role of adjustment costs (in the q literature) and uncertainty (in the Post Keynesian literature and, ironically, in its ideological opposite – the options theory literature). All these theories do embed quantity factors within them because of course future expected output and demand will inevitably determine future profitability. In this sense, Clark's original analysis and the later developments of accelerator theory form a lasting contribution to our understanding of fixed asset investment.

MICHELLE BADDELEY

See also:

Adaptive Expectations; Business Cycles: Keynesian Approach; Investment: Neoclassical Theories of; Keynes's *General Theory*; Multiplier-Accelerator Model.

Bibliography

Baddeley, M. (forthcoming), *The Analysis of Investment*, London: Palgrave.
Chenery, H.B. (1952), 'Overcapacity and the Acceleration Principle', *Econometrica*, **20**, January, pp. 1–28.
Clark, J.M. (1917), 'Business Acceleration and the Law of Demand: A Technical Factor in Economic Cycles', *Journal of Political Economy*, **25**, March, pp. 217–35.
Harrod, R.F. (1939), 'An Essay in Dynamic Theory', *Economic Journal*, **49**, March, pp. 14–33.
Jorgenson, D.W. (1963), 'Capital Theory and Investment Behaviour', *American Economic Review*, **53**, May, pp. 247–59.
Jorgenson, D.W. (1971), 'Econometric Studies of Investment Behaviour: A Survey', *Journal of Economic Literature*, **9**, December, pp. 681–712.
Jorgenson, D.W. (1996), *Investment*, Cambridge, MA: MIT Press.
Junankar, P.N. (1972), *Investment: Theories and Evidence*, London: Macmillan.
Keynes, J.M. (1936), *The General Theory of Employment, Interest and Money*, London: Macmillan.
Koyck, L.M. (1954), *Distributed Lags and Investment Analysis*, Amsterdam: North-Holland Publishing Company.
Matthews, R.C.O. (1959), *The Trade Cycle*, Cambridge: Cambridge University Press.
Tinbergen, J. (1938), 'Statistical Evidence on the Acceleration Principle', *Economica*, **5**, May, pp. 164–76.

Investment: Neoclassical Theories of

Investment in real capital goods by firms has been modelled in a variety of ways in recent years. In most studies firms are assumed to choose an optimal capital stock based on given technological knowledge and facing competitive credit, input and output markets. The derivation of an investment path usually requires some subsidiary assumptions about costs of adjustment or delivery lags. It is usually assumed that capital stock depreciates at a constant exogenous rate and that it is replaced by new capital goods of the same quality (or with the same level of technology). Since many capital goods are costly and long-lasting, firms have to consider how the future demand for its product will develop, what will happen to input and output prices, and so on. In other words, the firm invests on the basis of its expectations about the future. It is clear that expectations play a central role in our understanding of the determination of investment: how do firms form expectations about the future and what makes these expectations change? An issue that is important, and often ignored, is that of aggregation of firm-level investment decisions to give aggregate investment in the economy. It is clear that the underlying assumptions of most investment theories are unrealistic and their value must be determined by their success in explaining (in an econometric sense) investment expenditures.

Most neoclassical theories of investment begin with a firm maximizing (expected) profits or present values subject to a given production function. Many of these theories provide a justification for an optimal capital stock and then arbitrarily move to an investment (flow) equation. There are several variants of the theories depending on whether there are costs of adjustment, whether there is uncertainty, and whether credit, input and output markets are perfect or not.

In Jorgenson's (1967) neoclassical theory of investment a firm was postulated to maximize the present value of the flow of its returns subject to a (concave) production function which led to an optimal capital stock. Jorgenson then simply assumed that the investment function was derived from the difference between two alternative equilibrium paths of capital stock. The formal model can be specified as maximizing the following present value of future returns:

$$PV = \int_0^\infty e^{-rt}[pY - wL - qI]dt$$

$$\text{s.t.}$$

$$Y = Y(K, L)$$

$$NI_t = I_t - \delta K_{t-1}$$

subject to a production function and a definitional relationship that net investment equals gross investment less depreciation (= constant proportion of capital stock). This gives:

$$K_t^* = K_t^*(w_t, c_t, p_t)$$

and

$$I_t^* = I_t^*(w_t, c_t, p_t, K_{t-1}),$$

where I is gross investment, NI is net investment, Y is output, p is output price, K is capital stock, L is labour, w is the wage rate, c is the user cost of capital (see below), r is the rate of interest, q is the price of investment goods, and asterisks denote planned values. Note that for simplicity I have not included the time subscripts. The user cost of capital, c, is:

$$c_t = q_t(r_t + \delta) - (dq_t/d_t).$$

In words, the user cost of capital is the opportunity cost of tying funds (q_t) in the capital good plus the amount of the capital good that depreciates, minus any capital gain due to an increase in the price of capital goods. In the Jorgenson theoretical framework plans are always realized. Given static expectations and reversible capital, we get a myopic decision: firms only look at current prices as they can costlessly adjust their capital stock. In empirical work, Jorgenson allowed for various lag distributions.

This framework was criticized by Eisner and Strotz (1963) who set up a model of maximizing present values subject to a production function and a quadratic adjustment cost function. These adjustment costs could be 'internal' or 'external'. Internal costs of adjustment are the costs that the firm faces in installing new capital goods in terms of lost output during the installation (as some inputs like labour may be diverted from production to installation). External costs of adjustment are those that, during the process of investment, lead to the supply price of capital goods increasing; see Keynes (1936). It is critical that these costs of adjustment are convex (increasing marginal costs of adjustment) otherwise there would be a so-called 'bang-bang' solution and capital would adjust instantaneously. This model gives investment as a function of relative prices and lagged output (for further details see Junankar, 1972; Nickell, 1978).

An important aspect of investment is whether it is reversible (that is, whether we can sell an old capital good at its physically depreciated value) or irreversible (that is there is no second hand market for used capital goods). Investment expenditures are sunk costs when they are firm- or industry-specific and cannot be recovered. Irreversibility can arise from the 'lemons problem' when selling a capital good (the quality of which is uncertain to potential buyers: if it is being sold it must be bad!) or owing to institutional reasons such as capital controls (where a firm cannot sell its assets and reinvest in that country). Similarly, investment in human capital is affected by hiring and firing costs of labour. In an early paper, Arrow (1968) showed that if investment was irreversible then the simple theory of investment did not hold.

Another significant development came with Tobin (1969), who showed that investment was a positive function of the ratio of the stock market value of the firm to its capital stock: Tobin's q. The firm is postulated to decide whether it is going to invest in a capital good by comparing the market value of an *additional* unit of capital to its replacement cost; in other words, it was the marginal q that was relevant. Under certain conditions (where the production function and adjustment cost function are linear and homogeneous in capital and labour) marginal and average q are identical: see Hayashi (1982).

The next major innovation in this literature came with treating investment under uncertainty like a financial market 'option' by, *inter alia*, Abel (1983), Bernanke (1983), and McDonald and Siegel (1986). This approach was elegantly formalized and 'codified' in Dixit and Pindyck (1994) that looks at investment under uncertainty. It treats investment as a financial option with irreversible investment: a firm can either invest now or wait to see how the future unravels. There is an opportunity cost of waiting, and there is an expected return from waiting. In everyday life, consumers who are planning to buy a computer for their household may decide whether to buy it now or wait to see if the price of the computer is going to fall or whether to buy a more powerful model. There is an opportunity cost (loss of its use while waiting) but a potential benefit (a lower price or a more powerful computer).

Note that in this framework it is no longer optimal for a firm to maximize its net present value without taking account of the possibility of the necessity to sell capital if the future turns out worse than previously expected or the possibility that, if the future is favourable, additional capital stock will be purchased. Abel *et al.* (1996) provide an interesting account that shows the relationship between Tobin's q and the options approach of Dixit and Pindyck.

An important implication of this theory was that it led to hysteresis in investment: present investment was dependent on the previous time-path of investment. Uncertainty, in theory, has an ambiguous effect on investment but, in general, the greater the uncertainty the lower the investment as firms set up a higher hurdle rate for investment. Most econometric results find that investment is negatively affected by uncertainty although there are some problems about the measures of uncertainty.

There have been several econometric estimates provided of investment (both at a firm level and an aggregate macro level). A very rough summary of the results (see Jorgenson, 1971; Chirinko, 1993; Carruth *et al.* 2000) is that output is an important determinant of investment while relative prices (including interest rates and tax rates) play a very limited role in explaining investment. In addition, with irreversible investment we find that uncertainty leads to a lower level of investment. Several important issues involved include the problems of specification of models (including whether we should have interrelated factor demands), measurement of key variables, dynamic lag structures and the role of expectations.

There has been much discussion about what policies a government could use to stimulate investment. In the Jorgenson type of model, tax concessions would lower the cost of capital and hence stimulate investment. However, most of the econometric work found the impact of tax changes to be statistically insignificant or relatively small. In the modern view, the options approach suggests that decreasing uncertainty via stable interest rates, prices and exchange rates would help to increase investment. In general, stable (unchanging) credible government policies are better for investment.

Some important neglected issues

The role of technological change in affecting investment is an important but neglected area. There have been some attempts at treating capital as a putty–clay good, that is, there is *ex ante* substitution between capital and labour but, once the capital good is installed, there are no substitution possibilities. This leads to several complications in deriving investment functions in an uncertain world. Thus investment in particular types of capital goods may decrease production uncertainty (for example, labour-replacing investment may decrease production uncertainty or quality uncertainty). With rapid technological change there may be advantages to the 'wait-and-see' strategy for firms. Similarly, a firm may reduce uncertainty by buying out a competing producer or by vertical integration of its intermediate input producers.

There are serious problems of aggregation: theory derives an investment function for a firm and simply 'blows' it up to get an aggregate function. However, if there are externalities (one firm's investment decision is affected by another firm's behaviour) then aggregate investment is not simply the sum of individual firms' investment: see Abel *et al.* (1996). Further, there are externalities that are usually ignored: private investment may depend upon public investment in infrastructure. Depreciation and replacement investment are typically simply treated as if they take place at a constant exponential rate, which is clearly too *simpliste*. The role of strategic elements in investment is usually neglected in this field. Finally, we have much to learn about the way to model the role of expectations in influencing investment decisions, especially in an empirical manner.

To summarize, neoclassical theories of investment are still evolving as theory and evidence lead to small changes in the way models attempt to explain an important variable in the macro economy.

P.N. JUNANKAR

Bibliography

Abel, A.B. (1983), 'Optimal Investment under Uncertainty', *American Economic Review*, **73**, March, pp. 228–33.

Abel, A.B., A.K. Dixit, J.C. Eberly and R.S. Pindyck (1996), 'Options, the Value Capital, and Investment', *Quarterly Journal of Economics*, **111**, August, pp. 753–77.

Arrow, K. (1968), 'Optimal Capital Policy with Irreversible Investment', in J.N. Wolfe (ed.), *Value, Capital and Growth: Essays in Honour of Sir John Hicks*, Edinburgh: Edinburgh University Press.

Bernanke, B.S. (1983), 'Irreversibility, Uncertainty and Cyclical Investment', *Quarterly Journal of Economics*, **98**, February, pp. 85–106.

Caballero, R.J. (1999), 'Aggregate Investment', in J.B. Taylor and M. Woodford (eds), *Handbook of Macroeconomics, Volume 1B*, Amsterdam: North-Holland, Elsevier.

Carruth, A., A. Dickerson and A. Henley (2000), 'What do we Know about Investment under Uncertainty?', *Journal of Economic Surveys*, **14**, April, pp. 119–53.

Chirinko, R.S. (1993), 'Business Fixed Investment Spending: Modeling Strategies, Empirical Results, and Policy Implications', *Journal of Economic Literature*, **31**, December, pp. 1875–911.

Dixit, A.K. (1992), 'Investment and Hysteresis', *Journal of Economic Perspectives*, **6**, Winter, pp. 107–32.

Dixit, A.K. and R.S. Pindyck (1994), *Investment under Uncertainty*, Princeton: Princeton University Press.

Eisner, R. and R. Strotz (1963), 'Determinants of Investment Behavior', *Commission on Money and Credit: Impacts of Monetary Policy*, Englewood Cliffs, NJ: Prentice Hall.

Hayashi, F. (1982), 'Tobin's Marginal *q* and Average *q*: A Neoclassical Interpretation', *Econometrica*, **50**, January, pp. 213–24.

Jorgenson, D.W. (1967), 'The Theory of Investment Behavior', in R. Ferber (ed.), *Determinants of Investment Behavior*, New York: Columbia University Press.

Jorgenson, D.W. (1971), 'Econometric Studies of Investment Behavior: A Survey', *Journal of Economic Literature*, **9**, December, pp. 1111–47.

Junankar, P.N. (1972), *Investment: Theories and Evidence*, London: Macmillan.

Keynes, J.M. (1936), *The General Theory of Employment, Interest and Money*, London: Macmillan.

McDonald. R. and D. Siegel (1986), 'The Value of Waiting to Invest', *Quarterly Journal of Economics*, **101**, November, pp. 707–28.

Nickell, S.J. (1978), *The Investment Decisions of Firms*, Welwyn: Cambridge University Press.

Pindyck, R.S. (1991), 'Irreversibility, Uncertainty, and Investment', *Journal of Economic Literature*, **29**, September, pp. 1110–48.

Tobin, J. (1969), 'A General Equilibrium Approach to Monetary Theory', *Journal of Money, Credit and Banking*, **1**, February, pp. 15–29.

Involuntary Unemployment in Keynes's *General Theory*

While Keynes did not invent the involuntary unemployment concept, he has been responsible for its becoming a 'hot' issue in economic theory (see, for example, Corry, 1996). Involuntary unemployment, he recognized, was a phenomenon whose real existence was compelling yet for which economic theory could find no room. Bridging this gap was the task he set himself.

As far as the definitional aspect is concerned, Keynes stated that involuntary unemployment is a breaching of the classical second postulate, what amounts to stating that involuntary unemployment exists whenever agents can be observed as non-participating in labour exchange in spite of the fact that they are willing to work at the going wage (Keynes, 1936, p. 15). Involuntary unemployment must then be viewed as a case of 'forced leisure'. As it characterizes the fate of some individual agent, it refers to a case of 'individual disequilibrium'. That is, the agent in point is unable to make his optimizing plan come through. Excess of supply over demand or market rationing is its corollary at the labour market level.

Keynes wanted his involuntary unemployment concept to have a narrow scope. Therefore he excluded other forms of unemployment from its domain of relevance – frictional unemployment, unemployment due to imperfect competition, unemployment due to an exogenous wage floor, and chosen leisure (ibid., p. 6). Rather ambiguously, he put all of these other forms under the voluntary unemployment label. In fact, sticking to the model contained in the *General Theory* and leaving aside Keynes's metatheoretical commentaries, only two categories should be retained: involuntary unemployment and chosen leisure, the latter term not being used by Keynes.

We now turn to Keynes's attempt to explain the cause of involuntary unemployment (for a more detailed analysis, see De Vroey, 1997). What is striking in this respect is his recurrent skipping between the themes of involuntary unemployment and demand deficiency. He devotes the first five sections of Chapter 2 of the *General Theory* to the subject of involuntary unemployment, after which in section VI, he abruptly switches to aggregate demand in his criticism of Say's Law. Eventually, the two threads are brought together in section VII, in which the equivalence of involuntary unemployment and effective demand deficiency is stated. Afterwards (that is, from Chapter 3 onwards) the involuntary unemployment theme gradually fades away, whereas the twin notions of lack of full employment and effective demand deficiency come to the fore. As a matter of fact, in the subsequent chapters, involuntary unemployment intervenes only incidentally and then just as the corollary of the claim made about effective demand.

To Keynes, effective demand designates the intersection between the aggregate supply and the aggregate demand functions. This intersection, he claims, can occur at different employment levels, full employment being only one of them. Effective demand deficiency arises whenever the level of employment needed to produce the amount of output corresponding to the matching of aggregate demand and supply in the goods market falls short of full employment. It can be overcome (and employment increased) thanks to autonomous increases in aggregate demand.

Keynes's claim is that involuntary unemployment and effective demand deficiency are two faces of the same coin. Let us call this the claim of equivalence. If it is valid, Keynes's shifting away from involuntary unemployment to focus on demand deficiency is justified, since any result about aggregate demand deficiency can also be considered as valid for involuntary unemployment.

The central character of this claim has been recognized by many Keynesian authors – Seymour Harris, James Tobin, Axel Leijonhufvud, Paul Davidson and many others. However, amazingly enough, it has usually been taken for granted rather than scrutinized. Let us put it to the test in a twofold way, first, conceptually and, second, against the subsequent unfolding of economic theory.

As far as the first aspect is concerned, the task at hand is to probe the meaning of full employment, the concept that makes the link between involuntary unemployment and aggregate demand deficiency. In Chapter 2, Keynes states that any state of affairs characterized by the absence of involuntary unemployment shall be described as full employment (Keynes, 1936, pp. 15–16). Full employment is thus defined as the converse of involuntary unemployment. In Chapter 3, he claims that full employment exists whenever employment is inelastic in response to an increase in the effective demand for its output (ibid., p. 26). Keynes claims that these two definitions are the very same. At first sight, nobody would object to this statement. Unfortunately, it turns out to be false.

With reference to the first definition, full employment is synonymous with market clearing. More precisely, it designates the quantity component of market equilibrium. In fact, it is a useless concept, since it is redundant with market clearing. Be that as it may, it is an endogenous variable. Only exceptionally, when agents are choosing zero leisure, can it be equated to maximum employment. In reference to the second definition, the matter is quite different. Full employment now refers to the maximum feasible employment level, supposedly an exogenous magnitude, to which the endogenous level of employment is then compared.

Keynes's claim to the contrary notwithstanding, these two definitions of full employment fail to coincide. States can exist which can be characterized as full employment according to the first definition, while constituting lack of full employment according to the second. Assume, for example, a standard labour market (with flexible wages). If aggregate demand for produced goods decreases in favour of an increase in demand for non-produced goods, the equilibrium level of employment will also decrease. In this case, we still have full employment in the market-clearing sense, yet certainly not full employment in the second sense.

The recent history of macroeconomics confirms this conclusion. The claim of equivalence is invalidated as soon as it proves possible to demonstrate cases of involuntary unemployment unaccompanied by a deficiency in effective demand or the inverse. This is precisely what modern Keynesian theory is witness to (see the entry, 'Involuntary Unemployment in

Keynesian Economics'). Contrary to what Keynes assumed, involuntary unemployment and demand deficiency do not fall and stand together, and do not logically involve each other. Neither should demand deficiency be considered as a sufficient condition for involuntary unemployment, or the contrary.

Next, let us consider the role of wage rigidity in Keynes's argumentation. As he admits, most of the *General Theory* discussion takes place under the assumption of nominal wage rigidity. This may suggest that the underlying cause of involuntary unemployment is nothing else than an exogenous wage floor, an explanatory line that cannot but make Keynes's argumentation trivial. Keynes tried to avoid this criticism by arguing that this assumption is made only on a provisional basis. Dropping it, he claimed, does not change the conclusion reached. His justification is provided in Chapter 19, which Patinkin considered the climax of the book (Patinkin, 1987, p. 28).

Can we accept this claim? The answer is 'No'. Note first that it is necessary to separate adjustment as pertaining to a given trading round ('point in time adjustment') and adjustment across trading rounds ('intertemporal adjustment'). When speaking of adjustment it must always be made clear which of these is of concern. Here, the rigidity factor that needs to be removed pertains to adjustment at a given trading round. To be effective, Keynes's claim must be that the market non-clearance result stills prevail after a replacement of the 'point in time rigidity' assumption with the 'point in time flexibility' assumption.

The snag of Chapter 19 then becomes visible. Keynes's reasoning, it turns out, is not concerned with this replacement. It bears on a different subject, namely 'intertemporal rigidity', 'point in time rigidity' remaining unchanged. In other words, the question addressed is: would a decrease in the existing wage floor, at t_1 as compared to t_0, increase employment – a rigid nominal wage being assumed at each trading round, yet a different one at each round? Keynes may well have a point in stating that intertemporally rigid prices might be more desirable than intertemporally flexible prices, yet this is not the same as removing the point in time rigidity assumption. So, contrary to what Keynes, Patinkin and many others have argued, the rigid wage assumption is not abandoned for what concerns the trading round analysis.

The conclusion to be drawn is that Keynes may well have set in motion a new research programme, demonstrating the existence of involuntary unemployment while departing as minimally as possible from the classical theoretical construction. Yet he was unable to implement it in any solid way. This task has been left to his successors

A last question to be addressed is the following: if we are right in asserting that Keynes failed to provide a robust theory of involuntary unemployment, what explains his failure having escaped attention for so long? The methodological issue that is at stake here is as follows. In the context of the Great Depression, all economists would have endorsed the statement that the unemployment they were observing could be qualified as involuntary. The point, however, is whether real-world existence, by itself, is sufficient to make the phenomenon concerned theoretically admissible. To all intents and purposes, Keynes answered positively. Yet this viewpoint, which is still widely held today, is wrong. The 'real world' and the fictitious world of theory should not be amalgamated. Discourses about the former are concerned with empirical assertions about the 'real existence' of a phenomenon, whereas discourses about the latter are concerned with the deductive demonstration of 'logical existence'. One may put forward solid arguments for the empirical existence of the involuntary unemployment category, while not being able to succeed in the theoretical acceptability task. Conversely, a cogent demonstration as to the unacceptability of involuntary unemployment in the theoretical parable does not permit the assertion that this category does not exist in reality. Thus real-world existence may serve as a motivation for attempting to introduce the corresponding concept in economic theory, as soon as it is recognized that it has no room within the latter. Yet the 'authority of reality', that is, the undisputed existence of a phenomenon in the real world, cannot by itself warrant its theoretical acceptability. To this end, the concept has to be introduced in what is deemed to be a 'methodologically correct' way.

MICHEL DE VROEY

See also:

Involuntary Unemployment in Keynesian Economics; Keynes's *General Theory*.

Bibliography

Corry, B. (1996), 'Unemployment in the History of Economic Thought: An Overview and Some Reflections' in B. Corry (ed.), *Unemployment and the Economists*, Cheltenham, UK and Brookfield, US: Edward Elgar.
De Vroey, M. (1997), 'Involuntary Unemployment: The Missing Piece in Keynes's *General Theory*', *The European Journal of the History of Economic Thought*, **4**, Summer, pp. 258–83.
Keynes, J.M. (1936), *The General Theory of Employment, Interest and Money*, London: Macmillan.
Patinkin, D. (1987), 'Keynes, John Maynard' in J. Eatwell, M. Milgate and P. Newman (eds), *The New Palgrave: A Dictionary of Economics*, London: Macmillan, pp. 19–41.

Involuntary Unemployment in Keynesian Economics

In the entry on involuntary unemployment in the *General Theory* it was claimed that Keynes was unable to demonstrate involuntary unemployment in any robust way. The aim of the present entry is to gauge whether the next generation of Keynesian economists has been able to improve on him (for a more detailed analysis, see Lindbeck and Snower, 1988, ch. 2; De Vroey, 1998).

We start with what have probably been the two most influential papers in shaping Keynesian economics: Hicks (1937) and Modigliani (1944). These papers are assessed in De Vroey (2000). Hicks's paper, celebrated for its introduction of the IS–LM graph, postulates the existence of a rigid money wage, which is implicitly assumed to be above the market-clearing wage magnitude. Hicks's aim is to assess the conditions under which either fiscal policy (branded as Keynesian) or monetary policy (defined as classical) can increase the employment level. His paper comprises no reference to involuntary unemployment. In fact, it aims to assess the persistence of a postulated state of involuntary unemployment rather than to explain its emergence.

Turning to Modigliani's article, it claims that the Keynesian model is characterized less by a lack of investment than by a maladjustment between the quantity of money and the money wage, the latter being too high relative to the quantity of money. Modigliani also assumes a rigid money wage, supposedly reflecting workers' resistance to a wage cut mentioned by Keynes (1936) in Chapter 2 of the *General Theory*. It finds its expression in an inverse-L-shaped supply curve. The term 'involuntary unemployment' is mentioned only *in passim*. Full employment is declared to be lacking as long as the demand for labour intersects the supply schedule on its horizontal section. Modigliani's paper cannot be considered as offering a robust theory of involuntary unemployment because of its wage rigidity assumption and its failure to separate involuntary unemployment and less than maximum employment.

Most of the textbooks that flourished in the 1950s and 1960s have taken up Hicks's or Modigliani's accounts (or a mix of them). While they often refer to involuntary unemployment, they hardly care to define it rigorously and demonstrate little awareness of the conceptual problems that its use involves. Wage rigidity remains the main explanatory factor. However, in the same period, a few authors – in particular, Patinkin, Clower and Leijonhufvud – developed more original insights, offering a reappraisal of Keynesian theory. Their views are the object of a specific entry (see 'Keynesian Economics: Reappraisals of').

Barro and Grossman (1971, 1976) synthesize Patinkin's and Clower's models. Their work sparked important developments, to the point of making it possible to speak of the 'disequilibrium school' (a label which was to prove misleading). The names of Benassy, Drèze, Grandmont and Malinvaud can be evoked as being amongst its main proponents (for later synthetic expositions, see Benassy, 1993; Picard, 1993). All these authors rightly perceived that the gist of Keynes's intuition about unemployment lay in the claim that it was due to some flaw in market interdependency. In other words, they saw him as an unwitting general equilibrium analyst. As they conceived of only one way of doing general equilibrium analysis, the Walrasian one, they set forth to reformulate his project of demonstrating involuntary unemployment in a Walrasian framework.

Taking a model of general equilibrium in which prices are formed under the aegis of the auctioneer, Barro and Grossman suppose that the process of price formation is blocked before its normal end. It is as if the auctioneer cries out a first price vector, but that afterwards nothing else occurs, with the result that prices are stuck at this initial vector. Most plausibly, they will be 'false prices'. Different configurations for the economy can be distinguished according to the type of price vector obtained. Drawing on Barro and Grossman, Malinvaud (1977) puts forward a typology separating three states of the economy, 'classical unemployment', 'Keynesian unemployment' and 'repressed inflation'. The contrast between the first two types is deemed to be especially interesting. Classical unemployment arises when the cause of unemployment lies in the fact that the actual real wage is higher than the Walrasian market-clearing real wage. The policy to be followed is to decrease the real wage, the very policy that classical economists have always been supposed to vindicate. In contrast, Keynesian unemployment can arise even when the actual real wage is equal to its Walrasian value. In this case, the policy to be pursued is to increase the demand for goods rather than decreasing wages. This last type fits well Keynes's objective: while it takes his definition of involuntary unemployment, it prompts an exogenous stimulation of the demand for goods as its remedy. Moreover, the real wage is exonerated from any responsibility in causing unemployment.

For a while, the disequilibrium approach looked like a promising research programme, yet it declined almost as quickly as it arose. Barro and Grossman were soon to change their mind and recant their earlier views. Lucas played a central role in its dismissal, by advancing two arguments against it. First, he flatly dismissed the usefulness of the involuntary unemployment concept. In his words:

> Nor is there any evident reason why one would *want* to draw this distinction [between involuntary unemployment and voluntary unemployment]. . . .Thus there is an involuntary element in all unemployment in the sense that one chooses bad luck over good; there is also a voluntary element in all unemployment, in the sense that, however miserable one's current work options, one can always choose to accept them. . . . Involuntary unemployment is not a fact or a phenomenon which it is the task of theorists to explain. (Lucas [1978] 1981, pp. 242–3)

Second, Lucas outflanked the disequilibrium theorists, who were all pledging allegiance to the Walrasian approach, by lecturing them on its limitations and indicting them for not taking these into account. The Walrasian approach, he insisted, is entirely unable to conceptualize notions such as an employment relationship, a job or unemployment, owing to the fact that it rests on the assumption of *tâtonnement*. If it has no room for unemployment, *a fortiori* there is none for involuntary unemployment (Lucas, 1987, pp. 52–3).

Of course, Lucas's criticism did not stop the debate. Yet it put Keynesian economists in a defensive position (at least those who considered themselves as neoclassical economists as well). Now they had to realize that a concept such as involuntary unemployment, whose real-world relevance seemed beyond question, was an intruder in the theoretical discourse.

Among the different attempts at retorting to Lucas's indictment, two are worth considering here: first, the implicit contract and, second, Shapiro and Stiglitz's (1984) efficiency wage model. Significantly enough, their authors agree to wage the battle on Lucas's terms. That is, they agree to take the micro foundation requirement as the *sine qua non* of any admissible theoretical proposition.

Azariadis (1975) is the best-known implicit contract model. It argues that, in a context of uncertainty, assuming that workers are risk-averse and firms risk-neutral, it is optimizing behaviour for workers to enter into a contract implying the possibility of their being left out of work in case of an unfavourable state of world. The main criticism levelled against it is that its results depend on particular hypotheses, such as the indivisibility of labour time and the exclusion of the possibility that firms can pay indemnities to workers without work. But even if these flaws were absent, the question ought to be raised of whether Azariadis's result matches Keynes's objective. It is true that it abides by Keynes's definition of involuntary unemployment – certain agents are without work, even though at the prevailing wage they wish to be employed. To have got this result with robust micro foundations is a feat. However, whether this result serves the Keynesian cause is a different question. The answer is that it does not. In Azariadis's model, the involuntary unemployment concept receives a more restricted meaning. In fact it becomes deprived of what to Keynes must have been its central characteristic, the idea that unemployment arises through no fault of the unemployed. The only substantial content associated with it is the frustration idea. That is, the involuntary unemployed *à la* Azariadis have rationally entered a lottery yet they have lost. Azariadis's involuntary unemployment is efficient: involuntary unemployment dominates full employment in terms of agents' utility!

Shapiro and Stiglitz's (1984) seminal 'shirking' model aims at bringing to the fore the consequences of the inability of employers to observe costlessly workers' on-the-job effort. Equilibrium involuntary unemployment ensues. The basic story is well known. Work is disagreeable. So, without control, workers prefer shirking to exerting effort. Monitoring them is difficult (or costly) for firms. As a result, to have them working requires both a carrot and a stick. The carrot is a wage higher than the market-clearing wage. The stick is the fear of becoming unemployed. In this context, the market-clearing wage is no equilibrium or, put differently, equilibrium requires a wage entailing the existence of unemployment.

Unfortunately, Shapiro and Stiglitz have hardly succeeded in realizing Keynes's programme. First, it is questionable whether the lack of responsibility element is present. As in implicit contract theory, involuntary unemployment means nothing more than the fact that some agents are frustrated. Second, in their model involuntary unemployment is less a problem than the solution to a problem, namely shirking and moral hazard. Hence it may be an evil, but then it is a necessary one. Third, Shapiro and Stiglitz's result hardly vindicates a Keynesian policy of demand stimulation.

The irony is that when, at last, Keynes's aim of demonstrating involuntary unemployment is achieved, it turns out that this realization hardly serves the purpose which motivated Keynes in launching this concept! The question should then be raised as to whether abandoning the involuntary unemployment concept would be so dramatic for Keynesian economists. Probably it would not.

MICHEL DE VROEY

See also:

Involuntary Unemployment in Keynes's *General Theory*; Keynesian Economics; Keynesian Economics: Reappraisals of.

Bibliography

Azariadis, C. (1975), 'Implicit Contracts and Underemployment Equilibria', *Journal of Political Economy*, **83**, December, pp. 1183–2002.
Barro, R. and H. Grossman (1971), 'A General Disequilibrium Model of Income and Employment', *American Economic Review*, **61**, March, pp. 82–93
Barro, R. and H. Grossman (1976), *Money, Employment and Inflation*, Cambridge: Cambridge University Press
Benassy, J-P. (1993), 'Nonclearing Markets: Microeconomic Concepts and Macroeconomic Applications', *Journal of Economic Literature*, **XXXI**, June, pp. 736–61.
De Vroey, M. (1998), 'Accounting for Involuntary Unemployment in Neoclassical Theory: Some Lessons from Sixty Years of Uphill Struggle', in R. Backhouse, D. Hausman, U. Mäki and A. Salanti (eds), *Economics and Methodology: Crossing Boundaries*, London: Macmillan, pp. 177–224.
De Vroey, M. (2000), 'IS–LM "à la Hicks" versus IS–LM "à la Modigliani"', *History of Political Economy*, **32**, Summer, pp. 293–316.

Hicks, J.R. ([1937] 1967), 'Mr Keynes and the "Classics"', *Critical Essays in Monetary Theory*, Oxford: Clarendon Press, pp. 126–42.

Keynes, J.M. (1936), *The General Theory of Employment, Interest and Money*, London: Macmillan.

Lindbeck, A. and D. Snower (1988), *The Inside–Outsider Theory of Employment and Unemployment*, Cambridge, MA: MIT Press.

Lucas, R.E. Jr ([1978] 1981), 'Unemployment Policy', *Studies in Business Cycle Theory*, Cambridge, MA: MIT Press, pp. 240–7.

Lucas, R.E. Jr, (1987), *Models of Business Cycles*, Oxford: Basil Blackwell.

Malinvaud, E. (1977), *The Theory of Unemployment Reconsidered*, Oxford: Basil Blackwell.

Modigliani, F. (1944), 'Liquidity Preference and the Theory of Interest and Money', *Econometrica*, **12**, January, pp. 44–88.

Picard, P. (1993), *Wages and Unemployment: A Study in Non-Walrasian Macroeconomics*, Cambridge: Cambridge University Press.

Shapiro, C. and J. Stiglitz (1984), 'Equilibrium Unemployment as a Worker Discipline Device', *American Economic Review*, **74**, June, pp. 433–44.

IS–LM Model: Closed Economy

The purpose of IS–LM analysis was to provide a simple representation of the analytic structure of Keynes's (1936) *General Theory*. After the publication of the *General Theory*, several economists attempted to provide simplified versions which would make comprehensible what most found difficult to follow. Among these was John Hicks, whose 1937 article was easily the most influential. It has had a permanent influence on the way macroeconomic theory is formulated. While being an interpretation, the IS–LM approach did not, and does not, offer a complete or detailed account of what Keynes had to say. But it was certainly helpful as a form of technical apparatus in the early stages of the development of modern macroeconomics, and nowadays, therefore, exists in its own right. There is also a general sense in which IS–LM appears in a variety of guises in pretty well all contemporary macroeconomic theorizing. (A few economists, for example David Romer, 2000, appear to take a different view of the value of the *LM* curve, but, as Romer himself admits, they are very much in the minority.) It does this in at least three ways. Firstly, no matter how sophisticated and complex its microeconomic underpinnings are claimed to be, macroeconomics still ends up largely presented as a straightforward, rather simple equation system. Secondly, within any such system the distinction is usually made between goods and money market equilibria, and the need for compatibility between the two. Thirdly, while the subject is enormously more mathematically advanced than it was in 1936, there is still a great yearning on the part of economists to present it in the form of two-dimensional diagrams.

The IS part of the subject comes from goods market equilibrium. In the most elementary version the demand for output comprises investment, I, and consumption, C. In equilibrium the sum of the two must equal the supply of output, which is also the same as income earned from that supply, Y, that is,

$$I + C = Y \tag{1}$$

Investment is postulated to be determined by the rate of interest, r:

$$I = I(r). \tag{2}$$

Consumption is determined by income:

$$C = C(Y). \tag{3}$$

It follows that

$$I(r) + C(Y) = Y. \tag{4}$$

Saving is defined as income minus consumption:

$$S = Y - C. \tag{5}$$

In equilibrium, investment equals saving:

$$I(r) = S(Y). \tag{6}$$

Hence IS.

Two further postulates are that investment varies inversely with the rate of interest and saving increases as income increases. It follows that, if income is higher, making S higher, r must be lower so that I rises by the same amount. This implies an inverse relationship between r and Y if there is to be goods market equilibrium. This is the *IS* curve, which is illustrated in Figure 1.

The LM part of the subject comes from money market equilibrium, and so-called 'liquidity preference'. Assets may be held in the form of bonds which yield interest, or money which pays no interest but yields liquidity. Money will be demanded for a variety of motives, which may be connected with, and be captured within the theory by, the level of income. The higher the level of income, the more the demand for money. Holding money means forgoing the interest on bonds; that is, interest is the opportunity cost of holding a stock of money. The higher the rate of interest, therefore, the

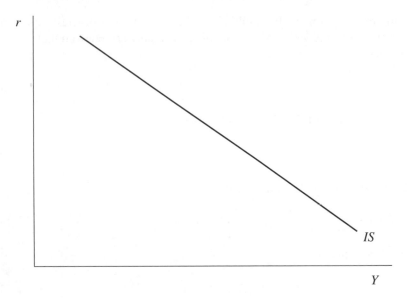

Figure 1 The IS curve

lower the demand for money. In sum, the demand for money, M_d, is deter-mined by the level of income and the rate of interest:

$$M_d = L(Y, r). \tag{7}$$

The L is there to remind us of liquidity preference. If the supply of money, M, is given, money market equilibrium implies:

$$L(Y, r) = M. \tag{8}$$

An increase in Y leads to an increase in the demand for money. This must be offset by an increase in r if total demand is to equal supply. In other words, if there is to be money market equilibrium, there must be a positive relationship between r and Y. For obvious reasons, this is called the *LM* curve. It is depicted in Figure 2.

Since full equilibrium requires both goods and money market equilib-rium, the levels of r and Y must be the same on each curve. Obviously, equi-librium will occur where the curves intersect. This is shown in Figure 3. The equilibrium level of interest is r^* and of income Y^*.

It is easy to see that the curves may shift for a variety of reasons. As one example, an increase in the propensity to invest means a higher level of I for any level of r. Thus income must be higher to generate the corresponding

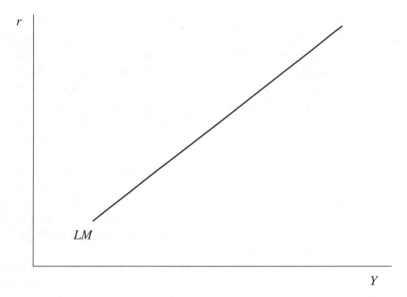

Figure 2 The LM curve

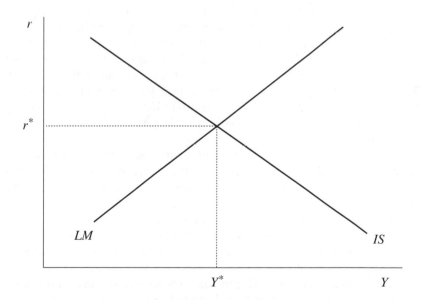

Figure 3 Equilibrium in the IS–LM model

level of savings. In other words, the *IS* curve will shift to the right. As a second example, an increase in the supply of money means, for any level of *r*, income must be higher so that the demand for money rises to equal the increased supply. This will be pictured as the *LM* curve shifting to the right.

In the first example, the rightward shift of the *IS* curve implies an intersection with the given *LM* curve leading to higher *Y* and higher *r*. In the second example, the rightward shift of the *LM* curve implies an intersection with the given *IS* curve once again leading to higher *Y*, but now lower *r*.

Many more comparative static exercises are possible. In addition, attention is often paid to how steep or flat the curves are. That depends on the interest and income sensitivity of the underlying behavioural relationships. As an example of the significance of the shape of the curves, revert to the example of the shift of the *IS* curve. It is easily seen that, the flatter the *LM* curve, the more the effect will be on *Y* and the less on *r*.

In the elementary form as set out above only private consumption and investment are included. It is easy to add public expenditure, both current and capital, to aggregate demand. In the present context, fiscal policy, involving an increase in such public expenditure, shifts the *IS* curve to the right, raising output and employment. We have already referred to an increase in the money supply, and that may be regarded as an example of monetary policy. An alternative, and possibly more realistic, example would be one in which the central bank fixes the interest rate and provides as much money as is demanded. That would be represented in the diagram by a horizontal *LM* curve at whatever level the policy rate of interest is set. The relative efficacy of the two forms of policy can then be examined in terms of how the slopes of both curves are influenced by the sensitivity of the underlying behavioural relationships to the rate of interest and the level of income.

Finally, in placing IS–LM in context, some additional comments must be made. Any reading of Keynes and *a fortiori* of recent theory would stress that each curve is dependent on expectations. A rise in uncertainty, for example, would lower the propensity to invest, shifting the *IS* curve to the left. It would also raise the demand for money, shifting the *LM* curve also to the left. This would certainly lower income, but the rate of interest could move either way. Secondly, the equilibrium examined here must be regarded as a temporary one, if only because investment is positive, and, therefore, capacity output is growing. Thirdly, the expenditure variables are at constant prices (or real terms). If there is no inflation, the interest rate is both the nominal and the real rate. But if there is inflation, the nominal and the real rates differ, the former exceeding the latter. It is normally demonstrated that investment is determined by the real rate of interest, and the demand for money by the nominal rate. In that case IS–LM analysis as usually formulated will not work. Fourthly, it should be noted that, once the public sector is introduced, the fiscal position, whether there is a budget surplus or deficit will affect the government's need to borrow or lend. The form in which this happens, whether long-term or short-term, will affect the money supply. The *IS* and *LM* curves will then no longer be independent of each other. Lastly, in the present day much of what is called money, that is, an asset which cannot lose nominal value and is immediately available for any purchase, frequently earns interest. This somewhat complicates the theory of liquidity preference and the *LM* curve.

In sum, as an introductory static model, IS–LM is extremely helpful. However, a good deal needs to be added to it merely to cope with such elementary possibilities as inflation and growth.

MAURICE PESTON

See also:

Demand for Money: Keynesian Approach; Keynes's *General Theory*; Keynesian Economics; Multiplier.

Bibliography

Hicks, J.R. (1937), 'Mr. Keynes and the "Classics": A Suggested Interpretation', *Econometrica*, **5**, April, pp. 147–59.
Keynes, J.M. (1936), *The General Theory of Employment, Interest and Money*, London; Macmillan.
Patinkin, D. (1990), 'On Different Interpretations of the *General Theory*', *Journal of Monetary Economics*, **26**, October, pp. 205–43.
Romer, D. (2000), 'Keynesian Macroeconomics without the LM curve', *Journal of Economic Perspectives*, **14**, Spring, pp. 149–69.

IS–LM Model: Open Economy

The openness of the economy arises in several ways. The sources of aggregate demand may be abroad: that is, we may export some of the goods and services produced here. In addition, home demand may be for foreign goods and services: we may import some goods and services from abroad. On the financial side, domestic savings may be used to acquire foreign assets of all sorts, and foreign savings used to acquire domestic assets. The borrowing and lending involved may be long- or short-term. In general terms, the stock of financial wealth held by domestic households and firms will include some foreign assets of varying liquidity. (In what follows we shall assume for the sake of simplicity that there is no domestic holding of foreign money. But it should be borne in mind that this is not always the case in the real world.) It follows that the analysis of closed economy money market equilibrium must be extended somewhat. Finally, it should be added that, strictly speaking, the extension to the open economy should include international labour mobility as well as capital mobility. That will be ignored in what follows, since it does not relate directly to the IS–LM approach.

Two obvious consequences follow from openness. One is that, since foreign goods and services and assets are priced in foreign currency terms, a decision whether or not to buy or sell them must depend on how their prices compare with domestic ones. The rate of exchange, defined as the purchase price of foreign currency, is the means by which foreign prices are converted into units of domestic currency. In the simplest terms, a decision to buy anything abroad involves an intermediate step of buying foreign currency (or of incurring a foreign debt). Similarly, a sale abroad involves the receipt of foreign currency.

A second consequence of openness is that deciding whether to borrow or lend abroad involves comparing the returns from a domestic asset with a comparable foreign one. That means comparing the interest earned on each asset. But asset returns also include capital gains. The price of a foreign asset will usually (but not inevitably) be expressed in foreign currency terms. When it is sold, its domestic value will depend on the rate of exchange prevailing at the time. Thus the rate of exchange is relevant to both goods and money market equilibrium.

All of this rather complicates IS–LM analysis. There are nonetheless some simple results that can be derived. (The classic contributions to this topic are Fleming, 1962; Mundell, 1962, 1963.) Assume the rate of exchange is fixed (as, for example, the result of central bank intervention in the foreign exchange market). Aggregate demand now includes exports, *EX*, in addition to investment and consumption. Aggregate supply is now made up of imports, *M*, as well as domestic output. It is still the case that in equilibrium demand must equal supply:

$$I + C + EX = Y + M. \tag{1}$$

or

$$I + C + EX - M = Y. \tag{2}$$

The *IS* curve may still be derived in the usual way, and will continue to be downward sloping. Suppose now that income rises in foreign countries. They will buy more goods and services, including those produced by us. In other words, they will import more from us; which is the same as saying that we will export more to them. For any rate of interest that means *Y* will be higher, so that the *IS* curve shifts to the right. It has the usual consequences that, in the new equilibrium, both *r* and *Y* will be higher.

This enables us to throw light on what happens if a currency is devalued, that is, if there is an increase in the purchase price of foreign exchange. Foreign goods will appear dearer to us and domestic goods cheaper to foreigners, causing both domestic and foreign demand to switch to domestic supply. Exports will rise and imports fall, and this increase in aggregate demand overall will shift the *IS* curve to the right, with the same result as before. (The usual word of caution needs to be uttered. Whether expenditure on exports net of imports rises depends on the elasticity of demand for each of them. It is possible that, if the elasticities are low, the net expenditure which is reflected in the balance of payments may fall.)

We turn now to the *LM* curve. In the closed economy, the alternative to holding a non-interest-bearing asset, money, is to hold an interest-bearing one, domestic bonds. Now there is another possibility, holding a foreign bond. Thus the demand for money will be inversely related to the domestic rate of interest, *r*, and the foreign rate of interest, *r**.

The equation for the demand for money becomes:

$$M_d = L(Y, r, r^*). \tag{3}$$

In equilibrium, the demand for money equals the supply of money:

$$L(Y, r, r^*) = M. \tag{4}$$

Assume that foreign interest rates rise. Foreign assets now look more attractive relative to domestic ones. The demand for domestic interest-bearing bonds will fall to a degree, depending on how close they and foreign bonds are as substitutes. To maintain domestic financial equilibrium will mean that the domestic rate of interest will tend to rise for any given level of income. In other words, the *LM* curve will shift to the left, with the usual consequences. Two points are worth noting. The move into foreign assets implies an outflow of capital and a (possibly temporary) worsening of the capital account. The decline in income implies a fall in imports and an improvement in the current account of the balance of payments.

With the exchange rate fixed, there is now the important special case of perfect international capital mobility to be referred to. Assume (a) that domestic asset holders are free to acquire assets or liabilities anywhere in the world, (b) that the risks of doing so do not depend on the international nature of the assets, and (c) transactions cost differences are low enough to be ignored. It must then be true that the return on identical assets are equalized throughout the world. This means in the simplest case that a country's interest rate will be set in a world market, and not at home. The *LM* curve is a horizontal line reflecting an interest rate not dependent on domestic monetary policy. It also means that, if the world interest rate rises, the domestic one must rise to the same degree, with a resulting fall in domestic output.

Consider what happens if domestic expenditure rises. There would be an immediate tendency for the interest rate to rise. That would cause an inflow of foreign capital to acquire domestic bonds. There would be a tendency for the exchange rate to appreciate. The central bank would purchase the foreign currency proceeds of the bond sale, keeping the exchange rate constant and, thereby, increasing the domestic money supply while leaving the interest rate at world levels. In terms of policy, the increase of domestic expenditure could be government expenditure. What we have shown is that, in this case, public expenditure is effective.

Suppose instead that the central bank attempts to increase the money supply. This would cause the domestic interest rate to tend to fall as holders of the additional money stock used it to acquire foreign bonds. The foreign recipients of those proceeds would sell them, causing the exchange rate to fall. To maintain the exchange rate, the home central bank would have to acquire these funds. At the same time the price of domestic bonds would rise, causing the interest rate to return to its initial world level. Thus the attempt to increase the money supply would fail, and monetary policy would have no effect.

As a contrast, consider what happens if there is perfect international capital mobility and a floating exchange rate. Suppose there is a rise in domestic expenditure, notably public expenditure. The *IS* curve will shift to the right and the interest rate will rise. That will cause a tendency towards an inflow of foreign capital and an exchange appreciation. With a floating exchange rate, the overall balance of payments will balance so that there will be no net inflow or outflow of funds and no change in the money supply. But the currency appreciation will cause aggregate demand at home to fall as exports decline and imports rise. The *IS* curve will start to fall back to where it was. The process will go on until the interest rate falls to its initial position. The result of the exchange rate appreciation will be a decline in the balance of trade exactly offsetting the rise in public expenditure.

If, instead, the money supply increases, the initial impact will be a fall in the rate of interest, an outflow of capital and an exchange rate depreciation. The improvement in the trade balance will shift the *IS* curve to the right so that income rises further. The rate of interest rises too. This goes on until income has risen sufficiently to cause all the new supply of money to be demanded. When that happens, the rate of interest will be back at the world level. In full equilibrium a rise in the money supply will cause income to rise and the exchange rate to depreciate. The trade balance will have improved, so that overall monetary policy will be exceptionally effective.

To summarize, given perfect international capital mobility, when the exchange rate is fixed, fiscal policy works and monetary policy does not. When the exchange rate floats, monetary policy works and fiscal policy does not. In this latter case, while the immediate effect of a monetary expansion is a fall in the interest rate, the policy works because of the effect it has on the exchange rate.

The analysis so far is close to what was originally set out by Fleming and Mundell. It may usefully be extended by introducing an element of exchange rate expectation into the model (see Dornbusch, 1980). If someone holds a foreign asset, he will earn interest on it. He will also make a capital gain if the domestic value of the foreign assets price rises. An important way in which that might happen is when the foreign currency appreciates in value (or the domestic currency is devalued).

Let E_t be the rate of exchange at time t and $\hat{E}_{t+1}$ the rate expected to rule at time $t+1$. The capital gain expected to result from holding a foreign asset is $(\hat{E}_{t+1} - E_t)/E_t$.

In addition there is interest r^* to be received. The domestic asset yields r. In a perfect capital market the investor will be indifferent between the two:

$$(\hat{E}_{t+1} - E_t)/E_t + r^* = r. \tag{5}$$

This is called uncovered interest parity. It should be noted that since $\hat{E}_{t+1}$, may differ from E_{t+1}, the investor is subject to some risk. If the exchange rate is expected to stay the same, domestic and overseas interest rates must be equal. If, however, the exchange rate is expected to depreciate, the capital gain term on the left-hand side will be positive, that is, $\hat{E}_{t+1}$ will be greater then E_t. This means that r must be larger than r^*. In essence, an expectation of a capital gain from holding overseas bonds will cause a capital outflow and a rise in the return from domestic bonds.

This leads to an interesting result on the effects of monetary policy. Start from a situation in which this period's exchange rate is expected to persist. In other words, $\hat{E}_{t+1}$ and E_t are equal. Suppose now the money supply is increased: the *LM* curve will move to the right, and there will be a decrease in the domestic rate of interest. This will cause interest-sensitive expenditure and income to rise, as shown by the *IS* curve. If expectations remain fixed, the only way interest parity can be met is by the current rate of exchange depreciating: that is, E_t must rise. In other words, the exchange rate depreciates, and for fixed expectations is then expected to appreciate. This depreciation results from the capital outflow caused by the fall in r.

The currency depreciation will cause a rise in net exports, and add to the interest effect on investment. There will be two forces, therefore, causing output to rise. Both of these are built into the *IS* curve, which now treats the interest effect on the exchange rate as endogenous. This, however, cannot be the end of the matter. It is obvious that, with the money supply up and the exchange rate down, expectations will change. One possibility is that the expected exchange rate jumps immediately to the depreciated value corresponding to full equilibrium. If that happens, the actual exchange rate must depreciate even further. Recall that, as long as interest parity holds, and the domestic interest rate is below the world level, the exchange rate must actually be expected to appreciate. In sum, both the actual and expected purchase prices of foreign currency rise, the former rising more than the latter. This is the phenomenon of overshooting (see Dornbusch, 1976).

Lastly, it must be recognized that, if there is to be full equilibrium, eventually the actual and expected exchange rates must converge to equality. Holders of assets must assume that this convergence happens, and that the expected capital gain from holding domestic assets or loss from holding foreign ones will diminish. There will be a tendency, therefore, for domestic bonds to become less attractive. There will be a fall in their price and a rise in the domestic interest rate. This will continue until the domestic interest rate equals the world level, and the expected and actual exchange rates are equal.

MAURICE PESTON

See also:

Fixed Exchange Rate System; Flexible Exchange Rate System; IS–LM Model: Closed Economy.

Bibliography

Dornbusch, R. (1976), 'Expectations and Exchange Rate Dynamics', *Journal of Political Economy*, **84**, December, pp. 1161–76.
Dornbusch, R. (1980), *Open Economy Macro-Economics*, New York: Basic Books.
Fleming, J.M. (1962), 'Domestic Financial Policies under Fixed and Floating Exchange Rates', *IMF Staff Papers*, November, pp. 369–79.
Mundell, R.A. (1962), 'The Appropriate Use of Monetary and Fiscal Policy for Internal and External Balance', *IMF Staff Papers*, March, pp. 70–79.
Mundell, R.A. (1963), 'Capital Mobility and Stabilisation Policy under Fixed and Flexible Exchange Rates', *Canadian Journal of Economics and Political Science*, **29**, November, pp. 475–85.

John Bates Clark Medal

Instituted in 1947 by the American Economic Association, the John Bates Clark Medal (named after the American economist John Bates Clark, 1847–1938) is awarded every two years to an American economist under the age of 40 who is adjudged to have made 'a significant contribution to economic thought and knowledge'. Recipients of the award, who have made notable contributions to macroeconomics, have included Paul A. Samuelson (1947), Milton Friedman (1951), James Tobin (1955), Lawrence R. Klein (1959), Robert M. Solow (1961), Dale W. Jorgenson (1971), Martin Feldstein (1977), Joseph E. Stiglitz (1979) and Lawrence H. Summers (1993).

See also:
American Economic Association.

Johnson, Harry G. (1923–79)

Harry Johnson (b.1923, Toronto, Canada) obtained a BA (1943) and MA (1947) from the University of Toronto, a BA (1946) and MA (1951) from the University of Cambridge, and an MA (1948) and PhD (1958) from Harvard University. His main posts included Assistant Lecturer (1949) and Lecturer (1950–56) at the University of Cambridge; Professor at the University of Manchester, 1956–9; Professor at the University of Chicago, 1959–74; Professor at the London School of Economics, 1966–74; and Professor at the Graduate Institute of International Studies, Geneva, 1976–9. He was president of the Canadian Association of Economic and Political Sciences, 1965–6, and editor of the *Journal of Political Economy*, 1960–66, 1969–77; *Economica*, 1969–70; and the *Journal of International Economics*, 1969–76. He is best known for his work on international economics, in particular the neoclassical theory of international trade and the monetary approach to the balance of payments; monetary economics; and synthesizing the contributions made in a range of fields of economic theory, including within the field of macroeconomics those involving the monetarist–Keynesian debate. Among his best known books are *International Trade and Economic Growth: Studies in Pure Theory* (George Allen & Unwin, 1958); *Money, Trade and Economic Growth: Survey Lectures in Economic Theory* (George Allen & Unwin, 1962); *Essays in Monetary Economics* (George Allen & Unwin, 1967); *Aspects of the Theory of Tariffs* (George Allen & Unwin, 1971); *Further Essays in Monetary Economics* (George Allen & Unwin, 1972); *Inflation and the Monetarist*

Controversy (North-Holland, 1972); *The Monetary Approach to the Balance of Payments* (ed. with J.A. Frenkel) (George Allen & Unwin, 1976); and *The Economics of Exchange Rates* (ed. with J.A. Frenkel) (Addison-Wesley, 1978). His most widely read articles include 'The Keynesian Revolution and the Monetarist Counter-Revolution' (*American Economic Review*, **61**, May 1971).

See also:

Balance of Payments: Monetary Approach.

Jorgenson, Dale W.

Dale Jorgenson (b.1933, Bozeman, Montana, USA) obtained his BA from Reed College in 1955 and his MA (1957) and PhD (1959) from Harvard University. His main past posts have included Assistant Professor (1958–61), Associate Professor (1961–3) and Professor (1963–9) at the University of California, Berkeley. Since 1969 he has been Professor at Harvard University where he is currently the Frederic Eaton Abbe Professor of Economics. In 1971 he was awarded the John Bates Clark Medal of the American Economic Association (AEA). Between 1967 and 1969 he was editor of the *American Economic Review*; he was president of the Econometric Society in 1987 and president of the AEA in 1999. He is best known for his contributions to: investment and capital theory, in particular a model of capital as a factor of production involving the concept of the cost of capital; econometrics; and economic growth. Among his best known books are *Productivity and US Economic Growth* (co-authored with F.M. Gollop and B.M. Fraumeni) (Harvard University Press, 1987); *International Comparisons of Economic Growth* (MIT Press, 1995); *Capital Theory and Investment Behavior* (MIT Press, 1996); and *Tax Policy and the Cost of Capital* (MIT Press, 1996). His most widely read articles include 'Capital Theory and Investment Behavior' (*American Economic Review*, **53**, May 1963); 'The Explanation of Productivity Change' (co-authored with Z. Griliches) (*Review of Economic Studies*, **34**, July 1967); 'Econometric Studies of Investment Behavior: A Survey' (*Journal of Economic Literature*, **9**, December 1971); and 'Information Technology and the US Economy' (*American Economic Review*, **91**, March 2001).

See also:

American Economic Association; Econometric Society; Investment: Neoclassical Theories of; John Bates Clark Medal.

Kahn, Richard F. (1905–89)

Richard Kahn (b.1905, London, England) obtained his BA (1927) and MA (1931) from the University of Cambridge. His main posts included Lecturer (1933–51) and Professor of Economics (1951–72) at the University of Cambridge; First Bursar of King's College, Cambridge, 1946–51; and Retired Professor of Economics at the University of Cambridge, 1972–89. He is best known for his work on the development of Keynesian economics, in particular his famous 1931 article on the employment multiplier. Among his best known books are *Selected Essays on Employment and Growth* (Cambridge University Press, 1972); and *The Making of Keynes's General Theory* (Cambridge University Press, 1984). His most widely read articles include 'The Relation of Home Investment to Unemployment' (*Economic Journal*, **41**, June 1931); 'Some Notes on Ideal Output' (*Economic Journal*, **45**, March 1935); and 'Some Aspects of the Development of Keynes's Theory' (*Journal of Economic Literature*, **16**, June 1978).

See also:

Keynesian Economics; Multiplier.

Kaldor, Nicholas (1908–86)

Nicholas Kaldor (b.1908, Budapest, Austro-Hungary) obtained his BSc from the London School of Economics in 1930. His main posts included: Assistant Lecturer (1932–41) and Reader in Economics (1942–7) at the London School of Economics; Fellow of King's College, Cambridge, 1949–86; Reader in Economics (1952–65) and Professor of Economics (1966–75) at the University of Cambridge; and Professor, Emeritus, Fellow, at King's College, Cambridge, 1975–86. Between 1964–8 and 1974–6 he was a Special Adviser to the UK (Labour) Chancellor of the Exchequer, and was created a life peer in 1974. He is best known for his contributions to taxation policy; the theory of trade cycles, income distribution, growth and development; and being a leading founder of the Post Keynesian school of economics. Among his best known books are *An Expenditure Tax* (George Allen & Unwin, 1955); *Causes of the Slow Rate of Economic Growth of the UK Economy* (Cambridge University Press, 1966); *Collected Economic Essays*, vols 1–9 (Gerald Duckworth, 1960, 1964, 1978, 1980, 1989); and *The Scourge of Monetarism* (Oxford University Press, 1982). His most widely read articles include 'A Model of the Trade Cycle' (*Economic Journal*, **50**, March 1940); 'The Relation of Economic Growth and Cyclical

Fluctuations' (*Economic Journal*, **64**, March 1954); 'Alternative Theories of Distribution' (*Review of Economic Studies*, **23**, 1956); and 'A Model of Economic Growth' (*Economic Journal*, **67**, December 1957).

See also:

Post Keynesian Economics.

Kalecki, Michal (1899–1970)

Michal Kalecki (b.1899, Lodz, Russia – now Poland) was a student at the Warsaw and Gdansk Polytechnics. His main posts included economic journalist; economist at the Institute of Research on Business Cycles and Prices in Warsaw, 1929–36; employee at the Oxford University Institute of Statistics, 1940–45; economist at the United Nations in New York, 1945–54; and economic adviser to the Polish government, 1955–70. He is best known for his influential work on business cycle theory, including developing (independently of Keynes) the theory of effective demand, and a theory of the political business cycle; the theory of economic dynamics and growth; and for having played a key role in influencing the subsequent development of the Post Keynesian school of economics. Among his best known books are *Essays in the Theory of Economic Fluctuations* (George Allen & Unwin, 1939); *Studies in Economic Dynamics* (George Allen & Unwin, 1943); *Studies in the Theory of Business Cycles, 1933–1939* (Basil Blackwell, 1966); *Dynamics of the Capitalist Economy, 1933–1970* (Cambridge University Press, 1971); and *Selected Essays on the Economic Growth of the Socialist and the Mixed Economy* (Cambridge University Press, 1972). His most widely read articles include 'Political Aspects of Full Employment' (*Political Quarterly*, October–December 1943).

See also:

Post Keynesian Economics.

Keynes Effect

The Keynes effect refers to the *indirect* stimulus to aggregate demand (most notably investment expenditure), induced by a fall in the rate of interest, which results from an increase in real money balances following a fall in the general price level (see Keynes's *General Theory*, ch. 19, p. 266). In terms of the IS–LM model, the Keynes effect is illustrated by a shift in the *LM* curve downwards to the right. The Keynes effect will fail to operate in two limiting or special cases, namely if the economy is in the liquidity trap or if investment is interest-inelastic (see Keynes's *General Theory*, ch. 18, p. 250). In *theory*, the economy could still automatically self-equilibrate at full employment equilibrium in these two limiting cases through the real balance effect. In contrast to the Keynes effect, the real balance effect, which shifts the *IS* curve to the right, refers to the *direct* stimulus to consumption expenditure that occurs when a fall in the general price level increases real money balances.

See also:

IS–LM model: Closed Economy; Keynes's *General Theory*; Keynesian Economics; Liquidity Trap; Real Balance Effect.

Keynes, John Maynard (1883–1946)

Much has been written about Keynes as intellectual, statesman, teacher, philosopher, logician, mathematician, reformer, negotiator and, of course, liberal economist and political scientist. Numerous biographies, including Roy Harrod's (1951), Robert Skidelsky's (1983, 1992, 2000) and Donald Moggridge's (1992), describe, among other aspects of his life, his childhood, education, social commitment to theatre and the arts, active role as college bursar, participation in the insurance business, interests in the stock exchange, and influential political involvement. To an already very rich literature focused particularly on his theoretical contributions, these few paragraphs will add some reflections on Keynes the macroeconomist.

Undeniably, from the time he joined the India Office in 1906 at the young age of 23, to his death in 1946, Keynes was a relentlessly active participant in the economics of Britain's domestic and international politics. He witnessed first hand the intricacies as well as the social, political and economic implications of World War I, the fall of the British pound standard, the Great Depression of 1929, World War II and the two wars' reparations. Very few academics have had the privilege of holding high civil service positions in the British government; even fewer had the ears of the restrictive circle of political decisionmakers in that very turbulent world of the first half of the twentieth century. Keynes's privileged education at Eton, then at Cambridge, his tremendous experience in government, broad interest in the improvement of society's well-being and awareness of the dangers of contemporary political trends in Europe's market economies towards an extreme *laissez-faire* economy by capitalists and totalitarianism by leftists, all contributed to making him a thinker effective, skilled and persuasive in putting forward original, ambitious macroeconomic policies which advocated measured government intervention in a market economy.

Keynes's ideas about politics, economic policies and theories are found in an impressive number of his publications. A quick look at his bibliography reveals that, apart from the *Treatise on Probability* (1921), which stems from the period of the writing of his thesis on the theory of probability when he was a student of Marshall and when mathematics was the subject in which he excelled, most of his economics writings were particularly related to the issues of money, finance and trade. It is from these topics that all the other economics problems he discussed followed. Unlike his fellow economists (from Ricardo to Pigou, whom he grouped as 'the classics') who relegated money to secondary importance, creating thus a dichotomy between the real sector and the monetary economy, Keynes made money the central variable of his own macro theory.

Not surprisingly, Keynes's economic theories derived directly from his concern with practical problems: how to finance a war; how to conserve the supply of foreign currencies during a war; how Germany could finance reparations; how to deal with the British foreign exchange and balance of payments; what to do with the pound and the international standard; what, in negotiating US loans to Britain, would be fair terms; what reforms would make the international monetary system effective. These questions were always assessed by him in terms of their broad implications for employment, inflation, prosperity and fair income distribution. To a large extent, Keynes was very Marshallian in his methodology. Having the application of economic policies ever in mind, he always had to juggle between the ideal and the feasible, to balance what he thought theoretical and universal, on the one hand, and in the interests of the United Kingdom in a competitive world, on the other. For example, in theory, he considered free trade the ideal, but in practice he acknowledged that real circumstances demanded a more complex approach.

While Cambridge was Keynes's academic work base and his home, on three occasions he occupied positions in London: at the India Office in Whitehall from 1906 to 1908, at the Treasury from 1915 to 1919, and as advisor to the chancellor from 1940 to 1945.

At the India Office, Keynes spent most of his time working on his thesis on probability theory which subsequently earned him a Fellowship at King's College. In 1913, he was asked to serve as secretary of a commission examining Indian finance and currency which led to the publication of his first book *Indian Currency and Finance* (1913) in which he examined the gold exchange standard.

Although by the outbreak of hostilities Keynes had written a couple of articles, his academic publication was interrupted until the end of World War I. In 1915, he was called to work on finance and currencies for the Treasury in a powerful position which propelled him close to the inner circle of government and led to his participation in the Versailles Peace Conference as advisor to Prime Minister Lloyd George. Unhappy about the quarrels among the current political leaders and the unfeasible war-reparations burden imposed on Germany, Keynes resigned from the Treasury and returned to Cambridge. In that same year, 1919, he published *The Economic Consequences of the Peace* in which he questioned the conclusions of the Conference and criticized its political leaders for their lack of realistic economic vision. Although the book was well received domestically and made Keynes famous internationally, it earned him the mistrust of British government officials and politicians.

As the preoccupations of World War I subsided, Keynes turned his attention back to theoretical issues and first submitted his *Treatise on Probability* for publication in 1921. With probability defined as a measure of 'degree of belief', Keynes provided an alternative to the frequentist theory, in a thesis which puzzled philosophers. The *Treatise on Probability* provided the basic foundation for Keynes's conception of risk and uncertainty underlying his economic theory of monetary instability.

The European economies of post World War I were riddled with instability, inflation and deflation, and their implications for employment argued for reforms. In *A Tract on Monetary Reform* (1923), Keynes would provide his blueprint for a stable monetary environment, a matter he would address in many publications throughout that decade. In the *Tract,* he rejected the long-run equilibrium perspective advocated by classical economists and insisted on emphasizing short-term analysis of the dynamics between public finance and changes in the value of money, and the theory of money and foreign exchange. When the purchasing power parity of the exchange rate is too high, as it was in the 1920s, Keynes suggested, in order to avoid fluctuation in the labour market, devaluation rather than deflation as a means of correction. It is no surprise that in 1925 he was against Britain's return to the prewar gold standard (Keynes, 1925). His fears of unemployment are expressed in many articles throughout the 1920s. The Great Depression would urge him on to even more work on theoretical aspects of money and employment.

Keynes's views on money culminated in the publication of the two-volume *A Treatise on Money* (1930). In addition to his analysis of money and index numbers, Keynes also had a very interesting approach to the savings–investment relationship. In his fundamental equations in which he related the price level to the cost of production as well as to the level of profitability in money terms, he proposed a hybrid theory that integrates both short- and long-term analysis through an original macro theory of value, an aspect of the *Treatise* which is yet to be explored.

Keynes's best known and most dissected work is *The General Theory of Employment, Interest and Money* (1936) in which he attempted 'to show that an economy had no natural tendency to full employment' (Skidelsky, 1992 p.XXIV). His ideas on equilibrium and underemployment, effective demand and the consumption function, savings and investment, the multiplier and aggregate demand, the marginal efficiency of investment and liquidity preference, tax incidence and public spending, finance and government deficits, the money supply and the price level have all generated both prolonged controversies among critics and vigorous schools of thought from followers (see, for example, Patinkin, 1990).

Although his health deteriorated rapidly after 1937, Keynes continued to be very innovative. His participation at the Bretton Woods conference on the reform of the international monetary system which, although the ensuing institutions were not quite in line with the type of Central World Bank that Keynes had had in mind, led to the creation of the World Bank and the IMF.

Not long ago the profession celebrated *The General Theory* 50 years after its publication, and soon it will reassess Keynes's contributions one hundred years after the work's publication, and so on. Just as A. Smith's and D. Ricardo's legacies are constantly being re-evaluated, so too will Keynes's.

OMAR HAMOUDA

See also:

Absolute Income Hypothesis; Bretton Woods; Gold Standard; Great Depression; Keynes's *General Theory*; Keynesian Economics.

Bibliography

Harrod, R. (1951), *The Life of John Maynard Keynes*, London: Macmillan.
Keynes, J.M. (1913), *Indian Currency and Finance*, London: Macmillan.
Keynes, J.M. (1919), *The Economic Consequences of the Peace*, London: Macmillan.
Keynes, J.M. (1921), *A Treatise on Probability*, London: Macmillan.
Keynes, J.M. (1923), *A Tract on Monetary Reform*, London: Macmillan.
Keynes, J.M. (1925), *The Economic Consequences of Mr. Churchill*, London: Hogarth Press.
Keynes, J.M. (1930), *A Treatise on Money*, London: Macmillan.
Keynes, J.M. (1936), *The General Theory of Employment, Interest and Money*, London: Macmillan.
Moggridge, D. (1992), *Maynard Keynes: An Economist's Biography*, London: Routledge.
Patinkin, D. (1990), 'On Different Interpretations of the General Theory', *Journal of Monetary Economics*, **26**, October, pp.205–43.
Skidelsky, R. (1983), *John Maynard Keynes: Hopes Betrayed 1883–1920*, London: Macmillan.
Skidelsky, R. (1992), *John Maynard Keynes: The Economist as Saviour 1920–1937*, London: Macmillan.
Skidelsky, R. (2000), *John Maynard Keynes: Fighting for Britain 1937–1946*, London: Macmillan.

Keynes's *General Theory*

The General Theory of Employment, Interest and Money (hereafter GT) by John Maynard Keynes was published in February 1936. Its significance to the development of economics as a discipline remains unsurpassed and is rivalled only by Smith's *The Wealth of Nations*. Keynes's GT created the field of macroeconomics, defining the basic concepts, setting out the key theoretical issues, providing the framework for the development of national income accounting and macroeconometrics, and promoting the need for government intervention to ensure full employment.

Keynes's GT consists of 24 chapters organized into six books. Book I consists of three chapters that set out Keynes's essential arguments. Chapter 1 is a one-paragraph justification of the book's title. Keynes states that 'the postulates of the classical theory are applicable to a special case only and not to the general case, the situation which it assumes being a limiting point of the possible positions of equilibrium' (1936, p.3). By classical theory, Keynes means the early classical theory of Smith and Ricardo as well as the subsequent neoclassical theory of Jevons, Menger and Edgeworth. Although the analytical frameworks differ, Keynes believes that there is a fundamental continuity in the belief that the economy is self-adjusting towards a full employment equilibrium.

Chapter 2 sets out the two fundamental postulates of classical theory. The first postulate is that the wage is equal to the marginal product of labour. The second postulate is that the utility of the wage is equal to the marginal disutility of employment. The first postulate represents the supply-side condition of profit maximization. Within neoclassical theory, it is interpreted as a demand-for-labour curve. The second postulate represents the supply-of-labour condition. Keynes rejects the second postulate. The significance of this break with classical theory is fundamental to understanding Keynes's GT. In essence, the rejection of the second postulate is the rejection of the notion of the aggregate labour market that self-adjusts towards the full-employment equilibrium via changes in the real wage. From this perspective, below-full-employment outcomes are primarily due to wage rigidities. Keynes rejects this conception of the causal process in the macro economy. He argues that classical theory only allows for frictional and voluntary unemployment, with the latter defined to include unemployment caused by the effects of collective bargaining. Keynes proposes a very different conception of the causal process. Employment and the real wage are not determined simultaneously in an allocative process. The real wage is a residual outcome, not a causal driver. Money wages are determined in the wage bargain. The price level and the level of output depend on effective demand. Given the level of output, the first postulate (that is, proft-maximizing production), represents the aggregate supply conditions that determine the level of employment. If the equilibrium level of employment is below full employment, this is the non-classical general case of involuntary unemployment.

Chapter 3 sets out the principle of effective demand, reinforcing the arguments of chapter 2 that the aggregate level of employment depends ultimately on demand-side conditions. Keynes shows that the rejection of the second postulate and the recognition of the possibility of involuntary unemployment are both equivalent to the rejection of Say's Law that supply creates its own demand. Keynes inverts the causal process; demand creates its own supply. Specifically, employment depends on the propensity to consume, the volume of investment and the aggregate supply function. The core of Keynes's GT is a detailed analysis of the determinants of consumption and investment, and their interaction through the multiplier process.

Book II consists of four chapters on definitions and ideas. Chapter 4 deals with the choice of units. It is argued that the wage unit should be used as the principal monetary unit of measurement. The aggregate supply function is also derived. Chapter 5 focuses on the notion of expectations. In particular, Keynes defines short-term expectations as those expectations associated with the daily production process and subject to continuous revision. Mistaken short-term expectations, specifically underestimation of market demand, can cause temporary falls in employment that Keynes defines as a form of frictional unemployment. Mistaken short-term expectations do not cause involuntary unemployment. Chapters 6 and 7 provide detailed definitions of income, saving and investment. Chapter 6 includes an appendix on user cost.

Book III consists of three chapter on the propensity to consume; that is, the relationship between consumption and income. Keynes recognizes that consumption decisions are very complex, affected by many factors. Chapter 8 details the objective factors, including changes in the wage unit, windfall gains, changes in the discount rate and changes in expectations of future income. Chapter 9 considers the subjective factors that Keynes summarizes as eight motives: precaution, foresight, calculation, improvement, independence, enterprise, pride and avarice. Chapter 10 defines the marginal propensity to consume and derives the multiplier relationship, first introduced by Kahn (1931). Keynes shows that the equilibrium level of demand (and hence output and employment) depends on the volume of investment and the multiplier, the latter in turn depending on the marginal propensity to consume. The multiplier process provides a non-allocative means of regulation by which the macro economy adjusts by changes in the level of income towards the equilibrium position defined by the equality of aggregate planned savings and investment. If the objective and subjective factors affecting consumption are assumed to be relatively stable, it follows that the multiplier is relatively stable. Hence aggregate employment ultimately depends on the volume of investment, the subject of Book IV.

Book IV, on the inducement to invest, consists of eight chapters. Chapter 11 and 12 deal with the marginal efficiency of capital (MEC) and the state of long-term expectation, respectively. Chapters 13–17 focus on the rate of interest and related concerns. Chapter 18 provides a short restatement of the principal arguments of Keynes's GT. Keynes defines the MEC as the expected monetary yield of an investment project. Entrepreneurs will undertake those projects for which the MEC exceeds the rate of interest. However, the concept of the MEC has been a source of confusion, often wrongly interpreted as equivalent to the neoclassical notion of marginal physical product of capital, and hence subject to all of the theoretical and measurement problems subsequently raised by the capital controversy. This line of criticism misinterprets the MEC and ignores Keynes's recognition elsewhere of the fundamental problems with the notion of aggregate capital.

The MEC is a prospective monetary yield and as such depends on future expectations. Keynes defines the state of long-term expectations as those expectations affecting the investment decision in contrast to short-term expectations that affect the production decision. The state of long-term expectations consists of both the most probable forecast and the state of confidence. The state of confidence represents the degree of uncertainty and it is in this context that Keynes refers to the concept of the weight of argument (that is, the degree of knowledge and ignorance associated with a probability) in his earlier book, *A Treatise on Probability* (1921). Keynes argues that private business recognizes the fragility of the MEC based on uncertain expectations of future outcomes, with the consequence that investment is not solely a matter of rational calculation but is also driven by animal spirits and the conventional belief in the continuity of existing conditions (in the absence of specific reasons to expect a change). This leads to the important policy implication that, by itself, a monetary policy of influencing the rate of interest is unlikely to be successful in maintaining a sufficient volume of investment to support full employment.

The key remaining issue for Keynes is the determination of the rate of interest. The principle of effective demand implies the rejection of the classical loanable funds theory of the rate of interest as the equilibrating mechanism ensuring that investment equals savings. Keynes proposes the liquidity preference theory in which the rate of interest equilibrates the demand for money with the supply of money as fixed by the central bank. For Keynes, the rate of interest is a monetary phenomenon ensuring equilibrium in the money and financial markets, not the aggregate goods market. Keynes recognizes three motives for the demand for money: transactions, precautionary and speculative. The speculative motive relates to the demand for money as a store of wealth (as distinct from the transactions demand for money as a medium of exchange). He argues that the choice between money and other financial assets is a trade-off between liquidity and monetary return that is regulated by the rate of interest in an allocative market process.

Books V and VI consider some of the further implications of Keynes's basic theory. Book V deals with changes in money wages (chapter 19, with an appendix on Pigou's theory of unemployment), the employment function (chapter 20) and the theory of prices (chapter 21). Particularly noteworthy is Keynes's exploration of the possible impact of a fall in money wages, the orthodox remedy for mass unemployment. Keynes shows that there would be a complex set of often conflicting impacts on effective demand and concludes that, on balance, it is likely that a fall in money wages is more likely to have a net negative effect on output and employment levels.

Book VI provides a set of notes on the trade cycle (chapter 22), mercantilism and underconsumption theories (chapter 23) and the social philosophy implications (chapter 24). Keynes reiterates that the problem with classical theory is not one of logical error but rather that its tacit assumptions are rarely satisfied. Classical theory is a special case providing a theory of the allocation of scarce (that is, fully utilized) resources via the price mechanism. Keynes's basic proposition is that classical theory cannot explain the aggregate underutilization of resources (that is, involuntary unemployment) due to the lack of effective demand. Hence the need for government intervention on the demand side to ensure a sufficient volume of investment and effective demand. This leads Keynes to the conclusion that, 'if our central controls succeed in establishing an aggregate volume of output corresponding to full employment as nearly as is practicable, the classical theory comes back into its own again from this point onwards' (1936, p. 378). Keynes's GT is the rejection of classical theory as a general theory. Keynes establishes the limitations of classical theory as a special theory of allocation and shows the necessity of encompassing classical theory within a more general theory that also provides a theory of resource utilization. This ultimately is the revolutionary message of Keynes's GT.

BILL GERRARD

See also:

Classical Economics; Demand for Money: Keynesian Approach; Involuntary Unemployment in Keynes's *General Theory*; Kahn, Richard F.; Keynes, John Maynard; Multiplier; Say's Law.

Bibliography

Kahn, R.F. (1931), 'The Relation of Home Investment to Unemployment', *Economic Journal*, **41**, June, pp. 173–98.

Keynes, J. M. (1921), *A Treatise on Probability*, London: Macmillan.

Keynes, J. M. (1936), *The General Theory of Employment, Interest and Money*, London: Macmillan.

Keynesian Cross

The Keynesian cross, otherwise known as the '45°-line model', provides the simplest representation of the Keynesian theory of income determination. As shown in Figure 1, the expenditure function ($E = I + A + bY$, where E is expenditure, I is investment, A is autonomous consumption and b is the marginal propensity to consume) intersects the $E = Y$ line at Y_0, the equilibrium level of income or output. This is equivalent to a diagram showing the intersection of investment and saving ($S = -A + (1-b)Y$) curves, also shown in Figure 1. It shows how the level of output adjusts to bring expenditure and output into equilibrium. To the left of Y_0, expenditure exceeds output, which means that firms' inventories are being reduced, causing

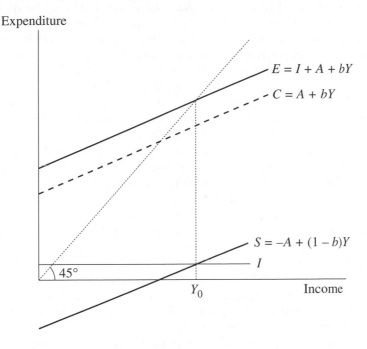

Figure 1

them to increase production. Conversely, to the right of Y_0, unplanned inventory accumulation is causing firms to reduce production. It is called the Keynesian cross to indicate a parallel with the Marshallian cross: the supply-and-demand diagram used in microeconomics to describe an individual market.

This version of the Keynesian cross appears to originate with Paul Samuelson. He used it, between 1937 and 1940, in Harvard's Fiscal Policy Seminars to show people like Alvin Hansen what their insights really were. It served to resolve the puzzle caused by economists such as Robinson (1937) saying both that savings were identically equal to investment and that income adjusted to make them equal. It appeared in print in Samuelson (1939, p. 790) and formed the basis for the macroeconomics section of the textbook that Samuelson wrote after 1940 at MIT, which became *Economics* (1948), the cover of which was decorated with the $S = I$ version of the diagram. During this period it also appeared in Mabel Timlin's *Keynesian Economics* (1942, p. 102) and was used in teaching Keynesian economics outside Harvard and MIT, for example by Oskar Lange in Chicago. By the time it appeared in Samuelson's textbook it had also appeared in Lawrence Klein's *The Keynesian Revolution* (1947, p. 115) and the second edition of Kenneth Boulding's *Economic Analysis* (1948, p. 405).

The Keynesian cross diagram is not in Keynes's *General Theory*. He referred instead to aggregate supply and demand functions (1936, ch. 3). The aggregate supply function, or the aggregate supply price (Z) of the output from employing N men, was 'the expectation of proceeds which will make it worth the while of the entrepreneurs to give that employment' (1936, p. 24). He denoted this $Z = \phi(N)$. The aggregate demand function, or the proceeds (D) that entrepreneurs expect to receive from employing N men, was $D = f(N)$. Though he did not draw a graph to show these two functions, he argued that D would rise by less than income, and that the gap between $\phi(N)$ and $f(N)$ would increase as employment and output rose. It can therefore be argued that the revolutionary element in Keynes's analysis is the part described by the Keynesian cross.

The difference between the Keynesian and Samuelsonian models is that the latter ignores the aggregate supply function. In the *General Theory*, the aggregate supply function was entirely conventional and most economists were content to focus on the demand side. However, a decade or so later, some Keynesians, notably Sidney Weintraub (1961), argued that the Keynesian cross oversimplified Keynes's theory and that supply factors were important in determining the level of income. This view was consistent with Keynes's (1936, p. 29) statement that the volume of employment depended on the propensity to consume, the volume of investment and the aggregate supply function.

By this time, however, the Keynesian cross had become established, along with the Hicks–Hansen IS–LM model, as the standard textbook version of Keynes's theory. It was extremely easy to teach, encapsulating Keynesian economics in a simple diagram that could be used for comparative–static exercises. The ease with which the Keynesian cross could be used to provide clear policy conclusions no doubt contributed to the rapid spread of the Keynesian revolution (Colander and Landreth, 1996). It was displaced from this position only in the late 1970s when the need to analyse inflation led textbook writers (for example, Dornbusch and Fischer, 1978) to bring in the modern aggregate supply and demand analysis. The IS–LM model and the Keynesian cross were retained simply to derive the aggregate-demand side of this model.

ROGER E. BACKHOUSE

See also:

IS–LM Model: Closed Economy; Keynes's *General Theory*; Keynesian Economics; Samuelson, Paul A.

Bibliography

Ambrosi, G.M. (1981), 'Keynes and the 45 Degree Cross', *Journal of Post Keynesian Economics*, **3**, Summer, pp. 503–9.
Boulding, K. (1948), *Economic Analysis*, 2nd edn, London: Hamish Hamilton.
Colander, D.C. (1988), 'The Evolution of Keynesian Economics: From Keynesian to New Classical to New Keynesian', in O.F. Hamouda and J.N. Smithin (eds), *Keynes and Public Policy after Fifty Years*, vol, 1: *Economics and Policy*, Aldershot, UK and Brookfield, US: Edward Elgar.
Colander, D.C. and H. Landreth (1996), *The Coming of Keynesianism to America*, Cheltenham, UK and Brookfield, US: Edward Elgar.
Dornbusch, R. and S. Fischer (1978), *Macroeconomics*, New York: McGraw Hill.
Keynes, J.M. (1936), *The General Theory of Employment, Interest and Money*, London: Macmillan.
Klein, L.R. (1947), *The Keynesian Revolution*, New York: Macmillan.
Pearce, K. and K.D. Hoover (1995), 'Paul Samuelson and the Textbook Keynesian Model', *History of Political Economy*, **27**, annual supplement, pp. 183–216.
Robinson, J. (1937), *Essays in the Theory of Employment*, London: Macmillan.
Samuelson, P.A. (1939), 'A Synthesis of the Principle of Acceleration and the Multiplier', *Journal of Political Economy*, **47**, December, pp. 786–97.
Samuelson, P.A. (1948), *Economics*, New York: McGraw Hill.
Timlin, M.F. (1942), *Keynesian Economics*, Toronto: University of Toronto Press.
Weintraub, S. (1961), *Classical Keynesianism, Monetary Theory and the Price Level*, Philadelphia: Chilton.

Keynesian Economics

Following the publication of the *General Theory* in 1936, and within a remarkably short period of time, there was an amazing transformation in the way the world perceived economic issues. Modem macroeconomics was born and the prevailing dichotomy between the theory of value and the theory of money was jettisoned in favour of the micro/macro distinction. There was also a remarkable change in attitudes. The inherent pessimism of the dismal science was swept away in the confident belief that the business cycle was now a thing of the past and that governments could actively intervene so as to control the economic destinies of their peoples. In short, the rationale for interventionist demand management policies had now been established and given a theoretical credence. Implicitly, this carried with it the rejection of the philosophy of the annually balanced budget and in so doing transformed the status of fiscal policy. The demise of the traditional quantity theory of money was soon to follow.

Now whilst there can be no doubting that this remarkable transformation occurred, and whilst equally it is beyond question that this transformation was due to John Maynard Keynes, there is precious little agreement upon what constitutes the basis of such an overwhelming reassessment of economics. It is remarkable that, more than 65 years after the appearance of the *General Theory*, its central message is still being widely debated and disputed despite the fact that its endorsement had seemingly been virtually complete within a decade of its appearance. (This apparent paradox is taken up by Patinkin, 1990, and likewise Gerrard, 1991, offers an explanation for the competing interpretations.)

The explanation for this situation lies in the timing. Keynesian economics emerged in the wake of the decline of the classical paradigm which maintained that the economy would, given the assumption of competition, reveal an inherent tendency to adjust to full employment income. In this view there was no need for government intervention, other than to ensure that a climate of competition prevailed throughout the economy. Now there are really two aspects of the *General Theory*: first, the theoretical argument that the classical theory was flawed and could not account for the persistence of unemployment upon such an extensive scale as characterized the 1930s; and secondly, the policy implications which stemmed from this analysis. In the conditions prevailing in the 1930s the first proposition seemed almost self-evident. There was no need to subject the argument to exhaustive examination. Provided one could be persuaded of the value of the Keynesian model, it did not really matter upon what grounds Keynes had denied the classical contention as long as it was believed that he had shown the classical thesis to be false. What caught the imagination was the implicit policy conclusions. And indeed, in the years immediately following, the essential debate between Keynes and the classics turned more upon the policy implications – the relative efficacy of fiscal and monetary intervention, for example – rather than upon the theoretical niceties.

Classical economics had relied upon impediments to competition to account for sustained unemployment. In the depressed conditions of the Great Depression it became increasingly difficult to posit explanations depending upon the monopoly power of trade unions or similar hindrances to market clearing. Keynesian economics postulated a new explanation, namely demand deficiency. The market economy was revealed to be inherently flawed in the sense that it could not be relied upon to generate sufficient demand to maintain a full employment economy. At its most elementary level, the Keynesian $Y = C + I$ framework, which underpins the economics of the *General Theory*, argued that consumption was a stable and predictable function of income. It follows that, for any given target income level, Y^*, implying a known volume of consumption spending C^*, we would need a determinate volume of investment spending I^*. But investment demand was largely autonomously determined. This is the nature of the Keynesian dilemma. There was no guarantee that the required amount of investment demand would be forthcoming. Moreover, there were compelling reasons advanced in the Keynesian analysis to explain why investment spending was likely to reveal a shortfall. Speculative influences would maintain interest rates at too high a level, whilst unduly pessimistic and unstable long-term business expectations would deter investment. Moreover, the difficulties are compounded for the more advanced economy in that the Keynesian consumption function implies that the savings ratio would rise with increasing income (necessitating increasing investment in both absolute and percentage terms), whilst the incentive to invest (the marginal efficiency of capital) would decline with an increasing capital stock.

Keynesian economics focused the debate firmly upon the side of aggregate demand. The classical consensus that both the cause and the cure for unemployment lay in the labour market was replaced by the assertion that the relevant market was really the market for goods. Equilibrium – not necessarily full employment equilibrium – would be determined by the level of aggregate demand in the goods market. Indeed, Keynesian economics readily became identified with the 45° cross diagram introduced in Samuelson's famous textbook (Samuelson, 1948). What that diagram portrayed was that equilibrium would be brought about by adjustments in output and employment. Seemingly incompatible saving and investment decisions are brought into equality by changes in the level of output and not by changes in prices (interest rate). In particular, if output exceeds demand, both output and demand will fall. Equilibrium is regained because the fall in output is greater than the fall in aggregate demand owing to the fact that the marginal propensity to consume is less than one. If the marginal propensity to consume were unity, no equilibrating mechanism would exist: both income and demand would decline by equivalent amounts. 'The fundamental psychological law . . . that men are disposed, as a rule and on the average, to increase their consumption as their income increases, but not by as much as the increase in their income' (Keynes, 1936 p. 96) is crucial to the adjustment process. We have a demand-determined model of the economy to which supply passively reacts and the theory of 'effective demand' remains the distinctive analytical feature of the *General Theory*.

As indicated, the emergence of Keynesian economics was timely, coinciding, as it did, with the inability of the classical framework to account adequately for the empirical evidence of the Great Depression. In itself, however, this would have been insufficient to explain the success of Keynesian economics not only in academia but also in business and government circles. It was the fact of a new explanation for recession *combined with* an apparently devastating critique of classical economics and, more importantly, with a proposed solution in terms of greater government intervention in the economy which ensured the Keynesian ascendancy. The Keynesian Revolution ushered in the philosophy of demand management, the belief that governments could and should intervene so as to ensure an adequate level of aggregate demand.

With regard to the critique of classical economics, there were three essential elements of the Keynesian thesis: namely the denial of Say's Law, a repudiation of the Treasury View and a dismissal of the assertion that money wage cuts were the solution to unemployment. The attempted denial of Say's Law was arguably misplaced. Say's Law had attempted to demonstrate that there was no limit to long-term economic growth or, in Ricardo's interpretation, no limit to the extent of possible capital accumulation in an economy. It was not intended to deny the phenomenon of short-term gluts and associated unemployment. By interpreting Say's Law as a denial of demand deficiency Keynes was arguably erecting a straw man which he immediately proceeded to demolish. The dismissal of the Treasury View was on firmer footing. The Treasury View had contended that public sector spending to stimulate employment would be effectively crowded out by withdrawing resources from the private sector. The Keynesian multiplier concept was instrumental in denying this thesis by showing that such public expenditure programmes would be partially self-financing by raising incomes (and thus savings and taxes) in excess of the initial expenditures. With regard to wage cuts, the Keynesian thesis was effectively denied by the logic of the Pigou effect. The latter showed that, given unlimited wage and price flexibility, there would be an automatic tendency for the economy to adjust towards full employment income regardless of any liquidity trap considerations. It was never convincingly demonstrated that Keynes had successfully denied the classical thesis on strictly theoretical grounds.

But this fact did not hinder the adoption of Keynesian economics. It was the spectre of a solution to the problem of persistent unemployment which ensured the success of the Keynesian analysis. It was not so much a victory in terms of theoretical supremacy; rather it was the sanctioning of interventionist demand management policies and the belief that one could effectively fine-tune the economy to the benefit of all classes in society, and in so doing ensure the future of capitalism, that guaranteed the Keynesian ascendancy.

This is revealed in the fact that what became widely accepted as encompassing the essence of Keynesian economics, especially in the postwar period, is the analysis presented by Hicks in his famous paper 'Mr. Keynes and the "Classics": A Suggested Interpretation' (Hicks, 1937). In this seminal contribution, Hicks suggested a reconciliation between classical and Keynesian models. Essentially, Hicks sought to graft onto the classical analysis the Keynesian monetary determination of interest and in so doing to present a simultaneous determination of interest and income, where the latter need not correspond to full employment income. A full employment outcome would be but a special case where aggregate demand was just sufficient to sustain full employment income.

Initially, the Hicksian statement was seen to be very much in keeping with the emphasis in Keynes. The implication of a stable equilibrium below full employment was quickly seized upon by Keynesian disciples as confirming Keynes's central message. In addition, the apparatus bristled with policy implications. Either monetary policy (shifting the *LM* schedule) or fiscal policy (shifting the *IS* curve) would be appropriate in moving the economy closer to the full employment objective. Finally, the theory of interest determination demolished the classical dichotomy; a change in the money stock could, by influencing the rate of interest, feed back upon investment spending and thereby influence employment and output levels in the real sector of the economy.

However, it soon became apparent that the IS–LM framework did not rule out all tendencies towards automatic adjustment. If a situation of unemployment led to a fall in nominal wages, which in turn generated a decrease in prices, then there would be repercussions in both money and commodity markets. Given unlimited wage and price flexibility the IS–LM model implies that the economy will ultimately adjust to full employment income. This was made clear in the work of Modigliani (1944) and Patinkin (1948) and leads to the view that the Keynesian unemployment equilibrium is but a special case – namely the case of wage and price inflexibility. And yet the IS–LM analysis was widely accepted as being representative of Keynesian economics. Keynesians were busily applauding a theoretical construct which, in the last resort, had vindicated classical employment theory!

What evolved then into the Keynesian economic orthodoxy involved a compromise. Upon the one hand, there was the conviction that the classical tendency to self-adjustment required too long a time horizon to substitute for direct interventionist measures. This was combined with the belief that the economy was substantially demand-determined and that the government could, by judicious demand management, substantially hasten the process of adjustment. In this context there was a marked preference for fiscal as opposed to monetary intervention on the grounds that the former provided more direct control when compared with the rather uncertain response to interest rate changes. This was combined with a general tendency to discount the financial implications stemming from budget deficits reflecting the belief that in periods of depression supply conditions were sufficiently elastic to enable changes in aggregate demand to be translated primarily into output and employment changes as opposed to changes in prices.

The foregoing is but one interpretation of Keynesian economics. It is arguably the view reflecting the conventional wisdom of mainstream economics, but it would not command universal respect. And it will be appreciated that it is a view which ignores Keynes's other major contributions, notably the *Tract on Monetary Reform* (1923) and the *Treatise on Money* (1930) which together with the *General Theory* (1936) constitute a remarkable trilogy (Patinkin, 1987).

G.K. SHAW

See also:

Absolute Income Hypothesis; Aggregate Demand Management; Classical Model; Great Depression; IS–LM Model: Closed Economy; Involuntary Unemployment in Keynes's *General Theory*; Involuntary Unemployment in Keynesian Economics; Keynes, John Maynard; Keynes's *General Theory*; Keynesian Cross; Keynesian Economics: Reappraisals of; Liquidity Trap; Multiplier; Say's Law; Pigou Effect.

Bibliography

Gerrard, B. (1991), 'Keynes's *General Theory*: Interpreting the Interpretations,' *Economic Journal*, **101**, March, pp. 276–87.
Hicks, J.R. (1937), 'Mr. Keynes and the "Classics": A Suggested Interpretation', *Econometrica*, **5**, April, pp. 147–59.
Keynes, J.M. (1936), *The General Theory of Employment, Interest and Money*, London: Macmillan.
Modigliani, F. (1944), 'Liquidity Preference and the Theory of Interest and Money', *Econometrica*, **12**, January, pp. 45–88.
Patinkin, D. (1948), 'Price Flexibility and Full Employment', *American Economic Review*, **38**, September, pp. 543–64.
Patinkin, D. (1987), 'Keynes, John Maynard (1883–1946)' in J. Eatwell, M. Milgate and P. Newman (eds), *The New Palgrave: A Dictionary of Economics*, London: Macmillan Press, pp. 19–42.
Patinkin, D. (1990), 'On Different Interpretations of the *General Theory*', *Journal of Monetary Economics*, **26**, October, pp. 205–43.
Samuelson, P.A. (1948), *Economics*, New York: McGraw-Hill.

Keynesian Economics: Reappraisals of

This entry is devoted to the reappraisals of Keynes's (1936) *General Theory* offered by Patinkin, on the one hand, and Clower and Leijonhufvud, on the other (another non-orthodox interpretation of Keynes is Post Keynesian theory; see the eponymous entry).

Patinkin

The overriding aim of Patinkin's (1965) celebrated book, *Money, Interest and Prices*, is to study the integration of monetary and value theory in a general equilibrium framework. However, in Chapters 13 and 14, Patinkin also broaches the issue of the interpretation of Keynes's *General Theory*. In particular, he demonstrates the possibility of involuntary unemployment.

Realizing that the corpus within which such an integration has to take place is general equilibrium theory, Patinkin easily admits that involuntary unemployment is an inconceivable outcome as long as the analysis is confined to the domain of the existence of equilibrium. Still, according to him, one way for grounding it remains open: that is, to consider it as a disequilibrium phenomenon arising in-between positions of equilibria. In this perspective, the disequilibrium notion should be understood as referring to the adjustment process through which the general equilibrium result is obtained, rather than to some end-state of the economy. The occurrence of involuntary unemployment then hinges on the assumption that the price mechanism operates slowly. Of course, this view has the drawback that the existence of involuntary unemployment is transitory, since market forces will progressively eliminate it.

Patinkin gives no model of involuntary unemployment, in the strict sense of the term. Rather he tells his readers a reasoned story, a sort of theoretical scenario, about how it arises. Starting from a state of equilibrium, some increase in the demand for bonds is supposed to have occurred, resulting in a decrease in the demand for commodities. Its effects are studied in two alternative contexts. In the first, the adjustment process in the goods market is supposed to operate quickly. As a result, a new equilibrium is rapidly established. In the second context where, according to Patinkin, involuntary unemployment is bound to arise, this adjustment process is assumed to occur at a slow pace. The proximate effect of the decrease in demand for goods is that its supply exceeds its demand. Firms' first reaction is to pile up inventories. However, after a while, when inventories become too great, they have no choice but to decrease production. As a result, their demand for labour also diminishes; that is, the 'notional' demand for labour, to use later terminology, ceases to be operative. Trading in the labour market takes place off the supply curve, which is tantamount to involuntary unemployment.

Excess supply in the labour market thus results from excess supply in the goods market. As it may coexist with the Walrasian real wage, too high a wage can no longer be viewed as its culprit.

Unfortunately, for all its appeal, this scenario is wanting (for a more detailed analysis, see De Vroey, 2001). First, Patinkin confuses quick and instantaneous adjustment. Therefore, he has no qualms in introducing the slow adjustment hypothesis in an otherwise unchanged Walrasian framework, failing to realize its incongruency. According to the Walrasian conception of price formation, at each trading, the equilibrium prices are supposed to be formed instantaneously or in logical time. No room is left for the occurrence of the false trading phenomena which Patinkin wants to bring to the fore. Nor can Patinkin have recourse to the Marshallian model of the working of markets, since market clearing is also one of its recurrent features. The reader is then at a loss to see which trade technology underpins Patinkin's reasoning. A second flaw is that Patinkin presumes that, after a shock, the economy will go back to the earlier equilibrium. This result, which is just stated but not demonstrated, cannot be accepted.

Transforming Patinkin's story into a model has proven to be an insuperable task. This drawback goes beyond the issue of involuntary unemployment itself. It follows from the fact that, to date, its prerequisite (a general equilibrium theory of disequilibrium behaviour of agents and disequilibrium states of the economy) is still lacking. Were such a general theory to exist, the analysis of involuntary unemployment could be derived as a particular case.

Two further remarks should be made. First, through all his long research career, Patinkin steadfastly defended the view that the disequilibrium line he adopted corresponds to what Keynes expounded in the *General Theory* (see, for example, Patinkin, 1987). Little support for this claim can be found – nor for the linked argument that Chapter 19 of the *General Theory* is its climax. Second, there is the question of Patinkin's influence. The judgment to be made here is mixed. True, many authors (for example, Tobin, Malinvaud, Modigliani, Barro and Grossman) have paid tribute to Patinkin, seemingly taking up his claim that rationing is due to slow adjustment. However, such an endorsement is usually confined to metatheoretical commentaries. When it comes to the models these authors have constructed, it turns out that the slow adjustment argument is absent from them.

Clower and Leijonhufvud

Clower's ([1965] 1984) renowned article, 'The Keynesian Counter-Revolution: A Theoretical Appraisal', is a criticism of standard Keynesianism, which, to him, includes Hicks and Patinkin and which he views as a betrayal of Keynes. His precise target is Walras's Law, and he does not hesitate to claim – quite boldly and at a high risk of backfiring – that 'either Walras's law is incompatible with Keynesian economics, or Keynes had nothing fundamentally new to add to orthodox economic theory' (ibid., p.41).

The underlying narrative is as follows. Households are unable to sell the quantity of labour they wish to trade for the current wage. As a result, their demand on the goods market is smaller than what it would otherwise have been. Their 'notional demand' for goods is supplanted by an 'effective demand' schedule, while a fixed parameter – the quantity of labour traded – enters their budget constraint. In Clower's model, the goods markets end up in a state that could be qualified as a 'pseudo-equilibrium', where firms' notional supply of goods matches households' effective demand for goods rather than their notional demand. The price and quantity emerging at this pseudo-equilibrium differ from the Walrasian magnitudes and are suboptimal with respect to them. Walras's Law is violated because only the labour market features non-market clearance.

Clower's article can be read in two different ways. Looking at the model it contains, one finds a scenario close to that of Patinkin, a case of rationing in a market which has a spillover effect on another market. Only this time the rationing arises in the labour market, the result of the wage rate being 'false', and spreads to the goods market. Moreover, Clower addresses the issue of the possibility of involuntary unemployment at equilibrium, rather than claiming that it exists only during the price formation process, as Patinkin did. But it contains another thread of reasoning, surfacing when it is read in the light of Clower and Leijonhufvud's (1975) joint posterior work. It then appears that Clower wished to emphasize price signalling problems and, beyond the latter, the possibility of coordination failure in a decentralized economy – in particular, the phenomenon of self-fulfilling predictions locking the economy into inefficient states.

Leijonhufvud's (1968) *On Keynesian Economics and the Economics of Keynes* has been a highly successful book. Leijonhufvud claims that standard Keynesian economics (that is, the IS–LM apparatus) is a totally inadequate vehicle for the interpretation of Keynes's ideas. Two basic reasons for this are its adoption of the wage rigidity assumption and its neglect of the role of money.

To understand Keynes, Leijonhufvud argues, one must abandon Walras and return to Marshall. The auctioneer *deus ex machina* needs to be removed. As a result, information problems come to the forefront, prompting 'effective demand failures' and involuntary unemployment, as its further result. Central to this possibility is Keynes's alleged inversion of the ranking of price and quantity adjustment velocities underlying Marshall's distinction between the market day and the short period. It explains that the initial response to a decline in demand is a quantity adjustment (thereby filling in the gap of Patinkin's lack of explanation as to the initial rationing outcome). To this end, no assumption of wage rigidity, Leijonhufvud asserts, is necessary. It suffices to give up the equally strong assumption of instantaneous price adjustment. Imperfect wage flexibility is thus proposed as an alternative to wage rigidity, a position that brings him close to Patinkin. Oddly enough, Leijonhufvud pays little tribute to Patinkin and considers him as belonging to the 'Keynesian school'.

In their joint work or separately, Clower and Leijonhufvud have tried to develop the positive side of their criticism, developing the theory of a trade technology alternative to the auctioneer hypothesis and taking the main characteristics of real-world decentralized economies better into account. Their starting point is Marshallian theory, which they try to improve in a twofold way. First, it needs to be generalized, from a partial to an economy-wide analysis. Second, they consider that a shift in emphasis from the study of the logical existence of equilibrium to that of the equilibration process is needed. Under the Marshallian 'general process analysis' label, they have proposed a theory of the decentralized economy, which

> (1) lacks a central information-processing and bill-collecting agency; (2) has, instead, middlemen trying to coordinate production and consumption activities in each output market separately; (3) makes the management of stocks of inventories essential to the coordination of these activities; and (4) has the system potentially subject to commercial crises associated with expansions and contractions of the volume of bank and nonbank credit. All this might be J.S. Mill or Alfred Marshall. (Clower and Leijonhufvod [1975] 1984, p. 217)

Unfortunately, it has proved highly difficult to push Clower and Leijonhufvud's views beyond the blueprint stage. To date, their scenario about the working of a really decentralized economy has hardly been transformed into a full-fledged theory.

MICHEL DE VROEY

See also:

Clower, Robert W.; Keynes's *General Theory*; Leijonhufvud, Axel; Patinkin, Don; Post Keynesian Economics.

Bibliography

Barro, R. and H. Grossman (1971), 'A General Disequilibrium Model of Income and Employment', *American Economic Review*, **61**, March, pp. 82–93.
Clower, R. ([1965] 1984), 'The Keynesian Counter-Revolution: A Theoretical Appraisal', in D. Walker (ed.), *Money and Markets: Essays by Robert W. Clower*. Cambridge: Cambridge University Press, pp. 34–58.

Clower, R. and A. Leijonhufvud ([1975] 1984), 'The Coordination of Economic Activities: A Keynesian Perspective', in D. Walker (ed.), *Money and Markets: Essays by Robert W. Clower*, Cambridge: Cambridge University Press, pp. 209–17.
De Vroey, M. (2001), 'Price Rigidity and Market Clearing. A Conceptual Clarification', *Cambridge Journal of Economics*, **25**, September, pp. 639–55.
Keynes, J.M. (1936), *The General Theory of Employment, Interest and Money*, London: Macmillan.
Leijonhufvud, A. (1968), *On Keynesian Economics and the Economics of Keynes*, Oxford: Oxford University Press.
Patinkin, D. (1965), *Money, Interest and Prices*, 2nd edn, New York: Harper & Row.
Patinkin, D. (1987), 'Keynes, John Maynard' in J. Eatwell, M. Milgate and P. Newman (eds), *The New Palgrave: A Dictionary of Economics*, London: Macmillan pp. 19–41.

Kindleberger, Charles P.

Charles Kindleberger (b.1910, New York City, New York, USA) obtained his BA from the University of Pennsylvania in 1932 and his MA (1934) and PhD (1937) from Columbia University. His main past posts have included research economist at the Federal Reserve Bank of New York, 1936–9 and at the Board of Governors of the Federal Reserve System, 1942–3; economist at the US Department of State, 1945–8; and Associate Professor (1948–51) and Professor (1951–76) at Massachusetts Institute of Technology (MIT). Since 1976, he has been Ford International Professor of Economics, Emeritus, at MIT. In 1986 he was elected president of the American Economic Association. He is best known for his work on international economics, in particular major problems and issues surrounding the dollar shortage, exchange rates, financial stability, international payments, liquidity and the international monetary system. His best known books include *International Short-Term Capital Movements* (Columbia University Press, 1937); *The Dollar Shortage* (MIT Press, 1950); *Europe and the Dollar* (MIT Press, 1966); *Europe's Postwar Growth: The Role of Labour Supply* (Harvard University Press, 1967); *Manias, Panics and Crashes: A History of Financial Crises* (Basic Books, 1978); *International Economics* (co-authored with P. Lindert) (Richard D. Urwin, 6th edn, 1978); *International Money: A Collection of Essays* (George Allen & Unwin, 1981); and *International Capital Movements* (Cambridge University Press, 1987).

See also:

American Economic Association; Federal Reserve System.

Klein, Lawrence R.

Lawrence Klein (b.1920, Omaha, Nebraska, USA) obtained his BA from the University of California, Berkeley in 1942 and his PhD from Massachusetts Institute of Technology in 1944. His main past posts have included Research Associate at the Cowles Commission, 1944–7; Research Associate at the National Bureau of Economic Research, 1948–50; Research Associate at the Survey Research Centre, University of Michigan, 1948–54; Senior Research Officer at the Oxford University Institute of Statistics, 1954–8; Reader at Oxford University, 1956–8; and Professor at the University of Pennsylvania, 1958–48. Since 1968 he has been the Benjamin Franklin Professor of Economics, Emeritus, at the University of Pennsylvania. His many offices and honours have included the award of the John Bates Clark Medal of the American Economic Association (AEA) in 1959; president of the Econometric Society in 1960; president of the AEA in 1977; and the award of the Nobel Prize in Economics in 1980 for his numerous contributions to econometric model building and applied econometrics. He is best known for his pioneering work on econometric modelling, including constructing (with A.S. Goldberger) in the early 1950s the first econometric model of the United States, and helping to construct in the early 1960s the Brookings–Social Science Research Council model of the US economy. Among his best known books are *The Keynesian Revolution* (Macmillan, 1947); *Economic Fluctuations in the United States: 1921–1941* (John Wiley, 1950); *An Econometric Model of the United States: 1929–1952* (co-authored with A.S. Goldberger) (John Wiley, 1955); *An Econometric Model of the United Kingdom* (co-authored with R.J. Ball *et al.*) (Basil Blackwell, 1961); *The Brookings Quarterly Econometric Model of the United States* (co-edited with J. Duesenberry, G. Fromm and E. Kuh) (Rand McNally, 1965); *The Wharton Econometric Forecasting Model* (co-authored with M.K. Evans) (Wharton School of Finance and Commerce, 1967); and *A History of Macroeconometric Model-Building* (co-authored with R.G. Bodkin and K. Marwah) (Edward Elgar, 1991).

See also:

American Economic Association; Cowies Commission; Econometric Society; Macroeconometric Models; National Bureau of Economic Research; Nobel Prize in Economics.

Kuznets, Simon S. (1901–85)

Simon Kuznets (b.1901, Pinsk, Russia) obtained his BSc (1923), MA (1924) and PhD (1926) from Columbia University. His main posts included member of the National Bureau of Economic Research (NBER) 1927–61; Professor at the University of Pennsylvania, 1930–54; Professor of Political Economy at Johns Hopkins University, 1954–60; and Professor of Economics at Harvard University, 1960–71. He was elected president of the American Statistical Association in 1949 and of the American Economic Association in 1954, and was awarded the Nobel Prize in Economics in 1971 for his work in collecting, estimating and interpreting statistical data relevant to economic development. He is best known for his influential work on developing the system of national income accounts; business cycles (including identifying so-called 'Kuznets' cycles); and the causes of economic growth and its consequences for income distribution. Among his best known books are *Secular Movements in Production and Prices: Their Nature and their Bearing upon Cyclical Fluctuations* (Houghton Mifflin, 1930); *National Income, 1929–1932* (NBER, 1934); *National Income and Capital Formation, 1919–1935* (NBER, 1941); *National Income and its Composition, 1919–1938* (co-authored with E. Jenks and L. Epstein) (NBER, 1941); *National Product Since 1869* (co-authored with E. Jenks and L. Epstein) (NBER, 1946); *Modern Economic Growth: Rate, Structure and Spread* (Yale University Press, 1966); *Economic Growth of Nations: Total Output and Production Structure* (Harvard University Press, 1971); and *Growth, Population and Income Distribution: Selected Essays* (W.W. Norton, 1979).

See also:

American Economic Association; National Bureau of Economic Research; Nobel Prize in Economics.

Kydland, Finn E.

Finn Kydland (b.1943, Norway) obtained his Sivilokonom (Business Administration) from the Norwegian School of Economics in 1968, and his MS (1972) and PhD (1973) from Carnegie-Mellon University. His main past posts have included Assistant Professor of Economics at the Norwegian School of Economics and Business Administration, 1973–6; Visiting Scholar at the University of Minnesota, 1976–7; and Visiting Fellow (1977) and Associate Professor of Economics (1978–82) at Carnegie-Mellon University. Since 1982, he has been Professor of Economics at Carnegie-Mellon University. He is best known for his influential work on time inconsistency; and the real business cycle approach to economic fluctuations. His most widely read articles, co-authored with E.C. Prescott, include 'Rules Rather than Discretion: The Inconsistency of

Optimal Plans' (*Journal of Political Economy*, **85**, June 1977); 'Time to Build and Aggregate Fluctuations' (*Econometrica*, **50**, November 1982); 'Business Cycles: Real Facts and a Monetary Myth' (*Federal Reserve Bank of Minneapolis Quarterly Review*, **14**, Spring 1990); 'The Econometrics of the General Equilibrium Approach to Business Cycles' (*Scandinavian Journal of Economics*, **93**, 1991); 'Hours and Employment Variation in Business Cycle Theory' (*Economic Theory*, **1**, January 1991); and 'The Computational Experiment: An Econometric Tool' (*Journal of Economic Perspectives*, **10**, Winter 1996).

See also:

Business Cycles: Real Business Cycle Approach; Time Inconsistency.

Laffer Curve

Complete the analogy: Oil is to water as:
a. Milton Friedman is to Friedrich Hayek
b. Adam Smith is to the invisible hand
c. The Chicago School is to John Maynard Keynes
d. Arthur Laffer is to napkins. (Nobel Prize Quiz, *The Economist*, 25 June 2001)

The Laffer curve graphs the relationship between tax rates and tax revenues. It is usually drawn as a backward bending curve with tax revenues on the horizontal axis as a function of tax rates on the vertical axis. Tax revenues increase up to a maximum at some critical tax rate. After that rate, raising tax rates further actually lowers tax revenues which, at ever-higher tax rates, will fall back to zero.

This illustrates an idea that can be a very important tool for any political macroeconomist's toolkit. The Laffer curve can provide a framework for technical analysis of tax structures, it can support political advocacy of tax reform, and it can help understand the humour in mock Nobel Prize quizzes proffered by the profession's favourite news magazine.

This famous curve made its modern debut, and gained its name, on 4 December 1974, at a luncheon in Two Continents Restaurant in Washington, DC. Arthur Laffer (then an Associate Professor of Business at the University of Chicago) drew a curve on a napkin to demonstrate a tax reform strategy. Among others present at its birth, Jude Wanniski, a journalist, subsequently popularized this napkin-drawing episode, and the curve, under Laffer's name (Wanniski, 2001).

The curve had a curious appeal for those who advocated tax reductions. As part of a supply-side programme of fiscal policy, it could be used to show that, under special conditions, a tax reduction could be self-financing. This idea enthralled tax-cut advocates and their converts, while frustrating their opponents, who were reduced to disputing whether the special conditions were present or demonizing supply-siders and the supply-side paradigm (for a recent example, see Krugman, 1998).

In the 1970s, such criticism by Laffer Curve opponents and sceptics had little appeal in the ensuing ideological battle over tax reform and tax reductions, which characterized the early years of the Reagan candidacy and presidency. George Bush, running against Reagan for the Republican nomination in 1980, characterized Reagan's programme of supply-side tax reform as 'Voodoo Economics'. Then, on losing the nomination to Reagan, Bush performed an act of political 'black magic' worthy of any 'voodoo mama' by becoming Reagan's vice-president and supply-side, cheerleading 'zombie' – at least until he took over the presidency in his own right, giving everyone a chance to, in his words, 'Read my lips, no new taxes.'

The 'curve' off Bush's lips was not by Laffer. New taxes were enacted under Bush. Voters were subsequently unforgiving as a result, denying him a second term as president.

After the millennium, ex-President Bush's son, George W. Bush, Jr, won the presidency and then delivered a Reaganesque tax reduction as one of his first significant acts. Ironically, George junior's own vice-president, and *de facto* CEO, Dick Cheney, was the one for whom the now famous curve was drawn on the now notorious napkin in 1974. In the mid-1970s, Cheney used Laffer's argument to convince President Gerald Ford to switch from a tax increase to a small tax cut (Wanniski, 2001). In 2000–2001, Cheney may have also used the Laffer Curve to champion and rationalize George junior's tax cut. Apparently, the evolution of political economy can turn a curve into a full circle.

Such political fashion in tax reform, especially tax cutting, was not confined to the late twentieth and early twenty-first centuries. Laffer (1981, p. 10) traces the origin of the ideas on which his curve is based back to an obscure Arab philosopher in the fourteenth century. Certainly, Adam Smith and J.B. Say in the late eighteenth and early nineteenth centuries were also aware of the concept. Indeed, as Laffer cites (ibid.), they wrote several memorable quotes that verbally describe what the Laffer curve graphs.

Of course, that was before the total tax burden escalated to modern levels of 30–50 per cent of GDP. In Smith's day, governments relied largely on land taxes and tariffs, the excess rates of which might drive farmers off the land or turn importers into smugglers. Peacetime tax revenues in Smith and Say's day were generally less than 10 per cent of GDP, as a consequence (Tanzi and Schuknecht, 1997).

Since few modern macroeconomics textbooks even mention the Laffer Curve, much less go into any detail of its nature and significance, some technical perspectives will be briefly explored here. Several important distinctions can be made: (1) 'upside' versus 'downside' of the curve; (2) 'revenue' versus 'deficit' effects; (3) 'short-run' versus 'long-run' shape; (4) 'supply-side' versus 'demand-side' derivation; (5) 'marginal' versus 'average' tax rate relevance; (6) 'micro' versus 'macro' effects. These will be discussed in turn in, with an emphasis on political economy aspects.

As regards distinction (1) the most basic political use of the Laffer curve is to support lobbying for a tax rate decrease – or, paradoxically, and as yet unexploited, for a tax rate increase. Its intrinsic logic can be immediately explained by lobbyists and grasped by politicians, or even by voters. For example, a simple mind experiment asks how much income tax revenue would be collected at tax rates of zero per cent and at 100 per cent of income. A moment's thought suggests the answer is the same – zero! At positive tax rates between those limits, however, it is also obvious that (a) tax revenues will be positive, (b) at some tax rate, tax revenue will be maximized, and (c) at lower revenue levels, the same revenue can be collected by two different tax rates – one lower than the other, and, hence, preferable. A government tax regime that employs that lower rate to collect its revenue is appropriately on the 'upside' of the curve. Contrarily, using the higher tax rate puts the government tax regime inappropriately on the 'downside' of the curve.

If an economy is already on the downside of the curve, lowering tax rates can *increase* tax revenues. This is a perfectly plausible neoclassical result that to some appears like magic or voodoo because it seems like promising something for nothing, or a 'free lunch'. However, it is exactly analogous to a business firm's total revenue increasing when the firm lowers price in the range where its product demand is elastic. (Paradoxically, economists are habituated to discovering such 'free lunches', that is, surpluses or 'rents', while simultaneously declaring that 'there is no such thing', because surpluses are dissipated by 'rent-seeking' costs.) Conversely, when on the upside of the curve, lowering tax rates will decrease tax revenue and vice versa. This is what most casual observers would regard as normal. There is a trade-off between two desiderata, tax-financed public goods and tax rate reductions. On the downside of the curve there is no trade-off – more of both is possible.

The key question is then: 'Which side of the curve is an economy on?' The answer is debatable and difficult to prove – even in retrospect, as has turned out to be the case for the Kennedy, Reagan and, soon, Bush, Jr cuts and for the Bush, Sr and Clinton tax increases. However, voters can easily reflect on their own voluntarily forgone opportunities for formal sector income with burdensome tax obligations, which tend to be more numerous and objectionable at ever higher tax rates, and judge accordingly. Thus higher tax rates tend to make 'the downside of Laffer curve' argument more believable and, hence, more politically appealing, regardless of whether it is true.

As regards distinction (2), attempts at proof sometimes become confused over measurement issues. The Laffer curve gives the relationship between tax rates and *tax revenues*, only promising an *eventual* increase in tax revenues with decreases in tax rates when on the downside of the curve. However, opponents of this idea often look at what happens to the government deficit (spending minus revenues) rather than to tax revenue, *per se*.

This mistake is one source of confusion over the Reagan tax cuts, which were not matched by spending cuts. Indeed, spending increased. In addition, an unusually restrictive monetary policy induced abnormal increases in interest rates, which substantially raised debt service costs. Consequently, the deficit increased for both these reasons. This caused some opponents to claim that the economy had been on the upside of the curve all along. The short-run data for tax revenues also supported that claim (Feldstein, 1986; Modigliani, 1988). However, there were confounding factors, such as the aforementioned deflationary monetary policy, which limited the economy's capacity for expansion, and, hence, limited revenue expansion from Reagan's earliest tax cuts.

The longer-run outcome for tax revenues tends to support the claim that pre-Reagan tax rates were on the downside of the curve. For example, income tax revenue actually increased by 76 per cent during Reagan's term of office (Sowell, 1996, p.82). Further, Hsing (1996) estimated from 1959–91 US data that there was a bell-shaped Laffer curve with a tax-maximizing rate between 32.67 per cent and 35.21 per cent for total personal income tax revenue. US marginal tax rates were above that range before Reagan's tax cuts and were approaching that range with the Clinton tax increases.

In retrospect, the early tax revenue-increasing (and deficit-reducing) potential for the Reagan tax cuts may have been overhyped by political supporters. However, without the hype, aided and abetted by the Laffer curve imagery, the Reagan tax cuts and reforms might not have occurred at all.

This is analogous to the political use of some Keynesian concepts, like the 'liquidity trap', 'inelastic investment' and 'rigid money wages', to urge a more active fiscal policy stance by the US government during the 1930s. In retrospect, there was more professional disagreement about the existence or relevance of such Keynesian concepts than there was about the appropriateness of increased government fiscal activism. Ironically, the liquidity trap notion has recently been revived as an argument for 'targeting inflation' in some modern economies (Krugman, 1999). Similarly, the Laffer curve may again prove useful politically as well as analytically.

Recently, Agell and Persson (2001) attributed 'seemingly contradictory' Laffer curve results to 'the alternative ways of defining a *ceteris paribus* tax cut in a dynamic model'. Using their preferred definition of the 'transfer-adjusted' tax rate, rather than the tax rate, *per se*, they showed the feasibility of self-financing tax rate cuts, *à la* Laffer. They also estimated that, among OECD countries, those 'with the most potential for self-financing tax cuts are the welfare states in Northern and Western Europe' (ibid., p. 410).

Finally, the measurement issue is further complicated under a rational expectations perspective, where the entire impact of anticipated tax cuts might occur *before* the cuts! Measuring the effect after the tax cuts would then miss detecting the true shape of the Laffer curve.

We now come to distinction (3). Since institutions and habits developed for one tax regime may be costly to change quickly in reaction to, and to accommodate, a new tax regime, the short-run Laffer curve may be flatter than the long-run curve. Indeed, the short-run curves may not even have the backward-bending shape of the long-run Laffer Curve. If policy makers typically base tax policy on their estimates of short-run curves, it is easy to demonstrate how the economy might come to be on the wrong side of the long-run curve after a series of apparently rational short-run trade-off decisions (see Buchanan and Lee, 1982). The shifting short-run curve always presents a more attractive trade-off than the long-run curve – just as for the short- and long-run Phillips curves that led policy makers blindly into excessive inflation during the 1970s.

As regards distinction (4), the main focus of proponents of the Laffer curve is the 'supply-side' of an economy. The reaction of production functions and factor supplies to tax changes are central to determining their impact and effect both on tax revenues and real output. For Laffer curve proponents, even when the economy is on the upside of the 'tax revenue' Laffer curve, tax cuts may still be desirable to stimulate the growth of real output and to reduce inflationary pressures. That is, the economy may still be on the downside of a 'real-output' Laffer curve (or a 'growth-rate Laffer curve'), which relates tax rates to real output (or to growth rate; see Barro, 1990; Chao and Grubel, 1998). The tax rate that maximizes real output (or growth rate) may be considerably lower than that which maximizes tax revenue and, implicitly, government size.

The supply-side analysis of such phenomena is best developed for labour supply as a factor of production. A tax reduction that increases the net wage to workers can have two effects: an 'income effect' which decreases labour supply and a 'substitution effect' which increases it. The sum of these gives the 'total effect' which, in the normal range, will be positive. That is, normally a tax rate cut will increase labour supply. Unless constrained by labour market institutions, an increased labour supply will increase employment, output and aggregate income. Increased income will increase tax revenue – perhaps enough to offset the revenue loss due to the tax cut at the initial income. If so, the economy was on the downside of both the real output and tax revenue Laffer curves.

Similar analyses can be explored for other factors or for the production function itself. Of particular interest for the 'official' production function is the effect tax rates can have on whether economic activity takes place 'unofficially', or 'underground' to escape taxation. Tax evasion, and avoidance activities, are a direct function of the level of tax rates (Mirus and Smith, 1994). Thus lower tax rates might yield higher tax revenues without a change in the total economy, as unofficial activities become official.

Finally, it should be recalled that Keynesian, or 'demand-side', macroeconomics also shows how a cut in tax rates will not necessarily decrease, and may increase, tax revenues. The Keynesian idea of the 'paradox of thrift' here might be relabelled the 'paradox of tax rate reductions'. In the Keynesian model with government spending a positive function of aggregate income, a cut in the marginal tax rate will increase equilibrium income. It will also increase government spending and its balancing item, taxes. Since this shifts the aggregate demand curve outwards, the equilibrium outcome depends on what happens to its interaction with the aggregate supply curve. If the supply-side effects of the tax cut shift out the aggregate supply curve as well, income will definitely increase, as will tax revenues.

Under distinction (5), the usual interpretation of the Laffer curve has the tax rate as an 'average', or possibly as a 'representative', tax rate, very much like the use of 'the interest rate' in macroeconomic analyses. However, from a supply-side perspective, the marginal rate is the key tax rate for productive factors within a tax jurisdiction (though relative average tax rates may give the appropriate 'margin' with respect to decisions about factor migration between tax jurisdictions).

Lowering the marginal tax rate might have more of a favourable impact and effect on tax revenues and output than lowering the average rate, given that the latter might have a less favourable balance between the 'income effect' and the 'substitution effect' than the former (Goolsbee, 1999). Lowering the maximum marginal tax rate would also be expected to have a more favourable effect on tax avoidance and tax evasion for taxpayers (Mirus and Smith, 1994; Palda, 2001) and on tax corruption for revenue service bureaucrats (Sanyal *et al.*, 2000). Typically, the maximum marginal tax rate in modern fiscal systems (especially those subject to inflation-induced 'bracket creep') applies not only to the super-rich but also to upper-middle-income earners, all of whom may have more flexibility in arranging their work, entrepreneurial and tax avoidance activity than low, and lower-middle, income groups.

Of course, lowering the maximum marginal rate is often the most difficult to achieve politically in a populist democracy because it is often damned as favouring 'the rich', even though, eventually, everyone would benefit. Populist politicians instead favour tax reductions for 'the poor' and/or 'the ordinary taxpayer'. Such tax concessions often have less favourable prospects for increasing work effort, output and tax revenue, but more favourable electoral prospects for those politicians and their parties. Perhaps the worst policy from a supply-side perspective is the much favoured, universal, lump-sum tax rebate. At best, that might have a positive, Keynesian-style, demand-side impact on the economy. More importantly, it would have the maximum possible electoral impact for those politicians under whose signatures the rebate cheques are mailed.

Finally, we come to distinction (6). The simple 'micro foundations of macroeconomics' can sometimes be misleading because of aggregation phenomena. In particular, not everyone experiences a tax cut uniformly, given the differing composition of personal incomes. Also everyone may not have the same facility to vary economic behaviour. Further, changing tax composition, tax base, and/or government spending simultaneously may entail confounding and offsetting effects causing a shift of the Laffer curve, instead of, or as well as, a movement along the long-run (and short-run) Laffer curve(s). The possibilities, and the words to explain them, are endless – too endless for this context.

So this summary must stop far short of a complete story of the robustness of the Laffer curve (or of its critics). Its usefulness has proved far wider than in its original application. It is especially applicable with respect to a government's choice of the inflation rate that maximizes its seigniorage on money and/or minimizes its interest expense on debt (Claessens, 1990). It has been applied in many innovative contexts, such as to life-saving rescue (Clark and Lee, 1997), and even to 'life's other choices' (Felkins, 1996). Its evolving ubiquity may be accounted for by its visualization of the ancient Greek principle of 'moderation' and/or the Classical idea of the 'golden mean'.

Oh, yes. *The Economist*'s answer to its question posed above is 'c'. However, under 'special conditions', 'd' is plausible. As oil floats on water, Arthur Laffer's fame 'floats' on a napkin.

ZANE A. SPINDLER*

(*Thanks are due to R.J. Sandilands, X. de Vanssay, H.G. Grubel and the editors for helpful suggestions.)

See also:

Fiscal Policy: Role of; Liquidity Trap; Supply-Side Economics.

Bibliography

Agell, J. and M. Persson (2001), 'On the Analytics of the Dynamic Laffer Curve', *Journal of Monetary Economics*, **48**, October, pp. 397–414.

Barro, R.J. (1990), 'Government Spending in a Simple Model of Endogenous Growth', *Journal of Political Economy*, **98**, October, pp. S103–25.

Buchanan, J.M. and D.R. Lee (1982), 'Tax Rates and Tax Revenues in Political Equilibrium: Some Simple Analytics', *Economic Inquiry*. **20**, July, pp. 344–54.

Chao, J.C.P. and H.G. Grubel (1998), 'Optimal Levels of Spending and Taxation in Canada', in H.G. Grubel (ed.), *How To Use the Fiscal Surplus: What is the Optimal Size of Government?*, Vancouver, B.C.: Fraser Institute.

Claessens, S. (1990), 'The Debt Laffer Curve: Some Estimates', *World Development*, **18**, pp. 1671–7.

Clark, J.R. and D.R. Lee (1997), 'Too Safe to Be Safe: Some Implications of Short- and Long-Run Rescue Laffer Curves', *Eastern Economic Journal*, **23**, pp. 127–37.

Feldstein, M. (1986), 'Supply-Side Economics: Old Truths and New Claims', *American Economic Review*, **76**, May, pp. 26–36.

Felkins, L. (1996), 'Using the Laffer Curve for Life's Other Choices' (*http://www.magnolia.net/~leonf/common/laffer.html*).

Goolsbee, A. (1999), 'Evidence on the High-income Laffer Curve from Six Decades of Tax Reform', *Brookings Papers on Economic Activity*, **99**, pp. 1–47.

Hsing, Y. (1996), 'Estimating the Laffer Curve and Policy Implications', *Journal of Socio-Economics*, **25**, pp. 395–401.

Krugman, P. (1998), 'Supply-Side Virus Strikes Again' and 'Supply-Side's Silly Season', in *The Accidental Theorist*, New York: W.W. Norton.

Krugman, P. (1999), 'Thinking About the Liquidity Trap' (*http://web.mit.edu/krugman/www/trioshrt.html*).

Laffer, A.B. (1981), 'Government Exactions and Revenue Deficiencies', *Cato Journal*, **1**, Spring, pp. 1–22.

Mirus, R. and R.S. Smith (1994), 'Canada's Underground Economy Revisited: Update and Critique', *Canadian Public Policy*, **20**, June, pp. 235–52.

Modigliani, F. (1988), 'Reagan's Economic Policies: A Critique', *Oxford Economic Papers*, **40**, October, pp. 397–426.

Palda, F. (2001), 'Why Fairness Matters: A New Look at the Laffer Curve and the Displacement Loss From Tax Evasion', CERGE-EI Discussion Paper 2001–65.

Sanyal, A., I.N. Gang and O. Goswami (2000), 'Corruption, Tax Evasion and the Laffer Curve', *Public Choice*, **105**, October, pp. 61–78.

Sowell, T. (1996), *The Vision of the Anointed: Self-Congratulation As a Basis for Social Policy*, New York: Basic Books.

Tanzi, V. and L. Schuknecht (1997), 'Reforming Government: An Overview of Recent Experience', *European Journal of Political Economy*, **13**, August, pp. 395–417.

Wanniski, J. (2001), 'Memo To: Website Fans, Browsers, Clients', 4 January (*http://www.polyconomics.com/*).

Leijonhufvud, Axel

Axel Leijonhufvud (b.1933, Stockholm, Sweden) obtained his Fil. kand. from the University of Lund in 1960, his MA from the University of Pittsburgh in 1961 and his PhD from Northwestern University in 1967. His main past posts have included Acting Assistant Professor (1964–7), Associate Professor (1967–71) and Professor (1971–94) at the University of California, Los Angeles. Since 1994, he has been Professor of Monetary Economics at the University of Trento, Italy. He is best known for his work on Keynesian economics and the economics of Keynes; coordination problems; and the costs and consequences of inflation. Among his best known books are *On Keynesian Economics and the Economics of Keynes: A Study in Monetary Theory* (Oxford University Press, 1968); *Keynes and the Classics: Two Lectures on Keynes's Contribution to Economic Theory* (Institute of Economic Affairs, 1969); *Information and Coordination: Essays in Macroeconomic Theory* (Oxford University Press, 1981); and *High Inflations* (co-authored with D. Heymann) (Oxford University Press, 1995). His most widely read articles include 'Keynes and the Keynesians: A Suggested Interpretation' (*American Economic Review*, **57**, May 1967); 'The Coordination of Economic Activities: A Keynesian

Perspective' (co-authored with R.W. Clower) (*American Economic Review*, **65**, May 1975); 'Three Items for the Macroeconomics Agenda' (*Kyklos*, **51**, 1998); and 'Mr. Keynes and the Moderns' (*European Journal of the History of Economic Thought*, **5**, Spring 1998).

See also:

Keynesian Economics: Reappraisals of.

Lender of Last Resort

One of the main functions of a central bank is to act as lender of last resort to banks in a financial crisis, ensuring that banks have sufficient reserves to meet the demands of depositors for currency and/or banks' reserve requirements.

Lerner, Abba P. (1903–82)

Abba Lerner (b.1903, Bessarabia, Russia) obtained his BSc (1932) and PhD (1943) from the University of London. His main posts included Assistant Lecturer at the London School of Economics, 1935–7; Assistant Professor at the University of Kansas City, 1940–2; Associate Professor (1942–6) and Professor of Economics (1946–7) at the New School for Social Research, New York; Professor of Economics at Roosevelt University, 1947–59; Professor at Michigan State University, 1959–65; Professor at the University of California, Berkeley, 1965–71; Professor at Queen's College, New York, 1971–8; and Professor at Florida State University, 1978–80. He is best known for his work on monopoly power; interpreting and extending Keynesian economics, including the principles of functional finance; and devising (with D.C. Colander) a plan for controlling inflation in a mixed economy. His best known books include *The Economics of Control: Principles of Welfare Economics* (Macmillan, 1944); *The Economics of Employment* (McGraw-Hill, 1951); *Essays in Economic Analysis* (Macmillan, 1953); *Flation: Not Inflation of Prices, not Deflation of Jobs* (Quadrangle Books, 1972); and *MAP, A Market Anti-Inflation Plan* (co-authored with D.C. Colander) (Harcourt Brace Jovanovich, 1980.

See also:

Keynesian Economics.

Lewis, W. Arthur (1915–91)

Arthur Lewis (b.1915, St Lucia, West Indies) obtained his BA from the London School of Economics in 1937, his MA from the University of Manchester in 1940 and his PhD from the University of London in 1942. His main past posts included Lecturer at the London School of Economics, 1938–48; Professor of Economics at the University of Manchester, 1948–58; Vice Chancellor of the University College of West Indies, 1959–63; Professor of Economics at Princeton University, 1963–70; President of the Caribbean Development Bank, 1970–73; and Professor of Economics at Princeton University, 1973–91. He was knighted in 1963; awarded (jointly with T.W. Schultz) the Nobel Prize in Economics in 1979; and elected president of the American Economic Association in 1983. He is best known for his influential work on the theory of economic development, in which he analysed a 'dual economy' composed of a modern sector which reinvested profits and which absorbed an unlimited supply of labour from a traditional sector. Among his best known books are *The Theory of Economic Growth* (George Allen & Unwin, 1955); *Development Planning: The Essentials of Economic Policy* (George Allen & Unwin, 1966); *Growth and Fluctuations: 1870–1913* (George Allen & Unwin, 1978); *The Evolution of the International Economic Order* (Princeton University Press, 1978); and *Selected Economic Writings of W. Arthur Lewis*, ed. M. Gersovitz (Columbia University Press, 1980). His most widely read articles include 'Economic Development with Unlimited Supplies of Labour' (*Manchester School of Economic and Social Studies*, **22**, May 1954); and 'The Slowing Down of the Engine of Growth' (*American Economic Review*, **70**, September 1980).

See also:

American Economic Association; Nobel Prize in Economics.

Life Cycle Hypothesis

The life cycle hypothesis of consumption is a body of theory associated with work undertaken by Franco Modigliani, and his collaborators Albert Ando and Richard Brumberg; see, for example, F. Modigliani and R. Brumberg, 'Utility Analysis and the Consumption Function: An Interpretation of Cross-Section Data', in K.K. Kurihara (ed.) *Post-Keynesian Economics* (Rutgers University Press, 1954) and A. Ando and F. Modigliani, 'The Life Cycle Hypothesis of Saving: Aggregate Implications and Tests' (*American Economic Review*, **53**, March 1963). According to the hypothesis, an individual's current consumption depends on, and is some fraction of (depending on tastes and preferences), the present value of his or her lifetime resources, which are composed of the person's wealth and lifetime earnings (both current income and expected future income from employment). It is assumed that an individual will maximize his or her utility by maintaining a stable or smooth pattern of consumption over their entire lifetime.

In what follows we outline a simple version of the hypothesis in order to illustrate how income and saving will vary over the life cycle of a typical individual. In the early years of working life, an individual's income will be relatively low and an individual will typically be a dissaver or net borrower, for example, to finance house purchase and consumer durables. Over the course of his or her working life, as income increases, an individual will typically seek to accumulate assets in order to repay earlier debts and save to finance consumption over the period of the individual's lifetime from retirement to death. The hypothesis is able to explain evidence from budget studies of a cross-section of the population that the marginal propensity to consume (MPC) is less than the average propensity to consume (APC), and that the APC declines as income increases. A typical cross-section of the population (for whom wealth is constant) will include a disproportionately large number of individuals on low levels of income who are in the early years of their working lives or in retirement. These individuals have a high APC and are typically engaged in dissaving. In contrast, high-level income brackets will include a disproportionately large number of individuals in the middle stage of their life cycle who typically save a larger fraction of their current income (low APC) in order to repay earlier debt or save for retirement when income is low.

The life cycle hypothesis can also explain evidence from short-run aggregate time-series data (a positive MPC which is less than unity and less than the APC) and long-run time series data (a constant APC = MPC). If the income distribution and age distribution (working and retired people) of the population remain relatively stable over time, individual consumption functions can be aggregated to produce a stable aggregate consumption function and explain why evidence points to the APC being constant in the long run. Aggregate consumption (C) is held to depend on both income (Y) and wealth (W):

$$C = \alpha W + \beta Y,$$

where α and β are the MPC out of wealth and income respectively. The APC (C/Y) can be found by dividing throughout by Y, so that

$$C/Y = \alpha(W/Y) + \beta.$$

In the short run, wealth (which provides the intercept of the short-run consumption function) is approximately constant so that APC falls as *Y* rises. In the long run, however, as wealth and income grow steadily together, the short-run consumption function will shift upward and result in a constant APC as *Y* rises.

The reader is referred to Franco Modigliani's article, 'Life Cycle, Individual Thrift, and the Wealth of Nations' (*American Economic Review*, **76**, June 1986) for a fuller discussion of the origin and implications of the life cycle hypothesis.

See also:

Absolute Income Hypothesis; Modigliani, Franco; Permanent Income Hypothesis; Relative Income Hypothesis.

Lipsey, Richard G.

Richard Lipsey (b.1928, Victoria, British Columbia, Canada) obtained his BA from the University of British Columbia in 1950, his MA from the University of Toronto in 1953 and his PhD from the University of London in 1957. His main past posts have included Assistant Lecturer, Lecturer, Reader and Professor at the London School of Economics, 1955–63; Professor of Economics at the University of Essex, 1964–70; and the Sir Edward Peacock Professor of Economics at Queen's University, Kingston, Ontario, 1970–85. Since 1986 he has been Professor of Economics, Emeritus, at Simon Fraser University in Vancouver. Between 1961 and 1964 he was editor of the *Review of Economic Studies* and from 1980 to 1981 president of the Canadian Economics Association. He is best known for his work on the general theory of second best; and the Phillips curve, in particular its micro underpinnings and place in macroeconomic models. Among his best known books are *The Theory of Custom Unions: A General Equilibrium Analysis* (Weidenfeld & Nicolson, 1973); and *The Selected Essays of Richard G. Lipsey, Volume One: Microeconomics, Growth and Political Economy; Volume Two: Macroeconomic Theory and Policy; Volume Three: On the Foundations of Monopolistic Competition and Economic Geography* (Edward Elgar, 1977). His most widely read articles include 'The Relation Between Unemployment and the Rate of Change of Money Wage Rates in the United Kingdom, 1862–1957: A Further Analysis' (*Economica*, **27**, February 1960); 'The Theory of Customs Unions: A General Survey' (*Economic Journal*, **70**, September 1960); 'Incomes Policy: A Reappraisal' (coauthored with J.M. Parkin) (*Economica*, **37**, May 1970); end 'The Understanding and Control of

Inflation: Is There a Crisis in Macroeconomics?' (*Canadian Journal of Economics*, **14**, November 1981).

See also:
Phillips Curve.

Liquidity

The ease and speed at which an asset can be converted into cash without loss.

Liquidity Preference

The term used by Keynes to denote the demand for money.

See also:
Demand for Money: Keynesian Approach.

Liquidity Trap

The liquidity trap refers to a situation where the interest rate is very low and the authorities are unable to reduce it any further by increasing the money supply. Any increase in the money supply would be absorbed entirely into idle/speculative balances as the demand for money became perfectly elastic with respect to the rate of interest.

The possibility of a liquidity trap was put forward by Keynes in 1936 in Chapter 15 (p. 207) of his *General Theory* and derives from his analysis of the motives that lead people to hold money. In the *General Theory*, Keynes emphasized three main motives for holding money, namely the transactions, precautionary and speculative motives. The demand for transactions balances, which derives from the function money serves as a medium of exchange, was considered to be mainly dependent on and be proportional to the level of income. The demand for precautionary balances, to provide for unforeseen circumstances and also 'to hold an asset of which the value is fixed in terms of money to meet a subsequent liability fixed in terms of money' (*General Theory*, p. 196), was also seen to be largely dependent upon the level of income. The demand for speculative or idle balances, which derives from money being not only a medium of exchange but also a store of value, was held to depend on the relationship between the current level of the rate of interest and the level regarded as normal.

In his analysis, Keynes focused attention on two alternative ways of holding financial assets: money whose value is fixed given the assumption of a stable price level, and long-term bonds whose value varies with changes in the rate of interest. A person's decision to allocate his wealth between either money or bonds will depend on his expectations about the future rate of interest in relation to the level regarded as normal. Keynes postulated that different people will have different expectations about the future course of the rate of interest and was able, in consequence, to postulate an *aggregate* speculative demand for money function which is a smooth and negative function of the current rate of interest. The higher is the current level of the rate of interest (relative to the level regarded as normal) so more and more individuals will expect future reductions in the rate of interest and will wish to hold bonds, rather than money. Not only can a high rate of interest be earned on bond holdings, but those individuals expecting the rate of interest to fall will also anticipate a capital gain on their bond holdings.

Conversely, as the current rate of interest falls relative to the normal level, so more and more individuals will expect the rate of interest to rise. More and more individuals will have a preference for money, rather than bonds, as they will anticipate that the capital losses on their bond holdings will outweigh the yield that can be earned on bonds.

Keynes put forward the theoretical possibility that, at low rates of interest, which would be expected to prevail in conditions of underemployment equilibrium, the demand for money could become perfectly elastic with respect to the rate of interest: the so-called liquidity trap. In this situation the rate of interest is so low that expectations converge and everyone expects that the only future course of the rate of interest is upwards. In consequence, individuals will be either unwilling to hold bonds (the expected capital loss on bonds outweighing interest received) or indifferent between money and bonds (the expected capital loss being matched by the interest received).

Although Keynes only put forward the liquidity trap as a theoretical possibility, and even commented that he was not aware of its ever having been operative in practice, it became important to the analysis of underemployment equilibrium in the orthodox Keynesian model. In the case of the liquidity trap monetary policy becomes impotent as a means of increasing aggregate demand and therefore the level of output and employment, as the authorities are unable to reduce the interest rate. Furthermore, any fall in prices which increases the real value of the money supply will fail to reduce the interest rate and increase aggregate demand; that is, the Keynes effect will fail to operate in the liquidity trap. Aggregate demand will only increase following a fall in the price level if increased real money balances make consumers wealthier and induce them to spend more: the so-called 'real balance or Pigou effect'.

While the results of a large number of empirical studies undertaken on the demand for money prior to the 1990s provide little evidence to support the existence of a liquidity trap, economists 'now know that the liquidity trap is not a historical myth'. In an article entitled 'It's Baaack: Japan's Slump and the Return of the Liquidity Trap' (*Brookings Papers on Economic Activity*, no. 2, 1998) Paul Krugman argues that Japan, the second biggest economy in the world, has been suffering from a liquidity trap problem during the last decade. Despite a decade of low interest rates, the economy has remained in depression relative to potential. Furthermore, Krugman has warned economists that the 1990s have witnessed *The Return of Depression Economics* (Penguin, 1999) and, if a liquidity trap can happen in Japan, 'perhaps it can happen elsewhere'. The interested reader should also refer to B.S. Bernanke (2000), 'Japanese Monetary Policy: The Case of Self-Induced Paralysis' in R. Mikitani and A.S. Posen (eds), *Japan's Financial Crisis and its Parallels to US Experience*, Institute of International Economics.

See also:

Demand for Money: Keynesian Approach; Keynes Effect; Keynes's *General Theory*; Keynesian Economics; Real Balance Effect.

Loanable Funds Theory

A theory of the rate of interest associated with a number of classical writers, including Knut Wicksell, in which the market rate of interest is determined by the demand for, and supply of, loanable funds. The demand for loanable funds consists of investment demand (I) plus the net hoarding (ΔH) demand for inactive money balances. The supply of loanable funds consists of savings (S) plus any net increase in the money supply (ΔM) through net credit creation. The theory recognizes that both real and monetary factors influence the rate of interest, the market rate of interest being determined where:

$$I + \Delta H = S + \Delta M.$$

In consequence, in equilibrium, when $I = S$, $\Delta M = \Delta H$ and the real rate of interest, or what Wicksell referred to as the natural rate of interest (determined by productivity and thrift), will be equal to the market rate of interest.

See also:

Wicksell, Knut.

Long-run Phillips Curve

The relationship between inflation and unemployment that exists in the long run. The general consensus is that while an inflation–unemployment trade-off exists in the short run along a given short-run Phillips curve, once agents have fully adjusted their inflationary expectations the trade-off disappears, resulting in a vertical long-run Phillips curve at the natural rate of unemployment.

See also:

Expectations-augmented Phillips Curve; Natural Rate of Unemployment; Phillips Curve; Short-run Phillips Curve.

Lucas Critique

During the 1970s, Robert Lucas, along with other 'New Classical' economists spearheaded a 'rational expectations revolution' that dramatically changed the future course of macroeconomic modelling and policy analysis. At the centre of this methodological transformation was the explicit incorporation of 'rational expectations' theory into theoretical and empirical macroeconomic models used for evaluating the economic effects of changes in fiscal and monetary policies. The core principle of rational expectations theory, as laid out initially by John Muth (1960), maintains that individuals and firms are forward-looking and seek to use all available information, including both past economic behaviour and expected future economic policy, when making predictions of economic events that affect their behaviour. Lucas's emphasis on rational expectations theory led to a fundamental shift in macroeconomic modelling that focused on the role of expectations in determining economic behaviour and the way that behaviour was affected by changes in economic policies. Because the behaviour of 'rational' economic agents is based on expectations of future economic events, including future policy changes, individuals' and firms' economic behaviour is likely to change in important ways when macroeconomic policy changes. Such changes in economic behaviour, in turn, alter the underlying aggregate structure of the macroeconomic models that were developed to describe that behaviour.

Macroeconomic model parameters and policy invariance
Prior to the mid-1970s, most large-scale macroeconomic models used for policy analysis were constructed on the assumption that the models' equations summarizing the relationships among economic aggregates were themselves invariant to the policy changes. In this setting, determining the economic effects of alternative macroeconomic policies was reduced to simply mapping out the dynamic responses of the model's variables to discrete changes in policy variables, such as the growth rate of the money supply or the level of government spending and taxation. Lucas's work during the 1970s, and in particular his 1976 article, 'Econometric Policy Evaluation: A Critique' – later referred to simply as the 'Lucas critique' – clearly illustrated that models based on this policy-invariance assumption were inherently flawed and were likely to lead to incorrect policy conclusions. The reason, according to Lucas, is that rational, optimizing economic agents will change their economic behaviour as expected future policy changes, in turn changing the relationships defining aggregate economic behaviour in macroeconomic models. The inclusion of rational expectations theory in large-scale macroeconomic models produces inter-relationships among the coefficients of the models' equations that explicitly link economic policy changes, not only to changes in the values of the policy variables, but to the coefficients themselves. Traditional models used prior to the mid–1970s assumed that these coefficient values were policy-invariant.

To be useful for policy analysis, according to Lucas, economists needed to describe explicitly how the model parameters, which were based on 'deep' behavioural relationships such as consumer preferences, were affected by changes in macroeconomic policy. Without such a description, traditional macroeconomic models were likely to give misleading results. For example, simply changing the level of the money supply, or its growth rate, and tracing out the dynamic response of the model's variables to this change in the policy variable using model parameters estimated from past data, would not provide accurate indications of the policy's effect on the economy because the model parameters themselves were likely to change at the same time that the policy variables changed. Because rational economic agents are forward-looking and base their expectations not only on immediate policy actions but also on those expected in the future, New Classical economists maintained that macroeconomic policy should be viewed as setting a policy *rule* rather than simply selecting new values for the policy variables. Lucas's major contribution was to show that, given economic agents with rational expectations, changes in the policy rule are inextricably linked to the parameters governing the dynamic behaviour of the model's variables. As a result, Lucas argued, meaningful policy analysis is only possible if economists can determine the explicit structure relating the two and incorporate that structure into their macroeconomic models.

Building on the general insights of Marschak (1953), Lucas's critique of econometric policy evaluation had a profound effect on macroeconomic model building and policy analysis for both theoretical and empirical reasons. Lucas was the first to develop well-defined macroeconomic models based on microeconomic foundations and rational expectations that explicitly illustrated the linkage between model parameter values and changes in macroeconomic policy rules. The internal logical consistency of such models provided a strong theoretical argument against the more 'ad hoc' structure of traditional macroeconomic models used at the time for macroeconomic policy analysis. Lucas's critique led Lucas and Sargent (1978) to argue that Keynesian macroeconomic models 'are of *no* value in guiding policy and that this condition will not be remedied by modifications along any line which is currently being pursued'. In addition, Lucas's arguments gained important empirical support from the dramatic failure of the large-scale macroeconomic models widely used to forecast inflation and unemployment in the early 1970s. These traditional models assumed a policy-invariant 'Phillips curve' relationship between inflation and unemployment that led to serious forecasting errors during this period. The combination of logically consistent theoretical arguments and real-world empirical support for Lucas's critique provided compelling evidence against the use of traditional (Keynesian) macroeconomic models for policy analysis and spurred the development of new macroeconomic models that were consistent with microeconomic foundations and could also explain observed real-world business cycle behaviour.

New directions in macroeconomic modelling
Following Lucas's (1976) critique of traditional macroeconometric policy analysis, macroeconomic model building developed along three separate, but related, fronts. Economists such as Lucas and Thomas Sargent initiated a wide-reaching research programme that sought to develop fully articulated, stochastic, dynamic rational expectations models that could be used to predict accurately how economic agents would react when government policy rules changed. These models were developed from basic microeconomic principles and employed a general equilibrium approach, in contrast to the static equilibrium framework used in traditional macroeconomic models dominant at the time. An important outgrowth of this line of

research was the 'real business cycle' approach to business cycle modelling, which was advocated by New Classical economists in the 1980s and 1990s. Kydland and Prescott (1982) were among the first to fully develop representative real business cycle models, which were aimed at meeting Lucas's (1977) goal of constructing 'a fully articulated artificial economy which behaves through time so as to imitate closely the time series behaviour of actual economies'.

At the same time, Keynesian macroeconomists responded to Lucas's critique by developing 'new Keynesian' macroeconomic models that incorporated rational expectations as well as wage or price rigidities that kept markets from reaching general equilibrium. The rigidities embedded in these models, such as long-term labour contracts and efficiency wage theory, while allowing a greater role for macroeconomic stabilization policies, were criticized by Lucas and others for being 'ad hoc' rather than the result of maximizing behaviour by individuals and firms. As a consequence, Lucas argued, such models were still subject to the policy analysis critique despite these models' ability to describe historical data.

Taking a different approach, Christopher Sims (1982) challenged Lucas and Sargent's insistence on developing fully-specified rational expectations models, instead promoting the use of 'atheoretical' vector autoregressions for policy analysis. While Sims's approach shared the same rational expectations foundations as those of Lucas and Sargent, his argument for the use of statistical reduced-form models whose parameters were largely unconstrained by economic theory was based on the belief that 'a policy action is better portrayed as implementation of a fixed or slowly changing rule', rather than a permanent shift in the policy rule. In Sims's framework, a set of relatively simple reduced-form equations, that did not require the identification of deep behavioural parameters, could be used to analyse accurately policy actions that were not too different from those experienced in the past.

Another challenge to Lucas's arguments was posed by Taylor (1989), who argued that, while the Lucas critique was methodologically important, its quantitative importance was less clear. Using a quantitative rational expectations econometric framework, Taylor found that macroeconomic model parameters were surprisingly stable across widely differing policy regimes. Taylor's results call into question the quantitative magnitude of the Lucas critique and the need to develop fully-specified macroeconomic models tied to deep behavioural parameters to carry out meaningful policy analysis. They suggest that traditional macroeconomic models, which are based on policy-invariant parameters, may be effective for empirically analysing the economic effects of macroeconomic policy changes, Lucas's theoretical arguments notwithstanding.

Summary

Despite continuing disagreement about the empirical relevance of Lucas's critique of macroeconometric policy analysis, his arguments have profoundly influenced macroeconomic model building and policy analysis since the 1970s. Both new Keynesian and New Classical economists now devote careful attention in their models to the expectations formation of rational individuals and firms, and the ways that those expectations are affected by economic policies. In addition, Lucas's arguments shed new light on the inherent interdependence between changes in economic policy and economic behaviour, highlighting the need to understand that relationship better in order to carry out meaningful policy analysis. As a consequence, both economists and policy makers today are more careful in carrying out macroeconomic policy analysis and more aware that predicted policy outcomes rely on empirical models whose structure may be affected by the very policies whose effects they are trying to analyse.

SCOTT SIMKINS

See also:

Business Cycles: Real Business Cycle Approach; Lucas, Robert E. Jr; Macroeconometric Models; New Classical Economics; New Keynesian Economics; Rational Expectations; Vector Autoregressions.

Bibliography

Kydland, F.E. and E.C. Prescott (1982), 'Time to Build and Aggregate Fluctuations', *Econometrica*, **50**, November, pp. 1345–70.
Lucas, R.E., Jr (1976), 'Econometric Policy Evaluation: A Critique', in K. Brunner and A. H. Meltzer (eds), *The Phillips Curve and Labor Markets*, Carnegie-Rochester Conference Series on Public Policy, 1, Amsterdam: North-Holland.
Lucas, R.E., Jr (1977), 'Understanding Business Cycles', in R.E. Lucas, Jr (ed.), *Studies in Business Cycle Theory*, Cambridge, MA: MIT Press.
Lucas, R.E., Jr (1981), *Studies in Business Cycle Theory*, Cambridge, MA: MIT Press.
Lucas, R.E., Jr and T.J. Sargent (1978), 'After Keynesian Macroeconomics', reprinted in P. Miller (ed.) (1994), *The Rational Expectations Revolution: Readings from the Front Line*, Cambridge, MA: MIT Press.
Lucas, R.E., Jr and T.J. Sargent (eds) (1981), *Rational Expectations and Econometric Practice*, Minneapolis: University of Minnesota Press.
Mankiw, N.G. (1988), 'Recent Developments in Macroeconomics: A Very Quick Refresher Course', *Journal of Money, Credit and Banking*, **20**, August, pp. 436–49.
Marschak, J. (1953), 'Economic Measurements for Policy and Prediction', in W. Hood and T. Koopmans (eds), *Studies in Econometric Method*, Cowles Foundation for Research in Economics, New Haven and London: Yale University Press.
McCallum, B.T. (1980), 'Rational Expectations and Macroeconomic Stabilization Policy: An Overview', *Journal of Money, Credit and Banking*, **12**, November, pp. 716–46.
McCallum, B.T. (1988), 'Postwar Developments in Business Cycle Theory: A Moderately Classical Perspective', *Journal of Money, Credit and Banking*, **20**, August, pp. 459–71.
Miller, P. (1994), *The Rational Expectations Revolution: Readings from the Front Line*, Cambridge, MA: MIT Press.
Muth, J. (1960), 'Optimal Properties of Exponentially Weighted Forecasts', reprinted in R.E.

Lucas and T.J. Sargent (eds) (1981), *Rational Expectations and Econometric Practice*, Minneapolis: University of Minnesota Press.
Sargent, T.J. (1984), 'Autoregressions, Expectations and Advice', *American Economic Review*, **74**, May, pp. 408–15.
Sims, C.A. (1982), 'Policy Analysis with Econometric Models', *Brookings Papers on Economic Activity*, **1**, pp. 107–64.
Taylor, J.B. (1989), 'Monetary Policy and the Stability of Macroeconomic Relationships', *Journal of Applied Econometrics*, **4**, December, pp. S161–78.

Lucas, Robert E. Jr

Robert Lucas was born in 1937 in Yakima, Washington and obtained his BA (in history) and his PhD in economics from the University of Chicago in 1959 and 1964, respectively. During the period 1963–74 he was Assistant Professor, Associate Professor and Professor of Economics at Carnegie-Mellon University. In 1974, Lucas returned to the University of Chicago, where he now holds the position of John Dewey Distinguished Service Professor of Economics. Professor Lucas is widely acknowledged as the originator and central figure in the development of what has come to be popularly known as the New Classical approach to macroeconomics. In recognition of Lucas's seminal research in macroeconomics, in October 1995, the Royal Swedish Academy of Sciences announced its decision to award him the Nobel Prize in Economics, 'For having developed and applied the hypothesis of rational expectations, and thereby having transformed macroeconomic analysis and deepened our understanding of economic policy.'

The award of this prestigious prize to Lucas came as no surprise to economists since, without doubt, his important contributions have made him the most influential macroeconomist of the past quarter-century (see Fischer, 1996; Hall, 1996; Svensson, 1996; Chari, 1998; Snowdon and Vane, 1998, 1999; Hoover, 1988, 1992, 1999). In addition to his work on business cycles, Lucas has made many other important contributions including those, for example, in investment theory (Lucas and Prescott, 1971), the theory of finance (Lucas, 1978b), monetary theory (Lucas and Stokey, 1987), recursive methods in economic dynamics (Lucas *et al.*, 1989) and, in recent years, growth theory (Lucas, 1988, 1990, 1993, 2001). While some commentators see Lucas's contributions to business cycle analysis as 'part of the natural progress of economics' (Chari, 1998), or as 'part of the steady accumulation of knowledge' (Blanchard, 2000), others make frequent reference to 'revolution' or counter-revolution when discussing the influence of Lucas's contributions to macroeconomics (Tobin, 1996; Woodford, 2000).

Building on the insights developed by Milton Friedman (1968) and

Edmund Phelps (1968), concerning the neglect of endogenous expectations in Keynesian macro models, the work of Lucas (1972, 1973, 1975, 1976) was crucial in introducing macroeconomists to Muth's (1961) rational expectations hypothesis, together with its enormous implications for theoretical and empirical work (Lucas and Sargent, 1981). In particular, with the introduction of rational expectations, the standard Keynesian models seemed unable to deliver their traditional policy conclusions. It soon became apparent that (what Blinder refers to as) the 'Lucasian revolution' represented a much more powerful and potentially damaging challenge to the Keynesian mainstream than the monetarist critique, which was of longer standing (see Snowdon, 2001). Although orthodox monetarism presented itself as an alternative to the standard Keynesian model, it did not constitute a radical theoretical challenge to it (see Laidler, 1986). Thus, while the mark I 1970s version of new classical macroeconomics initially evolved out of monetarist macroeconomics, it is clear that New Classical economics should be regarded as a separate school of thought from orthodox monetarism (Hoover, 1984).

Lucas recalls that he was 'raised as a monetarist in the 1960s' and that Friedman 'has been an enormous influence'. Indeed, Lucas still thinks of himself as a 'monetarist' (Lucas, 1994; Snowdon and Vane, 1998). While the New Classical school during the 1970s was undoubtedly 'monetarist' in terms of its policy prescriptions, according to Hoover (1984) the more radical tone to New Classical conclusions stems from key theoretical differences between Lucas and Friedman. And the roots of this theoretical divide are methodological: while Friedman is a Marshallian, Lucas is a Walrasian.

In his critique of Keynesian macroeconomics, Lucas took the position that the mainstream Keynesian model of the neoclassical synthesis period could not be patched up or modified, as suggested by Keynesians such as Alan Blinder (1988) or monetarists such as David Laidler (1986). According to Lucas, the problems facing Keynesian-style theorizing were much more fundamental and related in particular to (a) inadequate micro foundations which assume non-market clearing; and (b) the incorporation in both Keynesian and monetarist models of a hypothesis concerning the formation of expectations which was inconsistent with maximizing behaviour; that is, the use of adaptive rather than rational expectations. One of Lucas's major objectives has been to restore to mainstream macro theorizing classical modes of equilibrium analysis by building models involving continuous market clearing within a framework of competitive markets. However, the assumption of continuous market clearing, which implies perfectly and instantaneously flexible prices, remains one of the most controversial aspects of New Classical theorizing.

Although Lucas had made explicit use of the rational expectations hypothesis in analysing optimal investment behaviour as early as 1965, it was not until he began to wrestle with aggregate supply issues, within a general equilibrium framework, that the real significance of this hypothesis became clear (see Fischer, 1996). While Kevin Hoover (1988) argues that the Lucas and Rapping (1969) contribution is 'surely the first paper to deserve to be called new classical' because of its emphasis on the (voluntary) equilibrium nature of unemployment and its use of the intertemporal labour substitution hypothesis, it was the series of papers written by Lucas and published in the period 1972–6 that established the analytical base of the rational expectations-equilibrium approach to macroeconomics (Lucas, 1972, 1973, 1975, 1976, 1981). Collectively, these papers had a huge influence on macroeconomic research conducted during the 1970s and on the direction that macroeconomics has taken subsequently. Lucas's papers during the 1970s, combined with the work of other prominent new classicists such as Robert Barro, Finn Kydland, Edward Prescott, Thomas Sargent and Neil Wallace, helped to produce a 'rational expectations revolution' that swept through macroeconomics in the 1970s. As Hoover (1992) notes, 'whether for or against, the views of the new classical school have been the ones to debate; the problems it set have been the ones to solve; the techniques it used have been the ones to adopt'. We can get some idea of the influence of Lucas on macroeconomics by looking at citation counts as recorded by the Social Sciences Citation Index (see Snowdon and Vane, 1998). Between 1971 and 1997 three of Lucas's papers (1972, 1973 and 1976) received 2101 citations.

In classifying Lucas's published papers in macroeconomics, Fischer (1996) has distinguished between the 'fundamental analytic contributions' of 'Expectations and the Neutrality of Money' (Lucas, 1972) at the one extreme and the polemical 'After Keynesian Macroeconomics' (Lucas and Sargent, 1978) at the other. These two papers illustrate the range and diversity of Lucas's contribution to the field. Robert Hall (1996) has described Lucas's (1972) paper as 'probably the most significant paper in theoretical macroeconomics since Keynes'. In this paper, Lucas incorporated the Friedman–Phelps natural rate hypothesis in a continuous market-clearing context where all economic agents formed rational expectations. As a result, Lucas was able to demonstrate that a Phillips curve displaying non-neutrality can emerge even in an economy where 'all agents behave optimally in the light of their objectives and expectations'. Since a short-run 'trade off' between a real variable (unemployment or output) and a nominal variable (inflation or the general price level) breaks the classical dichotomy, Lucas's 1972 paper was crucial in that it demonstrated that a classical market-clearing model is compatible with the empirical Phillips curve phenomena providing the classical assumption of perfect information is abandoned.

Because Lucas's 1972 paper was exceedingly formal and mathematically complex, in order to reach a larger audience it was very important for Lucas to produce a more accessible paper. This was accomplished with the publication of his highly influential *American Economic Review* paper, 'Some International Evidence on Output–Inflation Tradeoffs' (Lucas, 1973).

An important result contained in these early papers is the demonstration that *unanticipated* monetary shocks can be shown to have only a *temporary* influence on real variables; that is, unanticipated money is non-neutral. Since, strictly speaking, monetary disturbances should be approximately neutral in a flexi-price equilibrium framework, Lucas's explanation of short-run monetary non-neutrality stands as a considerable intellectual achievement. Indeed, Lucas (1996) himself regards the finding that anticipated and unanticipated changes in monetary growth have very different effects as the key idea in postwar macroeconomics (Snowdon and Vane, 1999). Furthermore, Lucas (1996) notes that this distinction between anticipated and unanticipated monetary changes is a feature of all rational expectations-style models developed during the 1970s to explain the monetary non-neutrality exhibited in short-run trade-offs. Developing this idea, Lucas (1975, 1977) attempted to construct an equilibrium monetary explanation of the business cycle based on monetary shocks combined with a propagation mechanism (for example, a long-lived capital stock, accelerator effects, imperfect information). This attempt turned out to be highly influential methodologically even if it eventually proved to be theoretically and empirically unsatisfactory.

Moreover, although the emerging group of economists, inspired by Lucas, who set about transforming macroeconomics were referred to as 'rational expectationists' it is now clear that the incorporation of John Muth's (1961) rational expectations hypothesis into macroeconomics is not the uniquely defining characteristic of New Classical economics. For example, by the late 1970s, rational expectations models with Keynesian features also began to appear (see Snowdon *et al.*, 1994). The controversial component of new classical models relates to the assumption of continuous market clearing which implies perfect and instantaneous price flexibility (Tobin, 1996). In such a non-Keynesian world, all unemployment is voluntary, a notion difficult to swallow for committed Keynesians (Lucas, 1978a; Snowdon, 2001).

In contrast to Lucas's 1972 paper, the Lucas and Sargent (1978) contribution is a brilliant exercise in the use of rhetoric (Backhouse, 1997). While many economists did not accept that the case against Keynesian economics had been made conclusively, Lucas and Sargent argued that the flaws in Keynesian economics were fatal and that such models had been subject to 'econometric failure on a grand scale'. This conclusion is linked to another of Lucas's highly influential papers. Lucas (1976) argued that the traditional (Keynesian dominated) methods of policy evaluation do not adequately take into account the impact of policy on expectations. In Lucas's words, 'given that the structure of an econometric model consists of optimal decision rules of economic agents, and that optimal decision rules vary systematically with changes in the structure of series relevant to the decision maker, it follows that any change in policy will systematically alter the structure of econometric models'. Therefore the key parameters of large-scale Keynesian inspired macroeconometric models may not remain constant when policy changes because economic agents may adjust their behaviour in response to the new environment.

This criticism is known as the 'Lucas critique'. Lucas and Sargent (1978) concluded from this that the Keynesian solution to the problem of identifying a structural model 'has become increasingly suspect as a result of developments of both a theoretical and statistical nature'. Therefore Keynesian macroeconometric models are 'incapable of providing reliable guidance in formulating monetary, fiscal and other types of policy'. The prime example of econometric failure on a grand scale, given by Lucas and Sargent, is the breakdown during the 1970s of the Phillips curve, which had initially been interpreted as a possible long-run stable negative relationship between inflation and unemployment. To Lucas and Sargent, the Keynesian interpretation of the Phillips curve as a structural relationship had proved disastrous to policy formulation and had thereby contributed to the acceleration of inflation in the 1970s.

While the equilibrium approach to modelling macroeconomic dynamics has been Lucas's most important legacy to macroeconomic theory, Fischer (1996) argues that the development and application of rational expectations has been 'the most important contribution to the analysis of economic policy'. The new classical monetary models of the 1970s and early 1980s reinforced Friedman's arguments in favour of a rules-based framework for the conduct of macroeconomic policy. When agents have rational expectations, policy makers 'cannot ignore the interaction between their policy rules and the behaviour of rational agents'. Therefore, because the expectations of economic agents depend on many things, including the economic policies being pursued by the government, policy makers must design their strategies taking that interaction into account. The current approach to thinking about monetary and fiscal policy has absorbed Lucas's argument that economic behaviour is forward-looking. Therefore it is now widely accepted that the impact of government actions on the expectations of economic agents will crucially affect policy outcomes. The present emphasis among central bankers on the importance of credibility, reputation and commitment in the conduct of a rules-based monetary policy owes much to the influence of Lucas (Taylor, 1999; Woodford, 2000).

Although Lucas's influence on the course of macroeconomics during the 1970s was pervasive, and his work has transformed macroeconomic analysis forever, by 1980 his attempt to build a satisfactory equilibrium monetary theory of the business cycle was deemed by many, including those most sympathetic to the new classical research programme, to have failed (see Snowdon *et al.*, 1994). The resultant 'crisis' in macroeconomics fed the development of two very different routes of enquiry (Blanchard, 2000). In the post-1980 period of new exploration, one group of theorists, labelled as new Keynesians, concentrated on deepening our understanding of the impact of market imperfections (for example, price stickiness, imperfect information). Another group, led by Finn Kydland and Edward Prescott (1982), and known as real business cycle theorists, adopted the new classical methodology to begin exploring how far equilibrium theorizing could go in explaining aggregate fluctuations without resorting to monetary shocks and without introducing imperfections into the analysis. The real business cycle theorists have made an important methodological contribution by developing stochastic dynamic general equilibrium models based on preferences, resource endowments and technology. This research programme is remarkably similar to the one advocated by Lucas (1980) in his paper, 'Methods and Problems in Business Cycle Theory'. Here Lucas puts forward the case for building 'fully articulated, artificial economic systems' in order better to understand business cycle phenomena.

Since the mid–1980s there has been a resurgence of interest in the analysis of economic growth. To a large extent this renaissance has been stimulated by the new theoretical insights inspired by the research of Paul Romer and Robert Lucas. These insights led to the development of endogenous growth theory and renewed explorations in growth empirics (Temple, 1999). In his recent work, Lucas (2000) has presented a numerical simulation of world income dynamics in a simple model which captures certain features of the diffusion of the industrial revolution across the worlds' economies. In discussing prospects for the twenty-first century, Lucas concludes from his simulation exercise that 'the restoration of inter-society income equality will be one of the major economic events of the century to come'. In other words, in the twenty-first century we may well witness convergence big-time!

Paul Samuelson (1946) once remarked that 'the *General Theory* caught most economists under the age of thirty-five with the unexpected virulence of a disease first attacking and decimating an isolated tribe of South Sea islanders. Economists beyond fifty turned out to be quite immune to the ailment'. Samuelson's comment on the reaction within the economics profession to Keynes's *General Theory* might also be used to describe the 1970s reaction to Lucas's advocacy of adopting an equilibrium approach to the analysis of aggregate instability.

BRIAN SNOWDON
HOWARD R. VANE

See also:

Business Cycles: New Classical Approach; Lucas Critique; New Classical Economics; Nobel Prize in Economics; Rational Expectations.

Bibliography

Backhouse, R.E. (1997), 'The Rhetoric and Methodology of Modern Macroeconomics', in B. Snowdon and H.R. Vane (eds), *Reflections on the Development of Modern Macroeconomics*, Cheltenham, UK and Lyme, US: Edward Elgar.

Blanchard, O. (2000), 'What Do We Know About Macroeconomics that Fisher and Wicksell Did Not?', *Quarterly Journal of Economics*, **115**, November, pp. 1375–411.

Blinder, A.S. (1988), 'The Fall and Rise of Keynesian Economics', *Economic Record*, **64**, December, pp. 278–94.

Chari, V. (1998), 'Nobel Laureate Robert E. Lucas, Jr: Architect of Modern Macroeconomics', *Journal of Economic Perspectives*, **12**, Winter, pp. 171–86.

Fischer, S. (1996), 'Robert Lucas's Nobel Memorial Prize', *Scandinavian Journal of Economics*, **98**, March, pp. 11–31.

Friedman, M. (1968), 'The Role of Monetary Policy', *American Economic Review*, **58**, March, pp. 1–17.

Hall, R.E. (1996), 'Robert Lucas, Recipient of the 1995 Nobel Memorial Prize in Economics', *Scandinavian Journal of Economics*, **98**, March, pp. 33–48.

Hoover, K.D. (1984), 'Two Types of Monetarism', *Journal of Economic Literature*, **22**, March, pp. 58–76.

Hoover, K.D. (1988), *The New Classical Macroeconomics: A Sceptical Inquiry*, Oxford: Basil Blackwell.

Hoover, K.D. (ed.) (1992), *The New Classical Macroeconomics*, Aldershot, UK and Brookfield, US: Edward Elgar.

Hoover, K.D. (ed.) (1999), *The Legacy of Robert Lucas Jr*, Cheltenham, UK and Northampton, MA, USA: Edward Elgar.

Kydland, F.E. and E.C. Prescott (1982), 'Time to Build and Aggregate Fluctuations', *Econometrica*, **50**, November, pp. 1345–70.

Laidler, D.E.W. (1986), 'The New Classical Contribution to Macroeconomics', *Banca Nazionale Del Lavoro Review*, **156**, March, pp. 27–55.

Lucas, R.E. Jr (1972), 'Expectations and the Neutrality of Money', *Journal of Economic Theory*, **4**, April, pp. 103–24.

Lucas, R.E. Jr (1973), 'Some International Evidence on Output–Inflation Tradeoffs', *American Economic Review*, **63**, June, pp. 326–34.

Lucas, R.E. Jr (1975), 'An Equilibrium Model of the Business Cycle', *Journal of Political Economy*, **83**, December, pp. 1113–44.

Lucas, R.E. Jr (1976), 'Econometric Policy Evaluation: A Critique', in K. Brunner and A.H. Meltzer (eds), *The Phillips Curve and Labour Markets*, Amsterdam: North-Holland.

Lucas, R.E. Jr (1977), 'Understanding Business Cycles', in K. Brunner and A.H. Meltzer (eds), *Stabilisation of the Domestic and International Economy*, Carnegie-Rochester Conference Series in Public Policy, Amsterdam: North-Holland.

Lucas, R.E. Jr (1978a), 'Unemployment Policy', *American Economic Review*, **68**, May, pp. 353–7.

Lucas, R.E. Jr (1978b), 'Asset Prices in an Exchange Economy', *Econometrica*, **46**, November, pp. 1429–45.

Lucas, R.E. Jr (1980), 'Methods and Problems in Business Cycle Theory', *Journal of Money, Credit and Banking*, **12**, November, pp. 696–717.

Lucas, R.E. Jr (1981), *Studies in Business Cycle Theory*, Oxford: Basil Blackwell.

Lucas, R.E. Jr (1987), *Models of Business Cycles*, Oxford: Basil Blackwell.

Lucas, R.E. Jr (1988), 'On the Mechanics of Economic Development', *Journal of Monetary Economics*, **22**, July, pp. 3–42.

Lucas, R.E. Jr (1990), 'Why Doesn't Capital Flow From Rich To Poor Countries?', *American Economic Review*, **80**, May, pp. 92–6.

Lucas, R.E. Jr (1993), 'Making a Miracle', *Econometrica*, **61**, March, pp. 251–72.

Lucas, R.E. Jr (1994), 'Review of Milton Friedman and Anna J. Schwartz's *A Monetary History of the United States 1867–1960*', *Journal of Monetary Economics*, **34**, August, pp. 5–16.

Lucas, R.E. Jr (1996), 'Nobel Lecture: Monetary Neutrality', *Journal of Political Economy*, **104**, August, pp. 661–82.

Lucas, R.E. Jr (2000), 'Some Macroeconomics for the 21st Century', *Journal of Economic Perspectives*, **14**, Winter, pp. 159–68.

Lucas, R.E. Jr (2001), *Lectures on Economic Growth*, Cambridge, MA: Harvard University Press.

Lucas, R.E. Jr and E.C. Prescott (1971), 'Investment Under Uncertainty', *Econometrica*, **39**, September, pp. 659–81.

Lucas, R.E. Jr and L.A. Rapping (1969), 'Real Wages, Employment and Inflation', *Journal of Political Economy*, **77**, September/October, pp. 721–54.

Lucas, R.E. Jr and T.J. Sargent (1978), 'After Keynesian Macroeconomics', *After the Phillips Curve: Persistence of High Inflation and High Unemployment*, Boston, MA: Federal Reserve Bank of Boston.

Lucas, R.E. Jr and T.J. Sargent (eds.) (1981), *Rational Expectations and Econometric Practice*, Minneapolis: University of Minnesota Press.

Lucas, R.E. Jr and N.L. Stokey (1987), 'Money and Interest in a Cash in Advance Economy', *Econometrica*, **55**, May, pp. 491–514.

Lucas, R.E. Jr, N.L. Stokey and E.C. Prescott (1989), *Recursive Methods in Economic Dynamics*, Cambridge, MA: Harvard University Press.

Muth, J. (1961), 'Rational Expectations and the Theory of Price Movements', *Econometrica*, **39**, July, pp. 315–34.

Phelps, E.S. (1968), 'Money Wage Dynamics and Labour Market Equilibrium', *Journal of Political Economy*, **76**, August, pp. 678–711.

Samuelson, P.A. (1946), 'Lord Keynes and the General Theory', *Econometrica*, **14**, July, pp. 187–200.

Snowdon, B. (2001), 'Keeping the Keynesian Faith: An Interview with Alan Blinder', *World Economics*, **2**, April–June, pp. 105–40.

Snowdon, B. and H.R. Vane (1998), 'Transforming Macroeconomics: An Interview with Robert E. Lucas Jr.', *Journal of Economic Methodology*, **5**, June, pp. 115–46.

Snowdon, B. and H.R. Vane (1999), *Conversations With Leading Economists: Interpreting Modern Macroeconomics*, Cheltenham, UK and Northampton, MA, USA: Edward Elgar.

Snowdon, B., H.R. Vane and P. Wynarczyk (1994), *A Modern Guide to Macroeconomics: An Introduction to Competing Schools of Thought*, Aldershot, UK and Brookfield, US: Edward Elgar.

Svensson, L. (1996), 'The Scientific Contributions of Robert E. Lucas, Jr.', *Scandinavian Journal of Economics*, **98**, March, pp. 1–10.

Taylor, J.B. (ed.) (1999), *Monetary Policy Rules*, Chicago: University of Chicago Press.

Temple, J. (1999), 'The New Growth Evidence', *Journal of Economic Literature*, **37**, March, pp. 112–56.

Tobin, J. (1996), *Full Employment and Growth: Further Keynesian Essays on Policy*, Cheltenham, UK and Brookfield, US: Edward Elgar.

Woodford, M. (2000), 'Revolution and Evolution in Twentieth-Century Macroeconomics', in P. Gifford (ed.), *Frontiers of the Mind in the Twenty-First Century*, Cambridge, MA: Harvard University Press.

Lucas 'Surprise' Supply Function

During the 1970s, Robert E. Lucas Jr formulated an equilibrium monetary theory of the business cycle which combined three main sub-hypotheses: the rational expectations hypothesis, continuous market clearing, and the 'surprise' aggregate supply hypothesis. The latter is a key element in Lucas's (1972, 1973, 1975, 1977) attempt to explain both the systematic (Phillips curve) relationship between the rate of inflation and the level of real output (employment) and the business cycle as equilibrium phenomena. Building on Friedman's (1968) natural rate theory, Lucas assumes a world where agents' decisions depend on relative prices only. However, although agents form rational expectations they have imperfect information and therefore face a *signal extraction problem* since they have to distinguish between changes in prices that are real, and changes in prices that are nominal. In the case of an *unanticipated* rise in the general price level, agents are likely to interpret this as an increase in the price for their product/service (that is, as a relative price rise) and supply more goods/services. Therefore aggregate real output (supply) and employment will increase in response to an unanticipated rise in the absolute (nominal) price level. This relationship between aggregate output (Y_t) and the price level (P_t) has come to be known as the Lucas surprise aggregate supply function and is shown in equation (1):

$$Y_t = Yn_t + \alpha\left[P_t - E(P_t|\Omega_{-1})\right] + \varepsilon_t, \quad \alpha > 0. \tag{1}$$

Equation (1) shows that current aggregate supply (Y_t) is equal to a permanent component, that is, the natural or equilibrium level of aggregate supply (Yn_t), plus a component dependent on the price surprise, where P_t is the actual price level and $E(P_t|\Omega_{t-1})$ is the rational expectation of the price level subject to the information available up to the previous period (Ω_{t-1}), and ε_t is a random error process. For any given expectation of the price level, the aggregate supply curve will slope upwards in $P - Y$ space, and the greater the value of α, the more elastic will be the 'surprise' aggregate supply curve and the bigger will be the impact on real variables of an unanticipated rise in the general price level. Therefore, according to Lucas, countries where inflation has been relatively stable should show greater supply response to an inflationary impulse and vice versa. In his famous empirical paper, Lucas (1973) confirmed that, 'In a stable price country like the United States, then, policies which increase nominal income tend to have a large initial effect on real output, together with a small positive effect on the rate of inflation. . . . In contrast, in a volatile price country like Argentina, nominal income changes are associated with equal, contemporaneous price movements with no discernible effect on real output.' Equation (1) can be reformulated to include a lagged output term ($Y_{t-1} - Yn_{t-1}$) and this version was used by Lucas (1973) in his empirical work to deal with the problem of persistence (serial correlation) in the movement of economic aggregates. This reformulation of the surprise aggregate supply function is shown in equation (2):

$$Y_t = Yn_t + \alpha\left[P_t - E(P_t|\Omega_{-1})\right] + \beta(Y_{t-1} - Yn_{t-1}) + \varepsilon_t. \qquad (2)$$

The Lucas surprise aggregate supply equation is essentially an alternative representation of the rational expectations augmented Phillips curve shown in equation (3).

$$\dot{P}_t = E(\dot{P}_t|\Omega_{-1}) - \lambda\,(U_t - Un_t), \qquad \lambda > 0, \qquad (3)$$

Where $\dot{P}_t$ is the current rate of inflation, $E(\dot{P}_t|\Omega_{-1})$ is the rational expectation of inflation, U_t is the current rate of unemployment and Un_t is the natural rate of unemployment. Rearranging (3) we get equation (4):

$$U_t = Un_t - 1/\lambda\left[\dot{P}_t - E(\dot{P}_t|\Omega_{-1})\right]. \qquad (4)$$

In this formulation an inflation surprise leads to a temporary reduction of unemployment below the natural rate. In equations (1) and (4) a real variable is linked to a nominal variable. But, as Lucas demonstrated, the classical dichotomy only breaks down when a change in the nominal variable is a 'surprise' (see M. Friedman, 1968, 'The Role of Monetary Policy,' *American Economic Review*, **58**, March; R.E. Lucas, Jr, 'Expectations and the Neutrality of Money', *Journal of Economic Theory*, **4**, April 1972; R.E. Lucas, Jr, 'Some International Evidence on Output–Inflation Tradeoffs', *American Economic Review*, **63**, June 1973; R.E. Lucas, Jr, 'An Equilibrium Model of the Business Cycle', *Journal of Political Economy*, **83**, December 1975; R.E. Lucas, Jr, 'Understanding Business Cycles', in K. Brunner and A.H. Meltzer (eds), *Stabilisation of the Domestic and International Economy*, *Carnegie Rochester Conference Series in Public Policy*, North-Holland, 1977).

See also:

Business Cycles: New Classical Approach; Natural Rate of Unemployment; New Classical Economics; Rational Expectations.

Macroeconometric Models

Traditional modelling

The history of econometric modelling goes back to the work of Tinbergen (1939) who is usually credited with constructing the earliest econometric models. After World War II, the work of Klein and his various associates (for example, Klein and Goldberger, 1955) led to econometric models being estimated for the United States and most other industrialized countries. These models were used for *ex ante* forecasting and also policy analysis.

The approach adopted in constructing these models has been referred to as the Cowles Foundation approach or 'traditional' econometric modelling and can be stylized as consisting of the following stages:

1. Use the appropriate economic theory to decide which variables are of interest in explaining macroeconomic behaviour. These variables are then classified as those to be explained by the model (endogenous) and those to be determined outside the model (exogenous).
2. Formulate the theory as a series of equations linking together the variables. This requires the choice of a unit time interval, decisions about the precise timing of the variables (so that leads and lags are selected) and the use of some method of forming the expectational variables.
3. Obtain data on each of the variables. This involves relating the theoretical concepts to the available series.
4. Apply appropriate econometric techniques to the equations and the data to obtain numerical estimates of the parameters.
5. Examine the results to see if they are satisfactory. Should this not be the case, the earlier stages are repeated with appropriate changes until the results become satisfactory.
6. Given the estimated values of the parameters and projections of the future values of the exogenous variables, the future values of the endogenous variables can be forecast. Also the effects of alternative policies can be investigated.

This statement of the traditional approach to econometric modelling helps to indicate some of the problems that occur when it is applied in particular circumstances. The conclusion that a model is inadequate usually leads to a reconsideration of the earlier stages in the procedure. A review of the economic theory can suggest alternative formulations involving different variables. Problems with the data can lead to new information being utilized. The presence of autocorrelation or other violations of the assumptions can imply that different specifications or estimation methods should be used. Eventually, this process of repeating stages (1) to (5) will result in a model

455

which satisfies the main criteria of being consistent with the theory and accepted by the data.

It is at the point of producing forecasts that one of the most controversial adjustments takes place, since the forecaster generally does not accept the crude forecasts from the model but decides to use judgment to change them. This is known as applying 'tender loving care' (see Howrey *et al.*, 1974) and involves the forecaster taking account of the many factors, such as the effects of strikes and policy announcements, which are not covered by the model. Also any forecast for the recent past will differ from the observed outcome and a 'residual adjustment' may be made to get the model back on track.

Perhaps the most important objection to the methods of econometric modelling is the Lucas (1976) critique, which essentially says that the parameters of a model are derived under certain assumptions about the policy behaviour. If these assumptions change, so will the parameters, and hence any forecasts (and policy simulations) will be misleading.

Modern techniques

Before considering some recent developments in modelling it is worth mentioning two important limitations which applied to early econometric models. First, the data were scarce so that, for example, Tinbergen (1939) had 14 annual observations, the Klein and Goldberger (1955) model had 20 annual observations while the Brookings Project (Duesenberry *et al.*, 1965), had 30 quarterly observations. Secondly, the computing facilities were extremely limited until the 1970s so that estimating a multiple regression equation using matrix algebra could take several hours. These two limitations meant that there was a strong emphasis on prior theory and also the treatment of lagged terms was rudimentary.

In the 1970s and 1980s these two limitations ceased to be important. Quarterly data became available for most industrialized economies going back to the 1950s, so that by 1980 at least 100 quarterly observations could be used in empirical estimation. Personal computers, and remote access to mainframe computers, along with user-friendly software, allowed estimation to become almost instantaneous, speeding the process of specification, estimation and diagnostic testing.

These developments encouraged new approaches to econometric modelling. Hendry and his co-workers (for example, Davidson *et al.* 1978) criticized the traditional approach to economic modelling as being 'specific to general' in that economic theory is claimed to lead to a specific equation which, if it is found to be unsatisfactory, is then expanded to take account of particular empirical problems. The result is that a more complex model is found which is consistent with the data. Hendry points out that such an approach cannot test whether the theory is correct, since the final model must be accepted by the data. While recognizing that this procedure could end up with the correct model, this is unlikely. Other critics, including Leamer (1983), call the whole process 'data mining' or 'fishing' for the required results.

As an alternative procedure, Hendry proposes starting with a general model, which incorporates all the relevant variables from economic theory, and which has unrestricted dynamics. This model must be accepted by the data (and so have white noise residuals) and will have a large number of parameters. It would not be a sensible final model. Next, this general model is rearranged to reduce multicollinearity and to include patterns of variables which relate to equilibrium conditions, such as the error correction formulation discussed below. The model is estimated and, by testing the significance of the coefficients, is reduced to the smallest size which is compatible with the data. The accepted model is evaluated extensively by an analysis of residuals, structural stability and predictive performance, before finally being used for forecasting. In the United Kingdom, this extensive testing of the model has had a big impact on the way models are reported and, by implication, on their properties and forecasting performance.

The 'general to specific' approach relies on (a) the use of economic theory to indicate which variables are to be included in the general model, (b) the data set being extensive enough to discriminate between the alternative formulations of the model, and (c) there being a unique order in which the possible restrictions on the general model are tested. Of these, perhaps the third is the least likely to be correct.

As mentioned above, the 'general to specific' approach distinguishes between the long-run properties of the model – on which economic theory is generally informative – and the short-run dynamics – on which economic theory is rather vague. This links with the concept of cointegration (see Engle and Granger, 1987) where, for non-stationary variables, an error-correction model gives the short-run relationship while the cointegration vector gives the long-run relationship.

Another important development is the use of statistical or atheoretic models based on the data. Sims (1980) argues that the restrictions imposed by economic theory are frequently not credible and that the parameters of the resulting models are not identified. Any attempts at policy simulations are therefore misleading. As an alternative, Sims proposes estimating unrestricted reduced forms in which all the variables are treated as being endogenous. These are known as vector autoregressions (VARs) and Bayesian inference provides an efficient means of estimation.

Modelling in practice

Macroeconometric models are now widely used by governments and industry for forecasting and policy analysis. Many of the models were initially for academic research but have now become part of the commercial forecasting industry. Examples are those used by Wharton Econometric Forecasting Associates Inc., based on Klein's models of the USA, and the National Institute of Economic Research, London, model of the UK. Full details of the Bank of England's models are available on their website (*http://bankofengland.co.uk*).

KEN HOLDEN

See also:

Cowles Commission; Forecasting; Klein, Lawrence R.; Lucas Critique; Tinbergen, Jan; Vector Autoregressions.

Bibliography

Davidson, J.E.H., D.F. Hendry, F. Srba and S. Yeo (1978), 'Econometric Modelling of the Aggregate Time-Series Relationship Between Consumers' Expenditure and Income in the United Kingdom', *Economic Journal*, **88**, December, pp. 661–92.
Dusenberry, J.S., G. Fromm, L.R. Klein and E. Kuh (eds) (1965), *The Brookings Quarterly Econometric Model of the United States Economy*, Chicago: Rand McNally.
Engle, R.F. and C.W.J. Granger (1987), 'Cointegration and Error Correction: Representation, Estimation and Testing', *Econometrica*, **55**, March, pp. 251–76.
Howrey, E.P., L.R. Klein and M.D. McCarthy (1974), 'Notes on Testing the Predictive Performance of Econometric Models', *International Economic Review*, **15**, June, pp. 366–83.
Klein, L.R. and A.S. Goldberger (1955), *An Econometric Model of the United States 1929–1952*, Amsterdam: North-Holland.
Leamer, E.E.(1983), 'Lets Take the Con out of Econometrics', *American Economic Review*, **73**, March, pp. 31–43.
Lucas, R.E. Jr (1976), 'Econometric Policy Evaluation: A Critique' in K. Brunner and A.H. Meltzer (eds), *The Phillips Curve and Labour Markets*, vol. 1, Carnegie-Rochester Conferences on Public Policy, supplement to *Journal of Monetary Economics*, Amsterdam: North-Holland, pp. 19–46.
Sims, C.A.(1980), 'Macroeconomics and Reality', *Econometrica*, **48**, January, pp. 1–48.
Tinbergen, J. (1939), *Statistical Testing of Business Cycle Theories*, Geneva: League of Nations.

Malinvaud, Edmond

Edmond Malinvaud (b.1923, Limoges, France) obtained his Diplôme Ecole Polytechnique in 1946 and his Diplôme Ecole Nationale de la Statistique et de l'Administration Economique (ENSAE) in 1948. His main past posts have included Statistician (1948–56), Research Adviser (1967–71) and Director General (1974–87) at the Institut National de la Statistique et des Etudes Economiques (INSEE) in Paris; and

Professor–Director at ENSAE, 1957–66. Since 1987 he has been Professor at the College de France in Paris. He has been president of the Econometric Society (1963), the International Economic Association (1974–7) and the International Statistics Institute (1979–81). He is best known for his influential work on econometric theory; and the causes of unemployment, in particular developing a rationing model within a framework which allows for general equilibrium with involuntary unemployment in which he distinguishes between two forms of unemployment, Keynesian and classical. Among his best known books are *The Theory of Unemployment Reconsidered* (Basil Blackwell, 1977); *Statistical Methods of Econometrics* (3rd edn, North-Holland, 1980); *Profitability and Unemployment* (Cambridge University Press, 1980); *Mass Unemployment* (Basil Blackwell, 1984); and *Diagnosing Unemployment* (Cambridge University Press, 1994).

See also:
Econometric Society.

Managed Float

See:
Dirty Float.

Mankiw, N. Gregory

Gregory Mankiw (b.1958, Trenton, New Jersey, USA) obtained his AB from Princeton University in 1980 and his PhD from Massachusetts Institute of Technology in 1984. His main past posts have included Assistant Professor of Economics at Harvard University, 1985–7. Since 1987 he has been Professor of Economics at Harvard University. He is best known for his work on price adjustment; the determinants of consumer spending; the theory and empirics of economic growth; and is widely acknowledged as being a leading exponent of the new Keynesian school of economics. Among his best known books are *New Keynesian Economics, Volume One: Imperfect Competition and Sticky Prices; Volume Two: Coordination Failures and Real Rigidities* (co-edited with D. Romer) (MIT Press, 1991); *Monetary Policy* (ed.) (University of Chicago Press, 1994); and *Macroeconomics* (4th edn, Worth Publishers, 2000). His most widely read articles include 'Hall's Consumption Hypothesis and Durable Goods' (*Journal of Monetary Economics*, **10**, November 1982); 'Small Menu Costs and Large Business Cycles: A Macroeconomic Model of Monopoly'

(*Quarterly Journal of Economics*, **100**, May 1985); 'A Contribution to the Empirics of Economic Growth' (co-authored with D. Romer and D. Weil) (*Quarterly Journal of Economics*, **107**, May 1992); 'The Growth of Nations' (*Brookings Papers on Economic Activity*, 1995); and 'The Inexorable and Mysterious Trade-off Between Inflation and Unemployment' (*Economic Journal*, **111**, May 2001).

See also:
New Keynesian Economics.

Marginal Efficiency of Capital

The rate of discount which will just equate the present value of an expected income stream from an investment in a capital asset with the cost (or supply price) of the capital asset. The marginal efficiency of capital schedule depicts the relationship between the desired capital stock and the rate of interest. The schedule slopes downward to the right because with each additional unit of capital the marginal efficiency of capital declines, since expected net returns decline owing to diminishing marginal product of capital.

Marginal Efficiency of Investment

The rate of discount which will just equate the present value of an income stream from an investment in a capital asset with the cost of the capital asset, where the price of the capital asset can increase in the short run; also known as the internal rate of return. The marginal efficiency of investment schedule indicates the rate (or flow) of investment spending, per time period, at each possible market rate of interest.

Marginal Propensity to Consume

The change in consumption expenditure resulting from an additional unit of income; the slope of the consumption function. The marginal propensity to consume can be expressed as the propensity to consume out of either aggregate disposable income or national income.

See also:
Consumption Function.

Marginal Propensity to Import

The change in import expenditure resulting from an additional unit of income.

Marginal Propensity to Save

The change in saving resulting from an additional unit of income. The marginal propensity to save can be expressed as the propensity to save out of either aggregate disposable income or national income.

Marginal Propensity to Withdraw

The fraction of an additional unit of income which is withdrawn from circular flow of income.

Marginal Tax Rate

The amount of tax paid on an additional unit of income.

Marshall–Lerner Condition

The Marshall-Lerner condition (also called the Marshall–Lerner–Robinson, hereafter MLR, condition) is at the heart of the elasticities approach to the balance of payments. It is named after the three economists who discovered it independently: Alfred Marshall (1842–1924), Abba Lerner (1903–82) and Joan Robinson (1903–83). The condition seeks to answer the following question: when does a real devaluation (in fixed exchange rates) or a real depreciation (in floating exchange rates) of the currency improve the current account balance of a country?

For simplicity, assume that trade in services, investment-income flows and unilateral transfers are equal to zero, so that the trade account is equal to the current account. In its simplest version, the MLR condition states that a real devaluation (or a real depreciation) of the currency will improve the trade balance if the sum of the elasticities (in absolute values) of the demand for imports and exports with respect to the real exchange rate is greater than one ($\varepsilon + \varepsilon^* > 1$).

(*Note*: the real exchange rate is the relative price of foreign goods in terms of domestic goods. A real depreciation is equal to a nominal depreciation if the domestic price and the foreign price levels remain unchanged).

To see this, suppose that the trade balance is expressed in units of home currency. At one extreme, if the demand for imports has zero elasticity, the value of imports in home currency will go up by the full percentage of the real devaluation/depreciation. For the trade balance to improve, the value of exports in home currency has to go up by more than the full percentage of the real devaluation/depreciation. This is the case when the export elasticity is greater than one.

At the other extreme, suppose the elasticity of demand for exports is zero. Then, following a real devaluation/depreciation, the value of exports in home currency will remain the same. For the trade balance to improve following a real devaluation/depreciation, the value of imports in home currency has to go down. This is the case when the elasticity of demand for imports is greater than one.

So what the MLR condition states is that, in the event of a real devaluation, if each elasticity is less than one, but the sum is greater than one, the increase in imports (measured in home currency) will be more than offset by the increase in exports (also measured in home currency) and the trade balance will improve. The algebraic proof of this can be found in any respectable textbook on international economics (for example, Caves *et al.*, 2002).

This elementary condition rests on two assumptions. The first assumption is that we start from a situation of balanced trade. The second assumption is that the supply elasticities are infinite. It remains to examine each of these assumptions in turn.

If the initial situation is a trade deficit, the MLR condition is a necessary, but not sufficient, stability condition (when measured in home currency). Indeed, consider (again) the case where the elasticity of demand for imports is zero. The value of imports in home currency will go up by the full percentage of the real devaluation/depreciation. But, because of the trade deficit, the initial value of imports was greater than the value of exports. To improve the trade balance, the required percentage increase in exports has to be larger than the percentage of the real devaluation (in part to compensate for the relative smaller size of exports). It should be noted that, when the trade balance is expressed in foreign currency, and if the initial situation is a trade deficit, the MLR condition is a sufficient, but not necessary, stability condition.

A more complex version of the MLR condition involves supply elasticities that are less than infinite. It can easily be shown that the smaller the sum of the supply elasticities, the more likely it is that the MLR condition will be met (even if $\varepsilon + \varepsilon^* < 1$). Marshall (1923, p. 354), who was the first to formulate this stability condition, could not imagine that it would not be met. 'Nothing approaching to this has ever occurred in the real world: it is not inconceivable, but it is absolutely impossible.' He did not, however, supply any proof for his affirmation. Early econometric estimates found trade elasticities to be too low to satisfy the MLR condition (Chang, 1951). This led to the fear of 'elasticity pessimism' (Machlup, 1950). After a careful re-examination of the statistical problems involved, these early pessimistic estimates were refuted by Orcutt (1950) and others.

Hooper *et al.* (2000, pp. 8–9) have estimated the short-run and the long-run price elasticities of exports and imports for the Group of Seven (G7) countries (see Table 1).

Table 1

Country	Short-run export price elasticity	Short-run import price elasticity	Long-run export price elasticity	Long-run import price elasticity
Canada	−0.5*	−0.1	−0.9*	−0.9*
France	−0.1	−0.1	−0.2	−0.4*
Germany	−0.1	−0.2*	−0.3	−0.06*
Italy	−0.3*	−0.0	−0.9*	−0.4*
Japan	−0.5*	−0.1	−1.0*	−0.3*
United Kingdom	−0.2*	−0.0	−1.6*	−0.6
United States	−0.5*	−0.6	−1.5*	−0.3*

Note: *Denotes statistical significance at the 5 per cent level.

The message of this table is that trade elasticities increase over time. Based on the long-run elasticities, the MLR condition is met for nearly all the G7 countries. France and Germany are the exceptions. However, in the short run, the elasticities are very small and do not satisfy the MLR condition. The distinction between short-run and long-run elasticities is crucial and leads to what is known as the J-curve effect. A real devaluation (or depreciation) will worsen the current account balance in the short run, but will improve it in the longer run when the MLR condition is satisfied.

As a theory, the MLR condition lacks general equilibrium foundations. In particular, it considers the two markets (for importables and exportables) to be independent of each other. In a budget constraint, not all markets can be independent. So there must be at least one other market not accounted for by the MLR condition. In addition, from the absorption approach, we know that a country that has a current account surplus produces more than it spends. The MLR condition is silent on the mechanism by which this expenditure switching would operate following a devaluation. Dornbusch (1975) explicitly introduces a non-traded goods sector and fiscal policy in an attempt to reconcile the MLR condition with the absorption approach.

XAVIER DE VANSSAY

See also:

Absorption Approach to the Balance of Payments; Elasticities Approach to the Balance of Payments; Expenditure Switching Policy; Fixed Exchange Rate System; Floating Exchange Rate System.

Bibliography

Caves, R.E., J.A. Frankel and R.W. Jones (2002), *World Trade and Payments: An Introduction*, 9th edn, New York: Addison-Wesley.
Chang, T.C. (1951), *Cyclical Movements in the Balance of Payments*, Cambridge: Cambridge University Press.
Dornbusch, R. (1975), 'Exchange Rates and Fiscal Policy in a Popular Model of International Trade', *American Economic Review*, **65**, December, pp. 859–71.
Hooper, P., *et al.* (2000), 'Trade Elasticities for the G-7 Countries', Princeton Studies in International Economics, no. 87, Department of Economics, Princeton University.
Lerner, A. (1944), *The Economics of Control*, New York: Macmillan.
Machlup, F. (1950), 'Elasticity Pessimism in International Trade', *Economia Internazionale*, **III**, February, pp. 118–41.
Marshall, A. (1923), *Money, Credit and Commerce*, London: Macmillan and Co.
Orcutt, G.H. (1950), 'Measurement of Price Elasticities in International Trade', *Review of Economics and Statistics*, **XXXII**, May, pp. 117–32
Robinson, J. (1937), 'The Foreign Exchanges', reprinted in H. Ellis and L.A. Metzler (eds) (1950) *Readings in the Theory of International Trade*, Homewood: Irwin, pp. 83–103.

Marxian Macroeconomics: An Overview

The Marxian approach in economics stems from Karl Marx's analysis of the working of the capitalist economy, especially in his main investigation, *Capital* (three volumes, 1867, 1885, 1894). Although these works are interesting for the specialist, they can hardly serve as an introduction to current research in Marxian economics. For over a hundred years its research themes, methods and techniques have been in continuous revision (the same applies of course to Jevons and Marshall for the Neoclassicals, or Keynes for the Post Keynesians – at some point, however, it is rewarding to read the classics).

Since heterodox minority views in economics, including Marxian economics, are not generally taught in a large number of universities, several basic characteristics of Marxian theory should first be noted (for general introductory accounts of Marxian economics, see Foley, 1986, or the earlier Desai, 1979, and Fine and Harris, 1979; for current controversies and more advanced study, one might turn to Bellofiore, 1998).

First, central to the Marxian paradigm is that the capitalist system is a historically specific mode of production, allocation and distribution. Capitalism is not merely an allocating and distributing *market economy*; more than that, each historically specific economic system necessarily operates through a specific 'social form' as the dominant criterion and measure of *production*. For capitalism this is the monetary value form; it dominates not merely *market exchange* but also the *process of production*. Hence techniques of production and technological trajectories are not 'naturalistic' phenomena; for capitalism, they are determined by the value form (see Murray, 2002).

Second, key capitalist criteria of production deriving from the value form are *profit* and the *rate of profit* (these two do not always move in the same direction). Together, they determine the (rate of) accumulation of capital – the growth of capital – that is the lever for more profits. Thus profit and the growth of capital, rather than other possible criteria, such as human needs and use value, determine production. Note, however, that, as with technology, human needs are not 'naturalistic'; they are themselves determined within and as part of a social formation, in this case the capitalist system (see Campbell, 1993).

Third, profit is the result of exploitation of labour (the product of labour is larger than its wages, profit being the difference). However, the level of the wage rate is only one of the two factors determining the distribution of income. The other factor is the *labour process* at the point of production, which entails a particular intensity of labour. Hence we see a regular struggle between capital and workers, both over the wage and at the point of production (that is, over working conditions).

Many Marxists would add to these three factual theses normative judgments about each: the value form, the profit criterion and exploitation. In principle, however, moral and political judgments about these can be separated from the three analytical issues. Thus it is possible to accept the Marxian analytical apparatus as superior to the neoclassical, for example, without sharing the normative judgments. (Conversely, one might accept the analytical side of the neoclassical apparatus while being vigorously opposed to the capitalist system.)

We now move on to macroeconomics specifically. Although J.M. Keynes and his followers most influentially set out the principles of macroeconomics, macroeconomics originates independently in Marx's *Capital*. Apart from a theory of money and a general critique of Say's Law early on in *Capital I*, this work contains three main macroeconomic building blocks.

First is a model of *The Circuit of Capital* (Marx, 1885, Part One). This model emphasizes capital's continuous movement through four manifestations, or shapes, together constituting the macroeconomic circuit of capital.

$$\left(\underbrace{ \mathbf{M} \,-\epsilon-\, \mathbf{C} <\text{mp};\text{lp}> \,.....\, \mathbf{P} \,.....\, \mathbf{C}^* \,-\epsilon-\, (\mathbf{M}+\mathbf{\Delta M}) }_{\longleftarrow \qquad\qquad \longleftarrow \qquad\qquad \longleftarrow} \right)$$

Starting with the monetary finance of capital, the shape of 'money capital' (**M**), is transformed in the exchange process ($-\epsilon-$) into the shape of 'commodity capital' (**C**), specifically means of production (mp) and labour power (lp); the latter work up the former in the process of production (...). In production we have the shape of 'capital in process' (**P**), which constitutes a metamorphosis again into the shape of 'commodity capital' (**C***), with **C*** different qualitatively from **C**, as well as quantitatively in value terms (**C***>**C**). Finally, we have another market exchange ($-\epsilon-$) transforming the expanded commodity value **C*** into a monetary value equivalent **M**+**ΔM**, the shape of expanded 'money capital'. The process now resumes on an expanded scale. Note that in a sectoral breakdown of the macro conception, the exchange of **M**$-\epsilon-$**C** is at the same time for other capitals the exchange phase of **C***$-\epsilon-$(**M**+**ΔM**). (For more on this circuit, see Arthur, 1998.)

The second main building block is a *reproduction schema* of the capitalist economy (Marx, 1885, Part Three). In modern terms it would be called a dynamic two-sector macroeconomic model of production and realization (Marx was the first economist to develop such a model; up to about 1950 the term 'model' was not used in economics; 'schema' was a name adopted from Marx, for example by Tinbergen). The first sector in the model produces means of production (investment goods) and the second sector consumer goods. On the basis of the model, Marx was able to specify a number of dynamic interconnections in the functioning of the capitalist economy. In particular, he showed that, in the context of economic growth, proportionality, or balance, between the two major sectors of the economy is most unlikely. In other words, disproportional or disequilibrium growth, together with its potentialities for economic crisis, is the normal case. Over 50 years later, Harrod and Domar confirmed this result on the basis of their famous 'knife edge' models of economic growth. Empirically, the schema may explain the extreme volatility of investment (capital formation) that we perceive still today. (For more on this model, see Reuten, 1998.)

In the middle part of *Capital II*, we find a long and tedious (and therefore difficult) treatment of 'turnover time', a much neglected issue in economics generally (though not in 'financial accounting'), but also in Marxian economics (see, however, Mandel, 1975, ch. 7; Smith, 1998; and, especially for its monetary aspects, Campbell, 1998).

The third main building block is not this turnover treatment, but rather that of the *development of the average rate of profit* (to be found in *Capital III*, Part Three). This particular theory is controversial amongst Marxian economists (for a recent appreciation, see Reuten, 2002). Be that as it may, the evolution of the rate of profit remains central to any variant of Marxian macroeconomics – an interesting contrast with mainstream economics where the profit rate plays hardly any role, or gets reduced to the interest rate.

The most influential of Marx's economics on macroeconomics in the early twentieth century was the *Capital II* reproduction model. One of the first authors to adopt it was the business cycle researcher Tugan-Baranowski, writing around 1900. Via his work, the *Capital II* framework influenced a number of important non-Marxian economists of the first half of the twentieth century, such as Spiethoff, Cassel, Aftalion, W. Mitchell, Schumpeter, J.M. Keynes and Leontief.

The same *Capital II* model, sometimes combined with the third mentioned building block, also inspired the early twentieth-century macroeconomics of Marxists such as Otto Bauer, Rosa Luxemburg, Henryk Grossman, Maurice Dobb, Paul Sweezy, Michal Kalecki and, to some extent, also Joan Robinson. (See Howard and King, 1989, 1992, for a history of Marxian economics, with an overview of recent macroeconomic themes in Chapter 16 of the latter book; the latter chapter might also be combined with the earlier 90-page overview of Hardach *et al.*, 1978.)

In current Marxian macroeconomics, all three building blocks play a role, though variously developed. Increasingly this is coupled with macro monetary and macro financial matters. Marx's own work on this – especially in *Capital III*, Parts Four to Five – is sketchy, albeit he wrote some 350 pages on the issue (cf. Crotty, 1985; Campbell, 2002; Reuten, 2002). Although Hilferding developed Marx's analysis in his *Finance Capital* (1910), for long a standard text amongst Marxists, it is really only from the 1970s onwards that these issues become more prominent in Marxian macroeconomics: for example, through the work of Susanne de Brunhoff (1976) and Michel Aglietta (1976), with an explicit link from Marx's circuit approach to finance made by Augusto Graziani (see Bellofiore and Realfonzo, 1997). On all of these matters a thorough connection from Marx to the present is Harvey (1982). Itoh and Lapavitsas (1999) provide a general introduction.

A good starter for 'Marxian macroeconomics' is Laibman (1997) which contains further references. From a macroeconomic perspective, Brenner (1998) provides a theoretical and empirical record of capitalist development in the second half of the twentieth century. Combined with Fine *et al.* (1999), the 'Symposium on Brenner' (1999) provides a pattern-card of current Marxian positions and debates as well as further references.

Alternatively, one might move on from Laibman (1997) to the edited collection of Albritton *et al.* (2001) for papers on the long-term development of capitalism, especially in the past five decades.

GEERT REUTEN

See also:

Business Cycles: Marxian Approach; Marxian Macroeconomics: Some Key Relationships.

Bibliography

Aglietta, M. ([1976] 1979), *Régulation et Crises du Capitalisme*, Calmann-Lévi, Engl. trans. D. Fernbach, *A Theory of Capitalist Regulation; The US Experience*, London: NLB.
Albritton, R., M. Itoh, R. Westra and A. Zuege (eds) (2001), *Phases of Capitalist Development: Booms, Crises and Globalizations*, Basingstoke/New York: Palgrave.
Arthur, C.J. (1998), 'The Fluidity of Capital and the Logic of the Concept', in C.J. Arthur and G. Reuten (eds), pp. 95–128.
Arthur, C.J. and G. Reuten (eds) (1998), *The Circulation of Capital: Essays on Volume II of Marx's 'Capital'*, London/New York: Macmillan.
Bellofiore, R. (ed.) (1998), *Marxian Economics: A Reappraisal*, two vols, London/New York: Macmillan.
Bellofiore, R. and R. Realfonzo (1997), 'Finance and the Labour Theory of Value: Toward a Macroeconomic Theory of Distribution from a Monetary Perspective', *International Journal of Political Economy*, **27**, pp. 97–118.
Brenner, R. (1998), 'Uneven Development and the Long Downturn: The Advanced Capitalist Economies from Boom to Stagnation, 1950–1998; or, the Economics of Global Turbulence', *New Left Review*, **229** (special issue), pp. 1–265.
Brunhoff, S. de ([1976] 1978), *État et Capital*, Engl. trans. *The State, Capital and Economic Policy*, London: Pluto Press.
Campbell, M. (1993), 'Marx's Concept of Economic Relations and the Method of "Capital"', in F. Moseley (ed.), pp. 135–55.
Campbell, M. (1998), 'Money in the Circulation of Capital,' in C.J. Arthur and G. Reuten (eds), pp. 129–58.
Campbell, M. (2002), 'The Credit System', in M. Campbell and G. Reuten (eds), pp. 212–27.
Campbell, M. and G. Reuten (eds) (2002), *The Culmination of Capital: Essays on Volume III of Marx's 'Capital'*, Basingstoke/New York: Palgrave–Macmillan.
Crotty, J. (1985), 'The Centrality of Money, Credit and Financial Intermediation in Marx's Crisis Theory: An Interpretation of Marx's Methodology', in S. Resnick and R. Wolff (eds), *Rethinking Marxism*, Brooklyn: Autonomedia, pp. 45–81.
Desai, M. (1979), *Marxian Economics*, Oxford: Basil Blackwell.
Duménil, G. and D. Lévy (1993), *The Economics of the Profit Rate: Competition, Crises and Historical Tendencies in Capitalism*, Aldershot, UK and Brookfield, US: Edward Elgar.
Fine, B. and L. Harris (1979), *Rereading Capital*, London: Macmillan.
Fine, B., C. Lapavitsas and D. Milonakis (1999), 'Addressing the World Economy: Two Steps Back', *Capital and Class*, **67**, Spring, pp. 47–90.
Foley, D. (1986), *Understanding Capital*, Cambridge, MA/London: Harvard University Press.
Hardach, G., D. Karras and B. Fine (1978), *A Short History of Socialist Economic Thought*, London: Edward Arnold.
Harvey, D. ([1982] 1999), *The Limits to Capital*, London/New York: Verso.
Hilferding, R. ([1910] 1981), *Finance Capital; A Study of the Latest Phase of Capitalist Development*, London: Routledge & Kegan Paul.
Howard, M.C. and J.E. King (1989–1992), *A History of Marxian Economics; Volume I, 1883–1929; Volume II, 1929–1990*, London: Macmillan.
Itoh, M. and C. Lapavitsas (1999), *Political Economy of Money and Finance*, London/New York: Macmillan.

Laibman, D. (1997), *Capitalist Macrodynamics: A Systematic Introduction*, London: Macmillan.

Mandel, E. (1975), *Late Capitalism*, London: New Left Books.

Marx, K. ([1867–1885–1894], 1976–1978–1981), *Capital. Vol.I* [The Production Process of Capital]; *Vol.II* [The Circulation Process of Capital]; *Vol.III* [The Process of Capitalist Production as a Whole], Harmondsworth: Penguin.

Moseley, F. (ed.) (1993), *Marx's Method in 'Capital'; A Reexamination*, Atlantic Highlands, NJ: Humanities Press.

Murray, P. (2002), 'The Illusion of the Economic: The Trinity Formula and the "Religion of Everyday Life"', in M. Campbell and G. Reuten (eds), pp.246–72.

Reuten, G. (1998), 'The Status of Marx's Reproduction Schemes', in C.J. Arthur and G. Reuten (eds), pp.187–229.

Reuten, G. (2002), 'The Rate of Profit Cycle and the Opposition Between Managerial and Finance Capital', in M. Campbell and G. Reuten (eds), pp.174–211.

Smith, T. (1998), 'The Capital/Consumer Relation in Lean Production', in C.J. Arthur and G. Reuten (eds), pp.67–94.

Symposium on Brenner and the World Crisis (1999); Part 1, by A. Callinicos, G. Carchedi, S. Clarke, G. Duménil and D. Lévy, C. Harman, D. Laibman, M. Lebowitz, F. Moseley, M. Smith, E.M. Wood (in *Historical Materialism*, **4**, pp 3–179); Part 2, by W. Bonefeld, A. Freeman, M. Husson, A. Shaikh, T. Smith, R. Walker, J. Weeks (in *Historical Materialism*, **5**, pp 3–230).

Marxian Macroeconomics: Some Key Relationships

This entry sets out some key aspects of a Marxian approach to the macro-economics of capitalist economies. The account here is often simplifying, with no intention to present a model; the relations presented are rather general conceptual schemes for a model. The focus is on four aspects that differentiate the Marxian approach from other treatments: its account of production (section B); its 'disequilibrium' view (section C); its account of investment in relation to finance (section F); and its emphasis on the importance of the rate of profit (section G). Hence the casual account of, for example, government and consumption (section D and section E), or the absence of international relations, docs not imply that these play no role in Marxian theory. Note further that, on account of brevity, the presentation below may deviate in some details from usual Marxian presentations.

A Institutional conditions: property and labour market

One main institution characterizing capitalism is that workers do not own the means of production they work with, but that these are instead owned by capitalists firms. A counterpart of this that a market exists where workers offer their labour for sale to the owners of means of production or their managers. In what follows, it is assumed for simplicity that all firms have a corporate structure and that all finance operates via banks (thus banks are the locus of the finance 'market').

The existing macroeconomic stock of means of production (**K**), as owned by business corporations, is financed by the existing stock of share capital (**S**), retained profits (reserves, **Þ**), bank credit (**B**), and other loans (obligations, **O**) – all, including **K**, in monetary form.

$$\mathbf{K} = \mathbf{S} + \mathbf{Þ} + \mathbf{B} + \mathbf{O}. \tag{1}$$
[balance identity]

Throughout, all stock variables (in bold) are measured at the beginning of the year (flows into stock during the year are not in bold). The implicit time reference for all flows is the year (t). The right-hand side of (1) is the aggregated 'passive' side of the balance sheet of corporations; on the left we have its 'active' side (with trade credit cancelling out, and with a liquidity component being neglected – or **B** is net credit to business corporations). Although any changes in **K** are conditioned on changes in the stock of finance (the right-hand side of 1) the latter are not the impetus to the former.

We have a going technique of production $\langle\!\langle K/L \rangle\!\rangle$, which, given **K**, determines the employment of labour L (measured in labour years):

$$K/L \| \ L = \mathbf{K}/\langle\!\langle K/L \rangle\!\rangle. \tag{2}$$
[accounting device]

The money wage rate (w, per labour year) depends on (a) custom and tradition in an economic region, itself the result of past struggle; (b) relative labour shortage/abundance, both structural and cyclical, and bargaining positions following from that; (c) legislation. We take the first and third factor to be autonomous (*), and measure the second by the rate of unemployment (U, the latter's effect operating within a bound ε):

$$w = w^* + U^\varepsilon, \qquad \text{[approximation]} \ (3)$$

$$U = (N^* - L)/N^*, \qquad \text{[definition]} \ (4).$$

where N^* is the available labour (determined by social–demographic factors, including demographic policy, such as import of labour). Henceforth all Greek superscripts are variables or parameters; Roman superscripts are indices (p, r, as indicated below).

B Production
In what follows a representation of production is introduced that looks like a particular 'production function'. It must be borne in mind that the con-

ceptualization (especially as to what are variables and as to how a 'technique' is defined) is different from orthodox meanings.

K is a *specific* stock of fixed and circulating means of production (again, measured in monetary terms: prices times quantities). The calculation of the part of it used up in a year (μ) is a complex accountancy device, determined by technical, economic–technical and economic–strategic factors. Although this applies most of all to the fixed part, μ is a weighted composite over all means of production. Circulating means of production are replaced during the year according to the turnover time of production. Thus μK can be treated as a flow, whence $\mu K/L$ is the flow counterpart of the technique of production, which is taken to be 'almost' fixed in the short run: $\langle\!\langle \mu K/L \rangle\!\rangle$. In other words we are within a particular state of technology – or within a technological trajectory – in which only small variations in $\mu K/L$ (say within a 5 per cent bound) can be profitably applied (that is, macroeconomically; micro variations may be larger). There is no blue book of techniques that can profitably be used – no substitution in the orthodox sense – for we are on a one-way trajectory. In its most simple form we can then present production (X^p), the gross product in monetary terms, as

$$\mu K/L \parallel X^p = \langle\!\langle \mu K/L \rangle\!\rangle L^\beta. \qquad [1 > \mu > 0; \beta > 1] \qquad (5)$$
$$[\text{approximation}]$$

L is the economic scale counterpart of **K** (eqn 2). Within fairly narrow limits β is a *variable*. On the right-hand side of (5) we have the predetermined means of production per labourer ($\mu K/L$); this should be envisaged as the production plant when workers have just entered its gate, without, yet, having worked. In the actual labour process, labour works up the means of production to something qualitatively different. This qualitative transformation is one aspect of labour's power. The other aspect is the quantity of transformation. Beta (β) is the 'parameter' of transformation: the *power of labour* in both these aspects. In general, the power of labour faces physical, social and technical constraints; hence it is a variable within a bound (moreover, it is not easily comparable between technologies – a bound of β is attached to each major technology).

Whereas $\mu K/L$ is shorthand for the technology or the *possible production*, the power of labour determines how much output is actually produced. In fact this is *the* big economic leap. Behind it is the wider *subsumption of labour* to capitalist relations of production, which is an ideological complex of degree of acceptance of, or resistance to, capitalist norms – monetary, managerial and technical, all directed to the profit making of corporations – against the threat of unemployment.

For the purposes of this entry, we take the rate of unemployment (U) as a simple measure for the bounded variation (^{u}) in the power of labour.

$$\beta^* \text{ at } \langle\!\langle \mu K/L \rangle\!\rangle \| \ \beta = \beta^* + U^u. \tag{6}$$
[approximation]

In sum, referring back to (5), within a macroeconomic state of technology the K/L proportions in $\mu K/L$ cannot be varied at will: a labourer (or rather a group of labourers) cannot 'possibly' work up any amount of means of production; relatively small variations, though, are possible. The same boundedness applies to the power of labour. (Neither the operator of a production line nor the supermarket cashier can operate two lines at the same time, though within a technological trajectory the line can be speeded up both technically and organizationally. In fact we thus have some approximation in (5). Although the fixed part of μK is indeed fixed, an increase in β might require more circulating means of production, or would imply an increase in turnover time. In a more complicated account we would have the circulating part as a function of β.) The key point of this vision about production is that capital investment and technology do not fix production, but that, at each level of investment, production varies with the actual power of labour as determined by labour's subsumption to capitalist relations.

Of course the physical construction of means of production (**K** and μK in monetary terms) with which the process starts (eqn 1), is itself a product of previous labour (and nature). Equally, the technology is a product of previous subsumed labour.

At the end of the production period, with X^p finalized, one can in principle make the balance sheet operation of

$$R^p = X^p - (\mu K + wL), \tag{7}$$
[accounting identity]

where R^p are produced profits and μK and wL are costs. Both R^p and X^p are 'ideal', not yet realized, values – in fact circulating stocks. A maximum R^p is the purpose of the production process in representation (5).

C Realization: categories

In most of Marxian economics, a degree of *overproduction* with respect to realization is seen to be endemic to the capitalist economy. Competition presupposes overproduction – competitive pressure is only experienced when there is overproduction. Here we bracket cyclical implications of overproduction and proceed by assuming a state of the economy at a realization ratio near to its current structural value ($\ddot{o}$). Thus, in general, the realized production (X^r), or sales, is some fraction of X^p:

$$X^r = \ddot{o} X^p \quad [\ddot{o} < 1] \tag{8}$$
[postulated definition]

The categories of realization are the same as the conventional expenditure categories:

$$X^r = C_W + C_R + G + \mu K + \Delta K, \tag{9}$$
[balance identity]

with C_W and C_R consumption out of wages and profits, G government expenditure and μK and ΔK replacement and net investment. In what follows we will expand on the investment function only and keep the other categories as simple as possible.

Given realization we will get as the outcome for realized macro profits (R^r):

$$R^r = X^r - (\mu K + wL). \tag{10}$$
[accounting identity]

D Distribution of profits: financiers and government

Analogous to representation (1), profits are distributed into interest to banks (I_B), interests to holders of bonds ('obligations', I_o), dividends (D), retained profits ($\flat$) as well as taxes (T). (Hence of these, only $\flat$ is a direct flow to the stock $\flat$.)

$$D + \flat + I_B + I_o + T = R^r \tag{11}$$
[accounting identity]

In Marxian theory, this view of the matter (including a right to left determination in 11) is crucial. None of the left-hand side categories are 'costs'; they are indeed the categories into which realized profits (or total 'surplus value') are distributed.

For simplicity of presentation, a single tax (T) on profits is assumed (that is, no after distribution taxes).

$$T = tR^r. \tag{12}$$
[simplifying assumption]

Hence we have for realized net of tax profits:

$$R^{rN} = R^r - T. \qquad \text{[definition] (13)}$$

Government spending includes expenditures on the legal system, infra-structural institutions, 'social wages' such as health care as well as unemployment benefits. For simplicity, these are all taken to be autonomous (G^*). The government budget is taken to be balanced. (This should not give the impression that more detailed and complicated accounts of these issues are of no concern to Marxian economists. The presentation here is a matter of choice within limited space.)

$$G = G^* = T. \qquad (14)$$
$$\text{[simplifying assumption]}$$

E Consumption
Workers consume a fraction c out of wages:

$$C_W = cW = cwL. \qquad \text{[approximation] (15)}$$

Capitalists consume a fraction ç of anticipated after tax profits:

$$C_R = çR^{rN}. \qquad \text{[approximation] (16)}$$

The consumption out of distributed interest (I_o) and dividends (D) needs no explication. Interests to banks accrue in part to their creditors and in part to the bankers (see below), each consuming the same fraction. For the retained profits this consumption is the part accruing to the management via bonuses and so on.

F Accumulation of capital, finance and banks
Substituting (10) and (14)–(16) into (13) we have as an intermediate result:

$$R^{rN} = -(1-c)W + C_R + \Delta K. \qquad \text{[implication] (13a)}$$

Here we see a variant of Kalecki's dictum, 'capitalists earn what they spend': crucially, the determination of realized profits by the accumulation of capital itself.

The accumulation of capital is equal to the investment ΔK, which again is equal to, or accomplished through, its finance. In general there are two components of finance: internal (that is, retained profits, þ) and external.

As a core approximation we reduce the latter to bank credit (*B*). Each flow adds to the stocks of Þ and **B** (cf. eqn 1). Banks then operate as intermediary for corporate bonds and additional share capital. We assume that banks are the leading party in this respect, and may, at their discretion, substitute part of their credit to corporations for additional share capital or bonds: λ**B**=Δ**S**+Δ**O** (note that this simply 'shortens' both sides of the bank's balance sheet). Thus we have:

$$\Delta K = \Delta K_{Þ} + \Delta K_{B}. \tag{17}$$
[stylizing approximation]

Bank credit is a simple matter – though crucial. However, macroeconomically Þ involves a double move: expenditure (a ΔK fraction)=realization (Þ accumulated)=its finance. (And this is how one finds it microeconomically on the balance sheet of corporations: an equivalent on the active side and the passive side of the balance sheet; note that empirically the retained profits constitute the bulk of finance – in major capitalist countries, 69 to 97 per cent over the 1970–89 period; cf. Glyn, 1997, quoting Corbett and Jenkinson. But, again, this magnitude does not make bank credit less crucial; it is required to set accumulation of capital into motion.)

Investment is determined by four elements: (a) the realization ratio in the previous year ö; (b) the change in the rate of profit in the previous year Δr (its precise definition is amplified upon in section G); (c) the accumulated retained profits of the previous year Þ; (d) banks' accommodation of finance demanded.

$$\Delta K_{Þ} = \left[(1 + \ddot{o}_{t-1} - \underline{\ddot{o}}) + \chi(r_{t-1} - r_{t-2}) \right] \left[(1 - \varsigma)Þ_{t-1} \right], \tag{18}$$
[approximation]

where $\underline{\ddot{o}}$ is the current structural ratio of realization (indicating structural overproduction or mismatch), such as 0.85. If the going $\ddot{o}_{t-1}$ is above that, this effects increasing growth of $K_{Þ}$, and vice versa. The second determinant is the change in the rate of profit (with χ as parameter), which may of course be negative in a particular phase of the cycle. Accumulation might then still be positive ($\Delta K_{Þ} > 0$) depending on the realization effect. (Note that, in times of recession, part of the stock of retained profits (Þ) may be liquidated.)

Economic growth, and a growth of means of production in particular (ΔK), requires its accommodation by the banking system (part of the matter is that the quantity of money/credit must increase if price deflation and its depressing effects are to be avoided). In the current presentation this requirement operates solely directly, that is via the banks' finance of net investment. We suppose that interest (I) and dividends (D), after consuming a share ς out of it, are fed into the banking system, so that the banking system is full intermediary. All of savings out of wages, $(1-c)W$, are also fed into the banking system. Hence we have:

$$\Delta K_B = \{(1 + \ddot{o}_{t-1} - \ddot{o}) + \psi(r_{t-1} - r_{t-2}) + (\varphi r_{t-1})\} \tag{19}$$

$$[(1-\varsigma)(I_o + I_B + D)_{t-1} + (1-c)W_{t-1}]. \quad \text{[approximation]}$$

Here the part in curly brackets acts as the credit multiplier. For the bank-financed part of accumulation (ΔK_B) we have similar determinants as in (18), plus the level of the rate of profit, r_{t-1}, (with ψ and φ as parameters). Implicitly this last factor, r_{t-1}, compares with the banks' going rate of interest. Note that in a particular phase of the cycle the rate of profit might be decreasing, but still sufficiently large to service the debts; and even if r is smaller than the rate of interest (which is relevant for business corporations) the absolute R^{rN} (for which $\ddot{o}$ is an indicator) might still be sufficient to pay interests (which is relevant for banks). (Given ςR^{rN}, the banks' decision to provide less credit than the part in square brackets in (19), means in fact 'hoarding'. Conversely, in a more complicated presentation including the general price level, we have the credit multiplier as major lever of the rate of inflation – a De Brunhoff, 1976, type of approach, as in Reuten and Williams, 1989, chs 2 and 5.)

Note finally that in (19) we have 'new' savings (out of I_o, I_B, D, W) as a determinant. Each year we have the following flow addition to the banks' saving accounts: $(1-\varsigma)(I_o + D) + (1-c)W$. We also have each year the flow $(1-\varsigma)I_B$. It has two destinations: first, from it banks pay interest to the stock of their savings accounts (of which $1-\varsigma$ remains); second, the remaining part adds to the bank reserves (their capital). This remaining part is in fact the interest sum accruing to the sum of the 'credit multiplied' in the past.

With the accumulation of capital (ΔK), then, the realized profits R^r (10) or R^{rN} (13) are determined. The conventional *ex post* magnitudes of value added and net income result as outcomes:

$$Y = X^r - \mu K, \tag{20}$$
[definition of value added]

$$Y = W + R^r. \tag{20a}$$
[definition of net income]

G Profit and the rate of profit

The after-tax profit rate (r) is defined as

$$r = R^{rN}/\mathbf{K}, \qquad \text{[definition] (21)}$$

where $\mathbf{K}$ is the value of capital accumulated (taken to be equal to the stock of means of production; a liquidity component is neglected and the formulation presupposes that wages are paid out of revenue). Substituting (12), (13), (10), (8) and (5) into (21) we have

$$r = \frac{\{1 - t\}\ \{[\ddot{o}\ \langle\!\langle \mu K/L \rangle\!\rangle\ L^\beta] - [\mu K + wL]\}}{\mathbf{K}} \qquad \begin{array}{c}(21a)\\ \text{[implication]}\end{array}$$

which is the after-tax $(1-t)$, realized ($\ddot{o}$) production minus the costs of production, divided by capital invested. $\mathbf{K}$ and L measure the scale of the economy. Note again that, in the short run, $\langle\!\langle \mu K/L \rangle\!\rangle$ is fixed within narrow bounds, that β is a bounded variable and that t and $\ddot{o}$ are also variables; μ is in fact an efficiency factor.

In Marxian economics the rate of profit is the key dynamic factor. It is the thermometer, so to speak, of the capitalist system. On the one hand, *as result*, it is the concentration of many determinants: of the wage contract (w), of production (K/L and β), of realization and finance (summarized in $\ddot{o}$) and of taxation (t). On the other hand it is a major *prospective* determinant: of the accumulation of capital through both retained profits and bank credit to accommodate further accumulation. ΔK in turn is the major determinant of the growth of production and income (that is, *ceteris paribus*, K/L, β and $\ddot{o}$).

H A short-run story

The presentation above is too abbreviated and simplified to make rigorous statements. However, in the scarce model aspects of the presentation there is nevertheless some story to tell. (Let g_x be the growth rate of x.) At $g_K < g_{N*}$ unemployment $U\uparrow$; $w\uparrow$ dampens or we even have $w\downarrow$; at the same time the power of labour moves towards the upper bound, $\beta\uparrow$; $\rightarrow X^p\uparrow$ and $R^p\uparrow$; $\rightarrow$ the realization gap $\ddot{o}\uparrow$ (its degree depending also on the implicit unemployment benefits). Initially, ΔK keeps on increasing, first, because R^r is not affected (see 13a) and, second, owing to the accumulation lag (see 18, 19) – implicitly a micro optimism due to $\beta\uparrow$ and w dampening. Next, however, the gap increasingly works onto ΔK via ($\ddot{o}-\underline{\ddot{o}}$) and r (thus *on* R^r but not via R^r). Thus, so far, the initial unemployment rise is aggravated. However, when β reaches the maximum of its bound and w its minimum, the gap lessens.

At $g_K > g_{N*}$ unemployment $U\downarrow$; $\to w\uparrow$ and $\beta\downarrow$ towards the lower bound; $\to X^p\downarrow$ and $R^r\downarrow$; $\to ö\downarrow$; again the effect on ΔK is lagged. Again the initial condition $(U\downarrow)$ is reinforced. However, since in comparison with the previous case there are different limits on $w\uparrow$ and $\beta\downarrow$, it is this time especially the decreasing rate of profit that dampens ΔK.

Behind this aborted story are general Marxian conclusions about the functioning of the capitalist economy, namely that it is inherently a disequilibrium system (without, however, exploding), that it leaves workers insecure about their employment and income, and that it moves beyond their will: capitalist profit motives decide what happens generally, and at the point of production, where workers spend their daily life, specifically.

I Some long-run considerations

The 'short run' is a notion that is variously interpreted. Here it is in fact defined by the technological trajectory, or the boundedness of $\mu K/L$ and β. For some 'long-run' considerations we first define the before-tax share of profits in value added,

$$\ddot{e} = R/Y = R/(X - \mu K).\qquad\text{[definition] (22)}$$

Dividing through the right-hand side of (21a) by L and substituting $\ddot{e}$ we have:

$$r = \frac{\{1 - t\}\ \{\langle\!\langle\mu K/L\rangle\!\rangle(öL^{\beta-1} - 1)\ddot{e}\}}{K/L} \qquad\begin{array}{l}(21b)\\ \text{[implication]}\end{array}$$

which is the after-tax profit share in the realized net product per worker (or the after-tax realized net product per worker, minus the wage rate) divided by the capital per worker.

Thus the rate of profit depends on (1) the power of labour (L^β) in relation to (2) the technique of production ($\mu K/L$); (3) the capital–labour distribution of income (measured by w or $\ddot{e}$); (4) the rate of realization (ö); and (5) the tax rate (t). In the long run, all these are variables. Can we say something about their development over time?

One long-standing strand within Marxism (revived around 1970 through the work of Mattick, Yaffe and, in a way, through Fine and Harris, 1979) focuses on the K/L ratio, L^β and $\ddot{e}$, freezing so to speak t and ö (in fact their vantage point is the rate of 'produced profit' $r^P = R^P/K$, which comes down to (21a) or (21 b) with $t=0$ and ö$=1$). Within this strand it is posited, first, that K/L (and $\mu K/L$) increase in the long run. This may seem plausible. Second, it is posited (often implicitly) that the power of labour L^β cannot indefinitely keep pace with the increase in the ratio of K/L (or

$\mu K/L$). The intuitive idea behind this is that labour cannot indefinitely work up more means of production at the same pace. Thus increases in the latter ratio are offset by decreases in the power of labour. Then, with a constant share of labour in net product ($\ddot{e}$ constant), the rate of profit would fall.

Although this idea makes sense *within* a state of technology (a technological trajectory), it does not for inter-technology states. So-called 'long wave theory' (Mandel, 1995) applies this idea to successions of states of technology, each reaching an end with minimal profit rates. Then, after a cataclystic period, a new technological trajectory sets in a new long upswing. (In the past some trajectories have taken up to 50 years to 'mature'; it would seem, though, that this is contingent.)

Conversely, a second main strand (cf. Sweezy, 1942; Baran and Sweezy, 1966), focuses on ö, $\ddot{e}$ and t, 'freezing' technology (though it should be added that their time focus seems shorter than that of the previous strand). The Baran and Sweezy variant argues that over time the intensity of labour (something like L^β) tends to increase, with the growth of the wage rate being pushed down (at least lagging behind productivity rise) because of labour abundance. This would cause structural realization problems. Countering the latter, however, are so-called 'unproductive expenditures' on the part either of business corporations or of government. Unproductive expenditures are those that absorb capacity but themselves generate no production capacity-increasing effect; major ones, according to Baran and Sweezy, are the complex of advertisement and packing for business, and military expenditures for government.

Although these strands have different theoretical and empirical focuses, they are in principle not incompatible. A particular combination can be found in Moseley (1991; 1997); it embarks from the first approach but takes elements from the second into account. Another (Reuten and Williams, 1989) argues for a synthetical approach. Still other long-run approaches (variously indicated as 'phases', 'regimes' or 'social structure' of accumulation) combine the above-mentioned factors with long-run institutional changes, including international dimensions; Albritton *et al.* (2001) provides a good overview of these. After a reading of Laibman (1997) as a brief introduction to Marxian macroeconomics, the Albritton collection offers a good idea of what is going on within this approach to the study of capitalist economies.

GEERT REUTEN

See also:

Business Cycles: Marxian Approach; Marxian Macroeconomics: An Overview.

Bibliography

Albritton, R., M. Itoh, R. Westra and A. Zuege (eds) (2001), *Phases of Capitalist Development: Booms, Crises and Globalizations*, Basingstoke/New York: Palgrave.
Baran, P. and P. Sweezy (1966), *Monopoly Capital*, Harmondsworth: Penguin.
Brunhoff, S. de ([1976] 1978), *État et Capital*, Engl. tr. *The State, Capital and Economic Policy*, London: Pluto Press.
Fine, B. and L. Harris (1979), *Rereading Capital*, London: Macmillan.
Glyn, A. (1997), 'Does Aggregate Profitability Really Matter?', *Cambridge Journal of Economics*, **21**, pp. 593–619.
Laibman, D. (1997), *Capitalist Macrodynamics: A Systematic Introduction*, London: Macmillan.
Mandel, E. (1995), *Long Waves of Capitalist Development: A Marxist Interpretation* (revised edn; 1st edn. 1980), London: Verso.
Moseley, F. (1991), *The Falling Rate of Profit in the Postwar United States Economy*, London: Macmillan.
Moseley, F. (1997), 'The Rate of Profit and the Future of Capitalism', *Review of Radical Political Economics*, **29**, pp. 23–41
Reuten, G. and M. Williams (1989), *Value-form and the State: The Tendencies of Accumulation and the Determination of Economic Policy in Capitalist Society*, London/New York: Routledge.
Sweezy, P.A. (1942), *The Theory of Capitalist Development*, New York/London: Modern Reader Paperbacks.

Mayer, Thomas

Thomas Mayer (b.1927, Vienna, Austria) obtained his BA from Queens College, New York in 1948, and his MA (1949) and PhD (1953) from Columbia University. His main past posts have included Visiting Assistant Professor at the University of West Virginia, 1953–4; Assistant Professor at Notre Dame University, 1954–6); Assistant and then Associate Professor at Michigan State University, 1956–61; Visiting Associate Professor at the University of California, Berkeley, 1961–2; and Professor at the University of California, Davis, 1962–93. Since 1993 he has been Professor, Emeritus, at the University of California, Davis. He is best known for his work on the lags of monetary policy; the Keynesian–monetarist debate; and the methodology of economics. Among his best known books are *The Structure of Monetarism* (with others) (W.W. Norton, 1978); *Monetarism and Macroeconomic Policy* (Edward Elgar, 1990); *Truth versus Precision in Economics* (Edward Elgar, 1993); and *Doing Economic Research: Essays on the Applied Methodology of Economics* (Edward Elgar, 1995). His most widely read articles include 'Tests of the Relative Importance of Autonomous Expenditure and Money' (co-authored with M. De Prano) (*American Economic Review*, **55**, September 1965); 'The Structure of Monetarism' (*Kredit und Kapital*, 1975); and 'David Hume and Monetarism' (*Quarterly Journal of Economics*, **95**, August 1980).

See also:
Monetarism.

Meade, James E. (1907–95)

James Meade (b.1907, Swanage, Dorset, England) obtained his BA (1930) by incorporation and MA (1957) from the University of Cambridge, and his BA (1930) and MA (1933) from the University of Oxford. His main posts included Fellow of Hertford College, Oxford, 1930–37; Member of the Economics Section of the League of Nations, 1938–40; Economics Assistant (1940–45) and Director (1946–7) to the Economic Section of the UK Cabinet Office; Professor of Commerce at the London School of Economics, 1947–57; Professorial Fellow (1959–69) and Nuffield Research Fellow (1969–74) at Christ's College, Cambridge; and Professor of Political Economy at the University of Cambridge, 1957–68. He was president of the Royal Economic Society from 1964 to 1966, and was awarded (with B. Ohlin) the Nobel Prize in Economics in 1977 for his work on international trade. He is best known for his influential work on 'double-entry' national income accounts (with R. Stone); international economics, in particular the relationship between trade, protection and welfare; and economic policy, including analysing the necessary conditions for achieving internal and external balance. Among his best known books are *An Introduction to Economic Analysis and Policy* (Oxford University Press, 1936); *National Income and Expenditure* (co-authored with R. Stone) (Oxford University Press, 1944); *The Theory of International Economic Policy, Volume One: The Balance of Payments; Volume Two: Trade and Welfare* (Oxford University Press, 1951, 1955); *A Geometry of International Trade* (George Allen & Unwin, 1952); *The Theory of Customs Unions* (North-Holland, 1955); *A Neo-Classical Theory of Economic Growth* (George Allen & Unwin, 1961); and *Principles of Political Economy, Volume One: The Stationary Economy; Volume Two: The Growing Economy; Volume Three: The Controlled Economy; Volume Four: The Just Economy* (George Allen & Unwin, 1965, 1968, 1971, 1976).

See also:
Royal Economic Society; Nobel Prize in Economics.

Meltzer, Allan H.

Allan Meltzer (b.1928, Boston, Massachusetts, USA) obtained his BA from Duke University in 1948, and his MA (1955) and PhD (1958) from the University of California, Los Angeles. His main past posts have included Lecturer at the Wharton School, University of Pennsylvania, 1956–7; Assistant Professor (1957–61) and Associate Professor (1961–4) at the Graduate School of Industry and Administration, Carnegie Institute of Technology; Ford Foundation Visiting Professor at the University of Chicago, 1961–5; and Professor at the Carnegie Institute of Technology, 1964–80. Since 1980 he has been Professor of Political Economy and Public Policy at Carnegie-Mellon University. He is best known for his work on monetary theory and policy, in particular strongly criticizing discretionary monetary policy and advocating rules; and contributions to monetarism. Among his best known books are *An Analysis of Federal Reserve Monetary Policymaking* (co-authored with K. Brunner) (US Government Printing Office, 1964); *Keynes's Monetary Theory: A Different Interpretation* (Cambridge University Press, 1988); and *Money and the Economy: Issues in Monetary Analysis* (Cambridge University Press, 1993). His most widely read articles include: 'The Behaviour of the French Money Supply, 1938–1954' (*Journal of Political Economy*, **67**, June 1959); 'The Demand for Money: The Evidence from Time Series' (*Journal of Political Economy*, **71**, June 1963); 'Monetary and Other Explanations of the Start of the Great Depression' (*Journal of Monetary Economics*, **2**, November 1976) and 'Money and Credit in the Monetary Transmission Process' (*American Economic Review*, **78**, May 1988).

See also:

Monetarism.

Menu Costs

The significance of menu costs in economic analysis has changed considerably in the last two decades. In the inflationary 1970s, menu costs were among the adverse effects of inflation to which monetarists drew particular attention as one reason for seeking to eliminate inflation even at the cost of rising unemployment. The current importance of menu costs is much wider, particularly for new Keynesian macroeconomists, who see menu costs, admittedly small in themselves, as a possible cause of much larger economic phenomena, namely recessions and the increases in unemployment they bring with them.

For many years economists were interested in menu costs as one of the costs of inflation. As such they have two things in common with shoe leather costs: they are incurred even if inflation is perfectly anticipated and they have an intuitive appeal based on the behaviour of economic agents under hyperinflation. As part of the inflationary process, economic agents change nominal prices. In doing so they employ scarce resources and thereby incur costs. For example, it is known that during hyperinflation restaurateurs have sometimes raised the prices on the menu during the course of the day. No more meals are being produced but costs have risen because labour, ink and paper are used up in revising the menu. The same is true of catalogues, price tags, vending machines and so on. Menu costs also include the costs of gathering information about market conditions, when nominal price changes may or may not reflect changing relative scarcities, and management time devoted to making decisions about whether or not to change nominal prices. Nevertheless, Smithin (1990) expressed a widely held sceptical view of the importance of the menu costs of inflation in commenting that 'it is hard to see how these costs could really be all that significant' (p. 144).

Minford and Hilliard (1978) offer a reason for taking the menu costs of inflation more seriously. There is one price, the price of labour, which is not so easily revised. Adjusting nominal wage rates is not like rewriting a menu; a potentially lengthy and acrimonious process of negotiation is involved and output might be lost through industrial action. In attempting to measure the non-monetary or menu costs of moderate inflation, Minford and Hilliard calculated the number of days lost because of wage disputes as a proportion of total days worked in order to estimate the costs of wage negotiations. They also analysed data from a representative manufacturing firm to work out the salary costs of those employees who were responsible for publishing price rises and the costs of printing new price lists. The menu costs of known inflation are the sum of the costs of adjusting wages and the costs of changing prices. Bootle's (1981) verdict was that 'these estimated losses, although not insignificant, are hardly substantial and . . . increase much less than proportionately with the level of inflation' (p. 38).

Furthermore, as with shoe leather costs, there are reasons for believing that even this low estimate of menu costs may exaggerate their importance. First, to the extent that inflation is anticipated, firms will choose the method of disseminating price information that minimizes the costs of changing prices. Under high inflation in Israel, for example, many supermarkets' coded goods trigger a computerized estimate of the latest prices at the checkout (Brown, 1984, pp. 124–5). Second, wage negotiations ostensibly concerned with adjusting nominal wage rates for price inflation may provide an arena for a struggle over the relative rewards of workers and shareholders, which would still have to be resolved if prices were stable.

More recent work on menu costs suggests that, even if such costs are small in themselves, they may have large effects. In the first place this approach may lead to a reappraisal of the significance of menu costs as costs of inflation (see Ball and Mankiw, 1994a). Reinterpreting menu costs in this way contributes to the explanation of nominal price rigidity and hence the non-neutrality of money; that is, the idea that changes in the money supply have effects on the 'real' economy of growth and employment. Menu cost models assume that firms operate in imperfectly competitive markets and are therefore able to exercise some discretion over prices. As price makers they may choose to delay a price rise in response to the acceleration in inflation initiated by the expansionary shock. Firms may be assumed to change nominal prices only at regular intervals or only when actual prices diverge too far from their optimal level – see Blanchard (1983), Blinder (1991), Ball and Mankiw (1994b). The costs of changing prices – the menu costs – do not warrant constant monitoring and instant revision. Consequently, the pattern of relative prices that prevailed before the monetary shock may be disturbed. Relative price variability may therefore be the outcome of the inflationary process itself, even when the inflation is perfectly anticipated (Briault, 1995, p. 36). If so, menu costs reinforce the 'inflationary noise' argument that inflation leads to a misallocation of resources. An increase in the variability of relative prices undermines the role of price signals in disseminating information about relative scarcities. The implication is that the optimal rate of inflation is zero.

Recent studies of menu costs are of wider significance, seeing them as part of the process causing recessions. This literature is associated with new Keynesian macroeconomists, who have sought to use menu costs to rectify one of the most damaging perceived weaknesses of traditional Keynesianism, namely its lack of sound microeconomic foundations (see Akerlof and Yellen, 1985; Mankiw, 1985; Rotemberg, 1987). The problem is that there is no justification within the rational optimizing framework of neoclassical microeconomics for the price and wage stickiness that Keynesians had relied upon to explain the slowness of labour market adjustment to equilibrium in the face of excess labour supply. Menu costs offer a route by which decisions to leave prices and wages unchanged that are rational for each individual firm may have aggregate effects that are far from optimal for society as a whole. The core intuition is that, even if menu costs are small, it may be optimal for the firm to incur no such costs at all by leaving prices and wages unchanged, making quantity adjustments to output and employment instead.

Menu cost models share the assumption of imperfect competition, which affords firms some discretion over the prices they charge and opens up the possibility of a gap between actual and optimal prices at least in the short run. In the context of explaining recessions, the firm faces the problem of how to respond to a leftwards shift of its demand curve. The assumption of imperfectly competitive markets is usually justified on the grounds of realism and tends to be associated with the assumption of constant marginal costs (MC) on the same grounds. Other things being equal, these circumstances will lead to a fall in profits because, in the absence of a price reduction in response to the decline in demand, sales will fall. A price reduction will be optimal only if the increase in profits from higher sales is greater than the costs of making the adjustment, that is, the menu costs entailed by the cut in price. Whether the increase in profits is larger or smaller than the menu costs is an empirical question. After the fall in demand, the decline in profits from lost sales is less under the assumption of constant MC than it would have been with the rising MC curve of perfect competition. There is, therefore, a lower incentive to reduce price and, consequently, even small menu costs will be sufficient to persuade the firm to leave prices unchanged.

If all firms in the sector affected by the initial fall in demand behave in the same way, this will transmit it throughout the wider economy. The existence of small menu costs is therefore sufficient to magnify a sectoral fall in demand into a deficiency of aggregate demand. This has been interpreted as an aggregate demand externality, menu costs causing a divergence between the optimal decision for the individual firm and the optimal outcome for society as a whole (Blanchard and Kiyotaki, 1987). An economy where firms in imperfectly competitive markets face menu costs will not be self-adjusting. In this way the new Keynesians have sought to reinstate the grounds for the traditional Keynesian policy prescription of expansionary fiscal or monetary policy to make good a deficiency of aggregate demand. However, Blinder *et al.* (1998), who attempted to identify the reasons for price stickiness, found that menu costs are not among the most important reasons for the failure of firms to adjust nominal prices in the face of a decline in demand.

GRAHAM DAWSON

See also:

Inflation: Costs of; New Keynesian Economics; Shoe Leather Costs.

Bibliography

Akerlof, G.A. and J.L. Yellen (1985), 'A Near-Rational Model of the Business Cycle, with Wage and Price Inertia', *Quarterly Journal of Economics*, **100**, Supplement, pp. 823–38.

Ball, L. and N.G. Mankiw (1994a), 'A Sticky-Price Manifesto', *Carnegie-Rochester Series on Public Policy*, **41**, December, pp. 127–51.

Ball, L. and N.G. Mankiw (1994b), 'Asymmetric Price Adjustment and Economic Fluctuations', *Economic Journal*, **104**, March, pp. 247–61.

Blanchard, O.J. (1983), 'Price Asynchronisation and Price Inertia', in R. Dornbusch and M. Simonsen (eds), *Inflation, Debt and Indexation*, Cambridge, MA: MIT Press.

Blanchard, O.J. and N. Kiyotaki (1987), 'Monopolistic Competition and the Effects of Aggregate Demand', *American Economic Review*, **77**, September, pp. 647–66.

Blinder, A.S. (1991), 'Why are Prices Sticky? Preliminary Results from an Interview Study', *American Economic Review*, **81**, May, pp. 89–100.

Blinder, A.S., E. Canetti, D. Lebow and J. Rudd (1998), *Asking About Prices: A New Approach to Understanding Price Stickiness*, New York: Russell Sage Foundation.

Bootle, R. (1981), 'How Important is it to Defeat Inflation? The Evidence', *Three Banks Review*, **132**, pp. 23–47.

Briault, C. (1995), 'The Costs of Inflation', *Bank of England Quarterly Bulletin*, February, pp. 33–45.

Brown, C.V. (1984), *Unemployment and Inflation*, Oxford: Basil Blackwell.

Mankiw, N.G. (1985), 'Small Menu Costs and Large Business Cycles: A Macroeconomic Model of Monopoly', *Quarterly Journal of Economics*, **100**, May, pp. 529–39.

Mankiw, N.G. (1990), 'A Quick Refresher Course in Macroeconomics', *Journal of Economic Literature*, **XXVIII**, December, pp. 1645–60.

Minford, A.P.L. and G.W. Hilliard (1978), 'The Costs of Variable Inflation', in M. Artis and A.R. Nobay (eds), *Contemporary Economic Analysis*, London: Croom Helm.

Rotemberg, J.J. (1987), 'The New Keynesian Microfoundations', *NBER Macroeconomics Annual*, pp. 69–104.

Smithin, J.N. (1990), *Macroeconomics After Thatcher and Reagan*, Aldershot, UK and Brookfield, US: Edward Elgar.

Minsky, Hyman P. (1919–96)

Hyman Minsky (b.1919, Chicago, Illinois, USA) obtained his BS from the University of Chicago in 1941 and his MA (1947) and PhD (1954) from Harvard University. His main posts included Assistant Professor at Brown University, 1949–57; Associate Professor at the University of California, Berkeley, 1957–65; and Professor of Economics (1965–90) and Professor, Emeritus (1990–96) at Washington University of St. Louis. He is best known for work on financial instability; and his contributions to the Post Keynesian school of economics. Among his best known books are *John Maynard Keynes* (Columbia University Press, 1975); *Can 'It' Happen Again? Essays on Instability and Finance* (M.E. Sharpe, 1982); and *Stabilizing an Unstable Economy* (Yale University Press, 1986). His most widely read articles include 'The Financial Instability Hypothesis: A Restatement' (*Thames Papers in Political Economy*, Autumn 1978); 'Money, Financial Markets and the Coherence of a Market Economy' (*Journal of Post Keynesian Economics*, **3**, Fall 1980); and 'The Financial Instability Hypothesis: Capitalist Processes and the Behaviour of the Economy', in C.P. Kindleberger and J.-P. Laffargue (eds), *Financial Crises: Theory, History and Policy* (Cambridge University Press, 1982).

See also:

Financial Instability; Post Keynesian Economics.

Mismatch Unemployment

See:
Structural Unemployment.

Mitchell, Wesley C. (1874–1948)

Wesley Mitchell (b.1874, Rushville, Illinois, USA) obtained his BA (1896) and PhD (1899) from the University of Chicago. His main posts included Professor at the University of California, 1903–13; Professor at Columbia University, 1913–19, 1922–44; and Director of the New School of Social Research, 1919–31. Between 1920 and 1945 he was Director of the National Bureau of Economic Research (NBER). He is best known for helping to found the NBER in 1920 and his pioneering work on business cycles. His best known books include *Business Cycles* (University of California Press, 1913); *Business Cycles: The Problem and Its Setting* (NBER, 1927); and *Measuring Business Cycles* (co-authored with A.F. Burns) (NBER, 1946).

See also:
National Bureau of Economic Research.

Modigliani, Franco

Franco Modigliani was born in Rome on 18 June 1918. At the age of 17 (two years younger than normal) he entered the University of Rome to study Law, where in his second year of study he won a national essay competition in economics on price controls. After receiving his degree in Law in 1939, and being strongly opposed to the Fascist regime of Mussolini, he emigrated at the start of World War II to the United States, where he obtained a scholarship to study economics at the New School for Social Research, New York City in the autumn of 1939. Between 1942 and 1944 he was an Instructor in Economics and Statistics at Bard College, Columbia University. In 1943, he returned to the New School for Social Research (from where he received his doctoral degree in 1944), first as a lecturer (1943–4) and then as Assistant Professor of Mathematical Economics and Econometrics (1946–8), before leaving New York to join the Cowles Commission as a Research Consultant (1949–54). In 1949, he joined the University of Illinois as an Associate Professor and subsequently became Professor of Economics (1950–52). Between 1952 and 1960 he was

Professor of Economics and Industrial Administration at Carnegie Institute of Technology (now Carnegie-Mellon University) and, after a brief spell at Northwestern University (1960–62) as Professor of Economics, moved in 1962 to Massachusetts Institute of Technology (MIT) as Professor of Economics and Finance, teaching at MIT until his retirement in 1988. He is currently Institute Professor, Emeritus, at MIT.

Between 1964 and 1972 he was a consultant to the Secretary to the Treasury of the USA and since 1966 has been a consultant to the Board of Governors of the Federal Reserve System. Since 1971 he has been a Senior Adviser to the Brookings Panel on Economic Activity. His many offices and honours have included president of the Econometric Society (1962), the American Economic Association (1976), the American Finance Association (1981) and honorary president of the International Economic Association (1983). In 1985, he was awarded the Nobel Prize in Economics in recognition of his work on 'the construction and development of the life cycle hypothesis of household saving and the formulation of the Modigliani–Miller theorems of the valuation of firms and of capital costs' (see Kouri, 1986; Merton, 1987; Modigliani, 1995).

While noted for the breadth and depth of his research output, which has manifested itself in the prodigious number of books and top-ranked journal articles he has had published, he is best known for his seminal contributions in three main areas, namely macroeconomic and monetary theory, the theory of saving, and the theory of finance. His published research output in macroeconomics and monetary theory began with his highly influential 1944 *Econometrica* article, 'Liquidity Preference and the Theory of Interest and Money'. This article which 'marked a milestone in the formal integration of money into the Keynesian system' (Blaug, 1998) is largely based on his doctoral dissertation. In the article, Modigliani argued that wage rigidity is the crucial hypothesis for explaining underemployment equilibrium in the Keynesian system and that, apart from the special case of the liquidity trap, the main weapon for stabilization policy is monetary policy, not fiscal policy. In a subsequent article, Modigliani (1963) refined his analysis, returning to address the issue of 'The Monetarist Controversy or, Should We Forsake Stabilisation Policies?' (Modigliani, 1977) in his 1976 Presidential Address to the American Economic Association. In addition to his theoretical contributions in this area he also sought to test the effects of policy changes on the economy. Working in collaboration with Albert Ando (University of Pennsylvania) in the mid-1960s, he designed and constructed an econometric model of the US economy for the Federal Reserve known as the FMP model (Federal Reserve–MIT–University of Pennsylvania model) to be used for forecasting and stabilization purposes. In helping to extend Keynesian economics,

Modigliani has consistently argued that a market economy '*needs* to be stabilized, *can* be stabilized, and therefore *should* be stabilized by appropriate monetary and fiscal policies' (Modigliani, 1977; see also Modigliani, 1988).

His research into the theory of saving began in the early 1950s, while at the University of Illinois, in collaboration with Richard Brumberg, then a graduate student at the university. Their work, which has come to be referred to as the 'life cycle hypothesis' of saving and consumption, was developed in two seminal papers (1954, 1980) which were published after both had left the University of Illinois. Although the second paper was completed before Richard Brumberg died prematurely in 1955, upset by the death of his friend, Modigliani did not look at the paper for a long time afterwards and it was not published until 1980. According to the life cycle hypothesis, an individual's current consumption depends on, and is some fraction of (depending on tastes and preferences), the present value of his or her lifetime resources, which are composed of the person's wealth and lifetime earnings (both current income and expected future income from employment). The theory assumes that an individual will maximize his or her utility by maintaining a stable or smooth pattern of consumption over their entire lifetime. A joint article with Albert Ando published in 1963 in the *American Economic Review* sought to test the hypothesis and examine its implications.

The third area of research for which Modigliani is best known is the theory of finance. In two joint articles, Modigliani and Merton Miller produced what has come to be known as the 'Modigliani–Miller theorems' of the modern theory of finance. In the first of these two papers, Modigliani and Miller (1958) showed that, in a competitive market with rational investors, ignoring the effects of taxes, the financial structure (debt–equity ratio) of a firm has no effect on its market value. In the second paper, Modigliani and Miller (1961) argued that dividend policy has no effect on the market value of a firm's shares. In other words, the market value of a firm's shares will be independent of its policy choice between paying dividends to shareholders or retaining earnings.

In addition to his influential contributions to these three areas (see the collection of papers gathered together by Abel, 1980) Modigliani has had numerous papers published on 'Monetary and Stabilisation Policies' and 'Savings, Deficits, Inflation and Financial Theory' (these have been gathered together by Johnson, 1989).

BRIAN SNOWDON
HOWARD R.VANE

See also:

American Economic Association; Cowles Commission; Econometric Society; Federal Reserve System; Keynesian Economics; Life Cycle Hypothesis; Liquidity Trap; Macroeconometric Models; Nobel Prize in Economics.

Bibliography

Abel, A. (ed.) (1980), *The Collected Papers of Franco Modigliani*, vol. 1, *Essays in Macroeconomics*; vol. 2, *The Life Cycle Hypothesis of Saving*; vol. 3, *The Theory of Finance and Other Essays*, Cambridge, MA: MIT Press.

Ando A. and F. Modigliani (1963), 'The "Life Cycle" Hypothesis of Saving: Aggregate Implications and Tests', *American Economic Review*, **53**, March, pp. 55–84.

Blaug, M. (1998), *Great Economists Since Keynes*, 2nd edn, Cheltenham, UK and Lyme, US: Edward Elgar.

Johnson, S. (ed.) (1989), *The Collected Papers of Franco Modigliani*, vol. 4, *Monetary and Stabilisation Policies*; vol. 5, *Savings, Deficits, Inflation and Financial Theory*, Cambridge, MA: MIT Press.

Kouri, P.J.K. (1986), 'Franco Modigliani's Contributions to Economics', *Scandinavian Journal of Economics*, **88**, pp. 311–34.

Merton, R.C. (1987), 'In Honour of Nobel Laureate, Franco Modigliani', *Journal of Economic Perspectives*, **1**, Fall, pp. 145–55.

Modigliani, F. (1944), 'Liquidity Preference and the Theory of Interest and Money', *Econometrica*, **12**, January, pp. 45–88.

Modigliani, F. (1963), 'The Monetary Mechanism and its Interaction with Real Phenomena', *Review of Economics and Statistics*, **45**, February, pp. 79–107.

Modigliani, F. (1977), 'The Monetarist Controversy or, Should We Forsake Stabilization Policies?', *American Economic Review*, **67**, March, pp. 1–19.

Modigliani, F. (1988), *The Debate Over Stabilization Policy*, Cambridge: Cambridge University Press.

Modigliani, F. (1995), 'Ruminations on my Professional Life', in W. Breit and R.W. Spencer (eds), *Lives of the Laureates: Thirteen Nobel Economists*, 3rd edn, Cambridge, MA: MIT Press, pp. 139–64.

Modigliani F. and R. Brumberg (1954), 'Utility Analysis and the Consumption Function: An Interpretation of Cross-Section Data', in K.K. Kurihara (ed.), *Post-Keynesian Economics*, New Brunswick, NJ: Rutgers University Press.

Modigliani F. and R. Brumberg (1980), 'Utility Analysis and Aggregate Consumption Functions: An Attempt at Integration' in A. Abel (ed.), *The Collected Papers of Franco Modigliani*, vol. 2, *The Life Cycle Hypothesis of Saving*, Cambridge, MA: MIT Press.

Modigliani, F. and M.H. Miller (1958), 'The Cost of Capital, Corporation Finance and the Theory of Investment', *American Economic Review*, **48**, June, pp. 261–97.

Modigliani, F. and M.H. Miller (1961), 'Dividend Policy, Growth and the Valuation of Shares', *Journal of Business*, **34**, October, pp. 411–33.

Snowdon, B. and H.R. Vane (1999), 'Interview with Franco Modigliani', in *Conversations With Leading Economists*, Cheltenham, UK and Northampton, MA, USA: Edward Elgar.

Monetarism

Monetarism can be traced back at least to the work of David Hume, and in 1911 Irving Fisher reformulated the quantity theory of money that is at the heart of it. But it went into eclipse after 1936 with the start of the Keynesian revolution. After that, most economists considered the money supply just one of several factors – and far from the most important one – determining nominal income. They believed that changes in interest rates had little effect on nominal income because the interest elasticity of expenditures was very low, so that the primary effect of a change in the money supply was an offsetting change in velocity. Given the still fresh experience of the Great Depression, they also believed that the maintenance of full employment should be the central goal of macro policy. If this required some inflation, so be it. These beliefs were based more on casual reasoning and simple observations than on rigorous theory and econometric evidence.

Despite the earlier criticisms of Clark Warburton (1950) it was not until the mid-1950s that these beliefs faced a serious challenge in the work of Milton Friedman and his students. Friedman (1956) reformulated the quantity theory as a theory of the demand for money along the lines of a demand function for a durable good, and argued that this demand function was stable. Whether this reformulation is closer to the traditional quantity theory than to Keynesian theory has been debated (see, for instance, Patinkin, 1969). But what is beyond debate is that Friedman's reformulation – in conjunction with his empirical work – yielded the traditional quantity-theory results. It also showed that the validity of the quantity theory can only be determined by empirical tests. This is congruent with Friedman's emphasis on testing the implications of theories, a position that was gaining increasing acceptance at that time.

Friedman's empiricist focus is well illustrated by his treatment of fiscal policy. While the prevailing Keynesian theory considered it obvious that fiscal policy is a much more important determinant of income than is monetary policy, Friedman and Meiselman (1963), without much discussion of the underlying theory, presented regression results showing the opposite. Anderson and Jordan (1968) subsequently obtained similar results in a study that avoided some (but not all) of the problems that critics had raised about the Friedman–Meiselman paper. Specifically, they regressed income on the growth rate of money (or of the monetary base, that is currency and bank reserves) and on measures of fiscal policy. They found that monetary policy explained much of income change, while fiscal policy was important only in the very short run. This paper generated an extensive debate, focusing largely on whether in such regressions money can be treated as exogenous.

Karl Brunner (who coined the term 'monetarism'), together with Allan Meltzer, developed a variant of monetarism with a much richer theoretical structure. While Friedman focused on the demand for money and treated the demand for everything else as a residual, Brunner and Meltzer included bonds and capital in their analysis. They also paid attention to the government budget constraint, because unless the budget is balanced the stock of government debt is changing, so that the economy is not in equilibrium. Full equilibrium also requires that the economy be on its long-run, and hence vertical, Phillips curve. This theoretical model, which has a significant role for fiscal policy, is similar to some models that are labelled 'Keynesian'. But

Brunner and Meltzer used it alongside their extensive empirical work that shows the demand function for money, or more recently for the monetary base (currency plus reserves), to be stable, so that changes in the money supply are the dominant factor in economic fluctuations.

An important aspect of any macroeconomic theory is its treatment of the short-run/long-run dichotomy. Both monetarists and Keynesians take prices to be sticky, although in monetarist models markets clear faster than in typical Keynesian models. Hence monetarists agree with Keynesians that an increase in the growth rate of money initially lowers interest rates and unemployment. But they argue that, after two years or so, monetary neutrality prevails. They therefore criticize Keynesians for failing to maintain the crucial distinction between nominal and real interest rates.

Monetarists could readily demonstrate in the 1960s and 1970s a strong correlation between the growth rates of money and of nominal income. What proved difficult was imputing causality. Here monetarists put much emphasis on narrative history. In their *A Monetary History of the United States*, Milton Friedman and Anna Schwartz (1963) showed that for the major fluctuations in the US economy from 1867 to 1960 the preceding changes in the money supply could be traced to some exogenous cause, such as an improvement in refining gold. But they did not deal with the smaller fluctuations that constitute most business cycles.

Until the appearance of *A Monetary History of the United States* in 1963 most economists had explained the Great Depression in Keynesian terms of expenditure motives. And, they argued, since the Federal Reserve had kept short-term interest rates extremely low, the length and severity of the Depression demonstrated the weakness of monetary policy and the need for fiscal policy. But Friedman and Schwartz argued that, on the contrary, the Fed was responsible for the length and severity of the Depression. Instead of intervening with massive open market purchases it stood by while bank failures and rising currency/deposit and reserves/deposits ratios reduced the (broadly defined) money supply by one third. And well into the 1930s the sharp decline in nominal Treasury bill rates and commercial paper rates merely masked a sharp rise in the real interest rates on business borrowing. Hence the Great Depression demonstrates the importance of changes in the money supply.

Subsequently Brunner and Meltzer (1964) demonstrated that, in the early postwar years, the Fed's ideas on monetary policy were incoherent and misleading. They, along with other monetarists, showed the danger inherent in trying to stabilize interest rates by accommodating changes in the demand for money.

Monetarists also challenged the then-prevailing Keynesian consensus that there is an exploitable inflation–unemployment trade-off, and that policy should focus primarily on unemployment. They argued that the goal of monetary policy should preferably be a stable price level, or at least a stable inflation rate. Since the long-run Phillips curve is vertical and the costs of inflation are high, attempts to maintain unemployment below its natural rate can only end in costly failure.

Owing to long lags in the effects of its policy, a central bank needs a more proximate target than the price level. Monetarists argued that this should be the growth rate of money or the base, and not interest rates, because the expected real interest rate that would maintain price stability is unknown. Moreover, the short-term nominal rate that the central bank controls is an inadequate proxy for the expected real rate on securities of various maturities and risk classes. Monetarists advocated that money grow at a stable and hence predictable rate, so that monetary policy is transparent and central bank discretion is reduced. Some went further and required central banks to change the money stock (or reserves) at a fixed rate, thus eliminating all discretionary policy.

The current consensus embraces many important elements of monetarism, while rejecting others. Few mainstream economists now deny that the growth rate of money plays the central role in long-run inflation, and also has an important role in cyclical fluctuations. Economists no longer brush aside the long run, or the distinction between nominal and real interest rates, and they accept the long-run vertical Phillips curve. That monetary policy should focus on inflation and not unemployment is widely accepted, and many economists also accept much of Friedman and Schwartz's explanation of the Great Depression. Central banks now understand the destabilizing effects of accommodating changes in the demand for money and the importance of central bank transparency. Explicit inflation targeting is not only widely advocated, but is practised by some countries.

But not all of monetarism has been accepted. Both econometric models and many theoretical models usually work within a Keynesian paradigm by paying much attention to such Keynesian variables as the propensity to consume and the marginal efficiency of capital. Moreover, given the short-run instability of velocity, few economists now advocate that money grow at a fixed rate, or that central banks target money and not interest rates. However, much of the case for such policies underlies the belief that central banks should follow an explicit policy of linking interest rates (or reserves or the base) to the lagged inflation rate and a measure of output.

Thomas Mayer

See also:

Brunner, Karl; Demand for Money: Friedman's Approach; Discretionary Policy; Federal Reserve System; Fisher, Irving; Friedman, Milton; Great Depression; Hume, David; Inflation

Targeting; Keynesian Economics; Macroeconometric Models; Meltzer, Allan H.; Natural Rate of Unemployment; Neutrality of Money; Phillips Curve; Quantity Theory of Money; Schwartz, Anna J.; Velocity of Circulation.

Bibliography

Anderson, L. and J. Jordan (1968), 'Monetary and Fiscal Actions: A Test of Their Relative Importance in Economic Stabilization', *Federal Reserve Bank of St. Louis Review*, November, pp. 11 –24.

Brunner, K. and A.H. Meltzer (1964), *Some General Features of the Federal Reserve Approach to Policy*, US Congress, House Committee on Banking and Currency, Subcommittee on Domestic Finance, 88th Congress, 2nd session, Washington, DC.

Brunner, K. and A.H. Meltzer (1989), *Monetary Economics*, Oxford: Blackwell.

Brunner, K. and A.H. Meltzer (1993), *Money and the Economy: Issues in Monetary Analysis*, Cambridge: Cambridge University Press.

De Long, J.B. (2000), 'The Triumph of Monetarism', *Journal of Economic Perspectives*, **14**, Winter, pp. 83–94.

Fisher, I. (1911), *The Purchasing Power of Money*, New York: Macmillan.

Friedman, B. and K. Kuttner (1988), 'Money, Income, Prices and Interest Rates', *American Economic Review*, **82**, June, pp. 472–92.

Friedman, M. (1956), *Studies in the Quantity Theory of Money*, Chicago: University of Chicago Press.

Friedman, M. (1968), 'The Role of Monetary Policy', *American Economic Review*, **58**, March, pp. 1–17.

Friedman, M. and D. Meiselman (1963), 'The Relative Stability of Monetary Velocity and the Investment Multiplier in the United States, 1837–1958', *Commission on Money and Credit: Stabilization Policies*, Engelwood Cliffs, NJ :Prentice-Hall.

Friedman M. and A.J. Schwartz (1963), *A Monetary History of the United States, 1867–1960*, Princeton: Princeton University Press.

Laidler, D. (1982), *Monetarist Perspectives*, Cambridge, MA: Harvard University Press.

Mayer, T. *et al.* (1978), *The Structure of Monetarism*, New York: W.W. Norton.

Mayer, T. (1997), 'Monetarists and Keynesians on Central Banking: A Case Study of a Flawed Debate', in R. Backhouse, D. Hausman, U. Maki and A. Salanti (eds), *Economics and Methodology: Crossing Boundaries*, London: Macmillan, in association with the International Economic Association, pp. 254–302.

Patinkin, D. (1969), 'The Chicago Tradition, the Quantity Theory and Friedman', *Journal of Money, Credit and Banking*, **1**, February, pp. 46–70.

Warburton, C. (1950), 'The Theory of Turning Points in Business Fluctuations,' *Quarterly Journal of Economics*, **64**, November, pp. 525–49.

Monetary Approach to Exchange Rate Determination

See:

Exchange Rate Determination: Monetary Approach.

Monetary Approach to the Balance of Payments

See:

Balance of Payments: Monetary Approach.

Monetary Base

See:
High-Powered Money.

Monetary Policy: Role of

Monetary policy has become the predominant macroeconomic stabilization tool because it has several advantages over fiscal policy. One advantage is that in most developed countries it is administered by a more or less independent central bank and is less subject than fiscal policy to the political pressures that generate overly expansionary policies. A second advantage is that changes in fiscal policy often take longer to enact and become effective than do changes in monetary policy. And long lags combined with substantial errors in long-run forecasts are a dangerous combination.

In calling monetary policy stabilization policy, the latter should not be defined narrowly as a policy that stabilizes an inherently unstable private sector. It should be defined broadly enough to include the possibility that the private sector is more or less stable, and the main problem for monetary policy is to avoid being a source of instability.

Characterizing monetary policy as stabilization policy raises two questions. First, what does stabilization mean? Second, what is it that monetary policy should stabilize? Thus the phrase 'stabilizing GDP' is sometimes used loosely to mean maintaining GDP at its full employment level, rather than in its more correct sense of reducing the variance of GDP around its mean. In many neoclassical models this does not matter because the mean level of real GDP is taken to approximate the full employment level. However, in some Keynesian models, mean GDP is often well below its full employment level. In these models monetary policy can, by raising aggregate demand, raise the mean level of real GDP.

The question of what it is that monetary policy should stabilize has received different answers over time. Although in a general sense the founding of the first monetary standard, as well as medieval debasements of the coinage, already represented monetary policies, in the modern sense of the term monetary policy originated in nineteenth-century Britain. One answer then given was that monetary policy should stabilize the price of gold – and thus the exchange rate and the price level (see Eichengreen, 1992). A second answer was that it should stabilize the financial system by having the central bank act as a lender of last resort during financial crises. The demise of the gold standard as well as the establishment of deposit insurance have modified, but not entirely invalidated, these answers. Even in countries with extensive deposit insurance, such as the United States, monetary policy is still supposed to back up deposit insurance by providing banks with liquidity if systemic bank failure threatens.

Another role assigned to monetary policy has been to stabilize nominal (but not necessarily real) interest rates, a role that can conflict with the other roles of monetary policy. This has been much more popular among central bankers than among academic economists. For example, until the end of the 1970s, the Federal Reserve in practice often put short-term interest rate stability ahead of macroeconomic stability, though generally not showing any awareness of such a trade-off. However, nominal interest-rate stabilization has now been discredited because it results in a procyclical policy when aggregate demand shifts.

The nineteenth-century role of defending the gold standard has now evolved into a more general idea of maintaining exchange rate stability in the belief that this fosters international trade and investment. It also provides a barrier against the inflationary bias that is, rightly or wrongly, attributed to governments. It does so because adoption of a more inflationary policy puts pressure on the exchange rate, and that becomes readily apparent to the public. The benefits from exchange rate stabilization depend on a country's circumstances. Small, open economies, particularly those with a single dominant trading partner whose economy faces similar shocks, and countries that want to assure foreign investors, or their own citizens, that they will follow low inflation policies, have more reason to emphasize this role of monetary policy.

Exchange-rate stabilization may conflict with the other roles of monetary policy. Suppose that a country pegs its currency to the Euro. Then, if there is a recession, or else an inflationary shock, in Euroland, it will tend to import this shock. Moreover, if it experiences a shock that Euroland does not, it cannot use monetary policy to ameliorate it. In addition, with a pegged exchange rate a currency may be more vulnerable to speculative attack (see Mishkin, 2000).

It is therefore not surprising that the Keynesian revolution, inspired as it was by the Great Depression, assigned another primary role to monetary policy, achieving and maintaining full employment. Although even at the high tide of Keynesianism price stability and exchange rate stability were considered useful goals, many countries relegated them to distinctly secondary roles. Among the major industrialized economies, Germany, with its memory of hyperinflation, was the only exception. Many others relied on what they believed to be a workable Phillips curve trade-off between inflation and unemployment. For example, from the end of World War II until the 1980s, Britain followed a full employment policy that generated high inflation and periodic balance of payment crises that led to currency depreciations. The Bank of England would then reverse course and adopt a restrictive policy, but would abandon this policy after the crisis ended. In the United States, from the mid-1960s until the end of the 1970s, the Federal Reserve followed expansionary policies that resulted in accelerating inflation, interrupted by episodes of restrictive policy (see Mayer, 1999).

By the 1980s, several factors had combined to shift monetary policy back towards its traditional role. One was the European drive towards a common currency. As a precondition, countries had to use monetary policy to keep their exchange rates aligned. Another factor was that they, as well as the United States, had become disappointed with the results of focusing monetary policy on full employment. A public perception developed that inflation was reducing living standards, so that inflationary monetary policies lost political support. Moreover, although by and large economists had previously not considered the losses resulting from even high single-digit inflation to be substantial, by the 1990s they had detected various ways in which inflation seriously distorts resource allocation and reduces economic growth. Furthermore, they no longer believed that a monetary policy aimed at full employment could succeed: in many countries it had not prevented the rise in unemployment subsequent to the supply shocks of the 1970s that popularized the term 'stagflation'. Largely influenced by the rational-expectations revolution, many now argued that, since, except in the quite short run, the Phillips curve is vertical, inflation cannot be used to lower unemployment significantly (see Lucas, 1996). And, as time went on, and more and more observations from the 1970s entered the sample, even the expectations- augmented Phillips curves fitted by Keynesians showed less and less of an inflation–unemployment trade-off. The subsequent application of hysteresis theory to unemployment modified these findings only to some extent. Real business cycle theorists went even further by arguing that unemployment was an appropriate response to productivity shocks. Beyond this, time-inconsistency theory suggested that central banks have a systemic inflationary bias that generates inflation without in the longer run reducing unemployment.

The current understanding of the role of monetary policy combines various elements. Some economists advocate fixed exchange rates, and many small economies pursue this policy, while 12 European countries have carried exchange-rate fixity to the extreme of unifying their currencies. But exchange rate considerations play only a secondary role in the policies of the Bank of England and the European Central Bank, while the Federal Reserve pays very little, if any, attention to exchange rates. Moreover, many countries that peg their exchange rates abandon these pegs when they come under serious pressure; examples are the ERM crisis in the UK in 1992 and the East Asian crisis of 1997–8.

Employment and real income, while dethroned from the leading roles they once held in many countries, still play an important role. In a drastic recession most central banks would still focus on reducing unemployment. Secondly, even if a central bank cannot lower the average unemployment rate over the long run, it can lower its variance by accepting a higher variance of inflation. This is so because, when inflation deviates from its target, the central bank has to decide how quickly to return it to target so as to reduce the variance of inflation (see Taylor, 1998). And the faster it does so, the greater the fluctuations in unemployment that it generates. Some economists therefore advocate a publicly announced rule that responds to deviations of both real GDP and inflation from their targets. In one prominent rule, the Taylor rule, the response coefficients for inflation and unemployment are equal. This rule, which has attracted much attention, gives a good representation of Federal Reserve policy in recent years. Similarly, some economists advocate targeting nominal income, and this too implies an equal weight for percentage deviations of real income and prices from their targets.

But for the longer run the main role now widely assigned to monetary policy is keeping the inflation rate low, perhaps in the 1 to 3 per cent range, with some countries, such as Britain, Canada and New Zealand, as well as Euroland, having set explicit inflation targets. That makes monetary policy more transparent and central banks more accountable for failure to meet their targets. American monetary policy, while not formally targeting inflation, also focuses primarily on keeping inflation low (see Bernanke *et al.*, 1999).

Some economists advocate stabilizing the price level rather than the inflation rate, because even with 2 per cent inflation prices double every 35 years. Besides, they think it easier to maintain political support for a price stability rule than for a rule of, say, 2 per cent inflation. On the other hand, given the upward bias of many price indexes it is not clear whether a, say, 1 per cent rise in the index denotes inflation. Moreover, stabilizing the price level implies offsetting any increases in it, including those due to supply shocks, with subsequent deflations, and that may involve substantial unemployment. In addition, given inflexible money wages, negative demand shocks are more likely to generate unemployment at zero inflation than at, say, 3 per cent inflation, because with 3 per cent inflation real wages can be cut by up to 3 per cent without cutting nominal wages (see Akerlof *et al.*, 1996). Furthermore, since nominal interest rates cannot fall below zero, zero inflation sets a lower limit to the reductions in the real interest rate that a central bank can achieve. This, some economists argue, could make monetary policy impotent in a deep recession, as some claim happened in Japan in the late 1990s. In practice, central banks generally do not aim at price stability but at low inflation.

One more potential role of monetary policy needs mentioning; generating seigniorage (the government's profit from issuing currency and bank reserves). Earning seigniorage is generally not considered a valid role for monetary policy, but in a failed state that cannot collect taxes it may be the best of several bad choices.

THOMAS MAYER

See also:

Central Bank Independence; Euro; Expectations-augmented Phillips Curve; Federal Reserve System; Fiscal Policy: Role of; Fixed Exchange Rate System; Gold Standard; Hysteresis; Inflation Targeting; Phillips Curve; Taylor's Rule; Time Inconsistency.

Bibliography

Akerlof, G.A., W.T. Dickens and G.L. Perry (1996), 'The Macroeconomics of Low Inflation', *Brookings Papers on Economic Activity*, pp. 1–76.
Bernanke, B.S., T. Laubach, F.S. Mishkin and A.S. Posen (1999), *Inflation Targeting*, Princeton: Princeton University Press.
Blinder, A. (1998), *Central Banking in Theory and Practice*, Cambridge, MA: MIT Press.
Eichengreen, B. (1992), *Golden Fetters: The Gold Standard and the Great Depression*, New York: Oxford University Press.
Federal Reserve Bank of Kansas City (1984), *Price Stability and Public Policy*, Kansas City: Federal Reserve Bank of Kansas City.
Lucas, R.E. Jr (1996), 'Nobel Lecture: Monetary Neutrality', *Journal of Political Economy*, **104**, August, pp. 661–82.
Mankiw, N.G. (1994), *Monetary Policy*, Chicago: University of Chicago Press.
Mayer, T. (1999), *Monetary Policy and the Great Inflation in the United States*, Cheltenham, UK and Northampton, MA, USA: Edward Elgar.
Mishkin, F.S. (2000), 'What Should Central Banks Do?', *Federal Reserve Bank of St. Louis Review*, **82**, November/December, pp. 7–13.
Taylor, J.B. (1998), 'Monetary Policy Guidelines for Employment and Inflation Stability', in R.M. Solow and J.B. Taylor, *Inflation, Unemployment and Monetary Policy*, Cambridge, MA: MIT Press.

Money Illusion

This occurs where people mistake money or nominal changes for real changes. For example, if workers are not aware that prices are increasing more rapidly than their money wages, they will mistake money wage increases as real wage increases and suffer from money illusion. See P. Diamond, E. Shafir and A. Tversky's article, 'Money Illusion' (*Quarterly Journal of Economics*, **112**, May 1997).

Money Supply: Endogenous or Exogenous?

It has for a long time been conventional in macroeconomic modelling to classify the money supply as exogenous. This practice continued from IS–LM models, to monetarist models, to rational expectations models. The money supply thus acquired an important causal role in these models, which were then used to support the focus of policy makers on the money supply as a policy target variable. What is conventionally meant by the money supply in these models is real money balances. But the actual experience of money supply targeting confirmed doubts about how far the money supply was exogenous in a policy sense: that is, determined outside the private sector. The monetary policy literature was thus less sanguine about the capacity of the central bank to control the money supply (see, for example Goodhart, 1994; Dow and Saville, 1990). Meanwhile, real business cycle theory was distracting attention from the issue by suggesting that it was real shocks, rather than monetary shocks, which were the primary cause of the cycle.

Except in the still substantial area of traditional macro models, then, there is now a consensus that the money supply is in some sense endogenous. The interesting questions then surround the issue of what does determine the money supply. The key idea is that money comes into existence almost exclusively as the counterpart to new credit. The focus thus shifts to the other side of the balance sheet, to a consideration of credit supply. New Keynesian theory considers the possibility that information constraints induce banks to ration credit (see Stiglitz and Weiss, 1981). The credit market (specified only in terms of loan rates and credit levels) does not clear when interest rates rise if banks do not have access to full information for assessing default risk. Rather, they employ the rule of thumb that a rise in interest rates would cause lower return/lower risk borrowers to drop out, or induce them to switch to higher risk/higher return projects. Credit therefore may be lower than it would have been under full information when interest rates rise. But this is a very limited form of endogeneity, with banks choosing not to be fully lent up.

The arguments for a more general understanding of endogeneity have a long pedigree, building on Keynes's (1930) *Treatise on Money* and the Radcliffe (1959) *Report*. The active research into money supply endogeneity is centred on the Post Keynesian literature (see Cottrell, 1994; Hewitson, 1995, for surveys). Before the practical application of monetarism took hold, Davidson and Weintraub (1973) and Weintraub (1978) were arguing that the money supply did not play a causal role in inflation, but rather changed as a result of credit supply accommodating changes in the demand for credit to finance an inflationary process. But, further, Kaldor

(1982) argued that the authorities were not free to control credit supply, and thus the money supply, even if they wanted to. First, the central bank's lender-of-last-resort facility meant that excess demand for borrowed reserves was met (albeit at a potentially penal rate). Any attempt to remove the facility would threaten confidence in the banking system. Second, even if the central bank succeeded in controlling the money stock according to a particular definition, innovation in the financial sector would generate money substitutes such that the original definition of money assets was no longer relevant. The argument that attempts at controlling the money supply would thus continually be thwarted was enshrined in Goodhart's Law. Kaldor's arguments were extended, and detailed for the US case, by Moore (1988).

Kaldor and Moore's theory, that the demand for credit is accommodated at the rate of interest specified by the central bank, became known as horizontalism, in contrast to the verticalism of the exogenous money view. Attempts at money supply control were doomed to failure, and in any case addressed the symptom rather than the cause of inflationary pressures. It also held the implication that the demand for money, as opposed to credit, was of little consequence, since any change in the demand for money could be accommodated by the rate at which loans were repaid.

There is, however, another body of thought in Post Keynesian economics, called structuralism, which, while preserving the endogeneity of the money supply, also retains Keynes's emphasis on liquidity preference and sees banks meeting their liquidity needs through liability management first, and recourse to the central bank only as a last resort (see, for example, Wray, 1990; Pollin, 1991.) The banks are not seen as passively accommodating the demand for credit, as in horizontalism, but rather playing an active role themselves in the process. In particular, while the horizontalist argument is expressed in terms of the supply of credit to credit-worthy customers, the structuralists focus on changing perceptions of credit-worthiness over the business cycle and also on the banks' changing willingness to lend over the cycle, analysed in terms of banks' own liquidity preference. The emphasis then is on the importance for banks' risk assessment of shifting expectations, and confidence in expectations, in the absence of objective risk measures. This is a characteristic difference between Post Keynesian economics and the imperfect information assumption of new Keynesian economics.

Both supply of and demand for credit are determined by liquidity preference, understood broadly to refer to the size as well as the disposition of portfolios (see Dow and Dow, 1989). This in turn generates a volume of credit and thus deposits, while liquidity preference as more conventionally understood influences demand for deposits. The credit supply curve is expressed in terms of a range of credit levels over time relative to the loan rate, with an upward slope explained by increasing perceived lender's risk putting a premium on the mark-up over the cost of funds. At the same time, the willingness of the non-bank public to become indebted to banks in order to finance expenditure is also a function of liquidity preference. Minsky's (1982) work, which has inspired much of the structuralist approach, shows how the money market and credit market interact under changing economic conditions. It is not clear, however, how well the traditional supply and demand framework can capture the *process* of credit creation in real time (see Winnett, 1992). Arestis and Howells (1996) have suggested a framework with shifting supply and demand curves tracing out a horizontal path to represent this process.

Embedded in the difference between the horizontalist and structuralist views on endogenous money is a different perception of money itself. Horizontalists see money as a flow which is the passive counterpart to the flow of credit. The emphasis is all on the asset side of the banks' balance sheet, the dual of the monetarist emphasis on the liabilities side. This is also central to the circuitist/circulation approach to endogenous money (see Delaplace and Nell, 1996). Money is created in response to the demand for credit to finance investment, and traced by means of a circuit to its destruction when the loan is repaid. This one-sided treatment of the two sides of the banks' balance sheet – either only assets or only liabilities – has had the unfortunate consequence that the terms 'money' and 'credit' are often used interchangeably, or even conflated, since one is regarded as the passive mirror-image of the other. Thus horizontalists often refer to 'money' when credit is seen as the causal vehicle.

Since structuralists see the demand for money more as a stock demand, they are more inclined to see independent forces at work behind demand and its supply, which is a by-product of developments in the credit market. Money is demanded, not just to finance expenditure, but also as a safe asset in times of uncertainty. It is one of the currently active areas of debate how far the horizontalist, circuitist and structuralist approaches to endogenous money can be compatible (see Chick, 2000, for a comparison). Attempts are being made to synthesize them into a complete stock-flow framework (see, for example, Lavoie and Godley, 2000; Fontana, 2000).

SHEILA C. DOW

Bibliography

Arestis, P. and P. Howells (1996), 'Theoretical Reflections on Endogenous Money: The Problem with "Convenience Lending"', *Cambridge Journal of Economics*, **20**, September, pp. 539–52.

Chick, V. (2000), 'Money and Effective Demand', in J. Smithin (ed.), *What is Money?*, London: Routledge.

Cottrell, A. (1994), 'Post Keynesian Monetary Economics', *Cambridge Journal of Economics*, **18**, December, pp. 587–605.

Davidson, P. and S. Weintraub, (1973), 'Money as Cause and Effect', *Economic Journal*, **83**, December, pp. 1117–32.

Delaplace, G. and E.J. Nell, (eds) (1996), *Money in Motion: The Post Keynesian and Circulation Approaches*, London: Macmillan.

Dow, A.C. and S.C. Dow (1989), 'Endogenous Money Creation and Idle Balances', in J. Pheby (ed.) *New Directions in Post Keynesian Economics*, Aldershot, UK and Brookfield, US: Edward Elgar, reprinted in M. Musella and C. Panico (eds) (1995), *The Supply of Money in the Economic Process: A Post Keynesian Perspective*, Aldershot, UK and Brookfield, US: Edward Elgar.

Dow, J.C.R. and I.D. Saville (1990), *A Critique of Monetary Policy*, Oxford: Clarendon.

Fontana, G. (2000), 'Post Keynesians and Circuitists on Money and Uncertainty: An Attempt at Generality', *Journal of Post Keynesian Economics*, **23**, Fall, pp. 27–48.

Goodhart, C.A.E. (1994), 'What Should Central Banks Do? What Should be their Macroeconomic Objectives and Operations?', *Economic Journal*, **104**, November, pp. 1424–36.

Hewitson, G. (1995), 'Post Keynesian Monetary Theory: Some Issues', *Journal of Economic Surveys*, **9**, July, pp. 285–310.

Kaldor, N. (1982), *The Scourge of Monetarism*, Oxford: Oxford University Press.

Keynes, J.M. (1930), *A Treatise on Money*, vols. I and II, London: Macmillan.

Lavoie, M. and W. Godley (2000), 'Kaleckian Models of Growth in a Stock Flow Monetary Framework: A Neo-Kaldorian Model', *Levy Institute Working Paper*, no. 302, June.

Minsky, H.P. (1982), *Inflation, Recession and Economic Policy*, Brighton: Wheatsheaf.

Moore, B.J. (1988), *Horizontalists and Verticalists: The Macroeconomics of Credit Money*, Cambridge: Cambridge University Press.

Pollin, R. (1991), 'Two Theories of Money Supply Endogeneity: Some Empirical Evidence', *Journal of Post Keynesian Economics*, **13**, Spring, pp. 366–95.

Radcliffe, Lord (1959), *Report of the Committee on the Workings of the Monetary System*, London: HMSO.

Stiglitz, J. and M. Weiss (1981), 'Credit Rationing with Markets with Imperfect Competition', *American Economic Review*, **71**, March, pp. 22–44.

Weintraub, S. (1978), *Keynes, Keynesians and Monetarists*, Philadelphia: University of Philadelphia Press.

Winnett, A. (1992), 'Some Semantics of Endogeneity', in P. Arestis and V. Chick (eds), *Recent Developments in Post-Keynesian Economics*, Aldershot, UK and Brookfield, US: Edward Elgar.

Wray, L.R. (1990), *Money and Credit in Capitalist Economies*, Aldershot, UK and Brookfield, US: Edward Elgar.

Multiplier

It is, however, to the general principle of the multiplier to which we have to look for an explanation of how fluctuations in the amount of investment, which are a comparatively small proportion of the national income, are capable of generating fluctuations in aggregate employment and income so much greater in amplitude than themselves. (John Maynard Keynes, 1936, p. 122)

The apparent inability of capitalist market economies to provide for sustained full employment during the inter-war period was the main blemish on a system that John Maynard Keynes otherwise held in high regard. As early as 1929, Keynes was arguing forcefully in support of government programmes to expand aggregate demand via deficit financing. In his famous 1929 pamphlet, co-authored with Hubert Henderson, Keynes argued the case for public works programmes in support of Lloyd George's 1929 election pledge to the nation to reduce unemployment 'in the course of a single year to normal proportions' (see Skidelsky, 1992). However, Keynes and Henderson were unable convincingly to rebuff the orthodox 'Treasury dogma', expressed by the Chancellor of the Exchequer in 1929 as 'whatever might be the political or social advantages, very little additional employment can, in fact, and as a general rule, be created by State borrowing and State expenditure' (see Keynes, 1929).

Implicit in Keynes and Henderson's arguments in favour of public works programmes to reduce unemployment was the idea of an employment multiplier. However, the concept of the multiplier made its first influential appearance in a memorandum from Richard Kahn to the Economic Advisory Council during the summer of 1930. Kahn's more formal presentation appeared in his famous 1931 paper, published in the *Economic Journal*. Kahn's article analysed the impact of an increase in government investment expenditure on employment assuming that (a) the economy had spare capacity, (b) there was monetary policy accommodation, and (c) money wages remained stable. Kahn's article was written as a response to the Treasury's 'crowding out' objections to loan-financed public works expenditures as a method of reducing unemployment. The following year Jens Warming (1932) criticized, refined and extended Kahn's analysis. It was Warming who first brought the idea of a consumption function into the multiplier literature (see Skidelsky, 1992, p.451). The first coherent presentation of the multiplier by Keynes was in a series of four articles published in *The Times* in March 1933, entitled 'The Means to Prosperity', followed by an article in the *New Statesman* in April, entitled 'The Multiplier'.

However, the idea of the multiplier met with considerable resistance in orthodox financial circles and among fellow economists wedded to the classical tradition. By 1933, Keynes was attributing this opposition to the multiplier concept to

> the fact that all our ideas about economics . . . are, whether we are conscious of it or not, soaked with theoretical pre-suppositions which are only applicable to a society which is in equilibrium, with all its productive capacity already employed. Many people are trying to solve the problem of unemployment with a theory which is based on the assumption that there is no unemployment . . . these ideas, perfectly valid in their proper setting, are inapplicable to present circumstances. (Quoted by Meltzer, 1988, p. 137; see also Dimand, 1988, for an excellent survey of the development of the multiplier in this period)

There is no doubt that the multiplier process plays a key role in Keynesian economics. In Patinkin's (1976) view, the development of the multiplier represented a 'major step towards the *General Theory*' and Skidelsky (1992) describes the concept of the multiplier as 'the most notorious piece of Keynesian magic'. Keynes (1936) defines the investment multiplier (k), as the ratio of a change in income to a change in autonomous expenditure which brought it about: 'when there is an increment of aggregate investment, income will increase by an amount which is k times the increment in investment' (p. 115).

Keynes's argument can be illustrated most easily in a hypothetical closed economy in which there is no government sector. The output (Y) of such an economy would be split between the production of consumption (C) and investment (I) goods:

$$Y = C + I. \qquad \text{(equilibrium condition)} \quad (1)$$

Assume that consumption expenditure depends positively on income and that the form of the consumption function can be represented by a simple linear behavioural equation:

$$C = \alpha + \beta Y, \qquad \text{(behavioural equation)} \quad (2)$$

where α is autonomous consumer expenditure and β is the marginal propensity to consume ($\Delta C / \Delta Y$). Investment is assumed to be autonomously determined.

Substituting (2) into (1) we obtain:

$$Y = \alpha + \beta Y + I. \qquad (3)$$

Rearranging (3) and factorizing we obtain:

$$Y(1 - \beta) = \alpha + I. \qquad (4)$$

Finally, dividing both sides of (4) by $(1 - \beta)$ we obtain the familiar reduced form equation:

$$Y = (\alpha + I)\frac{1}{1 - \beta}. \qquad (5)$$

Equation (5) determines the equilibrium level of income. For this hypothetical economy the multiplier is equal to the reciprocal of 1 minus the marginal propensity to consume (β) (that is, $k = 1/1 - \beta$); or the reciprocal of the marginal propensity to save.

Starting from a position of less than full employment, suppose there occurs an increase in the amount of autonomous investment undertaken in the economy. The increase in investment spending will result in an increase in employment in firms producing capital goods. Newly employed workers in capital goods industries will spend some of their income on consumption goods and save the rest. The rise in demand for consumer goods will in turn lead to increased employment in consumer goods industries and result in further rounds of expenditure. In consequence an initial rise in autonomous investment produces a more than proportionate rise in income, a process known as the multiplier: that is, $\Delta Y = \Delta I \times k$. From the initial increase in investment spending (ΔI) we observe an increase in aggregate demand (ΔAD) in the form of a series of induced expenditures that become progressively smaller, as shown in (6):

$$\Delta AD = \Delta I + \beta \Delta I + \beta^2 \Delta I + \beta^3 \Delta I + \ldots = \Delta I(1 + \beta + \beta^2 + \beta^3 + \ldots) \qquad (6)$$

Clearly, the above analysis needs to be modified once we both introduce a government sector and consider an economy which engages in international trade. While an initial increase in investment spending will lead in exactly the same way to successive rounds of increased expenditure, some part of the *extra* income will be withdrawn not only in the form of savings (marginal propensity to save $= \Delta S/\Delta Y = s$) but also as import (M) spending (marginal propensity to import $= \Delta M/\Delta Y = m$) and taxes (T) paid to the government (marginal tax rate $= \Delta T/\Delta Y = t$). The multiplier will, in consequence, depend on the fraction of extra income which is withdrawn from the circular flow of income (the marginal propensity to withdraw $= \omega = s + m + t$) via savings, imports and taxes and can be generalized as the reciprocal of the marginal propensity to withdraw (ω). The multiplier for an open economy with a government sector is given by (7):

$$k = 1/\omega = 1/s + m + t \text{ and } \Delta Y = \Delta A 1/\omega, \qquad (7)$$

where A = autonomous expenditure. *Ceteris paribus*, the multiplier will be larger (a) the smaller the marginal propensity to save; (b) the smaller the marginal propensity to import; and (c) the smaller the marginal tax rate. The same multiplier process will apply following a change not only in investment expenditure but also in autonomous consumer expenditure, exports or government expenditure. In terms of the Keynesian cross model, the AD schedule will be steeper the larger the value of the multiplier, and vice versa. Within the Keynesian IS–LM model the multiplier affects the slope of the *IS* curve. The *IS* curve will be flatter the larger the value of the multiplier, and vice versa.

Keynes was well aware of the various factors that could limit the size of the multiplier effect of his proposed public expenditure programmes, including 'the effect of increasing the rate of interest . . . unless the monetary authority take steps to the contrary' thereby crowding out 'investment in other directions'; the potential for an adverse effect on 'confidence'; and the leakage of expenditures into imports in an open economy such as the UK (see Keynes, 1936, pp. 119–20). In the case of a fully employed economy, Keynes recognized that any increase in investment will 'set up a tendency in money-prices to rise without limit, irrespective of the marginal propensity to consume'.

Finally, we should also note that the multiplier plays a key role in the Keynesian approach to business cycles. In short, the interaction of the multiplier process and the accelerator explains why periods of economic expansion and contraction will tend to develop their own momentum. Following an initial increase in autonomous investment, the rise in income due to the multiplier process will be reinforced by an increase in new investment, via the accelerator, which will in turn have a further multiplier effect on income, and so on. Combining the so-called 'multiplier–accelerator model' with an analysis of 'ceilings' and 'floors' allows exponents of the Keynesian approach to account for both upper and lower turning points in the business cycle.

BRIAN SNOWDON
HOWARD R.VANE

See also:

Balanced Budget Multiplier; Business Cycles: Keynesian Approach; Crowding Out; IS–LM Model: Closed Economy; Keynesian Cross; Keynesian Economics; Marginal Propensity to Consume; Marginal Propensity to Import; Marginal Propensity to Save; Marginal Propensity to Withdraw; Marginal Tax Rate.

Bibliography

Dimand, R.W. (1988), *The Origins of the Keynesian Revolution*, Aldershot, UK: Edward Elgar.
Kahn, R.F. (1931), 'The Relation of Home Investment to Unemployment', *Economic Journal*, **41**, June, pp. 173–98.
Kahn, R.F. (1984), *The Making of the General Theory*, Cambridge: Cambridge University Press.
Keynes, J.M. (1929), 'A Programme of Expansion', reprinted (1963) in *Essays in Persuasion*, New York: W.W. Norton.
Keynes, J.M. (1936), *The General Theory of Employment, Interest and Money*, London: Macmillan.
Keynes, J.M. and H. Henderson (1929), *Can Lloyd George Do It?*, London: Hogarth Press.
Meltzer, A.H. (1988), *Keynes's Monetary Theory: A Different Interpretation*, Cambridge: Cambridge University Press.

508   *Multiplier–accelerator model*

Patinkin, D. (1976), *Keynes's Monetary Thought: A Study of its Development*, Durham, NC: Duke University Press.
Skidelsky, R., (1992), *John Maynard Keynes, Vol 2: The Economist as Saviour, 1920–1937*, London: Macmillan.
Warming, J. (1932), 'International Difficulties Arising Out of the Financing of Public Works During a Depression', *Economic Journal*, **42**, June, pp. 211–24.

Multiplier–Accelerator Model

The multiplier–accelerator model seeks to explain fluctuations in the level of economic activity through interactions between the multiplier and the accelerator.

Suppose, for example, that an economy is operating below full employment and there occurs an autonomous increase in the amount of investment undertaken. According to the multiplier process, a rise in autonomous investment will produce a *more than* proportionate rise in income. The rise in income will *induce* a further increase in investment as new capital equipment is required to meet the increased demand for output. Since the cost of capital equipment is usually greater than the value of its annual output, new investment will be *greater than* the increase in output which brought it about: a phenomenon referred to as the 'accelerator'. In short, following an initial increase in autonomous investment, the rise in income, due to the multiplier process will be reinforced by a further increase in new investment, via the accelerator, which will in turn have a multiplier effect on income, and so on. The interactions of the multiplier process and the accelerator can therefore explain both expansionary and contractionary phases of the business cycle.

The most famous exposition of the multiplier–accelerator interaction was put forward by Paul Samuelson ('Interactions between the Multiplier Analysis and the Principle of Acceleration', *Review of Economics and Statistics*, **21**, May 1939). Samuelson showed that, given a change in autonomous expenditure, income will follow different paths (including regular, damped and explosive) for different combinations of the marginal propensity to consume and the accelerator coefficient. The multiplier–accelerator model has been combined with Hicks's (*A Contribution to the Theory of the Trade Cycle*, Oxford University Press, 1950) analysis of 'ceilings' (due to resource constraints) and 'floors' (eventually, as existing capital equipment wears out, it will need replacing in order to produce the current demand for annual output) to form a central element of the Keynesian approach to business cycles. As such it can account for both upper and lower turning points in the business cycle.

See also:

Business Cycles: Keynesian Approach; Investment: Accelerator Theory of; Multiplier; Samuelson, Paul A.

Mundell, Robert A.

Robert Mundell was born in Kingston, Ontario, Canada in 1932. He obtained a BA from the University of British Columbia in 1953 and an MA from the University of Washington in 1954. After studying at the London School of Economics and the Massachusetts Institute of Technology (MIT) he received his PhD from MIT in 1956. His doctoral thesis concerned aspects of international capital movements, a topic that was to become a focus of much of his subsequent research. He held a Post-Doctoral Fellowship in Political Economy at the University of Chicago (1956–7), taught at Stanford University (Assistant Professor of Economics, 1958–9) and the Johns Hopkins University School of Advanced International Studies in Bologna, Italy (Professor of Economics, 1959–61), before joining the research department of the IMF (Senior Economist, 1961–3), which at that time was headed by Marcus Fleming. Subsequent posts included Visiting Professor of Economics at McGill University (1963–4); Visiting Research Professor of International Economics at the Brookings Institution (1964–5); (summer) Professor of International Economics at the Graduate Institute of International Studies in Geneva, Switzerland (1965–75); Professor of Economics at the University of Chicago (1966–71), where he was editor of the *Journal of Political Economy* (1966–70); and Professor of Economics at the University of Waterloo, Ontario (1972–4). Since 1974 he has been Professor of Economics at Columbia University in New York. His many offices and honours have included being awarded the title of Distinguished Fellow of the American Economic Association in 1997 and being made a Fellow of the American Academy of Arts and Science in 1998. In 1999, he was awarded the Nobel Prize in Economics 'for his analysis of monetary and fiscal policy under different exchange rate regimes and his analysis of optimum currency areas'.

Robert Mundell's pioneering contributions to open economy or international economics can be divided into three main areas: the development of the so-called Mundell–Fleming model and its implications for the effectiveness of fiscal and monetary policy under different exchange rate regimes; his work emphasizing the importance of monetary dynamics; and the development of the concept of an optimum currency area. While these pathbreaking contributions (which are drawn together in Mundell, 1968,

1971a) date from the 1960s, their lasting significance is reflected in the key part they still play at the heart of open economy macroeconomic courses. Furthermore, his contributions have provided fertile ground for researchers since the 1960s to extend and refine his original analyses.

The Mundell–Fleming model derives its name from the analysis contained in two papers by Robert Mundell (1963b) and Marcus Fleming (1962). Writing independently, while at the IMF, both researchers incorporated international trade and capital movements into the IS–LM model of a closed economy. Mundell demonstrated that for a *small* open economy, with *perfect* capital mobility, the effects of monetary and fiscal policy critically depend on whether the exchange rate is fixed or flexible. Under a fixed exchange rate the money supply is endogenous and monetary policy becomes totally ineffective in changing the level of domestic economic activity. Any attempt to increase the money supply by open market purchases of securities will merely lead to an offsetting loss of foreign exchange reserves. In contrast, fiscal policy becomes effective as there is no crowding out since the domestic interest rate is tied to the rate ruling abroad. Under a flexible exchange rate the money supply is exogenous and monetary policy becomes effective in changing the level of domestic economic activity. An increase in the money supply *implies* lower interest rates, which results in capital outflows and a depreciation of the exchange rate. This in turn causes an increase in aggregate demand (through an increase in net exports) and higher output. In contrast, fiscal policy becomes totally ineffective. An increase in government expenditure puts upward pressure on the domestic interest rate, resulting in an inflow of capital and an appreciation of the exchange rate. As the exchange rate appreciates net exports decrease, completely offsetting the effects of increased government expenditure. In this way fiscal expansion crowds out net exports and there is no change in output.

A second key contribution made by Mundell to open economy macroeconomics relates to his work emphasizing the importance of monetary dynamics. This can be seen in three main uses. First, Mundell analysed how persistent international payments imbalances could arise and how they would eventually be eliminated. In his approach the private sector's money holdings (and thereby its *stock* of wealth) change in response to balance of payment surpluses or deficits (*flows*). For example, under fixed exchange rates with a low degree of capital mobility, an increase in the money supply will reduce interest rates, increase domestic demand and cause a balance of payments deficit. The deficit will result in monetary outflows and a fall in demand until the balance of payments deficit is eliminated. Mundell's approach was subsequently adopted by others and was developed into the monetary approach to the balance of payments. One important conclusion that derives from his analysis is that attempts by the authorities to sterilize balance of payments deficits/surpluses will disrupt the adjustment mechanism. Second, Mundell (1962) used dynamic principles to solve the so-called 'assignment problem'. Employing a Keynesian model operating under a fixed exchange rate with imperfect capital mobility he considered the appropriate use of monetary and fiscal policy for internal and external stability. He demonstrated how monetary policy should be assigned to achieve external balance and fiscal policy to achieve internal balance. With the reverse assignment, the economy would be dynamically unstable, experiencing progressively rising unemployment and a deteriorating balance of payments situation. The explanation for this is related to his 'principle of effective market classification' (Mundell, 1960), in that policy instruments should be assigned to the objectives on which they have the most direct influence.

In his 1962 paper, Mundell also advocated a policy mix involving low taxes to stimulate employment and a tight monetary policy to protect the balance of payments. It should be noted that in 1962 this was the opposite policy mix to that being advocated by President Kennedy's Council of Economic Advisers who wanted low interest rates to spur growth and a budget surplus to prevent inflation (see Mundell, 2000). Third, Mundell's work on monetary dynamics results in his 'incompatibility trinity' whereby, given capital mobility, monetary policy can either be directed towards an external objective (such as the exchange rate) or an internal objective (such as the price level) but *not both* at the same time.

The third area in which he has made a major contribution to open economy macroeconomics is in the development of the concept of an optimum currency area. At the time of the Bretton Woods regime of fixed exchange rates, Mundell (1961) posed the then radical and far-sighted question 'when is it advantageous for a number of regions to relinquish their monetary sovereignty in favour of a common currency?' Addressing this question he considered both the advantages (for example, lower transactions costs) and disadvantages (for example, the problem of maintaining employment when 'asymmetric shocks' necessitate a reduction in real wages in a particular region) of a common currency. He found an optimum currency area to be a set of regions within which the degree of labour mobility is high enough to ensure full employment when one particular region experiences a disturbance. Surprisingly, given Europe's inflexible labour market, Mundell has been a strong supporter of European Monetary Union (EMU). For many economists the EMU project remains a 'gamble' (Obstfeld, 1997; Feldstein, 1997). Although it would be wrong to call Mundell the father of the Euro, he has accepted that 'maybe' he could be considered as 'one of several godfathers' (*Guardian*, 14.10.99).

In addition to the three main contributions noted above, Mundell has also made a number of other important contributions to macroeconomic theory and the theory of trade. These include, in the former case, the 'Mundell–Tobin effect', where a higher rate of inflation may induce people to reduce their real cash balances and invest more in real capital assets (see Mundell, 1963a; Tobin, 1965) and, in the latter case, the argument that factor mobility tends to equalize goods prices, even if international trade is restricted by trade barriers (Mundell, 1957).

In the 1970s his enthusiasm for tax cuts (see Mundell, 1971b) helped found supply-side economics. This approach has emphasized a policy mix of monetary discipline to control inflation, combined with lower taxes and regulatory reforms to promote employment and growth. Furthermore, Mundell has played an important part in the debate on the future of the international financial system (see, for example, Mundell, 1972). In more recent years he has been working on the history of the international monetary system (see Mundell, 2000).

BRIAN SNOWDON
HOWARD R. VANE

See also:

Balance of Payments: Monetary Approach; Bretton Woods; Crowding Out; Euro; European Monetary Union; Fixed Exchange Rate System; Flexible Exchange Rate System; IS-LM Model: Closed Economy; IS-LM Model: Open Economy; Nobel Prize in Economics; Optimum Currency Area; Supply-side Economics.

Bibliography
Dornbusch, R. (2000), 'Robert A. Mundell's Nobel Memorial Prize', *Scandinavian Journal of Economics*, **102**, June, pp. 199–210.
Feldstein, M. (1997), 'The Political Economy of the European Economic and Monetary Union: Political Sources of an Economic Liability', *Journal of Economic Perspectives*, **11**, Fall, pp. 23–42.
Fleming, J.M. (1962), 'Domestic Financial Policies under Fixed and Floating Exchange Rates', *IMF Staff Papers*, November, pp. 369–79.
Mundell, R.A. (1957), 'International Trade and Factor Mobility', *American Economic Review*, **47**, June, pp. 321–35.
Mundell, R.A. (1960), 'The Monetary Dynamics of International Adjustment under Fixed and Flexible Exchange Rates', *Quarterly Journal of Economics*, **84**, May, pp. 227–57.
Mundell, R.A. (1961), 'A Theory of Optimum Currency Areas', *American Economic Review*, **51**, November, pp. 509–17.
Mundell, R.A. (1962), 'The Appropriate Use of Monetary and Fiscal Policy for Internal and External Stability', *IMF Staff Papers*, March, pp. 70–79.
Mundell, R.A. (1963a), 'Inflation and Real Interest', *Journal of Political Economy*, **71**, June, pp. 280–83.
Mundell, R.A. (1963b), 'Capital Mobility and Stabilisation Policy under Fixed and Flexible Exchange Rates', *Canadian Journal of Economics and Political Science*, **29**, November, pp. 475–85.
Mundell, R. A. (1968), *International Economics*, New York: Macmillan.
Mundell, R.A. (1971a), *Monetary Theory: Interest, Inflation and Growth in the World Economy*, Pacific Palisades, CA: Goodyear.

Mundell, R.A. (1971 b), 'The Dollar and the Policy Mix', *Essays in International Finance*, no. 85, Princeton, NJ: Princeton University Press.

Mundell, R.A. (1972), 'The Future of the International Financial System', A. Acheson, J. Chant and M. Prachowny (eds), *Bretton Woods Revisited*, Toronto: University of Toronto Press, pp. 91–104.

Mundell, R.A. (2000), 'A Reconsideration of the Twentieth Century', *American Economic Review*, **90**, June, pp. 327–40.

Obstfeld, M. (1997), 'Europe's Gamble', *Brookings Papers on Economic Activity*, no. 2, pp. 241–317.

Rose, A.K. (2000), 'A Review of Some of the Economic Contributions of Robert A. Mundell, Winner of the 1999 Nobel Memorial Prize in Economics', *Scandinavian Journal of Economics*, **102**, June, pp. 211–22.

Tobin, J. (1965), 'Money and Economic Growth', *Econometrica*, **33**, October, pp. 671–84.

Mundell–Fleming Model

See:

IS–LM Model: Open Economy; Mundell, Robert A.

Muth, John F.

John Muth (b.1930, Chicago, Illinois, USA) obtained his BS from Washington University in 1952 and his MS (1954) and PhD (1962) from Carnegie-Mellon University. His main past posts have included Senior Research Fellow, Assistant Professor and Associate Professor at Carnegie-Mellon University, 1956–64; Professor of Management at Michigan State University, 1964–9; and Professor of Operations Management at Indiana University, 1964–94. Since 1994 he has been Professor of Operations Management, Emeritus, at Indiana University. He is best known for his work on modelling expectations and in particular for his seminal article, 'Rational Expectations and the Theory of Price Movements' (*Econometrica*, **29**, July 1961).

See also:

Rational Expectations.

NAIRU

The rate of unemployment at which inflation is stable; the non-accelerating inflation rate of unemployment.

See also:

Natural Rate of Unemployment.

National Bureau of Economic Research

Founded in 1920, the NBER is a private, non-profit, non-partisan research organization whose main aim is 'to promote a greater understanding of how the economy works' by 'undertaking and disseminating unbiased economic research among policymakers, business professionals, and the academic community'. Its publications include the *NBER Macroeconomics Annual*. In the early years, research undertaken at the NBER concentrated on the macro economy and included pioneering work by Simon Kuznets, on developing the system of national income accounts; Wesley Mitchell, on business cycles; Milton Friedman, on the theory of the consumption function; and Milton Friedman and Anna Schwartz, on money and business cycles. Today the Bureau's empirical research is focused on four main areas: developing new statistical measurements, estimating quantitative models of economic behaviour, assessing the effects of public policies on the US economy, and projecting the effects of alternative policy proposals. The main office of the NBER is located in Cambridge, Massachusetts and its president and chief executive is Martin Feldstein. For more information the reader is referred to the official website of the NBER (http://www.nber.org/).

See also:

Feldstein, Martin; Friedman, Milton; Kuznets, Simon S.; Mitchell, Wesley C.; Schwartz, Anna J.

National Income

The income that originates in the production of goods and services supplied by residents of a nation.

Natural Rate of Unemployment

The term 'natural rate of unemployment' refers to a level of unemployment which is compatible with a constant rate of inflation. In fact it is the only level of unemployment which is compatible with a constant rate of inflation. This is best illustrated by referring to the expectations-augmented Phillips curve in its price formulation:

$$\pi_t = \alpha + \beta(u_t - u^*) + \gamma E\pi \qquad \beta < 0, \gamma = 1, \tag{1}$$

where π is the actual rate of inflation, $E\pi$ is the expected rate of inflation, u_t is actual unemployment and u^* is the level of unemployment associated with capacity output, and was called the natural rate of unemployment by Friedman (1968).

The gap between actual unemployment and the natural rate represents the degree of excess demand and can be equivalently described in terms of output. This leads to the equivalent specification:

$$\pi_t = \alpha + \beta(y_t - y^*) + \gamma E\pi \qquad \beta > 0, \gamma = 1, \tag{1a}$$

where y_t is actual output and y^* capacity output.

Note that, for the sake of ease of exposition, both these formulations of the Phillips curve ignore productivity changes and influences other than domestic demand. Introduction of these other factors will not significantly change the predictions of the model.

Given the assumption that $\gamma = 1$, equating π and $E\pi$ in equation (1) produces

$$\pi_t - E\pi = \alpha + \beta(u_t - u^*). \tag{2}$$

Equilibrium requires the expected rate of inflation to be equal to the actual rate of inflation, otherwise agents would alter their behaviour pattern. Consequently, reference to equation (2) illustrates that equilibrium is only possible where $u = u^*$; that is, the actual rate of unemployment equals the natural rate. At this point it is worth emphasizing that the natural rate refers to some positive rate of unemployment. Workers will be unemployed during the time that they are searching for another job after relinquishing one job voluntarily or after being dismissed.

Any attempt by the authorities to maintain unemployment below the natural rate will be associated with 'accelerating' inflation. This process is illustrated in Figure 1, with linear Phillips curves being used for ease of exposition, noting that each short-run Phillips curve is associated with a different expected rate of inflation. The natural rate is shown as *UN*.

Starting the process with employment at the natural rate and an expected inflation rate of zero, any attempt to reduce unemployment permanently, to, say, *A* will cause the short-run Phillips curve to shift upwards continuously. First of all, it will shift upwards to *SRPC2* (with expected inflation = *OB*) with the fall in unemployment from *UN* to *A* resulting from the *unanticipated* expansion of aggregated demand. Subsequently, given maintenance of the government's desire to keep the level of unemployment at *A*, the Phillips curve will shift upwards again to *SRPC3* (with expected inflation = *OC*). This process of *accelerating* inflation (that is, *OB* to *OC* and so on) would continue while unemployment was held below the natural rate at, say, *A* and would cease only when unemployment returned to the natural rate, so that the Phillips curve in the long run is vertical at the natural rate of unemployment. Conversely, at levels of unemployment greater than the natural rate, the rate of inflation will decelerate. This process explains the alternative but less elegant term for the natural rate: the non-accelerating inflation rate of unemployment (NAIRU).

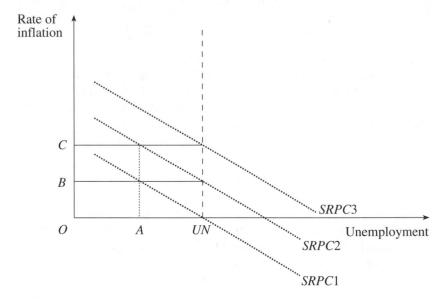

Figure 1   The expectations-augmented Phillips curve and the natural rate

It is important to realize that the natural rate is not immutable. It is dependent on the structural characteristics of the economy as a whole and the labour market in particular. General influences include such factors as the growth of productivity and all the determinants of the demand for and supply of labour functions, such as unemployment benefits, the minimum wage and strength of trade unions. To quote from Friedman (1968), 'it is the level [of unemployment] that would be ground out by the Walrasian system of general equilibrium equations'.

The policy prescriptions of the natural rate hypothesis are quite subtle. It is not possible for the authorities to lower actual unemployment permanently below the natural rate through demand management policies without continuously accelerating inflation. Conversely, governments must raise unemployment temporarily above the natural rate if they wish to lower the rate of inflation. It might also be objected that demand management policies could be directed towards maintaining the actual level of unemployment at or near the natural rate. The problem with this suggestion is that such fine-tuning of the economy requires a fairly precise estimate of the natural rate itself, apart from the structure of the rest of the economy. The required degree of precision seems to be lacking, as evidenced by estimates across a wide range of countries. To take just one example, Staiger *et al.* (1997a) estimate the natural rate for the United States to be 6.2 per cent, but with a 95 per cent confidence interval of 5.1 per cent to 7.7 per cent. This lack of both a long-run trade-off between unemployment and inflation, and also knowledge of the level of the natural rate does not *per se* debar government intervention in the economy. Supply-side policies to lower the 'natural' rate are feasible as long as they are directed towards the determinants of the natural rate.

This view of government macroeconomic policy is critically dependent on the assumption that the natural rate itself is not influenced by the actual current rate of unemployment. This is in itself controversial, since lower current unemployment may also alter the natural rate through the process of 'hysteresis' (see Ball, 1999). Consequently, attempts to cure inflation by raising unemployment above the natural rate may also raise the natural rate itself, so as to leave a permanent scar on the economy (see Mankiw, 2001, p. 48).

The natural rate hypothesis underpins the 'classical dichotomy' and the view that money is neutral in the long run. This is not a new idea as Hume (1752) wrote, 'In my opinion, it is only in this interval or intermediate situation, between the acquisition of money and rise of prices, that the increasing quantity of gold and silver is favourable to industry.' Friedman, drawing on Wicksell's concept of the natural rate of interest, formalized the concept of the natural rate of unemployment.

JOHN L. THOMPSON

See also:

Classical Dichotomy; Expectations-augmented Phillips Curve; Hysteresis; Okun's Law; Phillips Curve; Supply-side Economics.

Bibliography

Ball, L. (1999), 'Aggregate Demand and Long-Run Unemployment', *Brookings Papers on Economic Activity*, pp. 189–251

Cross, R. (ed.) (1995), *The Natural Rate of Unemployment: Reflections on 25 Years of the Hypothesis*, Cambridge: Cambridge University Press.

Friedman, M. (1968), 'The Role of Monetary Policy', *American Economic Review*, **58**, March, pp. 1–17.

Gordon, R.J. (1997), 'The Time-Varying NAIRU and its Implications for Economic Policy', *Journal of Economic Perspectives*, **11**, Winter, pp. 11–32.

Hume, D. (1752), 'Of Money', reproduced in K.A. Chrystal (ed.), (1990), *Monetarism*, vol. 1, Aldershot, UK and Brookfield, US: Edward Elgar, p. 8.

Mankiw, N.G. (2001), 'The Inexorable and Mysterious Trade-Off between Inflation and Unemployment', *Economic Journal*, **111**, May, pp. 45–61.

Staiger, D., J.H. Stock and M.W. Watson (1997a), 'How Precise are the Estimates of the Natural Rate of Unemployment?', in C.D. Romer and D.H. Romer (eds), *Reducing Inflation: Motivation and Strategy*, Chicago: University of Chicago Press, pp. 195–246.

Staiger, D., J.H. Stock and M.W. Watson (1997b), 'The NAIRU, Unemployment and Monetary Policy', *Journal of Economic Perspectives*, **11**, Winter, pp. 33–49.

Neoclassical Growth Model

The neoclassical model of economic growth is supply-dominated. Its basic assumption is that the unemployment rates of labour and capital are constant. They are not, of course; but the assumption is partially justified by the observation that unemployment and capacity-utilization rates in advanced economies tend to be confined within a fairly narrow range. With few exceptions, in any 25-to-50-year interval to which the model might be applied, the change in aggregate output from beginning to end would measure largely the growth of potential output, and reflect only slightly variations in effective demand.

Once this assumption is accepted, the evolution of the aggregative model is straightforward. At the beginning of a period the model economy has a stock of capital goods inherited from past investment and depreciation, and a supply of labour determined by demography and custom. (It is a harmless simplification that labour is taken to be supplied inelastically. A positive real-wage elasticity of supply can be included, but that changes nothing important and complicates exposition.) Current technology translates the supply of capital goods and labour into aggregate (potential) output. Normal market mechanisms determine the division of output between current consumption and gross investment. Allowance for depreciation and population growth then leads to the stock of capital goods and the labour force for the next period, and the model can start again.

The bland phrase 'normal market mechanisms' can cover a broad variety of economic processes. At one extreme is the assumption that the economy is tracing out the infinite-horizon plan of an immortal, foresighted household that maximizes a time-additive utility function, defined over consumption paths, constrained only by current and future technology and identities. Under favourable assumptions, this process can be decentralized to perfectly competitive markets. At the other extreme, the economy could be centrally planned according to arbitrary rules. In between are various combinations of perfect and imperfect competition in goods and factor markets, more or less empirically plausible supply functions for labour and capital goods, and consumption or savings functions summarily describing household behaviour. The same institutional assumptions will yield factor prices: real wage rates and rental rates for capital. The commonest assumption has been universal perfect competition. The basic assumption is maintained throughout that consumption and investment add up to potential output; that is, that savings equals investment identically at the fixed and constant level of utilization.

At this level of generality, the main conclusions that emerge from the neoclassical growth model are (a) with reasonable savings-investment functions, if the unchanging technology exhibits constant returns to scale in labour and capital, and enough diminishing returns to each factor, every path tends to a steady state in which output, capital stock and employment grow exponentially at the same rate; (b) thus the long-run growth rate is demographically determined, and steady-state productivity (output per person) is constant; (c) a permanent increase in the rate of investment can increase the growth rate only temporarily, but can increase the level of output permanently; (d) with technological progress of a special 'labour-augmenting' kind, (a) has to be modified to say that, in the eventual steady state, output and capital grow at the same rate, equal to the sum of the growth rate of the labour force and the rate of labour-augmenting technological progress, so that steady-state labour productivity and income per person grow at the rate of technological progress; (e) even with labour-augmenting technological progress, (c) remains true; (f) the model can accommodate increasing or decreasing returns to scale, but the steady-state property is retained only if non-constant returns to scale take a particular labour-enhancing form; (9) with increasing (decreasing) returns to scale, steady-state output per worker is rising (falling), and (c) remains true (see Solow, 2000; 2001).

This model has been extended in several different directions. Perhaps the most important is the introduction of human capital as a third factor of production, modelled analogously to physical capital (see Mankiw *et al.*, 1992). This does not alter the tone of the basic conclusions. Other extensions include allowance for two (or more) distinct produced goods (for instance, a consumer good and an investment good, or an agricultural good and an industrial good), introduction of a renewable or non-renewable natural resource and extension to a system of two or more growing and trading economies. Special mention should be made of Arrow's (1962) model of 'learning by doing', which makes the level of technology endogenously dependent on cumulative gross investment, but otherwise stays within the neoclassical model and leads to conclusions similar to those sketched above. The later so-called 'endogenous growth models' represent a larger departure in that conclusion (c) ceases to hold for them (see Barro and Sala-i-Martin, 1995; Jones, 1998; Valdés, 1999).

The main deficiencies of the neoclassical growth model include the absence of a well-developed aggregate demand side. This has the effect of separating the growth model from any consideration of short-run or medium-run macroeconomic fluctuations, except insofar as exogenous variations in the rate of investment affect the path of the model economy. This characteristic is usually expressed in terms of the absence of an independent investment function that would allow *ex ante* discrepancies between saving and investment.

One way to start creating an organic connection between a growth model and short-run macroeconomics would be to introduce explicit utilization rates for labour $(1-u)$ and capital $(1-v)$. Then a distinction can be drawn between potential output $Y_p = F(K,L,t)$ and current output $Y = F((1-v)K, (1-u)L,t)$ where F is a production function with the standard properties mentioned earlier. Then short-run equilibrium can be represented by IS–LM or any other appropriate model of aggregate demand that can be solved to give $Y = Y(M,F,Y_p)$, $r = r(M,F,Y_p)$ and $I = I(M,F,Y_p)$, where M and F are indicators of the stance of monetary and fiscal policy. Y_p enters because consumption and investment could plausibly be taken to depend on something like Y/Y_p. If I is interpreted as net investment, the growth process requires $dK/dt = I$. As before, it is simplest to take $L = L(t)$ as exogenous and exponential, though employment $(=(1-u)L)$ is endogenous. If $u=v=0$, then $Y = Y_p = C + dK/dt + \text{depreciation}$ and this reduces to the simplest neoclassical growth model.

The contentious part of this kind of construction would centre on $r(t)$ and its relation to the marginal product of capital as calculated from $F(.,.,.)$, on the determination of the price level (taken as given for the short-run model) and on the relation between u and v. It is to be noted that if aggregate saving is represented by $S(Y,Y_p)$, then $I = S$ for every t, but Y is not necessarily equal to Y_p.

The other obvious gap in the neoclassical growth model has already been mentioned. In a steady state the growth rate of income per head is determined solely by the rate of labour-augmenting technological progress. Thus if $Y_p(t) = F(K(t),A(t)L(t))$, the long-term growth rate of Y_p is the sum of the growth rates of A and L. Since $A(t)$ is exogenous, like $L(t)$, the model can be said to leave an important outcome exogenous. This is not quite true, as the earlier reference to 'learning by doing' suggests. But normal policy tools have no effect on the steady-state growth rate, though they do affect the level of the long-term trend. Many attempts have been made to extend the neoclassical model by making $A(t)$ explicitly the outcome of economically motivated decisions by agents, while remaining in other respects within the neoclassical framework (see Romer, 1990; Aghion and Howitt, 1998).

All such attempts seem to run into the limitation that they depend critically on a crucial linearity assumption, and thus tend to be non-robust. In effect, they require that increments to $A(t)$ be 'produced' by a relation like $dA/dt = G(A,X)$ where X is a 'level' variable that responds to economic incentives (and thus potentially to policy). If $G(A,X)$ has the form $Ag(X)$, then the growth rate of A (and Y_p) is determined by X, as desired. But if the elasticity of G with respect to A is even slightly above or below one, the model fails to deliver an endogenous steady-state growth rate.

The same formulation exhibits the so-called 'scale effect'. Let g be an increasing function of X. A 'larger' economy (for example, one with greater population) ought to be able to achieve a larger value of X, whatever X is, and thus faster growth. But it is not the case that large economies tend to grow faster. Reasonable solutions have been proposed for this difficulty, but the larger puzzle remains.

ROBERT M. SOLOW

See also:

Endogenous Growth Theory.

Bibliography

Aghion, P. and P. Howitt (1998), *Endogenous Growth Theory*, Cambridge, MA: MIT Press.

Arrow, K.J. (1962), 'The Economic Implications of Learning by Doing', *Review of Economic Studies*, **29**, June, pp. 155–73.

Barro, R.J. and X. Sala-i-Martin (1995), *Economic Growth*, New York: McGraw-Hill.

Jones, C.I. (1998), *Introduction to Economic Growth*, New York: W.W. Norton.

Mankiw, N.G., D. Romer and D.N. Weil (1992), 'A Contribution to the Empirics of Economic Growth,' *Quarterly Journal of Economics*, **107**, May, pp. 407–37.

Romer, P.M. (1990), 'Endogenous Technological Change', *Journal of Political Economy*, **98**, October, pp. S71–102.

Solow, R.M. (2000), *Growth Theory: An Exposition*, 2nd edn, Oxford: Oxford University Press.

Solow, R.M. (2001), *Landmark Papers in Economic Growth*, Cheltenham, UK and Northampton, MA, USA: Edward Elgar.

Valdés, B. (1999), *Economic Growth: Theory, Empirics and Policy*, Cheltenham, UK and Northampton, MA, USA: Edward Elgar.

Neoclassical Synthesis

The neoclassical synthesis is a term, attributed to Samuelson (1955, pp. vi, 212), denoting the mainstream professional consensus on the theory of the whole economy which was current from the 1940s to the early 1970s. It was composed of two elements: the debate on what were perceived to be the principal innovations introduced by J.M. Keynes in the *General Theory of Employment, Interest and Money* (1936), and the extent to which these innovations could be reconciled within the existing framework of neoclassical economics. Typically, it was assumed that a decentralized market economy subject to a deflationary shock would, in time, adjust to full employment equilibrium unless prevented by 'Keynesian' rigidities, at which point corrective macroeconomic policy would become relevant.

The achievement of professional consensus was a considerable step forward and the era of the neoclassical synthesis saw major advances in both theoretical and applied economics. It also coincided with a period of exceptional economic prosperity – a golden age of full employment, unprecedented high growth and low inflation – which served to confirm the confident feeling that macroeconomics had come of age.

For Keynes, however, the implications of the neoclassical synthesis were more complex. On the one hand, what became the standard interpretation of Keynesian economics could be associated with the successful management of the economy. On the other hand, and more profoundly, it represented the failure of the Keynesian revolution. Keynes had sought to provide a theory relevant to the real world, in which agents took decisions – on consumption, investment and the demand for money – under conditions of uncertainty and in which the level of effective demand so determined would in turn determine output and employment. Thus constrained, the economy would move forward in shifting equilibrium, with full employment equilibrium to be viewed as a limiting case governed by the assumptions of neoclassical economics. In an attempt to ensure the acceptance of his more general theory, Keynes had laid stress on his points of departure from orthodoxy and had consequently been criticized for his overtly controversial style of argument. It was therefore ironic that the neoclassical synthesis confirmed the validity of orthodox theory and subsumed Keynesian economics as a special case, albeit one relevant to policy making in an imperfectly adjusting real world (see Fletcher, 1987, pp. 17–19, 25–6, 29–36, 58–67).

The problem began with Keynes himself, who not only retained neoclassical elements within his theoretical scheme (an attempt at reconciliation between old and new that was bound to attract imitators) but also expressed his highly complex ideas in a form that did not readily lend itself to modern notions of economic analysis. It was inevitable, therefore, that more attention would be paid to parts that were testable than to those that were not.

The first and best known attempt at reconciliation was that of Hicks (1937), who sought to minimize the extent of Keynes's departures from his Marshallian roots, except in the peculiar circumstance of the 'liquidity trap' (in which the rate of interest is prevented by absolute liquidity preference from falling to the full employment level) which Hicks identified as 'Mr. Keynes's *special theory*' (Hicks 1937, p. 141).

Hicks also, famously, captured the central mechanism of Keynes's theory with his IS–LL model, which was later modified by Hansen (1949, ch. 5) to produce the IS–LM system familiar to generations of economics students. It was a brilliant simplification, with just two curves relating equilibrium interest and income, via money, investment and saving, but one which emasculated Keynesian economics by excluding its most characteristic features. Hicks also assumed money wages to be given, so that there was no distinction between real and monetary variables and, in the spirit of Keynes's original, placed the emphasis very clearly on the side of aggregate demand. The contributions of Hicks also heralded the beginning of the mathematization of the *General Theory* (see Skidelsky, 1992, ch. 16, pp. 610–24).

Hicks received Keynes's general approval for his formulation, though Keynes did in the same year publish an article (Keynes, 1937) that emphasized just those features that IS–LL omitted. In particular, the stress this article placed on the economic significance of uncertainty inspired aspects of the Post Keynesian response to the neoclassical synthesis (see Davidson, 1972, chs 1–2; Harcourt, 1987b). For orthodox economists, however, the crucial omissions lay elsewhere. Modigliani, in an influential article (Modigliani, 1944), supplemented Hicks's analysis with the addition of a competitive labour market, together with money wages and prices to produce a general equilibrium system in two parts. On the real, supply side, the labour market adjusts to produce an equilibrium real wage and output at full employment. On the money, demand side, the IS–LL system determines nominal income and the interest rate. The ratio of real to nominal income determines the price level which, in conjunction with the money wage, gives the equilibrium real wage.

Keynesian underemployment equilibrium will only occur in the presence of obstacles to adjustment in the form of the liquidity trap, which prevents nominal income from expanding to the full employment level, and of rigid money wages. Labour is assumed perfectly elastic in supply at some historically given money wage up to the full employment level. With the money wage fixed, monetary variables determine real values and the actual level of employment will only be known once aggregate demand, nominal income and the price level are determined. Therefore, Keynesian underemployment will be for a reason (wage rigidity) perfectly comprehensible to orthodox economists – except in the limiting case of absolute liquidity preference.

A different interpretation was given by Patinkin (1948, 1956), with a mixed message for Keynes. On the one hand, the concept of underemployment equilibrium was dismissed as logically impossible. With labour on its supply curve at the going real wage there is full employment equilibrium. If labour is off its supply curve with an excess supply of labour at the going real wage, we have a state of underemployment *disequilibrium*. That is, Keynesian involuntary unemployment is a disequilibrium phenomenon. This must be the case whether wages and prices are rigid or flexible. On the other hand, Patinkin was able to explain how unemployment could persist in the absence of rigidities by appealing to the Keynesian concept of inadequate aggregate demand. Though wage–price inflation would eventually correct the disequilibrium via the indirect or direct real balance effect, the process could be protracted, especially given adverse effects on expectations, so that there is scope for Keynesian policy measures, especially of the public works variety.

The possibilities offered for economic management shaped the neoclassical synthesis research programme and considerable advances were made on the study of the behavioural functions, of consumption, investment and the demand for money by, for example, Friedman, Modigliani, Jorgenson and Tobin (see Blanchard, 1987, p.635 and references). These in turn became components of more comprehensive schemes as the emphasis shifted towards the building of large-scale macroeconometric models of the economy such as those developed by Klein and Goldberger (1955) and the MPS model associated with Modigliani (see Beaud and Dostaler, 1997, ch. 5). This work carried out during the 1950s and 1960s might be considered a period of normal science in the Kuhnian sense.

The neoclassical synthesis was always an uneasy alliance of incompatible systems and critics were ready to point to inherent misrepresentations of Keynes (see, for example, Chick, 1983; Clarke, 1988, chs 12–13; Togati, 1998). The most visible critic was Leijonhufvud (1968) who, building on work by Clower (1965), drew an eye-catching distinction between Keynesian economics and what he took to be the 'economics of Keynes'. Because he employed a Walrasian general equilibrium system, however, and interpreted unemployment as a disequilibrium phenomenon, the ultimate significance of his contribution is debatable.

A more serious challenge was posed by the inability of theory to explain economic events. First, there were doubts as to how far the postwar prosperity was due to macroeconomic management and how far the product of thc growth of world trade and favourable economic circumstances stemming from the postwar reconstruction. There was also increasing concern that simple demand management models were inadequate and relied too much on *ad hoc* theorizing (Shaw, 1988, pp. 28–47). The most dramatic illustration of this was the Phillips curve (Phillips, 1958) which, viewed as the missing link of the IS–LM model, was eagerly seized upon as a means of promoting full employment policies without unacceptable inflation. It was not, however, a theory but a statistical relation, which failed in the face of the stagflation of the 1970s. In the crisis of macroeconomics that followed, the neoclassical synthesis gave way to monetarist and rational expectations models which seemed better able to explain contemporary events (see, for example, Friedman, 1971; Lucas, 1980).

GORDON FLETCHER

See also:

IS–LM Model: Closed Economy; Keynes, John Maynard; Keynesian Economics; Keynesian Economics: Reappraisals of; Macroeconometric Models; Phillips Curve; Post Keynesian Economics; Real Balance Effect.

Bibliography

Beaud, M. and G. Dostaler (1997), *Economic Thought since Keynes*, London and New York: Routledge.
Blanchard, O.J. (1987), 'Neoclassical Synthesis' in J. Eatwell, M. Milgate and P. Newman (eds) *The New Palgrave: A Dictionary of Economics*, vol. 3, London and Basingstoke: The Macmillan Press, pp. 634–6.
Chick, V. (1983), *Macroeconomics After Keynes: A Reconsideration of the General Theory*, Deddington: Philip Allan.
Clarke, P. (1988), *The Keynesian Revolution in the Making 1924–1936*, Oxford: Clarendon Press.
Clower, R.W. (1965), 'The Keynesian Counter-Revolution: A Theoretical Appraisal' in F.H. Hahn and F. Brechling (eds), *The Theory of Interest Rates*, London: Macmillan.
Davidson, P. (1972), *Money and the Real World*, London and Basingstoke: The Macmillan Press.
Fletcher, G.A. (1987), *The Keynesian Revolution and Its Critics: Issues of Theory and Policy for the Monetary Production Economy*, Basingstoke and London: Macmillan.
Friedman, M. (1971), *A Theoretical Framework for Monetary Analysis*, New York: National Bureau of Economic Research.
Greenaway, D., M. Bleaney and I.M.T Stewart (eds) (1991), *Companion to Contemporary Economic Thought*, London: Routledge.
Hansen, A. (1949), *Monetary Theory and Fiscal Policy*, New York: McGraw-Hill.
Harcourt, G.C. (1987a), 'Bastard Keynesianism', in J. Eatwell, M. Milgate and P. Newman (eds), *The New Palgrave: A Dictionary of Economics*, vol. 1, London and Basingstoke: The Macmillan Press, pp. 204–4.
Harcourt, G.C. (1987b), 'Post-Keynesian Economics', in J. Eatwell, M. Milgate and P. Newman (eds), *The New Palgrave: A Dictionary of Economics*, vol. 3, London and Basingstoke: The Macmillan Press, pp. 924–8.
Hicks, J. (1937), 'Mr Keynes and the "Classics"; A Suggested Interpretation', *Econometrica*, 5, April, pp. 147–59.
Hillard, J. (ed.), (1988), *J.M. Keynes in Retrospect: The Legacy of the Keynesian Revolution*, Aldershot, UK and Brookfield, US: Edward Elgar.

Keynes, J.M. (1936), *The General Theory of Employment, Interest and Money*, London: Macmillan.

Keynes J.M. (1937), 'The General Theory of Employment', *Quarterly Journal of Economics*, **51**, February, pp. 209–23.

Klein, L.R. and A.S. Goldberger (1955), *An Econometric Model of the United States: 1929–52*, New York: John Wiley.

Leijonhufvud, A. (1968), *On Keynesian Economics and the Economics of Keynes: A Study of Monetary Theory*, New York: Oxford University Press.

Lucas, R.E. Jr (1980), 'Methods and Problems in Business Cycle Theory', *Journal of Money, Credit and Banking*, **12**, November, pp. 696–715.

Modigliani, F. (1944), 'Liquidity Preference and the Theory of Interest and Money', *Econometrica*, **12**, January, pp. 45–88.

Patinkin, D. (1948), 'Price Flexibility and Full Employment', *American Economic Revue*, **38**, September, pp. 543–64.

Patinkin, D. (1956), *Money, Interest and Prices*, New York: Harper & Row.

Phillips, A.W. (1958), 'The Relation between Unemployment and the Rate of Change of Money Wage Rates in the United Kingdom, 1861–1957', *Economica*, **25**, November pp. 283–99.

Samuelson, P. (1955), *Economics*, 3rd edn, New York: McGraw-Hill.

Shaw, G.K. (1988), *Keynesian Economics: The Permanent Revolution*, Aldershot, UK and Brookfield, US: Edward Elgar.

Skidelsky, R. (1992), *John Maynard Keynes: The Economist as Saviour 1920–1937*, London: Macmillan.

Togati, T.D. (1998), *Keynes and the Neoclassical Synthesis: Einsteinian versus Newtonian Macroeconomics*, London: Routledge.

Young, W. (1987), *Interpreting Mr. Keynes: The IS–LM Enigma*, Cambridge: Polity Press.

Net Capital Flows

Capital flows from the rest of the world to a country minus capital flows from that country to the rest of the world. A net capital outflow occurs where outflows are greater than inflows, while a net capital inflow occurs where inflows are greater than outflows.

Net Exports

Exports of goods and services minus imports of goods and services; also known as the trade balance.

See also:

Trade Balance.

Neutrality of Money

The question whether money is 'neutral' with respect to the so-called 'real' economy, in other words, whether money is a 'veil', has been one of the recurrent themes in the economics debate over the last two-and-a-half centuries. The use of the term 'neutral', however, is of more recent origin. To all appearances it was first used by Wicksell to describe a situation where the market rate of interest is equal to the natural rate, that is the rate that would be found in a barter economy (Wicksell, 1898, p. 93; 1936, p. 102). Wicksell actually did not discuss neutral money but neutral interest. The idea, however, also implies neutral money in the sense that it describes a situation where money is indeed no more than a veil. Koopmans (1933 p. 228, n. 1) tells us that the term 'neutral money' was coined in 1919 by the German economist L. von Bortkiewicz and that at the end of the 1920s it more or less formed part of the standard vocabulary of Dutch monetary economists (see also Fase, 1992). It gained currency in the early 1930s through the publications of Hayek (1967) and Koopmans (1933) (see Klausinger, 1989; Patinkin and Steiger, 1989). The term 'neutral money' is, however, somewhat confusing as it has been used for different concepts:

1. the situation that money is a veil in the sense that the economy behaves as if it were a barter economy;
2. the situation of absence of disturbances from the monetary sphere, that is, maintenance of monetary equilibrium at all times;
3. neutrality in a comparative static sense, that is, the quantity theory of money;
4. superneutrality, that is the phenomenon that the 'real' economy is indifferent to the rate of inflation.

If money is a veil, the monetary economy behaves exactly like a barter economy. Relative prices of goods and services and quantities traded would not differ. Koopmans (1933, p. 230) and Hayek (1967, p. 130) emphasized that neutrality in this sense does not refer to real-world situations, but only serves as a kind of benchmark that helps to study the disturbances that may follow from the use of money. The barter economy they refer to is frictionless. The problem with this approach, is that, if barter is frictionless, there is no rationale for using money and the whole exercise seems futile. It is simply inconceivable that the use of money does not make a difference; that it is, in the happy phrase coined by Samuelson (1968), qualitatively neutral.

What Koopmans and Hayek and their Swedish predecessors Wicksell and Davidson in fact did was study the circumstances under which no excess supply of or demand for money would manifest itself; that is, they studied the conditions for monetary equilibrium (on Davidson, see Myrdal, 1933, pp. 436–8 and Thomas, 1935). This is equivalent to Say's Equality, or Say's Law seen as an equilibrium condition. Wicksell, Davidson and Hayek saw the constancy of a term or a combination of terms from the equation of exchange as a condition for monetary equilibrium. However, Koopmans demonstrated that this need not be the case, as it all depends on what happens in the real sector of the economy. In a stationary economy M, V, P and T of course have to remain constant for monetary equilibrium. Davidson argued that Wicksell's criterion of a constant P no longer holds in the case of productivity increases. These are tantamount to an increase in the natural rate of interest. A constant M with the price level falling, and thus a rise in the real interest rate, would be required to maintain monetary equilibrium. Davidson developed his views in a review of Wicksell (1898). Wicksell analyzed a so-called 'pure credit' economy, that is an economy without base money, where all money is created by the banks through credit creation. The banks will increase the volume of credit, and thus the volume of money, if the market rate of interest is lower than the natural rate. Thus the need for a constant M and a falling P in the case of productivity increases, according to Davidson.

Hayek did not bother about the way money is created, but simply asked himself how much money is required to maintain monetary equilibrium. He noted that changes in the degree of integration of the production process, as, for instance, when spinning and weaving are divided into two independent firms, have an impact on the demand for cash balances. Such a change implies a change in the velocity of money and any such change calls for a compensating change in the money supply to maintain Say's Equality. His criterion for the neutrality of money consequently is a constant MV (Hayek, 1967, pp. 121, 123). In this case V is defined as the income velocity of money, not the transactions velocity. Koopmans finally wondered what happens when the supply conditions of goods change. If, for instance, in an economy with three goods, A, B and C, the supply of A suffers from a bad harvest, no constancy of any item or combination of items from the equation of exchange may ensure monetary equilibrium. If the demand for good A is inelastic, its price will rise. B and C producers spend more on A and less on each other's products. Monetary equilibrium will only be maintained if A producers immediately increase their spending on B and C. Monetary equilibrium requires that MV increases, while T or y has fallen and P has increased (Koopmans, 1933, pp. 298–303; see also De Jong, 1973).

An older strand in the literature is the quantity theory. The quantity theory implies neutrality in a comparative-statics sense. This is a case of what Samuelson calls 'quantitative neutrality'. In the first fully developed analysis of the quantity theory, David Hume showed how an increase in the money supply increases spending and first results in higher employment (Hume, 1955 [1752]). Prices increase only gradually and money obviously affects the real sector during the transition between one equilibrium situation and the other. In later mathematical representations of the quantity theory, however, there is a dichotomy between the real and monetary sectors of the economy, in the sense that quantities and relative prices are determined in the real sector and the price level, and hence money prices, in the monetary sector (for instance, Walras, 1965, pp. 315–24; Divisia, 1962, p. 169). The economy is represented by a general equilibrium system specifying equilibrium conditions for all markets. The dichotomy implies that demand and supply are functions of real variables only, including relative prices. If equilibrium is found at some set of relative prices, this equilibrium is not affected by any proportional change in absolute prices. While the equation system may be mathematically irreproachable in the sense that the number of unknowns equals the number of independent equations, it lacks an economic mechanism linking individual prices to the money supply.

Patinkin (1965, pp. 75, 175) showed conclusively that, in a general equilibrium model, the price level can only be determined if the excess demand functions for goods contain real money balances as an argument. In this way an economic mechanism is built in which transmits monetary impulses to the real sector: if the money supply increases, real balances grow larger. This will stimulate demand and the monetary impulse will work its way into higher prices. In more recent approaches, in particular in New Classical Economics, real effects of changes in the money supply follow from unexpected monetary shocks that are mistakenly seen at first by economic agents as real shocks (cf. Lucas, 1996). Otherwise changes in the money supply would feed quasi-immediately into higher prices, as rational economic agents would know the new equilibrium prices and, through competition, be forced to trade at those prices. The transition period from one equilibrium to another would be asymptotically approaching zero.

Patinkin gave a mathematical expression to Hume's insight that money can be neutral in the sense of the quantity theory, that is, quantitatively neutral in a comparative-statics sense. A change in the money supply leads to another price level and in the new equilibrium situation quantities and relative prices may have reverted to their original values. There is no reference to a barter economy. Nonetheless, there is something inherently unsatisfactory in mathematical general equilibrium models of a monetary economy, such as Patinkin's. Price determination takes place essentially as a Walrasian tâtonnement mechanism, that is, without any friction. In other words, the transactions technology in such an economy is not different from a barter economy and the use of money does not really make a difference. It is difficult to justify the use of money in such models. Verbal expositions of the quantity theory, such as Hume's, do not suffer from this defect as they do not presuppose a tâtonnement pricing mechanism.

During the transition from one equilibrium situation to another, real variables are affected by monetary impulses and it is easy to imagine that the new equilibrium may differ from the original one. New money usually is not distributed proportionally to existing cash holders as a gift, like the dropping of bank notes from a helicopter envisaged by Friedman (1969, p.4). Money enters the economy through inflationary financed spending by the government, through a balance of payments surplus of the non-bank sector or through bank loans taken out by borrowers. If people borrow to finance consumption, that will drive up the rate of interest, but if businessmen receive net foreign payments their cash balances increase and they are likely to lend out some of the money, in the process reducing the rate of interest, as Richard Cantillon explained (Cantillon, 1964, pp.212–23). A change in the rate of interest may have lasting consequences. The structure of the economy may, for instance, change if aggregate investments increase as a result of the lower rate of interest. The same may hold for any change in the structure of relative prices and its consequent change in the structure of spending (for a meticulous analysis of the way changes in the money supply or money demand work their way through the economy, in the process changing relative prices, see also Keynes, 1971, ch. 17). In general, a number of conditions must be fulfilled for money to be fully neutral in a comparative statics analysis:

1. full price flexibility;
2. absence of money illusion, so that people do not mistake price level increases for relative price increases;
3. distribution of new money over economic agents proportional to existing money holdings;
4. absence of destabilizing price expectations, as when price increases fuel fears of further inflation and thus a scramble for inflation-proof assets such as real estate, jewellery and foreign assets;
5. no change in the ratio between base money and the total money supply, as that would imply a different relationship between bank money and total money and thus a change in the real volume of bank loans and, consequently, in the rate of interest;
6. absence of open market policies, as open market purchases, for instance, increase the money supply and the price level and thus leave the general public poorer; this may lead to higher savings and thus to a fall in the rate of interest;
7. absence of debt denominated in nominal, rather than real, terms;
8. money is fiat money, as, with full-blooded silver or gold coins, a change in the money supply and a consequent change in the price level would imply a change in the relative prices of silver or gold and all other goods and services.

Of course, neutrality in this strict sense can never be achieved in the real world. In assessments of real world developments, for instance by classical authors such as Ricardo, the criterion of neutrality therefore is used in a weaker sense; it refers to the level of output, not its composition (Humphrey, 1991). Neutrality in this sense would require that spending increases by actors who see their real wealth increase through an increase in the real value of their holdings of fixed nominal value assets (thanks to a larger than average increase in their holdings of helicopter-dropped money or through deflation) or a fall in the real value of their fixed nominal value debt (through inflation) are just offset by a fall in spending by actors who see their real wealth decrease as a result of an uneven distribution of new money and of price level changes. It goes without saying that neutrality, not only in the strict sense but also in the weaker one, is far removed from the world of Keynes's *General Theory*. With underutilization of resources the normal state of affairs, changes in the money supply can hardly fail to have an impact on real variables, unless the system is stuck in a liquidity trap.

Even if changes in the money supply were neutral, changes in the growth rate of money need not be neutral. If they are, we have superneutrality. This, of course, is a case of quantitative neutrality again. Different growth rates of the money supply are associated with different inflation rates. As long as no interest is received on money, or at least no interest rate that keeps pace with the rate of inflation, real effects on the economy are likely. For instance, people may react to a higher rate of inflation by reducing their real cash balances and investing more in other assets, such as common stock. The investment ratio increases. This phenomenon is known as the Tobin effect or the Mundell–Tobin effect, called after the pioneers of the monetary growth models featuring this trait (Mundell, 1963; Tobin, 1965). A fundamental problem with this kind of model is that it depicts a one-good economy where trade between economic agents does not play a role and a rationale for the use of money is absent. This implies that the harm inflicted by high inflation on the efficiency of the payments system is neglected (Orphanides and Solow, 1990).

In the 1930s, neutrality of money in the sense of the maintenance of monetary equilibrium was seen by the main protagonists as a desirable state of affairs, as it meant that the economic system would be free from shocks originating from the monetary sphere. Koopmans, however, showed conclusively that, in the case of shocks from the real sphere, no policy advice could follow from the norm of neutrality. The norm of monetary equilibrium loses all attractiveness if we move from a stable economy with more or less unchanging demand and supply functions, or a Davidsonian kind of steady-state growth, to the world of Schumpeter. In his epoch-making *The*

Theory of Economic Development (1961), Schumpeter argued that money creation is part and parcel of the transformation process which an economy undergoes as a result of entrepreneurial activities. Bank credit allows entrepreneurs to draw factors of production away from other applications and thus to realize innovations (ibid., p. 106; Trautwein, 2000). The question of neutrality in the quantity theory sense is, however, of great practical importance for macroeconomic policy. If money is not neutral, in the weak sense that aggregate economic activity is not affected, or if transition periods between one equilibrium situation to another are long, monetary policy could conceivably play a role in fighting unemployment.

Neutrality of money in a strict sense is well-nigh impossible. It may, however, be valid in an approximate way, in the sense that aggregate production is not affected by changes in the money supply. There are strong indications that the quantity theory is not a bad approximation of reality if we look at decades rather than years. But there is little evidence that price ratios and the composition of production are unaffected. It would be hard to prove, or disprove, that they would be, if longer periods are studied where everything in an economy, in particular technology, is in a flux. Situations of hyperinflation have provided useful cases to test the validity of the quantity theory over shorter time periods, but here distribution effects are prominent and the distribution of wealth, and with it equilibrium quantities and price ratios, could hardly return to their pre-inflation values. Compared with empirical studies of the quantity theory, tests of superneutrality are thin on the ground. Support for long-run superneutrality does not appear to be very strong (for a survey of empirical research, see Bullard, 1999).

HANS VISSER

See also:

Classical Dichotomy; Equation of Exchange; Hume, David; New Classical Economics; Quantity Theory of Money; Say's Law; Schumpeter, Joseph A.; Velocity of Circulation; Wicksell, Knut.

Bibliography

Bullard, J. (1999), 'Testing Long-Run Monetary Neutrality Propositions: Lessons from the Recent Research', *Review*, Federal Reserve Bank of St. Louis, **81**, November/December, pp. 57–77.
Cantillon, R. (1964), *Essai sur la Nature du Commerce en Général*, ed. H. Higgs, with an English translation, New York: Kelley; first published in this edn. 1931, originally published 1755, London: Fletcher Gyles.
De Jong, F.J. (1973), *Developments of Monetary Theory in the Netherlands*, Rotterdam: Rotterdam University Press.
Divisia, F. (1962), *Traitement Économétrique de la Monnaie, l'Intérêt, l'Emploi*, Paris: Dunod.
Fase, M.M.G. (1992), 'A Century of Monetary Thought in the Netherlands', in J. van Daal and A. Heertje (eds), *Economic Thought in the Netherlands: 1650–1950*, Aldershot, UK and Brookfield, US: Edward Elgar.

Friedman, M. (1969), 'The Optimum Quantity of Money', *The Optimum Quantity of Money and Other Essays*, London: Macmillan.
Hayek, F.A. (1967), *Prices and Production*, 2nd edn, London: Routledge & Kegan Paul; first published 1931.
Hume, D. (1955), 'Of Money', *Writings on Economics*, ed. E. Rotwein, Edinburgh: Nelson; first published in D. Hume (1752), *Political Discourses*, Edinburgh.
Humphrey, T.M. (1991), 'Nonneutrality of Money in Classical Monetary Thought', *Economic Review*, Federal Reserve Bank of Richmond, **77**, March/April, pp. 3–15.
Keynes, J.M. (1971), *A Treatise on Money*, London: Macmillan; first published 1930.
Klausinger, H. (1989), 'On the History of Neutral Money', in D.A. Walker (ed.), *Perspectives on the History of Economic Thought*, vol. II, Aldershot, UK and Brookfield, US: Edward Elgar.
Koopmans, J.G. (1933), 'Zum Problem des "Neutralen" Geldes', in F.A. Hayek (ed.), *Beiträge zur Geldtheorie*, Vienna: Julius Springer.
Lucas, R.E. Jr (1996), 'Nobel Lecture: Monetary Neutrality', *Journal of Political Economy*, **104**, February, pp. 661–82.
Mundell, R.A. (1963), 'Inflation and Real Interest', *Journal of Political Economy*, **71**, June, pp. 280–83.
Myrdal, G. (1933), 'Der Gleichgewichtsbegriff als Instrument der geldtheoretischen Analyse', in F.A. Hayek (ed.), *Beiträge zur Geldtheorie*, Vienna: Julius Springer.
Orphanides, A. and R.M. Solow (1990), 'Money, Inflation and Growth', in B.M. Friedman and F.H. Hahn (eds), *Handbook of Monetary Economics*, vol. I, Amsterdam: North Holland.
Patinkin, D. (1965), *Money, Interest and Prices*, 2nd edn, New York: Harper & Row.
Patinkin, D. and O. Steiger (1989), 'In Search of the "Veil of Money" and the "Neutrality of Money": A Note on the Origin of Terms', *Scandinavian Journal of Economics*, **91**, March, pp. 131–46.
Samuelson, P.A. (1968), 'What Classical and Neo-Classical Monetary Theory Really Was', *Canadian Journal of Economics*, **1**, pp. 1–15; reprinted in R.W. Clower (ed.) 1969, *Monetary Theory*, Harmondsworth: Penguin.
Schumpeter, J.A. (1961), *The Theory of Economic Development*, Oxford: Oxford University Press; first published 1934 by Harvard University Press as a translation of *Theorie der wirtschaftlichen Entwicklung*, 1911.
Thomas, B. (1935), 'The Monetary Doctrines of Professor Davidson', *Economic Journal*, **45**, March, pp. 36–50.
Tobin, J. (1965), 'Money and Economic Growth', *Econometrica*, **33**, October, pp. 671–84.
Trautwein, H.-M. (2000), 'The Credit View, Old and New', *Journal of Economic Surveys*, **14**, April, pp. 155–89.
Walras, M.E.L. (1965), *Elements of Pure Economics*, London: George Allen & Unwin, translation by W. Jaffé of the Édition Definitive of *Eléments d'économie politique pure*, 1926.
Wicksell, K. (1898), *Geldzins und Güterpreise*, Jena: Gustav Fischer.
Wicksell, K. (1936), *Interest and Prices*, translation of Wicksell (1898); repr. (1965), New York: Kelley.

New Classical Economics

The new classical approach to macroeconomics evolved out of monetarism during the 1970s and replaced it as the main rival to Keynesian economics. Although it incorporates certain elements of monetarism (such as the monetarist explanation of inflation) it should be seen as a separate school of thought from orthodox monetarism (see, for example, Hoover, 1984;

Laidler, 1986). A predominantly American school of thought (at least initially), the development of the first phase of new classical theorizing is often taken to be synonymous with the work, most notably, of Robert E. Lucas Jr, Thomas Sargent, Robert Barro, Edward Prescott and Neil Wallace.

Underlying the approach is the joint acceptance of three main sub-hypotheses. First is the rational expectations hypothesis which is associated with the work of John Muth in the context of microeconomics. In his seminal article, Muth (1961) suggested 'that expectations since they are informed predictions of future events are essentially the same as the predictions of the relevant economic theory'. The crucial implication of this hypothesis is that 'forward-looking' rational economic agents will not form expectations which are *systematically* wrong over time. Second, new classical models are Walrasian in that all observed outcomes are viewed as 'market-clearing' at each point in time. This in turn implies complete wage and price flexibility. Given the assumption that markets continuously clear, all possible gains from trade have been exploited and utility has been maximized. Third, new classical models incorporate an aggregate supply hypothesis based on two orthodox microeconomic assumptions, namely that rational decisions by workers and firms reflect optimizing behaviour on their part and that the supply of labour by workers, and output by firms, depends upon relative prices (see Lucas and Rapping, 1969; Lucas, 1972, 1973).

The hypothesis that aggregate supply depends upon relatives prices is crucial to the new classical explanation of fluctuations in output and employment. In the new classical approach *unanticipated monetary shocks* cause errors in (rationally formed) price expectations and result in output and employment deviating from their long-run (full information) equilibrium (natural) levels. These errors are held to result from workers and firms having *incomplete information*, so that they mistake general price changes for relative price changes and react by changing the supply of labour and output (see Lucas, 1975, 1977, 1981, 1987, 1996). In new classical *equilibrium* business cycle theory, economic agents respond optimally to the prices they perceive, and markets continuously clear.

The combination of the rational expectations, continuous market clearing and aggregate supply hypotheses within new classical models produces five highly controversial policy implications. First, the so-called 'policy ineffectiveness proposition' (Sargent and Wallace, 1975, 1976) implies that only random or arbitrary monetary policy actions undertaken by the authorities can have short-run real effects because they cannot be anticipated by rational economic agents. Given that such actions would only increase the variation of output and employment around their natural levels, increasing uncertainty in the economy, the proposition provides an argument against discretionary policy activism in favour of rules.

Second, in contrast to both Keynesianism and monetarism, the new classical approach implies that, as long as announced monetary contraction is believed to be credible, rational economic agents will immediately revise their inflationary expectations downwards, enabling the authorities to engineer painless disinflation.

Third, the influential work of Finn Kydland and Edward Prescott (1977) on the issue of dynamic time inconsistency has provided another argument in the case for monetary policy being conducted by rules rather than discretion. Their analysis, exemplified by reference to the Phillips curve trade-off between inflation and unemployment, illustrates how the authorities, having announced a policy of monetary contraction to reduce inflation, will – if the policy is believed and agents reduce their inflation expectations – have an incentive to renege or cheat on their previously announced policy and implement expansionary monetary policy in order to reduce unemployment temporarily. In circumstances where the authorities have discretion to vary the strength of monetary policy, and have in consequence an incentive to cheat, the credibility of announced policy will be significantly weakened. Thus the analysis implies that economic performance could be improved if discretionary powers are taken away from the authorities and has further highlighted the importance of establishing the credibility and reputation of policy and policymakers.

Fourth, associated with the work of Robert Barro (1974) is the highly controversial Ricardian debt equivalence theorem limiting the usefulness of tax changes as a stabilization instrument. According to the theorem, a bond-financed tax cut will leave consumption unchanged as the private sector will fully anticipate the future tax liability required to meet interest payments on, and redemption of, the debt.

Finally, following the 'Lucas critique' of econometric policy evaluation, Lucas (1976) undermined confidence that traditional Keynesian-style macroeconometric models could be used to predict accurately the consequences of various policy changes on key macroeconomic variables since the parameters of such models may change as economic agents adjust their expectations and behaviour to the new policy environment.

Ironically, while the new classical contributions have had an enormous methodological influence on the development of modern macroeconomics (see Lucas, 1980), the early 1980s witnessed the demise of the 'monetary surprise' equilibrium explanation of the business cycle. This was due in large part to the problem of reconciling the magnitude and length of business cycles – supposedly caused by incomplete information – with the fact that aggregate price level and money supply data are readily available to economic agents at a relatively low cost (Tobin, 1980). In addition, while early empirical work, in particular the seminal papers by Robert Barro (1977, 1978), seemed to support the policy ineffectiveness proposition, a number of subsequent studies, most notably those by Frederic Mishkin (1982) and Robert Gordon (1982), found evidence suggesting that both unanticipated *and* anticipated monetary policy affect output and employment. The events of the early 1980s also provided ammunition for critics of the new classical approach who pointed to the depth of the recessions in both the United States (1981–2) and the United Kingdom (1980–81), economies associated with the Volcker/Reagan and Thatcher 'announced' monetary disinflations. As a result of these developments, 'the idea that information limitations play a central role in how monetary policy affects output in the real world has largely fallen by the wayside' (Chari, 1998).

Despite the demise of the mark I version of the new classical approach to macroeconomics, the first phase of theorizing sowed the seeds for the development of a mark II version in the 1980s. This second phase of equilibrium theorizing was initiated by the seminal contribution of Finn Kydland and Edward Prescott (1982) which, following John Long and Charles Plosser (1983), has come to be referred to as real business cycle theory. Leading exponents and/or contributors to the real business cycle approach to macroeconomics include Edward Prescott, Finn Kydland, Charles Plosser, John Long, Robert King and Robert Barro. Proponents of this approach view economic fluctuations as being predominantly caused by persistent real (supply-side) shocks, rather than unanticipated monetary (demand-side) shocks, to the economy. The focus of these real shocks involves large random fluctuations in the rate of technological progress that result in fluctuations in relative prices to which rational economic agents optimally respond by altering their supply of labour and consumption.

Perhaps the most controversial feature of this approach is the claim that fluctuations in output and employment are Pareto-efficient responses to real technology shocks to the aggregate production function. This implies that observed fluctuations in output are fluctuations in the natural rate of output, not deviations of output from a smooth deterministic trend. Consequently, the government should not attempt to reduce these fluctuations through stabilization policy, not only because such attempts are unlikely to achieve their desired objective but also because reducing instability would reduce welfare (Prescott, 1986). The 'bold conjecture' of real business cycle theorists is that each stage of the business cycle, boom and slump, is an equilibrium. 'Slumps represent an undesired, undesirable, and unavoidable shift in the constraints that people face; but, given these constraints, markets react efficiently and people succeed in achieving the best outcomes that circumstances permit . . . every stage of the business cycle is a Pareto efficient equilibrium' (Hartley, *et al.*, 1998).

Needless to say, the real business cycle approach has proved to be highly controversial and has been subjected to a number of criticisms (see, for example, Summers, 1986; Mankiw, 1989). One important criticism, to give just one example, relates to the nature of the deterioration of a country's production capabilities in a recession: what are the negative technological shocks that cause recessions? (See Mankiw, 1989.) Despite the numerous criticisms, real business cycle theorists have made several important and lasting contributions to modern macroeconomics. First, real business cycle theory has challenged the conventional approach in which growth and fluctuations are studied separately using different analytical tools. Until the early 1980s the conventional wisdom, accepted by Keynesian, monetarist and new classical economists alike, was to interpret fluctuations in output as being short-run fluctuations, around a rising long-term trend, primarily caused by aggregate demand shocks. By integrating the theory of economic growth and fluctuations, the real business cycle approach has irreversibly changed the direction of modern business cycle research and helped further to refocus macroeconomists' attention to the supply side of the economy.

Second, the real business cycle research programme has highlighted the intertemporal and dynamic characteristics which necessarily need to be incorporated into macroeconomic analysis. Any analysis of key macroeconomic variables such as consumption, saving, labour supply and investment has an intertemporal dimension. Third, rather than attempting to provide models capable of conventional econometric testing, real business cycle theorists, inspired by the work of Kydland and Prescott (1982), have developed the calibration method in which the simulated results of their specific models (when hit by random shocks) in terms of key macroeconomic variables are compared with the actual behaviour of the economy. In doing this, real business cycle theorists have provided a new research methodology for macroeconomics involving quantitative 'general equilibrium' dynamic models.

Finally, it is interesting to note that new classical ideas are now widely presented in mainstream macro texts, most of which have been written by economists who would certainly not regard themselves as new classical economists. A discussion of such issues as rational expectations, policy ineffectiveness, time inconsistency, credibility, reputation, Ricardian equivalence and equilibrium business cycles (both monetary and real) can be found in all the most recent editions of modern intermediate macroeconomic textbooks. As is the case with most 'revolutions' in economics, exaggerated claims have been made on behalf of new classical macroeconomics. However, thanks to the seminal contributions of leading new classical economists, Keynesian macroeconomists have learned Samuelson's lesson that 'you learn less from those who agree with you than from those intelligent analysts who are critical. Water cannot rise above its own source' (Samuelson, 1996, p. 1680). While, following the new classical contributions, macroeconomics became 'famously controversial' during the 1970s (see Woodford, 2000), according to Blanchard (2000) macroeconomics today at the frontier of research is surprisingly non-ideological. Along similar lines, Goodfriend and King (1998) argue that macroeconomics is moving towards 'a New Neoclassical Synthesis' containing new classical and new Keynesian elements.

BRIAN SNOWDON
HOWARD R. VANE

See also:

Business Cycles: New Classical Approach; Business Cycles: Real Business Cycle Approach; Calibration; Credibility and Reputation; Inflation: Costs of Reducing; Keynesian Economics; Lucas Critique; Lucas, Robert E. Jr; Macroeconometric Models; Monetarism; Natural Rate of Unemployment; New Neoclassical Synthesis; Policy Ineffectiveness Proposition; Rational Expectations; Ricardian Equivalence; Rules Versus Discretion; Schools of Thought in Macroeconomics; Time Inconsistency.

Bibliography

Barro, R.J. (1974), 'Are Government Bonds Net Wealth?', *Journal of Political Economy*, **82**, November/December, pp. 1095–117.
Barro, R.J. (1977), 'Unanticipated Money Growth and Unemployment in the United States', *American Economic Review*, **67**, March, pp. 101–15.
Barro, R.J. (1978), 'Unanticipated Money, Output, and the Price Level in the United States, *Journal of Political Economy*, **86**, August, pp. 549–80.
Blanchard, O. (2000), 'What Do We Know About Macroeconomics that Fisher and Wicksell Did Not?', *Quarterly Journal of Economics*, **115**, November, pp. 1375–411.
Chari, V. (1998), 'Nobel Laureate Robert E. Lucas, Jr: Architect of Modern Macroeconomics', *Journal of Economic Perspectives*, **12**, Winter, pp. 171–86.
Goodfriend, M. and R.G. King (1998), 'The New Neoclassical Synthesis and the Role of Monetary Policy', *NBER Macroeconomics Annual*, pp. 231–95.
Gordon, R.J. (1982), 'Price Inertia and Policy Ineffectiveness in the United States, 1890–1980', *Journal of Political Economy*, **90**, December, pp. 1087–1117.
Hartley, J.E., K.D. Hoover and K.D. Salyer (eds) (1998), *Real Business Cycles: A Reader*, London: Routledge.
Hoover, K.D. (1984), 'Two Types of Monetarism', *Journal of Economic Literature*, **22**, March, pp. 58–76.
Hoover, K.D. (1988), *The New Classical Macroeconomics: A Sceptical Inquiry*, Oxford: Basil Blackwell.
Hoover, K.D. (ed.) (1992), *The New Classical Macroeconomics*, Aldershot, UK and Brookfield, US: Edward Elgar.
Kydland, F.E. and E.C. Prescott (1977), 'Rules Rather than Discretion: The Inconsistency of Optimal Plans', *Journal of Political Economy*, **85**, June, pp. 473–91.
Kydland, F.E. and E.C. Prescott (1982), 'Time to Build and Aggregate Fluctuations', *Econometrica*, **50**, November, pp. 1345–70.
Laidler, D.E.W. (1986), 'The New Classical Contribution to Macroeconomics', *Banca Nazionale Del Lavoro Review*, **156**, March, pp. 27–55.

Long, J.B. and C.I. Plosser (1983), 'Real Business Cycles', *Journal of Political Economy*, **91**, February, pp. 39–69.

Lucas, R.E. Jr (1972), 'Expectations and the Neutrality of Money', *Journal of Economic Theory*, **4**, April, pp. 103–24.

Lucas, R.E. Jr (1973), 'Some International Evidence on Output–Inflation Tradeoffs', *American Economic Review*, **63**, June, pp. 326–34.

Lucas, R.E. Jr (1975), 'An Equilibrium Model of the Business Cycle', *Journal of Political Economy*, **83**, December, pp. 1113–44.

Lucas, R.E. Jr (1976), 'Econometric Policy Evaluation: A Critique', in K. Brunner and A.H. Meltzer (eds), *The Phillips Curve and Labour Markets*, Amsterdam: North-Holland.

Lucas, R.E. Jr (1977), 'Understanding Business Cycles', in K. Brunner and A.H. Meltzer (eds), *Stabilisation of the Domestic and International Economy*, Carnegie Rochester Conference Series in Public Policy, Amsterdam: North-Holland.

Lucas, R.E. Jr (1980), 'Methods and Problems in Business Cycle Theory', *Journal of Money, Credit and Banking*, **12**, November, pp. 696–717.

Lucas, R.E. Jr (1981), *Studies in Business Cycle Theory*, Oxford: Basil Blackwell.

Lucas, R.E. Jr (1987), *Models of Business Cycles*, Oxford: Basil Blackwell.

Lucas, R.E. Jr (1996), 'Nobel Lecture: Monetary Neutrality', *Journal of Political Economy*, **104**, August, pp. 661–82.

Lucas, RE.Jr and L.A. Rapping (1969), 'Real Wages, Employment and Inflation', *Journal of Political Economy*, **77**, September/October, pp. 721–54.

Mankiw, N.G. (1989), 'Real Business Cycles: A New Keynesian Perspective', *Journal of Economic Perspectives*, **3**, Summer, pp. 79–90.

Mishkin, F.S. (1982), 'Does Anticipated Monetary Policy Matter? An Econometric Investigation', *Journal of Political Economy*, **90**, February, pp. 22–51.

Muth, J. (1961), 'Rational Expectations and the Theory of Price Movements', *Econometrica*, **39**, July, pp. 315–35.

Prescott, E.C. (1986), 'Theory Ahead of Business Cycle Measurement', *Federal Reserve Bank of Minneapolis Quarterly Review*, Fall, pp. 9–22.

Samuelson, P.A. (1996), 'Gottfried Haberler (1900–1995)', *Economic Journal*, **106**, November, pp. 1679–87.

Sargent, T.J. and N. Wallace (1975), 'Rational Expectations, the Optimal Monetary Instrument and the Optimal Money Supply Rule', *Journal of Political Economy*, **83**, April, pp. 241–54.

Sargent, T.J. and N. Wallace (1976), 'Rational Expectations and the Theory of Economic Policy', *Journal of Monetary Economics*, **2**, April, pp. 169–83.

Snowdon, B. and H.R. Vane (1999), *Conversations With Leading Economists: Interpreting Modern Macroeconomics*, Cheltenham, UK and Northampton, MA, USA: Edward Elgar.

Snowdon, B., H.R. Vane and P. Wynarczyk (1994), *A Modem Guide to Macroeconomics: An Introduction to Competing Schools of Thought*, Aldershot, UK and Brookfield, US: Edward Elgar.

Summers, L.H. (1986), 'Some Sceptical Observations on Real Business Cycle Theory', *Federal Reserve Bank of Minneapolis Quarterly Review*, Fall, pp. 23–7.

Tobin, J. (1980), 'Are New Classical Models Plausible Enough to Guide Policy?', *Journal of Money, Credit and Banking*, **12**, November, pp. 788–99.

Woodford, M. (2000), 'Revolution and Evolution in Twentieth-Century Macroeconomics', in P. Gifford (ed.), *Frontiers of the Mind in the Twenty-First Century*, Cambridge, MA: Harvard University Press.

New Economy

The enormous transformation of economic activity which started in Great Britain in the middle of the eighteenth century has become popularly known as the 'first industrial revolution'. This 'revolution' was based on major improvements in science and technology which laid the basis for inventions in steam power and wrought iron production. These inventions facilitated the mechanization of production via the emergence of 'a new general purpose technology' applicable to the manufacturing, transport, communications, agricultural and construction sectors of the economy. Towards the end of the nineteenth century a new series of significant inventions led to a 'second industrial revolution', this time based on the internal combustion engine, electricity, steel, plastics and petrochemicals. During the late 1990s several commentators argued that computers and information technology were transforming the US economy by raising the underlying rate of productivity growth. According to Alan Blinder and Janet Yellen (*The Fabulous Decade*, The Century Foundation Press, 2001), productivity growth was 'a full percentage point higher in the years 1996–99 than during the earlier 1991–95 period'.

Since, for a given distribution of income, the growth of real wages in the long run is mainly determined by the rate of productivity growth, a permanent jump in the rate of productivity growth will have dramatic long-run consequences for living standards. Consequently, economists during the last few years have debated whether or not the higher rates of productivity growth observed in the United States after 1995 represented the unveiling of a 'new economy'. Sometimes discussions of the 'new economy' are extended to include the improved macroeconomic performance of the US 'Goldilocks' economy with respect to successfully achieving a combination of falling unemployment and inflation during the 1990s (see R.J. Gordon, 'Foundations of the Goldilocks Economy: Supply Shocks and the Time-Varying Nairu', *Brookings Papers on Economic Activity*, no. 2, 1998; R.J. Gordon, 'US Economic Growth Since 1870: One Big Wave?', *American Economic Review*, **89**, May, 1999; R.J. Gordon, 'Does the New Economy Measure Up to the Great Inventions of the Past?', *Journal of Economic Perspectives*, **14**, Fall, 2000; K. Stiroh, 'Is There a New Economy?', *Challenge,* July–August, 1999; D.W. Jorgenson, D.K. Stiroh, 'Raising the Speed Limit: US Economic Growth in the Information Age', *Brookings Papers on Economic Activity*, no. 1., 2000; D.W. Jorgenson, 'Information Technology and the US Economy', *American Economic Review*, **91**, March, 2001; S.B. Wadhami, 'Do We Have a New Economy?', *Bank of England Quarterly Bulletin*, Winter, 2001).

Although the rise and spread of knowledge relating to microelectronics and the computer constitutes a possible 'third industrial revolution', Gordon (1999) believes that the 'inventions of the late nineteenth century and early twentieth century were more fundamental creators of productivity than the electronic/internet era of today . . . Much of what we are seeing now is second order'. For an alternative assessment, see Jorgenson and Stiroh (2000); Jorgenson (2001); M. Abramovitz and P. David (2001), 'Two Centuries of American Macroeconomic Growth: From Exploitation of Resource Abundance to Knowledge Driven Development', *Stanford Institute for Economic Policy Research Discussion Paper*, no. 01–05.

New Keynesian Economics

The new Keynesian economics developed in response to the new classical macroeconomics. Like the new classicals (NCs), new Keynesians (NKs) build macroeconomics on explicit microfoundations governing individual wage, price and expectation formation. They also typically share the NC view that these microfoundations should be based on an assumption of individual optimizing behaviour. Despite these similarities, the NKs produce an analysis of the macroeconomy that revives Keynesian insights and so lends support to forms of government activism.

It does some injustice to the variety of NK ideas, but there is one key to these differences: NKs recognize some information problems which the NCs do not. The remainder of this entry will sketch how the presence of these problems can create the scope for government activism to stabilize unemployment at a low level in a market economy (see Gordon, 1990; Hargreaves Heap, 1995, for more detailed accounts).

Where the NCs assume that agents are price takers and that prices move to clear markets, the NKs typically have agents that set prices and markets that fail to clear. There are many possible sources of this switch to imperfectly competitive microfoundations but one is the fact that information is rarely freely available. For example, in a market where knowledge of prices is not freely available, individuals face varying search costs and are unlikely to desert *en masse* a firm which raises its price modestly. Hence the firm faces a downward-sloping demand curve and has discretion over what price to set.

In a similar fashion, when a firm lacks information over the effort expended by its workers, it may set a wage above the market-clearing value even though the labour market is in other respects perfectly competitive. This is because a firm may respond to this lack of information by attempting to raise its wage relative to others in order to create a cost to shirking when there is at least some chance of a shirker being caught *ex post* and fired. Of course, when all firms attempt this, relative wages will not change. But as each firm boosts its wage, the general wage is bid up above the market-clearing value and, when this happens sufficiently, the pressure to increase wage subsides because the prospect of involuntary unemployment, once fired, now supplies the incentive against shirking. This is one version of the efficiency wage argument (see Shapiro and Stiglitz, 1984; for another, see Akerlof, 1982).

The switch to imperfect competition at the microfoundations is extremely important for at least two reasons. First, it alters the incentive of any firm to change price when there is an aggregate demand shock with the result that the adjustment of the general level of prices to the shock can be complex and slow, rather than instantaneous. Consider a deflationary monetary shock which requires an equiproportionate change in all prices to restore equilibrium at the initial real values. Each firm's demand curve shrinks, but what happens next?

When the firm is a price taker and the individual firm demand curve is infinitely elastic at the market price, the question is easily answered: no firm can afford to do other than change price in line with the falling market price because it would lose all its customers. In comparison, when a firm faces a contracting but downward-sloping demand curve, the same cannot be said: the failure to lower price would *not* lead to a loss of *all* customers. Since there are always some costs associated with changing prices (for example, menu costs), it therefore cannot be assumed that the gains from immediate price adjustment will necessarily outweigh those from non-adjustment (see Mankiw, 1985).

In general, the size of the gain from adjustment will depend not just on the size of the shock but also on the behaviour of other firms (because any non-adjusting firm's demand curve shrinks by more when other firms lower their prices). So the individual decisions of whether to adjust (and hence the fate of the general level of prices) here may depend on how firms solve what is a coordination problem (see Blanchard and Kiyotaki, 1987). Nor is this the only strategic complication affecting how the general level of prices responds to the shock. Suppose firms do not know precisely how their individual demand curves have been affected and so do not know how any alteration of the price might affect their sales. There is now potentially some advantage in delaying the price change until some other firms have changed theirs in order to see how their sales change in response. Of course, if all firms must adjust at the same time, it is not possible for all to wait on the change of others without all failing to adjust. Alternatively, each could learn from the experience of others before setting its own price if price setting by firms is staggered. However, when such a staggered arrangement is the equilibrium, the general price level only adjusts gradually to a shock (see Ball and Cecchetti, 1988).

In short, there are several reasons for supposing that, unlike the situation under perfect competition, prices will not adjust immediately to their new equilibrium values under conditions of imperfect competition. The adjustment process of prices may be long-drawn-out and in the meantime quantities will shoulder some of the burden with falling output and rising unemployment. In these circumstances, it is natural to wonder whether a judicious manipulation of aggregate demand in the first place to compensate for the monetary shock might not be the better solution (see Buiter, 1980; Clarida *et al.*, 1999).

The second important influence of the switch to imperfect competition concerns the long-run equilibrium position of a macroeconomy (that is, the position once prices have adjusted fully): it is likely to be inefficient. The efficiency wage model above gives one illustration of this possibility (the existence of involuntary unemployment in equilibrium). There are others. We focus on two to illustrate how the government might be called upon in new ways to improve matters.

One comes from comparing a decentralized wage bargaining system (where each firm faces a single but different union) with one where there is centralized bargaining (with all firms facing the same union). Consider the perceived cost of pushing the wage up (and losing jobs) under both systems. Under decentralization, the loss of jobs is tempered by the fact that the workers may get a job elsewhere and, if they do not, then they will receive unemployment benefit. Under a centralized system, there is no job elsewhere and any increase in the payment of unemployment benefits must be paid for through higher taxes. In effect, decentralization causes an externality so that the perceived local cost of wage militance is below the true social cost and as a result the wage is likely, *ceteris paribus*, to be higher (see Calmfors and Driffil, 1988).

The other illustration comes from a model of the economy as a trading game (see Diamond, 1982; Cooper and John, 1988). Suppose that each firm produces goods which it brings to the market to trade with other firms who have produced different goods. Each must decide how much to produce in advance of going to the market. Their decision will naturally depend on whether they expect to be able to trade their produced output. If each expects the other firms to produce 'high' levels of output then the markets will be thick with goods, the trading opportunities will be correspondingly large and so it makes sense for an individual firm to produce a 'high' level of output. Conversely, when other firms are expected to bring 'low' levels of output to the market, the trading opportunities are poor and the individual firm will produce a 'low' level of output. It will be evident that there could be at least two rational expectations equilibria in this economy: one where each expects others to produce 'low' levels and so each decides to produce a 'low' level; and one where each expects others to produce 'high' and so each produces 'high'.

This is one of many examples of multiple equilibria in the NK literature (for example, see also Bhaskar, 1990, Geanakopolos and Polemarchakis, 1986) and it raises a question of how economies actually select an equilibrium. If this was better understood, there might be scope for government action directed at shifting the economy towards an efficient equilibrium. There are no easy answers here because the task is to understand and influence the way expectations are coordinated. There is, though, an interesting possibility that it may lead NKs (as in the previous illustration with wage bargaining systems) to look more closely at the way institutions affect equilibrium selection in the economy. In short, the NK argument may come to focus on institutions in much the same way as the manipulation of expectations has led NCs to argue, for instance, for the institution of an independent central bank (for example, Barro and Gordon, 1983).

We have highlighted the role played by informational problems in the NK analysis as it connects with Keynes's own preoccupation with uncertainty and with the emphasis given by some of his earlier interpreters (for example, Leijonhufvud, 1968). Nevertheless, while Keynes spoke eloquently about uncertainty with respect to the future (because an economy occupies historical time, to pick up on the theme of post-Keynesian economics), this is not the aspect of uncertainty which NKs develop. Epistemic uncertainty about the future still plays a role in NK analysis (for instance, in explaining why economies are likely to be subjected to unanticipated shocks), but it is not central. Instead, as the examples here suggest, the NKs focus on the uncertainty associated with the behaviour of others that arises when they are strategically interdependent. This was, of course, the point of Keynes's famous discussion of the beauty contest in relation to the behaviour of financial markets and it has now, in effect, moved centre stage in macroeconomics with the NKs.

SHAUN P. HARGREAVES HEAP

See also:

Efficiency Wage Theory; Menu Costs; New Classical Economics; Shirking Model.

Bibliography
Akerlof, G. (1982), 'Labour Contracts as Partial Gift Exchange', *Quarterly Journal of Economics*, **97**, November, pp. 543–69.
Ball, L. and S. Cecchetti (1988), 'Imperfect Information and Staggered Price Setting', *American Economic Review*, **78**, December, pp. 999–1018.
Barro, R. and D. Gordon (1983), 'Rules, Discretion and Reputation in a Model of Monetary Policy', *Journal of Monetary Economics*, **12**, July, pp. 101–21.
Bhaskar, V. (1990), 'Wage Relativities and the Natural Range of Unemployment', *Economic Journal*, **100**, Supplement, pp. 60–66.
Blanchard, O and N. Kiyotaki (1987), 'Monopolistic Competition and the Effects of Aggregate Demand', *American Economic Review*, **77**, September, pp. 647–66.
Buiter, W. (1980), 'The Macroeconomics of Dr Pangloss: A Critical Survey of the New Classical Macroeconomics', *Economic Journal*, **90**, March, pp. 34–50.

Calmfors, L. and J. Driffill (1988), 'Centralisation of Wage Bargaining and Economic Performance', *Economic Policy*, **6**, pp. 13–61.

Clarida, R, J. Gali and M. Gertler (1999), 'The Science of Monetary Policy: A New Keynesian Perspective', *Journal of Economic Literature*, **XXXVII**, December, pp. 1661–1707.

Cooper, R. and A. John (1988), 'Coordinating Coordination Failures in Keynesian Models', *Quarterly Journal of Economics*, **103**, August, pp. 441–63.

Diamond, P. (1982), 'Aggregate Demand Management in Search Equilibrium', *Journal of Political Economy*, **90**, October, pp. 881–94.

Geanakopolos, J. and H. Polemarchakis (1986), 'Walrasian Indeterminacy and Keynesian Macroeconomics', *Review of Economic Studies*, **53**, October, pp. 755–79.

Gordon, R. (1990), 'What is the New-Keynesian Economics?', *Journal of Economic Literature*, **XXVIII**, September, pp. 1115–71.

Hargreaves Heap, S. (1995), *The New Keynesian Macroeconomics*, Aldershot, UK and Brookfield, US: Edward Elgar.

Leijonhufvud, A. (1968), *On Keynesian Economics and the Economics of Keynes*, London: Oxford University Press.

Mankiw, N.G. (1985), 'Small Menu Costs and Large Business Cycles: A Macroeconomic Model of Monopoly', *Quarterly Journal of Economics*, **100**, May, pp. 529–37.

Shapiro, C. and J. Stiglitz (1984), 'Equilibrium Unemployment as a Discipline Device', *American Economic Review*, **74**, June, pp. 433–44.

New Neoclassical Synthesis

A unifying theme in the evolution of modern macroeconomics has been an 'ever-evolving classical-Keynesian debate'. The synthesis of the ideas of the classical economists with those of Keynes dominated mainstream economics at least until the early 1970s. The standard textbook approach to macroeconomics during the period following World War II until the early 1970s relied heavily on the interpretation of the *General Theory* provided by John Hicks and modified by the contributions of economists such as Modigliani, Patinkin and Tobin. Paul Samuelson's best-selling textbook popularized the synthesis of Keynesian and classical ideas, making them accessible to a wide readership and successive generations of students. It was Samuelson who introduced the label 'neoclassical synthesis' into the literature in the third edition of *Economics* in 1955. This synthesis of classical and Keynesian ideas, captured by the IS–LM AD–AS framework, represented the consensus view prior to the 1970s and was the standard approach to macroeconomic analysis both in textbooks and in professional discussion.

During periods of consensus in macroeconomics, divisions among economists naturally become less intense and less visible in the literature. However, the 1970s and 1980s were a period of highly visible and intense disagreement among academic economists. In particular, this was a result of controversies stirred up by the 'new classical' revolution in macroeconomics and the reaction to it by mainstream Keynesians. During the 1980s, the disarray in macroeconomics was most evident in the disagreements between the real business cycle theorists and a broader group of more mainstream economists referred to as 'new Keynesians' (see B. Snowdon, H.R. Vane and P. Wynarczyk, *A Modern Guide to Macroeconomics: An Introduction to Competing Schools of Thought*, Edward Elgar, 1994; B. Snowdon and H.R.Vane (eds), *A Macroeconomics Reader*, Routledge, 1997). However, according to Marvin Goodfriend and Robert King ('The New Neoclassical Synthesis and the Role of Monetary Policy', *National Bureau of Economic Research Macroeconomics Annual*, 1998), the intellectual currents of the last ten years are moving modern macroeconomics towards a 'New Neoclassical Synthesis' (see also O. Blanchard, 'What Do We Know About Macroeconomics that Fisher and Wicksell Did Not?', *Quarterly Journal of Economics*, **115**, November, 2000).

The new synthesis 'inherits the spirit of the old in that it combines Keynesian and classical elements'. This can be seen by noting that the key elements in the new synthesis comprise intertemporal optimization, rational expectations, imperfect competition in goods, labour and credit markets, and nominal rigidities and costly price adjustment. In their analysis, Goodfriend and King conclude that the New Neoclassical Synthesis suggests several important conclusions about the role of monetary policy. First, monetary policy has real effects in the short run. Second, there is little by way of a long-run trade-off between inflation and real activity. Third, inflation is costly and it is important to eliminate it. Fourth, the credibility of policy actions has an important impact on monetary policy outcomes. Goodfriend and King argue that these conclusions point the way to a rules-based monetary policy framework with inflation targeting acting as the nominal anchor.

See also:

Credibility and Reputation; Inflation: Costs of; Inflation Targeting; Monetary Policy: Role of; Neoclassical Synthesis; New Classical Economics;

New Political Macroeconomics

New political macroeconomics uses the conceptual and analytical tools of economics to examine the interaction of politics and economics in democratic systems, emphasizing the choice of policies as well as how (and how effectively) they influence economic outcomes. In this analysis, government does not assume the role of social planner, benignly maximizing a social welfare function. Instead, conflicts of interest and the exercise of power result in macroeconomic policies with outcomes that benefit some and disadvantage others. The political preferences of the party in power are pursued subject to prevailing political realities, including the desire to be re-elected. Thus the government is viewed as endogenous to the politico-economic system.

The idea of government acting in the interest of a particular group is found in earlier work, notably Kalecki's (1943) political business cycle theory. Kalecki assumes (a) policy and the cyclical mechanism to be rooted in class conflict, and (b) that business and *rentier* interests control the political system whatever party is in power. The new political macroeconomics gives government a more active role. It began in the mid-1970s, when two streams appeared simultaneously. Nordhaus (1975) used the term 'political business cycle' for his model of policy choice in which re-election is the prime concern of governments. Using the inflation–unemployment trade-off as his example, Nordhaus assumes that unemployment affects a large fraction of households with more severe effects than inflation. Then governments attempting to maximize votes generate a business cycle by lowering unemployment as the election approaches; the inflationary effects are reversed by raising unemployment after the election. This opportunistic behaviour is common to all political parties. Partisan theory was proposed by Hibbs (1977), and assumes that the objective of political parties is to implement policies that benefit their core constituencies. In this view, 'down-scale' socioeconomic classes whose income depends almost solely on wages are less tolerant of unemployment than of inflation, and are represented by left-of-centre parties. 'Up-scale' classes hold the bulk of financial wealth, giving them greater exposure to inflation; they find representation in right-of-centre parties that tolerate high unemployment to keep inflation low. *Ceteris paribus*, shifts in policy reflecting these preferences are expected when there is a change in government.

Since governments can shift between opportunistic and ideological motives for policy choice, both approaches offered insight. Frey and Schneider (1978) proposed a model in which a government would switch from ideological to opportunistic behaviour in response to a fall in popularity. Instead of continued development of the field, a hiatus followed the ascendancy of rational expectations theory, and its policy ineffectiveness proposition. A decade later, a second generation of models incorporated versions of rational expectations that permit policy to effect transitory change in real variables, either because expectations are based on inadequate information or because of policy surprises. Cukierman and Meltzer (1986) and Rogoff and Sibert (1988) provide rational expectations versions of the opportunistic model, in which asymmetric information allows governments to create political business cycles; only 'competent' governments achieve pre-electoral booms, thus ensuring their re-election. Unlike the case of the Nordhaus model, there is no post-election recession: rational expectations ensure that real effects are temporary, and tight money is used to reduce inflation. Alesina (1987) uses uncertain election results in systems with multi-period, non-indexed, nominal wage contracts to provide the surprises necessary for policy effectiveness in a rational partisan theory. The model predicts that the lower unemployment and higher growth under left-wing governments are transitory, unlike the more lasting effects found in the Hibbs version. As Hibbs (1992) notes, the assumption that labour repeatedly accepts such wage contracts introduces a theoretical inconsistency.

The inclusion of rational expectations in models of policy choice creates some problems. As noted, the assumptions needed to generate temporary policy effectiveness may stretch credulity. But perhaps it is more important to note that the political conflict stressed in the new political macroeconomics must include, not only conflict of interest, but also conflicting views about how the economy works. Rational expectations rules out this second class of conflict entirely, raising questions about its application in this context.

Other work has considered apparently irrational behaviour resulting in socially suboptimal policies, with failure or delay in adopting reforms. Explanations have included policy choice where there is uncertainty about the distribution of the benefits of reform (Fernandez and Rodrik, 1991; Rodrik, 1996) and conflict caused by where the burden of reform is expected to fall (Drazen and Grilli, 1993). The distribution of power among various segments of society is the ultimate source of seeming suboptimality. Garrett (1998) considers both opportunistic and ideological models in the context of changing power relationships among business, government and labour caused by increasing globalization. Both of these areas throw into sharp relief the heterogeneity and conflicts of interest that are a primary focus of this field.

The recent expansion of new political macroeconomic theory has not been matched by comparable growth of empirical testing. Moreover, a frequent shortcoming of empirical work in this field is its tendency to ignore influences on the current value of an economic variable other than its past values and the party in power (see, for example, Alesina *et al.*, 1997). The implicit assumption is that party preferences alone determine which economic policies are implemented, overlooking the possibility that policies often have adverse side-effects or encounter institutional barriers that restrict their use. In short, these models consider political power and preferences, whether opportunistic or ideological, but ignore the constraints. In the case of unemployment and inflation, and assuming that there is at least a short-run exploitable Phillips curve, these constraints determine the tradeoff, that is, the position of the Phillips curve. A second source of constraints is the prevailing state of the economy. Adverse economic conditions are likely to limit policy choice, regardless of the party in power; variables to account for this are not included. The weak results in much empirical work can be traced to omitted variables that define these constraints on policy.

Drazen (2000, ch. 5) discusses laws, social norms and other institutions, accurately identifying these as important sources of constraints on policy choice. Improved specification would include institutional and other variables as measures of political and economic constraints, and a more sensitive measure of power than the simple dummy variable commonly used. Although many institutional variables change little over time, cross-country studies can yield useful insights and serve as a preliminary step for in-depth country studies. For example, Cornwall (1999) estimates the reduced form unemployment equation $U = U(V_1, V_2)$ for 16 OECD economies. The vector V_1 is from the political preference function, and V_2 is from the Phillips curve which defines the set of possible inflation–unemployment outcomes. *Effective* political preferences are measured by the proportion of left-of-centre votes. The higher this proportion, the greater is the tolerance of inflation and the stronger the preference for low unemployment; the simple left–right dummy variable cannot show this gradation. Institutions also influence choice, for example inflation aversion; measures include central bank independence and membership of monetary unions. The position of the Phillips curve is influenced by the degree of industrial conflict, measured by the volume of strikes, and by economic conditions, such as international demand. These measures of power, institutional variation and economic conditions ensure that both preferences and constraints are represented. This equation yielded statistically significant estimates of the sources of unemployment differences among countries over the post-World War II period and provided strong support for partisan behaviour. Empirical tests of new political macroeconomic theories would benefit from this approach.

The new political macroeconomics provides a broad spectrum of opportunities for valuable research. This value derives from its concern with real economies and the political mechanisms that drive policy choice and outcomes, a concern that makes empirical testing of new theory especially relevant. The breadth of application of this very active field is illustrated by Drazen (2000), who covers distributional issues, public goods, international topics and economic transition as well as the topics discussed here. Snowdon and Vane (1999) provide a survey of work over the past 25 years. This brief entry has dealt with only a very small part of the large literature, chosen to suggest the possibilities (and some of the pitfalls) the field offers.

WENDY CORNWALL

See also:

Alesina, Alberto; Business Cycles: Political Business Cycle Approach; Central Bank Independence; Globalization; Kalecki, Michal; Phillips Curve; Policy Ineffectiveness Proposition; Rational Expectations.

Bibliography

Alesina, A. (1987), 'Macroeconomic Policy in a Two-Party System as a Repeated Game', *Quarterly Journal of Economics*, **102**, August, pp. 651–78.
Alesina, A., N. Roubini and G. Cohen (1997), *Political Cycles and the Macroeconomy*, Cambridge, MA: MIT Press.
Cornwall, W. (1999), 'The Institutional Determinants of Unemployment', in M. Setterfield (ed.), *The Political Economy of Growth, Employment and Inflation*, London: Macmillan.
Cukierman, A. and A. Meltzer (1986), 'A Positive Theory of Discretionary Policy, the Cost of Democratic Government, and the Benefits of a Constitution', *Economic Inquiry*, **24**, July, pp. 367–88.
Drazen, A. (2000), *Political Economy in Macroeconomics*, Princeton, NJ: Princeton University Press.
Drazen, A. and V. Grilli (1993), 'The Benefit of Crises for Economic Reforms', *American Economic Review*, **83**, June, pp. 538–607
Fernandez, R. and D. Rodrik (1991), 'Resistance to Reform: Status Quo Bias in the Presence of Individual Specific Uncertainty', *American Economic Review*, **81**, December, pp. 1146–55.
Frey, B.S. and F. Schneider (1978), 'A Politico-Economic Model of the United Kingdom', *Economic Journal*, **88**, June, pp. 243–53.
Garrett, G. (1998), *Partisan Politics in the Global Economy*, Cambridge: Cambridge University Press.
Hibbs, D. (1977), 'Political Parties and Macroeconomic Policy', *American Political Science Review*, **71**, December, pp. 1467–87.
Hibbs, D. (1992), 'Partisan Theory after Fifteen Years', *European Journal of Political Economy*, **8**, October, pp. 361–73.
Hibbs, D. (1994), 'The Partisan Model of Macroeconomic Cycles: More Theory and Evidence for the United States', *Economics and Politics*, **6**, March, pp. 1–24.
Kalecki, M. (1943), 'Political Aspects of Full Employment', reprinted in M. Kalecki (1971), *Selected Essays on the Dynamics of the Capitalist Economy*, Cambridge: Cambridge University Press.
Nordhaus, W. (1975), 'The Political Business Cycle', *Review of Economic Studies*, **42**, April, pp. 169–90.
Rodrik, D. (1996), 'Understanding Economic Policy Reform', *Journal of Economic Literature*, **34**, March, pp. 9–41.
Rogoff, K. and A. Sibert (1988), 'Elections and Macroeconomic Policy Cycles', *Review of Economic Studies*, **55**, January, pp. 1–16.
Saint-Paul, G. (2000), 'The "New Political Economy": Recent Books by Drazen and by Persson and Tabellini', *Journal of Economic Literature*, **38**, December, pp. 915–25.
Snowdon, B. and H.R. Vane (1999), 'The New Political Macroeconomics: An Interview with Alberto Alesina', *American Economist*, **43**, Spring, pp. 19–34.

Nobel Prize in Economics

The prestigious 'Sveriges Riksbank (Bank of Sweden) Prize in Economic Sciences in Memory of Alfred Nobel', more popularly known as the Nobel Prize in Economics, was first awarded in 1969. The Nobel Prize in

Economics is awarded annually by the Royal Swedish Academy of Sciences in accordance with the same principles as those for the other five Nobel Prizes (chemistry, literature, medicine/physiology, peace, and physics) which have been awarded since 1901. The prize which consists of a gold medal, diploma and a sum of money (in recent years a million dollars) rewards 'specific discoveries or breakthroughs, and the impact of these on the discipline'. To date, the prize has been awarded, either singly or jointly, to scholars for their major contributions to the following broad fields of study: microeconomics, macroeconomics, econometrics, financial economics, monetary economics, international economics, economic growth, economic development, public sector economics, and economic history. Reflecting the leading role the United States has played in pioneering economic research since 1969 (the award cannot be given posthumously), more than 60 per cent of the awards, as of 2002, have gone to US citizens.

Not surprisingly, the Nobel laureates were affiliated, when the Prize was awarded, with some of the most famous universities in the world, including the University of Chicago (9 awards), Harvard University (4 awards); University of Cambridge (4 awards), University of California, Berkeley (4 awards), Massachusetts Institute of Technology (3 awards), Columbia University (3 awards), Stanford University (3 awards), Princeton University (2 awards), and Yale University (2 awards). The economists who have been awarded the Nobel Prize, and who have made significant contributions to macroeconomics, include (in alphabetical order): George Akerlof, Milton Friedman, Ragnar Frisch, Friedrich von Hayek, John Hicks, Lawrence Klein, Simon Kuznets, Athur Lewis, Robert Lucas Jr, James Meade, Franco Modigliani, Robert Mundell, Paul Samuelson, Robert Solow, Joseph Stiglitz, Richard Stone, Jan Tinbergen and James Tobin (see entries on these individuals in this volume). For more information the reader is referred to the official website of the Nobel Foundation (*http://www.nobel.se*).

Nominal Exchange Rate

The number of units of foreign currency that residents of a country can purchase in exchange for one unit of their own currency; the price of one currency in terms of another.

Nominal GDP

The value of gross domestic product measured in terms of the prices prevailing at the time; also known as GDP in current prices.

See also:
Gross Domestic Product.

Nominal Interest Rate

The nominal or market rate of interest measured in current prices with no adjustment for inflation.

Nominal Rigidity

A fundamental question in macroeconomics is whether it should be assumed that nominal prices and wages are temporarily rigid. This entry will review the evidence for, and discuss explanations of, the existence of nominal rigidities, consider their implications and assess directions for further research.

A first attempt to define nominal rigidity might be that it exists if the nominal price of good X stays constant in spite of excess supply or demand in the market for X. A better definition might recognize that, for many goods, prices are determined by price-setting agents rather than by an anonymous market. Suppose the 'optimal' or desired real price an agent would like to set, given his environment, is p^*/P, where p^* is the optimal nominal price and P is the current value of a relevant price index (outside the control of the agent); suppose p^* is also the current price. Then, following Ball and Romer (1990), real rigidity is characterized by the failure of p^*/P to adjust (by much) in response to shocks, and the degree of real rigidity in the economy might be characterized by how little p^*/P changes. Nominal rigidity means that the actual nominal price chosen fails to adjust. It is clear that real rigidity does not necessarily imply nominal rigidity, or vice versa. It is important to distinguish between the two types of rigidity, for perhaps two main reasons. The first is that it is nominal rigidity, and not real rigidity, which is crucial for the non-neutrality of money. The second is that explanations of nominal rigidities are usually very different from explanations of real rigidities.

Evidence for the existence of nominal rigidities
First, there is survey evidence. For the United States, the results of an extensive study by Blinder are reported in Blinder (1994) and Blinder *et al.* (1998); for the United Kingdom, see Hall *et al.* (2000). Such evidence shows how infrequently many prices are changed. Blinder also seeks to evaluate 12 different explanations of price rigidity. However, it might be pointed out

that neither of these studies tries to distinguish nominal from real price rigidity, and that some of the theories Blinder tests are in fact theories of real rigidities.

Second, there is evidence based on the non-neutrality of money. The evidence that monetary changes affect output and employment in the short run (for example, over a period of six months to two years) is powerful. Such evidence includes the 'narrative' approach of Friedman and Schwartz (1963), updated by Romer and Romer (1989). There are more formal tests based on statistical and econometric techniques (for example, Christiano *et al.*, 1999, review the evidence and conclude that 'after a contractionary monetary policy shock . . . aggregate output, employment, profits and various monetary aggregates fall', ibid., p. 69). While sticky-price models do not provide the only possible explanation for short-run monetary non-neutrality, they do arguably offer the most plausible explanation.

Third, there are studies using data on individual transactions prices: 'The degree of price rigidity in many industries is significant. It is not unusual . . . for prices . . . to remain unchanged for several years' (Carlton, 1986, p. 636).

Fourth, Poterba *et al.* (1986) conduct an ingenious test based on the effects of shifts between direct and indirect taxation.

Fifth, there is evidence from open economy macroeconomics: 'For anyone who looks even casually at international data . . . the idea that nominal price rigidities are irrelevant seems difficult to sustain' (Obstfeld and Rogoff, 1996, p. 606). Most striking is the correlation between nominal and real exchange rates, for which nominal price rigidity is an obvious explanation.

Finally, a number of studies (for example, Nickell and Quintini, 2001) have used panel data to investigate the distribution of nominal wage changes. The existence of a 'spike' at zero suggests some degree of nominal rigidity; however, another result is that some workers do in fact receive nominal wage cuts, suggesting that the degree of nominal wage rigidity is modest.

Explanations of nominal rigidities
Explanations for *real* wage and price rigidities abound; these include efficiency wage theories, insider–outsider theories, implicit contracts, imperfect competition and customer markets. However, these are not explanations for nominal rigidities, the main explanations for which will be reviewed in this section.

Menu costs
These are the costs incurred in changing the price of a good; such costs may include the costs of relabelling goods, the costs of reprinting catalogues,

and so forth. It might be contended that menu costs are too small to explain large effects of monetary changes. There are a number of points that might be made in response. First, as argued by Mankiw (1985) and others, small menu costs may have large economic effects. A related point is made by Akerlof and Yellen (1985): in a wide variety of models, the cost to a price-setting agent of deviating slightly from the optimal price may be trivial. It may only need a small menu cost, or a small deviation from rationality, for him not to adjust the price when the optimal price changes. However, the costs to the economy of this decision may be much greater than the costs to the individual agent.

Second, the costs of changing prices may not, in fact, be trivial. One attempt to measure menu costs (by Levy *et al.*, 1997) for some large American supermarkets concluded that such costs were 0.70 per cent of revenues – not huge, but not entirely insignificant. One cost of changing prices which emerged from this study was that of rectifying the mistakes which inevitably arise after price changes.

Third, it has been argued, especially by Ball and Romer (1990), that small menu costs may be much more important in the presence of real rigidities.

Fourth, some prices, such as the minimum wage, may be determined by legislation. The menu cost in this case may be very high indeed.

Finally, there may be interdependencies between prices: prices may be set as a mark-up on costs, so that a nominal rigidity in one sector may worsen nominal rigidities elsewhere.

Imperfect information
A firm may well not know how the optimal nominal price for its good has changed in response to a shock. Acquisition of relevant information may be slow and costly. For this reason, firms might normally review pricing decisions only at particular points of time (say once a year) and consequently change prices infrequently.

Disruptive effects of frequent price changes
Customers may adjust their purchasing behaviour if a firm changes prices frequently by, for example, trying to anticipate increases in prices and purchasing accordingly. This might be costly for a firm; for example, a retailer might need to increase its holdings of inventories and/or its costs of processing orders might be such that it prefers a fairly steady flow of orders.

Interdependencies between price setters
Consider a colluding oligopolistic industry producing a homogenous good, which experiences a negative demand shock, with this reducing the optimal nominal (and real) price for each firm. Each firm may be reluctant to reduce

its price if others do not, so the price may not fall. We might describe this as a coordination failure. This explanation gains considerable support from Blinder's study. Keynes (1936, p. 14) gives a similar explanation for the failure of workers to agree to (nominal) wage cuts in a time of unemployment: whereas workers overall might be willing to accept a reduction in real wages owing to a rise in prices, no individual group of workers will agree to a reduction in its own wage, as this means a reduction in its real wage relative to other workers.

Characteristics of the specific medium of exchange in which prices are quoted
This is a category intended to capture a number of effects such as the following. The medium of exchange, although highly divisible, is not infinitely divisible. In the UK the price (in pence) must be an integer. So even if the optimal price changes continuously, the actual price cannot, because of the integer constraint – instead, we might expect it to stay constant for a period of time, and then jump to a new level. Also some prices (for example, £9.99) may be preferred by consumers for a variety of reasons – they may be easier to remember and/or have some salience or psychological appeal. Some price structures may enable retailers to economize on their holdings of change. It might be asserted that these costs and benefits are trivial; however, we can respond to this criticism in the same way as we responded above to the criticism that menu costs are trivial. For example, a retailer may be almost indifferent over which price he sets within a certain range. One of these considerations may hence be decisive in explaining which price he actually chooses.

Implications of the existence of nominal rigidities and directions for further research
Blanchard and Kiyotaki (1987) stress that introducing imperfect competition *per se* into an otherwise standard macroeconomic model does not destroy the neutrality of money. For non-neutrality it is necessary to add another distortion, such as menu costs. Then an increase in aggregate demand facing firms may result in higher output with no change in prices. Imperfect competition means price is above marginal cost, so a firm would be willing to supply extra output at the current price, and this may in certain circumstances be preferable to incurring the menu cost and raising the price to its optimal level. It seems clear, then, that it is necessary to analyse sticky prices in a framework with imperfect competition.

One criticism of many menu cost models is that they are static; nominally rigid prices do not stay unchanged for ever, so it is necessary to study how and why prices change. While dynamizing menu cost models is highly desirable, this is not easy, and the conclusions derived from dynamic menu cost models are often model-specific. For example, Caplin and Spulber (1987) give an ingenious example in which money is neutral even with menu costs and imperfect competition, but this example does not seem to generalize.

A promising direction for research is provided by models of staggered price and/or wage setting (reviewed by Taylor, 1999, for example). In such a framework, a wage setter chooses a nominal wage to last for a period of time (perhaps a year), aware that other wages will be set over this period by other wage setters. The fact that wage changes are not synchronized gives rise to wage inertia, and if the wage setter does not wish to change his real wage by a large amount when changing his wage, this can give rise to a fair degree of nominal inertia. Developing models along these lines with both wage setting and consumer and firm behaviour determined by optimization seems very promising and offers hope of a more satisfactory, unified, macroeconomics which combines the insights of both Keynesian economics and real business cycle theory. However, one problem such models encounter is that they have difficulty accounting for the persistence of monetary shocks (Ascari, 2000; Chari *et al.*, 2000).

An extension of this approach to open economy macroeconomics would seem highly desirable, as well. An important paper, Obstfeld and Rogoff (2000), presents an open macroeconomic model with imperfect competition, temporary price rigidity and intertemporal optimization, and this paper has generated a huge literature, surveyed by Lane (2001). The price dynamics of the original Obstfeld–Rogoff model are very crude; this is probably the main drawback of their model, and incorporating more plausible wage and price behaviour seems highly desirable. However, in an open economy there is the further question of whether it is the foreign-currency or domestic-currency prices of goods that are rigid. Both cannot be rigid if the exchange rate changes. Obstfeld and Rogoff (2000) provide a compelling critique of one particular assumption made about the pricing-to-market version of price rigidity incorporated into some recent open macroeconomic models.

Conclusion

In conclusion, it might be stated that there is a significant amount of nominal price and wage rigidity in the economy, but it is uncertain what the best explanation for such rigidity is. Perhaps all the explanations reviewed have at least an element of truth. We would also argue that we should certainly not just add an assumption of exogenous price or wage rigidity to a standard macroeconomic model. It is necessary to explain how prices, which are rigid in nominal terms for a period of time, are adjusted, and consider the implications of such an adjustment mechanism for the macro economy. It is clear that there is still much more to do in theoretical macroeconomics.

JOHN FENDER

See also:

Menu Costs; New Keynesian Economics; Real Rigidity.

Bibliography

Akerlof, G.A. and J.L.Yellen (1985), 'A Near-Rational Model of the Business Cycle, with Wage and Price Inertia', *Quarterly Journal of Economics*, **100**, Supplement, pp. 823–38.

Ascari, G. (2000), 'Optimising Agents, Staggered Wages and Persistence in the Real Effects of Money Shocks', *Economic Journal*, **110**, July, pp. 664–86.

Ball, L. and D. Romer (1990), 'Real Rigidities and the Nonneutrality of Money', *Review of Economic Studies*, **57**, April, pp. 183–203.

Blanchard, O.J. and N. Kiyotaki (1987), 'Monopolistic Competition and the Effects of Aggregate Demand', *American Economic Review*, **77**, September, pp. 647–66.

Blinder, A.S. (1994), 'On Sticky Prices: Academic Theories Meet the Real World', in G. Mankiw (ed.), *Monetary Policy*, Chicago and London: University of Chicago Press.

Blinder, A.S., E. Canetti, D. Lebow and J. Rudd (1998), *Asking about Prices: A New Approach to Understanding Price Stickiness*, New York: Russell Sage Foundation.

Caplin, A.S. and D.F. Spulber (1987), 'Menu Costs and the Neutrality of Money', *Quarterly Journal of Economics*, **102**, November, pp. 703–25.

Carlton, D.W. (1986), 'The Rigidity of Prices', *American Economic Review*, **76**, September, pp. 637–58.

Chari, V., P. Kehoe and E. McGrattan (2000), 'Sticky Price Models of the Business Cycle: Can the Contract Multiplier Solve the Persistence Problem?', *Econometrica*, **68**, September, pp. 1151–79.

Christiano, L.J., M. Eichenbaum and C. Evans (1999), 'Monetary Policy Shocks: What have we Learned and to what End?', in J.B. Taylor and M. Woodford (eds), *Handbook of Macroeconomics*, vol. 1A, Amsterdam: North-Holland.

Friedman, M. and A.J. Schwartz (1963), *A Monetary History of the United States, 1867–1960*, Princeton: Princeton University Press.

Hall, S., M. Walsh and A. Yates (2000), 'Are UK Companies' Prices Sticky?' *Oxford Economic Papers*, **52**, pp. 425–46.

Keynes, J.M. (1936), *The General Theory of Employment, Interest and Money*, London: Macmillan.

Lane, P. (2001), 'The New Open Economy Macroeconomics: A Survey', *Journal of International Economics*, **54**, August, pp. 235–66.

Levy, D., M. Bergen, S. Dutta and R. Venable (1997), 'The Magnitude of Menu Costs: Direct Evidence from Large U.S. Supermarket Chains', *Quarterly Journal of Economics*, **112**, August, pp. 791–825.

Mankiw, N.G. (1985), 'Small Menu Costs and Large Business Cycles: A Macroeconomic Model of Monopoly', *Quarterly Journal of Economics*, **100**, May, pp. 529–39.

Nickell, S. and G. Quintini (2001), 'Nominal Wage Rigidity and the Rate of Inflation', Centre for Economic Performance Discussion Paper no. 489, March.

Obstfeld, M. and K. Rogoff (1996), *Foundations of International Macroeconomics*, Cambridge, MA: MIT Press.

Obstfeld, M. and K. Rogoff (2000), 'New Directions for Stochastic Open Economy Models', *Journal of International Economics*, **50**, February, pp. 117–53.

Poterba, J., J. Rotemberg and L. Summers (1986), 'A Tax-Based Test for Nominal Rigidities', *American Economic Review*, **76**, September, pp. 659–75.

Romer, C.D. and D.H. Romer (1989), 'Does Monetary Policy Matter? A New Test in the Spirit of Friedman and Schwartz', *NBER Macroeconomics Annual*, **4**, pp. 121–70.
Taylor, J.B. (1999), 'Staggered Price and Wage Setting in Macroeconomics', in J.B. Taylor and M. Woodford (eds), *Handbook of Macroeconomics*, vol. 1B, Amsterdam: North-Holland.

North American Free Trade Agreement

A free trade agreement signed in 1993 by the United States, Canada and Mexico to eliminate, over a 15-year period, all duties, tariffs and non-tariff barriers between the three countries.

Okun, Arthur M. (1928–80)

Arthur Okun (b.1928, Jersey City, New Jersey, USA) obtained his BA (1949) and PhD (1956) from Columbia University. His main posts included instructor of economics (1952–6), Assistant Professor (1956–60), Associate Professor (1960) and from 1963 Professor of Economics at Yale University. Between 1961 and 1962 he worked as a staff economist for the Council of Economic Advisers (CEA) and was a member of the Council during 1964–8, before chairing the CEA in 1968–9. In 1969, he joined the Brookings Institution as a Senior Fellow and in 1972 helped to co-found the *Brookings Papers on Economic Activity*, which he co-edited until his death in 1980. He is best known for his work on forecasting with the CEA; and the empirical relationship between unemployment and the gap between actual and potential GNP, popularly known as Okun's Law. Among his best known books are *The Political Economy of Prosperity* (Brookings Institution, 1970); *Equality and Efficiency: The Big Tradeoff* (Brookings Institution, 1975); *Prices and Quantities: A Macroeconomic Analysis* (Brookings Institution, 1981); and *The Economics of Policy-Making* (ed. J.A. Pechman) (MIT Press, 1983). His most widely read articles include 'Potential GNP: Its Measurement and Significance' (*Proceedings of the Business and Economics Statistics Section*, American Statistical Association, 1962).

See also:

Brookings Institution; Council of Economic Advisers; Okun's Law.

Okun's Law

A rule of thumb developed by Arthur Okun (1928–80) when he served as a staff economist (1961–2) on President Kennedy's Council of Economic Advisers (see A.M. Okun, 'Potential GNP: Its Measurement and Significance', *Proceedings of the Business and Economics Statistics Section*, American Statistical Association, 1962). Estimating that in the postwar period potential GNP for the US economy (a measure of the economy's productive capacity) corresponded with a 4 per cent unemployment rate, Okun's Law states that, on average, each 1 per cent increase in the unemployment rate above 4 per cent is associated with a 3 per cent decrease in actual GNP relative to potential GNP. In consequence 'a reduction in unemployment, measured as a percentage of the labour force, has a much larger proportionate effect on output' (Okun, 1962).

Up to the mid-to-late 1970s the law provided a crude, but reasonably accurate, rule of thumb for estimating the loss in real GNP associated with an increase in unemployment. While some economists (for example, Keynesians) still apply such a rule of thumb (albeit having revised Okun's original results of a 3:1 ratio downwards to a current 2:1 ratio), other economists (for example, real business cycle theorists) question Okun's Law as they view fluctuations in GNP as fluctuations in the natural (trend) rate of output, rather than deviations of actual GNP from potential GNP.

See also:

Business Cycles: Real Business Cycle Approach; Council of Economic Advisers; Okun, Arthur M.

Open Economy Trilemma

An open liberalized capital market forces governments to confront what Obstfeld and Taylor (1998) call the 'open-economy trilemma', or 'inconsistent trinity'; that is, 'a country cannot simultaneously maintain fixed exchange rates and an open capital market while pursuing a monetary policy toward domestic goals' (Obstfeld, 1998). Governments can only combine two of the above at any one time. If a government decides to use monetary policy instruments to target domestic macroeconomic objectives, it must either abandon its commitment to free capital mobility or allow the exchange rate to float. If, on the other hand, a government decides that it wishes to target the exchange rate and liberalize capital mobility, it cannot use monetary policy to achieve domestic objectives. To simultaneously target domestic objectives and the exchange rate is only possible if controls on capital mobility are imposed. How this open economy trilemma problem has been resolved under different monetary regimes is summarized in Table 1.

In a world of capital mobility, many economists have warned of the dangers of attempting to adopt 'soft-peg exchange rate regimes' and, as Fischer (2001) has shown, the world does seem to be moving towards a corner (bipolar) solution with respect to the choice of exchange rate regime in response to this trilemma problem (that is, by adopting either hard pegs, including currency unions and dollarization, or by moving to a floating exchange rate regime). (See S. Fischer 'Exchange Rate Regimes: Is the Bi-Polar View Correct?', *Journal of Economic Perspectives*, **15**, Spring, 2001; M. Obstfeld, 'The Global Capital Market: Benefactor or Menace?', *Journal of Economic Perspectives*, **12**, Fall, 1998; M. Obstfeld and A. Taylor, 'The Great Depression as a Watershed: International Capital Mobility over the Long Run', in M. Bordo, C. Goldin and E. White (eds), *The Defining*

Table 1   The trilemma and major phases of capital mobility

| Era | Resolution of the trilemma: countries choose to sacrifice | | | |
	Activist policies	Capital mobility	Fixed ex-change rate	Notes
Gold standard	Most	Rare	Rare (crises)	Broad consensus
Inter-war (off gold)	Rare	Several	Most	Capital controls (e.g. Latin America)
Bretton Woods	None (?)	Most	Rare (crises)	Broad consensus
Float	Rare	Increasingly rare	Increasingly common	Some consensus; except currency boards

Source: Obstfeld and Taylor (2001).

Moment: The Great Depression and the American Economy in the Twentieth Century, Chicago University Press, 1998; M. Obstfeld and A. Taylor 'Globalisation in Capital Markets', in M. Bordo, A. Taylor and J.G. Williamson (eds), *Globalisation in Historical Perspective*, University of Chicago Press, 2001).

See also:
Fixed Exchange Rate System; Flexible Exchange Rate System.

Open Market Operations

Purchases or sales of government securities made by the central bank in order to increase or decrease the money supply.

Optimum Currency Area

'No single currency regime is right for all countries or at all times' (Jeffrey Frankel, 1999a).

In 1999, Robert Mundell received the Nobel Prize in Economics 'for his analysis of monetary and fiscal policy under different exchange rate regimes and his analysis of optimum currency areas'. Mundell's (1961a) contribution to the 'Theory of Optimum Currency Areas' (OCA), building on earlier work in international economics (Mundell, 1957, 1960, 1961b), formed the organizing framework for subsequent research into this field. Following the publication of his 1961 paper the OCA issue has, over the years, been frequently revisited and elaborated on by many distinguished scholars, and often linked to the question of exchange rate arrangements in general and European Monetary Union (EMU) in particular. These studies have been both theoretical and empirical (for example, see McKinnon, 1963; Johnson, 1971; Krauss, 1973; Mundell, 1973a, 1994, 1997a; Tavlas, 1993; Eichengreen, 1998; Frankel and Rose, 1998, 2002; De Grauwe, 2000; Alesina and Barro, 2001, 2002; McKinnon, 2001, forthcoming).

To put the OCA discussion in context we should note that in general, economic integration can take a variety of forms, as indicated in Table 1. A monetary union in the form of a single currency clearly relates to countries which have decided to move towards complete economic integration involving a unified economic policy.

Table 1   Alternative forms of economic integration

Forms of integration	Free trade between members	Common external tariff	Free mobility of factors	Harmonized economic policy	Unified economic policy
Free trade area	*				
Customs union	*	*			
Common market	*	*	*		
Economic union	*	*	*	*	
Complete economic integration	*	*	*	*	*

Source: Adapted from Balassa (1973) and Hitiris (1998).

We should also note that in reality there are several possible monetary arrangements between countries of which full monetary union with a single currency is just one. Frankel (1999a) distinguishes nine alternative forms of currency regime. Moving from the most rigid to the most flexible form of exchange rate arrangement, these are (a) single currency union (including 'dollarization'); (b) currency board arrangement for example, Argentina prior to the 2001 crisis; (c) 'truly fixed' exchange rate, for example, currencies pegged to the dollar; (d) adjustable peg arrangement, for example, the Bretton Woods regime; (e) crawling peg regime; (f) basket peg regime; (g) target zone or band, for example, the ERM system in the EEC/EU; (h) managed or 'dirty float'; (i) free float, for example, the United States is the closest to this regime. Frankel notes that the 'currently fashionable view is that countries are being pushed to choose between the extremes', that is, to join a currency union (or truly fixed exchange rate regime) or to move towards a free float (see Eichengreen, 1999; Fischer, 2001). The main cause of this move towards a bipolar world of exchange rate arrangements is the so-called 'open economy trilemma', 'impossible trinity' or 'integration trilemma' (see Obstfeld, 1998; Frankel, 1999a, 1999b; Summers, 1999). This 'trilemma' relates to the difficulty facing any country wishing to achieve simultaneously exchange rate stability, monetary independence and full financial integration, that is, free capital mobility. A country can attain any two at a given time but not all three. With financial integration expanding across the world, the choice is becoming increasingly one between exchange rate stability via truly fixed exchange rates, or currency union (that is, giving up monetary independence), or pure float (that is, giving up exchange rate stability). According to the modern theory of optimum currency areas, there is a set of criteria to guide countries in their choice of exchange rate arrangements and it is important for countries to evaluate the costs and benefits of joining a particular exchange rate regime, especially a monetary union. To date (March, 2002) the majority of European Union (EU) members (12 out of 15) have opted to join a currency union based on the Euro. This raises the crucial question: is the EU an optimal currency area? (See De Grauwe and Vanhaverbeke, 1993.)

The early research on OCAs highlighted the relevant issues that need to be considered when a particular group of countries are considering the formation of a currency union or fixed exchange rate system. According to Tavlas (1993), the main exchange rate arrangements that characterize countries intending to adopt a monetary union in either single currency, or separate currency, form are (a) the total liberalization of capital and current transactions, (b) the complete absence of exchange controls, (c) the irrevocable fixing of parity rates, and (d) the elimination of margins of fluctuation between exchange rates. However, before embarking on such arrangements the following factors need to be carefully considered as they all affect the costs and benefits of participating in a single currency system. These factors include the degree of openness and size of the economy; the extent of labour and other factor mobility; price and wage flexibility; the diversification of the economy and extent of financial market integration; the extent of fiscal integration between the currency union economies; and the level of goods market integration.

The conventional wisdom is that an optimum geographic coverage for a common currency (an optimal currency area) will be a region 'that is neither too small that it would be better off pegging its currency to a neighbor, nor so large that it would be better off splitting into sub-regions with different currencies' (Frankel, 1999a). In other words, the size of participating economies should be optimal. The OCA is also influenced by openness to trade because the benefits resulting from having a fixed exchange rate increases with the degree of economic integration, while the advantages of a flexible exchange rate diminish. Also, for high inflation-prone economies, a fixed exchange rate is likely to provide a credible nominal anchor and succeed in reducing and stabilizing the inflation bias associated with discretionary policies (providing of course that the currency is pegged to a country with a strong anti-inflation reputation). A fixed exchange rate monetary regime also becomes a better bet for more open economies, since nominal exchange rate depreciation may not lead to improved real competitiveness if domestic prices and wages rise in response to a depreciation.

The extent of labour mobility is of crucial importance to the success of a currency union, as Mundell clearly recognized and earlier writers had already discussed (see Meade, 1957; Skitovsky, 1958). In a seminal paper, Mundell (1961a) put the question, 'What is the appropriate domain of a currency area?' He concluded that an optimum currency area is 'the region'. Thus the question of EMU 'reduces to whether or not Western Europe can be considered a single region, and this is essentially an empirical problem'. The 'essential ingredient of a common currency is that the currency area should exhibit a high degree of internal factor mobility'. As Mundell (ibid.) notes: 'if the world can be divided into regions within each of which there is factor mobility and between which there is factor immobility, then each of these regions should have a separate currency which fluctuates relative to all other currencies'.

High labour mobility, combined with extensive goods market integration and flexible prices and wages between regions, will greatly diminish the need for exchange rate adjustment to deal with the unemployment and inflation consequences of asymmetric shocks across different regions (Gros, 1996). The extent of goods market integration and diversification between members is therefore very important because countries with diverse economic structures are much more likely to be hit by asymmetric shocks. Providing the countries forming a regional currency union are affected symmetrically by economic shocks, and labour and other factors of production flow freely between them, these countries may gain by moving to a single currency and its corollary, a single monetary authority. A higher level of fiscal integration between regions also helps to mitigate the adverse consequences of economic shocks by allowing fiscal transfers from booming to depressed regions, as occurs in the US monetary union. Although the USA established its monetary union in 1788, according to Rockoff (2000) it 'was not until the 1930s that all regions, including the South, could be said to be parts of a single optimal currency area'. It is hoped that it takes a much shorter time in Europe!

Relating to these considerations, the early literature on OCAs analysed the potential costs and benefits to a nation of participating in a currency union. The main cost to joining a monetary union for any particular country is the loss of monetary sovereignty: the central bank loses control of monetary policy when exchange rates are fixed or a common currency is adopted. However, as Tavlas (1993) and De Grauwe (2000) discuss, the demise of the stable long-run Phillips curve and the modern consensus view relating to Friedman's natural rate hypothesis means that independent monetary authorities cannot in any case target real variables such as unemployment in the long run.

The most important benefits of adopting a single currency are related to the elimination of the exchange rate risk, which is equivalent to a transaction cost for a risk-averse trader, reductions in the cost of acquiring information, and increased price transparency. Reducing risk and uncertainty is likely to encourage investment and hence growth. According to Tavlas (1993), other cost-reducing benefits include enlargement of the foreign exchange rate market, elimination of speculative capital flows within the area, and economizing on the need to hold foreign exchange reserves through the pooling of reserves. In considering the formation of a currency area, policy makers need to balance the benefits of having a single currency against the consequences of diminished policy autonomy following the loss of the exchange rate and monetary policy as instruments used to offset the impact of economic shocks. That loss will be more costly the more economic shocks are region-specific. Taking a cost–benefit approach, countries should only consider membership of a currency union if the benefits outweigh the costs, although we need to note that political motives may often outweigh economic considerations (see Feldstein, 1997a).

In addition to the above considerations, Mundell (1997a) lists some of the circumstances which may lead to a country deciding against membership of a fixed exchange rate zone or currency union. For example, a country may want to have a different inflation rate than that of other members of the currency area; it may be reluctant to give up domestic monetary policy and the use of the exchange rate as instruments of employment policy; the country may wish to use monetary expansion (an inflation tax) to finance government spending; the government may be corrupt and wish to disguise this fact; the country may not want to lose national (political) independence; the country may wish to maintain its monetary independence in the event of a war; a country may wish to protect the secrecy of its data/statistics; the country may fear immigration from other countries. For all of these and other reasons, a country may decide not to participate in a currency union. On the other hand, a country may choose to join a monetary union in order to benefit from the low inflation rate of the currency area; to reduce its transaction costs from trading with a major partner; to eliminate the costs of printing and maintaining a separate national currency; to establish an automatic mechanism and to remove discretion from its monetary and fiscal authorities; and to help build an economic power block to rival the USA.

Although Mundell's initial analysis provides much ammunition for those who are currency union sceptics, he now believes that in many cases the benefits of joining a monetary union exceed the costs (see Mundell, 1973a, 1973b). In order to explain his intellectual journey, Mundell (1997a, p. 2) states that his famous (1961a) article 'presented a qualification to the case for flexible exchange rates, which, provided the basic argument was valid, works best when currency areas are regions'. However, by the late 1960s, he had become more sceptical about the applicability of flexible exchange rates as an adjustment mechanism in many situations, and explored the implications of adjustment mechanisms under fixed exchange rates. Mundell also recognizes that there are exceptions to his preference for fixed exchange rate arrangements. These include cases where countries are very unstable with large budget deficits financed by the banking system; and, for very large countries such as the USA, where the adoption of a fixed exchange rate is not feasible.

The theory of optimum currency areas has received increasing attention over recent years mainly because of debates relating to EMU and the introduction of the Euro (see Feldstein, 1997a, 1997b; Obstfeld, 1997; Wyplosz, 1997; Allsopp and Vines *et al.*, 1998; Frankel, 1999a, 1999b; Mundell, 1999, 2000; McKinnon, 2001, 2002). In particular, consideration of the economic costs and benefits of EMU relates to the theory of optimum currency areas and this has undoubtedly contributed to a revival of interest in this part of international economics. In the EMU literature, several important questions are highlighted with respect to the relationships between the countries intending to participate in a currency union, including, first, the extent to which economic shocks are likely to be symmetric across EMU members. The European Commission believes that, following the completion of the 'Single Market', integration will deepen and the likelihood of asymmetric shocks will decline. Therefore, if member states have similar economic structures, produce similar products and have a similar degree of economic diversification, the need for exchange rate adjustments between EU members as a method for restoring equilibrium is substantially reduced (see Frankel and Rose, 1998, 2002). If the economic cycles are highly correlated across EMU members then a single 'one-size-fits-all' monetary policy, operated by the European Central Bank (ECB), will be appropriate. However, Krugman (1991) argues that when economies of scale are important, increasing integration will lead to more regional concentration of economic activities (see also Kenen, 1969). Thus sector-specific shocks (for example, to the motor industry) may become country-specific asymmetric shocks (see De Grauwe, 2000). A second question concerns the extent to which participants in EMU have relatively common economic institutions enabling the free movement of capital and labour across borders. The greater the factor mobility between members of EMU, the easier it is for countries to adjust to economic shocks. Thirdly, it is also important that member states share a general consensus on the priorities for economic policy laid down for EMU, such as the priority given to achieving price stability and the coordination of fiscal policy (see Eijffinger and Haan, 2000).

However, the question of how far the EMU conforms to the characteristics of an optimum currency area, as laid out in the literature on OCAs, remains highly controversial. At first glance, many empirical studies seem to support the sceptics' view that the EMU is not an optimum currency area, for two main reasons. First, EMU countries have experienced frequent and often large shocks over recent years. A well-known example is German reunification. Second, persistent high unemployment rates throughout Europe suggest that the labour market in EMU economies is highly inflexible and therefore slow to adjust to economic disturbances (Feldstein, 1997a, 1997b). Some sceptics therefore argue that common monetary policy actions will be damaging to some member countries because the EMU is a long way from being an optimum currency area. For example, McKinnon (2001) considers that the 12 members do not satisfy the classic criteria for an optimum currency area as well as the 50 American states do.

Nevertheless, trade integration and labour mobility within Europe are increasing over time and the correlation of national business cycles can be expected to increase as well. Thus the EMU optimists hope that European countries will, with the passage of time, come increasingly to satisfy the criteria for a common currency. Meanwhile, the Euro, dollar and yen should continue in the future to float freely against each other. In addition, an increasing number of scholars believe that the dollar's continued vehicle-currency role is unlikely to be displaced by the extended currency area role of the Euro in today's more globalized world.

Finally, recent work by Alesina and Barro (2001, 2002) and Alesina and

Spolare (2002) draws attention to the increasing number of countries in the world: 76 in 1947 and 193 in 2001. This has resulted in a substantial increase in the number of currencies in circulation. Unless by definition a country is an optimal currency area, either 'there were too few currencies in 1947 or there are too many today'. Alesina and Barro argue that there must be too many today, since the 'increasing integration of international markets implies that the optimal number of currencies would tend to decrease'. They conclude that, 'in a world of small highly integrated countries, where the benefits of low and stable inflation are highly valued, one should observe a collapse of the one-country-one-money identity and a move toward a world with relatively few currencies'.

DILEK DEMIRBAS

See also:

Bretton Woods; Euro; European Central Bank; European Monetary Union; European Union; Exchange Rate Mechanism; Fixed Exchange Rate System; Flexible Exchange Rate System; Mundell, Robert A.; Nobel Prize in Economics; Open Economy Trilemma.

Bibliography

Alesina, A. and R.J. Barro (eds) (2001), *Currency Unions*, Cambridge, MA: MIT Press.
Alesina, A. and R.J. Barro (2002), 'Currency Unions', *Quarterly Journal of Economics*, **117**, May, pp. 409–36.
Alesina, A. and E. Spolare (2002), *The Size of Nations*, Cambridge, MA: MIT Press.
Allsopp, C. and D. Vines *et al.* (1998.), 'Symposium: Macroeconomic Policy After EMU', *Oxford Review of Economic Policy*, **14**, Autumn, pp. 1–167.
Balassa, B. (1973), *The Theory of Economic Integration*, London: George Allen & Unwin.
De Grauwe, P. (2000), *Economics of Monetary Union*, Oxford: Oxford University Press.
De Grauwe, P. and W. Vanhaverbeke (1993), 'Is Europe an Optimum Currency Area? Evidence From Regional Data', in P.R. Masson and M.P. Taylor (eds), *Policy Issues in the Operation of Currency Unions*, Cambridge: Cambridge University Press.
Dornbusch, R. (2000), *Keys to Prosperity: Free Markets, Sound Money and a Bit of Luck*, Cambridge, MA: MIT Press.
Eichengreen, B. (1998), *European Monetary Unification: Theory, Practice and Analysis*, Cambridge, MA: MIT Press.
Eichengreen, B. (1999), 'Kicking the Habit: Moving from Pegged Rates to Greater Exchange Rate Flexibility', *Economic Journal*, **109**, March, pp. 1–14.
Eijffinger, C.W. and J. De Haan (2000), *European Monetary and Fiscal Policy*, Oxford: Oxford University Press.
Feldstein, M. (1997a), 'The Political Economy of the European Economic and Monetary Union: Political Sources of an Economic Liability', *Journal of Economic Perspectives*, **11**, Fall, pp. 23–42.
Feldstein, M. (1997b), 'EMU and International Conflict', *Foreign Affairs*, **76**, November/December, pp. 60–73.
Fischer, S. (2001), 'Exchange Rate Regimes: Is the Bi-Polar View Correct?', *Journal of Economic Perspectives*, **15**, Spring, pp. 3–24.
Frankel, J. (1999a), 'No Single Currency Regime is Right for all Countries or at all Times', *Essays in International Finance*, no. 215, Princeton, NJ: Princeton University Press.
Frankel, J. (1999b), 'The New International Financial Architecture: Exchange Rate Regimes and Financial Integration', *Policy Brief*, no. 51, June, Washington, DC: Brookings Institution.

Frankel, J. and A. Rose (1998), 'The Endogeneity of the Optimal Currency Area Criteria', *Economic Journal*, **108**, July, pp. 1009–25.

Frankel, J. and A. Rose (2002), 'An Estimate of the Effect of Common Currencies on Trade and Income', *Quarterly Journal of Economics*, **117**, May, pp. 437–66.

Gros, D. (1996), 'A Reconsideration of the Optimum Currency Area Approach: The Role of External Shocks and Labour Mobility', *National Institute Economic Review*, October, pp. 108–17.

Hitiris, T. (1998), *European Union Economics*, 4th edn, London: Prentice Hall Europe.

Johnson, H.G. (1971), 'Problems of European Monetary Union', *Journal of World Trade Law*, **5**, August, pp. 377–87; reprinted in H.G. Johnson (1972), *Further Essays in Monetary Economics*, London: George Allen & Unwin.

Kenen, P. (1969), 'The Theory of Optimum Currency Areas: An Eclectic View', in R. Mundell and A. Swoboda (eds), *Monetary Problems of the International Economy*, Chicago: University of Chicago Press.

Krauss, M.B. (1973), *The Economics of Integration: A Book of Readings*, London: George Allen & Unwin.

Krugman, P. (1991), *Geography and Trade*, Cambridge, MA: MIT Press.

McKinnon, R.I. (1963), 'Optimum Currency Areas', *American Economic Review*, **53**, September, pp. 717–24.

McKinnon, R.I. (2001), 'Optimum Currency Areas and the European Experience', October, (*http://www.stanford.edu/~mckinnon/*), pp. 1–20.

McKinnon, R.I. (forthcoming), 'Mundell, the Euro, and Optimum Currency Areas', in T. Courchene (ed.), *Essays in Honor of Robert Mundell*.

Meade, J.E. (1957), 'The Balance-of-Payments Problems of a Free Trade Area', *Economic Journal*, **67**, September, pp. 379–96.

Mundell, R.A. (1957), 'Transport Costs in International Trade Theory', *Canadian Journal of Economics and Political Science*, **23**, August, pp. 331–48.

Mundell, R.A. (1960), 'The Monetary Dynamics of International Adjustment Under Fixed and Flexible Exchange Rates', *Quarterly Journal of Economics*, **84**, May, pp. 227–57.

Mundell, R.A. (1961a), 'A Theory of Optimum Currency Areas', *American Economic Review*, **51**, November, pp. 657–65.

Mundell, R.A. (1961b), 'The International Disequilibrium System', *Kyklos*, **14**, pp. 154–72.

Mundell, R.A. (1973a), 'Uncommon Arguments for Common Currencies', in H.G. Johnson and A.K. Swoboda (eds), *The Economics of Common Currencies*, London: Allen & Unwin.

Mundell, R.A. (1973b), 'A Plan for a European Currency', in H.G Johnson and A.K. Swoboda (eds), *The Economics of Common Currencies*, London: Allen and Unwin.

Mundell, R. A. (1994), 'The European Monetary System 50 years after Bretton Woods: A Comparison Between Two Systems' (*http://www. columbia.edu/cu/economics*).

Mundell, R.A. (1997a), 'Optimum Currency Areas' (*http://www.columbia.edu/cu/economics*).

Mundell, R.A. (1997b), 'The International Monetary System in the 21st Century: Could Gold Make a Comeback?' (*http://www.columbia.edu/cu/economics*).

Mundell, R.A. (1999), 'The Euro and the Stability of the International Monetary System' (*http://www.columbia. edu/cu/economics*).

Mundell, R. (2000), 'A Reconsideration of the Twentieth Century', *American Economic Review*, **90**, June, pp. 327–40.

Obstfeld, M. (1997), 'Europe's Gamble', *Brookings Papers on Economic Activity*, no. 2., pp. 241–317.

Obstfeld, M. (1998), 'The Global Capital Market: Benefactor or Menace?', *Journal of Economic Perspectives*, **12**, Fall, pp. 9–30.

Rockoff, H. (2000), 'The History of the US as a Monetary Union', *NBER Working Paper*, Historic Paper, no. 124, April.

Scitovsky, T. (1958), *Economic Theory and Western European Integration*, London: George Allen & Unwin.

Summers, L.H. (1999), 'Reflections on Managed Global Integration', *Journal of Economic Perspectives*, **13**, Spring, pp. 3–18.

Tavias, G.S. (1993),'The Theory of Optimum Currency Areas Revisited', *Finance and Development*, **30**, June, pp. 32–5.
Wyplosz, C. (1997), 'EMU: Why and How It Might Happen', *Journal of Economic Perspectives*, **11**, Fall, pp. 3–22.

Organization for Economic Cooperation and Development

The Organization for Economic Cooperation and Development (which replaced the Organization for European Economic Co-Operation in 1961) is an intergovernmental organization, based in Paris, which provides a policy forum for the major industrialized countries for the promotion of economic growth, expansion of multinational trade and provision of foreign aid to developing countries. For more information, the reader is referred to the OECD website (*http://www.oecd.org/*).

Organization of Petroleum-exporting Countries

Established in 1960, OPEC's current members, in addition to the five founding members of Iran, Iraq, Kuwait, Saudi Arabia and Venezuela, include Algeria, Indonesia, Libya, Nigeria, Qatar and the United Arab Emirates. Between them OPEC members produce approximately 40 per cent of the world's oil and hold in excess of 77 per cent of the world's proven oil reserves. The organization seeks to coordinate and negotiate policy on production and price between member petroleum-exporting countries. Some economists believe that the two oil price hikes made by OPEC in the 1970s (1973–4 and 1979) significantly contributed to the stagflation of that period.

See also:
Stagflation.

Outside Lag

The time lag between the implementation of a policy change and when the policy change starts to affect the economy. The outside lag is a distributed lag, as the effects of a policy change on the economy will be spread out over time. The length of the outside lag will depend on a number of factors, including whether fiscal or monetary policy changes are implemented; the state of the economy at the time when the policy change is implemented; and the way the private sector responds to the policy change.

Outside Money

Money which is a direct debt of the public sector (for example, currency circulating within the private sector) and/or which is based on public sector debt (for example, bank deposits which are matched by banks' holdings of cash reserves or reserves at the central bank). In contrast to inside money, there is no offsetting private sector liability with outside money.

See also:

Inside Money.

Passive Policy Rule

A pre-specified rule for the conduct of policy which is not linked to prevailing economic circumstances. An example of a passive policy rule would be where the money supply is targeted to grow at a rate of, say, 3 per cent per annum regardless of the state of the economy.

See also:

Rules Versus Discretion.

Patinkin, Don (1922–95)

Don Patinkin (b.1922, Chicago, Illinois, USA) obtained his BA (1943), MA (1945) and PhD (1947) from the University of Chicago. His main posts included Assistant Professor at the University of Chicago, 1947–8; Associate Professor at the University of Illinois, 1948–9; Lecturer (1949–52), Associate Professor (1952–6) and Professor (1956–95) at the Hebrew University of Jerusalem. Between 1956 and 1972 he was Director of the Maurice Falk Institute for Economic Research in Israel and, in 1974, president of the Econometric Society. He is best known for his work on monetary and macroeconomic theory, in particular integrating real and monetary theory by giving macroeconomics rigorous microfoundations in a general equilibrium model; and the development of Keynes's monetary theory. Among his best known books are *Money, Interest and Prices: An Integration of Monetary and Value Theory* (Row Peterson, 1956); *Studies in Monetary Economics* (Harper & Row, 1972); *Keynes's Monetary Thought: A Study of its Development* (Duke University Press, 1976); *Keynes, Cambridge and 'The General Theory': The Process of Criticism and Discussion Connected with the Development of 'The General Theory'* (co-edited with J.C. Leith) (University of Toronto Press, 1978); *Essays On and In the Chicago Tradition* (Duke University Press, 1981); and *Anticipation of 'The General Theory' and Other Essays on Keynes* (University of Chicago Press, 1982). His most widely read articles include 'Price Flexibility and Full Employment' (*American Economic Review*, **38**, September 1948); 'The Chicago Tradition, the Quantity Theory and Friedman' (*Journal of Money, Credit and Banking*, **1**, February 1969), and 'On Different Interpretations of the *General Theory*' (*Journal of Monetary Economics*, **26**, November 1990).

See also:

Econometric Society; Keynesian economics; Keynesian Economics: Reappraisals of; Real Balance Effect.

Peak

The upper turning point, following the expansionary phase of the business cycle, at which aggregate economic activity stops increasing and thereafter begins to fall.

See also:
Business Cycle.

Permanent Income Hypothesis

In the early 1950s, two similar, yet distinct, theories of consumption were advanced: the permanent income hypothesis and the life cycle hypothesis. Both of these theories can be viewed as a response to the failure of the absolute income hypothesis to receive support from all forms of empirical evidence.

The permanent income hypothesis (PIH) is attributable to Milton Friedman. This hypothesis evolved over a number of years. After some delay, it was published in the form of a book, entitled *A Theory of the Consumption Function* (ATCF) (Friedman, 1957). In the preface to this book, Friedman informs the reader that the development of the theory was a group effort. In particular, he acknowledges the contributions made by his wife, Rose Friedman, as well as Dorothy Brady and Margaret Reid.

The PIH is strictly a microeconomic theory of individual behaviour. The analysis performed by Friedman in chapter II of his book is founded upon Irving Fisher's (1907, 1930) theory of saving. The consumer unit plans consumption with the objective of maximizing utility over the long term, subject to a wealth constraint. When this constrained optimization problem is solved, current-period consumption is seen to depend upon both wealth and the rate of interest. In contrast to the absolute income hypothesis, under the PIH, a change in current income will only affect current consumption by way of altering wealth. Note that, in the context of Friedman's analysis, wealth comprises not only non-human wealth (for example, financial assets and property) but also human wealth, where the latter can be defined as the discounted sum of current and future labour income.

On pages 10 and 11 of ATCF, Friedman introduces and defines the concept of permanent income. Permanent income is defined as 'the amount a consumer unit could consume (or believes that it could) while maintaining its wealth intact' (ATCF, p. 10). Assuming an infinite life span, permanent income has the interpretation of the annuity value of household wealth. Mathematically, permanent income can be expressed as

$$y_{Pt} = iW_t.$$

In this equation, y_P and W denote permanent income and wealth, respectively. The t subscript signifies that the value of the associated variable relates to the current time period; i denotes the rate of interest, the value of which is assumed to be fixed over time. Thus permanent income can be regarded as the interest income that is derived from a household's holdings of human and non-human wealth.

Given the above relationship between permanent income and wealth, the outcome of solving the intertemporal utility maximization problem is the consumption function:

$$c_{Pt} = f(y_{Pt}/i, i),$$

where c_{Pt} denotes the value of the services that the individual plans to consume during the current period, referred to by Friedman as permanent consumption (ATCF, p. 11). In the above equation, permanent consumption is seen to depend upon two variables, namely, permanent income and the rate of interest. Hence, it is possible to present the consumption function as

$$c_{Pt} = g(y_{Pt}, i).$$

If the assumption is made that the dynamic utility function has the property of homotheticity then, more specifically, there is a proportional relationship between c_{Pt} and y_{Pt}. In terms of mathematics:

$$c_{Pt} = ky_{Pt},$$

where $0 < k < 1$.

Factors which affect the proportionality parameter, k, include the rate of interest, tastes, the age and the composition of the consumer unit, and income uncertainty. Also k is positively dependent upon the ratio of non-human wealth to permanent income on the understanding that non-human wealth provides more substantial collateral than human wealth. Importantly, though, k is independent of permanent income. *Ceteris paribus*, the average propensity to consume permanent income is the same for a wealthy household as it is for a poor household.

Given the factors affecting k, the proportional relationship between c_{Pt} and y_{Pt} can be presented as

$$c_{Pt} = k(i, z, u)y_{Pt}.$$

In this equation, z is used to denote the ratio of non-human wealth to permanent income and u is a portmanteau variable which represents utility factors.

The above equation describes the permanent consumption of a single consumer unit. To be able to use the same equation to characterize group consumption behaviour, the same functional relationship has to apply to all members of the group. Also it is necessary to assume that the distribution of consumer units by permanent income is independent of their distribution by i, z and u. Friedman (ATCF, p.19) recognizes that such an assumption is obviously false. However, he maintains that the interdependence between i, z and u and the distribution of y_{Pt} may not be important for aggregation. He asserts that the proportional relationship will serve as a useful approximation even when interdependence exists.

A problem which exists for the purpose of testing the PIH is that the proportional relationship, presented above, involves what are merely theoretical constructs. To compare the predictions of the PIH with empirical evidence, it is necessary to relate these conceptual variables to variables upon which data can be obtained. Consequently, Friedman decomposes measured or absolute disposable income into a permanent component and a transitory component, that is,

$$y_t = y_{Pt} + y_{Tt},$$

where y and y_T denote measured income and transitory income, respectively. The empirical definition of permanent income is the regular or expected income of the consumer. In contrast, transitory income is the income that arises accidentally or by chance.

Similarly, Friedman regards measured or actual consumption as consisting of permanent and transitory elements:

$$c_t = c_{Pt} + c_{Tt},$$

where c and c_T denote measured consumption and transitory consumption, respectively.

Note that, in the context of the PIH, consumption is defined to be the flow of services derived from current and past purchases of consumption goods. Permanent consumption and transitory consumption have the interpretations of planned consumption and unplanned consumption, respectively.

The two definitional equations for y_t and c_t that were constructed by Friedman still do not allow the PIH to be tested. The reason for this is that they introduce two unknowns, namely, the transitory components, y_{Tt} and c_{Tt}. To enable the PIH to be contradicted by observed data, Friedman makes assumptions about the properties of the probability distributions of transitory income and transitory consumption. Specifically, he assumes the transitory components to be uncorrelated with their respective permanent components:

$$\rho(y_{Tt}, y_{Pt}) = 0 \text{ and } \rho(c_{Tt}, c_{Pt}) = 0,$$

where ρ denotes the correlation coefficient corresponding to the two variables entering the parentheses.

Also Friedman assumes the transitory components of income and consumption to be uncorrelated:

$$\rho(y_{Tt}, c_{Tt}) = 0.$$

(Note that, following the publication of Friedman's theory, various studies were performed with the specific objective of testing the validity of this particular aspect of the PIH. Based upon the studies conducted using survey data by Bodkin (1959). Bird and Bodkin (1965), Kreinin (1961) and Attfield (1976), the evidence obtained has been mixed.)

In comparison to the absolute income hypothesis, a desirable feature of the PIH is that it is capable of explaining all forms of empirical evidence on the relationship between measured consumption and absolute income – the so-called 'stylized facts'. From both budget studies and short-run time-series data, there was found evidence of a non-proportional relationship between consumption and income. In contrast, long-run time-series data indicated a proportional relationship between these two variables.

Specified below is a linear, stochastic relationship between consumption and absolute income:

$$c = a + by + u,$$

where a and b are the parameters of the equation and u denotes a disturbance term. All variables relate to the current period. For convenience, time subscripts have been omitted.

If Friedman's PIH model has validity, then $a = 0$, $b = k$ and $u = c_T - ky_T$. Given the composition of the disturbance term and recalling the definition, $y = y_P + y_T$, there is a non-zero correlation between the disturbance term and the regressor in the consumption function. Specifically:

$$\text{Cov.}(u, y) = -k(\text{var.}(y_T)).$$

The consequence of the non-zero correlation between u and y is that the ordinary least squares estimators of the parameters of the consumption equation are biased and inconsistent. In particular, it can be demonstrated that

$$\text{Plim.}(b^*) = k[\text{var.}(y_P)/\text{var.}(y)]$$

and

$$\text{Plim.}(a^*) = k[1 - \text{var.}(y_P)/\text{var.}(y)]\mu_{yP}.$$

In the above equations, b^* and a^* denote the ordinary least squares estimators of b and a, respectively, and μ_{yP} is the mean value of permanent income. To produce these results, it has been assumed that the expected value of each of the transitory components of income and consumption is equal to zero.

The results show that, in the situation in which at least some of the variation in measured income is attributable to a variation in transitory income, the ordinary least squares estimator, b^*, is subject to downward bias, while the ordinary least squares estimator, a^*, is subject to upward bias. For both estimators, the greater is the contribution of transitory income to the variation in measured income, the more severe is the bias. Furthermore, the bias will be a feature of large as well as small samples.

Consequently, the finding from budget studies, that different income groups have different values of the average propensity to consume, can be explained by the contribution of transitory income to measured income. More specifically, it can be argued that the relatively small average propensity to consume that is associated with a high-income group arises from favourable transitory income effects outweighing negative transitory effects. Also the relatively large average propensity to consume that is associated with a low-income group stems from negative transitory income effects collectively being stronger than favourable transitory effects. (For a more detailed explanation, see ATCF, pp. 34–6.)

Using the PIH, the approximately constant value of the ratio of consumption to income that has been observed over the course of several business cycles can be explained by movements in measured income, over the long run, being dominated by movements in permanent income. In contrast, over a single business cycle, secular changes have less responsibility for fluctuations in income. The considerable contribution made by transitory income to the variation in absolute income over the short run results in the ordinary least squares estimate of the marginal propensity to consume being less than the long-run counterpart and the estimate of the intercept term being greater than zero.

In ATCF, Friedman performs empirical analysis using both cross-section data (Chapter IV) and time-series data (Chapter V). Concerning the analysis of time-series data, Friedman seeks to estimate the PIH consumption function,

$$c_t = k y_{Pt} + c_{Tt},$$

using annual data on the United States.

Given that transitory consumption can be treated as a conventional stochastic disturbance term, the principal problem confronting Friedman is the measurement of permanent income. In order to overcome this measurement problem, Friedman makes the implicit assumption that estimates of permanent income are formed using an adaptive expectations mechanism. However, following the critique by Lucas (1976) of econometric policy evaluation, there has been a preference amongst economic researchers for assuming rational expectations. Since the late 1970s, there have been published a considerable number of studies that have sought to consider and test the implications of combining the PIH with the assumption of rational expectations: for example, Hall (1978), Flavin (1981) and Campbell and Deaton (1989).

In a seminal paper, Robert Hall (1978) demonstrated that a consequence of combining the PIH with the rational expectations hypothesis is that consumption behaves in accordance with the stochastic process:

$$c_t = \beta_0 + \beta_1 c_{t-1} + \varepsilon_t.$$

In this equation, ε_t denotes an error term which has the property of being orthogonal to all information that is available in period $t-j$ ($j \geq 1$). Given this property of the error term, a straightforward means of testing the rational expectations–permanent income hypothesis (REPIH) is to add, as regressors, lagged variables to the above specification and to examine their joint significance. Such exclusion tests have been performed by Hall, himself, and in studies by Daly and Hadjimatheou (1981), Davidson and Hendry (1981), Cuddington (1982), Chatterji (1983), Johnson (1983) and Gausden and Whitfield (2000).

Another implication of the PIH, when combined with the assumption of rational expectations, is that consumption is responsive only to an unanticipated change in income. Any change in income which is anticipated is predicted to have no effect on consumption. Thus an approach that has been adopted in order to test the validity of the REPIH involves modelling jointly consumption and income. An examination then takes place of whether or not the sensitivity of consumption to a change in current-period income is in excess of that which is attributable to the new information contained within the latter. Such excess sensitivity tests have been performed by, amongst others, Bilson (1980), Flavin (1981) and Muellbauer (1983).

Combining the PIH and the rational expectations hypothesis also has an important policy implication. For a policy change, such as a reduction in the basic rate of personal income tax, to have a significant effect on consumption, two conditions must be satisfied. First, the policy change must be perceived by households to have a permanent effect on their disposable income. Second, the policy change must not have been anticipated. Furthermore, it will be the case that the response of consumption to the policy change will occur at the time of its announcement as opposed to the time of its implementation.

In general, the results obtained from both exclusion tests and excess sensitivity tests have refuted the REPIH. Popular explanations for the contradiction of the theory by the empirical evidence have included liquidity constraints and precautionary saving in the presence of uncertainty about the future. In a survey article, Muellbauer (1994) discusses both these and other factors which may account for the rejection of the REPIH by the data.

ROBERT GAUSDEN

See also:

Absolute Income Hypothesis; Adaptive Expectations; Friedman, Milton; Life Cycle Hypothesis; Rational Expectations.

Bibliography

Attfield, C.L.F. (1976), 'Estimation of the Structural Parameters in a Permanent Income Model', *Economica*, **43**, August, pp. 247–54.

Bilson, J.F.O. (1980), 'The Rational Expectations Approach to the Consumption Function. A Multi-Country Study', *European Economic Review*, **13**, pp. 273–99.

Bird, R.C. and R.G. Bodkin (1965), 'The National Service Life-Insurance Dividend of 1950 and Consumption: A Further Test of the "Strict" Permanent-Income Hypothesis', *Journal of Political Economy*, **73**, October, pp. 499–515.

Bodkin, R. (1959), 'Windfall Income and Consumption', *American Economic Review*, **49**, September, pp. 602–14.

Campbell, J. and A. Deaton (1989), 'Why is Consumption So Smooth?', *Review of Economic Studies*, **56**, July, pp. 357–73.

Chatterji, M. (1983), 'On Forecasting UK Consumption', *Applied Economics*, **15**, June, pp. 417–23.

Cuddington, J.T. (1982), 'Canadian Evidence on the Permanent Income–Rational Expectations Hypothesis', *Canadian Journal of Economics*, **15**, pp. 331–5.

Daly, V. and G. Hadjimatheou (1981), 'Stochastic Implications of the Life Cycle-Permanent Income Hypothesis: Evidence for the UK Economy', *Journal of Political Economy*, **89**, June, pp. 596–9.

Davidson, J.E.H. and D.F. Hendry (1981), 'Interpreting Econometric Evidence: The Behaviour of Consumers' Expenditure in the UK', *European Economic Review*, **16**, pp. 177–92.

Fisher, I. (1907), *The Rate of Interest*, New York: Macmillan.

Fisher, I. (1930), *The Theory of Interest*, New York: Macmillan.

Flavin, M. (1981), 'The Adjustment of Consumption to Changing Expectations about Future Income', *Journal of Political Economy*, **89**, October, pp. 974–1009.

Friedman, M. (1957), *A Theory of the Consumption Function*, Princeton: Princeton University Press.

Gausden, R. and I.A. Whitfield (2000), 'Testing the Stochastic Implications of the Life Cycle–Permanent Income Hypothesis Using UK Regional Time-Series Data', *Applied Economics*, **32**, August, pp. 1299–1310.

Hall, R.E. (1978), 'Stochastic Implications of the Life Cycle–Permanent Income Hypothesis: Theory and Evidence', *Journal of Political Economy*, **86**, December, pp. 971–87.

Johnson, P. (1983), 'Life-Cycle Consumption under Rational Expectations: Some Australian Evidence', *Economic Record*, **59**, December, pp. 345–50.

Kreinin, M.E. (1961), 'Windfall Income and Consumption – Additional Evidence', *American Economic Review*, **51**, June, pp. 388–90.

Lucas, R.E., Jr (1976), 'Econometric Policy Evaluation: A Critique', in K. Brunner and A. H. Meltzer (eds), *The Phillips Curve and Labor Markets*, Carnegie–Rochester Conference Series on Public Policy 1, Amsterdam: North-Holland.

Muellbauer, J. (1983), 'Surprises in the Consumption Function', *Economic Journal*, **93**, Supplement, pp. 34–50.

Muellbauer, J. (1994), 'The Assessment: Consumer Expenditure', *Oxford Review of Economic Policy*, **10**, pp. 1–41.

Phelps, Edmund S.

Edmund Phelps (b.1933, Evanston, Illinois, USA) obtained his BA from Amherst College in 1955 and his MA (1957) and PhD (1959) from Yale University. His main past posts have included Assistant Professor at Yale University, 1960–62; Visiting Associate Professor at Massachusetts Institute of Technology, 1962–3; Associate Professor at Yale University, 1963–6; Professor of Economics at the University of Pennsylvania, 1966–71; Professor at Columbia University, 1971–8; Professor at New York University, 1978–9; and Professor at Columbia University, 1979–82. Since 1982 he has been the McVickar Professor of Political Economy at Columbia University. He is best known for his work on the natural rate of unemployment; and the microfoundations of macroeconomics; and for being a leading influence on the development of the new Keynesian school. Among his best known books are *Microeconomic Foundations of Employment and Inflation Theory et al.* (W.W. Norton, 1970); *Inflation Policy and Unemployment Theory: A Cost–Benefit Approach to Monetary Planning* (W.W. Norton, 1972); *Studies in Macroeconomic Theory: Employment and Inflation* (Academic Press, 1979); *Seven Schools of Macroeconomic Thought* (Oxford University Press, 1990); and *Structural Slumps: The Modern Equilibrium Theory of Unemployment, Interest and Assets* (Harvard University Press, 1994). His most widely read articles include 'Phillips Curves, Expectations of Inflation and Optimal Unemployment over Time' (*Economica*, **34**, August 1967); 'Money Wage Dynamics and Labour Market Equilibrium' (*Journal of Political Economy*,

76, August 1968); 'Stabilizing Powers of Monetary Policy under Rational Expectations' (co-authored with J.B. Taylor) (*Journal of Political Economy*, **85**, February 1977); and 'Behind the Structural Boom' (*American Economic Review*, **89**, May 1999).

See also:

Expectations-augmented Phillips Curve; Natural Rate of Unemployment; New Keynesian Economics.

Phillips Curve

The *Phillips curve*, purporting to show a trade-off between inflation and unemployment, has been at the centre of the macroeconomic policy debate for well over 40 years. This is a highly sensitive issue in the political economy of capitalism. In particular, inflation is anathema to what Keynes (1936, p. 376) called the *rentier* interests, those individuals and institutions who have already accumulated substantial financial resources. Hence any suggestion that lower unemployment can be 'bought' with higher inflation tends to be fiercely resisted. So successful has this resistance been in recent times that, after the 'conservative revolution' (Smithin, 1990) in theory and policy making in the last quarter of the twentieth century, almost the opposite position became influential. That is, the argument that from a longer-term perspective a very *low* level of inflation is a prerequisite for higher growth and lower unemployment. The actual evidence for this, however, is weak (Barro, 1995; Temple, 2000).

The original Phillips curve was an empirical relationship documented by Phillips (1958) between the rate of change of money wages and unemployment in Britain from 1861 to 1957. As pointed out by Humphrey (1993), Phillips was actually not the first to suggest the relationship associated with his name. He was anticipated most famously by Fisher (1926), but also by classical writers, such as Law, Hume and Thornton, even further back.

Following Phillips's contribution, and given the close association between wage inflation and price inflation, the idea of a price-inflation/ unemployment trade–off seemed to follow. This concept was then taken up and propagated in such contributions as Lipsey (1960) and Samuelson and Solow (1960). During the 1960s it was therefore widely believed that there existed a permanent and stable negative trade-off between inflation and unemployment, which could be exploited for policy purposes. It would be possible for either monetary or fiscal policy to reduce unemployment permanently, but only at the cost of a permanently higher inflation rate or vice versa. Each society would therefore have to assess the relative costs of inflation and unemployment and choose some optimal mix of the two. At the time, the Phillips curve seemed to fill a gap on the supply side of the 'orthodox' Keynesian model (Snowdon *et al.*, 1994), which may account for its quick success.

However, the Phillips curve was soon in trouble in academia and among policy makers. There were two main problems, one theoretical, one empirical. First, the logic of the Phillips curve, as originally presented, was in conflict with one of the most basic precepts of neoclassical economics, namely that economic decisions should be based on real (inflation-adjusted) magnitudes rather than nominal magnitudes. This point was made in two influential articles by Phelps (1967) and Friedman (1968). Second, during the 1970s, the original Phillips curve trade-off seemed to be actively misleading owing to the occurrence of 'stagflation' in the real world data during that decade. There were episodes in which *both* inflation and unemployment increased in various jurisdictions. It is worth pointing out that the apparent empirical failures came well *after* the theoretical challenge. The former gave credence to the latter and was apparently decisive.

In the 1970s, then, belief in a permanent trade-off between inflation and unemployment declined. It was argued that the *short-run Phillips curve* (SRPC), also known as the *expectations-augmented Phillips curve*, could shift bodily whenever there is a change in inflationary expectations. In the mainstream macroeconomic models of the late 1970s, through the 1980s, and beyond, any postulated trade-off between inflation and unemployment was therefore explicitly short term. In the long run, any rate of inflation was thought compatible with the *natural rate* of unemployment, which later came to be called (more neutrally) the NAIRU (non-accelerating inflation rate of unemployment). The *long-run Phillips curve* (LRPC) was assumed to be vertical. This general framework changed the consensus evaluation of the relative costs of inflation and unemployment. Even if it is recognized that the impact of a disinflation will normally be a recession, if the lower inflation is expected to be permanent and the recession only temporary, it can be argued that the costs are not too onerous relative to the benefits. There may be some suspicion that those suffering the 'pain' (those most likely to lose their jobs) are not those who eventually 'gain' (typically those already financially comfortable). However, this point can be glossed over, and the opposite view is also argued (Romer and Romer, 1999). In any event, it is not too much to claim, for example, that the policy-induced recessions in both the early 1980s and early 1990s in many jurisdictions were deliberately provoked by monetary authorities whose actions were based on ideas of this kind.

For the 'monetarist experiments' (Smithin, 1990) of 1979–82, it was even the case that rational expectations *policy irrelevance* arguments, advanced by such authors as Lucas (1972), Sargent and Wallace (1975) and Barro (1976), had convinced some economists that a deflationary policy could be pursued without *any* short-run output effects, as long as the actions of the central bank were preannounced and 'credible'. A deliberate disinflationary policy would then carry no costs at all. Events since the early 1980s, however, have obviously not borne out this extreme view.

Contrary to the conventional wisdom as it stood around 20 years ago, more recent events must, if anything, have somewhat rehabilitated the notion of an inflation/unemployment trade-off, if not in the textbooks, at least in terms of *realpolitik*. Experience seems to show that the pain of the recessionary periods required for disinflation is severe, and more long-lasting than the expression 'short term' would suggest. In this regard, the concept of *hysteresis* (a term originally borrowed from physics) has been much discussed since the mid-1980s (Blanchard and Summers, 1986; Wyplosz, 1987; Setterfield, 1993; Ball, 1999). The suggestion is that the time path of an economic variable, such as the unemployment rate or the level of real GDP, may depend crucially on its own past history. For example, workers who are unemployed during a recession lose job skills, and the experience itself adversely affects them, both socially and emotionally. They may therefore become less 'employable'. Similarly, if an industrial firm closes down a plant during a recession, it is unlikely to be as efficient when it reopens as it was originally. Hence it may not be reasonable to assume that a policy-induced recession will leave no permanent scars. To recognize issues of hysteresis and path dependency does not restore a precise quantitative notion of a trade-off between inflation and unemployment, as in the original Phillips curve. However, it does tend to dispel the notion that the real effects of monetary policy can safely be ignored, even given a fairly orthodox understanding of the relationship between money and the economy.

The opposite view, that the LRPC, if not vertical, is positively sloped (that is, the longer-run association between inflation and growth is negative, at least for positive rates of inflation) has also been influential. This idea was originally floated by Friedman (1977) in his Nobel Prize lecture, and theoretical support is provided by some of the 'cash-in-advance' literature (Stockman, 1981; Abel, 1985), which treats inflation as a tax on economic activity. Similar arguments are also used informally by those advocating policies to reduce or eliminate inflation, as in Howitt (1990). Nonetheless, it would be fair to say that there is little evidence for this position comparable to that originally accumulated by Phillips. Moreover, as shown by Kam (2000), and previously by MacKinnon and Smithin (1993), it is a straightforward matter to devise models with a LRPC going the other way, and which are equally 'rigorous' from the viewpoint of neoclassical 'microfoundations'. (But see also Smithin, 2001, for a critique of this methodology.) A *negatively-sloped* LRPC would be a revival of the *Mundell–Tobin effect* (Mundell, 1963; Tobin, 1965), whereby inflation stimulates growth by discouraging the holding of financial assets in favour of 'real capital', or the earlier *forced saving* arguments of classical economics (Hayek, 1932).

A useful rhetorical device in introducing the Phillips curve to students is to argue (only slightly 'tongue-in-cheek') that professional economists seem to forget the lessons of 'Economics 101' when discussing this topic. In the context of an introductory course, no-one is surprised to find that sometimes price increases are associated with increases in output (for a demand expansion), but that prices can also rise when output is falling (for a reduction in supply). The syllabus will also cover such topics as increasing returns and imperfect competition, which impinge on these basic relationships. At the macroeconomic level, modern mainstream theory attempts to rule out such ideas by appeal to natural rates of unemployment, output and interest, and by the insistence that employment and output are ultimately determined on the supply side. However, the relative importance of the demand and supply sides for economic outcomes is actually *the* central debate in macroeconomics, and is unlikely to be solved for all time by the prevalence of one school or another at the present juncture. It can be argued, on the contrary, that any comprehensive theory of inflation and economic growth should be able to explain, equally convincingly, periods of high growth with high inflation, low growth with low inflation, low growth with high inflation, and high growth with low inflation (Smithin, 1997). All of these have occurred at various times and places.

JOHN SMITHIN

See also:

Expectations-augmented Phillips Curve; Hysteresis; Inflation: Costs of; Inflation: Costs of Reducing; NAIRU; Natural Rate of Unemployment.

Bibliography

Abel, A. (1985), 'Dynamic Behavior of Capital Accumulation in a Cash-In-Advance Model', *Journal of Monetary Economics*, **16**, July, pp. 55–71.

Ball. L. (1999), 'Aggregate Demand and Long-Term Unemployment', *Brookings Papers on Economic Activity*, **2**, pp. 189–236.

Barro, R. (1976), 'Rational Expectations and the Role of Monetary Policy', *Journal of Monetary Economics*, **2**, pp. 1–32.

Barro, R. (1995), 'Inflation and Economic Growth', *Bank of England Quarterly Bulletin*, May, pp. 39–52.

Blanchard, O.J. and L. Summers (1986), 'Hysteresis and the European Unemployment Problem', in S. Fischer (ed.), *NBER Macroeconomics Annual*, Cambridge, MA: MIT Press.

Fisher, I. (1926), 'A Statistical Relation Between Unemployment and Price Changes', *International Labour Review*, **13**, June, pp. 85–92.

Friedman, M. (1968), 'The Role of Monetary Policy', *American Economic Review*, **58**, March, pp. 1–17.

Friedman, M. (1977), 'Inflation and Unemployment', *Journal of Political Economy*, **85**, June, pp. 451–72.

Hayek, F.A. (1932), 'A Note on the Development of the Doctrine of Forced Saving', *Quarterly Journal of Economics*, **47**, pp. 123–33.

Howitt, P. (1990), 'Zero Inflation as a Long-Term Target', in R.G. Lipsey (ed.), *Zero Inflation: The Goal of Price Stability*, Toronto: C.D. Howe Institute.

Humphrey, T.M. (1993), *Money, Banking and Inflation: Essays in the History of Economic Thought*, Aldershot, UK and Brookfield, US: Edward Elgar.

Kam, A.E. (2000), 'Three Essays on Endogenous Time Preference, Monetary Non-Superneutrality and the Mundell–Tobin Effect', unpublished Ph.D thesis, York University, Toronto.

Keynes, J.M. (1936), *The General Theory of Employment, Interest and Money*, London: Macmillan.

Lipsey, R.G. (1960), 'The Relation Between Unemployment and the Rate of Change of Money Wages in the UK, 1862–1957: A Further Analysis', *Economica*, **27**, February, pp. 1–32.

Lucas, R.E. Jr (1972), 'Expectations and the Neutrality of Money', *Journal of Economic Theory*, **4**, April, pp. 103–24.

MacKinnon, K.T. and J. Smithin (1993), 'An Interest Rate Peg, Inflation and Output', *Journal of Macroeconomics*, **15**, Fall, pp. 769–85.

Mundell, R. (1963), 'Inflation and Real Interest', *Journal of Political Economy*, **71**, June, pp. 280–83.

Phelps, E.J. (1967), 'Phillips Curves, Expectations of Inflation and Optimal Inflation Over Time', *Economica*, **34**, August, pp. 254–81.

Phillips, A.W. (1958), 'The Relation Between Unemployment and the Rate of Change of Money Wages in the United Kingdom, 1861–1957', *Economica*, **25**, November, pp. 283–99.

Romer, C.D. and D.H. Romer (1999), 'Monetary Policy and the Well-Being of the Poor', *Federal Reserve Bank of Kansas City Economic Review*, **84**, Q1, pp. 21–49.

Samuelson, P.A. and R. Solow (1960), 'Analytical Aspects of Anti-Inflation Policy', *American Economic Review*, **50**, May pp. 177–94.

Sargent, T.J. and N. Wallace (1975), 'Rational Expectations, the Optimal Monetary Policy Instrument, and the Optimal Money Supply Rule', *Journal of Political Economy*, **83**, April, pp. 241–54.

Setterfield, M. (1993), 'Towards a Long-Run Theory of Effective Demand: Modelling Macroeconomic Systems with Hysteresis', *Journal of Post Keynesian Economics*, **15**, Spring, pp. 347–64.

Smithin, J. (1990), *Macroeconomics after Thatcher and Reagan: The Conservative Policy Revolution in Retrospect*, Aldershot, UK and Brookfield, US: Edward Elgar.

Smithin, J. (1997), 'An Alternative Monetary Model of Inflation and Growth', *Review of Political Economy*, **9**, October, pp. 395–409.

Smithin, J. (2001), 'Macroeconomic Theory, (Critical) Realism and Capitalism', in P.A. Lewis (ed.), *Transforming Economics: Perspectives on the Critical Realist Project*, London: Routledge.

Snowdon, B., H.R. Vane, and P. Wynarczyk (1994), *A Modern Guide to Macroeconomics: An Introduction to Competing Schools of Thought*, Aldershot, UK and Brookfield, US: Edward Elgar.

Stockman, A.C. (1981), 'Anticipated Inflation and the Capital Stock in a Cash-In-Advance Economy', *Journal of Monetary Economics*, **8**, November, pp. 387–93.

Temple, J. (2000), 'Inflation and Growth: Stories Short and Tall', *Journal of Economic Surveys*, **14**, pp. 395–426.

Tobin, J. (1965), 'Money and Economic Growth', *Econometrica*, **33**, October, pp. 671–84.

Wyplosz, C. (1987), 'Comment', in R. Layard and L. Calmfors (eds), *The Fight Against Unemployment*, Cambridge, MA: MIT Press.

Phillips, A. William H.

William Phillips (b.1914, Te Rehunga, Dannevirke, New Zealand) obtained his BSc (1949) and PhD (1952) from the University of London. His main posts included the Tooke Professor of Economic Science and Statistics at the London School of Economics, 1958–67; and Professor of Economics, Research School of Social Science, National University of Australia, 1967–70. He is best known for his work on the relation between the level of unemployment and the rate of change of money wage rates, popularly referred to as the Phillips curve; and optimal control theory. His most widely read articles include 'Mechanical Models in Economic Dynamics' (*Economica*, **17**, August 1950); 'Stabilisation Policy in a Closed Economy' (*Economic Journal*, **64**, June 1954); 'The Relation Between Unemployment and the Rate of Change of Money Wage Rates in the United Kingdom, 1861–1957' (*Economica*, **25**, November 1958); 'Employment, Money and Prices in a Growing Economy' (*Economica*, **28**, November 1961); and 'Employment, Inflation and Growth' (*Economica*, **29**, February 1962). For an interesting discussion of Phillips's contributions, see R. Leeson (ed.), *A.W.H. Phillips: Collected Works in Contemporary Perspective* (Cambridge University Press, 1999) and R. Leeson, 'A.W.H. Phillips MBE (Military Division), (*Economic Journal*, **104**, May 1994).

See also:
Phillips Curve.

Pigou Effect

See:
Real Balance Effect.

Pigou, Arthur C. (1877–1959)

Arthur Pigou (b.1877, Ryde, Isle of Wight, England) obtained his MA from the University of Cambridge in 1900. His main posts included Lecturer (1901), Fellow (1902) and Professor of Political Economy (1908–43) at King's College, Cambridge. He is best known for his work as one of the last great classical economists who initially, as a staunch opponent of the Keynesian revolution, spoke for the classical school; and having put forward what has come to be referred to as the real balance, or Pigou, effect. Among his best known books are *Unemployment* (Holt, 1914); *Industrial Fluctuations*

(Macmillan, 1927); and *The Theory of Unemployment* (Macmillan, 1933). His most widely read articles include 'Mr. J.M. Keynes's *General Theory of Employment, Interest and Money*' (*Economica*, **3**, May 1936); 'The Classical Stationary State' (*Economic Journal*, **53**, December 1943); and 'Economic Progress in a Stable Environment' (*Economica*, **14**, August 1947).

See also:
Classical Model; Keynesian Economics; Real Balance Effect.

Policy Ineffectiveness Proposition

According to the new classical policy ineffectiveness proposition, first presented by Thomas Sargent and Neil Wallace in two influential papers in the mid–1970s – 'Rational Expectations, the Optimal Monetary Instrument and the Optimal Money Supply Rule' (*Journal of Political Economy*, **83**, April 1975) and 'Rational Expectations and the Theory of Economic Policy' (*Journal of Monetary Economics*, **2**, April 1976) – only unanticipated changes in monetary policy can affect real variables, and then only in the short run. Anticipated changes in monetary policy will be ineffective, having no effect on output and employment. The proposition can be illustrated as follows.

Suppose the money supply is determined by the authorities according to some 'known' rule: for example, the authorities might adopt a monetary rule which allows for a given fixed rate of monetary growth of 6 per cent per annum. In this situation the authorities will be unable to influence output and employment, even in the short run, by pursuing a systematic monetary policy, as it can be anticipated by rational economic agents. In forming their expectations of inflation, rational economic agents would include the anticipated effects of the 6 per cent expansion of the money supply. Consequently, the systematic component (6 per cent) of the monetary rule would have no effect on real variables. If, in practice, the money supply grew at a rate of 8 per cent per annum the non-systematic (unanticipated) component of monetary expansion (2 per cent) would cause income and output to rise temporarily above their natural levels, owing to errors in inflation expectations. Alternatively, the authorities might allow the money supply to be determined by a feedback rule. Again changes in the rate of monetary growth, which arise from a known feedback rule, will be anticipated by agents, making the feedback rule ineffective. Only departures from a known monetary rule (such as policy errors made by the monetary authorities or unforeseen changes in policy) which are unanticipated will influence output, and then only in the short run.

The policy ineffectiveness proposition, that only unanticipated monetary surprises have real output effects, has been the subject of a number of empirical studies. Early work, in particular Robert Barro's two studies, 'Unanticipated Money Growth and Unemployment in the United States (*American Economic Review*, **67**, March 1977) and 'Unanticipated Money, Output and the Price Level in the United States' (*Journal of Political Economy*, **86**, August 1978) seemed to support the proposition. However, subsequent studies, most notably Frederic Mishkin's study, 'Does Anticipated Monetary Policy Matter? An Econometric Investigation' (*Journal of Political Economy*, **90**, February 1982) and Robert Gordon's study of 'Price Inertia and Policy Ineffectiveness in the United States, 1890–1980' (*Journal of Political Economy*, **90**, December 1982) found evidence that suggested that both unanticipated *and* anticipated monetary policy affect income and employment.

See also:

Feedback Rule; New Classical Economics; Rational Expectations; Sargent, Thomas J.; Wallace, Neil.

Post Keynesian Economics

Keynes, addressing *The General Theory of Employment, Interest and Money* chiefly to his 'fellow economists', insisted:

> The postulates of the classical theory are applicable to a special case only and not to the general case . . . Moreover, the characteristics of the special case assumed by the classical theory happen not to be those of the economic society in which we actually live, with the result that its teaching is misleading and disastrous if we attempt to apply it to the facts of experience. (Keynes, 1936, p. 3)

Keynes believed that he could logically demonstrate why 'Say's Law . . . is not the true law relating the aggregate demand and supply functions' (ibid., p. 26) when we model an economy possessing real-world characteristics. Until we get our theory to mirror accurately and apply to the 'facts of experience', there is little hope of getting our policies right.

Keynes compared those economists whose theoretical logic was grounded in Say's Law to Euclidean geometers living in a non-Euclidean world,

> who discovering that in experience straight lines apparently parallel often meet, rebuke the lines for not keeping straight – as the only remedy for the unfortunate collisions which are occurring. Yet, in truth, there is no remedy except to throw over the axiom of parallels and to work out a non-Euclidean geometry. Something similar is required today in economics. (Ibid., p. 16)

Following Keynes, Post Keynesians have identified the axioms of classical theory that Keynes's analysis rejects in developing a more general theory of employment, interest and money for an entrepreneurial economy. To throw over an axiom is to reject what the faithful believe are 'universal truths'. The Keynesian revolution in economic theory was therefore truly a revolt against what orthodoxy held to be universal truths. Keynes aimed at rejecting some fundamental axioms of orthodox theory to provide a general logical foundation for a model that was not tied to Say's Law but instead was closely related to the real world in which we happen to live. Unfortunately, since Keynes, mainstream macro theorists, seduced by a technical methodology that promised precision and unique results at the expense of applicability and accuracy, have reintroduced more sophisticated forms of the very axioms Keynes rejected almost a half-century ago. Consequently, the so-called 'Keynesian revolution' was almost immediately shunted onto a wrong track by Samuelson's (1947) *Foundations of Economic Analysis*, where the microfoundations of what Samuelson called 'neoclassical synthesis Keynesianism' were laid out. These microfoundations utilized more obtuse versions of the same classical axioms underlying a Say's Law world. Samuelson's classical axiomatic based microfoundations became the keystone of modern mainstream theory. Monetarists, new classical economists, neoclassical synthesis (or old) Keynesians, and new Keynesians have all reconstructed their brand of macro theory on the foundations of those 'universal truths' that Keynes struggled to overthrow.

Post Keynesian economics attempts to revive Keynes's revolutionary analysis. Post Keynesians create a model of a money-using, market-oriented entrepreneurial economy that does not rely on the restrictive axioms that are the logical foundations of the aforementioned orthodox schools of economic thought. The major classical axioms rejected by the Post Keynesians are (1) the gross substitution axiom, (2) the money-is-neutral axiom, and (3) the orthodox presumption of an ergodic economic system. (The ergodic axiom is the basis for the rational expectations hypothesis of stochastic models; the ordering axiom provides a foundation for subjective probability analysis in the non-stochastic models of expected utility theory.)

The characteristics of the real world which Keynes believed could be modelled only by overthrowing these three classical axioms are as follows. First, money matters in both the long and short run; that is, money is never neutral. Money and therefore liquidity considerations always affects real decision making. Despite Milton Friedman's use of the motto 'money matters', Friedman remains faithful to the neutral-money axiom and does not permit money to affect the long-run outcome of his system (Friedman, 1974).

Second, the economic system is moving through calendar time from an irrevocable past to an uncertain future. In Keynes's conception of uncertainty, decision-making agents 'know' that past economic evidence does not provide a reliable basis for calculating the probability of future economic outcomes (see Davidson, 1982–3). Keynes (1973) wrote: 'The sense in which I am using the term [uncertainty] is that . . . there is no scientific basis on which to form any calculable probability whatever. We simply don't know.' This sense of uncertainty violates the orthodox presumption of an ergodic economic system.

In a stochastic world, in order to predict future outcomes one must draw samples from the future. Since this is impossible, classical theorists invoke the ergodic axiom which presumes that samples drawn from the past are equivalent to samples drawn from the future. Thus, in an ergodic system, agents can reliably predict the future by studying the past data. In other words, the ergodic axiom implies that the future can be reliably predicted through calculating past probability distributions The future becomes merely the statistical shadow of past events.

Third, in a world where the future *cannot* be predicted on any scientific basis using either subjective or objective probability analysis, in entrepreneurial economies humans have developed the institution of forward contracts in money terms as a means of organizing time-consuming production and exchange processes (see Davidson, 1980). The money-wage contract is the most ubiquitous of these contracts. Modern production economies are organized on a money-wage contract-based system.

Fourth, involuntary unemployment, rather than full employment, is a common outcome in a *laissez faire* market-oriented, monetary production economy where the gross substitution axiom is not applicable to savers' choices between using liquid and non-liquid assets as a means of storing purchasing power over time.

The gross substitution axiom
The gross substitution axiom is the backbone of orthodox economics. It is the assumption that any good is a substitute for any other good. This axiom means that, if the demand for good x goes up, its price will rise, inducing demand to spill over to the now relatively cheaper substitute good, y. For an economist to deny this 'universal truth' is truly revolutionary heresy. As in the days of the Inquisition, the present-day College of Cardinals of mainstream economics destroys all non-believers – if not by burning them at the stake, then by banishing them from the mainstream professional journals. Yet Keynes's *General Theory* analysis, which rests on 'The Essential Properties of Interest and Money' (Keynes, 1936, ch. 17) propagates this heresy in rejecting the gross substitution axiom as a ubiquitous

phenomenon applicable to the relationship between liquid assets (including money) and the products of industry.

The essential properties that Keynes associated with money (and all other liquid assets, that is, assets readily resaleable for money in a well-organized market) are:

1. The elasticity of production of all liquid assets including money is (approximately) zero vis-à-vis the producible output of industry. In other words, the employment of labour by private-sector entrepreneurs can not be used to produce durable assets that are held for liquid store of value purposes.
2. The elasticity of substitution between money (and other liquid assets) and producible goods (goods possessing high elasticities of production) is (approximately) zero. In other words, the gross substitution axiom does not apply regarding the substitutability between money and producible goods as potential liquid stores of value over time.

The first essential property, a zero elasticity of production, can be translated as meaning that money does not grow on trees. If money grew on trees (that is, if money had a high elasticity of production), workers without current employment could always be hired to harvest the money trees. As long as the marginal utility of money exceeded the marginal disutility of reaching up to pluck the fruit of the money trees, unemployed workers could find a job and full employment would prevail. If money and other liquid assets are non-producible, and if people buy less out of current income to save more in the form of non-producible liquid assets, there will be a reduction in demand for workers to produce producible goods, while this increase in liquidity demand does not increase the demand for workers to harvest liquidity trees. Or, as Hahn writes, Say's Law is not applicable as long as there are 'resting places for saving other than reproducible assets' (Hahn, 1977, p. 31). The existence of 'any non-reproducible asset allows for a choice between employment inducing and non-employment inducing demand' (ibid.).

Any increase in demand by savers for non-producible assets will increase their price. If the gross substitution axiom was applicable, rising prices of non-producibles would induce savers to substitute reproducible durables for non-producibles in their wealth holdings. Consequently, non-producibles would not be the ultimate 'resting place' for saving (Davidson, 1972, 1977, 1980). Demand for a store of value would spill over into producible goods markets and restore employment opportunities. The assumption of a ubiquitous gross substitution axiom therefore assures the restoration of Say's Law and denies the logical possibility of involuntary unemployment. If the gross substitution axiom is rejected as not being universally applicable, increased aggregate saving without concomitant increased autonomous spending on the products of industry will cause involuntary unemployment. A change in relative market prices between non-producible assets and producible goods cannot cure unemployment unless gross substitution is presumed applicable.

To overthrow the axiom of gross substitution in an intertemporal context is truly heretical. It changes the entire perspective on what is meant by 'rational' or 'optimal' saving, on why people save or what object they use to carry their saving forward to the future. Hicks (1979) noted that all Keynes needed to say was that income was divided between current consumption and a vague provision for the uncertain future. Hicks added the mathematical assumption that 'planned expenditures at specified different dates in the future have independent utilities [and are gross substitutes] . . . this assumption I find quite unacceptable. . . . the normal condition is that there is strong complimentarily between them [consumption plans in successive periods]' (ibid., pp. 76–7). Indeed Danziger *et al.*, (1982–3) have shown that the facts regarding consumption and saving behaviour by the elderly are incompatible with the notion of intertemporal gross substitution of consumption plans. Yet this presumption underlies both life-cycle models and overlapping-generation models; models which are fundamental and popular in mainstream macroeconomic theory.

In the absence of the axiom of gross substitution, income effects (for example, the Keynesian multiplier) predominate and can swamp any hypothetical neoclassical substitution effects. Consequently, if the gross substitution axiom is not applicable for the saving decision between liquid non-producibles and non-liquid producible goods, then relative price changes via a flexible pricing mechanism will not be the cure-all snake-oil medicine usually recommended by many neoclassical doctors for the unfortunate economic maladies that are occurring in the real world.

The neutrality-of-money axiom

The neutrality-of-money axiom implies that money is a veil, and therefore all economic decisions are made on the basis of real phenomena and relative prices alone. Money does *not* matter. Money cannot affect employment and real-output outcomes. To reject this neutrality axiom does not require assuming that agents suffer from a money illusion (see Keynes, 1973, p. 411). It merely means that money can matter in both the short run and the long run, or as Keynes put it:

> The theory which I desiderate would deal . . . with an economy in which money
> plays a part of its own and affects motives and decisions, and is, in short, one of

the operative factors in the situation, so that the course of events cannot be predicted in either the long period or in the short, without a knowledge of the behaviour of money between the first state and the last. And it is this which we ought to mean when we speak of a monetary economy. (Ibid., pp. 108–9)

Can anything be more revolutionary? In this passage from an article entitled 'The Monetary Theory of Production' (and I emphasize the word 'monetary'), Keynes specifically rejects the neutrality axiom. Once we admit that money is a real phenomenon, that money matters, then orthodox economic analysis collapses and it is no longer possible to prove that a general clearing of all markets is an inevitable outcome of a freely flexible price system. Arrow and Hahn (1971, pp. 356–7) have argued as follows:

> The terms in which contracts are made matter. In particular, if money is the good in terms of which contracts are made, then the prices of goods in terms of money are of special significance. This is not the case if we consider an economy without a past or future. . . . If a serious monetary theory comes to be written, the fact that contracts are made in terms of money will be of considerable importance.

Moreover as Arrow and Hahn (ibid., p. 361) demonstrate, if contracts are made in terms of money (so that money affects real decisions) in an economy moving along in calendar time with a past and an uncertain future, then all existence theorems are jeopardized. The existence of money contracts – a characteristic of the world in which Keynes lived and in which we still do – implies that there need never exist, in the long run or the short run, any rational expectations equilibrium and/or general equilibrium market-clearing price vector.

The ergodic presumption

Most orthodox mainstream economists suffer from the pervasive form of what we may call the classical economist's disease. That is, these economists want to be considered first-class scientists dealing with a 'hard science' rather than be 'second-class' citizens of the scientific community dealing with a non-precise 'social' and 'political' science. These economists, mistaking precision (rather than accuracy) as the hallmark of 'true' science, prefer to be precise rather than accurate. Precision conveys the meaning of 'sharpness to minute detail'. Accuracy, on the other hand, means 'care to obtain conformity with fact or truth'. For example, if you phone the plumber to come and fix an emergency breakdown in your plumbing system and he responds by indicating he will be there in exactly 12 minutes, he is being precise but not exercising care to obtain conformity with fact or truth. If he says he will be there before the day is over, he is being accurate, if not necessarily precise.

Most economists prefer to be precisely wrong rather than roughly right or accurate. The presumption of an ergodic economic system permits economists to act as if they were dealing with a 'hard science' where data are homogeneous with respect to time. In such an ergodic world, observations of a time series realization (that is, historical data) are useful information regarding the probability distribution of the stochastic process that generated this realization. The same data also provide information about a universe of realization that exists at any point of time such as today. These observations are also reliable information regarding the future probability distribution of events. Hence, by statistically studying the past generated by an ergodic process, present and future events can be forecast in terms of statistically reliable probabilities (Davidson, 1982–3.) In the absence of an ergodic environment, there is no scientific basis for calculating the probabilities associated with possible future outcomes from an exiting data set.

Keynes (1936, pp. 149–50) rejected this view that past data sets provided reliable information about important future economic events. In a non-ergodic world – our economic world – the future cannot be reliably predicted and therefore liquidity matters. To store one's saving in money or other liquid assets is to refrain from exercising today's claims on resources. Instead, by utilizing liquid assets to store today's saving, the saver is able to defer to the indefinite future how he/she will use these claims. Liquidity is freedom to make a decision another day. When liquidity matters, money is never neutral, and neither Say's Law or Walras's Law is relevant. In such a world, Keynes's revolutionary analysis, Post Keynesians believe, is the applicable theory that explains real world phenomena.

Mainstream economic theory has not followed Keynes's revolutionary logical analysis to develop what Arrow and Hahn have called a 'serious monetary theory' in which contracts are made in terms of money in an economy moving from an irrevocable past to an uncertain, non-ergodic future. Post Keynesian economics has taken on the task of providing a serious monetary theory following the analytical leads provided by Keynes.

Some policy implications
How one interprets volatility in the international financial markets and therefore chooses a policy stance regarding these markets depends on the underlying economic theory that one explicitly, or implicitly, utilizes to explain the role of financial markets in a market-oriented entrepreneurial economy. There are two major alternative theories of financial markets: (1) the classical efficient market theory (hereafter EMT) and (2) Keynes's liquidity preference theory (hereafter LPT). Each produces a different set of policy prescriptions. EMT advocates call for a liquidity plumber to patch up some short-run stresses in today's efficient international financial

flow system. LPT proponents believe that the current system is structurally flawed. Consequently, it will require an architect to build a new international financial structure on more solid foundations.

EMT is the backbone of conventional economic wisdom. The mantra of EMT is 'the market knows best' how to allocate optimally scarce capital resources and promote maximum economic growth. This EMT view was succinctly epitomized in US Treasury Secretary Summers's statement: 'the ultimate social functions [of financial markets are] spreading risks, guiding the investment of scarce capital, and processing and disseminating the information possessed by diverse traders . . . prices will always reflect fundamental values . . . The logic of efficient markets is compelling' (Summers and Summers, 1989, p. 166).

In contrast, the logic of Keynes's LPT indicates that the primary function of financial markets is to provide liquidity not efficiency. (And a liquid market requires *orderliness*.) If Keynes's LPT of orderly financial markets is relevant, the real world's international capital markets may never deliver, in either the short run or the long run, the results claimed by EMT.

Peter L. Bernstein is the author of the best-selling book entitled *Against the Gods* (1996), a treatise on risk management, probability theory and financial markets. Bernstein argues that the LPT and not the EMT is the relevant theory for the world in which we live. He states, 'The fatal flaw in the efficient market hypothesis is *that there is no such thing as an [efficient] equilibrium price* . . . a market can never be efficient unless equilibrium prices exist and are known' (Bernstein, 1999, emphasis in original; also Bernstein, 1998). In other words, in Bernstein's view, EMT is not applicable to real-world financial markets.

If EMT theory is not applicable to the real world then there is an important role for rebuilding of the system to permit some degree of international capital flow regulation as a necessary but not sufficient condition for producing a golden age of economic development for the global economy of the twenty-first century. Since the 1970s, however, the compelling logic of EMT has provided the rationalization for nations to dismantle most of the ubiquitous regulations of postwar international financial markets. The justification for this 'liberalization' of financial markets is that it will produce lower real costs of capital, greater growth rates of output and productivity, and more employment opportunities compared to the rates experienced between World War II and 1973, when international capital flow controls were practised by most countries of the world, including the United States.

The facts do not support this EMT argument for financial liberalization. World economic growth since 1973 has slowed dramatically. The post-1973 period of capital market liberalization has not delivered what efficient market theorists claimed it would (see Davidson, 2000). Accordingly, the plumbing solutions recommended by EMT, (for example, more transparency, uniform bankruptcy laws, the Tobin Tax, currency boards) will not solve the growing global liquidity problems. Only an architectural solution similar to Keynes's Bretton Woods plan will (see Davidson, 2000).

PAUL DAVIDSON

See also:

Davidson, Paul; Involuntary Unemployment in Keynes's *General Theory*; Keynes, John Maynard; Keynes's *General Theory*; Keynesian Economics; Neoclassical Synthesis; Neutrality of Money; Say's Law; Weintraub, Sidney.

Bibliography

Arrow, K.J. and F. H. Hahn (1971), *General Competitive Analysis*, San Francisco: Holden-Day.
Bernstein, P.L. (1996), *Against the Gods*, New York: Wiley.
Bernstein, P.L. (1998), 'Stock Market Risk in a Post Keynesian World', *Journal of Post Keynesian Economics*, **21**, pp. 15–24.
Bernstein, P.L. (1999), 'The Efficient Market Offers Hope to Active Management', *Journal of Applied Corporate Finance*, **12**, pp. 129–36.
Danziger, S., J. Van der Gaag, E. Smolensky and M.K. Taussig (1982–3), 'The Life Cycle Hypothesis and Consumption Behaviour of the Elderly', *Journal of Post Keynesian Economics*, **5**, pp. 208–27.
Davidson, P. (1972), *Money and the Real World*, London: Macmillan.
Davidson, P. (1977), 'Money and General Equilibrium', *Economie Appliquée*, **30**, pp. 541–63.
Davidson, P. (1980), 'The Dual Nature of the Keynesian Revolution', *Journal of Post Keynesian Economics*, **2**, pp. 291–307.
Davidson, P. (1982–3), 'Rational Expectations: A Fallacious Foundation for Studying Crucial Decision Making Processes',' *Journal of Post Keynesian Economics*, **5**, pp. 182–98.
Davidson, P. (2000), 'Is a Plumber or a New Financial Architect Needed to End Global International Liquidity Problems?', *World Development*, **28**, June, pp. 1117–31.
Friedman, M. (1974), 'A Theoretical Framework for Monetary Analysis,' in R.J. Gordon (ed.), *Milton Friedman's Monetary Framework: A Debate with his Critics*, Chicago: University of Chicago Press.
Hahn, F.H. (1977), 'Keynesian Economics and General Equilibrium Theory: Reflections on Some Current Debates', in G.C. Harcourt (ed.), *The Microfoundations of Macroeconomics*, London: Macmillan.
Hicks, J.R. (1979), *Causality in Economics*, New York: Basic Books.
Keynes, J.M. (1936), *The General Theory of Employment, Interest and Money*, New York: Harcourt.
Keynes, J.M. (1973), 'The General Theory', *Quarterly Journal of Economics*, 1937; reprinted in D. Moggridge (ed.), *The Collected Writings of John Maynard Keynes*, London: Macmillan; all references are to the reprint.
Samuelson, P.A. (1947), *Foundations of Economic Analysis*, Cambridge, MA: Harvard University Press.
Summers, L.H. and V.P. Summers (1989), 'When Financial Markets Work Too Well: A Cautious Case for a Securities Transactions Tax', *Journal of Financial Services*, **3**, pp. 163–88.

Potential Output

The maximum output that can be produced in an economy, given its factor endowments, without generating accelerating inflation; also known as full employment output or the natural level of output.

Precautionary Balances

Money held by individuals in order to meet unforeseen expenditures.

See also:
Demand for Money: Keynesian Approach.

Prescott, Edward C.

Edward Prescott (b.1940, Glens Falls, New York, USA) obtained his BA (Maths) from Swarthmore College in 1962, his MS (Operations Research) from Case Institute of Technology and his PhD from Carnegie-Mellon University in 1967. His main past posts have included Assistant Professor of Economics at the University of Pennsylvania, 1966–71; Assistant Professor (1971–2), Associate Professor (1972–5) and Professor of Economics (1975–80) at Carnegie-Mellon University; and Professor of Economics at the University of Chicago, 1998–9. Since 1980 he has been Professor of Economics at the University of Minnesota. He is best known for his influential work on the implications of rational expectations in a variety of contexts; and the development of stochastic dynamic general equilibrium theory (in particular being a leading advocate of the real business cycle approach to economic fluctuations). Among his best known books are *Recursive Methods in Economic Dynamics* (co-authored with R.E. Lucas Jr and N.L. Stokey) (Harvard University Press, 1989); and *Barriers to Riches* (co-authored with S.L. Parente) (MIT Press, 2000). His most widely read articles include 'Investment Under Uncertainty' (co-authored with R.E. Lucas Jr) (*Econometrica*, **39**, September 1971); 'Rules Rather than Discretion: The Inconsistency of Optimal Plans' (co-authored with F.E. Kydland) (*Journal of Political Economy*, **85**, June 1977); 'Time to Build and Aggregate Fluctuations' (co-authored with F.E. Kydland) (*Econometrica*, **50**, November 1982); 'Business Cycles: Real Facts and a Monetary Myth' (co-authored with F.E. Kydland) (*Federal Reserve Bank of Minneapolis Quarterly Review*, **14**, Spring 1990); 'The Econometrics of the General Equilibrium Approach to Business Cycles' (co-authored with

F.E. Kydland) (*Scandinavian Journal of Economics*, **93**, 1991); 'Hours and Employment Variation in Business Cycle Theory' (co-authored with F.E. Kydland) (*Economic Theory*, **1**, January 1991); 'The Computational Experiment: An Econometric Tool' (co-authored with F.E. Kydland) (*Journal of Economic Perspectives*, **10**, Winter 1996); and 'Prosperity and Depression' (*American Economic Review*, **92**, May 2002).

See also:
Business Cycles: Real Business Cycle Approach; Rational Expectations; Time Inconsistency.

Present Value

The value of a future stream of incomes or costs expressed in terms of their current value.

Price Index

A measure of the average level of prices of a set of goods and services relative to the prices of the same goods and services in a particular base year.

Procyclical Variable

A variable (such as employment) that tends to move in the same direction as aggregate economic activity over the business cycle.

See also:
Business Cycles: Stylized Facts.

Productivity Slowdown

Growth accounting research shows that the rate of productivity growth in the United States (and elsewhere) slowed down during the late 1960s or early 1970s. This productivity slowdown was viewed with great concern because it also implies a slowdown in real wage growth (assuming labour has a constant share of GDP). Although economists remain uncertain about the causes of the productivity slowdown, they have offered a variety of explanations (see, for example, the contributions by Griliches, Jorgenson, Olson and Boskin to the 'Symposium on the Slowdown in

Productivity Growth' in the *Journal of Economic Perspectives*, Fall, 1988). Explanations include those emphasizing slower growth of capital inputs, reductions in the quality of the labour input, the impact of higher energy prices following the two OPEC price shocks in 1973 and 1979, adverse effects resulting from changes in the human and legal environment, a slowdown in the pace of technological innovation, and measurement errors (see E.F. Denison, *Trends in American Economic Growth, 1929–82*, Brookings Institution, 1985; M.N. Bailey and R.J. Gordon, 'The Productivity Slowdown, Measurement Issues, and the Explosion of Computer Power', *Brookings Papers on Economic Activity*, no. 2, 1988).

During the late 1990s, concern over the productivity slowdown 'faded from view' as productivity growth exhibited a strong recovery in the United States. This acceleration of productivity growth led to increasing speculation about the possible emergence of a 'New Economy' dynamic among the major industrial economies linked to the 'Information Technology Revolution' (see M. Abramovitz and P. David, 'Two Centuries of American Macroeconomic Growth: From Exploitation of Resource Abundance to Knowledge Driven Development', *Stanford Institute for Economic Policy Research Discussion Paper*, no. 01-05, 2001).

See also:
Growth Accounting; New Economy.

Public Sector Borrowing Requirement

The amount by which the expenditure of the public sector exceeds its revenue.

Purchasing Power Parity Theory

In its strictest form, as its name suggests, purchasing power parity (PPP) theory states that money has the same purchasing power, or real value, in any currency. Thus if one pound buys 4.86 US dollars, as it did in 1900, then according to the PPP theory the one pound would purchase exactly the same quantity of goods in Britain that the $4.86 would in the United States. Another way to express the same idea is to say that the price level is the same in all currencies, converted at the ruling exchange rate.

This theory is well known to be incorrect in this form. One reason is indirect taxation: new cars cost more in Denmark than in other European countries because they are more heavily taxed. Another reason is the existence of transport costs and trade barriers, which prevent arbitrage between identical goods selling at different prices in different places.

In modern economics, the idea of PPP has been supplanted by the looser concept of the equilibrium real exchange rate, which may be defined as the level of home prices relative to foreign prices that is consistent with balance-of-payments equilibrium (where balance-of-payments equilibrium is that level of the current account balance that is consistent with 'normal' long-term capital flows). Two questions in particular have been the subject of much discussion.

One is whether equilibrium real exchange rates (RERs) vary systematically across countries. The evidence suggests strongly that they do. Prices tend to be higher in countries with higher per capita GDP, with higher capital/labour ratios and with greater differentials in labour productivity between tradeables and non-tradeables (Bergstrand, 1991). Clague (1986) has shown that, amongst developing countries, price levels are positively correlated with the share of minerals production and of tourism in output. As has been known since Balassa (1964), greater productivity differences across countries in tradeables than in non-tradeables will make non-tradeables relatively expensive in rich countries, since relative wage costs reflect equilibrium in international trade which is based on tradeables sector relationships only. In developing countries in particular, the degree of trade protection can be an important influence on the equilibrium RER. With more import restrictions, the equilibrium RER is higher.

The other issue is whether RERs revert to equilibrium in the long run (and if so, how quickly). Economic theory would certainly suggest that RERs do ultimately revert to equilibrium, but demonstrating this proposition with empirical data has proved somewhat troublesome. One reason is that the equilibrium RER is not constant over time, because of variations in the degree of trade protection, changing world relative prices, and so on; yet statistical tests almost invariably assume that it is constant, for the simple reason that otherwise the hypothesis under test would then be a joint one of reversion to equilibrium *and* a particular theory of the path of the equilibrium. Some elementary evidence in favour of PPP comes from the fact that nominal exchange rates almost invariably move, on average, in the 'right' direction as determined by inflation differentials: in other words, currencies that are subject to higher inflation tend to depreciate. This is true, for example, amongst OECD countries in the post-1973 period, as well as in the case of extreme inflationary experiences.

The issue of whether RERs revert to equilibrium is, in modern econometric terms, equivalent to the question: are the series stationary or non-stationary? Standard tests of stationarity, such as Dickey–Fuller tests, do not reject the null of non-stationarity on the real exchange rates of any

OECD countries against the US dollar for the period of floating exchange rates since 1973, although the null is rejected at the 0.05 level for four out of 14 European currencies against the Deutschmark (Bleaney and Leybourne, 1998, Table 1). Since Dickey–Fuller tests (and alternatives) have limited power, researchers have reacted by trying to increase the sample size, either by going back into history to analyse a very long run of data (for example, Lothian and Taylor, 1996) or by aggregating individual exchange rate series into a panel (for example, Oh, 1996). In both cases much stronger evidence of stationarity is obtained.

Unfortunately, in both cases simple tests are open to criticism. Exchange rates clearly have very different dynamics in pegged and in floating regimes. Engel (2000) shows that ignoring this may lead to spurious rejections of the null of non-stationarity. In panel data a similar effect can arise if cross-correlations between exchange rate series are ignored (O'Connell, 1998), although Abuaf and Jorion (1990) and Bleaney and Leybourne (1998) both find in favour of stationarity after correcting for this effect. Bleaney and Leybourne pursue the idea that, if real exchange rates are truly stationary, autoregressive models should outperform a random walk in out-of-sample tests. They find that this is not the case for real exchange rates against the US dollar. They then perform some tests for a stochastic unit root, in which the autoregressive parameter is not fixed but variable (with a mean of one). A stochastic unit root process switches between non-stationary (possibly explosive) and stationary behaviour. These authors show that, if real exchange rates follow a stochastic unit root process, spurious rejections of the null occur in panel unit root tests. Their tests for a stochastic unit root (against the null of a fixed unit root) reject the null at the 0.10 level for all but three out of 17 US dollar RER series, which suggests that the stochastic unit root model has empirical merit.

An interesting idea which has been pursued by a number of authors recently is that real exchange rates display near-random-walk behaviour when they are within a certain distance of equilibrium, and increasingly strong mean-reversion outside this range. Because, if this hypothesis were true, most observations in any sample would be from within the range of near-random-walk behaviour, standard unit root tests would fail to reject the null. Studies of this kind include Bleaney and Mizen (1996), Michael *et al.* (1997), and Sollis *et al.* (2002). Bleaney and Mizen (1996) appeal to the idea of Frankel and Froot (1986) of tension between 'fundamentalists' and 'chartists' in the foreign exchange market, and test a model in which the rate of mean-reversion is a cubic function of deviations from the mean. Michael *et al.* (1997) attribute non-linearity to transactions costs and use a smooth transition autoregressive (STAR) model. Soilis *et al.* (forthcoming) adapt this model to allow for asymmetric effects in US dollar series according to whether the dollar is high or low. They kind much stronger mean-reversion when the dollar is undervalued than when it is overvalued. These results essentially reflect the great dollar bubble of 1980–86.

Although these non-linear tests generally yield results that are more favourable to stationarity, a word of caution is appropriate. Such a non-linear model is likely to work well when there has been *one* exchange rate bubble; the model will estimate the point at which mean-reversion starts to come into play to match the experience of that particular bubble. If a second bubble occurs, however, it needs to be very similar in magnitude to the first to be consistent with the estimated model. Thus one cannot dismiss the possibility that the apparently superior performance of non-linear models is an example of skilled data-mining.

MICHAEL BLEANEY

See also:

Fixed Exchange Rate System; Flexible Exchange Rate System.

Bibliography

Abuaf, N. and P. Jorion (1990), 'Purchasing Power Parity in the Long Run', *Journal of Finance*, **45**, March, pp. 157–74.
Balassa, B. (1964), 'The Purchasing Power Parity Doctrine: A Reappraisal', *Journal of Political Economy*, **72**, December, pp. 584–96.
Bergstrand, J.H. (1991), 'Structural Determinants of Real Exchange Rates and National Price Levels: Some Empirical Evidence', *American Economic Review*, **81**, March, pp. 325–34.
Bleaney, M.F. and S.J. Leybourne (1998), 'Real Exchange Rate Dynamics under the Current Float: A Re-examination', *School of Economics Discussion Paper* no. 98/9, University of Nottingham (forthcoming, *Manchester School*).
Bleaney, M.F. and P.D. Mizen (1996), 'Nonlinearities in Exchange Rate Dynamics: Evidence from Five Currencies, 1973–94', *The Economic Record*, **72**, March, pp. 36–45.
Clague, C. (1986), 'Determinants of the National Price Level: Some Empirical Results', *Review of Economics and Statistics*, **68**, May, pp. 321–3.
Engel, C. (2000), 'Long-Run PPP May Not Hold After All', *Journal of International Economics*, **51**, August, pp. 243–73.
Frankel, J.A. and K.A. Froot (1986), 'Understanding the US Dollar in the Eighties: The Expectations of Chartists and Fundamentalists', *Economic Record*, **62**, Supplement, pp. 24–38.
Lothian, J. and M.P. Taylor (1996), 'Real Exchange Rate Behaviour: The Recent Float from the Perspective of the Past Two Centuries', *Journal of Political Economy*, **104**, June, pp. 488–510.
Michael, P., R. Nobay and D.A. Peel (1997), 'Transactions Costs and Nonlinear Adjustment in Real Exchange Rates: An Empirical Investigation', *Journal of Political Economy*, **105**, August, pp. 862–79.
O'Connell, P.G.J. (1998), 'The Overvaluation of Purchasing Power Parity', *Journal of International Economics*, **44**, February, pp. 1–19.
Oh, K.-Y. (1996), 'Purchasing Power Parity and Unit Root Tests Using Panel Data', *Journal of International Money and Finance*, **15**, June, pp. 405–18.
Sollis, R., S.J. Leybourne and P. Newbold (forthcoming), 'Tests for Symmetric and Asymmetric Nonlinear Mean Reversion in Real Exchange Rates', *Journal of Money, Credit and Banking*.

Quantity Theory of Money

The phrase 'quantity of theory of money' came into general usage at the end of the nineteenth century, but the ideas to which it refers are much older. In the modern world they were developed in the sixteenth century in response to the monetary upheavals caused by the inflows of gold and silver from Central and South America (Grice-Hutchinson, 1978), and received one of their classic statements from David Hume (1752).

The quantity theory starts from the *equation of exchange* that notes the necessary equality at the level of the economy as a whole of the volume of money expenditures and money receipts. In the *income form* of the equation, which dominates modern expositions, receipts are equal to nominal national income, real income times the price level, PY, while expenditures are given by the quantity of money, M, times the income velocity of circulation, V, a measure of the rate at which money circulates. Specifically, V is defined as the ratio of money income to the quantity of money, so that:

$$MV = PY.$$

The quantity theory is derived from this accounting identity by supplementing it with empirical, and hence refutable, hypotheses about relationships among its variables. These vary in details among expositions, but always include the following: V is a parameter of the macro economy's structure, not simply a ratio that reconciles the two sides of the equation of exchange; though V and Y might vary over time, thus tending to cause movements in P, the dominant causes of the latter are changes in M; finally, feedbacks from prices to the quantity of money are small enough to be negligible.

Neoclassical economics always tries to explain behaviour as the outcome of maximizing choices made by individual agents, and as early as 1871 Alfred Marshall reformulated the quantity theory in terms of the interaction of variations in the stock of money with the desire of agents to hold it. The key to this reformulation is, as Wicksell (1898) noted, that the inverse of velocity is simply money's interval of rest, so that the quantity theory may be written as:

$$Ms = Md = k\,PY,$$

where k is $1/V$. This is the *Cambridge* version of the theory (Pigou, 1917). Irving Fisher's (1911) formulation, in which the volume of transactions, rather than of output, measures the amount of work money has to do, and in which transaction velocity refers to the actual frequency with which money turns over, may seem at first sight to be empirically more useful, being more closely related to real-world phenomena. However, no fundamental theoretical issues separate these two approaches (Laidler, 1991), and problems associated with actually measuring transactions volumes and money's turnover, combined with the advantages of the Marshallian theory's choice-theoretic basis, have caused Fisher's version to give way to it as the quantity theory's dominant formulation.

The key parameter in the Cambridge version of the theory is k. Even the theory's earliest exponents thought of k as potentially variable, being the outcome of choices made by maximizing agents, who would balance the usefulness of money holding against the returns forgone by not holding wealth in other forms. However, a precise statement that such choices involved the allocation of a portfolio in which an assessment of marginal costs and benefits was of the essence, was agonizingly slow to develop. A formulation along these lines that also caught widespread attention did not emerge until Keynes's (1930) exposition in the *Treatise on Money* of what soon came to be called 'liquidity preference' theory (Patinkin, 1974). Thus, when Milton Friedman (1956) 'restated' the quantity theory as a theory of the demand for money in which an inverse relationship between the demand for money and the opportunity cost of holding it played a central role, he was vulnerable to suggestions that his theoretical work was, in fact, in the tradition of Keynesian monetary theory, rather than of some earlier version of the quantity theory.

The quantity theory of money is sometimes thought of as a *sine qua non* of 'classical economics' as it existed before Keynes's (1936) *General Theory* but this is not the case. When classical value theory was dominated by the cost of production theory of value, and the world used commodity-convertible monies, the predominant long-run theory of the price level had it determined by the marginal cost of production of the precious metals. Until the 1870s, the quantity theory coexisted uneasily with this doctrine, being thought of as relevant to the special case of inconvertible paper money, and perhaps as providing insight into short-run adjustment mechanisms under commodity convertibility (Laidler, 1991). Even in these contexts it was not unchallenged. As commercial banks developed and their liabilities began to serve as money, the idea that the predominant direction of causation runs from prices and/or nominal income to money, rather than vice versa as the quantity theory would have it, developed. And serious questions about how to define 'money' for empirical purposes were raised.

These ideas also go back to the eighteenth century, but they are often referred to as *Banking School* doctrine, after the group of economists who advanced them during the debates that surrounded the passage of Sir

Robert Peel's 1844 Bank Charter Act in Britain. In recent debates they have worn the label *endogenous money*, and have been strongly associated with Post Keynesian economics. Some aspects of Banking School doctrine, notably those having to do with the influence of institutional change in the banking system on the measurement of the money stock, and hence on the quantity theory's empirical relevance, have proved to be of serious practical significance in recent years.

The quantity theory's influence on economic thought was at its peak between about 1870 and the outbreak of World War I (Laidler, 1991). During this period, the cost of production theory of value, with which Banking School ideas had become closely, albeit temporarily, associated in the monetary field, rapidly gave way to marginal utility theory and supply and demand analysis. By default, the quantity theory became the reigning theory of the price level in neoclassical economics, even though, in the United States, its reputation suffered from being associated with the bimetallist and inflationist populism of William Jennings Bryan during the 1880s and 1890s.

At this time the quantity theory also became the starting point for a body of business cycle theory, which explained this phenomenon as mainly caused by fluctuations in the quantity of money. However, even the quantity theory's most ardent supporters, for example Fisher (1911), noted that the interaction between money and prices over the course of the cycle involved price level fluctuations inducing changes in the quantity of bank deposits that in turn influenced prices. Though these cycle theories started from the quantity theory, therefore, they were understood to go beyond it. The quantity theory ruled out significant reverse causation from prices to money, and was therefore a theory of the secular interaction of money and prices, not of the role of money in the economic system more generally. Milton Friedman (1987) would later apply the label 'quantity theory' to a more general body of macroeconomic analysis that also included the *Fisher effect* of expected inflation on nominal interest rates, the doctrine of the *natural rate of unemployment*, as well as to the monetary theory of cyclical fluctuations that can be constructed from these components, a theory whose origins can be traced back to Fisher (1911) and Ralph Hawtrey (1913).

In the immediate aftermath of World War I, the dominant macroeconomic problems were inflation and international monetary instability. Keynes's (1923) *Tract on Monetary Reform*, which addressed these policy issues, is arguably the most distinguished work ever to deploy the Cambridge version of the quantity theory. Being a theory of the price level, however, the quantity theory had little to say about the deficient output and high unemployment that dominated the inter-war period as a whole, and it therefore lost influence after the mid-1920s.

There were also theoretical reasons for the decline in the quantity theory's influence. Knut Wicksell (1898), drawing heavily on earlier Banking School work, had tried to adapt it more closely to the analysis of monetary systems that used bank deposits as their means of exchange. Central here was the interaction of the 'money' interest rate at which banks would lend and hence create credit and money, and the economy's 'natural' interest rate, which Wicksell often (but not always) defined as the rate which would equate savings and investment at full employment. In the hands of others, this approach would shift the emphasis in monetary economics away from the influence of the quantity of money on prices, and towards the influence of the rate of interest on saving and investment, and hence the level of real economic activity. This new emphasis, the 'Wicksell connection' (Leijonhufvud, 1981), dominated those developments in inter-war monetary theory, which culminated in the 1936 publication of Keynes's *General Theory of Employment, Interest and Money* (Laidler, 1999).

It was only with the disappearance of high unemployment in the postwar years, and the advent of serious inflation in the 1960s and after, that, particularly as a result of the already-mentioned work of Milton Friedman, the quantity theory again attracted serious attention as a component of what came to be called 'monetarism'. This association with monetarism has led to the quantity theory being linked to a 'conservative' economic policy agenda in popular economic understanding, but the theory's central position in the radical populism of the late nineteenth-century USA shows that its political links are altogether more complicated than that. However, two points are worth noting here. First, the quantity theory is at its empirically most relevant in the case of a fully employed economy, so that those who believe market economies to have an inherent tendency to operate in this region kind it more relevant than those who regard chronic stagnation as a more likely state of affairs. Second, the theory's Cambridge version enables inflation to be analysed as a tax on money holding, resorted to by governments unable to finance their expenditures by more conventional means (Keynes, 1923; Bailey, 1956). In this respect, the quantity theory has an obvious appeal to those who favour a small role for government in economic life.

As monetarism gave way to new classical economics as the predominant orthodox macroeconomic doctrine in the last quarter of the twentieth century, the quantity theory's central implication about the *ceteris paribus* long-run proportionality of the price level to the quantity of money, with causation running from money to the price level, continued to command widespread assent. This belief has, however, been challenged within this camp by adherents of the so-called *backing* theory of money associated with Thomas Sargent, Neil Wallace and their associates (Wallace, 1988).

Like modern Post Keynesian theory, this approach also has roots in nineteenth-century Banking School doctrine, so there is a remarkable degree of historical continuity to modern discussions of the quantity theory.

DAVID LAIDLER

See also:

Classical Economics; Demand for Money: Friedman's Approach; Demand for Money: Keynesian Approach; Equation of Exchange; Fisher Effect; Monetarism; Money Supply: Endogenous or Exogenous?; Natural Rate of Unemployment; New Classical Economics; Post Keynesian Economics; Velocity of Circulation; Wicksell, Knut.

Bibliography

Bailey, M.J. (1956), 'The Welfare Costs of Inflationary Finance', *Journal of Political Economy*, **64**, February, pp. 93–110.

Fisher I. (1911), *The Purchasing Power of Money*, New York: Macmillan.

Friedman M. (1956), 'The Quantity Theory of Money, a Restatement', in M. Friedman (ed.), *Studies in the Quantity Theory of Money*, Chicago: University of Chicago Press.

Friedman, M. (1987), 'Quantity Theory of Money', in J. Eatwell, M. Milgate and P. Newman (eds), *The New Palgrave, a Dictionary of Economics*, London: Macmillan.

Grice-Hutchinson, M. (1978), *Early Economic Thought in Spain 1172–1740*, London: George Allen & Unwin.

Hawtrey, R.G. (1913), *Good and Bad Trade*, London: Constable.

Hume, D. (1752), 'Of Money', 'Of Interest' and 'Of the Balance of Trade', in *Essays Moral, Political and Literary*, reprinted London: Oxford University Press, 1963.

Keynes, J.M. (1923), *A Tract on Monetary Reform*, London: Macmillan.

Keynes, J.M. (1930), *A Treatise on Money*, 2 vols, London: Macmillan.

Keynes, J.M. (1936), *The General Theory of Employment, Interest and Money*, London: Macmillan.

Laidler, D. (1991), *The Golden Age of the Quantity Theory*, Hemel Hempstead: Philip Allan.

Laidler, D. (1999), *Fabricating the Keynesian Revolution*, Cambridge: Cambridge University Press.

Leijonhufvud, A. (1981), 'The Wicksell Connection', *Information and Coordination*, London: Oxford University Press.

Marshall, A. (1871), 'Money', in J. Whittaker (ed.) (1975) *The Early Economic Writings of Alfred Marshall*, 2 vols, London: Macmillan.

Patinkin, D. (1974), 'Keynesian Monetary Theory and the Cambridge School', in H.G. Johnson and A.R. Nobay (eds), *Issues in Monetary Economics*, London: Oxford University Press.

Pigou, A.C. (1917), 'The Value of Money', *Quarterly Journal of Economics*, reprinted in F.W. Lutz and L.W. Mints (eds) (1954), *Readings in Monetary Economics*, Homewood, IL: Richard Irwin, for the AEA.

Wallace, N (1988), 'A Suggestion for Oversimplifying the Theory of Money', *Conference Papers, Supplement to the Economic Journal*, **98**, March, pp. 25–36.

Wicksell, K. (1898), *Interest and Prices*, tr. R. Kahn (1936), for the Royal Economic Society, London: Macmillan.

Random Walk

The path of a variable whose changes over time are unpredictable.

Rational Expectations

In many areas, expectations of a variable are a significant determinant of economic behaviour. Examples abound, such as in the consumption function, the real rate of interest and the Phillips curve, to name just three. The way agents form expectations is also vital in examining the implications of economic relationships. Two main hypotheses about expectation formation exist in the literature, namely adaptive expectations and rational expectations, discussed here.

The concept of the rational expectations hypothesis (REH) was first put forward by Muth (1961) who suggested that agents form their expectations according to economic theory. The theory was further elaborated by Walters (1971), who offered the alternative term of 'consistent expectations' since such expectations were consistent with the relevant economic theory. The REH was first introduced into formal macroeconomic analysis by Lucas (1972).

In the REH, it is assumed that agents use the relevant information efficiently so that, for a one-period horizon,

$$Y_t = EY_t + \varepsilon_t, \tag{1}$$

where EY_t is the expected value formed previously of Y for the period t, Y_t is the actual value of Y for period t and ε_t is a random error term.

The conditions on ε are quite important. Its mean value is 0 although individual values may be quite large. In other words, the forecast is right 'on average' and contrasts with forecasts based on the adaptive expectations hypothesis, which exhibit large and increasing errors in the case of variables subject to a time trend. Also the error term, ε_t, is uncorrelated with any variable known at the time the expectation is formed and in particular any of its own lagged values. This latter condition implies that the rational expectation of Y is the best forecast of Y and could not be improved by incorporating any other information known at the time that the forecast is made. Note also that REH forecasts are forward-looking as compared with the adaptive expectations model, which is purely backward-looking.

Two assumptions underlie equation (1), namely:

1. Agents know the true model generating Y; for example, in the case of expected inflation, they would know the structure of the relevant

model, including the size of the parameters linking the explanatory variables to inflation.

2. The second assumption required to utilize the rational expectations hypothesis is that it is necessary that all agents have the same information set so that it is possible to talk about *the* expectation. In the case of separate groups of agents such as, for example, financial markets, each member of the group is required to have the same information set so that it is possible to talk about the group expectation. The existence of *the* expectation(s) is necessary for the solution of rational expectation models. These formal methods are beyond the scope of this note so the interested reader is referred to Holden *et al.* (1985).

These assumptions and conditions are quite restrictive and perhaps the most powerful criticism is that economic agents are assumed to know the *true* model, since many economic models are themselves the subject of controversy – see Shiller (1978) for a critique of the rational expectations hypothesis. Many (perhaps most) members of the general public do not possess the sophisticated knowledge of economic theory necessary to process data to produce REH forecasts. One line of defence to this critique is to argue that the general public receives forecasts via the media rather than preparing them for themselves. Nevertheless, this still requires the general public to distinguish between the forecasts produced by different agencies since (a) forecasts often exhibit quite wide variations and (b) no one forecasting agency produces consistently 'best' forecasts – see Holden and Thompson (1997) for the evidence regarding forecasts produced by econometric models of the United Kingdom.

In this connection a useful distinction is made by Feige and Pearce (1976) between pure rational expectations and *economically* rational expectations. This distinction is based on the recognition that processing information incurs costs. Consequently, it would be expected that agents gather new information up to the point where the marginal cost of acquiring new information equals the marginal benefit derived in the form of improved forecasting accuracy. This view recognizes the possibility that rational agents may accept large forecasting errors.

Since expectations are internal to the individuals, it is difficult to test directly any hypothesis of the way agents may form their expectations. However, one such direct method is to examine the rationality of the results of expectations surveys on the basis of the properties of the error term: that is, ε_t in equation (1). The conclusion reached in Holden *et al.* (1985) was that, 'in general, surveys of expectations do not support the rational expectations hypothesis'.

The REH has been utilised to derive a number of important propositions, including the following. First is the ineffectiveness of stabilization policy. The rational expectations hypothesis is one of the props of the 'New Classical Economics' in which it is often argued that stabilization policy would be ineffective unless it was unanticipated because the non-government sector would be able to forecast policy and take actions now to avoid the consequences of that policy. To take just one example, workers could demand wage increases now to offset any future inflation resulting from expansionary fiscal or monetary policies. In terms of the Phillips curve, this view argues that the Phillips curve is vertical in both the short and the long run. This stance is incorrect as a general proposition since it only applies to simple equilibrium models as monetary (or fiscal policy) will influence real variables including unemployment in models with a dynamic structure; that is, where continuous and complete market clearing does *not* occur. Even then the proposition has to be modified since macroeconomic stabilization policy influences employment in conditions where the authorities possess information superior to that possessed by the other agents. In other words, for all practical purposes, stabilization policy is likely to be effective, but it should be appreciated that public reaction to policy changes will be speeded up if expectations are formed according to the rational expectations hypothesis. The important distinction is between anticipated and unanticipated policy changes, which leads to the prediction that policy announcements will influence the behaviour of the public provided the policy changes are *credible*.

Second, the 'Lucas critique' is dependent on expectations being formed according to the rational expectations hypothesis. Third is the efficient market hypothesis (EMH), which suggests that prices in an efficient market would instantaneously reflect all available information. Clearly, the EMH is a subset of the rational expectations hypothesis. Financial markets are potentially 'rational' because (a) they are dominated by experts whose remuneration is likely to be dependent – at least in part – on the profitability of their operations, and (b) they are continuous. Nevertheless, the empirical evidence concerning the efficiency of the various financial markets is, to say the least, controversial.

What conclusions can we draw about the rational expectations hypothesis? The following seem pertinent:

1. Although the hypothesis predicts expectations, which are forward looking, the information criteria are too onerous to be taken literally. Nevertheless, it may be appropriate to view expectations as approximating the rational expectations hypothesis.
2. The hypothesis has stimulated economists to consider how the structure of models may be 'learned' by agents and how expectations may

be formed. This is the really important point and suggests that the value of the rational expectations hypothesis goes well beyond consideration of the efficacy of stabilization policies.

JOHN L. THOMPSON

See also:

Adaptive Expectations; Credibility and Reputation; Lucas Critique; Policy Ineffectiveness Proposition.

Bibliography

Feige, E.L. and D.K. Pearce (1976), 'Economically Rational Expectations: Are Innovations in the Rate of Inflation Independent of Innovations in Measures of Monetary and Fiscal Policy?', *Journal of Political Economy*, **84**, June, pp. 499–522.
Holden, K. and J.L. Thompson (1997), 'Combining Forecasts, Encompassing and the Properties of UK Macroeconomic Forecasts', *Applied Economics*, **29**, November, pp. 1447–58.
Holden, K., D.A. Peel and J.L. Thompson (1985), *Expectations: Theory and Evidence*, Basingstoke: Macmillan.
Lucas, R.E. Jr (1972), 'Expectations and the Neutrality of Money', *Journal of Economic Theory*, **4**, April, pp. 103–24.
Muth, J.F. (1961), 'Rational Expectations and the Theory of Price Movements', *Econometrica*, **29**, July pp. 313–35.
Shiller, R.J. (1978), 'Rational Expectations and the Dynamic Structure of Macroeconomic Models: A Critical Review', *Journal of Monetary Economics*, **4**, January, pp. 1–44.
Walters, A.A. (1971), 'Consistent Expectations, Distributed Lags and the Quantity Theory', *Economic Journal*, **81**, June, pp. 273–81.

Reaganomics

A term applied to the economic policies pursued by the Reagan administration (1981–8) which sought to stimulate the supply side of the US economy. The American approach to supply-side economics in the 1980s focused on incentives to encourage work effort, saving, investment and risk taking. Policies included less taxation; reduced government regulation of business; and less government interference in the workings of markets.

See also:

Laffer Curve; Supply-side Economics.

Real Balance Effect

The real balance effect or Pigou effect (or Pigou–Haberler–Scitovsky effect) is the influence of a change in real money balances on aggregate expenditure through the impact of changed wealth on consumption. A lower price level (or increased nominal quantity of money) increases real money balances, making consumers wealthier and, given an inverse relationship between saving and the wealth/income ratio, induces consumers to spend more (Pigou, 1943, 1947; Patinkin, 1948). The Keynes effect is the influence of a changed real money supply on interest rates and hence on investment (Keynes, 1936; Patinkin [1956] 1965). With the Keynes effect, a lower price level in an underemployed economy increases real money balances (M/P), shifting the *LM* curve to the right in Hicks's IS–LM diagram, so that equilibrium between money supply and money demand is restored at a lower interest rate (as people with an initial excess supply of money bid up bond prices) and a higher level of income. This is the main reason why the aggregate demand (*AD*) curve, relating the price level and real output, is downward-sloping even in a closed economy. If there were perfect flexibility of prices and nominal wages (a vertical aggregate supply curve), such a downward-sloping *AD* curve implies that a lower price level would restore full employment after a negative demand shock.

However, the Keynes effect can fail in a deeply depressed economy. Expectation of rapidly falling prices can bring the economy to a liquidity trap, where the nominal interest rate cannot fall below zero or a rate slightly above zero (Fischer Black's currency trap is the same phenomenon under another name). Further deflation, with nominal interest stuck at zero, would simply push up real interest rates, reducing investment and moving the economy further away from full employment. Pigou (1943) argued that, in theory, a lower price level would always restore full employment, even in a liquidity trap, because of the wealth effect on consumption of a higher real value of holdings of money and government bonds. In practice, Pigou preferred public works to wage cutting and price deflation as a response to depressions, so he presented the real balance effect only as a point of abstract theory.

Michal Kalecki (1944) pointed out that bank deposits are mostly backed by the loans made by the banks, so that a lower price level would increase the real value both of deposits owed by the banks to the public and of loans owed by the public to the banks. Such 'inside money' is not part of net private wealth (see also Gurley and Shaw, 1960), unlike 'outside money', the monetary base (currency in circulation plus reserves held with the central bank). Only net private wealth is relevant for the real balance effect on consumption. Pesek and Saving (1967) argued that, since inside money performs real transaction services, the capitalized value of those transaction services should be considered part of net wealth.

Keynes, who had demonstrated an understanding of the real balance effect as early as the correspondence about drafts of Robertson (1926) (see Presley, 1986), was not persuaded by Pigou's theoretical argument. In editorial correspondence (published in Patinkin, 1982) about Kalecki's comment on Pigou, Keynes and Kalecki agreed that government bonds are not part of net private wealth (and hence not relevant for the real balance effect) because the payments on the bonds are made by the taxpayers (see Dimand, 1991). Such debt neutrality, or Ricardian equivalence, together with the exclusion of inside money from net wealth, would restrict the real balance effect to a very narrow range of assets. This is consistent with findings that the real balance effect is not empirically significant (for example, Mayer, 1959). Nonetheless, the real balance effect convinced many macroeconomists (beginning with Haberler, Pigou and Patinkin) that the economy would, at least in theory and in the long run, be self-adjusting given price flexibility, so that they view Keynesian economics as a special case of classical economics with nominal rigidities added.

James Tobin (1980) rejects this, drawing on the debt–deflation process presented by Fisher (1933) and sketched more briefly by Keynes (1931) to argue that the effects of changes in the real value of inside debt do not wash out, that they are opposite in direction to the Pigou effect, and that, since there is so much more inside debt than outside money, the Pigou effect may be swamped. When an economy has a large amount of inside debt of fixed nominal value, unanticipated deflation increases the risk of bankruptcy and default. By increasing the real value of inside debt, unanticipated deflation transfers wealth to lenders from borrowers, who presumably became borrowers because they have a higher propensity to spend than the lenders. By reducing the opportunity cost of holding money, deflation increases demand for real money balances, exerting upward pressure on real interest rates (even more so if the nominal interest rate has been driven down to zero or close to zero), which reduces investment. These flow effects of deflation may plausibly be expected to dominate the Pigou effect. Taking these effects into account, it is by no means clear that the real balance effect ensures that the economy would be self-adjusting given wage and price flexibility, or even that increased wage and price flexibility would contribute to greater stability. An expectation that prices will fall would lead agents to postpone consumption and investment, causing unemployment to rise. Declines of 20 to 30 per cent in wages and prices in the early 1930s did not suffice to end the Great Depression.

Patinkin ([1956] 1965) stressed the real balance effect in his critique of the 'invalid dichotomy' between the determination of relative prices and of the general price level in classical and neoclassical economics. He found that many earlier economists wrote the demands for commodities as functions of relative prices but not of real money balances, implying that changing the prices of all goods in the same proportion would not affect any quantities. The money market, determining the general price level, was separated from the system of equations determining quantities and relative prices. Patinkin objected that this 'invalid dichotomy' left the general price level indeterminate, since equilibration depends on the real balance effect. If the price level is below its equilibrium level, the mechanism that raises it is that people find their real balances too high and increase their demands for goods, services and assets. In a 'valid dichotomy', changing all prices and the quantity of money in the same proportion leaves quantities unchanged, and money balances appear in demand functions for commodities. In this way, the real balance effect has a role in general equilibrium theory.

ROBERT W. DIMAND

See also:

IS–LM Model: Closed Economy; Keynesian Economics; Liquidity Trap; Ricardian Equivalence; Tobin, James.

Bibliography

Black, F. (1987), *Business Cycles and Equilibrium*, New York and Oxford: Basil Blackwell.
Dimand, R.W. (1991), 'Keynes, Kalecki, Ricardian Equivalence and the Real Balance Effect', *Bulletin of Economic Research*, **43**, June, pp. 289–92.
Fisher, I. (1933), 'The Debt–Deflation Theory of Great Depressions', *Econometrica*, **1**, October, pp. 337–57.
Gurley, J.G. and E.S. Shaw (1960), *Money in a Theory of Finance*, Washington, DC: Brookings Institution.
Haberler, G. (1941), *Prosperity and Depression*, 3rd edn, Geneva: League of Nations.
Haberler, G. (1952), 'The Pigou Effect Once More', *Journal of Political Economy*, **60**, April, pp. 240–46.
Kalecki, M. (1944), 'Professor Pigou on "The Classical Stationary State": A Comment', *Economic Journal*, **54**, February, pp. 131–2.
Keynes, J.M. (1931), 'An Economic Analysis of Unemployment', in Q. Wright (ed.), *Unemployment as a World Problem*, Chicago: University of Chicago Press, pp. 1–42.
Keynes, J.M. (1936), *The General Theory of Employment, Interest and Money*, London: Macmillan.
Mayer, T. (1959), 'The Empirical Significance of the Real Balance Effect', *Quarterly Journal of Economics*, **73**, May, pp. 275–91.
Melitz, J. (1967), 'Pigou and the "Pigou Effect": Rendez-vous with the Author', *Southern Economic Journal*, **43**, October, pp. 268–79.
Patinkin, D. (1948), 'Price Flexibility and Full Employment', *American Economic Review*, **38**, September, pp. 543–64.
Patinkin, D. ([1956] 1965), *Money, Interest and Prices*, 2nd edn, New York: Harper & Row.
Patinkin, D. (1982), *Anticipations of the General Theory? And Other Essays on Keynes*, Chicago: University of Chicago Press.
Pesek, B.P., and T.S. Saving (1967), *Money, Wealth and Economic Theory*, New York: Macmillan.
Pigou, A.C. (1943), 'The Classical Stationary State', *Economic Journal*, **53**, December, pp. 343–51.
Pigou, A.C. (1947), 'Economic Progress in a Stable Environment', *Economica*, **14**, August, pp. 180–88.
Presley, J.R. (1986), 'J.M. Keynes and the Real Balance Effect', *Manchester School of Economic and Social Studies*, **54**, March, pp. 22–30.
Robertson, D.H. (1926), *Banking Policy and the Price Level*, London: P.S. King & Son.

Scitovsky, T. (1941), 'Capital Accumulation, Employment, and Price Rigidity', *Review of Economic Studies*, **8**, February, pp. 69–88.

Tobin, J. (1980), *Asset Accumulation and Economic Activity*, Chicago: University of Chicago Press.

Real Business Cycle Model

A model in which fluctuations in aggregate output and employment are predominantly caused by persistent real (supply-side) shocks to the economy. The focus of the real shocks involves large random fluctuations in the rate of technological progress that result in fluctuations in relative prices to which rational economic agents optimally respond. Observed fluctuations in output are viewed as fluctuations in the natural rate of output, not deviations of output from a smooth deterministic trend. As such there is no role for stabilization policy, not only because government attempts to reduce fluctuations are unlikely to achieve their desired objective, but also because such policies could reduce welfare and distort output and employment from the optimal amounts chosen by firms and workers.

See also:

Business Cycles: Real Business Cycle Approach; Kydland, Finn E.; Prescott, Edward C.

Real Exchange Rate

The rate at which one country's goods trade in exchange for those of another country; also known as the terms of trade.

Real GDP

The value of gross domestic product measured in terms of the prices that prevailed in some particular base year; also known as GDP in constant prices.

See also:

Gross Domestic Product.

Real Interest Rate

The 'actual' real interest rate (or *ex post* real interest rate) is the nominal (or market) interest rate minus the rate of inflation, whereas the 'expected' real interest rate (or *ex ante* real interest rate) is the nominal interest rate minus the 'expected' rate of inflation. The actual and expected real interest rates will only be equal when the rate of inflation is perfectly anticipated.

See also:
Anticipated Inflation; *Ex ante*, *Ex post*.

Real Money Balances

The money supply divided by the price level (M/P).

Real Rigidity

The concept of real rigidity has played an important role in the history of economic thought. In particular it has provided an explanation for real wages not adjusting to their equilibrium value.

The concept of 'rigidity' means that *something* changes less than it ought to or less than it normally does. The rigidity can be real or nominal. If the rigidity is real, then the 'something' is a real variable, typically a price ratio. The most common example is the real wage (the ratio of nominal wage to nominal price). This contrasts to a nominal rigidity, in which a price or wage level is rigid.

So what does it mean to say that a variable changes less than it ought to? This requires a comparison with some standard equilibrium. For example, we could take the perfectly competitive equilibrium. Changes in exogenous parameters will imply shifts in demand and/or supply which in turn imply shifts in real variables. If we take the labour market, an increase in the energy price will lead to an inward shift in the demand for labour, which we would expect to lead to a fall in the real wage from W to W^1 and a move from A to B in Figure 1. We can say that a market exhibits some real wage rigidity if the real wage changes by less than this. In an extreme form, complete real wage rigidity would happen if the real wage was completely unaffected by the demand fall. In this case the real wage remains at W, and the equilibrium moves from A to C.

However, there can be real rigidity in a model where the equilibrium price is completely flexible, owing to some special feature of the model. For example, even in a competitive market, the real wage will be rigid if the labour supply is 'horizontal': that is, there is a fixed reservation wage common to all labour market participants. In this case, the labour market

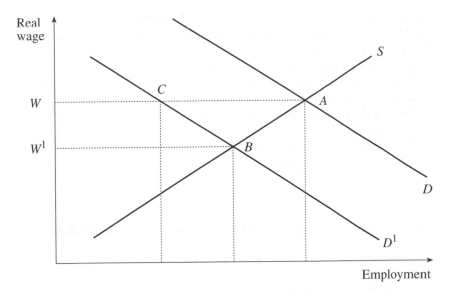

Figure 1: A fall in the demand for labour

will display less variation in the real wage than is 'normal' in terms of an upward-sloping labour supply curve.

One possible cause of real rigidity is *indexation*: this sets some nominal variable relative to the price index. In effect, full indexation results in complete real rigidity. For example, the legal minimum wage, unemployment benefit or pensions might be indexed to the price level, so that they are fixed in real terms. If the equilibrium wage is related to these variables, then their indexation can result in wages behaving as if they were indexed themselves. In times of (high) inflation, wage contracts might be indexed to the price level (inflation rate), to avoid the need to renegotiate wages simply because of the inflation.

The rigidity of relative prices or the real wage often implies that *quantities* are more variable. In the case of a completely rigid real wage, a demand shock will cause a bigger fall in employment than in the competitive case where the real wage falls. In terms of the labour market depicted in Figure 1, employment falls more when there is a rigid real wage (*A–C*) than when the real wage adjusts to its new equilibrium (*A–B*). Hence real rigidities are important because they may lead to quantities fluctuating more than they would if there were flexible real wages. Furthermore, because the market is no longer in competitive equilibrium after the fall in employment, there is some involuntary unemployment (more people would like to work at the going wage than are employed). At point *C*, the labour supply is still at the initial level A: it is just that labour demand has fallen, so that not all workers willing to work at W can work. The horizontal distance A–C measures the level of involuntary unemployment. Hence real rigidities can lead to deviations from the standard equilibrium concept and thus lead to different welfare results and interpretations. Furthermore, real rigidities can be used to explain why equilibrium is not attained.

Perhaps the most important theory of the real rigidity of wages is the *efficiency wage* model. This has a variety of forms. The simplest version is due to Robert Solow (1979). Suppose that the degree of effort a worker puts in is increasing in the real wage rate, w:

$$e = e(w).$$

Output depends on the number of workers hired, N, and their effort:

$$Y = f(N.e(w)).$$

The firm therefore chooses w to maximize profits:

$$Y(N.e(w)) - N.w.$$

The first order conditions are that

$$Y'e - w = 0, \ Y'Ne' - N = 0.$$

From the first equation we have the marginal product of effective labour equals the reciprocal of the efficiency wage w/e:

$$Y' = w/e.$$

Substituting this in the second equation and dividing through by N implies that

$$\frac{w}{e} \frac{de}{dw} = 1.$$

This states that the equilibrium wage set will be where the elasticity of effort with respect to the real wage is unity. The important point to note is that this condition determines the real wage *independently of labour market conditions* such as the labour supply (although it is assumed that labour demand does not exceed supply). If the efficiency wage is above the competitive wage, there will be involuntary unemployment.

There are several different versions of the efficiency wage theory. Perhaps the best known is the shirking model of Shapiro and Stiglitz (1984). In this model, because of problems in monitoring workers, employers pay an efficiency wage to ensure that workers will not shirk: a higher wage than the going rate elsewhere means that workers have more to lose if they shirk and are as a result thrown out of their job. Other efficiency wage models giving rise to real wage rigidity include the labour turnover model (Stiglitz, 1974), adverse selection models (Weiss, 1980) and sociological models (Akerlof, 1984).

There are other theories of real wage rigidity to the efficiency wage model. These include the insider–outsider model (Lindbeck and Snower, 1988). This approach emphasizes the power of insiders, those already employed, relative to those outsiders who might be seeking employment. The market power of insiders rests on hiring and firing costs and the threat of the withdrawal of cooperation by insiders.

Whilst the concept of real rigidity is important, most authors have chosen to emphasize *nominal rigidity* as a key to understanding unemployment and economic fluctuations. This emphasis dates back to Keynes's discussion of (downward) nominal rigidity in the *General Theory*, and is seen in more recent new Keynesian contributions (see Dixon, 2000, chs 4–5). The emphasis on nominal rigidity stems from a focus on the effect of nominal changes in demand on real output (the non-neutrality of money, for example). Real rigidities do not require any non-neutrality of money and can explain unemployment and related effects when there is no important nominal effect.

The concept of real rigidity has no *direct* relation to the notion of nominal rigidity. The fact that two prices have a fixed ratio does nothing to tie down their level. For example, the real wage is the ratio W/P: if this is fixed to some value, this tells us nothing about the level of either W or P.

However, nominal and real rigidities can interact. When there are real rigidities, nominal rigidities in one variable can spill over to other nominal prices or wages (for a discussion of this, see Ball and Romer, 1990; Dixon, 1994). If $W/P = w$, and the nominal wage is fixed, then so is the nominal price $P = W/w$. For example, if the efficiency wage ties down the real wage, and menu costs tie down the nominal price, the nominal wage will also be determined. Another example of the interaction of nominal and real rigidities is *real-wage resistance* in an open economy model (Dornbusch, 1980, ch. 4). Suppose that the price level depends on the price of both traded and non-traded goods. If the price of the traded good is fixed (owing to a fixed exchange rate), a real wage rigidity ties down the nominal wage and the nominal price of tradables.

Huw Dixon

See also:

Efficiency Wage Theory; Insider–Outsider Theory; Keynes's *General Theory*; New Keynesian Economics; Nominal Rigidity.

Bibliography

Akerlof, G. (1984), 'Gift Exchange and Efficiency Wage Theories: Four Views', *American Economic Review*, **74**, May, pp. 79–83.
Ball, L. and D. Romer (1990), 'Real Rigidities and the Non-Neutrality of Money', *Review of Economic Studies*, **57**, April, pp. 183–203.
Dixon, H. (1994), 'Macroeconomic Price and Quantity Responses with Heterogeneous Product Markets', *Oxford Economic Papers*, **46**, July, pp. 385–402.
Dixon, H. (2000), *Surfing Economics: Essays for the Enquiring Economist*, London: Palgrave.
Dornbusch, R. (1980), *Open Economy Macroeconomics*, New York: Basic Books.
Lindbeck, A. and D. Snower (1988), *The Insider–Outsider Theory of Employment and Unemployment*, Cambridge, MA: MIT Press.
Shapiro, C. and J.E. Stiglitz (1984), 'Equilibrium Unemployment as a Worker Disciplining Device', *American Economic Review*, **74**, June, pp. 433–44.
Solow, R.M. (1979), 'Another Possible Source of Wage Stickiness', *Journal of Macroeconomics*, **1**, Winter, pp. 79–82.
Stiglitz, J.E. (1974), 'Wage Determination in LDCs: The Labour Turnover Model', *Quarterly Journal of Economics*, **88**, May, pp. 194–227.
Weiss, A (1980), 'Job Queues and Layoffs in Labour Markets with Flexible Wages', *Journal of Political Economy*, **88**, June, pp. 526–38.

Real Wage

The money wage divided (or deflated) by a price index; the amount of goods and services a money wage can buy.

See also:

Price Index.

Recession

Usually defined as a decline in real GDP that lasts for at least two consecutive quarters of a year. In business cycle analysis the term is generally used to describe a slowdown in the growth rate of output below the trend growth rate.

See also:

Real GDP.

Recognition Lag

The time lag between when a disturbance or shock affects the economy and when the authorities recognize that some kind of corrective action is needed; also known as the detection lag.

See also:
Inside Lag.

Relative Income Hypothesis

The relative income hypothesis, which was most fully developed by James Duesenberry (*Income, Saving and the Theory of Consumer Behaviour*, Harvard University Press, 1949), represents an important early contribution to the theory of consumer behaviour.

Duesenberry's analysis is based on two hypotheses. First, at a moment in time, utility functions are socially determined; that is, they are *interdependent* between people. This can be illustrated by examining a cross-section of the population at a moment in time. Within any income group there will be some 'known' customary living standard. Households with an income below that of the norm will attempt to conform by spending a higher proportion of their income (that is, they 'attempt to keep up with the Joneses') so that their average propensity to consume is higher than the norm, and vice versa: a so-called 'demonstration effect'. Second, utility functions are *interdependent* for the same individual at different moments in time. For example, a household which experiences a rise in its income over time will learn to adjust to a new pattern of consumption. Having learned to appreciate a new, higher level of consumption, the household will not return to its previous original pattern of consumption if its income should return to its previous peak level: a so-called 'ratchet effect'.

Duesenberry sought to reconcile the conflicting evidence from various types of empirical study. Early empirical studies (both budget studies of a cross-section of the population and short-run aggregate time series studies) of the consumption–income relationship provided evidence that, in line with Keynes's absolute income hypothesis, the marginal propensity to consume (MPC) is less than the average propensity to consume (APC), and that the APC declines as income increases. However, empirical work involving long-run time-series data undertaken by Simon Kuznets (*National Product Since 1869*, NBER, 1946) suggested that in the long run the APC had not changed significantly and that the consumption–income relationship is best represented by a straight line through the origin with a slope of approximately 0.9 (that is, $MPC = APC$).

How can the relative income hypothesis reconcile the conflicting evidence from cross-section and long-run time-series data? As discussed earlier, a household's APC is in part determined by its *relative* income in the income distribution. The 'demonstration effect' explains why cross-section studies provide evidence that the APC differs between households on different income levels. Over time, if all incomes were to double, for example, a household's APC would remain unchanged. If the overall income distribution remains unchanged as national income increases in the long run, the APC will remain constant. In other words, over time, cross-section functions will move upwards, giving rise to a long-run consumption function with a constant APC.

Next, we consider how the relative income hypothesis can reconcile the conflicting evidence from short-run and long-run time-series data. As discussed earlier, household consumption is also in part a function of current income *relative* to peak income received in previous time periods. The 'ratchet effect' explains the specification of the short-run consumption function (along which the APC differs) and the long-run consumption function (best represented by a straight line through the origin). Over time, as national income increases, households learn to appreciate a higher level of consumption. If income always increased steadily in the long run the APC would remain constant. However, there are clearly fluctuations in the level of national income. In a recession, as incomes decline, households will seek to maintain their previous standard of living by reducing their consumption by less than their income has fallen. As a result, in the short run, APC increases as income decreases.

Despite its intuitive appeal, based as it is on interdependent utility functions, Duesenberry's theory has been superseded by the permanent and life cycle hypotheses.

See also:

Absolute Income Hypothesis; Duesenberry, James S.; Life Cycle Hypothesis; Permanent Income Hypothesis.

Replacement Ratio

The ratio of total benefits (such as unemployment benefit) paid to the unemployed, to the average after-tax (net) income of people in work.

Representative Agent Model

In macroeconomic models, the use of a representative agent as a proxy for a whole collection of heterogeneous individuals, all interacting in the economy, first became fashionable in an attempt to break with the fundamental Keynesian analytical categories of aggregate income and expenditure. In spite of the horrendous aggregation problems, the representative agent approach was used by Friedman in his earlier study of consumption. It appears also in his 'Optimum Quantity of Money' (1969). Indeed, there appeared no other way of beginning if the Keynesian income–expenditure categories were rejected. Dressing it up as 'micro foundations' is a *post factum* rationalization, making a virtue out of a necessity. It is worth emphasizing that Friedman was using the representative agent approach long before the debate on 'micro foundations' became a major concern.

Yet it is commonly perceived that the outcome of the debate on the so-called 'micro foundations of macroeconomics' was that macroeconomics can only be done 'properly' by starting with the behaviour of *micro* units, the household and the firm who are referred to as 'agents'. In the conclusion of his survey of 'Microfoundations', Roy Weintraub (1979, p. 161) states clearly that the question of what constitutes the appropriate foundations for macroeconomics is an open one.

According to Hoover (1988), Friedman was trying to construct 'an engine for analyzing concrete economic problems' (see Friedman, 1955, p. 904), as suggested by Cournot ([1938], 1927 p. 127). Hence Friedman, along with Cournot and Marshall, is concerned with the *first order* impacts of variables. On this basis, Hoover concludes that Friedman is a Marshallian, which would justify, perhaps, the use of a representative agent. This may be plausible, but the Marshallian method entails invoking the *ceteris paribus* assumption where everything else is locked up in the *ceteris paribus* pound (see Dore, 1985). Marshall's use of the representative firm is valid for short-period analysis only. But, as Hoover notes correctly, Friedman's analysis is of a long-period nature: 1867–1975, or some 108 years! Thus the validity of the Marshallian method for Friedman's work is questionable (see Negishi, 1985, ch. 14).

Without detailed argument, one may note that Friedman's main concern was operationally useful results with some predictive success, which can hardly be described as methodological purism. Thus the use of the representative agent in Friedman does not spring from a commitment to Marshall's method, but from a conscious decision to break with the Keynesian income and expenditure categories, just as he had earlier attempted to break with the Keynesian consumption function by inventing a transcendental and non-observable concept of *permanent income*

(Dore, 1993). The New Classical School of macroeconomics adopted Friedman's representative agent approach as the only correct methodological response to the Lucas Critique, which had argued that the use of demand and supply functions for policy purposes would yield biased results, as such functions typically do not take into account expectations. The gist of the Lucas Critique was that it was necessary to 'go behind' the demand and supply functions, to the primitive parameters of taste and technology. This can best be done by using the representative agent as an analytical device. Hence all models in the New Classical mode (for example, the models of real business cycles) rely on such a device. In this way it was suggested that, as these models have the appropriate 'micro foundations', they were superior to the whole class of Keynesian models, which they dubbed *ad hoc*.

A number of New Keynesians conceded that models *should* have the appropriate micro foundations and set out to demonstrate Keynesian results even when the model adopted the representative model as an analytical device. For example, New Keynesian business cycle theory explains the non-neutrality of money through nominal rigidities, where the rigidities are derived from optimizing or near-rational behaviour. The empirical work supports a framework of imperfect competition and market power (see Dore, 1993, ch. 7, for a survey). Hence prices are endogenously set without resorting to some mythical Walrasian auctioneer who arrives at equilibrium prices in a costless manner.

New Keynesian models rely on demonstrating the existence of price rigidity at the *micro* level, asserting implicitly that it is sufficient for aggregate *macro* level price rigidity. Is this warranted? Is a micro description adequate for explaining the business cycle, which is an aggregate phenomenon? While it is tempting to consider the entire question of the relationship between microeconomics and macroeconomics, such an undertaking is impossible here. But it is not possible to evade the issue completely: Friedman adopted the *representative agent* as an analytical starting point, in order to avoid the (aggregate) Keynesian expenditure categories, and the analysis that followed from it. Friedman did this allegedly to rehabilitate the classical quantity theory tradition, although the use of the representative agent or methodological individualism is alien to the classical tradition; it is specifically a *neo*-classical invention in economics. (Of course the influence of methodological individualism can be seen in other social sciences also.)

But there are New Keynesians and 'other Keynesians', who are not necessarily old-style Keynesians, in the Hicksian mould. Keynesians like Peter Diamond, Robert Solow and Takashi Negishi have explicitly rejected the Walrasian competitive auctioneer as the appropriate 'foundation' of their macro analysis (see, for example, Solow, 1998). Yet the representative agent persists in the analysis of New Keynesians. But the proposition that characteristics of the aggregate merely reflect characteristics of individual units may in fact be a fallacy of composition. Such a fallacy has been investigated, both in Europe and in North America, for example by Garretsen and Janssen (1989), Bertola and Caballero (1990), Caballero (1992). An important review article on the subject is that of Kirman (1992); see also the references given therein. The reader may also wish to consult Hartley (1997) and Gellegati and Kirman (1999).

Before returning to that question, it might be useful to define a fallacy of composition. *A Dictionary of Philosophy* by Angeles (1981, p. 97) defines it as

> Arguing (a) that what is true of each part of a whole is also necessarily true of the whole, or (b) that what is true of some parts of a whole is also necessarily true of the whole itself. Example: 'Each member (or some members) of the team is married; therefore the team also has (must have) a wife.' Inferring that a collection has certain characteristics merely on the basis that its parts have them erroneously proceeds from regarding the collection distributively to regarding it collectively.

Consequently, a whole host of propositions derived from the behaviour of micro units (price rigidity or excess capacity at the level of the firm, near-optimal or suboptimal behaviour) need have no significance for the analysis of the aggregate. Thus the existence of price rigidity due to menu costs at the level of the firm is quite consistent with complete aggregate price flexibility, as demonstrated by Caplin and Spulber (1987). It is clear from this work that the aggregate business cycle in New Keynesian literature results from aggregate price rigidity, which in turn rests on the positive menu cost at the firm level. But it is the representative-agent framework that leads to the fallacy of composition: when one firm fails to adjust the price, all firms are assumed to fail to adjust the price. This then is the basis of aggregate rigidity, which then leads to the non-neutrality of money in Akerlof and Yellen (1985). Once we depart from the representative agent, and consider *a distribution of firms*, the aggregate rigidity disappears.

Menu costs impose integer constraints in pricing; if the profit maximizing price is S, and the menu cost is z, then $S - z = s$, where s is the trigger point at which firms raise their prices back to S. This is called an (S,s) pricing policy (Barro, 1972; Sheshinski and Weiss, 1977, 1983). In a model similar in conception to the (S,s) pricing model, Caballero (1992) analysed the sources of several fallacies of composition in representative agent models. These fallacies arise because direct microeconomic arguments do not take into account the strong restrictions that probability theory puts on the joint behaviour of a large number of units whose actions are not fully synchronized.

Caballero (1992) uses the example of non-convex adjustment costs – with thresholds that prevent a firm from making smooth and continuous adjustments. These adjustment costs may be costs of changing prices (menu costs), the cost of hiring and firing labour, the costs of adjusting the capital stock to shocks that are particular to a given firm (called 'idiosyncratic shocks') or shocks that are common to all firms.

To begin with, assume that all firms have the same adjustment costs, and their shocks are perfectly correlated. Then, whatever the asymmetric microeconomic phenomenon (say firm-level price rigidity), it carries over to the aggregate phenomena (aggregate price level rigidity). However, here everything is exactly the same for every firm at *all* times. In effect, there is only one firm. Suppose next that the shocks are less than perfectly correlated across firms. Caballero shows that it is possible to construct examples in which any microeconomic asymmetry vanishes at the aggregate level. It is also possible to show that, provided there are idiosyncratic shocks, any microeconomic asymmetry does not carry over to aggregate data. Similarly, in the author's Monte Carlo experiments, microeconomic asymmetries do not carry over into aggregate level asymmetries and, even when they do, they are not necessarily the consequence of a microeconomic asymmetry.

Suppose firms adjust their factors of production, or prices, at different speeds in the upward and downward direction – this is the asymmetry. Then whichever is the slower speed will take a longer time to adjust. But the aggregate would exhibit substantially *less* asymmetry in its response to positive and negative shocks than individual firms would.

The conclusions of Caballero's paper are clear: asymmetric pricing policies at the firm level do not necessarily imply asymmetries at the aggregate level; and asymmetries at the aggregate price level need not come from asymmetries at the firm level. Similarly, asymmetric factor adjustment costs at the firm level need not imply asymmetric responses of the capital stock and the level of employment to positive and negative shocks. *To assert otherwise is to commit the fallacy of composition.*

To claim that both the New Classical and the New Keynesian are 'general equilibrium approaches' is wrong. In Arrow–Debreu general equilibrium, no specific functional form of the utility function is required; that is the beauty and generality of the Arrow–Debreu model: it is compatible with all agents having different utility functions, as long as the basic assumptions (such as diminishing marginal utility, and so on) are satisfied. By optimizing with respect to the given prices of all goods and the given endowments, demand functions are derived, which are then expressed as excess demand functions by subtracting the given initial endowments (supplies).

In contrast, in the representative agent models, it is necessary to start with a *specific* functional form of a utility function; it may be Cobb–Douglas, as in New Classical models, or some variant (Rotemberg, 1987) that yields a constant elasticity demand function for the representative consumer. This means that there is one consumer or that all consumers are alike. If they are all alike, why do they trade? In the Arrow–Debreu model, consumers trade because they have different preferences and different endowments.

In the New Keynesian representative agent models the demand function is not of the Arrow–Debreu type, for, in the latter, demand functions are homogeneous of degree zero, which leaves no role for money But the representative agent's demand is a function of relative prices as well as the real supply of money. Hence the homogeneity property of Arrow–Debreu demand functions is lost.

For these reasons it is not correct to describe the representative agent model as a 'general equilibrium' approach. We conclude that all models adopting the representative agent framework are seriously flawed.

MOHAMMED H.I. DORE

See also:

Friedman, Milton; Menu Costs; New Classical Economics; New Keynesian Economics.

Bibliography

Akerlof, G. and J. Yellen (1985), 'A Near-Rational Model of the Business Cycle, with Wage and Price Inertia', *Quarterly Journal of Economics*, **100**, Supplement, pp. 823–38; reprinted in N.G. Mankiw and D. Romer (eds) (1991), vol. 1.

Angeles, P.A. (1981), *Dictionary of Philosophy*, New York: Harper & Row.

Barro, R.J. (1972), 'A Theory of Monopolistic Price Adjustment', *Review of Economic Studies*, **39**, January, pp. 17–26.

Bertola, G. and R.J. Caballero (1990), 'Kinked Adjustment Costs and Aggregate Dynamics', *NBER Macroeconomics Annual*, pp. 237–88; also Columbia Department of Economics Working Paper, 465.

Caballero, R.J. (1992), 'A Fallacy of Composition', *American Economic Review*, **82**, December, pp. 1279–92; also National Bureau of Economic Research Working Paper Series no. 3735, 1991.

Caplin, A.S. and D.F. Spulber (1987), 'Menu Costs and the Neutrality of Money', *Quarterly Journal of Economics*, **102**, November, pp. 703–25; reprinted in N.G. Mankiw and D. Romer (eds) (1991), vol. 1.

Cournot, A.A. ([1938] 1927), *Researches into the Mathematical Principles of the Theory of Wealth*, trans. Nathaniel T. Bacon, New York: Macmillan.

Dore, M.H.I. (1985), 'The Concept of Equilibrium', *Journal of Post Keynesian Economics*, **III**, Winter, pp. 193–206.

Dore, M.H.I. (1993), *The Macroeconomics of Business Cycles: A Comparative Evaluation*, New York: Basil Blackwell; Japanese translation published by Bunka Shobou Hakubunsha, Tokyo, 1995.

Friedman, M. (1955), 'Leon Walras and his Economic System: A Review Article', *American Economic Review*, **45**, December, pp. 900–909.

Friedman, M. (1969), *Optimal Quantity of Money and Other Essays*, London: Macmillan.

Garretsen, H. and M.C.W. Janssen (1989), 'Two Fallacies of Composition in a Keynesian OLG model', *University of Groningen Research Memorandum*, no. 317.

Gellegati, M. and A. Kirman (eds) (1999), *Beyond The Representative Agent*, Cheltenham, UK and Northampton, MA: Edward Elgar.

Hartley, J.E. (1997), *The Representative Agent In Macroeconomics*, Frontiers of Political Economy Series, **10**, London and New York: Routledge.

Hoover, K.D. (1988), *The New Classical Macroeconomics*, Oxford: Basil Blackwell.

Kirman, A. (1992), 'Whom or What Does the Representative Individual Represent?', *Journal of Economic Perspectives*, **6**, Spring, pp. 117–36.

Mankiw, N.G. and D. Romer (eds) (1991), *New Keynesian Economics*, Cambridge, MA: MIT Press.

Negishi, T. (1985), *Economic Theories in a non-Walrasian Tradition*, Cambridge: Cambridge University Press.

Rotemberg, J. (1987), 'The New Keynesian Microeconomic Foundations', *NBER Macroeconomics Annual*, pp. 69–104.

Sheshinski, E. and Y. Weiss (1977), 'Inflation and Costs of Price Adjustment', *Review of Economic Studies*, **44**, June, pp. 287–303.

Sheshinski, E. and Y. Weiss (1983), 'Optimum Pricing Policy under Stochastic Inflation', *Review of Economic Studies*, **50**, July, pp. 513–29.

Solow, R.M. (1998), *Monopolistic Competition and Macroeconomic Theory*, Cambridge: Cambridge University Press.

Weintraub, E.R. (1979), *Microfoundations: The Compatibility of Microeconomics and Macroeconomics*, Cambridge: Cambridge University Press.

Reputation

See:

Credibility and Reputation.

Revaluation

A revaluation of a currency involves a deliberate increase in the value of one currency in terms of another when the currency in question is part of a fixed exchange rate system.

See also:

Fixed Exchange Rate System.

Ricardian Equivalence

Ricardian equivalence, also known as debt neutrality or the absence of fiscal illusion, holds that it makes no difference whether government spending is financed by current taxes or by borrowing against future tax revenues. The market value of the bonds sold by the government is equal to the present discounted value of the payments of interest and principal to which the bonds commit future taxpayers. If taxpayers are risk-averse and able to optimize intertemporally (as in Irving Fisher's two-period consumption diagram, Milton Friedman's permanent income hypothesis or Franco Modigiliani's life cycle theory of consumption), they will choose to smooth their consumption over time by saving in anticipation of future tax payments. A given amount of current government spending will thus reduce private consumption by the same amount, whether the taxpayers pay for the spending in current taxes or save the same amount in anticipation of the future tax liabilities implied by government borrowing. Under Ricardian equivalence, an increase in the stock of outstanding government bonds does not increase net private wealth, because the public, who own the bonds, are also conscious of the offsetting increase in their future tax liabilities.

The fiscal policy implications of Ricardian equivalence, noted by Robert Barro (1974, 1989), are that an increase in government spending will shift the *IS* curve in the standard macroeconomic model only by the balanced budget multiplier effect, regardless of how it is financed, and that a tax cut or an increase in transfer payments, if financed by borrowing, would have no effect whatsoever. During World War II, J.M. Keynes (1980, p. 320) had commented that 'a remission of taxation on which people could rely only for an indefinitely short period might have very limited effect in stimulating their consumption'. Debt neutrality would put any deficit-financed tax cut into that category. Barro's debt neutrality challenged the Keynesian countercyclical fiscal policy of budget deficits in recessions and surpluses in booms. With debt neutrality, only the level of government spending matters for aggregate expenditure, not the deficit or surplus. The crowding out of private investment through higher interest rates would also be no greater for debt-financed government spending than for tax-financed government spending.

After Barro (1974) propounded the debt neutrality theorem, James Buchanan (1976) noted that it could be found in the writings of David Ricardo (1817) and coined the term 'Ricardian equivalence'. However, Gerald O'Driscoll (1977) pointed out that Ricardo did not believe that debt neutrality held in the real world, holding instead that myopic taxpayers would misperceive a substitution of debt for tax finance as an increase in their net worth and so increase their consumption. Dimand and West (1989) note an earlier statement akin to debt neutrality by Ricardo's contemporary, Destutt de Tracy, published in English in 1817 but translated from an earlier unpublished French manuscript.

Debt neutrality also reduces the strength of the real balance effect, which A.C. Pigou invoked to argue that reducing wages and prices could restore full employment even in a liquidity trap. In correspondence in 1944 (published in Patinkin, 1982) about Kalecki's comment on Pigou, Michal Kalecki remarked that, 'If the interest on the [National] Debt is financed by taxation its existence does not affect the aggregate disposable income', to which Keynes replied that, 'Assuming that interest is paid on this out of taxation, it cannot affect the wealth of the community one way or another. Thus, it seems to me that Pigou is in reality depending entirely on the increase in the value of gold' (see Dimand, 1991; Tobin, 1980).

Debt neutrality may not hold if consumers are uncertain about their future income (whether income or life span is uncertain). Opinion is divided on the effect of uncertainty. Buchanan holds that confused signals may lead consumers to underestimate their future tax liabilities, while Barro posits that risk-averse consumers may overestimate their future tax payments and engage in precautionary saving. Barro's exposition of debt neutrality assumed that taxes are lump sum and that the future taxes to service a debt issue will be paid by the same taxpayers who benefit from the initial tax cut association with the issue of debt. A possible cause of failure of debt neutrality is that, if taxpayers have finite lives, they will choose to consume more thanks to the initial tax cut and not worry about the tax liabilities of future generations. Debt neutrality can still hold if consumers care enough about the welfare of their descendants and have a strong enough bequest motive, smoothing the consumption of an infinitely lived family and saving in anticipation of the tax liabilities of their distant descendants as though the liabilities were their own (see Weil, 1987).

Consumers may be liquidity-constrained, facing higher interest rates on their borrowing than they receive on their savings, so that their intertemporal consumption possibility frontier is kinked at current disposable income. If such a consumer has a tangency with the highest attainable indifference curve at the kink in the consumption possibility frontier, that consumer's consumption spending would depend only on current disposable income, as in the simple Keynesian consumption function, and debt neutrality would fail (see Hayashi, 1987). A related failure of debt neutrality due to a credit market imperfection would occur if the government could borrow at a lower interest rate than individuals, so that the public would be enriched by having the government borrow against their expected future income, rather than doing so themselves. Drazen (1978) noted that government debt might increase intertemporal efficiency by permitting evasion of the non-negativity constraint on bequests.

In view of uncertainty, the liquidity constraints facing some consumers, finite life spans, and the lower interest rates at which governments can borrow, it is agreed that Ricardian equivalence does not hold strictly. The empirical literature surveyed by John J. Seater (1993) is concerned with whether Ricardian equivalence holds as an approximation, and in particular whether it is a better approximation than the traditional Keynesian view that government debt exerts a positive wealth effect on consumption and that a debt-financed increase in government spending will have a larger multiplier effect than a tax-financed balanced-budget increase in government spending. The consensus is that, empirically, Ricardian equivalence is a better approximation than the traditional model, with government debt having no significant effect on any dependent variable (except for a few studies finding a puzzling negative relation between government debt and interest rates, which is not consistent with either model). The early tests of the effect of government debt on consumption yielded conflicting results, but econometricians tackled problems of measurement, specification, differencing, simultaneity and treatment of expectations until their results converged on the conclusion they expected, approximate Ricardian equivalence. In contrast to the consensus in the empirical literature, introductory textbooks continue to teach the multiplier effects of tax cuts and transfer payments, and in some books the real balance effect of changes in the value of public debt, bringing in Ricardian equivalence later as a special topic.

ROBERT W. DIMAND

See also:

Balanced Budget Multiplier; Crowding Out, Fiscal Policy: Role of; IS–LM Model: Closed Economy; Real Balance Effect.

Bibliography

Barro, R.J. (1974), 'Are Government Bonds Net Wealth?', *Journal of Political Economy*, **82**, December, pp. 1095–1117.
Barro, R.J. (1989), 'The Ricardian Approach to Budget Deficits', *Journal of Economic Perspectives*, **3**, Spring, pp. 37–54.
Buchanan, J.M. (1976), 'Barro on the Ricardian Equivalence Theorem', *Journal of Political Economy*, **84**, April, pp. 337–42.
Churchman, N. (1997), 'David Ricardo on Public Debt', PhD dissertation, University of Toronto.
Destutt de Tracy, A.C.L. (1817), *A Treatise on Political Economy*, translation revised and corrected by T. Jefferson, Georgetown, DC: Joseph Milligan.
Dimand, R.W. (1991), 'Keynes, Kalecki, Ricardian Equivalence and the Real Balance Effects', *Bulletin of Economic Research*, **43**, July, pp. 289–92.
Dimand, R.W. and E.G. West (1989), 'Destutt de Tracy: A French Precursor of the Virginia School of Public Finance', *History of Economics Society Bulletin*, **11**, Fall, pp. 210–15.
Drazen, A. (1978), 'Government Debt, Human Capital and Bequests in a Lifecycle Model', *Journal of Political Economy*, **86**, June, pp. 505–16.
Hayashi, F. (1987), 'Tests for Liquidity Constraints: A Critical Survey and Some New Observationss', in T. Bewley (ed.), *Advances in Econometrics, Fifth World Congress*, vol. 2, Cambridge: Cambridge University Press.

Keynes, J.M. (1980), *Collected Writings*, Volume XXVII, ed. D.E. Moggridge, London: Macmillan, and New York: Cambridge University Press, for the Royal Economic Society.

O'Driscoll, G.P. (1977), 'The Ricardian Nonequivalence Theorem', *Journal of Political Economy*, **85**, February, pp. 207–10.

Patinkin, D. (1982), *Anticipations of the General Theory? And Other Essays on Keynes*, Chicago: University of Chicago Press.

Ricardo, D. (1817), *On the Principles of Political Economy and Taxation*, London, reprinted in P. Sraffa with M. H. Dobb (eds) (1951), *The Works and Correspondence of David Ricardo*, Cambridge: Cambridge University Press for the Royal Economic Society.

Seater, J.J. (1993), 'Ricardian Equivalence', *Journal of Economic Literature*, **31**, March, pp. 142–90.

Tobin, J. (1980), *Asset Accumulation and Economic Activity*, Chicago: University of Chicago Press.

Weil, P. (1987), 'Love Thy Children: Reflections on the Barro Debt Neutrality Theorem', *Journal of Monetary Economics*, **19**, June, pp. 377–91.

Robinson, Joan (1903–83)

Joan Robinson (b. Joan Maurice 1903, Camberley, Surrey, England) obtained her MA from the University of Cambridge in 1925. Her main posts included Assistant Lecturer (1931–7), Lecturer (1937–49), Reader (1949–65) and Professor of Economics (1965–71) at the University of Cambridge. She is best known for her work on imperfect competition; defending, promoting and developing Keynesian economics; and the accumulation of capital and the theory of economic growth in which she extended Keynes's short-period analysis in dynamic terms, providing a foundation for Post Keynesian economics. Among her best known books are *Economics of Imperfect Competition* (Macmillan, 1933); *Essays in the Theory of Employment* (Macmillan, 1937); *Introduction to the Theory of Employment* (Macmillan, 1937); *The Rate of Interest and Other Essays* (Macmillan, 1952); *The Accumulation of Capital* (Macmillan, 1956); and *Essays in the Theory of Economic Growth* (Macmillan, 1962).

See also:

Keynes's *General Theory*; Keynesian Economics; Post Keynesian Economics.

Romer, Paul M.

Paul Romer (b.1955, Denver, Colorado, USA) obtained his BS (Maths, 1973) and his PhD (1983) from the University of Chicago. His main past posts have included Assistant Professor at the University of Rochester, 1982–8; Professor at the University of Chicago, 1988–90; and Professor at the University of California, Berkeley, 1990–96. Since 1996 he has been

Professor in the Graduate School of Business at Stanford University. He is best known for his influential contributions to the field of economic growth which have led to the renaissance of economic growth analysis and, in particular, the development of endogenous growth models which highlight the importance of ideas in driving economic growth. His most widely read articles include 'Increasing Returns and Long-Run Growth' (*Journal of Political Economy*, **94**, October 1986); 'Growth Based on Increasing Returns Due to Specialization' (*American Economic Review*, **77**, May 1987); 'Endogenous Technological Change' (*Journal of Political Economy*, **98**, October 1990); 'Idea Gaps and Object Gaps in Economic Development' (*Journal of Monetary Economics*, **32**, December 1993); and 'The Origins of Endogenous Growth' (*Journal of Economic Perspectives*, **8**, Winter 1994).

See also:

Endogenous Growth Theory.

Rostow, Walt W.

Walt Rostow (b.1916, New York City, USA) obtained his BA (1936) and his PhD (1940) from Yale University. His main past posts have included Professor of American History at Oxford University, 1946–7; Assistant to the Executive Secretary of the Economic Commission for Europe, 1947–9; Professor of American History at Cambridge University, 1949–50; Professor of Economic History at Massachusetts Institute of Technology, 1951–61; Chairman of the Policy Planning Council and Counsellor of the US Department of State, 1961–6; and Special Assistant to the US President for National Security Affairs, 1966–9. Since 1969 he has been the Rex G. Baker Jr Professor, Emeritus, of Political Economy at the University of Texas, Austin. He is best known for his work on growth and development, in particular his analysis of five stages of economic growth from the traditional society, to the preconditions for take-off, take-off, maturity and the age of high mass consumption. His best known books include *Essays on the British Economy of the Nineteenth Century* (Clarendon Press, 1948); *The Process of Economic Growth* (W.W. Norton, 1952); *The Stages of Economic Growth: A Non-Communist Manifesto* (Cambridge University Press, 1960); *How It All Began: Origins of the Modern Economy* (McGraw-Hill, 1975); *Why the Poor Get Richer and the Rich Slow Down: Essays in the Marshallian Long Period* (University of Texas Press, 1980); and *Theories of Economic Growth from David Hume to the Present* (Oxford University Press, 1990).

Rough Tuning

A term used to describe the occasional use of fiscal and monetary policy in response to a large divergence in output and employment from their full employment or natural levels; also known as coarse tuning.

See also:
Aggregate Demand Management; Discretionary Policy; Fine Tuning.

Royal Economic Society

Originally founded in 1890 as the British Economic Association, it became the Royal Economic Society in 1902, when it was granted a royal charter. The main purpose of the society is 'to promote the encouragement of the study of economic science in academic life, government service, banking, industry and public affairs'. Among its publications is the prestigious *Economic Journal* (first published in 1891), widely acknowledged as one of the leading journals in economics. Although originally published as a quarterly journal, since 1991 it has been published six times a year. The society has more than 3000 individual members, 60 per cent of whom live outside the United Kingdom. For more information the reader is referred to the official website of the RES (*http://www.res.org.uk/*).

Rules versus Discretion

'Enlightened discretion is the rule' Blinder (1998). The modern approach to stabilization policy evolved over the second half of the twentieth century following the devastating impact on the world economy of the Great Depression during the 1930s. It is widely recognized that it was this event that prompted Keynes (1936) to write *The General Theory of Employment, Interest and Money*, a book that gave birth to the subject of macroeconomics. Keynes was concerned that the massive unemployment problems experienced during the 1930s, reflecting what he considered to be market failure on a grand scale, might lead to the destruction of capitalism, and so he sought to provide an alternative solution involving greater involvement of the government in managing the economy. Keynes defended the enlargement of the functions of government 'as the only practicable means of avoiding the destruction of existing economic forms in their entirety and as the condition of the successful functioning of individual initiative' (ibid., p. 380). This outcome he considered to be a 'moderately conservative' implication of his analysis.

The first 25 years following the end of World War II were halcyon days for Keynesian macroeconomics. The Keynesian revolution stimulated research into national income accounting techniques as well as establishing the conceptual framework out of which developed the idea of conducting discretionary countercyclical stabilization policies. Initially, it seemed that the task of stabilizing the economy would be relatively easy. If an economy was seen to be moving into a recession, the authorities should respond to the decline in private spending by implementing expansionary fiscal and monetary policies. Conversely, in the case of an inflationary boom, the authorities should use contractionary fiscal and monetary policies. Despite some dissenting voices (most notably those of Milton Friedman and Friedrich von Hayek) the orthodox Keynesian (neoclassical synthesis) view dominated economists' vision of the need for, and conduct of, stabilization policy until the early 1970s. This vision consisted of the following key elements:

1. acceptance that the *long-run*, market clearing, general level of prices and quantities could be explained using orthodox neoclassical general equilibrium theory and that in the long run the market system was self-equilibrating;
2. acceptance that in the short run, various rigidities in the system prevented the typical industrial market economy from returning to 'full employment' with sufficient speed to be acceptable;
3. a general agreement that governments had a legitimate activist role to play in *managing* aggregate demand in order to stabilize a predominantly free enterprise economy and reduce the economic and human costs resulting from aggregate instability.

Many had concluded from the postwar Keynes–Classics debate that, although the classical economists appeared to have won the intellectual battle, Keynes and the Keynesians had won the policy debate. For example, it became more widely accepted that governments should adopt the principles of *functional finance* and balance their budgets over the economic cycle, rather than attempt to maintain a balanced budget at all times irrespective of the state of the economy (prior to the Great Depression, the US and other governments tended to borrow in times of war and pay off debt with peacetime surpluses). Few economists today would support any form of strict fiscal rule requiring a government to attempt continuously to balance its budget.

These general principles represented the 'new economics' mainstream view during the 1945–70 period. James Tobin, one of America's most distinguished Keynesian economists, explains the postwar consensus in terms of what he calls a two-regime model. 'Sometimes the economy is in a classical situation where markets are clearing and the economy's ability to produce is supply constrained . . . At other times the economy is in a Keynesian situation in which the constraint on actual output is *demand* – aggregate spending . . . That situation obtains a lot of the time, not always, and there are demand-increasing policies that will eliminate the social waste involved' (see Snowdon and Vane, 1999). Early Keynesianism became identified with 'fiscalism' and there was also intense debate between economists such as Friedman and Tobin on the likely division of the impact of fiscal and monetary policy on nominal and real variables. One key feature of the Keynesian–monetarist debate related to disagreement over the most effective way of managing aggregate demand so as to limit the social and economic waste associated with instability and also whether it was desirable for governments to try and 'fine-tune' the economy using countercyclical policies (see Snowdon *et al.*, 1994; Hammond, 1996).

Friedman was an early critic of activist discretionary policies and initially focused on some of the practical aspects of implementing such policies. As early as 1948, he noted that 'Proposals for the control of the cycle thus tend to be developed almost as if there were no other objectives and as if it made no difference within what framework cyclical fluctuations take place.' He also drew attention to the problem of *time lags* which, in his view, could in all likelihood 'intensify rather than mitigate cyclical fluctuations'. Friedman distinguished between three types of time lag: the recognition lag, the action lag and the effect lag. These inside and outside lags, by delaying the impact of policy actions, would constitute the equivalent of an 'additional random disturbance'. While monetary policy could be implemented relatively quickly, its effects were subject to a long and variable outside lag. Discretionary fiscal adjustments, particularly in a political system like the United States, could not realistically be implemented quickly. Moreover, the public choice literature suggested that structural deficits, with damaging effects on national saving and hence long-run growth, would be the likely result of discretionary fiscal policy operating within a democracy (see Buchanan and Wagner, 1977). Politicians may also deliberately create instability when they have discretion since, within a democracy, they may be tempted to manipulate the economy for political profit as suggested in the political business cycle literature (Alesina *et al.*, 1997).

Although theoretical and empirical developments in economics facilitated the development, by Klein, Goldberger, Modigliani and others, of the highly aggregative simultaneous-equation macroeconometric models used for forecasting purposes, many economists remained unconvinced that such forecasts could overcome the problems imposed by the problem of time lags and the wider political constraints. Friedman concluded that governments had neither the knowledge nor the information required to conduct fine-tuning forms of discretionary policy in an uncertain world and advocated instead that the monetary authorities adopt a passive form of monetary rule whereby the growth in a specified monetary aggregate would be predetermined at some stated known (k per cent) rate (Friedman, 1960, 1968, 1972). While Friedman (1960) argued that such a rule would promote greater stability, 'some uncertainty and instability would remain', because 'uncertainty and instability are unavoidable concomitants of progress and change. They are one face of a coin of which the other is freedom'. DeLong (1997a) also concludes that it is 'difficult to argue that "discretionary" fiscal policy has played any stabilising role at all in the post-World War II period' in the US economy. However, it is generally accepted that *automatic stabilizers* have an important role to play in mitigating the impact of economic shocks.

Towards the end of the 1960s, research began to focus more carefully on the importance for understanding macroeconomic phenomena of endogenous expectations, especially following the publication of the highly influential papers of Friedman (1968) and Phelps (1967, 1968). The 'Great Peacetime Inflation', combined with recession and rising unemployment, during the 1970s, was a tremendous shock to the confidence of policy makers who, in the 'shadow of the Great Depression', believed in the regular use of expansionary demand management policies in order to maintain a high level of economic activity (see DeLong, 1997a, 1997b). The orthodox Keynesian insistence that relatively low levels of unemployment are permanently achievable via the use of discretionary aggregate demand management was vigorously challenged, first by Milton Friedman, who launched a monetarist counterrevolution against policy activism during the 1950s and 1960s, and, later, during the 1970s, by the new classical critiques inspired by Robert Lucas.

There is no doubt that Friedman's demonstration of the complexity of implementing discretionary stabilization policies in a dynamic and uncertain world has influenced a whole generation of eminent macroeconomists, most notably Robert Lucas, who freely admits his intellectual debt to his former teacher (Snowdon and Vane, 1999). Moreover, the experience of what John Taylor (1992) labelled the 'Great Inflation' of the 1970s appeared to vindicate the views of the monetarist critics. As a result of the 'Great Peacetime Inflation' in the 1970s many key monetarist insights were absorbed within mainstream models (Mayer, 1997). According to DeLong (2000), the key aspects of monetarist thinking that now form a crucial part of mainstream thinking in macroeconomics are the natural rate of unemployment hypothesis, the analysis of fluctuations as movements about trend rather than deviations below potential, the acceptance that under normal circumstances monetary policy is 'a more potent and useful tool' for stabilization than fiscal policy, the consideration of macroeconomic policy within a rules-based framework, and the recognition of the limited possibilities for success of stabilization policies.

Building on the insights developed by Friedman and Phelps, the work of Robert Lucas was crucial in introducing macroeconomists to Muth's (1961) rational expectations hypothesis, together with its enormous implications for theoretical and empirical work. In particular, with the introduction of rational expectations, the standard Keynesian models seemed unable to deliver their traditional conclusions. It soon became apparent to the Keynesian mainstream that the new classical critique represented a much more powerful and potentially damaging challenge than the one launched by the monetarists. It was a series of papers written by Lucas and published in the period 1972–6 that established the analytical base of the rational expectations–equilibrium approach to macroeconomics (Lucas, 1972, 1973, 1976). Collectively these papers had an immense influence on macroeconomics research conducted during the 1970s and on the direction that macroeconomics has taken subsequently.

The new classical monetary models of the 1970s and early 1980s reinforced Friedman's arguments in favour of a rules-based framework for macroeconomic policy. When agents have rational expectations, policy makers cannot ignore the interaction between their policy rules and the behaviour of rational agents. Therefore, because the expectations of economic agents depend on many things, including the economic policies being pursued by the government, policy makers must design their strategies taking that interaction into account (Hoover, 1995; Fischer, 1990). Following the *Lucas critique* (Lucas, 1976), Lucas and Sargent (1978) concluded that Keynesian style macroeconometric models are 'incapable of providing reliable guidance in formulating monetary, fiscal and other types of policy'. Furthermore, policy making within a rational expectations framework becomes a strategic game between the policy maker and economic agents. The seminal paper by Finn Kydland and Edward Prescott (1977), which developed the idea of *time inconsistency* within a macroeconomic setting, showed how discretionary policy led to an 'inflation bias'. Within the Kydland and Prescott framework, the optimal combination of inflation and unemployment cannot be achieved under a discretionary monetary policy regime since there will always be a temptation for the policy maker to cheat. In order to gain policy credibility, the monetary authorities needed to be constrained by rules. However, the idea of implementing Friedman's k per cent monetary growth rate rule (hard core monetarism) is highly dependent on the stable velocity of money, and the instability of velocity observed during the 1980s led central bankers to 'distrust monetary aggregates as indicators' (DeLong, 2000). As a result of unstable velocity, the interest rate has now become the main instrument of monetary policy for most central banks (Blinder, 1998).

An important element of the growing consensus in macroeconomics in recent years is that low and stable inflation is conducive to growth, stability and the efficient functioning of market economies (Taylor, 1996, 1998a, 1998b). The consensus view is that inflation has real economic costs, especially unanticipated inflation. While the impact of inflation rates of less than 20 per cent on the rate of economic growth may be small, it is important to remember that small variations in growth rates have dramatic effects on living standards over relatively short historical periods (Snowdon, 2002). If a consensus of economists agree that inflation is damaging to economic welfare, it remains to be decided how best to control inflation. Since it is now widely accepted that the *primary long-run goal of monetary policy* is to control inflation and create reasonable price stability, and that expectations are endogenous to changes in policy, the clear task for economists is to decide on the exact form of *monetary regime* to adopt in order to achieve this goal. Monetary regimes are characterized by the use of a specific *nominal anchor*. Mishkin (1999) defines a nominal anchor as 'a constraint on the value of domestic money' or more broadly as 'a constraint on discretionary policy that helps weaken the time-inconsistency problem'. In recent years an increasing number of countries have begun to adopt inflation targeting as their nominal anchor, combined with greater central bank independence (see Bernanke and Mishkin, 1997; Bernanke *et al.*, 1999). However, Bernanke *et al.* insist that inflation targeting should be thought of as a broad framework for monetary policy making, '*constrained discretion*', rather than a strict rule in the classical sense. Nevertheless, as Taylor argues, a policy maker needs a set of procedures for changing the instruments of policy in response to economic shocks in order to achieve the inflation target. Thus we can think of a policy rule as a systematic decision-making process that makes the best use of available information in a consistent and predictable way. One such rule is the well-known 'Taylor Rule' that seems to describe accurately the monetary policy regime of the Fed during the Alan Greenspan era up to 1992. Taylor (1993) suggested a simple rule for monetary policy shown by

$$r = r^* + \pi + 0.5\,(\pi - \pi^*) + 0.5(y), \tag{1}$$

where r is the Federal Funds rate, r^* is the equilibrium *real* Federal Funds rate, π is average inflation over the current and previous three-quarters, π^* is the inflation target, and y is the output gap, that is, real GDP−potential

GDP. An important criticism of Taylor's rule is that it is backward-looking. Lars Svennson (1997a, 1997b) argues the case for 'inflation forecast targeting' as a forward-looking approach. In two recent papers, Clarida *et al.* (1999, 2000) set out what they consider to be some important lessons which economists have learned about the conduct of monetary policy. Economists' research in this field points towards some useful general principles about optimal policy. Clarida *et al.* identify their approach as new Keynesian because in their model nominal price rigidities allow monetary policy to have non-neutral effects on real variables in the short run, there is a positive short-run relationship between output and inflation (that is, a Phillips curve), and the *ex ante* real interest rate is negatively related to output (that is, an IS function). In their analysis of US monetary policy in the period 1960–96, Clarida *et al.* (2000) show that there is a 'significant difference in the way that monetary policy was conducted pre- and post-1979', being relatively well managed after 1979 compared to the earlier period. The key difference between the two periods is the magnitude and speed of response of the Federal Reserve to expected inflation. Under the respective chairmanships of William M. Martin, G. William Miller and Arthur Burns, the Fed was 'highly accommodative'. In contrast, in the years of Paul Volcker and Alan Greenspan, the Fed was much more 'proactive toward controlling inflation'.

Clarida *et al.* (2000) conduct their investigation by specifying a baseline policy reaction function of the form given by

$$r_t^* = r^* + \beta \big[E(\pi_{t,k} | \Omega_t) - \pi^* \big] + \gamma\, E[y_{t,q} | \Omega_t].$$ (2)

Here r_t^* represents the target rate for the Federal Funds (FF) nominal interest rate; $\pi_{t,k}$ is the rate of inflation between time periods t and $t+k$; π^* is the inflation target, $y_{t,q}$ measures the average deviation between actual GDP and the target level of GDP (the output gap) between time periods t and $t+q$; E is the expectations operator; Ω_t is the information set available to the policy maker at the time the interest rate is set; and r^* is the 'desired' nominal FF rate when both π and y are at their target levels. For a central bank with a quadratic loss function that specifies costs arising from deviations of inflation from target, and deviations of output from potential, this form of policy reaction function (rule) is appropriate in a new Keynesian setting. The policy rule given by equation (2) differs from Taylor's rule in that it is forward-looking. In the case of Taylor's rule the Fed reacts to *lagged* output and inflation, whereas equation (2) suggests that the Fed sets the Federal Funds rate according to its *expectation* of the future values of inflation and output gap. The Taylor rule is equivalent to a 'special case' of equation (2) where lagged values of inflation and the output gap provide sufficient information for forecasting future inflation. In the case of equation (2) the policy maker is able to take into account a broad selection of information about the future path of the economy.

According to Clarida *et al.* (2000), there was a clear and visible change to the conduct of monetary policy after 1979 when, following the Volcker disinflation via tight monetary policy, the real rate for most of the 1980s became positive. As a result of this marked change in the Fed's policy, inflation was successfully reduced, although as a consequence of the disinflation the USA suffered its worst recession since the Great Depression. Unemployment rose from 5.7 per cent in the second quarter of 1979 to 10.7 per cent in the fourth quarter of 1982. There seems little doubt that the lower inflation experienced during the past two decades owes a great deal to the more anti-inflationary monetary stance taken by the Fed and other central banks around the world.

While economists such as James Tobin (1996), Robert Solow (1998) and Alan Blinder (1998) remain unconvinced of the desirability, feasibility and necessity of conducting stabilization policy within a rules-based framework since in reality only discretion prevails, John Taylor believes that the much improved economic performance of the US economy since the mid-1980s is due to the better conduct of monetary policy which has become more transparent, systematic and credible (Taylor, 1999, 2000a, 2000b, 2001; for useful and detailed information on monetary policy rules see John Taylor's website (*http://www.stanford.edu/~johntayl/*).

BRIAN SNOWDON
HOWARD R. VANE

See also:

Aggregate Demand Management; Automatic Stabilizers; Central Bank Independence; Discretionary Policy; Federal Funds Rate; Federal Reserve System; Fine Tuning; Fiscal Policy: Role of; Great Depression; Great Inflation; Inflation Targeting; Inside Lag; Keynesian Economics; Lucas Critique; Monetary Policy: Role of; New Classical Economics; Outside Lag; Rational Expectations; Time Inconsistency.

Bibliography

Alesina, A. and N. Roubini, with G.D. Cohen (1997), *Political Cycles and the Macroeconomy: Theory and Evidence*, Cambridge, MA: MIT Press.
Bernanke, B.S. and F.S. Mishkin (1997), 'Inflation Targeting: A New Framework for Monetary Policy', *Journal of Economic Perspectives*, **11**, Spring, pp. 97–116.
Bernanke, B.S., T. Laubach, F.S. Mishkin and A.S. Posen (1999), *Inflation Targeting: Lessons from the International Experience*, Princeton, NJ: Princeton University Press.
Blinder, A.S. (1998), *Central Banking in Theory and Practice*, Cambridge, MA: MIT Press.
Buchanan, J. and R. Wagner (1977), *Democracy in Deficit: The Political Legacy of Lord Keynes*, New York: Academic Press.
Clarida, R., J. Gali and M. Gertler (1999), 'The Science of Monetary Policy: A New Keynesian Perspective', *Journal of Economic Literature*, **37**, December, pp. 1661–1734.

Clarida, R., J. Gali and M. Gertler (2000), 'Monetary Policy Rules and Macroeconomic Stability: Some Evidence and Some Theory', *Quarterly Journal of Economics*, **115**, February, pp. 147–80.

DeLong, J.B. (1997a), 'America's Fiscal Policy in the Shadow of the Great Depression', in M. Bordo, C. Goldin and E. White (eds), *The Defining Moment: The Great Depression and the American Economy in the Twentieth Century*, Chicago: University of Chicago Press.

DeLong, J.B. (1997b), 'America's Only Peacetime Inflation: The 1970s', in C. Romer and D. Romer (eds), *Reducing Inflation: Motivation and Strategy*, Chicago: University of Chicago Press.

DeLong, J.B. (2000), 'The Triumph of Monetarism?', *Journal of Economic Perspectives*, **14**, Winter, pp. 83–94.

Fischer, S. (1990), 'Rules versus Discretion', in B. Friedman and F. Hahn (eds), *Handbook of Monetary Economics*, Amsterdam: Elsevier.

Friedman, M. (1948), 'A Monetary Framework for Economic Stability', *American Economic Review*, **38**, June, pp. 245–64.

Friedman, M. (1960), *A Program for Monetary Stability*, New York: Fordham University Press.

Friedman, M. (1968), 'The Role of Monetary Policy, *American Economic Review*, **58**, March, pp. 1–17.

Friedman, M. (1972), 'Have Monetary and Fiscal Policies Failed?', *American Economic Review*, **62**, May, pp. 11–18.

Hammond, D. (1996), *Theory and Measurement: Causality Issues in Milton Friedman's Monetary Economics*, Cambridge: Cambridge University Press.

Hoover, K.D. (ed.) (1995), *Macroeconometrics: Developments, Tensions and Prospects*, Boston, MA: Kluwer Academic Publishers.

Keynes, J.M. (1936), *The General Theory of Employment, Interest and Money*, London: Macmillan.

Kydland, F.E. and E.C. Prescott (1977), 'Rules Rather Than Discretion: The Inconsistency of Optimal Plans', *Journal of Political Economy*, **85**, June, pp. 473–92.

Lucas, R.E. Jr (1972), 'Expectations and the Neutrality of Money', *Journal of Economic Theory*, **4**, April, pp. 103–24.

Lucas, R.E. Jr (1973), 'Some International Evidence on Output–Inflation Tradeoffs', *American Economic Review*, **63**, June, pp. 326–34.

Lucas, R.E. Jr (1976), 'Econometric Policy Evaluation: A Critique', in K. Brunner and A.H. Meltzer (eds), *The Phillips Curve and Labour Markets*, Amsterdam: North Holland.

Lucas, R.E. Jr and T.J. Sargent (1978), 'After Keynesian Macroeconomics', *After the Phillips Curve: Persistence of High Inflation and High Unemployment*, Boston, MA: Federal Reserve Bank of Boston.

Mayer, T. (1997), 'What Remains of the Monetarist Counter-Revolution?', in B. Snowdon and H.R. Vane (eds), *Reflections on the Development of Modern Macroeconomics*, Cheltenham, UK and Lyme, US: Edward Elgar.

Mishkin, F.S. (1999), 'International Experiences with Different Monetary Regimes', *Journal of Monetary Economics*, **43**, June, pp. 579–606.

Muth, J.F. (1961), 'Rational Expectations and the Theory of Price Movements', *Econometrica*, **29**, July, pp. 315–35.

Phelps, E.S. (1967), 'Phillips Curves, Expectations of Inflation and Optimal Unemployment Over Time', *Economica*, **34**, August, pp. 254–81.

Phelps, E.S. (1968), 'Money Wage Dynamics and Labour Market Equilibrium', *Journal of Political Economy*, **76**, August, pp. 678–711.

Snowdon, B. (2002), *Conversations on Growth, Stability and Trade: An Historical Perspective*, Cheltenham, UK and Northampton, MA, USA: Edward Elgar.

Snowdon, B. and H.R. Vane (1999), *Conversations With Leading Economists: Interpreting Modern Macroeconomics*, Cheltenham, UK and Northampton, MA, USA: Edward Elgar.

Snowdon, B., H.R. Vane and P. Wynarczyk (1994), *A Modern Guide to Macroeconomics: An Introduction to Competing Schools of Thought*, Aldershot, UK and Brookfield, US: Edward Elgar.

Solow, R.M. (1998), 'How Cautious Must the Fed Be?', in R.M. Solow and J.B. Taylor, *Inflation, Unemployment and Monetary Policy*, Cambridge, MA: MIT Press.

Solow, R.M. (1999), 'Interview with Robert Solow', in B. Snowdon and H.R. Vane, *Conversations with Leading Economists: Interpreting Modern Macroeconomics*, Cheltenham, UK and Northampton, MA, USA: Edward Elgar.

Svensson, L. (1997a), 'Optimal Inflation Targets, "Conservative" Central Banks, and Linear Inflation Contracts', *American Economic Review*, **87**, March, pp. 98–114.

Svensson, L. (1997b), 'Inflation Forecast Targeting: Implementing and Monitoring Inflation Targets', *European Economic Review*, **41**, June, pp. 1111–46.

Svensson, L. (1999), 'Inflation Targeting as a Monetary Policy Rule', *Journal of Monetary Economics*, **43**, pp. 607–54.

Taylor, J. (1992), 'The Great Inflation, the Great Disinflation, and Policies for Future Price Stability', in A. Blundell-Wignall (ed.), *Inflation, Disinflation and Monetary Policy*, Sydney: Ambassador Press.

Taylor, J.B. (1993), 'Discretion Versus Policy Rules in Practice', *Carnegie Rochester Conference Series on Public Policy*, Amsterdam: North-Holland.

Taylor, J.B. (1996), 'Stabilisation Policy and Long-Term Growth', in R. Landau, T. Taylor and G. Wright (eds), *The Mosaic of Economic Growth*, Stanford: Stanford University Press.

Taylor, J.B. (1998a), 'Monetary Policy Guidelines for Employment and Inflation Stability', in R.M. Solow and J.B. Taylor, *Inflation, Unemployment and Monetary Policy,* Cambridge, MA: MIT Press.

Taylor, J.B. (1998b), 'Monetary Policy and the Long Boom', *Federal Reserve Bank of St. Louis Review*, November/December, pp. 3–11.

Taylor, J.B. (1999), 'A Historical Analysis of Monetary Policy Rules', in J.B. Taylor (ed.), *Monetary Policy Rules*, Chicago: University of Chicago Press.

Taylor, J.B. (2000a), 'Reassessing Discretionary Fiscal Policy', *Journal of Economic Perspectives*, **14**, Summer, pp. 21–36.

Taylor, J.B. (2000b), 'Teaching Modern Macroeconomics at the Principles Level', *American Economic Review*, **90**, May, pp. 90–94.

Taylor, J.B. (2001), *Economics*, 3rd edn., New York: Houghton Mifflin.

Tobin, J. (1996), *Full Employment and Growth: Further Keynesian Essays on Policy*, Cheltenham, UK and Brookfield, US: Edward Elgar.

Sacrifice Ratio

The number of percentage points of annual output (real GDP) sacrificed or lost in order to reduce inflation by 1 per cent.

See also:

Inflation: Costs of Reducing.

Samuelson, Paul A.

In 1970, when Paul A. Samuelson was awarded the Nobel Memorial Prize in Economics, the Swedish Academy of Sciences wrote in their citation: '[he] has done more than any other contemporary economist to raise the level of scientific analysis in economic theory'. This statement summarizes all of Samuelson's work, which ranges over virtually every field of economics. Our focus here, however, is confined to his contributions to macroeconomics. Even this subset is huge, and what follows merely scratches the surface.

Samuelson was born in 1915 and was an undergraduate at the University of Chicago. After receiving his PhD from Harvard in 1941, Samuelson went to the Massachusetts Institute of Technology (MIT) where he has spent his entire professional career. Since 1986 he has been Institute Professor of Economics, Emeritus at MIT. In addition to being the first American to be awarded the Nobel Memorial Prize in Economics, his many offices and honours have included the award of the first John Bates Clark Medal of the American Economic Association (AEA) in 1947; president of the Econometric Society in 1951; president of the AEA in 1961; and president of the International Economic Association from 1965 to 1968.

Samuelson's contributions to the making of macroeconomic policy include service as an advisor to the National Resources Planning Board, the United States Treasury, the Council of Economic Advisors and the Federal Reserve. He also was a key advisor to President John F. Kennedy and authored the influential 1961 Task Force Report, *State of the American Economy*. Moreover, Samuelson's textbook, *Economics: An Introductory Analysis*, has educated an audience far beyond academicians. For over 50 years this classic has served to introduce millions of students to macroeconomic theory and policy issues, starting with the first edition in 1948 and continuing today with the seventeenth edition (since 1985 co-authored with William D. Nordhaus) in 2001. Samuelson's celebrated 'neoclassical synthesis', the insight that many of the results from classical economic theory are validated in an economy with monetary and fiscal policies operating to maintain high employment, was first introduced in the third edition of

Economics: An Introductory Analysis (1955, p.vi). It is extraordinary to find such an influential contribution in an introductory textbook.

Samuelson's first contributions to macroeconomics appear even before publication of his epic treatise, *Foundations of Economic Analysis*. By Samuelson's own account in his Preface to the first edition, 'most of the material presented [in 1941 to the David A. Wells Prize Committee at Harvard University] was already several years old, having been conceived and written primarily in 1937', though World War II delayed publication until 1947. Part II of *Foundations* contains three chapters that were instrumental in revolutionizing economics in general and macroeconomics in particular:

1. 'The Stability of Equilibrium: Comparative Statics and Dynamics', Chapter IX (with a section entitled 'Analysis of the Keynesian System');
2. 'The Stability of Equilibrium: Linear and Nonlinear Systems,' Chapter X;
3. 'Some Fundamentals of Dynamical Theory', Chapter XI (with a section entitled 'Nature of the Business Cycle'.

These three path-breaking chapters in *Foundations* stimulated all economists, and particularly macroeconomists, to deal explicitly with the fact that economic events unfold over time.

Some 35 years later, the 1983 Enlarged Edition of *Foundations* appeared including, among other things, an update to 'A Note on the Demand for Money', which was a section of his original Chapter V (pp. 496–503 in the 1983 Enlarged Edition contain this update). Of fundamental importance is Samuelson's (1983) conclusion, 'Neoclassical theory thus provides a rational theory of how money's velocity of circulation changes as the interest rate changes, in defiance of simplistic theories of ultra-monetarism.'

Turning now to Samuelson's journal articles, we will first provide an estimate for the number of his publications in macroeconomics and then select six exemplary contributions for brief comment.

Our quantity estimate is based on the *Collected Scientific Papers of Paul A. Samuelson* (volumes 1 to 5, covering the years up to 1986; no doubt his additional hundreds of papers in press for volumes 6 and 7 will contain more macroeconomic contributions). The various editors of these *Collected Scientific Papers* volumes grouped his publications by subject, though the groupings are necessarily arbitrary because many of Samuelson's papers could have been classified under more than one subject. And, of course, the subjects themselves are a matter of editorial judgment.

We have chosen those subject groupings that correspond to a broad definition of 'macroeconomics', and, for each of these, Table 1 reports the number of published papers. Of the 388 publications included in all five

volumes of *Collected Scientific Papers*, 66, or about 17 per cent, are
included in Table 1. This provides at least a good first approximation to
both the absolute and relative quantity of Samuelson's journal contributions to macroeconomics – at least up to 1986 – he is still an active
researcher today. As we shall see, however, some of his most important contributions to macroeconomics escaped the subject groupings of Table 1.

Table 1   Estimate for the number of macroeconomic papers included in
Collected Scientific Papers of Paul A. Samuelson

Subject grouping	Vols 1–2 (1966)	Vol. 3 (1972)	Vol. 4 (1977)	Vol. 5 (1986)
Dynamics and statics of income determination	10	3	n.a.	n.a.
Pure theory of public expenditure	3	4	n.a.	n.a.
Principles of fiscal and monetary policy	11	5	n.a.	n.a.
Theory of money and inflation	n.a.	n.a.	4	n.a.
Lectures and essays on current economic problems	n.a.	n.a.	6	n.a.
Current economics and policy	n.a.	n.a.	n.a.	20

Note: 'n.a.' indicates that the subject grouping is not contained in the corresponding
volume.

We now select six papers from *Collected Scientific Papers* to illustrate the
extraordinary breadth and depth of Samuelson's contributions to macroeconomics:

- 'Interactions between the Multiplier Analysis and the Principle of
  Acceleration' (*The Review of Economics and Statistics*, May 1939).
  This paper brought Samuelson youthful fame with readers in intermediate macroeconomics, and it played a role in the cycle literature
  of Hansen, Harrod, Kaldor, Goodwin, Hicks, and numerous others.
- 'Evaluation of Real National Income' (*Oxford Economic Papers*,
  1950). Here Samuelson provides a rigorous and elegant answer to the
  question, 'What can we learn about economic welfare from the aggregate data in national income accounts?'
- 'An Exact Consumption Loan Model with or without the
  Contrivance of Money' (*Journal of Political Economy*, 1958). In this
  paper Samuelson provided one of the first theoretically rigorous
  models of both interest rate determination over time and the role of

money, and in the process he introduced the overlapping generations model, which has become a workhorse of modern macroeconomics.

● 'Analytical Aspects of Anti-Inflation Policy' (co-authored with Robert M. Solow, *American Economic Review*, 1960). In 'Analytical Aspects of Anti-Inflation Policy', Samuelson and Solow were the first to examine the Phillips curve using US data, thereby spawning a whole new debate about both the short-run and long-run trade-offs between inflation and the unemployment rate.

● 'Proof that Properly Anticipated Prices Fluctuate Randomly' (*Industrial Management Review*, 1965). In this more obscure publication, Samuelson was the first to prove that a competitive equilibrium price series is a martingale ('fair game'), thereby establishing one of the most important properties of rational expectations models (including asset pricing models and stochastic growth models, both of which constitute part of 'modern macroeconomics'). While this paper is already central to finance, both it and financial economics have yet to have the major impact on mainstream macroeconomics that they are likely ultimately to achieve.

(*Note*: A *martingale* is a stochastic process for which $E[|\tilde{P}_n|] < \infty$ and $E[\tilde{P}_{n+1} | p_0, p_1, \ldots, p_n] = p_n$; a random walk with zero drift is a special case of a martingale.)

● 'What Classical and Neoclassical Monetary Theory Really Was' (*Canadian Journal of Economics*, 1968). Here Samuelson derives the equations and homogeneity properties that must hold for a valid quantity theory of money, thereby solving a problem that had been an enigma for centuries.

A significant aspect of Samuelson's work is revealed by the subject groupings into which the above selected papers were placed, a choice made by the various editors of *Collected Scientific Papers*; see Table 2. Only three of these six selected papers are included in the count of Table 1. This fact illustrates both the difficulty of classifying any particular paper as 'macroeconomics' and, more importantly, the extent to which many of Samuelson's contributions were sufficiently fundamental for their importance to extend to multiple subject areas.

Space limitations necessitate only a brief summary. Recognizing that others might justifiably make quite different choices, we conclude with a list of *some* of Samuelson's primary contributions to macroeconomics. He

1. provided the first rigorous foundations for dynamic economic models;
2. laid the theoretical foundations for the way to interpret national income accounts;

648   *Samuelson, Paul A.*

Table 2   Subject groupings for the six selected papers; only the three papers listed in bold typeface are included in the count of Table 1

Paper	Chapter, volume	Subject grouping
'Interactions between the Multiplier Analysis and the Principle of Acceleration'	**82 (2)**	**Dynamics and statics of income determination**
'Evaluation of Real National Income'	77 (2)	Welfare economics
'An Exact Consumption Loan Model with or without the Contrivance of Money'	21 (1)	The pure theory of capital and growth
'Analytical Aspects of Anti-Inflation Policy'	**102 (2)**	**Principles of fiscal and monetary policy**
'Proof that Properly Anticipated Prices Fluctuate Randomly'	198 (3)	Portfolio selection, warrant pricing and the theory of speculative markets
'What Classical and Neoclassical Monetary Theory Really Was'	**176 (3)**	**Principles of fiscal and monetary policy**

3. introduced the 'neoclassical synthesis' (in the third edition of *Economics: An Introductory Analysis*, 1955) and the Phillips curve (in the fifth edition of *Economics: An Introductory Analysis*, 1961) to mainstream economics;
4. set out the logical foundations for the role of money;
5. first proved one of the key theorems upon which the rational expectations revolution is based.

This is indeed a formidable list, and one stands in awe of Samuelson's monumental contributions not only to macroeconomics, but also to all of economics. Aptly, the 1996 National Medal of Science presented to Samuelson by the President of the United States carries the citation, 'For fundamental contributions to economic science, specifically general equilibrium theory and macroeconomics, and to economic education and policy over a period of nearly 60 years.'

EDWIN BURMEISTER

I am grateful to Stephen A. Ross and Robert M. Solow for comments on earlier drafts, as well as to Paul A. Samuelson for corrections to the penultimate draft.

See also:

American Economic Association; Econometric Society; John Bates Clark Medal; Keynesian Cross; Multiplier–Accelerator Model; Neoclassical Synthesis; Nobel Prize in Economics; Phillips Curve.

Bibliography

Samuelson, P.A. (1947), *Foundations of Economic Analysis*, Cambridge, MA: Harvard University Press.
Samuelson, P.A. (1948), *Economics: An Introductory Analysis*, 1st edn, New York: McGraw-Hill Book Company.
Samuelson, P.A. (1955), *Economics: An Introductory Analysis*, 3rd edn, New York: McGraw-Hill Book Company.
Samuelson, P.A. (1961), *Economics: An Introductory Analysis*, 5th edn, New York: McGraw-Hill Book Company.
Samuelson, P.A. (1966), *Collected Scientific Papers of Paul A. Samuelson*, vols 1 and 2, ed. Joseph E. Stiglitz, Cambridge, MA: MIT Press.
Samuelson, P.A. (1972), *Collected Scientific Papers of Paul A. Samuelson*, vol 3, ed. Robert A. Merton, Cambridge, MA: MIT Press.
Samuelson, P.A. (1977), *Collected Scientific Papers of Paul A. Samuelson*, vol 4, ed. Hiroaki Nagatani and Kate Crowley, Cambridge, MA: MIT Press.
Samuelson, P.A. (1983), *Foundations of Economic Analysis*, Enlarged Edition, Cambridge, MA: Harvard University Press.
Samuelson, P.A. (1986), *Collected Scientific Papers of Paul A. Samuelson*, vol 5, ed. Kate Crowley, Cambridge, MA: MIT Press.
Samuelson, P.A. and W.D. Nordhaus (2001), *Economics*, 17th edn, New York: McGraw-Hill Book Company.

Sargent, Thomas J.

Thomas Sargent (b.1943, Pasadena, California, USA) obtained his BA from the University of California, Berkeley in 1964 and his PhD from Harvard University in 1968. His main past posts have included Associate Professor at the University of Pennsylvania, 1970–71; and Associate Professor (1971–5), then Professor (1975–87) at the University of Minnesota. Since 1987 he has been Senior Fellow at the Hoover Institution of Stanford University. He is best known for his influential work on the implications of the rational expectations hypothesis, in particular the policy ineffectiveness proposition, and being a central figure, along with Robert Lucas Jr, in the development of the new classical approach to macroeconomics. Among his best known books are *Rational Expectations and Econometric Practice* (co-edited with R.E. Lucas Jr) (University of Minnesota Press, 1981); *Macroeconomic Theory* (Academic Press, 2nd edn, 1987); *Dynamic Macroeconomic Theory* (Harvard

University Press, 1987); *Rational Expectations and Inflation* (Harper Collins, 2nd edn, 1993); *The Conquest of American Inflation* (Princeton University Press, 1999); *Recursive Macroeconomic Theory* (co-authored with L. Ljungqvist) (MIT Press, 2000); and *The Big Problem of Small Change* (co-authored with F. Veld) (Princeton University Press, 2002). His most widely read articles include 'Rational Expectations, the Real Rate of Interest, and the Natural Rate of Unemployment' (*Brookings Papers on Economic Activity*, 1973); 'Rational Expectations, the Optimal Monetary Instrument and the Optimal Money Supply Rule' (co-authored with N. Wallace) (*Journal of Political Economy*, **83**, April 1975); 'A Classical Macroeconometric Model for the United States' (*Journal of Political Economy*, **84**, April 1976); 'Rational Expectations and the Theory of Economic Policy' (co-authored with N. Wallace) (*Journal of Monetary Economics*, **2**, April 1976); 'After Keynesian Macroeconomics' (co-authored with R.E. Lucas Jr) (*Federal Reserve Bank of Boston*, 1978); 'Some Unpleasant Monetarist Arithmetic' (co-authored with N. Wallace) (*Federal Reserve Bank of Minneapolis Quarterly Review*, Autumn 1981); 'The European Unemployment Dilemma' (co-authored with L. Ljungqvist) (*Journal of Political Economy*, **106**, June 1998); and 'Robust Control and Model Uncertainty' (co-authored with L. Hansen) (*American Economic Review*, **91**, May 2001).

See also:

New Classical Economics; Policy Ineffectiveness Proposition; Rational Expectations.

Say's Law

Say's Law is the term used by English-speaking economists to refer to what is known in French economics as 'la loi des débouchés' (the law of markets). Other shorthand descriptions include 'supply creates its own demand'; 'commodities are purchased with commodities'; and 'the impossibility of general overproduction'.

The modern understanding of this law, derived from Oskar Lange and Don Patinkin (see Becker and Baumol, 1952), involves distinguishing between three propositions:

1. Walras's Law states that if there are n markets in the economy, Σ_{i-1}^{n} $p_i(x_i^d - x_i^s) \equiv 0$, where p_i, x_i^d and x_i^s denote the price, quantity demanded and quantity supplied of the ith commodity. If commodity n is money, this implies that $\Sigma_{i-1}^{n-1} p_i(x_i^d - x_i^s) \equiv m^s - m^d$, where m^s and m^d are the supply of, and demand for, money. This is purely an identity.

2. Say's identity, which applies if money is purely a unit of account, as in a barter economy, is the proposition that $\sum_{i-1}^{n-1} p_i(x_i^d - x_i^s) = m^s - m^d = 0$. This states that, because there can never be an excess supply of money, the aggregate demand for commodities (other than money) must always equal the aggregate supply.
3. Say's equality is the proposition that, in equilibrium, $\sum_{i-1}^{n-1} p_i(x_i^d - x_i^s) \equiv m^s - m^d = 0$. This implies that, out of equilibrium, people may desire to increase or decrease their holdings of money and hence that total demand for commodities need not equal total supply. It leaves open the questions of what mechanisms exist to bring about equilibrium and how effective these mechanisms are.

This understanding of Say's Law emerged out of a long series of controversies. At the beginning of the nineteenth century, James Lauderdale, Simonde de Sismondi and Thomas Robert Malthus argued that it was possible for there to be general gluts of commodities. Jean-Baptiste Say, James and John Stuart Mill, and David Ricardo used the law of markets to argue that general gluts could not occur. Depressions might be serious but they arose because there was an imbalance in the goods being produced. In particular, for Say, depression in manufacturing arose because a bad harvest meant that more money had to be spent on agricultural goods, causing a fall in demand for manufactured goods. During the nineteenth century and the early twentieth century, this was the 'classical' orthodoxy, challenged by Karl Marx and by underconsumptionists (prominent amongst whom were John A. Hobson, William Truffant Foster and Waddil Catchings) who argued that recessions arose because too few goods were being consumed. In the twentieth century, controversy was re-ignited by John Maynard Keynes, who presented his *General Theory* (Keynes, 1936) as overthrowing Say's Law and rehabilitating the underconsumptionist tradition. For Keynes, Say's Law was 'equivalent to the proposition that there is no obstacle to full employment' (ibid., p. 26). This challenge to what Keynes chose to call 'classical economics' stimulated many attempts to make sense of the difference between Keynes and the 'classics'. In particular, Oskar Lange and Don Patinkin, using the Walrasian framework of multi-market equilibrium, were led to the interpretation of Say's Law outlined at the start of this entry.

Given this long history, the way in which Say's Law was understood varied considerably. It was used to encompass a great variety of propositions, the relationships between which were not fully understood. Elements of the doctrine can be found in eighteenth-century writing, notably Adam Smith and the Physiocrats (see Thweatt, 1979). For example, Smith argued that saving constitutes spending, which can be read as implying a form of Say's Law. However, Smith could also write of international trade as a means of disposing of surplus commodities, something that would not make sense in a world where Say's Law held. Smith's arguments were the basis for the work of Say and James Mill (who has some claim to have formulated the concept independently). Say's version of the law was not completely precise and James Mill simplified it to obtain what is defined above as Say's identity. He argued that no one would save money unless they were going to invest it (that is, hoarding would be zero) and that

> *The production of commodities creates, and is the one and universal cause which creates a market* for commodities produced . . . Whatever be the additional quantity of goods therefore which is at any time created in any country, an additional power of purchasing, exactly equivalent is at the same instant created; so that a nation can never be naturally overstocked either with capital or with commodities. (Mill [1808] quoted by Thweatt, 1980, p. 468)

It was not until the second edition of his Treatise (1814) that Say expressed the law in this way, though he still qualified the statement.

For all these economists, Say's Law was a proposition about economic growth rather than a statement about the business cycle and market clearing. It was used to argue that the capacity to consume would automatically rise alongside the capacity to produce. The importance of this is illustrated by the fact that even those arguing for the possibility of general gluts, such as Malthus, assumed that savings would automatically be invested. They were not interested in gluts caused by hoarding, which they assumed would be only a temporary phenomenon. Even later underconsumptionists, such as Hobson, treated saving and investment as equivalent.

In general, the classical economists perceived that Say's identity did not hold in a monetary economy. One of the clearest statements is by John Stuart Mill (1844). He argued that, in a world of barter, there could never be an excess of commodities: to offer something for sale was, by definition, to demand something of equal value. However, the existence of money allowed people to separate the acts of buying and selling. Whilst few people wanted money for its own sake, it was entirely possible that there would be times when people wished to sell goods but to postpone their consumption. The result would be a shortage of demand for commodities as a whole. To use the modern terminology, J.S. Mill accepted Say's equality. When discussing economic growth and capital accumulation, he argued that supply created demand: there could be no long-run shortage of aggregate demand. In the context of the cycle, on the other hand, there might be a shortage of demand. Depressions might involve a glut of all commodities because people, though they had the power to consume, were choosing to postpone their consumption, hoarding money instead of spending it.

J.S. Mill's argument that people might have the power to spend but choose not to use it undermines the strongest version of Say's Law. Neoclassical economists such as Marshall (see, for example, Marshall and Marshall, 1879) understood this argument. However, in their concern to rebut underconsumptionist arguments, they played down the implications of hoarding. The result was that Keynes was able to present Say's Law as the defining feature of 'classical' economics and his own theory as involving a radical break with it. However, in comparing his theory with the arguments of Malthus and Lauderdale in the general glut controversy (Keynes, 1936, pp. 358–71), Keynes overlooked the enormous theoretical differences.

ROGER E. BACKHOUSE

See also:

Classical Economics; Keynes's *General Theory*.

Bibliography

Baumol, W.J. (1977), 'Say's (at Least) Eight Laws, or What Say and James Mill May Really Have Meant', *Economica*, **44**, May, pp. 145–61.
Baumol, W.J. (1999), 'Say's Law', *Journal of Economic Perspectives*, **13**, Winter, pp. 195–204.
Becker, G.S. and W.J. Baumol (1952), 'The Classical Monetary Theory: The Outcome of the Discussion', *Economica*, **19**, November, pp. 355–76.
Beraud, A. (1992), 'Ricardo, Malthus, Say et les controverses de la "seconde génération"', in A. Beraud and G. Faccarello (eds), *Nouvelle histoire de la pensée économique*, Vol. 1: *Des Scolastiques aux Classiques*, Paris: Editions la Découverte, pp. 365–508
Blaug, M. (ed.) (1991), *Pioneers in Economics*, Vol. 15: *Jean-Baptiste Say (1776–1832)*, Aldershot, UK and Brookfield, US: Edward Elgar.
Hutchison, T.W. (1978), *On Revolutions and Progress in Economic Knowledge*, Cambridge: Cambridge University Press.
Jonsson, P.O. (1997), 'On Gluts, Effective Demand and the Meaning of Say's Law', *Eastern Economic Journal*, **20**, Spring, pp. 203–18.
Keynes, J.M. (1936), *The General Theory of Employment, Interest and Money*, London: Macmillan.
Marshall, A. and M.P. Marshall (1879), *The Economics of Industry*, London: Macmillan.
Mill, J.S. (1844), *Essays on Some Unsettled Questions of Political Economy*, London: John W. Parker; reprinted Bristol: Thoemmes Press, 1992.
O'Brien, D.P. (1975), *The Classical Economists*, Oxford: Clarendon Press.
Say, J.-B. (1971), *A Treatise on Political Economy*, New York: Augustus Kelley, trans. C.R. Prinsep.
Sowell, T. (1972), *Say's Law: An Historical Analysis*, Princeton: Princeton University Press.
Thweatt, W.O. (1979), 'Early Formulators of Say's Law', *Quarterly Review of Economics and Business*, **19**, Winter, pp. 79–96.
Thweatt, W.O. (1980), 'Baumol and James Mill on "Say's" Law of Markets', *Economica*, **47**, November, pp. 467–9.

Schools of Thought in Macroeconomics

To a much greater extent than microeconomics, macroeconomics contains alternative approaches sufficiently distinct to be viewed as competing schools of thought.

Macroeconomics has been divided into competing schools of thought ever since the field crystallized out of long-standing traditions of business cycle theory and monetary theory, with Keynes (1936) distinguishing Keynesian economics (with a role for government intervention to remedy unemployment due to insufficient aggregate demand) from classical economics (caricatured by Keynes as acceptance of Say's Law that 'supply creates its own demand'). Macroeconomists have often drawn eclectically on contributions from several schools, leading to predictions over the past half-century of the disappearance of distinct schools (for example, Solow *et al.*, 1997; Solow, 2000), but recognizably distinct approaches to aggregate economics persist (Phelps, 1990; Vercelli and Dimitri, 1992).

Keynesian economics dominated academic research and policy discussion for 25 years after World War II, in the form of what Paul Samuelson's textbook termed a 'neoclassical synthesis' between Keynesian macroeconomics and neoclassical microeconomics (so that, for example, Robert Solow contributed both to Keynesian short-run analysis and to long-run neoclassical growth theory). The Keynesian cross diagram, and the multiplier analysis associated with it, remain central to introductory economics textbooks, while the IS–LM diagram, in both closed and open economy versions, and the Phillips curve are still the basis of intermediate macroeconomics textbooks, emphasizing the role of aggregate demand in determining national income. Simultaneous inflation and rising unemployment in the early 1970s posed a challenge to the simple Keynesian cross, aggregate demand/aggregate supply model of the introductory textbooks, which prescribed demand stimulus in response to unemployment (a recessionary gap between actual and potential output) and demand contraction in response to inflation. Although the Lucas critique (that quantitative structural relationships among variables will change when the policy regime changes) has reduced the popularity of the large-scale simultaneous-equations macroeconometric models pioneered by American Keynesians such as Lawrence Klein, Project LINK continues to combine such national models into a world model (Hickman and Klein, 1998).

Monetarism, building on the pre-Keynesian tradition of the quantity theory of money, was developed by Milton Friedman and his students at the University of Chicago (Friedman, 1956), as well as by Karl Brunner and Allan Meltzer. In contrast to Keynesianism, monetarism stressed policy rules rather than discretion, the social costs of inflation rather than of unemployment, monetary rather than fiscal policy, and misguided government policy rather than volatile private investment as the source of instability. Together with their students, Friedman's Chicago colleagues Harry Johnson and Robert Mundell extended the monetary approach to the balance of payments and exchange rates. Friedman and Schwartz

(1963), the outstanding scholarly achievement of this school, marshalled historical evidence of the dominant influence of monetary changes on short-run output fluctuations, especially in the Great Depression of the 1930s (which Keynesians had regarded as evidence of the ineffectiveness of monetary policy). Friedman (1968) and Edmund Phelps argued that there is a natural rate of unemployment (voluntary investment in job search, consumption of leisure and household production) consistent with any correctly anticipated rate of inflation, and that people learn from forecast errors (adaptive expectations). Any deviation of unemployment above or below the natural rate would thus be the consequence of people being temporarily fooled while they learn how monetary shocks have affected the purchasing power of their wages. The natural rate hypothesis appealed especially to central bankers, absolving them of any responsibility for fighting unemployment beyond making their policy transparent by adopting a constant money growth rule.

Rules rather than discretion and the monetarist emphasis on controlling inflation have fared better than the constant money growth rule. That policy rule was introduced and then abandoned in Britain, Canada and the United States, in the face of Goodhart's law: targeting a particular monetary aggregate induces financial innovation that changes the relationship of that aggregate to other monetary aggregates and nominal income (DeLong, 2000). Similarly, the more general idea that expectations should be modelled as endogenous fared better than the adaptive expectations hypothesis. Adaptive expectations implied that people make forecasting mistakes forever, with the mistakes continually getting smaller, and introduced a disquieting element of arbitrariness, since adaptive expectations of the price level (associated with Irving Fisher) are not equivalent to adaptive expectations of the inflation rate (Friedman,1968) or of the rate of change of the inflation rate. Consequently, new classical economists such as Robert Lucas (1981) assumed rational expectations (no systematic mistakes by agents) in place of adaptive expectations in combination with a variant of Friedman's natural rate hypothesis (a link that led Tobin to refer to new classical economics as monetarism, mark II). However, some monetarists remain reluctant to accept instantaneous, or strong form, rational expectations (gathering and processing all relevant information is costless and instantaneous), and the empirical superiority of rational over adaptive expectations in explaining, for example, the term structure of interest rates continues to be subject to debate.

According to the monetary misperceptions stream of new classical economics (Lucas and Sargent, 1981; Hoover, 1992), no systematic aggregate demand policy will have real effects, because any systematic policy rule will be fully anticipated, with an observed upward-sloping aggregate supply curve resulting solely from unpredictable random demand shocks (the Lucas 'surprise' supply function). Mishkin (1983), testing the joint hypotheses of rationality and neutrality, found evidence that anticipated aggregate demand has real effects, contrary to the Lucas supply function. Persistence of output fluctuations was also difficult to explain within a theory that held that nominal shocks have no effect once they are known.

New classical economics stresses consistent microeconomic foundations in optimization by rational individuals, in contrast to the allegedly arbitrary aggregate functions of Keynesianism and monetarism (although optimizing micro foundations had been provided for particular sectors by Friedman's permanent income hypothesis and Modigliani's life cycle hypothesis for consumption, Jorgensen for investment, and Allais, Baumol and Tobin for money demand). However, Geweke (1985) and Kirman (1992) show that a wide class of new classical models is equally arbitrary in deriving microeconomic foundations by the assumption of representative agents (abstracting from heterogeneity of agents and requiring that there be no trade in equilibrium). Farmer (1999) and Guesnerie (2001) show that equilibrium paths may not be unique in rational expectations models, with outcomes subject to self-fulfilling prophecies or sun-spots (intrinsically irrelevant variables that affect expectations). New classical concern for endogeneity of expectations and for consistent, optimizing microeconomic foundations (manifested for example in the Lucas critique) has contributed to improving macroeconomic modelling and theorizing, but is not sufficient to establish policy ineffectiveness propositions or uniqueness of equilibrium paths.

Related to new classical economics, real business cycle theory (Plosser, 1989) interprets fluctuations of output and employment as driven by technology shocks that shift the aggregate supply schedule and the marginal product of labour schedule (the labour demand curve). This implies a procyclical pattern of real wages that is no more observable in the data than is the countercyclical pattern of real wages implied by Keynes (1936, ch. 2) and by the monetary misperceptions model of Lucas (1981). To replicate observed employment shifts by shocks to aggregate supply and labour demand requires assuming labour supply to be considerably more elastic than it is usually estimated to be by labour economists. Real business cycle theorists often rely on calibration rather than estimation, and have been criticized for theory ahead of measurement (Mankiw, 1989). A somewhat related approach, Phelps's *Structural Slumps* (1994), models shifts of the natural rate of unemployment.

The endogenous growth theory of Paul Romer, Lucas, Barro and Sala-i-Martin (1994), and Aghion and Howitt (1998) has affinities to real business cycle theory, with emphasis on stochastic trend rather than on fluctuations, and with attention to investment in research and development and in human capital formation. Aghion and Howitt emphasize Schumpeterian 'creative destruction', with new technologies reducing the value of physical and human capital embodying existing technologies. With the important exception of Grossman and Helpman (1991), endogenous growth theory has not developed open-economy extensions comparable to Keynesian and monetarist economics. Richard Nelson (1996) argues that the elements of this 'new growth theory' are not all that new, and the emphasis in this literature on formalization within the canons of general equilibrium theory has limited empirical understanding of growth as a disequilibrium process, as well as narrowing the institutional frameworks considered.

New Keynesian economics (Mankiw and Romer, 1991; Mankiw *et al.*, 1993) shares the new classical concern with explicit microeconomic foundations, but looks to imperfect markets to derive Keynesian results about demand shocks moving the economy between alternative, Pareto-ranked equilibria and about the scope for government stabilization policy. The leading strand within new Keynesian economics emphasizes asymmetric information and menu costs to explain the existence of nominal rigidities without assuming any irrationality on the part of agents. This strand of new Keynesian economics has largely absorbed a European tradition of examining the consequences of such nominal rigidities in general equilibrium models (Malinvaud, 1977; Benassy, 1986; Drèze, 1991). A few daring scholars have attempted to learn why wages and prices are sticky by asking wage and price setters (Blinder *et al.*, 1997; Bewley, 2000). Solow (1990) studies the labour market as a social institution, and considers how this may contribute to wage rigidity. Another strand of new Keynesian economics posits that increased wage and price flexibility might be destabilizing (also a theme of such a professed 'Old Keynesian' as James Tobin, in Mankiw *et al.*, 1993). Russell Cooper (1998) brings game theoretic analysis of strategic complementarities to bear on the question of why labour markets may fail to clear.

Post Keynesian economics, drawing on the contributions of Keynes's Cambridge followers Joan Robinson, Richard Kahn and Nicholas Kaldor, holds that the neoclassical synthesis and new Keynesian economics neglect Keynes's insights into fundamental uncertainty and money supply endogeneity and the work on income distribution, effective demand, mark-up pricing and the political business cycle of Keynes's younger contemporary Michal Kalecki (see Hewitson, 1995 for a survey of Post Keynesian monetary economics). Taking a self-consciously critical perspective outside the mainstream of the profession, Post Keynesian economics has less influence than new classical or new Keynesian economics. Perhaps the most productive area of Post Keynesian economics is work on the fragility of the financial system in the tradition of Hyman Minsky (Fazzari and Papadimitriou, 1992), which draws on the insights of Keynes and Fisher in ways that parallel the later work of James Tobin. Overlapping with Post Keynesian work based on Kalecki, the Marxian school of economics (Zarembka, 1999) takes a stand further outside the mainstream of economics, with the French regulation school its most active strand on macroeconomic issues. At the opposite end of the political spectrum, Austrian trade cycle theorists have revived Ludwig von Mises's and Friedrich Hayek's view of economic fluctuations as a disequilibrium process of entrepreneurial innovation and discovery.

Ever since Samuelson's neoclassical synthesis, the disappearance of schools of thought in macroeconomics has been predicted, with the valuable parts of each approach absorbed by the discipline. Nonetheless, distinguishable schools of thought remain much more evident in macroeconomics than in microeconomics.

ROBERT W. DIMAND

See also:

Adaptive Expectations; AD–AS Model; Balance of Payments: Keynesian Approach; Balance of Payments: Monetary Approach; Business Cycles: Austrian, Approach; Business Cycles: Keynesian Approach; Business Cycles: Monetarist Approach; Business Cycles: New Classical Approach: Business Cycles: Political Business Cycle Approach; Business Cycles: Real Business Cycle Approach; Classical Economics; Demand for Money: Friedman's Approach; Demand for Money: Keynesian Approach; Endogenous Growth Theory; Exchange Rate Determination: Monetary Approach; Friedman, Milton; Great Depression; IS–LM Model; Keynes, John Maynard; Keynesian Cross; Keynesian Economics; Life Cycle Hypothesis; Lucas Critique; Lucas, Robert E. Jr; Macroeconometric Models; Marxian Macroeconomics: An Overview; Marxian Macroeconomics: Some Key Relationships; Modigliani, Franco; Monetarism; Multiplier; Natural Rate of Unemployment; Neoclassical Growth Model; Neoclassical Synthesis; New Classical Economics; New Keynesian Economics; New Political Macroeconomics; Nominal Rigidity; Permanent Income Hypothesis; Phillips Curve; Policy Ineffectiveness Proposition; Post Keynesian Economics; Quantity Theory of Money; Rational Expectations; Real Rigidity; Representative Agent Model; Rules versus Discretion; Samuelson, Paul A.; Solow, Robert M.; Supply-side Economics; Tobin, James.

Bibliography

Aghion, P. and P. Howitt (1998), *Endogenous Growth Theory*, Cambridge, MA: MIT Press.
Barro, R.J. and X. Sala-i-Martin (1994), *Economic Growth*, New York: McGraw-Hill.
Benassy, J.-P. (1986), *Macroeconomics: An Introduction to the Non-Walrasian Approach*, Orlando, FL: Academic Press.
Bewley, T. (2000), *Why Wages Don't Fall During a Recession*, Cambridge, MA: Harvard University Press.
Blinder, A.S., E. Canetti, D. Lebow and J. Rudd (1997), *Price Stickiness in the United States: A Survey Approach*, New York: Russell Sage Foundation.
Cooper, R.W. (1998), *Coordination Games: Complementarities and Macroeconomics*, Cambridge, UK: Cambridge University Press.
DeLong, J.B. (2000), 'The Triumph of Monetarism?', *Journal of Economic Perspectives*, **14**, Winter, pp. 83–94.

Drèze, J.H. (1991), *Underemployment Equilibria: Essays in Theory, Econometrics and Policy*, Cambridge: Cambridge University Press.

Eisner, R. (1994), *The Misunderstood Economy: What Counts and How to Count It*, Boston: Harvard Business School Press.

Farmer, R.E.A. (1999), *Macroeconomics of Self-Fulfilling Prophecies*, 2nd edn, Cambridge, MA: MIT Press.

Fazzari, S. and D.B. Papadimitriou (eds) (1992), *Financial Conditions and Macroeconomic Performance: Essays in Honor of Hyman P. Minsky*, Armonk, NY: M.E. Sharpe.

Friedman, M. (ed.) (1956), *Studies in the Quantity Theory of Money*, Chicago: University of Chicago Press.

Friedman, M. (1968), 'The Role of Monetary Policy', *American Economic Review*, **58**, March, pp. 1–17, also in Snowdon and Vane (eds) (1997).

Friedman, M. and A.J. Schwartz (1963), *A Monetary History of the United States. 1867–1960*, Princeton, NJ: Princeton University Press for National Bureau of Economic Research.

Geweke, J. (1985), 'Macroeconometric Modeling and the Theory of Representative Agents', *American Economic Review*, **75**, May, pp. 206–10.

Grossman, G. and E. Helpman (1991), *Innovation and Growth in the World Economy*, Cambridge, MA: MIT Press.

Guesnerie, R. (2001), *Assessing Rational Expectations: Sunspot Multiplicity and Economic Fluctuations*, Cambridge, MA: MIT Press.

Hewitson, G. (1995), 'Post Keynesian Monetary Theory: Some Issues', *Journal of Economic Surveys*, **9**, September, pp. 285–310.

Hickman, B.G. and L.R. Klein (eds) (1998), *LINK Proceedings 1991, 1992: Selected Papers From Meetings in Moscow, 1991, and Ankara, 1992*, River Edge, NJ: World Scientific.

Honkapohja, S. (ed.) (1989), '90th Anniversary Symposium: Whither Macroeconomics?', *Scandinavian Journal of Economics*, **91**, June, pp. 207–516.

Hoover, K.D. (ed.) (1992), *The New Classical Macroeconomics*, 3 vols, Aldershot, UK, and Brookfield, US: Edward Elgar.

Keynes, J.M. (1936), *The General Theory of Employment, Interest and Money*, London: Macmillan.

Kirman, A.P. (1992), 'Whom or What Does the Representative Individual Represent?', *Journal of Economic Perspectives*, **6**, Spring, pp. 117–36.

Lucas, R.E. Jr (1981), *Studies in Business Cycle Theory*, Cambridge, MA: MIT Press.

Lucas, R.E. Jr and T. J. Sargent (eds) (1981), *Rational Expectations and Econometric Practice*, 2 vols, Minneapolis: University of Minnesota Press.

Malinvaud, E. (1977), *The Theory of Unemployment Reconsidered*, Oxford: Basil Blackwell.

Mankiw, N.G. (1989), 'Real Business Cycles: A New Keynesian Perspective', *Journal of Economic Perspectives*, **3**, Summer, pp. 79–90; also in Snowdon and Vane (eds) (1997).

Mankiw, N.G. and D. Romer (eds) (1991), *New Keynesian Economics*, 2 vols, Cambridge, MA: MIT Press.

Mankiw, N.G., D. Romer, B. Greenwald, J. Stiglitz, J. Tobin and R.G. King (1993), 'Symposium: Keynesian Economics Today', *Journal of Economic Perspectives*, **7**, Winter, pp. 3–82; Greenwald and Stiglitz and Tobin, also in Snowdon and Vane (eds) (1997).

Mishkin, F.S. (1983), *A Rational Expectations Approach to Macroeconometrics: Testing Policy Ineffectiveness and Efficient-Markets Models*, Chicago: University of Chicago Press.

Nelson, R.R. (1996), *The Sources of Economic Growth*, Cambridge, MA: Harvard University Press.

Phelps, E.S. (1990), *Seven Schools of Macroeconomic Thought*, Oxford: Clarendon Press.

Phelps, E.S. (1994), *Structural Slumps: The Modern Equilibrium Theory of Unemployment, Interest and Assets*, Cambridge, MA: Harvard University Press.

Plosser, C.I. (1989), 'Understanding Real Business Cycles', *Journal of Economic Perspectives*, **3**, Summer, pp. 51–77; also in Snowdon and Vane (eds) (1997).

Snowdon, B. and H.R. Vane (eds) (1997), *A Macroeconomics Reader*, London and New York: Routledge.

Solow, R.M. (1990), *The Labor Market as a Social Institution*, Cambridge, MA: Blackwell.

Solow, R.M. (2000), 'Toward a Macroeconomics of the Medium-Run', *Journal of Economic Perspectives*, **14**, Winter, pp. 151–8.
Solow, R.M., J.B. Taylor, M. Eichenbaum, A.S. Blinder and O. Blanchard (1997) 'Is There a Core of Practical Macroeconomics We Should All Believe In?', *American Economic Review: Papers and Proceedings*, **87**, May, pp. 230–46.
Taylor, J.B. and M. Woodford (eds) (1999), *Handbook of Macroeconomics*, 3 vols, Amsterdam: Elsevier/North-Holland.
Vercelli, A. and N. Dimitri (eds) (1992), *Macroeconomics: A Survey of Research Strategies*, Oxford: Oxford University Press.
Zarembka, P. (ed.) (1999), *Economic Theory of Capitalism and Its Crises*, vol. 17 of *Research in Political Economy*, Amsterdam: Elsevier/North-Holland.

Schumpeter, Joseph A. (1883–1950)

Joseph Schumpeter (b.1883, Triesch, Austro-Hungary, now Czech Republic) obtained his doctorate of law from the University of Vienna in 1906. His main posts included Teacher at the University of Czernowitz, 1909–11; Professor of Political Economy at the University of Graz, 1911–18; Austrian Minister of Finance, 1919–20; President of the Biederman Bank, 1920–24; Professor of Economics at the University of Bonn, 1925–32; and Professor at Harvard University, 1932–50. In 1949, he became the first non-American to be elected president of the American Economic Association. He is best known for his influential work on business cycles, in which he distinguished different types of cycles and their causes; and economic development, in particular his focus on the importance of entrepreneurship and innovation to the long-term development and success of capitalism. His best known books include *The Theory of Economic Development* (first published in 1912; Harvard University Press, 1954); *Business Cycles: A Theoretical, Historical and Statistical Analysis of the Capitalist Process* (McGraw-Hill, 1939); *Capitalism, Socialism and Democracy* (Harper, 1942); and *History of Economic Analysis* (Oxford University Press, 1954).

See also:

American Economic Association.

Schwartz, Anna J.

Anna Schwartz (b.1915, New York City, USA) obtained her BA from Barnard College in 1934 and her MA (1935) and PhD (1964) from Columbia University. Her main past posts have included Research Associate at Columbia University Social Science Research Council, 1936–41; and Staff Director of the US Gold Commission, 1981–2. Since

1941 she has been a Research Associate at the National Bureau of Economic Research. She is best known for her influential work, in collaboration with Milton Friedman, on money and business cycles and monetary policy. Her best known books include: *A Monetary History of the United States, 1867–1960* (co-authored with M. Friedman) (Princeton University Press, 1963); *Monetary Statistics of the United States* (co-authored with M. Friedman) (Columbia University Press, 1970); and *Monetary Trends in the United States and the United Kingdom: Their Relation to Income, Prices, and Interest Rates, 1867–1975* (co-authored with M. Friedman) (University of Chicago Press, 1982). Her best known articles include 'Money and Business Cycles' (co-authored with M. Friedman) (*Review of Economics and Statistics*, **45**, February 1963); and 'Understanding 1929–1933', in K. Brunner (ed.), *The Great Depression Revisited* (Martinus Nijhoff, 1981).

See also:

Business Cycles: Monetarist Approach; Friedman, Milton; National Bureau of Economic Research.

Search Unemployment

See:

Frictional Unemployment.

Seasonal Unemployment

Unemployment that occurs because of seasonal fluctuations in the supply of or demand for labour in certain industries, most notably the agricultural, construction and tourist industries.

Seigniorage

See:

Inflation Tax.

Shackle, George L.S. (1903–92)

George Shackle (b.1903, Cambridge, England) obtained his BA (1931) and PhD (1937) from the University of London. His main posts included member of the wartime statistical research committee assembled by Winston Churchill, 1939–45; member of the Economic Section of the Cabinet Office, 1945–50; Reader at the University of Leeds, 1950–51; and the Brunner Professor of Economic Science at the University of Liverpool, 1951–69. He is best known for his work on the role of expectations and uncertainty in decision making. His best known books include *Expectations, Investment and Income* (Oxford University Press, 1938, 1968); *Expectation in Economics* (Cambridge University Press, 1949, 1952); *Time in Economics* (North-Holland, 1958); *A Scheme of Economic Theory* (Cambridge University Press, 1965); *The Years of High Theory: Invention and Tradition in Economic Thought, 1926–1939* (Cambridge University Press, 1967); *Epistemics and Economics* (Cambridge University Press, 1972); and *Keynesian Kaleidics* (Edinburgh University Press, 1974).

Shirking Model

A model which suggests that in many occupations workers can exercise considerable discretion with respect to how well they perform their job, and that in consequence there is a real possibility that some workers will shirk their work effort. Such behaviour may be difficult to detect and/or costly to monitor, particularly where team work characterizes the workplace. The threat of dismissal will not be an effective deterrent to shirking in the labour market where workers can quickly find a job at the same wage rate. If, however, a firm pays a wage in excess of that available elsewhere, or if there is unemployment, there will be an incentive for workers not to shirk since, if they are caught shirking and are subsequently dismissed, they may experience a wage cut, or may not readily find employment elsewhere. In other words, by paying an efficiency wage above the market-clearing real wage, firms will discourage shirking and raise worker productivity. Not only will an efficiency wage act as a disciplinary device but it will also allow firms to reduce costs in monitoring workers' performance.

See also:
Efficiency Wage Theory.

Shoe Leather Costs

The costs, in time and effort, incurred in economizing on holdings of money balances. As no interest is paid on money balances (notes and coin), when the rate of inflation rises the opportunity cost of holding cash increases. In consequence, people have an incentive to make more trips to the bank, and other financial institutions, to withdraw cash as and when needed for transactions.

See also:

Inflation: Costs of.

Short-run Phillips Curve

The relationship between inflation and unemployment that exists for a given expected rate of inflation.

See also:

Expectations-augmented Phillips Curve; Phillips Curve.

Slump

The period of rapid contraction before the movement of output from trend begins to flatten out near the bottom of the business cycle.

See also:

Business Cycle.

Solow, Robert M.

In 1987, when Robert Solow became the fifteenth American (and third MIT staff member) to receive the Nobel Memorial Prize in Economics, the Swedish Academy of Science's citation was 'for his contributions to the theory of economic growth' (Prescott, 1988). These days, Solow prefers to emphasize his contributions to aggregative economics, observing in his entry in Blaug's *Who's Who in Economics* (1999, p. 1050) that 'Even my work on the economics of non-renewable resources originated from curiosity about the extent to which gradual resource scarcity becomes a drag on economic growth.'

Whilst it is as a growth economist that his reputation as a macroeconomist rests primarily, growth and capital theory were the springboard for him to take abstract concepts of equilibrium over time to add tools to economics' engine of analysis which he, and others, have then applied most productively to Keynesian macrodynamics, the economics of exhaustible resources, and to urban and labour economics. An indication of his significance to the discipline and the rarity of his gifts is given by Dixit (1990, p. 17) in an essay, one in a series contributed by his friends and former students, which uses a by now standard rhetorical device for economists: 'How many professors does it take to change a light bulb? The answer is that no number will suffice, because professors don't change light bulbs. They go on using the bulb they screwed in when they were graduate students, and when that burns out, they just sit in the dark. As Paul Samuelson [the first American and first MIT Nobel economics laureate] would say, Bob Solow is the exception that improves the rule. He has made a career out of *manufacturing* new light bulbs for himself and other professors to use. What is more, his bulbs last a very long time.'

With such wide interests and influence, Solow is thus a rare theorist and consequently difficult to categorize; and, perhaps, particularly difficult in this respect because, unlike many other Nobel laureates, he has been very resistant to efforts to tease out of him a life philosophy as he worries about the cult of personality in economics, the scarcity value of true rigorous economics research and about the propensity of economic ideas 'to turn to mush' (Solow, 1989, 1992, 1995, 2000a).

Biography
Born in Brooklyn, New York, in August 1924 to second generation immigrants, Solow admits to being a 'child of the depression' economist, although when he entered Harvard in 1940 he had no particular intention of studying economics, let alone becoming an economist. Like many also of that generation, his undergraduate studies were interrupted by war service: the first of three formative influences to which he admits. The other two were his service on the Council of Economic Advisers (1961–2) and his membership since 1950 of the MIT Economics Department, to which he moved after attaining his Harvard BA (1947), MA (1949) and PhD (1951) for a thesis modelling the dynamics of income distribution. Initially an assistant professor of statistics, he became a full professor of economics in 1958 and an Institute professor in 1973. The Nobel apart, notable honours along the way include the David A. Wells Prize (1951, for his PhD, never published), the John Bates Clark Medal (1961), the Presidencies of the Econometric Society (1964) and the American Economic Association (1979), Fellowships of the American Academy of Arts and Sciences and of the British Academy, visiting professorships and numerous honorary degrees. For five years he was a member, then chairman, of the Federal Reserve Bank in Boston, but, as with his CEA experience, day-to-day policy advice was not – as he would no doubt say – his comparative advantage.

Growth and capital
His Nobel citation listed three of his early papers (Solow, 1956, 1957, 1960). The first of these established the growth model, the second attempted empirical estimates of the contributions of various production factors to growth which, together with the third, laid the foundations for what quickly became (with Kendrick, 1961, and Denison, 1962) the growth-accounting or sources-of-growth method of analysis which continues today, indeed has become a veritable industry testing the conditional convergence hypothesis.

Solow (1956) was the first neoclassical version of the Harrod–Domar model. With an aggregate production function that assumed constant returns to scale, diminishing returns to each of two inputs and a positive elasticity of factor substitution between them, when combined with a constant-saving-rate rule, it produced a simple general equilibrium model of the economy. This was to prove enormously fertile for further theorizing and empirical testing: it opened up a whole field of study, via a framework which was soon accepted as the profession's common property, whilst the model appeared to explain parsimoniously the essential features of US economic growth. This latter property was opened up in the companion piece (Solow, 1957) which estimated that some seven-eighths of the US growth in output per worker (between 1909 and 1949) was accounted for by changes in the technology coefficient (later named the Solow residual) and only one-eighth by increases in fixed capital per worker. Contemporaneously, in cooperation with Dorfman and Samuelson, he began to make contributions to the optimal growth literature and to devote resources to expounding recent developments for the profession (Dorfman *et al.*, 1958; also Solow, 1970, 2000b, an intermediate textbook – the latter a new edition, including reflections on the development of growth theory since his pioneering work of the 1950s). Resulting work in the 1960s was in developing vintage growth models, in which he made important contributions to capital theory (Solow, 1963) but, of course, also, he became embroiled (with Samuelson, *contra* Joan Robinson and Kaldor) in the rather sterile Cambridge capital controversy. This also marked something of a transitional period as he developed parallel interests in macroeconomics and policy.

Macroeconomics and policy
Beginning with Samuelson and Solow (1960), which if it did not coin, did at least domesticate the phrase 'the Phillips curve', and was the first to examine US data, he has been a frequent contributor to debates about Keynesian stabilization policies. Since his Wicksell lecture (Solow, 1964), the failure of market forces to clear the labour market has been central to

his account of unemployment, whilst in Solow and Stiglitz (1968) he anticipated many later concerns with the short-run dynamics of employment and
output. However, it is Blinder and Solow (1974) which is his best known
macroeconomic paper as this made an important contribution to understanding the effects of the size of government debt on demand via crowding out.

Defining himself as an eclectic Keynesian, and having joined battle once
in the capital controversy, his predisposition to polemicism was then displayed in defending Keynesianism (albeit never the fashionable hydraulic
variant of the time) against the attacks of, first, the monetarists and, lat-
terly, the new classical economists. His American Economic Association
presidential address (Solow, 1980) on theories of unemployment was
important with respect to both, reiterating strongly his commitment to
Keynesian analysis when labour markets are not in equilibrium and his
opposition to the developing conservative macroeconomic policies of the
Reagan–Thatcher years. Elsewhere he has been and continues to be a
fervent opponent of 'natural rate' analyses, notably in his exploration of
the labour market as a social institution (Solow, 1990; Solow and Taylor,
1998). These interests widened in the 1990s with joint work criticizing the
welfare-reducing welfare reform policies of the Clinton administration
(Solow and Gutmann, 1998). Finally, the New Keynesians have also been
a target for his pugilistic scepticism: 'to my eye . . . a mixed bag. Its aims are
right and its techniques are nice. But sometimes the particular facts of life
it chooses to emphasize seem too farfetched or insignificant to bear the
weight that is placed upon them' (Solow, 1995, p. 198). Nevertheless his
(1979) paper was an important and influential contribution to new
Keynesian efficiency wage theory.

From Solow residual to Solow paradox
Although he has indicated that 'involvement in growth theory can be seen
as (and really was) an integral part of my education in macroeconomics'
(1995, p. 193), Solow has become to growth theory what Keynes is to
macroeconomic theory and policy. From the golden age of growth theory
of the 1960s through to the claims made for endogenous growth theory and
the 'new economy' at the beginning of the new millennium, it is the combination of Solow's theoretical contributions with his scepticism about fads
and fashions in macroeconomics that imbues his work with particular significance. It is, of course, somewhat ironic that his work has inspired so
many growth accounting (and now conditional convergence) exercises
when he has such deep reservations about their value in face of the risks
posed by omitted variables and possible reverse causations; ironic also that
his throwaway remark, that 'You can see the computer age everywhere these

days, except in the productivity statistics', should have been elevated to the status of Solow paradox when the US economy was about to embark upon one of its most substantial and sustained business cycle upturns of the twentieth century on the back of massive investments in productivity-enhancing information and communication technologies (and some rectification of the measurement errors which had previously understated the role of those technologies). (For an assessment of the paradox, see Triplett, 1999). Of course, as Solow would be one of the first to admit, economics is not a Science but should always aspire to be science.

ROGER MIDDLETON

See also:

American Economic Association; Council of Economic Advisers; Econometric Society; Growth Accounting; John Bates Clark Medal; Keynesian Economics; Neoclassical Growth Model; Nobel Prize in Economics.

Bibliography

Blaug, M. (ed.) (1999), *Who's Who in Economics*, 3rd edn, Cheltenham, UK and Northampton, MA, USA: Edward Elgar.
Blinder, A.S. and R.M. Solow (1974), 'Analytical Foundations of Fiscal Policy', in A.S. Blinder *et al.* (eds), *The Economics of Public Finance*, Washington, DC: Brookings Institution.
Denison, E F. (1962), *The Sources of Economic Growth in the United States and the Alternatives Before Us,* New York: Committee for Economic Development.
Dixit, A. (1990), 'Growth Theory after Thirty Years', in P. Diamond (ed.), *Growth/ Productivity/Unemployment: Essays to Celebrate Bob Solow's Birthday*, Cambridge, MA: MIT Press.
Dorfman, R., P.A. Samuelson and R.M. Solow (1958), *Linear Programming and Economic Analysis*, New York: McGraw-Hill.
Kendrick, J.W. (1961), *Productivity Trends in the United States*, Princeton, NJ: Princeton University Press.
Prescott, E.C. (1988), 'Robert M. Solow's Neoclassical Growth Model: An Influential Contribution to Economics', *Scandinavian Journal of Economics*, **90**, March, pp. 7–12.
Samuelson, P.A. and R.M. Solow (1960), 'Analytical Aspects of Anti-Inflation Policy', *American Economic Review*, **50**, May, pp. 177–94.
Solow, R.M. (1956), 'A Contribution to the Theory of Economic Growth', *Quarterly Journal of Economics*, **70**, February, pp. 65–94.
Solow, R.M. (1957), 'Technical Change and the Aggregate Production Function', *Review of Economics and Statistics*, **39**, August, pp. 312–20.
Solow, R.M. (1960), 'Investment and Technical Progress', in K.J. Arrow *et al.* (eds), *Mathematical Methods in the Social Sciences*, Stanford, CA: Stanford University Press.
Solow, R.M. (1963), *Capital Theory and the Rate of Return*, Amsterdam: North-Holland.
Solow, R.M. (1964), *The Nature and Sources of Unemployment in the United States*, Stockholm: Almqvist and Wicksell.
Solow, R.M. (1970), *Growth Theory: An Exposition*, Oxford: Clarendon Press.
Solow, R.M. (1979), 'Another Possible Source of Wage Stickiness', *Journal of Macroeconomics*, **1**, Winter, pp. 79–82.
Solow, R.M. (1980), 'On Theories of Unemployment', *American Economic Review*, **70**, March, pp. 1–10.
Solow, R.M. (1987), 'We'd Better Watch Out', *New York Times*, Book Review section, 12 July, p. 36.

Solow, R.M. (1989), 'How Economic Ideas Turn to Mush', in D.C. Colander and A.W. Coats (eds), *The Spread of Economic Ideas*, Cambridge: Cambridge University Press.
Solow, R.M. (1990), *The Labour Market as a Social Institution*, Oxford: Basil Blackwell.
Solow, R.M. (1992), 'Notes on Coping', in M. Szenberg (ed.), *Eminent Economists: Their Life Philosophies*, Cambridge: Cambridge University Press.
Solow, R.M. (1995), 'My Evolution as an Economist', in W. Breit and R.W. Spencer (eds), *Lives of the Laureates: Thirteen Nobel Economists*, 3rd edn, Cambridge, MA: MIT Press.
Solow, R.M. (2000a), 'Three Nobel Laureates on the State of Economics', *Challenge*, **43**, January–February, pp. 6–13.
Solow, R.M. (2000b), *Growth Theory: An Exposition*, 2nd edn, Oxford: Oxford University Press.
Solow, R.M. and A. Gutmann (eds) (1998), *Work and Welfare*, Princeton, NJ: Princeton University Press.
Solow, R.M. and J.E. Stiglitz (1968), 'Output, Employment and Wages in the Short Run', *Quarterly Journal of Economics*, **82**, November, pp. 537–60.
Solow, R.M. and J.B. Taylor (1998), *Inflation, Unemployment and Monetary Policy*, Cambridge, MA: MIT Press.
Triplett, J.E. (1999), 'The Solow Productivity Paradox: What do Computers do to Productivity?', *Canadian Journal of Economics*, **32**, April, pp. 309–34.

Speculative Balances

Money held as a store of wealth because people are uncertain about the return from other forms (such as bonds) in which they can hold their wealth.

See also:

Demand for Money: Keynesian Approach.

Speculative Bubbles

A speculative bubble occurs when an asset's price movements do not reflect changes in the asset's fundamental value, where the fundamental value is the discounted value of future expected returns from that asset. Kindleberger (1996) shows that economic history is littered with examples of speculative bubbles; to name just a few: the Dutch excitement over tulip bubbles during the seventeenth century (Tulipmania), the South Sea Bubble of the eighteenth century, the spectacular stock market crashes of 1929 and 1987, and the South East Asian financial crises of 1997/8.

Keynes was one of the first modern economists to analyse speculative behaviour within stock markets. He argued that, whilst financial markets do provide much needed liquidity, uncertainty compromises rational decision making. So professional speculators are unlikely to make profits from forecasting the likely profitability of financial assets; instead they will focus on outwitting the crowd and second-guessing public opinion. In addition, under conditions of uncertainty, amateur speculators will be unsure of their own judgments of the likely worth of the assets they are holding and therefore will tend to look to others in forming their judgments. This means that, in times of uncertainty when the state of confidence is low, the stock market becomes volatile, vulnerable and fragile. Movements in asset prices will be dictated by herd instincts and conventional behaviour. Keynes argues that speculation can bestow some benefits in capitalist economies as it is the inevitable by-product of liquid financial markets: if speculation is a bubble on the steady stream enterprise then the job of the stock market will be well done. But if speculation becomes a whirlpool, then uncertainty will feed upon itself. Keynes argues that financial markets will have a crucial impact on fixed asset investment, employment and unemployment and his ideas about the real effects of speculation have been developed in the models of Minsky (1982), Tobin (1969), Davidson (1972/1978, 1998) and Kaldor (1939), amongst many others. Shleifer (2000) presents a twenty-first-century version of Keynes's ideas in which he argues that the standard postulates of the mainstream financial literature, that is, the rational expectations hypothesis and efficient market hypothesis, have limited relevance to modern financial markets.

After Keynes, a number of economists tried to explain speculative episodes as *rational* phenomena. For example, Garber (1989, 1990) and Flood and Garber (1980) argued against the idea that speculative bubbles were truly speculative; instead, they argued that asset price bubbles reflect changes in the fundamental values of assets. However, these analyses were unconvincing defences of rational speculation because it seemed unlikely that changes in fundamental values could explain large yet ephemeral fluctuations in asset prices. The defence of speculation as a rational phenomenon gained credence with Blanchard and Watson's (1982) analysis of speculation that outlined circumstances in which speculative bubbles could emerge within a rational expectations world. Defending this position is difficult because the strict version of the efficient markets hypothesis states that asset prices fully reflect all available information and therefore provide an unbiased measure of the fundamental value of an asset. This approach seems to preclude the existence of rational bubbles. However, assuming rational expectations and starting with a weak version of the efficient markets hypothesis (that is, that no arbitrage opportunities exist), Blanchard and Watson showed that a number of possible equilibrium paths are possible. Only one of these equilibrium paths will track movements in the fundamental value of an asset and Blanchard and Watson therefore concluded that there were a large number of rational paths that were consistent with movements away from fundamental values.

In other words, Blanchard and Watson were arguing that there are a large number of speculative paths that are consistent with rational expectations and no arbitrage. This is because, in the case of stock markets, rational speculators realize that there are two opportunities for making money: first, returns from the assets such as dividends; and second, prospects for capital gains. In real-world asset markets, the latter is likely to predominate. Given liquid asset markets, for each period of time, rational agents will balance the probability of a speculative bubble growing against the probability of the bubble bursting. They will judge that the probability of a bubble continuing is relatively high if that bubble is short-lived and if the asset price has not deviated too far away from its fundamental value. In contrast, they will judge that the probability of the bubble bursting is relatively large if the bubble is old and big. So, even if rational agents know that the price of an asset is far away from the asset's fundamental value, they will continue to hold financial assets if they estimate that the probability of a bubble continuing is relatively high.

Topol (1991) relaxes the model presented by Blanchard and Watson and describes a world in which people are 'weakly rational'. Information constraints will mean that people will not concentrate solely on their own judgments of the fundamental value of assets. Instead they weight their own judgments together with information about other people's judgments as reflected in the asset prices paid by other agents. This is rational in a world of asymmetric information because other people may have access to better private information about the future value of assets. This mimicking behaviour means that changes in asset prices are contagious and financial investors exhibit herding behaviour. Topol shows that, under conditions of increasing uncertainty, people are more likely to look to other traders in deciding about asset prices, and their judgments of the 'efficient price' of an asset, that is, its fundamental value, are accorded a lower weight the higher is the degree of uncertainty. In more certain times, people are more likely to trust their own judgments and the asset prices paid by others are given less weight. In a world of completely symmetric information and no uncertainty, people are not forced to copy each other and the bubble collapses. So Topol argues that the key propagation mechanism in speculative episodes is mimicry.

Blanchard and Watson's analysis describes a world of rational representative agents. Topol analyses speculative bubbles in a world in which people are weakly rational: they do not all have access to the same information set and are therefore forced to copy each other. The key difference between speculative bubbles in Keynes's, Topol's and Blanchard and Watson's analyses is in the description of behaviour. In a world of symmetric information and strong rationality, Topol's model converts into Blanchard and Watson's model. In contrast, in a world of endemic uncertainty, there are numerous resonances between Topol's model and Keynes's analysis.

A large number of empirical analyses of speculative episodes have been conducted; for example, see Neal (1996), Garber (1989, 1990), Shleifer and Summers (1990), White (1990) and Flood and Hodrick (1990). However, as shown above, the range of theoretical explanations for speculative bubbles is wide. Speculative bubbles are consistent with a wide range of behaviours, from strictly rational to completely irrational behaviour. Therefore, it is difficult to establish the relative validity of the various theories because it is impossible to assess, at least using standard statistical techniques, whether or not people are being rational when they indulge in speculative behaviour. For this reason, some researchers have adopted a survey/questionnaire approach (for example, see Shiller, 1990) or an historical approach (for example, see Baddeley and McCombie, 2001) to the analysis of speculative bubbles.

MICHELLE BADDELEY

See also:

Financial Instability; Rational Expectations.

Bibliography

Baddeley, M. and J. McCombie (2001), 'An Historical Perspective on Speculative Bubbles: Tulipmania and the South Sea Bubble', *What Global Economic Crisis?*, London: Palgrave, pp. 219–43.

Blanchard, O.J. and M.W. Watson (1982), 'Bubbles, Rational Expectations and Financial Markets', in P. Wachtel (ed.), *Crises in Economic and Financial Structure*, Lexington: Heath, pp. 295–315.

Brunnermeier, M.K. (2001), *Asset Pricing under Asymmetric Information*, Oxford: Oxford University Press.

Davidson, P. (1972, 1978), *Money and the Real World*, London: Macmillan.

Davidson, P. (1998), 'Post Keynesian Employment Analysis and the Macroeconomics of OECD Unemployment', *Economic Journal*, **108**, May, pp. 817–31.

Flood, R.P. and R.J. Garber (1980), *Speculative Bubbles, Speculative Attacks and Policy Switching*, Cambridge, MA: MIT Press.

Flood, R.P. and R.J. Hodrick (1990), 'On Testing for Speculative Bubbles', *Journal of Economic Perspectives*, **4**, Spring, pp. 85–101.

Garber, P.M. (1989), 'Tulipmania', *Journal of Political Economy*, **97**, June, pp. 535–60.

Garber, P.M. (1990), 'Famous First Bubbles', *Journal of Economic Perspectives*, **4**, Spring, pp. 35–53.

Kaldor, N. (1939), 'Speculation and Economic Stability', *Review of Economic Studies*, **7**, October, pp. 1–27.

Keynes, J.M. (1936), *The General Theory of Employment, Interest and Money*, London: Macmillan.

Keynes, J.M. (1937), 'The General Theory of Employment', *Quarterly Journal of Economics*, **51**, February, pp. 209–23.

Kindleberger, C.P. (1996), *Manias, Panics and Crashes*, New York: John Wiley.

Minsky, H.P. (1982), *Can 'It' Happen Again? Essays on Instability and Finance*, Armonk, NY: M.E. Sharpe.

Neal, L.D. (1996), 'How the South Sea Bubble was Blown Up and Burst: A New Look at Old Data', in E.N. White (ed.) *Stock Market Crashes and Speculative Manias*, Cheltenham, UK and Brookfield, US: Edward Elgar, pp. 154–77.

Shiller, R.J. (1990), 'Speculative Prices and Popular Models', *Journal of Economic Perspectives*, **4**, Spring, pp. 55–65.

Shiller, R.J. (2000), *Irrational Exuberance*, Princeton: Princeton University Press.

Shleifer, A. (2000), *Inefficient Markets – An Introduction to Behavioural Finance*, Oxford: Oxford University Press.

Shleifer, A. and L. Summers (1990), 'The Noise Trader Approach to Finance', *Journal of Economic Perspectives*, **4**, Spring, pp. 19–33.

Smith, B.M. (2001), *Towards Rational Exuberance: the Evolution of the Modern Stock Market*, New York: Farrar Straus Giroux.

Tobin, J. (1969), 'A General Equilibrium Approach to Monetary Theory', *Journal of Money, Credit and Banking*, **1**, February, pp. 15–29.

Topol, R. (1991), 'Bubbles and Volatility of Stock Prices: Effect of Mimetic Contagion', *Economic Journal*, **101**, July, pp. 786–800.

White, E.N. (1990), 'The Stock Market Boom and Crash of 1929 Revisited', *Journal of Economic Perspectives*, **4**, Spring, pp. 67–83.

Stabilization Policy

Policy aimed at reducing the severity of short-term cyclical fluctuations in aggregate economic activity.

See also:

Aggregate Demand Management; Business Cycle.

Stagflation

The period 1950–73 is generally regarded as the 'golden age' of capitalism. During this era the major capitalist economies of the world experienced historically high rates of economic growth, combined with low inflation and low unemployment (see A. Maddison, *The World Economy: A Millennial Perspective*, OECD, 2001). In retrospect, we can see that this remarkable period of success with respect to the achievement of the three major macroeconomic objectives was coming to an end towards the end of the 1960s as inflation began to increase. By 1973–5, the acceleration of inflation had become a widespread phenomenon. However, not only was inflation rising, so too was unemployment. In addition, the 1970s witnessed a marked productivity slowdown, especially in the United States. The simultaneous phenomena of rising unemployment, slower economic growth and accelerating inflation became known as 'stagflation' (combining the words *stag*nation and in*flation*). Table 1 indicates how the 1973–83 period stands out.

Table 1   *Experience of unemployment and inflation in advanced capitalist countries, 1950–98*

	Level of Unemployment (per cent of labour force)				Changes in consumer price index (annual average compound growth rate)			
	1950–73	1974–83	1984–93	1994–98	1950–73	1973–83	1983–93	1994–98
Belgium	3.0	8.2	8.8	9.7	2.9	8.1	3.1	1.8
Finland	1.7	4 7	6.9	14.2	5.6	10.5	4.6	1.0
France	2.0	5.7	10.0	12.1	5.0	11.2	3.7	1.5
Germany	2.5	4.1	6.2	9.0	2.7	4.9	2.4	1.7
Italy	5.5	7.2	9.3	11.9	3.9	16.7	6.4	3.5
Netherlands	2 2	7.3	7.3	5.9	4.1	6.5	1.8	2.2
Norway	1.9	2.1	4.1	4.6	4.8	9.7	5.1	2.0
Sweden	1.8	2.3	3.4	9.2	4.7	10.2	6.4	1.5
United Kingdom	2.8	7.0	9.7	8.0	4.6	13.5	5.2	3.0
Ireland	n.a.	8.8	15.6	11.2	4.3	15.7	3.8	2.1
Spain	2.9	9.1	19.4	21.8	4.6	16.4	6.9	3.4
Western Europe Average	**2.6**	**6.0**	**9.2**	**10.7**	**4.3**	**11.2**	**4.5**	**2.2**
Australia	2.1	5.9	8.5	8.6	4.6	11.3	5.6	2.0
Canada	4.7	8.1	9.7	9.4	2.8	9.4	4.0	1.3
United States	4.6	7.4	6.7	5.3	2.7	8.2	3.8	2.4
Average	**3.8**	**7.1**	**8.3**	**7.8**	**3.4**	**9.6**	**4.5**	**1.9**
Japan	1.6	2.1	2.3	3.4	5.2	7.6	1.7	0.6

Source: A. Maddison (2001), *The World Economy: A Millennial Perspective*, Paris: OECD, Table 3-8.

Taking the 1950–98 period as a whole, we can see that on average in the 'Golden Age' both unemployment and inflation were low. In the period 1983/4–93, inflation had come down but unemployment remained stubbornly high in many countries, especially in Western Europe, where high unemployment has been attributed to hysteresis effects and/or various labour market rigidities. In the most recent period, 1994–8, inflation has been low but unemployment has remained high in Western Europe, while it declined in the USA. But only in the period 1973–83 do we see the *simultaneous* combination of high unemployment and high inflation, that is, stagflation.

There are a variety of explanations of the way the 'Great Peacetime Inflation' of the 1970s got started. These range from policy errors (Tobin, 1987) to the influence of the OPEC supply shocks (Blinder, 1979) and to the use of the wrong model for policy purposes (Taylor, 1997; Mayer, 1999). Bradford DeLong (1997) sees the 'Great Peacetime Inflation' as the inevitable result of what he calls the 'Shadow of the Great Depression'. Politicians, living in the 'Shadow of the Great Depression', simply tried to push unemployment down to too low levels during the 1960s. The debate over the relative importance of supply shocks, excessive demand and policy choices as the major source of stagflation during the 1970s has been, and remains, a major source of disagreement (see A.S. Blinder, *Economic Policy and the Great Stagflation*, Academic Press, 1979; J. Cornwall (ed.), *After Stagflation: Alternatives to Economic Decline*, Basil Blackwell, 1984; M. Bruno and J. Sachs, *The Economics of Worldwide Stagflation*, Harvard University Press, 1985; J. Tobin, *Policies for Prosperity: Essays in a Keynesian Mode*, ed. P.M. Jackson, Wheatsheaf, 1987; J.B. DeLong, 'America's Only Peacetime Inflation: The 1970s', in C.D. Romer and D. Romer (eds), *Reducing Inflation: Motivation and Strategy*, University of Chicago Press, 1997; J.B. Taylor, 'Comment', in C.D. Romer and D. Romer (1997); T. Mayer, *Monetary Policy and the Great Inflation in the United States*, Edward Elgar, 1999; R. Barsky and L. Kilian, 'Do We Really Know that Oil Caused the Great Stagflation', *National Bureau of Economic Research Macroeconomics Annual*, 2001).

See also:
Golden Age Growth; Hysteresis; Productivity Slowdown.

Staggered Wage Contracts

These occur where wage contracts are staggered or overlap, with different expiry dates. In consequence, wage adjustments for different workers will take place at different times and cannot be synchronized. When some wage contracts are near to expiry and need to be renegotiated, others will still have a period to run before they expire.

Steady State Growth

In the neoclassical theory of growth the *steady state* represents the long-run equilibrium balanced growth path of an economy. In 1956, Solow demonstrated that, in the absence of technological progress, an economy will reach a 'steady state' where output, consumption and capital per worker are constant (R.M. Solow, 'A Contribution to the Theory of Economic Growth', *Quarterly Journal of Economics*, **70**, February, 1956). According to the basic neoclassical growth framework, output per worker ($y = Y/L$) is positively dependent on capital per worker ($k=K/L$). The accumulation of capital evolves according to equation (1), which is the fundamental differential equation of the Solow model:

$$\Delta k = sf(k) - (n + \delta)k, \tag{1}$$

where Δk is the change in capital input per worker, s is the saving rate, $sf(k)$ is saving (investment) per worker, n is the rate of population (labour force) growth, and δ is the depreciation rate of the capital stock. The $(n + \delta)k$ term represents the 'investment requirements' per worker in order to keep the capital labour ratio constant. The *steady state condition* in the Solow model is given in equation (2):

$$sf(k^*) - (n + \delta)k^* = 0. \tag{2}$$

In the steady state equilibrium output per worker (y^*) and capital per worker (k^*) are constant and all economies, irrespective of their initial conditions, will converge towards their own steady state. However, although in the absence of technological progress there is no growth of output per worker in the steady state, there is growth of total output (Y) because population (and hence the labour input) is growing at a rate of n per cent per annum. Thus, in order for output per worker and the capital labour ratio to remain constant, both Y and K must also grow at the same rate as population. Changes in the saving rate (s), the depreciation rate (δ) and the population growth rate (n) will cause the steady state to change: for example, an increase in the saving rate will raise the steady state *level* of output per worker and capital–labour ratio, although it will have no permanent effect on raising the growth rate of output per worker. A *'golden rule steady state'* is one where the level of capital per worker maximizes consumption per worker. Once we allow for innovation-driven productivity improvements in the Solow model, steady state output and capital per worker will grow at a rate equal to the rate of technological progress (see C.I. Jones, *An Introduction to Economic Growth*, 2nd edn, W.W. Norton, 2001).

Although without technological progress output per worker is constant in the steady state, Solow (2000) emphasizes that 'a policy that does not touch the long-term growth rate, but simply lifts the steady-state path by one or two per cent above its original track, would be a genuine contribution to *growth*' (see R.M. Solow, *Growth Theory: An Exposition*, 2nd edn, Oxford University Press, 2000).

See also:

Neoclassical Growth Model.

Sterilization

Sterilization involves neutralizing the effects of balance of payments surpluses or deficits on the domestic money supply by making offsetting policy changes. Under a fixed exchange rate system, the monetary authorities are committed to buy and sell foreign exchange for the home currency at a fixed price. In the case of a balance of payments surplus, residents will sell foreign currency for home currency. In consequence, *ceteris paribus*, a balance of payments surplus results in an increase in residents' holdings of home currency and the domestic money supply. The converse holds in the case of a balance of payments deficit. One way the authorities may attempt to sterilize the effects of balance of payments surpluses or deficits on the domestic money supply is by engaging in open market operations. In the case of a balance of payments surplus, the central bank would need to sell bonds to domestic residents in order to reduce their holdings of home currency and offset the monetary effects of the balance of payments surplus. Conversely, in the case of a balance of payments deficit, the central bank would need to buy bonds from domestic residents in order to prevent a fall in residents' holdings of home currency and a decrease in the money supply. Although it is possible for the authorities to pursue such offsetting policy changes, sterilization is very difficult, if not impossible, in the long run. In contrast, under a flexible exchange rate system, the exchange rate should adjust to maintain balance of payments equilibrium with no effects on the domestic money supply.

See also:

Fixed Exchange Rate System.

Stiglitz, Joseph E.

Joseph Stiglitz (b.1943, Gary, Indiana, USA) obtained his BA from Amherst College in 1964 and his PhD from the Massachusetts Institute of Technology (MIT) in 1966. His main past posts have included Assistant Professor at MIT, 1966–7; Associate Professor (1967–70) and Professor (1970–74) at Yale University; Professor at Stanford University, 1974–6; Professor at Oxford University, 1976–9; Professor at Princeton University, 1979–88; Professor at Stanford University, 1988–2001; and since 2001 Professor at Columbia University. From 1997 to 1999 he was Chief Economist and Senior Vice-President, Development Economics, at the World Bank in Washington. He was the founding editor of the *Journal of Economic Perspectives*, co-editor of the *American Economic Review*

(1968–76), the *Review of Economic Studies* (1968–76), the *Journal of Public Economics* (1980–83) and associate editor of the *Journal of Economic Theory* (1968–73). In 1979, he was awarded the John Bates Clark Medal of the American Economic Association and he was a member (1993–5) and chairman (1995–7) of the US Council of Economic Advisers. In 2001, he was jointly awarded, with George Akerlof and Michael Spence, the Nobel Prize in Economics 'for their analyses of markets with asymmetric information'. He is best known for his work on market imperfections, in particular the economic consequences of incomplete information and uncertainty, and for being one of the leading architects of new Keynesian economics. Among his best known books is *Wither Socialism?* (MIT Press, 1994). His most widely read articles include 'On the Impossibility of Informationally Efficient Markets' (co-authored with S.J. Grossman) (*American Economic Review*, **70**, June 1980); 'Credit Rationing in Markets With Imperfect Information' (co-authored with A. Weiss) (*American Economic Review*, **71**, June 1981); 'Equilibrium Unemployment as a Worker Disciplinary Device' (co-authored with C. Shapiro) (*American Economic Review*, **74**, June 1984); 'Keynesian, New Keynesian and New Classical Economics' (co-authored with B.C. Greenwald) (*Oxford Economic Papers*, **32**, March 1987); 'Examining Alternative Macroeconomic Theories' (co-authored with B.C. Greenwald) (*Brookings Papers on Economic Activity*, 1988); 'Financial Market Imperfections and Business Cycles' (co-authored with B.C. Greenwald) (*Quarterly Journal of Economics*, **108**, February 1993); and 'Reflections on the Natural Rate Hypothesis' (*Journal of Economic Perspectives*, **11**, Winter 1997).

See also:

American Economic Association; Council of Economic Advisers; John Bates Clark Medal; New Keynesian Economics; Nobel Prize in Economics.

Stone, J. Richard N. (1913–91)

Richard Stone (b.1913, London, England) obtained his BA (1935) and MA (1938) from the University of Cambridge. His main posts included UK Office War Cabinet, Central Statistical Office, 1940–45; Director of the Department of Applied Economics at the University of Cambridge, 1945–55; and P.D. Leake Professor of Finance and Accounting at the University of Cambridge, 1955–80. His many offices and honours included president of the Econometric Society in 1955 and the Royal Economic Society from 1978 to 1980; being knighted in 1978; and being awarded the Nobel Memorial Prize in Economics in 1984. He is best known for his work on pioneering the development of national income accounting; the analysis of consumer demand; and the construction of a disaggregated model of the British economy. Among his best known books are *National Income and Expenditure* (co-authored with J.E. Meade) (Oxford University Press, 1944); *The Measurement of Consumers' Expenditure and Behaviour in the United Kingdom, 1920–1938* (co-authored with D.A. Rowe *et al.*) (Cambridge University Press, vol. One, 1954; vol. Two, 1966); *Quantity and Price Indexes in National Accounts* (OECD, 1956); and *A Computable Model of Economic Growth* (co-authored with A. Brown) (Chapman and Hall, 1962). His most widely read articles include 'The Marginal Propensity to Consume and the Multiplier' (co-authored with W.M. Stone) (*Review of Economic Studies*, **6**, October 1938); 'Definition and Measurement of the National Income and Related Totals', *Measurement of National Income and the Construction of National Accounts* (United Nations, 1947); 'Linear Expenditure Systems and Demand Analysis' (*Economic Journal*, **64**, September 1954); and 'The Accounts of Society' (*Journal of Applied Econometrics*, **1**, January–March 1985).

See also:

Econometric Society; Nobel Prize in Economics; Royal Economic Society.

Structural Budget Balance

See:

Full Employment Budget Balance.

Structural Unemployment

Unemployment that results from a mismatch between the skills or location of existing job vacancies and the present skills or location of the unemployed; also known as mismatch unemployment.

Summers, Lawrence H.

Lawrence Summers (b.1954 in New Haven, Connecticut, USA) obtained his BS degree from MIT in 1975 and his PhD from Harvard University in 1982. His main past posts have included Assistant and Associate Professor of Economics at MIT (1979–82); Professor of Economics at Harvard University (since 1983); Vice President of Development Economics and

Chief Economist at the World Bank (1991–3); Under-Secretary of the Treasury for International Affairs (1993–5); and Deputy Secretary of the Treasury (1995–9), before being promoted to Secretary of the Treasury in 1999. From January to July 2001, he served as the Arthur Okun Distinguished Fellow in Economics, Globalisation, and Governance at the Brookings Institution, before taking up his current post as President of Harvard University. In 1993, Professor Summers was awarded the prestigious John Bates Clark Medal. He is best known for his work on macroeconomics, finance, taxation, labour economics and development economics. Among his best known books is *Understanding Unemployment* (MIT Press, 1990). His most widely read articles include 'Some Skeptical Observations on Real Business Cycle Theory', (*Federal Reserve Bank of Minneapolis Quarterly Review*, **10**, Fall 1986); 'Hysteresis and the European Unemployment Problem' (co-authored with O. Blanchard) (*National Bureau Macroeconomics Annual*, 1986); 'Is Price Flexibility Stabilizing?' (co-authored with B. DeLong) (*American Economic Review*, **76**, December 1986); 'Did Henry Ford Pay Efficiency Wages?' (co-authored with D. Raff) (*Journal of Labour Economics*, **5**, October 1987); 'How Does Macroeconomic Policy Matter?' (co-authored with B. DeLong) (*Brookings Papers on Economic Activity*, 1988); 'Equipment Investment and Economic Growth: How Strong is the Nexus?' (co-authored with B. DeLong) (*Brookings Papers on Economic Activity*, 1992); 'Central Bank Independence and Macroeconomic Performance' (co-authored with A. Alesina) (*Journal of Money, Credit and Banking*, **25**, May 1993); 'Reflections on Managed Global Integration' (*Journal of Economic Perspectives*, **13**, Spring 1999); and 'International Financial Crises: Causes, Prevention and Cures' (*American Economic Review*, **90**, May 2000).

See also:

Brookings Institution; John Bates Clark Medal; World Bank.

Supply-side Economics

Modern macroeconomic thinking, a central feature of which is rational expectations, implies that the economy is converging on its 'natural rate' (that is, its equilibrium) at some speed determined by, for example, overlapping contracts or adjustment costs. Therefore the natural rates of output and unemployment become of central interest. These are commonly termed the 'supply side'.

Much of the literature on the supply side dwells on productivity and growth, but this neglects the important issue of unemployment which has been a particular problem in Europe. This has importance beyond the narrow issue of the number of people unemployed because of its social significance: politicians attach great importance to 'curing unemployment' because of its obvious unpopularity with voters. Unfortunately, they tend to alight on measures that address the symptoms, not the disease; notably 'work-sharing', reducing participation (by, for example, early retirement or 'family policies' designed to keep women at home), reducing working hours, or indeed reducing productivity growth and the penetration of new technology. The reason they pick such policies is that the original disease, as will be argued below, is due to erecting 'social' support mechanisms that raise labour costs; it follows that cures based on 'labour market deregulation' (that is, eliminating or bypassing such support) have no appeal to them. Instead they put their faith in measures that they think may mitigate the side-effects, in unemployment, of their (desirable) social policies. Thus, by the end of the 1990s, low participation and low working hours tended to accompany the high unemployment in Germany, France and Italy. In Italy, for example, were the participation rate to be at the US level, with no other changes, unemployment would be around 30 per cent. The evidence also shows that these countries have also experienced a relative slowdown in productivity growth in the 1980s and 1990s from the earlier postwar period; this suggests that their productivity growth too may have been held back by such policies.

Hence unemployment tends to breed policies that inhibit participation and productivity growth. Our discussion therefore begins with unemployment. It goes on to the optimal size of government. It ends with growth itself.

Unemployment
Our focus in this section is on the natural rate, not on the cyclical behaviour of unemployment. The latter has to be explained in the context of business cycle models. The natural rate is the equilibrium to which these cycles tend. Milton Friedman (1968) remarked in his AEA Presidential Address that it was the equilibrium 'ground out by the Walrasian system' of real demands and supplies. However, it never really occurred to macroeconomists to model it until much later; Friedman, Phelps (1970) and others using the natural rate concept effectively treated it like a natural constant. It was not until the early 1980s, in the United Kingdom, where unemployment rose above 10 per cent, with no apparent tendency to fall, that models began to be formulated of a changing natural rate. The first effort was Minford (1983); he took the classical labour supply and added the idea of a permanent unemployment benefit, payable without any check on work availability (a peculiarly European concept). The result was to tilt the

labour supply curve so that the real wage offer never fell below the benefit. This had the effect of creating the 'real wage rigidity' identified, for example, by Bruno and Sachs (1985) in their account of the 1973–4 oil crisis. Notice too that with such benefits one can account also for the cyclical behaviour of real wages and unemployment; real wages are procyclical, rising in the upswing and lifting people out of benefit, falling in the downswing so that people go onto benefit.

In this approach the normal marginal product of labour schedule can interact with this distorted labour supply schedule to generate equilibrium unemployment. Should the benefit rise relative to productivity, unemployment will result. That is, people will voluntarily refuse to take available wage offers because benefits are preferable. They are 'unemployed' in the sense that they are not working but are 'available for work': thus, in response to the usual survey questions, they would be counted as wanting work (if at the 'right wage', but this is not generally included in the assessment) and some governments also would count them as unemployed because they are in receipt of unemployment benefit. In any case the unemployment is recognizable as what causes social dissatisfaction.

The labour market model can be generalized to include the effects of union power, taxes of all sorts, and employer and employee national insurance contributions (which in Europe are largely taxes in nature). When these are placed within the general equilibrium of an open economy one obtains natural rates of output, real wages and the real exchange rate, as well as employment and unemployment. Later versions have proliferated; in the UK, Layard and Nickell (1985) estimated a similar model, and Bean *et al.* (1986) attempted to extend it to other European countries which began to experience rising unemployment UK-style during the late 1980s and 1990s. It turns out that in each country there are substantial idiosyncrasies in the social support mechanisms, complicating effective modelling of the natural unemployment rate. Nevertheless, a large amount of empirical work, both cross-section (Burda, 1988, was the first to exploit the variation across European countries and show the importance of long-duration benefits) and time-series (Layard *et al.* 1991, survey much of it) seemed to confirm that these mechanisms, particularly the length of time benefits were available and the ease of eligibility, were responsible for persistently high unemployment in Europe. By the end of the 1990s, a general consensus had appeared, embodied in the OECD secretariat, that 'labour market flexibility' was the key to reducing equilibrium unemployment (see also Siebert, 1997; Ljungqvist and Sargent, 1998).

Much of the traditional literature on unemployment emphasizes search behaviour (Lancaster, 1979; Nickell, 1979). In the absence of a permanent unemployment benefit, such behaviour would make sense; we could model a steady flow of job separations, with people searching for some average time determined in the usual search-optimizing manner. This would give rise to an unemployment equilibrium of the rate of flow times the length of search; for example, if 20 per cent of the workforce leave employment each year and spend three months searching, this will yield an unemployment rate of 5 per cent (0.2 × 0.25 = 0.05). We can think of this as a 'frictional' rate of unemployment; plainly, in a well-functioning economy, the natural rate should be such a frictional rate. The very high and long-lasting levels of unemployment seen in Europe during the late 1980s and early 1990s are not well explained in these terms, however; these high natural rates are better explained in terms of the model above, in which the long-term unemployed cannot be said in any meaningful way to be 'searching'.

Thus a first set of policies to generate high activity should be those of labour market flexibility.

The optimal role of government
It is plain that government provides some useful services. These services (such as law and order and infrastructure) could be provided privately, but it is more efficient in practice to provide them publicly; that is, for 'public goods' there is a direct saving of resources from eliminating the duplication, the transactions costs and the underuse from private provision. However, there is also a cost in public provision: that distorting taxes must be raised to pay for the service. Though lump-sum taxes without a distorting effect are possible, they are so unpopular that in practice governments do not raise them to any serious extent (when the UK government brought in the 'poll tax' in the late 1980s to replace the 'rate', a tax on property values, it contributed to the fall of Margaret Thatcher; subsequently, the tax was withdrawn in favour of a banded property tax).

We can model these two sides of public spending in terms of the labour market and the production function: public spending raises productivity but causes a distortion in labour supply. A helpful way of summarizing the twin effects as government spending rises as a fraction of GDP stems from the Laffer curve, which shows tax revenue as a function of the tax rate (tax revenue equals public spending). At low levels of spending, the tax rate is low and the marginal distortion cost of taxation (which rises with the square of the tax rate according to the standard consumer surplus formula) is correspondingly low, while the marginal benefit of government spending is high. With efficiency raised by the spending and low tax-distorting inefficiency, the revenue yield relative to the tax rate is high. As spending and the tax rate rise, this relative yield falls, as the marginal benefit of the spending falls and the marginal distorting cost rises. The optimal tax rate and size of government occurs where the marginal benefit and cost of higher tax intersect; as spending rises above this point, we move towards the revenue-maximizing tax rate where any further rise in the tax rate yields no extra revenue and so permits no extra spending. Thus, whatever its motives, no government can rationally operate to the right of this point.

This, useful as it is conceptually, tells us nothing in practice about where the optimal tax rate is. If we neglect very poor countries in Africa and elsewhere with poor infrastructure, there seem to be three main groups: Asian emerging-market countries with low tax rates (around 20 per cent), good basic infrastructure but limited provision of welfare services and social insurance like unemployment benefit and public health care; an Anglo-Saxon group with medium tax rates (35–40 per cent) and fairly extensive welfare services/social insurance; and a European group with high tax rates (around 50 per cent) and very extensive social insurance. The essential problem with the latter group is, as we saw in the last section, that generous social insurance distorts labour supply. Furthermore, the high marginal tax rates implied have substantial effects on work incentives for taxpayers on top rates at least; evidence from the United States (Lindsey, 1987a, 1987b; Feldstein, 1995) and the UK (Minford and Ashton, 1991) suggests that high earners' hours respond strongly to rising marginal rates so that higher-band tax revenues are likely to fall, putting them on the wrong side of the Laffer curve (this is without counting in tax avoidance/evasion and migration or 'brain drain' effects). It is true that a degree of social insurance may make workers more willing to be flexible in job choice and location (for example, the combination of no unemployment benefit and strong unions, as in Italy, may make it extremely difficult to close operations). Nevertheless, in a rich society, most people would be willing to pay for higher than basic levels of health insurance, pensions and education; if the state provides these basic levels but no more, there is a basis for cutting tax rates to somewhere between the Anglo-Saxon and the Asian rates. Such a move has proved to be popular in the UK with pensions, for example. If acceptable politically, it enables the economy to have a less distorting tax system, with the reduction in government provision offset by higher private provision.

Growth
Supply-side policy in principle extends to policies for growth. Classical economists always stressed the benefits of government policies that provided basic services such as law and order, but otherwise did not intervene in the market's workings. However, they offered no real analysis of the mechanisms involved. Until recently, growth theory has treated the proximate causes of growth (technological change and population growth) as exogenous. More recently, 'endogenous growth theory' has attempted to

sketch possible mechanisms by which these proximate causes could be triggered.

One can perhaps single out three mechanisms as front runners, though it must be stressed that empirical testing has lagged way behind the theory (not least because of the great difficulties of identification in this area where so many different mechanisms are at work, all of them related in both causal directions with growth) so that we are still largely in our armchairs on this issue.

The first is increasing returns to scale over sections of the production function (Romer, 1986). Suppose one accepts that in nature at some comprehensive level of description there are constant returns essentially on logical grounds: if you double every single ingredient that is producing something, then, in principle you should double output since all you are doing is replication – putting the same thing side by side with itself must give you double. Nevertheless, in practice not everything is included in the production function, there are always uncoated factors ('commons', resources that are uncharged for because they are not scarce in the given situation) and also, as size changes, so does the nature of the operation. For example, in 'virgin territories' land is free; then the increasing penetration of people can reap increasing returns as thresholds of exploitability are passed. A similar thing appears to happen with all new technologies (Mansfield, 1968); they follow an S-shaped curve of productivity. In the early stages productivity grows slowly because the technique is poorly implementable, with little learning and few users; as more users join and learning increases, productivity rises rapidly; finally, as all its uses are exploited, productivity growth tails off.

These ideas underpin specifications of the production function with increasing returns – most easily represented by making technology depend on size of output. Assuming that the stock of labour is exogenous, the increasing returns can be exploited by increasing the capital stock.

A second main route is to model technology as accumulated knowledge with knowledge production an industry in its own right (the R&D sector): see, for example, Romer (1990), Aghion and Howitt (1992), Grossman and Helpman (1991).

The third, closely related, route is to include human capital (skills of the workforce as opposed to pure technological knowledge) in the production function (Lucas, 1988). One can then treat it as investment requiring, like physical capital, savings to create it (though in this case not recorded financial savings but rather the substitution of 'creative' for non-creative leisure), in which case the model's behaviour is essentially like that of the Solow model; but, because it downgrades the contribution of 'pure labour' in favour of human capital, it implies that saving has a bigger effect on growth and so can account more easily for growth differences between countries (Romer, 1996, s. 3.11). Or we can attribute human capital to learning-by-doing, so that it increases with the level of output, say (more precisely with the accumulation of output experience). As with increasing returns, one can think of this as a way by which size improves technology.

The general implication of these models is that, with uncoordinated private agents, there are potentially massive externalities in activities generating 'growth agents' such as knowledge, human capital and agglomeration and other sources of increasing returns.

Suppose instead that private choices are coordinated in some way. This could happen in different ways. Government coordination is one; as it involves detailed knowledge of the potential gains from new technological applications and investments, this is not a main candidate except for rather basic elements of a joint strategy such as infrastructure. Plainly, however, in any coordination the government is likely to have some role to play, if only in agreeing to get out of the way (for example, in monopoly regulation). Probably the main way in which coordination might occur is in intra-industry joint ventures; there are many examples of such collaboration between competitors (such as in the airline industry to develop internet booking systems or in the telecommunications industry to develop the new generation of mobile phones and hand-held computers). One should also not discount popular coordination, now more achievable via the Internet.

The role for government in this case would be different from the externality case just considered. Here government has no business spending any resources since there are no ('external') opportunities not already exploited by the private sector/government coordination. In these circumstances, government regulations, taxes and other interventions would inhibit the private sector from exploiting available opportunities. In crude terms, where there are large incentives to exploit potential new technologies, the private sector will take larger risks and invest more resources than where taxes are high and regulations are stringent. Interestingly, Parente and Prescott (1999) concluded that some such x-factor of the degree of non-intervention promised the best hope of explaining the stylized facts of growth.

This emphasizes the importance of social institutions and policy frameworks, within which households in general take decentralized decisions in their own private interests but do have some limited opportunities for internalizing externalities. There is plenty of evidence that institutions evolve over time instead of being the direct object of social choice (Sugden, 1986). They are the result either of unprompted social interaction or of some political process: success and failure in producing institutions that are good for the supply side of the economy are a matter of political economy, to which we turn.

The political economy of the supply side
There is a massive literature on the creation and evolution of the institutions that favour or inhibit capitalist growth. In striking contributions, North (1981) charted the way in which Protestant dissent in the Low Countries and the UK produced the first industrial revolutions; while Lal (1998) has gone further back to show how competition in Europe between nation states under the shelter of Papal Christendom gave capitalism its secure basis. In two important books, *The Logic of Collective Action* and *The Rise and Decline of Nations*, Mancur Olson (1965 and 1982) set out the mechanism by which vested interest groups could prevent the general good (in the second, he argued that as nations become older they acquire more powerful vested interests, as networks and clubs have longer to form and become entrenched); essentially, they can exercise discipline over their members who have strong interests at stake, whereas the general public have too little incentive individually to understand how their own interests are prejudiced by the action of these groups. Hence for politicians to mobilize opinion in favour of reform is costly and uncertain, whereas these groups can offer them rewards, both personal and political, for pushing forward their own agendas – an activity known as 'rent seeking', in which existing rents are diverted instead of being augmented by productive action. This basic idea has led to a substantial applied research agenda (for example, see St. Paul, 1996, on the difficulties of modifying costly firing regulations in Europe, and Tullock *et al.*, 2000, for a survey of American work).

However, there are examples of supply-side reforms being taken in spite of vested interest opposition. Three such are the wide-ranging reforms of the Thatcher conservatives over the 1980s and 1990s in the UK, and in the USA the Carter deregulation of the 1970s and the Reagan tax reforms of the 1980s. On these occasions it proved possible for politicians to build a sufficient coalition in public opinion to support reform.

So there is a tension between the strengths of vested interests and the power of public opinion in asserting its general interests. As hints towards a possible model of this tension, we may reflect on the way downward shifts in general economic prosperity have triggered increased intervention (more benefits, taxation and regulation). The Great Depression in the USA famously unleashed both the Roosevelt New Deal interventions and massive protection. During the 1980s in continental Europe, as noted above, the rise of unemployment brought increased regulation of the labour market (for example, reduced working hours) that reduced participation as well. At the same time we may also note that crises and very poor economic performance can trigger reform because voters suspend their normal voting patterns; so obviously atrocious has the general state of the economy become that it pays them more to restore its health than to gain a rent-seeking interest.

This sort of voting behaviour might suggest a model for change in the political equilibrium according to some indicator of general economic performance, say unemployment. We might perhaps assume that at very low rates of unemployment (good performance) the floating voters are predominantly 'capitalist', with little concern for unemployment (because prosperity has enhanced holdings of non-human capital and reduced the risk to human capital); at high but not catastrophic rates they are predominantly 'workers', with high concern (the risk to human capital has risen and holdings of non-human capital have been devalued); and that, at catastrophic rates, they switch from normal voting patterns to become concerned with maximizing the general good. Suppose we focus on a representative supply-side issue, like the level and duration (overall 'generosity') of real unemployment benefits: then, initially, a rise in unemployment above some critical rate would trigger demands for higher benefits; but, as unemployment rose, the general good element would become more of a restraining factor, until ultimately voters demanded that reform and benefits be cut. One could postulate similar mechanisms affecting other supply-side policies. For example, the tax rate would tend to rise as benefit bills rose with intermediate unemployment, but be cut once the crisis had hit, while demands for regulations would tend to mirror demands for benefits. If we combine this with the unemployment model set out above, we can generate a tendency for the political equilibrium to add supply-side damage on top of a bad shock, perhaps from demand producing a 'vicious circle', but also the phenomenon of drastic reform prompted by disaster that causes vested interests to set their narrow aims aside. Depending on how rapidly the economy improves after such reform, a virtuous circle can result as unemployment drops sufficiently for demands for restored benefits to disappear. What is being suggested here is that good macroeconomic management has a crucial role in supporting good supply-side policy, just as poor supply-side policy may create pressures for inflationary macroeconomic policies. There are intimate linkages through political economy between the two sorts of policies, and these links have the capacity to create both vicious and virtuous circles of economic performance. It follows that good macro 'demand' policies may well be strongly linked with good supply-side policies – with good and bad in each reinforcing each other.

PATRICK MINFORD

See also:

Endogenous Growth Theory; Laffer Curve; Natural Rate of Unemployment; Neoclassical Growth Model.

Bibliography

Aghion, P. and P. Howitt (1992), 'A Model of Growth through Creative Destruction', *Econometrica*, **60**, March, pp. 323–51.

Bean, C., R. Layard and S. Nickell (1986), 'The Rise in Unemployment: A Multi-Country Study', in C. Bean, R. Layard and S. Nickell (eds), *The Rise in Unemployment*, Oxford: Basil Blackwell.

Bruno, M. and J.D. Sachs (1985), *The Economics of Worldwide Stagflation*, Oxford: Basil Blackwell.

Burda, M. (1988), 'Wait Unemployment in Europe', *Economic Policy*, **7**, October, pp. 391–416.

Feldstein, M. (1995), 'The Effect of Marginal Tax Rates on Taxable Income: A Panel Study of the 1986 Tax Reform Act', *Journal of Political Economy*, **103**, June, pp. 551–72.

Friedman, M. (1968), 'The Role of Monetary Policy', *American Economic Review*, **58**, March, pp. 1–17.

Grossman, G.M. and E. Helpman (1991), *Innovation and Growth in the Global Economy*, Cambridge, MA: MIT Press.

Lal, D. (1998), *Unintended Consequences: The Impact of Factor Endowments, Culture and Politics on Long-Run Economic Performance*, Cambridge, MA: MIT Press.

Lancaster, T. (1979), 'Econometric Models for the Duration of Unemployment', *Econometrica*, **47**, July, pp. 939–56.

Layard, R. and S. Nickell (1985), 'The Causes of British Unemployment', *National Institute Economic Review*, February, pp. 62–85.

Layard, R., S. Nickell and R. Jackman (1991), *Unemployment, Macroeconomic Performance and the Labour Market*, Oxford: Oxford University Press.

Lindsey, L.B. (1987a), 'Capital Gains Rates, Realizations and Revenues', in M. Feldstein (ed.), *The Effects of Taxation on Capital Accumulation*, Chicago: University of Chicago Press, for NBER.

Lindsey, L.B. (1987b), 'Individual Taxpayer Response to Tax Cuts, 1982–4; with Implications for the Revenue Maximising Tax Rates', *Journal of Public Economics*, **33**, pp. 173–206.

Ljungqvist, L. and T.J. Sargent (1998), 'The European Unemployment Dilemma', *Journal of Political Economy*, **106**, June, pp. 514–50.

Lucas, R.E. Jr (1988), 'On the Mechanics of Economic Development', *Journal of Monetary Economics*, **22**, July, pp. 3–42.

Mansfield, E. (1968), *The Economics of Technological Change*, New York: W.W. Norton.

Minford, A.P.L. (1983), 'Labour Market Equilibrium in an Open Economy', *Oxford Economic Papers*, Supplement, pp. 207–44.

Minford, A.P.L. and P. Ashton (1991), 'The Poverty Trap and the Laffer Curve: What can the GHS Tell Us?', *Oxford Economic Papers*, pp. 245–79.

Nickell, S.J. (1979), 'The Effect of Unemployment and Related Benefits on the Duration of Unemployment', *Economic Journal*, **89**, March, pp. 39–49.

North, D.C. (1981), *Structure and Change in Economic History*, New York: W.W. Norton.

Olson, M. (1965), *The Logic of Collective Action*, Cambridge, MA: Harvard University Press.

Olson, M. (1982), *The Rise and Decline of Nations: Economic Growth, Stagflation and Social Rigidities*, Newhaven, CT: Yale University Press.

Parente, S.L. and E.C. Prescott (1999), 'Monopoly Rights: A Barrier to Riches', *American Economic Review*, **89**, December, pp. 1216–33.

Phelps, E.S. (1970), 'The New Microeconomics in Employment and Inflation Theory', in E.S. Phelps *et al.* (eds), *Microeconomic Foundations of Employment and Inflation Theory*, New York: W.W. Norton.

Romer, D.H. (1996), *Advanced Macroeconomics*, 1st edn, New York: McGraw-Hill.

Romer, P.M. (1986), 'Increasing Returns and Long Run Growth', *Journal of Political Economy*, **94**, October, pp. 1002–37.

Romer, P.M. (1990), 'Endogenous Technological Change', *Journal of Political Economy*, **98**, October, S71–102.

Siebert, H. (1997), 'Labour Market Rigidities: At the Root of Unemployment in Europe', *Journal of Economic Perspectives*, **11**, Summer, pp. 37–54.

St. Paul, G. (1996), 'Exploring the Political Economy of Labour Market Institutions', *Economic Policy*, **23**, pp. 265–300.

Sugden, R. (1986), *The Economics of Rights, Co-operation and Welfare*, Oxford: Basil Blackwell.

Tullock, G., A. Seldon and G.L. Brady (2000), *Government: Whose Obedient Servant? A Primer in Public Choice*, London: Institute of Economic Affairs.

Taylor, John B.

John B. Taylor (b.1946, Yonkers, New York, USA) obtained his BA from Princeton University in 1968 and his PhD from Stanford University in 1973. His main past posts have included Assistant Professor (1973–7), Associate Professor (1977–9) and Professor of Economics (1979–80) at Columbia University; and Professor of Economics and Public Affairs at Princeton University, 1980–84. Since 1984 he has been the Mary and Robert Raymond Professor of Economics at Stanford University. He was a Senior Staff Economist (1976–7), Member (1989–91) of the US President's Council of Economic Advisers and since 2001 has been Treasury Under Secretary for International Affairs. Between 1985 and 1989 he was co-editor of the *American Economic Review* and associate editor of *Econometrica* (1981–4) and the *Journal of Monetary Economics* (1978–83). He is best known for his work on the development of rational expectations models with staggered wage setting; the design of monetary policy rules for the conduct of economic policy; and international policy coordination. Among his best known books are *Macroeconomic Policy in a World Economy* (W.W. Norton, 1993); *Macroeconomics* (co-authored with R.E. Hall) (5th edn, W.W. Norton, 1997); *Inflation, Unemployment and Monetary Policy* (co-authored with R.M. Solow) (MIT Press, 1998); *Monetary Policy Rules* (ed.) (University of Chicago Press, 1999); and *Handbook of Macroeconomics* (co-authored with M. Woodford) (North-Holland, 1999). His most widely read articles include 'Monetary Policy During a Transition to Rational Expectations' (*Journal of Political Economy*, **83**, October 1975); 'Stabilizing Powers of Monetary Policy Under Rational Expectations' (co-authored with E.S. Phelps) (*Journal of Political Economy*, **85**, February 1977); 'Staggered Wage Setting in a Macro Model' (*American Economic Review*, **69**, May 1979); 'Estimation and Control of a Macroeconomic Model With Rational Expectations' (*Econometrica*, **47**, September 1979); 'Establishing Credibility: A Rational Expectations Viewpoint' (*American Economic Review*, **72**, May 1982); 'Discretion Versus Policy Rules in Practice' (*Carnegie Rochester Conference Series on Public Policy*, **10**, 1993); 'A Core of Practical Macroeconomics' (*American Economic Review*, **87**, May 1997); and 'Reassessing Discretionary Fiscal Policy' (*Journal of Economic Perspectives*, **14**, Summer 2000).

See also:

Council of Economic Advisers; Rational Expectations; Rules versus Discretion; Taylor's Rule.

690

Taylor's Rule

A rule proposed by John B. Taylor of Stanford University (at the November 1992 Carnegie Rochester Conference), for central banks to follow in order to keep inflation low and stable, and avoid large fluctuations in output and employment. The policy rule for the federal funds rate (the interest rate charged on reserves lent by one bank to another) is:

federal funds rate = rate of inflation + 2 + 0.5 (percentage deviation of real GDP from trend real GDP) + 0.5 (rate of inflation − 2)

According to the rule, the federal funds rate should rise whenever inflation increases above a target of 2 per cent, or real GDP rises above trend real GDP. If both inflation is on target (at 2 per cent) and real GDP is on target (at its trend rate) then the federal funds rate will equal 4 per cent; that is, a real federal funds rate of 2 per cent. In short, if the monetary authorities followed this rule they would raise the short-term nominal interest rate if inflation or real GDP were above their target values, and vice versa. Interestingly, Taylor's rule closely approximates the Fed's behaviour over the last 15–20 years. Furthermore, while the Fed does not have a formal explicit target for inflation, most observers believe that it does have an implicit inflation target of somewhere between 1 and 2 per cent.

See also:
Federal Reserve System; Inflation Targeting; Rules versus Discretion.

Temin, Peter

Peter Temin (b.1937, Philadelphia, Pennsylvania, USA) obtained his BA from Swarthmore College in 1959 and his PhD from Massachusetts Institute of Technology (MIT) in 1964. His main past posts have included Assistant Professor (1965–7) and Associate Professor (1967–70) at MIT. Since 1970 he has been Professor of Economics at MIT. He is best known for his work on the forces behind the Great Depression. Among his best known books are *Causal Factors in American Economic Growth in the Nineteenth Century* (Macmillan, 1975); *Did Monetary Forces Cause the Great Depression?* (W.W. Norton, 1976); and *Lessons from the Great Depression* (MIT Press, 1989). His most widely read articles include 'The End of One Big Deflation' (co-authored with B.A. Wigmore) (*Explorations in Economic History*, **27**, October 1990); 'Transmission of the Great Depression' (*Journal of Economic Perspectives*, **7**, Spring 1993); and 'The

Gold Standard and the Great Depression' (co-authored with B. Eichengreen) (*Contemporary European History*, July 2000).

See also:
Great Depression.

Term Structure of Interest Rates

The relationship between yield and maturity for securities of different terms to maturity; also known as the yield curve. The most commonly observed shape for the yield curve is upward-sloping with lower yields for shorter-term assets than for longer-term assets. Attempts to explain the term structure of interest rates have included the expectations theory, the preferred market habitat theory and the market segmentation theory. The essence of the expectations theory is that long-term interest rates will be a geometric average of current known, and future expected, short-term rates and that the term structure depends on future expected rates of interest. For example, the theory predicts that the yield curve would slope upwards if short-term interest rates were expected to rise in the future. The preferred market habitat theory acknowledges the different preferred habitats of borrowers and lenders. Borrowers prefer to borrow long term to ensure greater security of funding. In contrast, lenders prefer to lend short term so that in the event of a shortage in cash they can more easily liquidate their loans. Reinforcing this difference in preferences is the fact that long-term lending is riskier since the value of long-term securities fluctuates more than that of short-term securities. Long-term lending therefore involves a greater degree of risk of the lender incurring a capital loss should there be a need to encash a security before maturity. The theory predicts that lenders will demand, and borrowers will be willing to pay, a risk premium for long-term lending over and above that for short-term lending. Thus the existence of a risk premium will ensure that the normal shape of the yield curve will be upward-sloping. The yield curve will only slope downwards when the expected fall in short-term interest rates offsets the risk premium. Finally, the essence of the market segmentation theory is that the market for securities of different maturities is segmented. With no substitution between markets, the shape of the yield curve reflects demand and supply conditions in the various markets. Higher long-term rates compared to short-term rates reflect that demand will be more and supply less at the long end of the market, and vice versa.

Terms of Trade

See:
Real Exchange Rate.

Thatcherism

A term applied to the economic and political philosophy adopted by the Thatcher government (1979–90) in the UK. The Thatcher government argued that its power to improve the overall performance of the economy was strictly limited, in that, while it could reduce inflation, it could only create the conditions in which sustainable growth of output and employment was possible. Underlying the economic policies that were pursued to achieve these two main objectives (which in the former case involved announced progressive reductions in the rate of growth of the money supply and the public sector borrowing requirement; and in the latter case cutting marginal income tax rates to increase the incentive to work, trade union reform to promote greater flexibility of wages and working practices and privatization to make the market for goods and services function more efficiently) lay a 'non-interventionist' political philosophy of minimal state interference with the workings of the free market system.

Theory and Measurement in Macroeconomics: Role of

For the past century, economists have engaged in a continuing debate over the role of theory and measurement in business cycle research, a debate that continues to shape the development of modern macroeconomic theory and research techniques. At the centre of this debate is the question of whether empirical–inductive or theoretical–deductive reasoning should take the lead role in guiding macroeconomic modelling; at times one or the other has dominated the research methodology in the discipline, although there appears to be a growing acknowledgment of the interdependence between the two today.

The empirical approach of Wesley Clair Mitchell and the NBER
The theory versus measurement debate has its origins in the business cycle analysis of Wesley Clair Mitchell, whose pioneering empirical analysis of business cycle behaviour undertaken at the National Bureau of Economic Research (NBER) in the 1920s to 1940s provided the empirical foundation for modern macroeconomic theory. Mitchell envisioned economics as a

'quantitative science,' with economic observation and measurement informing and suggesting theoretical hypotheses rather than simply verifying or testing them. Although Mitchell earned the respect of his colleagues for his careful empirical studies, the quantitative approach he advocated was at odds with those of mainstream economists in the 1920s. A growing number of economists maintained that theoretical modelling, followed by statistical estimation and testing, was the key to advancing macroeconomic knowledge rather than the inductive, empirical methodology that Mitchell proposed.

Mitchell's vision of a discipline ruled by careful empirical observation and analysis was driven by the lack of a dominant theory of cyclical fluctuations in the early 1900s. Mitchell's lifelong focus was to collect, measure and analyse masses of economic data in the hope of discovering empirical regularities that could support or refute competing explanations of cyclical behaviour and lead to the development of a comprehensive theory of the business cycle. Throughout, the primary role of observation and measurement in the development of analytical theories was always clear in Mitchell's work and it was this inductive–empirical approach that became the hallmark of Mitchell's lifelong research and that of the NBER, which Mitchell directed from 1920 to 1945.

The result of that research was the collection of hundreds of economic time series cataloguing the business cycle behaviour of the United States and international economies, the development of new statistical methods of business cycle analysis that allowed Mitchell (and former student Arthur F. Burns) to uncover a broad set of 'stylized business cycle facts', and the construction of a formal definition of the 'business cycle' based on these stylized facts. The business cycle research undertaken by Burns, Mitchell and their colleagues at the NBER culminated in the publication of *Measuring Business Cycles* (Burns and Mitchell, 1946), which outlined their pioneering methods of business cycle research and provided a comprehensive empirical analysis of business cycle behaviour in the US economy.

Measurement without theory and the Cowles Commission

Burns and Mitchell's *Measuring Business Cycles* generated immediate criticism from Tjalling Koopmans (1947), who accused Burns and Mitchell of carrying out 'measurement without theory'. Koopmans likened Burns and Mitchell's empirical methodology to the 'Kepler stage' of astronomy, which lacked the deductive logic that was necessary for causal interpretation of observed behaviour, and viewed it as inferior to the theoretical–statistical methodology of the nascent econometric programme being developed by the Cowles Commission, a research group centred first in Colorado Springs and later at the University of Chicago.

The Cowles Commission, whose research activities were directed by Koopmans from 1948 to 1954, advocated a singularly deductive approach to economic research – an approach that used economic theory to develop 'structural' econometric models whose parameters could be estimated and tested using statistical theory. In a series of exchanges with Koopmans following Mitchell's death in 1948, Rutledge Vining (1949, 1951), a colleague of Mitchell's at the NBER, defended Mitchell's empirical methodology against Koopmans's stinging attacks, arguing that the deductive methods advocated by the Cowles Commission placed a 'straitjacket on economic research' that overlooked the benefits of simple observation.

However, the debate between empirical economists, represented by Mitchell's NBER approach, and the econometricians, represented by the growing Cowles Commission approach, quickly ended following the Koopmans–Vining exchange. While the NBER continued to carry out the type of empirical analyses that Mitchell initiated, from the early 1950s on the Cowles Commission approach dominated macroeconomic research, with the development of large-scale structural macroeconometric models as its central focus. The formal structure of these models was rooted in Keynesian economic theory, which provided the theoretical underpinning for many of the model's equations. Important empirical support for these large-scale Keynesian structural models was provided by Frank and Irma Adelman (1959), who were the first to show that such models could qualitatively and quantitatively mimic the business cycle characteristics of the US economy. The success of these large-scale macroeconometric models in predicting the consequences of policy changes in the USA during the 1960s led to further support for the Cowles Commission approach to macroeconomic modelling. Throughout the 1960s these large econometric models were widely used by economists and policy makers to make national economic forecasts and analyse the effects of changes in fiscal and monetary policies.

Macroeconometric modelling under attack
By the early 1970s, however, the Keynesian macroeconometric models that formed the centrepiece of the Cowles Commission approach were being questioned for both theoretical and empirical reasons. Empirically, the same models that forecast so well in the 1960s began to forecast poorly in the 1970s. At issue was the explicit negative trade-off between inflation and unemployment that was a central feature of these models. This trade-off implied that expansionary monetary and fiscal policy could reduce unemployment rates at the expense of higher inflation. During the 1970s, however, *both* inflation *and* unemployment rates rose dramatically in most industrialized countries, leading economists to re-examine the models' theoretical underpinnings.

Lucas (1976) was the first to highlight the theoretical shortcomings of these models, illustrating how Keynesian model parameters were likely to change in response to expected future policy changes. Such parameter instability made meaningful policy analysis based on these models impossible, according to Lucas. In addition, Sims (1980) attacked the structural modelling approach of the Cowles Commission for its reliance on 'incredible restrictions' that were used to identify the models statistically. Sims maintained that such *ad hoc* restrictions, while statistically expedient, were inconsistent with economic theory based on the behaviour of rational decision makers.

Together, these incisive theoretical arguments, accompanied by the forecasting failures of Cowles-type macroeconometric models in the 1970s, led some economists to abandon traditional Keynesian structural modelling in search of alternative modelling strategies. The resulting theoretical turmoil produced two distinct responses during the 1980s, one focused on the development of distinctly 'atheoretical' statistical models of business cycle behaviour and the other centred on the construction of fully specified, internally consistent, theoretical models of the business cycle.

The measurement without theory debate – a reprise
In the absence of a dominant economic theory of the business cycle, Christopher Sims focused his attention on the development of small statistical models of the macro economy (vector autoregressions) that could be used to summarize business cycle behaviour compactly and analyse macroeconomic policy outcomes. These models differed markedly from the Cowles-type structural models, both in their structure and in their uses. Rather than focusing on the estimation and testing of large-scale models grounded in economic theory, Sims developed small reduced-form models that were used to map out the dynamic responses of the models' economic variables to stochastic shocks or policy interventions. Sims's statistical approach to business cycle analysis embodied the spirit of Mitchell's quantitative research, yet differed from Mitchell's in its use of formal statistical techniques. Sims and Mitchell, however, shared the view that careful statistical work, undertaken with a minimum of economic theory, provided valuable insights that could both suggest and test a wide range of theories of business cycle behaviour. Throughout the 1980s, support grew for using the reduced-form statistical models developed by Sims and they became a widely used tool for carrying out empirical macroeconomic research and policy analysis.

Like Mitchell, Sims was criticized for practising 'atheoretical economics', in contrast to mainstream econometric analysis. Cooley and LeRoy (1985), supporting the traditional econometric approach of the Cowles

Commission, echoed Koopmans's arguments that economic theory was not only beneficial, but necessary, for making meaningful structural interpretations of the dynamic behaviour generated by Sims's statistical models. Sims maintained that the relatively 'unstructured' models he advocated were not only more consistent with modern macroeconomic theory but were more useful for uncovering broad empirical regularities in economic data than the heavily restricted structural models promoted by the Cowles Commission.

The mutual interdependence of theory and measurement
Alongside the development of Sims's statistical models of business cycle behaviour, new classical economists such as Thomas Sargent, Robert Lucas, Finn Kydland and Ed Prescott were responding to the criticisms of Keynesian macroeconometric models by developing general equilibrium theoretical models based on microeconomic foundations and rational expectations theory. The result was the emergence of 'real business cycle' models that were capable of mimicking the broad qualitative features of observed business cycle behaviour. Unlike the Cowles Commission-type macroeconometric models, whose structural relationships lacked a consistent theoretical foundation, real business cycle models were developed from first principles to 'derive the quantitative implications of theory'. The latter was accomplished by simulating the equilibrium laws of motion from the models and comparing the sampling distributions of the resulting data with those computed for actual economies.

Real business cycle models also attracted criticism, most notably from Sims (1996), who argued that relatively unrestricted statistical models that 'let the data speak' are more likely to advance macroeconomics knowledge than either theoretical general equilibrium models or Cowles-type macroeconometric models. Sims's arguments are rooted in his views on scientific method, which hold that the goal of economics is continually to develop more efficient ways of 'compressing' or summarizing real-world data with a minimal loss of information. Sims sees little empirical pay-off in the results of purely theoretical general equilibrium models or heavily restricted structural models, and views progress as coming from *statistical* models that contain only a minimal amount of theoretical restrictions.

The theory versus measurement debate continues, but there appears to be a growing recognition of the mutual interdependence between the two, as evidenced by the development of 'structural' vector-autoregressive models that combine the statistical properties of Sims's approach with identifying restrictions drawn from economic theory, and increased support for research that seeks to determine the empirical regularities that theoretical models must account for. Hoover (1994) likens economics to astronomy, where theory and observation play complementary roles in advancing scientific knowledge. Like the astronomer's telescope, 'econometric calculations are the economist's telescope', with economic theory providing the rules for focusing the telescope's lenses. Economic theory determines how many data are allowed to pass through the econometrician's lenses, while simple observation suggests modifications to the theory that might be overlooked if the theoretical filter is too restrictive. The theory versus measurement debate in macroeconomics during the past century has been over how restrictive the theoretical lens should be, with statistical economists like Mitchell favouring a wide-angle lens that can take in as many observations as possible, and econometricians like Koopmans favouring a much narrower one. Macroeconomists in recent years appear to favour a middle ground, where both theory and observation interact to bring into better focus observed macroeconomic behaviour. The lasting lesson from the theory versus measurement debate is that the processes are mutually supportive, with both making significant contributions to the advancement of economic knowledge.

SCOTT SIMKINS

See also:

Burns, Arthur F.; Business Cycles: Real Business Cycle Approach; Business Cycles: Stylized Facts; Cowles Commission; Macroeconometric Models; Mitchell, Wesley C.; National Bureau of Economic Research; Vector Autoregressions.

Bibliography

Adelman, F. and I. Adelman (1959), 'The Dynamic Properties of the Klein–Goldberger Model', *Econometrica*, **27**, October, pp. 596–625.
Backus, D.K. and P.J. Kehoe (1992), 'International Evidence on the Historical Properties of Business Cycles', *American Economic Review*, **82**, September, pp. 864–88.
Biddle, J.E. (1998), 'Wesley Clair Mitchell', in J.B. Davis, D.W. Hands, and U. Mäki (eds), *The Handbook of Economic Methodology*, Cheltenham, UK and Lyme, US: Edward Elgar.
Burns, A.F. and W.C. Mitchell (1946), *Measuring Business Cycles*, New York: National Bureau of Economic Research.
Christ, C. (1994), 'The Cowles Commission's Contributions to Econometrics at Chicago, 1939–1955', *Journal of Economic Literature*, **32**, March, pp. 30–59.
Cooley, T.F. and S.F. LeRoy (1985), 'Atheoretical Macroeconometrics: A Critique', *Journal of Monetary Economics*, **16**, November, pp. 283–308.
Fabricant, S. (1984), *Toward a Firmer Basis of Economic Policy: The Founding of the National Bureau of Economic Research*, Cambridge, MA: National Bureau of Economic Research.
Friedman, M. (1950), 'Wesley C. Mitchell as an Economic Theorist', *Journal of Political Economy*, **58**, December, pp. 465–93.
Ginzberg, E. (1997), 'Wesley Clair Mitchell', *History of Political Economy*, **29**, Fall, pp. 371–90.
Hansen, A.H. (1949), 'Wesley Mitchell, Social Scientist and Social Counselor', *Review of Economics and Statistics*, **31**, November, pp. 245–55.
Hoover, K.D. (1994), 'Econometrics as Observation: The Lucas Critique and the Nature of Econometric Inference', *Journal of Economic Methodology*, **1**, June, pp. 65–80.

Koopmans, T.C. (1947), 'Measurement Without Theory', *Review of Economics and Statistics*, **29**, August, pp. 161–72.

Koopmans, T.C. (1949), 'Koopmans on the Choice of Variables to be Studied and the Methods of Measurement: A Reply', *Review of Economics and Statistics*, **31**, May, pp. 86–91.

Lucas, R.E., Jr (1976), 'Econometric Policy Evaluation: A Critique', in K. Brunner and A.H. Meltzer (eds), *The Phillips Curve and Labor Markets*, Carnegie-Rochester Conference Series on Public Policy, 1, Amsterdam: North-Holland.

Mills, F.C. (1928), 'The Present Status and Future Prospects of Quantitative Economics', Round Table Discussion, *American Economic Review*, **18**, March, pp. 28–45.

Mills, F.C. (1949), 'Wesley Clair Mitchell, 1874–1948', *American Economic Review*, **39**, June, pp. 730–42.

Mitchell, W.C. (1913), *Business Cycles*, Berkeley: University of California Press.

Mitchell, W.C. (1927, *Business Cycles: The Problem and its Setting*, New York: National Bureau of Economic Research.

Mitchell, W. C. (1951), *What Happens During Business Cycles: A Progress Report*, New York: National Bureau of Economic Research.

Schumpeter, J.A. (1950), 'Wesley Clair Mitchell (1874–1948)', *Quarterly Journal of Economics*, **64**, February, pp. 139–55.

Sims, C.A. (1980), 'Macroeconomics and Reality', *Econometrica*, **48**, January, pp. 1–48.

Sims, C.A. (1996), 'Macroeconomics and Methodology', *Journal of Economic Perspectives*, **10**, Winter, pp. 105–20.

Vining, R. (1949), 'Koopmans on the Choice of Variables to be Studied and the Methods of Measurement', *Review of Economics and Statistics*, **31**, May, pp. 77–86.

Vining, R. (1951), 'Economic Theory and Quantitative Research: A Broad Interpretation of the Mitchell Position', *American Economic Review*, **41**, May, pp. 106–18.

Working, H. (1927), 'The Use of the Quantitative Method in the Study of Economic Theory', *American Economic Review*, **17**, March, pp. 18–25.

Time Inconsistency

Time inconsistency problems arise in situations where a key player (for example, a policy maker) is perceived by others (for example, private agents) to lack the incentive/integrity to honour earlier promises. These promises then lack credibility, and the other agents react to this lack of credibility in a way that produces an outcome that everyone might have agreed, *ex ante*, was undesirable and almost certainly avoidable.

Typically, the policy maker might make a 'commitment' to act in a particular way, and if this promise is believed by the private-sector agents (that is, is credible), the latter will react to it in ways that would lead to a collectively 'good' outcome if the promise was subsequently honoured. But if the private agents were to act on the anticipation that the policy maker would honour his promise, then it might no longer be in the policy maker's own interest to keep his word, and there would be a danger that he might break his promise and that private agents would lose out as a result. However, because the private agents are rational, they appreciate that the policy maker would have an incentive to break his promise, so they disbelieve him and take action accordingly. The result is a suboptimal outcome that could have been avoided had the policy-maker's promise been credible: everyone loses out because the policy maker lacks credibility.

The basic time-inconsistency problem is a very general one: for example, it arises with investment or savings taxation, where the government may wish to induce inward investment or domestic saving by promising not to tax them, but is then tempted to tax them once the investments or savings are made; it arises with patent policy, where the government may promise patent protection to encourage invention, and then be tempted to remove patent protection once the inventions have become available.

The best known example arises in macroeconomic policy, where it arises because of the inability of the central bank to pre-commit itself credibly: see Kydland and Prescott (1977), Barro and Gordon (1983a, 1983b). This situation is illustrated in Figure 1.

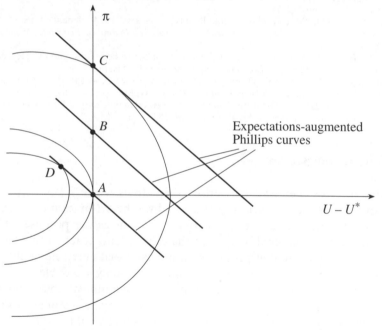

Figure 1 The time inconsistency of optimal monetary policy

Suppose the monetary authorities face an objective function with inflation (π) as one 'bad' and the deviation of unemployment (U) above its natural rate (U^*) as the other. The straight lines are expectations-augmented Phillips curves, and the curves are the central bank's indifference curves. The central bank wishes to maximize its objective function over time, but faces an expectations-augmented Phillips curve, the expectations in which are formed rationally. The social optimum, *A*, say, is for the central bank to engineer a permanent zero rate of inflation that also keeps unemployment at its natural rate. The problem is that *A* is not a privately optimal long-run outcome for the central bank because it does not equalize the central bank's marginal costs and benefits of inflation. If the economy were at *A*, the central bank would want to move from the indifference curve running through *A* by generating a 'surprise' inflation, so as to achieve a higher indifference curve (at point *D*). However, the public, being rational, would expect the central bank to do just that, and so the social optimum *A* cannot be a consistent (that is, long-run) equilibrium. Indeed, given the freedom of the central bank to do as it wishes, the only consistent equilibrium is that at which the marginal costs and benefits of inflation to the central bank are equal, and this outcome, *C*, say, involves higher inflation than the socially optimal inflation rate of zero. This can be verified visually by plotting central bank indifference curves and expectations-augmented Phillips curves, noting that the equilibrium must be on the vertical axis and involve no deviation of unemployment above the natural rate, and then finding the equilibrium *C* where a Phillips curve is tangential to a central bank indifference curve.

The source of the failure of the central bank to deliver the socially optimal outcome is the central bank's own discretion. Imagine that the central bank promised to deliver the socially optimal outcome *A*, and the public believed it. The public would then expect zero inflation, but the central bank would have no incentive to deliver it. It would therefore inflate, and the public's expectations would not be fulfilled. A rational public would therefore disbelieve the central bank's promise to deliver zero inflation, or, indeed, any promise to deliver any other inflation rate than the one implied by the central bank's own interests (as reflected in its own indifference curves). The central bank's problem is that it cannot pre-commit itself with the credibility needed to bring rational private-sector expectations of inflation down. Its ability to change its future policy – that is, its discretion – undermines its credibility, and in the absence of credibility it cannot deliver the socially optimal outcome.

A partial answer is for the central bank to try to build up a reputation for good behaviour. If a central bank promises low inflation and actually delivers it, it may become rational for the public to start believing it when it promises future low inflation. The central bank then acquires more credibility, and inflationary expectations fall. (Conversely, if the central bank misbehaves, it loses credibility and inflationary expectations rise again.) The central bank thus builds up a reputation, which it values because it enhances its credibility, and it offers this reputation as a hostage for its future good behaviour. We now get an intermediate outcome, *B*, which lies between the socially optimal outcome A and the earlier, fully discretionary, outcome C. The better the central bank's reputation, the greater its credibility and the lower the public's inflationary expectations – a better reputation therefore pushes B towards the socially optimal outcome and away from the fully discretionary (or zero reputation) one. While a good reputation can push the outcome towards the socially optimal one, it cannot actually deliver that outcome because there will always be *some* chance that the central bank would decide to cash in on its reputation and 'cheat'. Building up a reputation for good behaviour is therefore a partial, but not a complete, response to the time-inconsistency problem.

Since reputations typically evolve slowly over time, the reputational equilibrium will also give rise to a cycle. Imagine that the economy starts off in a position where the central bank has a good reputation for delivering low inflation (so B is relatively close to A). Since low inflation is credible, people buy government debt at relatively low interest rates, they bargain for relatively low pay rises, and so on. They therefore act in ways that expose themselves to inflation and so give the central bank considerable temptation to engineer a surprise inflation to catch them out. At some point, the central bank gives in to this temptation and inflation rises. The central bank's good reputation depreciates, inflationary expectations rise, and B drifts up towards the zero-reputation outcome C. The central bank then finds itself in a high inflation equilibrium, but a time comes when it decides to get serious about inflation again and disinflate. Of course, by this time it has a poor reputation and few people believe it, but it persists and over time gradually acquires a renewed reputation for monetary toughness. Inflationary expectations therefore fall, and the central bank rebuilds its reputation. Eventually, its reputation is more or less fully restored, and the economy returns to the point where it started. The temptation to inflate slowly rises again, and at some point the central bank gives in to this temptation and the process starts again.

We thus get a cycle, in which a central bank starts off with a good reputation, squanders it by going off on a monetary binge, then does its penance, gets inflation down again, and slowly restores its reputation; and then starts all over again. Interest rates, unemployment and other macroeconomic variables also cycle along with the inflation rate. Since the cycle is driven by the combination of the central bank's credibility problems and the central bank's unobservable concern (or lack of it) for its own reputation, private agents cannot easily predict the movements of these variables. The cycle is therefore damaging, not just because these variables move, but also, and more particularly, because they move in unpredictable and often erratic ways.

The broad sweep of historical evidence on discretionary monetary policy is largely consistent with these predictions. Monetary policy in most countries has been a series of monetary binges followed by 'mornings after' in which a short-lived attempt would be made to bring inflation back down. As Timberlake nicely summarized the history of US monetary policy,

> money stocks and price level fluctuations behaved similarly to a remorseful but irresolute alcoholic and his bottle. A period of monetary drunkenness would be followed by a weeping and wailing and gnashing of teeth and a return to monetary austerity. Then rationalizations would appear: 'High interest rates are hurting the fragile economic recovery.' . . . 'We need monetary relief from —.' (Here, the reader can furnish his favorite scapegoat policy, such as 'monetarism'.) With a happy gasp, the bottle would appear again. (Timberlake,1986, p. 753)

The advocates of discretionary monetary policy would say that this has all changed since the early 1990s: they would say that central banks have learned their lessons and inflation has been eliminated. There is of course no denying that central banks have been on the wagon for a good few years now, but time will ultimately tell whether monetary time-inconsistency problems have really been eliminated – and the theory of time-inconsistency certainly suggests not. The issue of who guards the (monetary) guardians may have gone dormant for a while, but it never truly goes away.

KEVIN DOWD

See also:

Credibility and Reputation; Expectations-augmented Phillips Curve; Natural Rate of Unemployment; Rational Expectations.

Bibliography

Barro, R.J. and D.B. Gordon (1983a), 'Rules, Discretion and Reputation in a Model of Monetary Policy', *Journal of Monetary Economics*, **12**, July, pp. 101–21.
Barro, R.J. and D.B. Gordon (1983b), 'A Positive Theory of Monetary Policy in a Natural Rate Model', *Journal of Political Economy*, **91**, August, pp. 589–610.
Kydland, F.E. and E.C. Prescott (1977), 'Rules Rather than Discretion: The Inconsistency of Optimal Plans', *Journal of Political Economy*, **85**, June, pp. 473–91.
Timberlake, R.H. Jr (1986), 'Institutional Evolution of Federal Reserve Hegemony', *Cato Journal*, **5**, Winter, pp. 743–63.

Tinbergen, Jan (1903–94)

Jan Tinbergen (b.1903, The Hague, Netherlands) obtained his Dr. in Physics from the University of Leiden in 1929. His main posts included Statistician at the Dutch Central Bureau of Statistics, 1929–45; Director of the Central Planning Bureau in The Hague, 1944–55; Visiting Professor at Harvard University, 1956–7; Professor at the Netherlands School of

Economics, 1957–73; and Professor at the University of Leiden, 1973–5. Among his many offices and honours he was an adviser to various governments of developing countries and the World Bank, and in 1969 was awarded, jointly with Ragnar Frisch, the first Nobel Memorial Prize in Economics for his contributions to the development of econometrics. He is best known for his pioneering work on econometric modelling, in particular the macroeconomic modelling of business cycles; and the theory of economic policy, in which he demonstrated the need for equality of instruments and targets. Among his best known books are *Statistical Testing of Business Cycle Theories*, 2 vols (League of Nations, 1939); *Business Cycles in the United Kingdom, 1870–1914* (North-Holland, 1951); *On the Theory of Economic Policy* (North-Holland, 1952); *Centralization and Decentralization in Economic Policy* (North-Holland, 1954); *Economic Policy: Principles and Design* (North-Holland, 1956); and *Development Planning* (McGraw-Hill, 1967).

See also:

Nobel Prize in Economics.

Tobin, James (1918–2002)

James Tobin was a self-described old-style Keynesian macroeconomist who consistently argued for an activist macro policy. He was involved with Keynesian economics from its beginning in the United States. He was an undergraduate at Harvard as Keynesian economics was being introduced, and further developed by graduate students and young professors there, and he continued his study of Keynesian economics in his graduate studies. After graduation he became a professor at Yale, where, together with Art Okun, he led what was known as the Yale school of macro, which was the dominant approach to macro in the 1960s.

Throughout his life, Tobin maintained a consistent approach to macro theory and policy. That approach centred around an expanded IS/LM analysis in theory, and countercyclical fiscal and monetary policy, supplemented by incomes policies, in policy. This brief entry discusses, first, Tobin's personal history, second, his policy contributions, and third, his theoretical contributions. It concludes with a discussion of his legacy and his view of modern developments.

Personal history
James Tobin was born in 1918 in Champaign, Illinois. He went to Harvard on a scholarship and there he received his bachelor's and master's degrees

in 1939 and 1940, respectively. He was in the US Navy from 1942 to 1946 and then returned to Harvard, where he received his PhD in 1947. He started teaching at Yale in 1950 and he remained there academically as the Sterling Professor of Economics throughout his teaching career. He was director of the Cowles Foundation during 1955–61 and 1964–5. He was a member of President Kennedy's Council of Economic Advisers in 1961–2.

Tobin received a variety of awards for his work, the most prestigious of which was the Nobel Prize in 1981 for 'his analysis of financial markets and their relations to expenditure decisions, employment, production and prices' (see Purvis, 1982). He also won the John Bates Clarke Medal, given by the American Economic Association to the best economists aged under 40, in 1955. A less distinguished, but certainly more novel, tribute to him is the fact that the novelist Herman Wouk, who met Tobin when they were in the Naval Reserve together, drew upon Tobin when he wrote the character 'Tobit' in *The Caine Mutiny*. In that novel, Tobit is a highly intelligent naval officer, superbly competent in everything he does, whose character is unimpeachable. Those who know Tobin say that the novelist's depiction is an accurate one.

Policy views and contributions
Tobin's policy views are best described as liberal activist. There is a consistent world-view underlying Tobin's activist policy positions; it is a pragmatic view that sees the market as sometimes working to coordinate individual decisions, but not always, and not always for the best, and when it does not, government needs to intervene. Consistent with this world-view, Tobin's approach to macro policy is a policy-oriented, pragmatic approach that sees possible roles for both monetary and fiscal policy (see Tobin, 1987a, 1996a). Its theoretical foundation is the neoclassical synthesis, which Tobin, together with Paul Samuelson, was instrumental in establishing as the reigning approach to macro in the 1960s.

The primary alternative approach advocated in the 1960s was monetarism, and Tobin was often contrasted with Milton Friedman in terms of both policy options and theory. Many of Tobin's famous debates with Friedman concerned the importance of money in macro policy (see, for example, Tobin, 1981). Tobin argued that money is important for Keynesian economics and that empirical evidence on money and inflation can be seen as consistent with a broad range of theories, not just monetarist theory, as Friedman suggested.

Tobin was a leader in bringing Keynesian economics out of depression economics and structuring it as a general theory appropriate for all times. He saw his policy approach as a synthesis approach – one that recognized the advantages of the neoclassical position, but also recognized the need for Keynesian-type policy. In an interview (Colander, 1999) he nicely summarized his views of policy:

> Sometimes the economy is characterized as being at, or close to, or maybe above, full employment. In that case, the opportunity-cost logic of neoclassical economics applies. At other times however, the economy is better described not as a perfectly competitive marketplace situation, but as a situation with general excess supply (particularly in the labor markets). In this case it is possible for monetary and fiscal policy to increase aggregate demand and increase output. That doesn't mean that opportunity cost calculations are ruled out, but it does change the nature of the calculation. The macro calculation concerns how you expand the economy. Since there are several different ways of getting to full employment from a situation of excess supply one should apply welfare analysis to choose the appropriate path. For example, you might want to recover by monetary expansion rather than fiscal expansion, if you were trying to do something to improve long-term growth while you restore full employment.

This policy position does not seem especially novel now, but it was when he first started espousing it. The neoclassical synthesis policy approach differed from the economics of many early Keynesians in that it saw a role for both monetary and fiscal policy, whereas some early Keynesians had emphasized fiscal policy as the only workable tool. Early Keynesians saw neoclassical rules as never applying.

In implementing policy, Tobin argued that, because the loss from unemployment is greater than the loss from inflation, an economy should err on the side of high real output, and should not worry inordinately about inflation. Should the economy develop inflationary problems, the correct policy response is to introduce incomes policies, perhaps tax-based, so that high employment can be maintained.

Internationally, Tobin is best known for his development and support of what has become known as the Tobin Tax (see Tobin, 1996b), an internationally uniform tax on all spot conversions of one currency into another, proportional to the size of the transaction. It is meant to deter short-term financial round-trip excursions into another currency, where the tax would offset much of the gain from interest rate differentials for short-term changes.

Theoretical views and contributions

Tobin's theoretical contributions to economics started when he was still an undergraduate. He wrote his honours thesis, which was published in the *Quarterly Journal of Economics* in 1941, on the influence of money wages on employment. In it he criticized the way Keynes connected the real and financial sectors. He continued developing these ideas as he went to Yale to teach.

The thread tying Tobin's theoretical work together is the idea that for Keynesian economics to be meaningful it must be integrated into the real world and it must shed light on policy. For Tobin, theory and policy were closely entwined. This tying together of theory and policy required money and financial markets to be integrated into the Keynesian system. Tobin achieved this by developing portfolio theory and the theory of liquidity preference into the Keynesian model (Tobin, 1958). These theories describe how individual households and firms determine the composition of their assets within a general equilibrium setting.

Portfolio theory integrated risk, and preferences towards risk, in the theory of money. It explained why individuals would hold money, even if it paid no interest. Money was held because it avoided the risk that bonds or stocks had. Portfolio theory allowed the financial sector to be linked to expenditure decisions, employment, production and price movements. In doing so it provided a transmission mechanism through which monetary policy could affect the economy. This work in portfolio theory helped spawn modern finance theory, and Tobin's 'separation theorem' is seen as a fundamental theorem in modern finance.

A complete summary of his theoretical framework is presented in 'A General Equilibrium Approach to Monetary Theory' (1969) where he set out a complete asset equilibrium model and related it to the flow of investment. That model makes the Q ratio, the ratio of the market value of the firm's capital to the replacement cost of the firm's capital (often called Tobin's Q), a key decision variable. When stock prices are above the replacement cost of the investment, stock finance is lucrative, and will tend to increase. In other work (Tobin, 1963) Tobin showed how monetary policy, through its effect on inflation, can influence the interest rate, and hence the rate of growth in the economy.

While Tobin is best known for his theoretical contributions to macro theory, he also made an important contribution in econometric theory. Specifically, he developed the Tobit method (named by Tobin via the Wouk character) for estimating econometric relationships involving limited or truncated dependent variables (see Tobin, 1987b).

Conclusion
Tobin is one of the pillars upon which modern macro stands. Despite this he was not enthralled with the way modern economics has developed, and the way in which his work has been used. His legacy is primarily in theory, not policy; much of his theoretical work is built into the core of modern macroeconomics and finance theory. The policies he advocated are not. This presents a problem, since Tobin saw theory and policy as intricately intertwined. Ironically, his primary opponent for much of the time, Milton

Friedman, has suffered a different fate. Friedman's Marshallian approach to theory has, in large part, been discarded, but Friedman's policy advice remains central to economics in the early 2000s.

When asked what he thought about real business cycle theory, Tobin answered, only somewhat jokingly, 'That's just the enemy.' He has a similarly negative view on new Keynesian economics. When asked about his views on new Keynesians he said, 'I'm not sure what that means. If it means people like Greg Mankiw, I don't regard them as Keynesians. I don't think they have involuntary unemployment or absence of market clearing. It is a misnomer to call Mankiw any form of Keynesian.' These views of modern macro follow from Tobin's vision: that policy and theory are related and that Keynesian theory provides a foundation for activist monetary and fiscal policy. Modern new Keynesians have little focus on policy, so it is not surprising that Tobin preferred to distinguish himself from them and see himself as an Old Keynesian (Tobin, 1993).

DAVID C. COLANDER

See also:

Council of Economic Advisers; Cowles Commission; Incomes Policy; John Bates Clark Medal; Keynesian Economics; Monetarism; Neoclassical Synthesis; New Keynesian Economics; Nobel Prize in Economics; Okun, Arthur M.

Bibliography

Colander, D. (1999), 'Conversations with James Tobin and Robert Shiller on the "Yale Tradition"', *Macroeconomic Dynamics*, **3**, March, pp.116–43.
Purvis, D.D. (1982), 'James Tobin's Contributions to Economics', *Scandinavian Journal of Economics*, **84**, January, pp.61–88.
Tobin, J. (1941), 'A Note on the Money Wage Problem', *Quarterly Journal of Economics*, **50**, May, pp.508–16.
Tobin, J. (1958), 'Liquidity Preference as Behaviour towards Risk', *Review of Economic Studies*, **25**, February, pp.65–86.
Tobin, J. (1963), 'Money and Economic Growth', *Econometrica*, **33**, October, pp.671–84.
Tobin, J. (1969), 'A General Equilibrium Approach to Monetary Theory', *Journal of Money, Credit and Banking*, **1**, February, pp.15–29.
Tobin, J. (1981), 'The Monetarist Counter-Revolution: An Appraisal', *Economic Journal*, **91**, March, pp.29–42.
Tobin, J. (1987a), *Policies For Prosperity: Essays in a Keynesian Mode*, Brighton: Wheatsheaf.
Tobin, J. (1987b), *Essays in Economics*, Cambridge, MA: MIT Press.
Tobin, J. (1993), 'Price Flexibility and Output Stability: An Old Keynesian View', *Journal of Economic Perspectives*, **7**, Winter, pp.45–65.
Tobin, J. (1996a), *Full Employment and Growth: Further Keynesian Essays on Policy*, Cheltenham, UK and Brookfield, US: Edward Elgar.
Tobin, J. (1996b), *The Tobin Tax: Coping with Financial Volatility: Prologue*, New York and Oxford: Oxford University Press, pp.ix–xviii.

Tobin's Q

The ratio of the market value of capital stock to its replacement cost.

Trade Balance

The difference between receipts from exports of goods and services and payments for imports of goods and services; also known as net exports. A trade deficit (or negative trade balance) occurs where imports are greater than exports, while a trade surplus (or positive trade balance) occurs where exports are greater than imports.

Trade Union Density

The percentage of the labour force that is unionized.

Transactions Balances

Money held by individuals in order to finance regular and planned purchases of goods and services.

See also:
Demand for Money: Keynesian Approach.

Transitory Income

Income that people do not expect they will continue to receive in the future; the difference between current (measured) income and permanent or normal income. For example, a worker may receive an unexpected bonus at work one year, but has no reason to believe that he or she will receive such a windfall gain in future years.

See also:
Permanent Income Hypothesis.

Trough

The lower turning point, following the contractionary phase of the business cycle, at which aggregate economic activity stops falling and thereafter begins to rise.

See also:

Business Cycle.

Unanticipated Inflation

The difference between the actual and the expected rate of inflation; also known as imperfectly anticipated inflation. For example, if economic agents expected the rate of inflation to be 6 per cent over some future time period (such as a year), but in reality the actual rate of inflation turned out to be 8 per cent over that period, then unanticipated inflation is 2 per cent. Debate exists about how best to model the way economic agents form their expectations.

See also:
Adaptive Expectations; Anticipated Inflation; Inflation: Costs of; Rational Expectations.

Unemployed

People who are available for work and are actively seeking jobs but cannot find them. Unemployment is measured at a point in time. Whether or not the level of unemployment changes over time depends on flows into and out of a pool of unemployed labour. There are six main inflows into this pool. Four of these involve people previously employed who become unemployed because they are made redundant, are fired or sacked, are temporarily laid off, or voluntarily quit their existing job. The other two inflows into the pool of unemployed labour involve new entrants (for example, people not previously in the labour force who are looking for work, such as school leavers) and re-entrants (for example, people who are returning to the labour force, such as those who have raised a family and are now actively seeking employment). In contrast, there are three main outflows from the pool of unemployed labour, previously unemployed people who find new jobs, people who are recalled after being temporarily laid off, and unemployed people who withdraw from the labour force (for example, because of retirement). Considerable debate exists over the cause of, and cure for, unemployment.

See also:
Demand-deficient Unemployment; Frictional Unemployment; Full Employment; Involuntary Unemployment in Keynes's *General Theory*; Involuntary Unemployment in Keynesian Economics; Seasonal Unemployment; Structural Unemployment.

Unemployment Rate

The percentage of the labour force who are unemployed.

Vector Autoregressions

Vector autoregressions (VARs) are simple time-series models in which every variable in the system is endogenous and appears in every equation, with each variable depending on its own past values and past values of all the other variables. The attraction of VARs for economists is their ease of specification and estimation. They are reduced-form equations and are particularly easy to use for forecasting.

A simple example for the two variables growth (y) and inflation (x) is

$$y_t = \alpha_1 + \beta_1 y_{t-1} + \beta_2 y_{t-2} + \delta_1 x_{t-1} + \delta_2 x_{t-2} + u_{1t} \tag{1}$$

$$x_t = \alpha_2 + \Phi_1 y_{t-1} + \phi_2 y_{t-2} + \gamma_1 x_{t-1} + \gamma x_{t-2} + u_{2t} \tag{2}$$

where there are two lags on each variable, giving a total of five unknown parameters in each equation. More generally, with k variables and a maximum lag of M there will be ($kM+1$) unknown parameters in each equation. Since the variables on the right-hand side in equations (1) and (2) are the same, ordinary least squares is a valid method of estimation for the system of equations.

Sources of VARs

There are three ways in which VARs can arise. First, following Zellner and Palm (1974), a dynamic simultaneous econometric model can be written:

$$A(L)Y + B(L)X = C(L)E, \tag{3}$$

where $A(L), B(L)$ and $C(L)$ are matrices of polynomials in the lag operator, L, Y and X are vectors of endogenous and exogenous variables, respectively, and E is a vector of white noise residuals. Now, if the path of the exogenous variables can be represented by an autoregressive moving-average (ARMA) process, and the various matrices are invertible, so that X can be replaced by its moving-average representation, then equation (3) can be written

$$J(L)Y = E, \tag{4}$$

where $J(L)$ is a matrix of lag polynomials. This is a VAR model in which the restrictions implicit in the definitions of A, B and C in the structural model (3) have been ignored but could, in principle, be imposed.

The second approach leading to a VAR model starts with the work of Box and Jenkins (1970), who proposed the univariate autoregressive moving-average (ARMA) model for a variable. The obvious multivariate generalization of the ARMA model is the vector ARMA (or VARMA) model which can be written in matrix form as

$$\Phi(L)Y_t = \theta(L)\varepsilon_t \tag{5}$$

If $\theta(L)$ is invertible then Y has a VAR representation.

The third approach feeding to VAR models follows from the work of Sims (1980), who argues that the restrictions arising from economic theory imposed on structural models (which are needed for identification) are incredible and cannot be taken seriously. First, Sims objects to the arbitrary normalizations which occur when an equation is claimed to 'explain' one of the several endogenous variables it includes. Next, he criticizes the 'one-equation-at-a-time' specification procedure for macroeconomic models where restrictions which are appropriate for partial equilibrium models are imposed, frequently resulting in undesirable systems properties. Similarly, policy variables are frequently assumed to be exogenous when in fact they are at least partly endogenous. The third area of concern is the treatment of expectations variables. Behaviour depends on the expected future values of variables and these can be affected by any information currently available. Thus any variable in the system can affect expectations and this results in problems over identification.

To deal with these criticisms of the traditional modelling approach, Sims proposes estimating unrestricted reduced forms in which each current endogenous variable is a function of lagged values of all the variables in the system. This is the unrestricted VAR model.

Sims does not discuss how the list of variables is selected, but a knowledge of macroeconomics would imply that, for a macroeconomic model of a national economy, variables such as national income, consumption, prices and unemployment are appropriate. Beyond this the inclusion of extra variables such as money and credit might be regarded as being controversial, since there is disagreement as to their importance.

Granger causality
Since the variables are all required to be endogenous, a Granger (1969) causality test can be used to check whether variables should be included. For two variables, x_t and y_t, the test requires the regression of each of the variables on past values of both variables, as, for example, in equations (1) and (2) above, but where the length of the maximum lag is chosen to make the disturbances random. Using a standard F-test of restrictions, if $\delta_1 = \delta_2 = 0$ then past values of x do not help to forecast current y, so x does not Granger-cause y. Hence y is exogenous with respect to x. Similarly, if $\phi_1 = \phi_2 = 0$, y

does not Granger-cause x and x is exogenous with respect to y. Variables which are not found to be exogenous will be included in the VAR model. The choice of the common lag length, L, is also arbitrary, but Sims suggests a likelihood ratio test for deciding whether the value of L can be reduced.

Bayesian VARs

One problem with the unrestricted VAR modelling procedure is the large number of variables (and hence unknown parameters) included in the model. Litterman (1986a, 1986b) reports that very good in-sample fits are obtained but, when VARs are used for forecasting, the out-of-sample forecasts are poor. This is because of the lack of precision in the coefficient estimates due to multicollinearity. Doan *et al.* (1984) have adopted a Bayesian framework in which the forecaster has prior ideas about the values of the parameters and the data are used to revise these ideas. This gives the Bayesian VAR (or BVAR) model.

Initially, each variable is modelled by a random walk with drift so that, for example,

$$y_t = y_{t-1} + c + \varepsilon_t,$$

where c is a constant and ε is a white noise disturbance. The coefficients on all the other lagged variables are set at a mean value of zero but have a non-zero variance, which is assumed to decline as the length of the lag increases. This results in a specification with a small number of parameters and the possibility of the data changing a zero coefficient to non-zero if there is a strong enough influence. Another aspect of the BVAR approach is that the parameters are re-estimated each period using the Kalman filter (see Doan and Litterman, 1988). Sims examines the properties of VARs using innovation analysis (see Holden, 1995, for an introduction).

Stationary series and cointegration

The discussion so far assumes that the variables (or their differences) are weak or covariance stationary. This requires the variable to have a constant mean, a constant and finite variance and constant covariances. Variables which are stationary are said to be integrated of order zero. If a variable can be transformed to be stationary by first-differencing, it is said to be integrated of order one. Whether a variable is stationary or integrated of order one can be tested by the Dickey–Fuller (1979) test or Phillips–Perron tests (see Phillips, 1987).

More generally, Engle and Granger (1987) consider the properties of two or more related variables, each of which is integrated of order one but has a resulting combination which is stationary. Such variables are said to be cointegrated. The implications of cointegration are far-reaching for economic modelling and forecasting. First, if the variables in an equation are not cointegrated, then, because the error term is non-stationary, the relationship is likely to be misspecified and, at a minimum, reliable estimation of the parameters will be difficult. Secondly, Engle and Granger have proved that, if x and y are both integrated of order one, have constant means and are cointegrated, then an error-correcting data-generating mechanism or error correction model exists and takes the form

$$\Delta y_t = -\rho_1 u_{t-1} + \text{lagged } (\Delta y, \Delta x) + d(L)\, \varepsilon_{1t} \tag{6}$$

$$\Delta x_t = -\rho_2 u_{t-1} + \text{lagged } (\Delta y, \Delta x) + d(L)\, \varepsilon_{2t},$$

where

$$u_t = y_t - \beta x_t \tag{7}$$

and Δ is the first difference operator. Here $d(L)$ is a finite polynomial in the lag operator, L, ε_i is a white noise error process and

$$|\rho_1| + |\rho_2| \neq 0 \tag{8}$$

The interpretation of equation (6) is helped by considering the equilibrium situation when the differenced terms in (6) are zero and it collapses to u_t equals zero. That is, in equilibrium, y is proportional to x. Hence, from equation (7), u measures the deviation from the equilibrium value and, since u is stationary with a mean of zero, deviations from equilibrium in period $t-1$ are partly corrected in period t. Thus the error correction mechanism, which has an economic interpretation, provides a link between structural models and time-series models. For forecasting, the error correction mechanism is important because it implies that a model which only includes first differences of variables will be misspecified if the levels of the variables are cointegrated. This could happen if, for example, a VAR model is fitted to first differenced data.

KEN HOLDEN

See also:

Forecasting; Macroeconometric Models.

Bibliography

Box, G.E.P. and G.M. Jenkins (1970), *Time-Series Analysis: Forecasting and Control*, San Francisco: Holden-Day.

Dickey, D.A. and W.A. Fuller (1979), 'Distribution of the Estimators for Autoregressive Time Series with a Unit Root', *Journal of the American Statistical Association*, **74**, June, pp. 427–31.

Doan, T.A. and R.B. Litterman (1988), *User's Manual for RATS*, Evanston: VAR Econometrics.

Doan, T.A., R.B. Litterman and C.A. Sims (1984), 'Forecasting and Conditional Projection Using Realistic Prior Distributions', *Econometric Reviews*, **3**, pp. 1–100.

Engle, R.F. and C.W.J. Granger (1987), 'Cointegration and Error Correction: Representation, Estimation and Testing', *Econometrica*, **55**, March, pp. 251–76.

Granger, C.W.J. (1969), 'Investigating Causal Relations by Econometric Models and Cross-Spectral Methods', *Econometrica*, **37**, July, pp. 424–38.

Holden, K. (1995), 'Vector Autoregression Modelling and Forecasting', *Journal of Forecasting*, **14**, May, pp. 159–66.

Litterman, R.B. (1986a), 'A Statistical Approach to Economic Forecasting', *Journal of Business and Economic Statistics*, **4**, January, pp. 1–4.

Litterman, R.B. (1986b), 'Forecasting with Bayesian Vector Autoregressions – Five Years of Experience', *Journal of Business and Economic Statistics*, **4**, January, pp. 25–38.

Phillips, P.C.B. (1987), 'Time Series Regression with Unit Roots', *Econometrica*, **55**, March pp. 277–302.

Sims, C.A. (1980), 'Macroeconomics and Reality', *Econometrica*, **48**, January, pp. 1–48.

Zellner, A. and F. Palm (1974), 'Time Series Analysis and Simultaneous Equation Econometric Models', *Journal of Econometrics*, **2**, pp. 17–54.

Velocity of Circulation

The speed at which money changes hands, or circulates, in the economy. In the equation of exchange, $MV = PT$, the quantity of money (M) times the transactions velocity of circulation (V) *must equal* the average price of all transactions (P) times the number of transactions that take place (T). Rearranging this identity, $V = PT/M$, so that the transactions velocity of circulation of money is equal to the average number of times money changes hands to finance *all* transactions (that is, both final and intermediate transactions). In Irving Fisher's transactions version of the quantity theory of money, the transactions velocity of circulation was treated as being independent of M, P and T, and was held to be determined by institutional arrangements. In contrast, in the Cambridge cash-balance version of the quantity theory of money, $MV = Py$, M is the quantity of money, P is the average price of final output, y is real income (final output) and V is the income velocity of circulation of money.

See also:

Equation of Exchange; Quantity Theory of Money.

Wallace, Neil

Neil Wallace (b.1939, New York City, USA) obtained his BA from Columbia University in 1960 and his PhD from the University of Chicago in 1964. His main past posts have included Professor of Economics at the University of Minnesota, 1969–94; and Barnett Banks Professor of Money and Banking at the University of Miami, 1994–7. Since 1997 he has been Professor of Economics at Pennsylvania State University. He is best known for his work with T.J. Sargent on the policy ineffectiveness proposition. His most widely read articles, co-authored with T.J. Sargent, include 'Rational Expectations, the Optimal Monetary Instrument and the Optimal Money Supply Rule' (*Journal of Political Economy*, **83**, April 1975); and 'Rational Expectations and the Theory of Economic Policy' (*Journal of Monetary Economics*, **2**, April 1976).

See also:
Policy Ineffectiveness Proposition.

Weintraub, Sidney (1914–83)

Sidney Weintraub (b.1914, New York City, USA) obtained his PhD from New York University in 1941. His main posts included Professor of Economics at the University of Pennsylvania, 1952–81. In 1978, he co-founded and co-edited (with Paul Davidson) the *Journal of Post Keynesian Economics*. He is best known for his important contributions to Post Keynesian economics, and his support for the introduction of a tax-based incomes policy to solve the problem of stagflation in the 1970s. Among his best known books are *Income and Employment Analysis* (Pitman, 1951); *A General Theory of the Price Level, Output, Income Distribution and Economic Growth* (Chilton, 1959); *Classical Keynesianism, Monetary Theory and the Price Level* (Chilton, 1961); *A Keynesian Theory of Employment, Growth and Income Distribution* (Chilton, 1966); *Capitalism's Inflation and Unemployment Crisis: Beyond Monetarism and Keynesianism* (Addison-Wesley, 1978); and *Our Stagflation Malaise: Ending Inflation and Unemployment* (Quorum Books, 1981). His most widely read articles include 'An Incomes Policy to Stop Inflation' (*Lloyd's Bank Review*, **99**, January 1971); 'A Tax-Based Incomes Policy' (co-authored with H.C. Wallich) (*Journal of Economic Issues*, **5**, June 1971); and 'Money as Cause and Effect' (co-authored with P. Davidson) (*Economic Journal*, **83**, December 1973).

See also:
Post Keynesian Economics; Stagflation; Incomes Policy.

Wicksell, Knut (1851–1926)

Knut Wicksell (b.1851, Stockholm, Sweden) obtained his BSc in Maths and Physics (1872) and his Dr. in Maths (1885) from the University of Uppsala. His main posts included Assistant Professor at the University of Uppsala, 1899; and Associate Professor (1900) and Professor (1903–17) at the University of Lund. He is best known for his work on monetary theory, in particular the relationship between the natural or real rate of interest and the market rate of interest which, he argued, explained the cumulative and self-generating processes of economic expansion and contraction. His best known books include *Interest and Prices* (1898; reprinted by Macmillan, 1936); and *Lectures on Political Economy, Volume Two: Money* (1906; reprinted by Routledge & Kegan Paul, 1935).

See also:
Loanable Funds Theory.

World Bank

In July 1944, representatives from 45 countries met at Bretton Woods in New Hampshire, USA, to discuss the postwar establishment of major international institutions whose purpose would be to facilitate international cooperation and to improve the stability of the world economy following the disastrous events and consequences of economic mismanagement during the interwar years (for a fascinating account of the role played by John Maynard Keynes at the Bretton Woods conference, see R. Skidelsky, *John Maynard Keynes: Fighting for Britain*, London: Macmillan, 2000). In retrospect, it seems that the 'Great War' which began in August 1914 finally came to an end in April 1945. Fortunately, by 1945, the lessons of 1919 and the inter-war experience had been learnt, but at an unimaginable price in terms of human life and physical destruction. As a result of depression and war, the world economy had also witnessed a massive decline in the volume of international trade and capital flows and the pre-1914 era of increasing globalization had been brought to an abrupt end.

The task facing those at Bretton Woods was to establish a framework of institutions that would help to put the world economy back on its feet. The meeting led to the creation of three new international institutions, the International Monetary Fund (IMF), the General Agreement on Tariffs and Trade (GATT), and the International Bank for Reconstruction and Development (IBRD). The latter is more popularly known as the World Bank (*http://www.worldbank.org/*) and was set up to provide loans (with conditionality) to the governments of United Nations countries for the purpose of promoting economic development. In this task the World Bank was viewed as playing a complementary role to the IMF (*http://www.imf.org/*) whose primary task was to monitor and stabilize the international financial system by providing short-term financial help to member countries experiencing balance of payments difficulties. The purpose of GATT was to promote trade liberalization by encouraging and facilitating the lowering of trade barriers. Since 1995 GATT has been replaced by the World Trade Organization (see *http://www.wto.org/*).

The World Bank's primary role has been to borrow funds on private capital markets in the developed countries and provide long-term loans on preferential terms to finance development projects in developing countries. For many developing countries who lack access to private capital markets, the World Bank remains virtually the sole source of long-term external capital apart from that coming from foreign direct investment and bilateral aid flows. However, the World Bank has also played another important role as a source of new ideas on development, particularly via the publication of the annual *World Development Report*. For example, there is now much greater recognition at the World Bank of the importance of institutional factors in the development process (see *Building Institutions for Markets*, World Bank, 2002). Influential senior economists who have worked at the World Bank and have helped to shape development thinking include Hollis Chenery (1972–82), Anne Krueger (1982–6), Stanley Fischer (1988–90), Michael Bruno (1989–96), Lawrence Summers (1991–3), Joseph Stiglitz (1997–9), and Nicholas Stern (2000 to date).

Although the World Bank has been the subject of much criticism (for example, with respect to its structural adjustment strategy and loan conditionality), it is likely to continue to play an important role in helping to solve global market failures and also in its role as provider of knowledge and technical assistance to those countries whose institutions and policy framework are acting as barriers to progress (see M. Gavin and D. Rodrik, 'The World Bank in Historical Perspective', *American Economic Review*, **85**, May 1995; A.O. Krueger, 'Whither the World Bank and the IMF?', *Journal of Economic Literature*, **36**, December 1998; C. Gilbert *et al.*, 'Positioning the World Bank', *Economic Journal*, **109**, November 1999; C. Gilbert and D. Vines, *The World Bank: Policies and Structure*, Cambridge University Press, 1999; J. Stiglitz, 'The World Bank at the Millennium',

Economic Journal, **109**, November 1999; B. Snowdon, 'Redefining the Role of the State: Joseph Stiglitz on Building a Post-Washington Consensus', *World Economics*, **2**, July–September 2001).

See also:

Bretton Woods; General Agreement on Tariffs and Trade; International Monetary Fund; World Trade Organization.

World Trade Organization

Established in 1995, the WTO was created by the Uruguay Round negotiations (1986–94) to succeed the General Agreement on Tariffs and Trade, and is located in Geneva, Switzerland. The main objective of the international organization, which has more than 130 member countries who between them account for more than 90 per cent of world trade, is 'to help trade flow smoothly, freely, fairly and predictably'. This objective is achieved by: administering trade agreements which have been negotiated, signed and ratified in all member nations' parliaments; providing a forum for trade negotiations; settling trade disputes; monitoring national trade policies; helping developing countries in trade policy issues by providing technical assistance and training; and cooperating with other international organizations. For more information the reader is referred to the official website of the WTO (*http://www.wto.org/*).

See also:

General Agreement on Tariffs and Trade.

Yield Curve

See:

Term Structure of Interest Rates.